THE CLARENDON EDITION OF
THE WORKS OF THOMAS HOBBES

VOLUME VI

THE CORRESPONDENCE

THOMAS HOBBES

THE CORRESPONDENCE

EDITED BY
NOEL MALCOLM

VOLUME I: 1622–1659

CLARENDON PRESS · OXFORD
1994

Oxford University Press, Walton Street, Oxford OX2 6DP

Oxford New York Toronto
Delhi Bombay Calcutta Madras Karachi
Kuala Lumpur Singapore Hong Kong Tokyo
Nairobi Dar es Salaam Cape Town
Melbourne Auckland Madrid
and associated companies in
Berlin Ibadan

Oxford is a trade mark of Oxford University Press

Published in the United States
by Oxford University Press Inc., New York

British Library Cataloguing in Publication Data
Data available

Library of Congress Cataloging in Publication Data
Hobbes, Thomas, 1588–1679
The correspondence / Thomas Hobbes : edited by Noel Malcolm.
— (The Clarendon edition of the works of Thomas Hobbes)
Includes bibliographical references
1. Hobbes, Thomas, 1588–1679—Correspondence.   2. Philosophers—
England—Correspondence.   I. Malcolm, Noel.   II. Title.
III. Series: Hobbes, Thomas, 1588–1679. Works. 1994.
B1246.A4   1994   192—dc20 [B] 93–41404
ISBN 0–19–824065–1 (v. 1)
ISBN 0–19–824099–6 (v. 2)

1 3 5 7 9 10 8 6 4 2

Typeset by Joshua Associates Ltd., Oxford
Printed in Great Britain
on acid-free paper by
Bookcraft (Bath) Ltd.,
Midsomer Norton, Avon

For S.R.L.

In memory

CONTENTS

VOLUME I: 1622–1659

General Introduction	xxi
Textual Introduction	xlii
A description of the main manuscripts	xlii
Principles of inclusion	xliv
Non-letters	xlvii
Missing letters	li
Principles of transcription	lvii
The arrangement of the notes	lxii
The Biographical Register	lxv
References	lxvi
Dates	lxvii
Translations	lxviii
Acknowledgements	lxix
Abbreviations Used in this Edition	lxxiii

LETTER 1: 10 [/20] DECEMBER 1622
Robert Mason to Hobbes   1

LETTER 2: 6 [/16] NOVEMBER 1628
Hobbes to Christian Cavendish, Countess of Devonshire   6

LETTER 3: 8 /18 NOVEMBER 1629
George Aglionby to Hobbes   7

LETTER 4: 19 /29 APRIL 1630
Hobbes to Sir Gervase Clifton   10

LETTER 5: 10 /20 MAY 1630
Hobbes to Sir Gervase Clifton   13

LETTER 6: 30 JUNE /10 JULY 1630
Hobbes to Robert Leeke   15

LETTER 7: 25 JULY /4 AUGUST 1630
Hobbes to Robert Leeke   16

LETTER 8: 2 [/12] NOVEMBER 1630
Hobbes to Sir Gervase Clifton   17

LETTER 9: 23 NOVEMBER [/3 DECEMBER] 1632
Hobbes to Sir Gervase Clifton   18

CONTENTS

LETTER 10: 26 JANUARY [/5 FEBRUARY] 1634
Hobbes to William Cavendish, Earl of Newcastle   19

LETTER 11: 27 MARCH [/6 APRIL] 1634
Hobbes to Sir Gervase Clifton   21

LETTER 12: 21 /31 OCTOBER 1634
Hobbes to ?   22

LETTER 13: 20 /30 JANUARY 1635
Hobbes to Sir Gervase Clifton   25

LETTER 14: 21 APRIL /1 MAY 1635
Hobbes to Sir Gervase Clifton   26

LETTER 15: [early AUGUST 1635]
Hobbes to Sir Gervase Clifton   27

LETTER 16: 15 /25 AUGUST 1635
Hobbes to William Cavendish, Earl of Newcastle   28

LETTER 17: 6 /16 APRIL 1636
Hobbes to Mr Glen   30

LETTER 18: 13 /23 JUNE 1636
Hobbes to William Cavendish, Earl of Newcastle   32

LETTER 19: 29 JULY /8 AUGUST 1636
Hobbes to William Cavendish, Earl of Newcastle   33

LETTER 20: 1 [/11] OCTOBER 1636
Sir Kenelm Digby to Hobbes   36

LETTER 21: 16 [/26] OCTOBER 1636
Hobbes to William Cavendish, Earl of Newcastle   37

LETTER 22: 26 OCTOBER [/5 NOVEMBER] 1636
Hobbes to William Cavendish, Earl of Newcastle   39

LETTER 23: 26 OCTOBER [/5 NOVEMBER] 1636
Robert Payne to Hobbes   40

LETTER 24: 25 DECEMBER 1636 [/4 JANUARY 1637]
Hobbes to William Cavendish, Earl of Newcastle   41

LETTER 25: 17 [/27] JANUARY 1637
Sir Kenelm Digby to Hobbes   42

LETTER 26: 11 [/21] SEPTEMBER 1637
Sir Kenelm Digby to Hobbes   50

LETTER 27: 4 [/14] OCTOBER 1637
Sir Kenelm Digby to Hobbes   51

LETTER 28: 22 AUGUST [/1 SEPTEMBER] 1638
Hobbes to the Hon. Charles Cavendish   52

LETTER 29: [11/] 21 JANUARY 1641
René Descartes to Marin Mersenne for Hobbes   54

CONTENTS

LETTER 30: [28 JANUARY/] 7 FEBRUARY 1641
Hobbes to Marin Mersenne   62

LETTER 31: [29 JANUARY/] 8 FEBRUARY 1641
Hobbes to Sir Charles Cavendish   80

LETTER 32: [8/] 18 FEBRUARY 1641
René Descartes to Marin Mersenne for Hobbes   86

LETTER 33: [22 FEBRUARY/] 4 MARCH 1641
René Descartes to Marin Mersenne for Hobbes   94

LETTER 34: [20/] 30 MARCH 1641
Hobbes to Marin Mersenne   102

LETTER 35: 2 /12 APRIL 1641
Hobbes to John Scudamore, first Viscount Scudamore   114

LETTER 36: [11/] 21 APRIL or [18/] 28 APRIL 1641
René Descartes to Marin Mersenne for Hobbes   116

LETTER 37: 23 JULY /2 AUGUST 1641
Hobbes to William Cavendish, third Earl of Devonshire   120

LETTER 38: [1/] 11 JULY 1645
Samuel Sorbière to Hobbes   121

LETTER 39: [29 JULY/] 8 AUGUST 1645
Hobbes to Edmund Waller   124

LETTER 40: [6/] 16 MAY 1646
Hobbes to Samuel Sorbière   125

LETTER 41: [11/] 21 MAY 1646
Samuel Sorbière to Hobbes   128

LETTER 42: [22 MAY/] 1 JUNE 1646
Hobbes to Samuel Sorbière   131

LETTER 43: [22 AUGUST/] 1 SEPTEMBER 1646
Samuel Sorbière to Hobbes   134

LETTER 44: [late SEPTEMBER] 1646
Samuel Sorbière to Hobbes   136

LETTER 45: [24 SEPTEMBER/] 4 OCTOBER 1646
Hobbes to Samuel Sorbière   138

LETTER 46: [12/] 22 OCTOBER 1646
Hobbes to Samuel Sorbière   141

LETTER 47: [21/] 31 OCTOBER 1646
Samuel Sorbière to Hobbes   144

LETTER 48: [1/] 11 NOVEMBER 1646
Hobbes to Samuel Sorbière   146

LETTER 49: [c. 1647]
Adrian May to Hobbes   148

CONTENTS

LETTER 50: [18/] 28 FEBRUARY 1647
Hobbes to Samuel Sorbière   152

LETTER 51: [22 FEBRUARY/] 4 MARCH 1647
Samuel Sorbière to Hobbes   154

LETTER 52: [12/] 22 MARCH 1647
Hobbes to Samuel Sorbière   155

LETTER 53: [2/] 12 AUGUST 1647
Samuel Sorbière to Hobbes   159

LETTER 54: [9/] 19 AUGUST 1647
Samuel Sorbière to Hobbes   161

LETTER 55: [24 SEPTEMBER/] 4 OCTOBER 1647
Samuel Sorbière to Hobbes   162

LETTER 56: [17/] 27 NOVEMBER 1647
Hobbes to Samuel Sorbière   163

LETTER 57: [7/] 17 FEBRUARY 1648
Hobbes to Marin Mersenne   165

LETTER 58: 2 / 12 MAY 1648
Hobbes to William Cavendish, third Earl of Devonshire   169

LETTER 59: [15/] 25 MAY 1648
Hobbes to Marin Mersenne   172

LETTER 60: [9/] 19 JUNE 1648
Hobbes to Marin Mersenne   173

LETTER 61: [4/] 14 JUNE 1649
Hobbes to Samuel Sorbière   176

LETTER 62: [12/] 22 SEPTEMBER 1649
Hobbes to Pierre Gassendi   178

LETTER 63: 27 MAY [/6 JUNE] 1651
Ralph Bathurst to Hobbes   180

LETTER 64: [25 OCTOBER/] 4 NOVEMBER 1653
François du Verdus to Hobbes   181

LETTER 65: [28 APRIL/] 8 MAY 1654
Samuel Sorbière to Hobbes   182

LETTER 66: 10 /20 JULY 1654
Hobbes to Pierre Gassendi   184

LETTER 67: [25 JULY/] 4 AUGUST 1654
François du Verdus to Hobbes   186

LETTER 68: [10/] 20 AUGUST 1654
François du Verdus to Hobbes   193

LETTER 69: [26 AUGUST/] 5 SEPTEMBER 1654
Thomas de Martel to Hobbes   198

LETTER 70: [4/] 14 SEPTEMBER 1654
Abraham du Prat to Hobbes 204

LETTER 71: [13/] 23 SEPTEMBER 1654
François du Verdus to Hobbes 206

LETTER 72: [14/] 24 APRIL 1655
Thomas de Martel to Hobbes 208

LETTER 73: 6 [/16] JUNE 1655
Henry Oldenburg to Hobbes 211

LETTER 74: [24 SEPTEMBER/] 4 OCTOBER 1655
Abraham du Prat to Hobbes 212

LETTER 75: [13/] 23 DECEMBER 1655
François du Verdus to Hobbes 216

LETTER 76: [20 FEBRUARY/] 1 MARCH 1656
François du Verdus to Hobbes 231

LETTER 77: [22 MARCH/] 1 APRIL 1656
Abraham du Prat to Hobbes 245

LETTER 78: [26 MARCH/] 5 APRIL 1656
François du Verdus to Hobbes 248

LETTER 79: [26 MARCH/] 5 APRIL 1656
François du Verdus to Hobbes 269

LETTER 80: 1 [/11] APRIL 1656
Henry Stubbe to Hobbes 271

LETTER 81: [9/] 19 APRIL 1656
Claude Mylon to Hobbes 272

LETTER 82: 13–14 [/23–4] MAY 1656
Philip Tanny or Tandy to Hobbes 276

LETTER 83: 13–14 [/23–4] MAY 1656
Philip Tanny or Tandy to Hobbes 277

LETTER 84: [14/] 24 MAY 1656
François du Verdus to Hobbes 281

LETTER 85: [18/] 28 MAY 1656
François Peleau to Hobbes 288

LETTER 86: 2 [/12] JULY 1656
Philip Tanny or Tandy to Hobbes 292

LETTER 87: 8 [/18] JULY 1656
Henry Stubbe to Hobbes 293

LETTER 88: [late JULY 1656]
Edmund Waller to Hobbes 294

LETTER 89: [17/] 27 AUGUST 1656
François du Verdus to Hobbes 297

LETTER 90: 18 /28 AUGUST 1656
François Peleau to Hobbes   300

LETTER 91: 7 [/17] OCTOBER 1656
Henry Stubbe to Hobbes   311

LETTER 92: [11/] 21 OCTOBER 1656
Claude Mylon to Hobbes   314

LETTER 93: [19/] 29 OCTOBER 1656
François Peleau to Hobbes   316

LETTER 94: [20/] 30 OCTOBER 1656
François du Verdus to Hobbes   319

LETTER 95: [22 OCTOBER/] 1 NOVEMBER 1656
François Peleau to Hobbes   329

LETTER 96: 25 OCTOBER [/4 NOVEMBER] 1656
Henry Stubbe to Hobbes   333

LETTER 97: 25 OCTOBER [/4 NOVEMBER] 1656
Henry Stubbe to Hobbes   337

LETTER 98: 9 [/19] NOVEMBER 1656
Henry Stubbe to Hobbes   338

LETTER 99: [12/] 22 NOVEMBER 1656
Abraham du Prat to Hobbes   342

LETTER 100 [23 NOVEMBER/] 3 DECEMBER 1656
François du Verdus to Hobbes   344

LETTER 101: 26 NOVEMBER [/6 DECEMBER] 1656
Henry Stubbe to Hobbes   378

LETTER 102: 29 NOVEMBER [/9 DECEMBER] 1656
Henry Stubbe to Hobbes   379

LETTER 103: [30 NOVEMBER/] 10 DECEMBER 1656
François Peleau to Hobbes   381

LETTER 104: 8 [/18] DECEMBER 1656
Henry Stubbe to Hobbes   383

LETTER 105: [13/] 23 DECEMBER 1656
Samuel Sorbière to Hobbes   386

LETTER 106: [13 /23 December 1656?]
Abraham du Prat to Hobbes   393

LETTER 107: 19 [/29] DECEMBER 1656
Henry Stubbe to Hobbes   394

LETTER 108: [22 DECEMBER 1656/] 1 JANUARY 1657
François du Verdus to Hobbes   397

LETTER 109: 23 DECEMBER 1656 [/2 JANUARY 1657]
Thomas Barlow to Hobbes   420

CONTENTS

LETTER 110: [25 DECEMBER 1656/] 4 JANUARY 1657
François Peleau to Hobbes   422

LETTER 111: 26 DECEMBER 1656 [/5 JANUARY 1657]
Henry Stubbe to Hobbes   425

LETTER 112: 29 DECEMBER 1656 /8 JANUARY 1657
Hobbes to Samuel Sorbière   427

LETTER 113: 13 [/23] JANUARY 1657
Henry Stubbe to Hobbes   430

LETTER 114: [23 JANUARY/] 2 FEBRUARY 1657
Samuel Sorbière to Hobbes   433

LETTER 115: [29 JANUARY/] 8 FEBRUARY 1657
François Peleau to Hobbes   438

LETTER 116: 30 JANUARY [/9 FEBRUARY] 1657
Henry Stubbe to Hobbes   439

LETTER 117: 6 [/16] FEBRUARY 1657
Hobbes to Samuel Sorbière   442

LETTER 118: 10 [/20] FEBRUARY 1657
Hobbes to Samuel Sorbière   447

LETTER 119: 14 [/24] FEBRUARY 1657
Henry Stubbe to Hobbes   448

LETTER 120: [1/] 11 MARCH 1657
François Peleau to Hobbes   450

LETTER 121: [12/] 22 MARCH 1657
François du Verdus to Hobbes   452

LETTER 122: 17 [/27] MARCH 1657
Henry Stubbe to Hobbes   455

LETTER 123: 11 [/21] APRIL 1657
Henry Stubbe to Hobbes   458

LETTER 124: [15/] 25 APRIL 1657
Thomas de Martel to Hobbes   461

LETTER 125: 6 [/16] MAY 1657
Henry Stubbe to Hobbes   464

LETTER 126: [17/] 27 MAY 1657
François du Verdus to Hobbes   467

LETTER 127: [5/] 15 JUNE 1657
Samuel Fermat to Hobbes   474

LETTER 128: [11/] 21 JULY 1657
Claude Mylon to Hobbes   476

LETTER 129: [29 JULY/] 8 AUGUST 1657
Thomas de Martel to Hobbes   479

xiii

CONTENTS

LETTER 130: [7/] 17 AUGUST 1657
Thomas de Martel to Hobbes   482

LETTER 131: 29 AUGUST /8 SEPTEMBER 1657
Claude Mylon to Hobbes   485

LETTER 132: [late 1657]
Claude Mylon to Hobbes   488

LETTER 133: [22 JANUARY/] 1 FEBRUARY 1658
Samuel Sorbière to Hobbes   491

LETTER 134: 1 [/11] MARCH 1658
Edward Bagshaw to Hobbes   497

LETTER 135: [22 JULY/] 1 AUGUST 1658
Samuel Sorbière to Hobbes   499

LETTER 136: 15 [/25] MAY 1659
Pierre Guisony to Hobbes   501

LETTER 137: 5 /15 SEPTEMBER 1659
Charles du Bosc to Hobbes   504

LETTER 138: 9 [/19] OCTOBER 1659
Henry Stubbe to Hobbes   505

LETTER 139: [21/] 31 DECEMBER 1659
M. de la Moulinière to Samuel Sorbière for Hobbes   507

VOLUME II

LETTER 140: 23 JANUARY [/2 FEBRUARY] 1660
Hobbes to Samuel Sorbière   513

LETTER 141: [21/] 31 MARCH 1660
Samuel Sorbière to Hobbes   515

LETTER 142: [2/] 12 MAY 1661
Samuel Sorbière to Hobbes   518

LETTER 143: 30 AUGUST [/9 SEPTEMBER] 1661
John Aubrey to Hobbes   520

LETTER 144: 21 SEPTEMBER [/1 OCTOBER] 1661
François du Prat to Hobbes   521

LETTER 145: 9 [/19] FEBRUARY 1662
Hobbes to Margaret Cavendish, Marchioness of Newcastle   524

LETTER 146: 3 [/13] MARCH 1662
Hobbes to Samuel Sorbière   525

LETTER 147: [17/] 27 MARCH 1662
Samuel Sorbière to Hobbes   527

CONTENTS

LETTER 148: AUGUST 1662
Christiaan Huygens to Andrew Crooke for Hobbes   530

LETTER 149: [10/] 20 DECEMBER 1662
Christiaan Huygens to Sir Robert Moray for Hobbes   534

LETTER 150: [23 DECEMBER 1662/] 2 JANUARY 1663
Samuel Sorbière to Hobbes   540

LETTER 151: early 1663
Samuel Sorbière to Hobbes   544

LETTER 152: early 1663
Samuel Sorbière to Hobbes   548

LETTER 153: 7 [/17] SEPTEMBER 1663
Hobbes to John Aubrey   554

LETTER 154: [11/] 21 SEPTEMBER 1663
Samuel Sorbière to Hobbes   555

LETTER 155: 19/29 SEPTEMBER 1663
François du Prat to Hobbes   558

LETTER 156: [30 OCTOBER/] 9 NOVEMBER 1663
Samuel Sorbière to Hobbes   560

LETTER 157: 4/14 NOVEMBER 1663
François du Prat to Hobbes   570

LETTER 158: 21 NOVEMBER/1 DECEMBER 1663
François du Prat to Hobbes   572

LETTER 159: [24 NOVEMBER/] 4 DECEMBER 1663
Samuel Sorbière to Hobbes   573

LETTER 160: 30 NOVEMBER/10 DECEMBER 1663
Hobbes to Samuel Sorbière   576

LETTER 161: 19 [/29] DECEMBER 1663
Hobbes to Samuel Sorbière   578

LETTER 162: [22–4 DECEMBER 1663/] 1–3 JANUARY 1664
Samuel Sorbière to Hobbes   585

LETTER 163: [28 DECEMBER 1663/] 7 JANUARY 1664
François du Verdus to Hobbes   587

LETTER 164: 7 [/17] MARCH 1664
Hobbes to Samuel Sorbière   596

LETTER 165: [20/] 30 APRIL 1664
Samuel Sorbière to Hobbes   610

LETTER 166: [21 JUNE/] 1 JULY 1664
Samuel Sorbière to Hobbes   617

LETTER 167: 30 JUNE [/10 JULY] 1664
Hobbes to John Aubrey   620

CONTENTS

LETTER 168: [24 JULY/] 3 AUGUST 1664
François du Verdus to Hobbes   621

LETTER 169: [13/] 23 AUGUST 1664
Samuel Sorbière to Hobbes   629

LETTER 170: [19/] 29 AUGUST 1664
François du Verdus to Hobbes   632

LETTER 171: [24 JANUARY/] 3 FEBRUARY 1665
Samuel Sorbière to Hobbes   668

LETTER 172: [10/] 20 APRIL 1665
François du Verdus to Hobbes   670

LETTER 173: [26 APRIL/] 6 MAY [1665?]
Alexandre Morus to Hobbes   674

LETTER 174: [25 SEPTEMBER/] 5 OCTOBER 1665
François du Verdus to Hobbes   676

LETTER 175: [11/] 21 DECEMBER 1665
François du Verdus to Hobbes   686

LETTER 176: 4 [/14] FEBRUARY 1666
François du Prat to Hobbes   687

LETTER 177: [27 MAY/] 6 JUNE 1666
François du Verdus to Hobbes   690

LETTER 178: 9 [/19] JUNE 1667
Hobbes to Joseph Williamson   692

LETTER 179: [29 NOVEMBER/] 9 DECEMBER 1667
Pieter Blaeu, on behalf of Johan Blaeu, to Hobbes   693

LETTER 180: [3/] 13 APRIL 1668
François du Verdus to Hobbes   696

LETTER 181: 30 JUNE [/10 JULY] 1668
Hobbes to Joseph Williamson   699

LETTER 182: [8/] 18 JULY 1668
Samuel Sorbière to Hobbes   700

LETTER 183: 20 [/30] OCTOBER 1668
Hobbes to John Brooke   701

LETTER 184: 24 OCTOBER [/3 NOVEMBER] 1668
Hobbes to the Hon. Edward Howard   704

LETTER 185: [22 JANUARY/] 1 FEBRUARY 1669
Samuel Sorbière to Hobbes   706

LETTER 186: [9/] 19 JULY 1669
Pieter Blaeu, on behalf of Johan Blaeu, to Hobbes   708

LETTER 187: 6 [/16] AUGUST 1669
Hobbes to Cosimo de' Medici   710

LETTER 188: [25 JANUARY /] 4 FEBRUARY 1670
Cosimo de' Medici to Hobbes   711

LETTER 189: 13 /23 JULY 1670
Gottfried Wilhelm Leibniz to Hobbes   713

LETTER 190: [28 APRIL /] 8 MAY 1671
François du Verdus to Hobbes   722

LETTER 191: 26 NOVEMBER [/6 DECEMBER] 1672
Hobbes to Henry Oldenburg   725

LETTER 192: 30 DECEMBER 1672 [/9 JANUARY 1673]
Henry Oldenburg to Hobbes   727

LETTER 193: 1 [/11] FEBRUARY 1673
Hobbes to Josiah Pullen   729

LETTER 194: 10 [/20] NOVEMBER 1673
Josiah Pullen to Hobbes   730

LETTER 195: [1674?]
Gottfried Wilhelm Leibniz to Hobbes   731

LETTER 196: [25 FEBRUARY /] 7 MARCH 1674
François du Verdus to Hobbes   736

LETTER 197: 20 [/30] APRIL 1674
Hobbes to Anthony Wood   744

LETTER 198: 24 FEBRUARY [/6 MARCH] 1675
Hobbes to John Aubrey   751

LETTER 199: 24 JUNE [/4 JULY] 1675
John Aubrey to Hobbes   753

LETTER 200: 14 [/24] AUGUST 1677
Hobbes to James Butler, first Duke of Ormonde   756

LETTER 201: 1678
Charles Blount to Hobbes   759

LETTER 202: 5 [/15] MARCH 1678
Hobbes to John Aubrey   766

LETTER 203: SEPTEMBER 1678
Thomas Shipman to Hobbes   768

LETTER 204: 25 MARCH [/4 APRIL] 1679
Hobbes to William Crooke   769

LETTER 205: 25 MARCH [/4 APRIL] 1679
Hobbes to John Aubrey   770

LETTER 206: 19 [/29] JUNE 1679
Hobbes to William Crooke   771

LETTER 207: 21 [/31] JULY 1679
Hobbes to William Crooke   772

LETTER 208: 18 [/28] AUGUST 1679
Hobbes to John Aubrey   772
LETTER 209: 18 [/28] AUGUST 1679
Hobbes to William Crooke   774
LETTER 210: undated
Hobbes to King Charles II   774
ADDENDUM. LETTER 62A: late SEPTEMBER 1649
Hobbes to Sir Charles Cavendish   776

Biographical Register of Hobbes's Correspondents
  George Aglionby   777
  John Aubrey   779
  Edward Bagshaw   782
  Thomas Barlow   785
  Ralph Bathurst   787
  Johan and Pieter Blaeu   789
  Charles Blount   790
  Charles du Bosc   795
  Sir John Brooke   797
  James Butler, first Duke of Ormonde   799
  Sir Charles Cavendish   801
  The Hon. Charles Cavendish   805
  Christian Cavendish, Countess of Devonshire   806
  Margaret Cavendish, Duchess of Newcastle   811
  William Cavendish, first Earl, first Marquess, and first
    Duke of Newcastle   812
  William Cavendish, third Earl of Devonshire   815
  Charles II   817
  Sir Gervase Clifton   820
  William Crooke   823
  René Descartes   825
  Sir Kenelm Digby   828
  Samuel Fermat   832
  Pierre Gassendi   834
  Mr Glen   837
  Pierre Guisony   837
  The Hon. Edward Howard   839
  Christiaan Huygens   840
  Robert Leeke   843
  Gottfried Wilhelm Leibniz   845

CONTENTS

Thomas de Martel   848
Robert Mason   855
Adrian May   857
Cosimo de' Medici, Grand Duke of Tuscany   860
Marin Mersenne   862
Alexandre Morus   865
M. de la Moulinière   867
Claude Mylon   868
Henry Oldenburg   869
Robert Payne   872
François Peleau   877
Abraham du Prat   878
François du Prat   881
Josiah Pullen   885
John Scudamore, first Viscount Scudamore   886
Thomas Shipman   888
René-François de Sluse   889
Samuel Sorbière   893
Henry Stubbe   899
Philip Tanny or Tandy   902
François du Verdus   904
Edmund Waller   913
Sir Joseph Williamson   915
Anthony Wood   917

Manuscript Sources   921
Bibliography   933
Index of Correspondents   973
General Index   974

xix

GENERAL INTRODUCTION

I

ALTHOUGH Thomas Hobbes was a very good letter-writer, he was not one of the great letter-writers of the seventeenth century. According to Aristotle a man cannot be described as beautiful if, however well-proportioned he may be, he is below the proper stature for a man; and perhaps something similar must be said of a letter-writer who, however well he writes, does not leave a substantial *œuvre* in epistolary form. The 211 surviving letters to and from Hobbes contrast pitifully with the 3,656 letters of the Locke correspondence, the 4,350 of Rivet, or the roughly 20,000 (no one yet knows the precise figure) of Leibniz. Among figures of comparable importance from this period, only Pascal seems to have left an even smaller legacy of correspondence than Hobbes.

Much (but not all) of the explanation of this state of affairs can be found in the practicalities and contingencies of Hobbes's biographical history. The flowering of his philosophical and scientific interests came famously late, in the 1630s; the first indication of such interests in his correspondence is in a letter written a couple of months before his forty-sixth birthday (Letter 10). Had Descartes tarried so long, we should have none of his philosophical or scientific correspondence before 1642—thus eliminating nearly 250 of his surviving 600-odd letters. The point is not that Hobbes was intellectually dormant before the 1630s—though we know frustratingly little, we do know that he had contacts with Bacon, that he pondered the appearance of a comet in 1618,[1] that he had experience of public affairs in the Virginia and Summer Island Companies,[2] and that he translated Thucydides—but merely that until the 1630s he was neither engaged in any large-scale philosophical project, nor closely connected with any particular circle of fellow researchers who might have stimulated him to correspond. The first such group to which Hobbes can confidently be attached is that of Walter Warner, Robert Payne, and Sir Charles Cavendish.[3] Although

[1] Hobbes, *Anti-White*, VIII. 1.
[2] See my 'Hobbes, Sandys, and the Virginia Company'.
[3] On Warner see Letter 16 n. 3; on Payne and Sir Charles see the Biographical Register.

this was hardly the self-enclosed 'Welbeck academy' portrayed by some writers (there is no evidence that Warner ever visited the Cavendish household at Welbeck), the fact that Hobbes had frequent opportunities to meet Payne and the Cavendish brothers, either in Nottinghamshire and Derbyshire or in London, must have reduced the need for correspondence between them; while the more distant Warner, on the other hand, was obviously of less intellectual interest to Hobbes.[4]

In the following decade, Hobbes was indeed involved in one of the most active and stimulating intellectual milieux of the age, the philosophical and scientific network which centred on that great letter-writer and *animateur* of correspondence Marin Mersenne. But here again sheer proximity removed the need for letter-writing. Had Hobbes remained in England in the 1640s, his intellectual development might have taken a different course; but at least we should now know more about it, assuming that Mersenne would have shown the same degree of interest in Hobbes as a correspondent that he did when Hobbes was a visitor and a friend. It is only thanks to Samuel Sorbière's removal to Holland (as the result of a religious scandal) that we have any significant sequence of personal correspondence from Hobbes during his Paris years. The letters he sent to Robert Payne would probably be far more revealing of Hobbes's private thoughts and intellectual enthusiasms, if they survived; but sadly they do not.

It was only after Hobbes's return to England at the beginning of 1652, therefore, that conditions were really ripe for a flourishing correspondence: now, at long last, he was both connected intellectually with a whole circle of people, and separated physically from them. Conditions were not as ideal as they might have been, of course: Mersenne had died in 1648, the Fronde caused disruptions for several years, and Gassendi was to succumb to a long illness in 1655. Hobbes's correspondence with some of his French friends seems to have taken several years to get going: Thomas de Martel's and Abraham du Prat's first surviving letters date from the autumn of 1654 (Letters 69, 70). But by 1656 his French correspondence was in full flood. This is the *annus mirabilis* of the Hobbes correspondence, with 37 surviving letters (or 32, if the year is calculated by the Gregorian calendar), 20 of which were from France. During this year Hobbes was receiving letters at an average rate of one nearly every ten days. Only one out of those 37 surviving letters is a letter from Hobbes (to Sorbière); but it contains the assurance that 'so far as I remember, I

---

[4] See Hobbes's comments in Letter 16.

have never received a letter from you, de Martel, du Bosc, or du Prat without sending a letter in reply'.[5] Out of all Hobbes's French correspondents, however, only Sorbière preserved the letters he received in a form that has survived to the present day. Mere contingency, it seems, has deprived us of dozens, perhaps scores, of letters: from Hobbes to de Martel, du Bosc, Abraham du Prat, François Peleau, and, above all, to his most faithful and devoted correspondent, François du Verdus.

After the mid-1650s, the spate of correspondence recedes considerably, with only Sorbière's letters steadying the flow. Thomas de Martel drifted off into obscurity; du Bosc and Abraham du Prat died in 1659 and 1660; and after Sorbière's farewell in his final and rather moving letter of 1669 (Letter 185), only du Verdus, now teetering between paranoia and religious exaltation, remained from Hobbes's original group of continental friends.

These facts are sufficient to explain in large part the tailing-off of Hobbes's correspondence during those years; but another contingency must also be mentioned. During the last three decades of his life, Hobbes suffered from a disease known as the 'shaking palsy'—something similar to, or perhaps identical with, Parkinson's disease. According to Aubrey, this 'began in France before the yeare 1650, and haz growne upon him by degrees, ever since, so that he haz not been able to write very legibly since 1665 or 1666, as I find by some of his letters to me'.[6] Hobbes's hand had never been very elegant or regular, and the last surviving example of his writing at any length (Letter 66, from June/July 1654) is cramped, jagged, and visibly shaky. As early as June 1655 we find Henry Oldenburg beginning a letter to Hobbes by insisting that 'I found no trouble at all in ye reading of y^r hand, wch in ye close of y^r letter you seemed to apprehend' (Letter 73). In the following year Hobbes enlisted the services of the Earl of Devonshire's baker at Chatsworth, James Wheldon, a writer of a neat, rounded italic script, who became his regular amanuensis. The first sign of his employment in Hobbes's correspondence comes in a letter from du Verdus of October 1656, which asks: 'But what am I to infer from the fact that, as I see, you are using an amanuensis or scribe and copyist? Have you been ill, or is it merely because of that infirmity which you told me

---

[5] 'Nullam vnquam, quod memini, Epistolam ad me, et à te, vel à Martello vel à Bosquio, vel à Prataeo perlatam esse cui non sit à me literis responsum' (Letter 112). For details of all these correspondents, see the Biographical Register.

[6] *ABL* i, p. 352.

about in a letter, the trembling of your hand?'[7] Probably as a result of his private employment by Hobbes, Wheldon also did some scribal work for the Earl of Devonshire: at Christmas in 1657 he was paid £1 for 'drawing a Catalogue of ye Bookes in ye Library at Hardwick, by yor Lordships Order from Mr Hobbes'.[8]

Eventually, the use of James Wheldon became so much Hobbes's normal practice that François du Prat, staying in Sorbière's house in Paris in 1663, could confidently identify a letter from Hobbes which 'I knew to be one of y.^rs, by ye superscription wch. is in Jame's hand'.[9] Wheldon's personal account book survives, with entries listing the total of gifts from Hobbes for each year from 1662 to 1679: it starts at £5. 2s. 6d., rises to a peak of £20. 12s. in 1669, and then settles to an average of £10 for each year from 1672 to 1679.[10] Hobbes was clearly making much use of his services; but however willing and helpful Wheldon may have been, the need for his assistance must have put something of a brake on Hobbes's letter-writing. How exactly Hobbes dictated letters in French and Latin to an uneducated and presumably monoglot baker can only be guessed at. A hint comes from Pieter Blaeu's letter to Hobbes of 1667, concerning Hobbes's translation of *Leviathan* into Latin: 'I fully understand that you are having it written down by someone else, because of the weakness of your hand, and that since he does not understand Latin, you are having it reread and corrected afterwards by someone else who understands it well.'[11] Hobbes may have followed a similar procedure with his letters; or he may, at least during the early years of Wheldon's employment, have provided him with rough copies in his own hand. Aubrey assures us that Hobbes could still write in 1665 or 1666;[12] but a description of Hobbes's condition from 1663 or 1664 suggests that his symptoms were then already quite severe. Robert Hooke, chancing upon Hobbes in an optical instrument-maker's shop in Long Acre, found him 'holding his

---

[7] Mais que doy-j'inferer de ce que je uoy que vous uous serués d'un amanuänse ou scribe et copyiste? Est ce que vous ayés esté malade; ou seulement pour cette incomodité que vous m'écriuites, que la main vous tremble?' (Letter 94).

[8] Chatsworth, MS Hardwick 14, entry for 26 Dec. 1657.

[9] Letter 155.

[10] Chatsworth, MS Hardwick 19. The starting-date is of no special significance; Wheldon only began keeping these accounts in 1661.

[11] 'J'ay bien compris que vous le faictes écrire par vn autre a cause de la foiblesse de vostre main, et puisque celuy là n'entend pas le latin, vous le faictes par aprés redire, et corriger par vn autre qui l'entend bien' (Letter 179).

[12] See above, n. 6.

spectakle in his hand, which shuk as fast one way as his head did the other'.[13]

One significant piece of evidence—significant in more than one way—can be added at this point. It is a letter written to a friend, Adam Barker, by James Wheldon from Hardwick in 1700, twenty-one years after Hobbes's death; and it is perhaps the most poignant statement that any Hobbes scholar could ever have stumbled across:

Mr Barker,

According to your earnest desire, I have sent you some of Mr. Hobbes's own hand-writing, towards the latter end of his time; but it is not fit to shew to any body; for his hand was so much given to shaking, for many years before he died, that he was ashamed his writing should be seen, so burned most of his own hand. With my kind respects, I remain your very loving friend,

James Whildon.[14]

Calligraphic embarrassment may have played some small part in this, but it seems an insufficient motive for such drastic action. A more likely explanation comes from Aubrey, who recalled: 'There was a report (and surely true) that in parliament, not long after the king was setled, some of the bishops made a motion to have the good old gentleman burn't for a heretique. Which he hearing, feared that his papers might be search't by their order, and he told me he had burn't part of them.'[15] Corroboration of Aubrey's dating of this incident comes from the evidence of Hobbes's manuscript tract on the law of heresy (written with the not disinterested intention of demonstrating that people should not be burned for heresy), which has been dated to *c.*1661.[16] On the other hand, the evidence from parliamentary sources suggests a date of October 1666: it was then that a committee considering a 'Bill against Atheisme Prophaneness and Swearing' was 'impowered to receive Informacion toucheing such bookes as tend to Atheisme Blasphemy or Prophanenesse or against the Essence or Attributes of God. And in perticular [. . .] the booke of Mr Hobbs called the Leuiathan.'[17] This date is certainly closer to what Wheldon calls 'the latter end of his time'. But whenever it was that

---

[13] Hooke to Boyle, in a transcript of a letter dated 'about the year 1664' (BL MS Add. 6193, fo. 69^r. Printed in Boyle, *Works*, v, p. 533, where it is dated '1663').

[14] *Gentleman's Magazine*, 54, part 2, no. 4 (Oct. 1784), p. 729.

[15] *ABL* i, p. 339.

[16] Chatsworth, MS Hardwick, drawer 145, no. 18 (see Mintz, 'Hobbes on the Law of Heresy', and, correcting his dating, Willman, 'Hobbes on the Law of Heresy').

[17] BL MS Harl. 7257 (journal of the House of Commons, 1665–6), p. 220 (17 [/27] Oct. 1666).

Hobbes's prudential *auto-da-fé* took place, we have no way of knowing what kind of writing it was that he consigned to the flames.

We can only guess, therefore, at the significance of the fact that not a single draft or copy of one of Hobbes's own letters survives among his papers. This is a striking fact, given that so large a proportion of the letters of so many philosophers and scientists of this period survives in the form of copies retained by them. Copies might be kept for obvious practical reasons—either because the writer had produced a rough draft anyway, or because it was judged a sensible precaution to retain a copy in case the letter miscarried. But increasingly, among learned men, copies were kept with the ulterior purpose of eventual publication. Pierre Chanut's advice to his brother-in-law Claude Clerselier, when the latter was sorting through Descartes's manuscripts after his death and planning his edition of the philosopher's correspondence, was that he thought it right to publish *only* those letters of which Descartes had retained the drafts: he had kept them, one could assume, because he intended eventually to publish them.[18] The practice of editing the correspondence of learned men was one of the boom industries of seventeenth-century publishing. A form of writing and publication which had once been largely the preserve of the humanist tradition, with its combination of moral *consilia* and the small change of classical scholarship, quickly broadened to include the letters of mathematicians, metaphysicians, and medical men. Clerselier's edition of Descartes's letters began to appear in 1657; when the edition of Gassendi's *Opera omnia* was produced in 1658, three years after his death, it was not thought strange that one of the six thick folio volumes should be devoted to his correspondence; and for the next few generations the reading public's taste for learned letters was satisfied by a whole series of important published collections, culminating in Brant's *Clarorum virorum epistolae* (1702) and Burman's *Sylloges epistolarum* (1727). One popular encyclopaedic reading-guide, Daniel Morhof's *Polyhistor* (1688), devoted two chapters to the letters, both published and unpublished, of learned men, recommending their study 'especially because more secret matters tend to be discussed in them'.[19]

Writers did not need to be dead before their letters could appear in print. In the same year as the appearance of the Gassendi *Opera omnia*, for example, John Wallis published his *Commercium epistolicum*, in which he

---

[18] See Paul Dibon's discussion of this point in 'Les Échanges épistolaires', p. 44.
[19] 'praesertim cum secretiora in illis tractari soleant' (p. 273).

printed letters which had circulated very recently between a number of English and French mathematicians. Behind such a volume as this, one senses the building up of that pressure for the instant publication of new ideas and research work which was to find release in the *Journal des sçavans* (from 1665), the *Philosophical Transactions* (also from 1665), the *Giornale de' letterati* (from 1668), and the *Acta eruditorum* (from 1682). It is often said that people such as Mersenne, who managed large networks of correspondence, were performing the function of a learned journal *avant la lettre*; there is much truth in this, but it must also be said that in one important sense they were creating the very problem which the learned journals were partly intended to solve. This was the problem of priority— and of how to prove it. Almost every major figure involved in the epistolary circulation of research during this period became embroiled sooner or later in squabbles over precedence and plagiarism. One thinks of Descartes's quarrels with Fermat and de Beaugrand, and his suspicions that Pascal had stolen ideas for his barometric experiments from his letters; of Roberval's quarrels with Torricelli (and with almost everyone else he ever dealt with); and of all the strange devices, anagrams and coded statements, by which scientists such as Pascal and Huygens sometimes tried to protect and circulate their discoveries at one and the same time.

Setting Hobbes against this background, we can sense how far removed such a way of doing things was from his own character and intellectual procedures. There is one exception that helps to prove the rule: his bruising encounter with Descartes in 1641. Readers can make up their own minds as to how the blame for this fracas should be apportioned. Despite the dignified style and measured humility of Letter 30, Hobbes's first surviving letter in the sequence—here, at least, one feels that he was writing for a potential audience as well—there are touches of intellectual cheekiness, such as his play of words on 'haereret',[20] which he must have known would rile the French philosopher. But the element of vicious scorn which entered into the exchange was Descartes's contribution; and so too was the suggestion of plagiarism. In fact Descartes must bear a double responsibility for the row about plagiarism here. Not only did he first suggest that Hobbes might have borrowed his theory of 'subtle body' from him (Letter 33), but he then misinterpreted Hobbes's reply to this point as a claim that he, Descartes, must have stolen the theory from Hobbes (Letter 36). When

---

[20] See pp. 63 and 71, where I translate it as 'I think he himself would be stuck'.

Descartes writes to Mersenne, 'I also beg you to communicate as little as possible to him of those of my opinions which you know, and which have not appeared in print',[21] this strikes an authentically Cartesian note. Hobbes's own view of the circulation of knowledge was set out in a grandiloquent but not absurdly self-justifying statement in his *Six Lessons*, when replying to a false accusation by Seth Ward that he had stolen his optical theories from unpublished manuscripts by Walter Warner:

But wheresoever you finde my Principles, make use of them, if you can, to demonstrate all the Symptomes of Vision; and I will do (or rather have done and meane to publish) the same; and let it be judged by that, whether those Principles be of mine, or other mens invention. I give you time enough, and this advantage besides, that much of my *Optiques* hath been privately read by others. For I never refused to lend my papers to my friends, as knowing it to be a thing of no prejudice to the advancement of Philosophy, though it be (as I have found it since) some prejudice to the advancement of my own reputation in those Sciences; which reputation I have alwayes postposed to the common benefit of the studious.[22]

In saying that the constant squabbles over priority in the letter-writing learned world were contrary to Hobbes's character and intellectual procedures, I do not mean to claim that he was either incapable of plagiarism or above accusing others of it. The suggestion, made by an anonymous correspondent of John Wallis (possibly none other than Hobbes's own friend John Vaughan), that Hobbes had borrowed ideas from Cavalieri without acknowledgement appears to be well founded;[23] and Hobbes in turn referred jokingly to Roberval's accusations of plagiarism (which he made against both Hobbes and Wallis) when he published a mathematical piece under the initials 'V.A.Q.R.'—meaning 'Un Autre Que Roberval', someone other than Roberval.[24] But what I do wish to suggest is that the constant needling

---

[21] 'Je vous prie aussy de ne luy communiquer que le moins que vous pourrez de ce que vous sçavez de mes opinions et qui n'est point imprimé' (see the general note to Letter 33).

[22] p. 59 (*EW* vii, pp. 342–3).

[23] See Letter 107 n. 1.

[24] This folio broadsheet, *La Duplication du cube*, was printed apparently in Paris. One copy survives at Chatsworth, classified as Hobbes MS, 'letters from foreign correspondents', letter 85. Hobbes discussed and defended it in the final section of his *Dialogus physicus*; Wallis described, translated, and refuted it in his *Hobbius heauton-timorumenos*, pp. 128–32. Hobbes discusses Roberval's peculiar obsession with plagiarism in *Examinatio et emendatio*, pp. 121–2 (*OL* iv, p. 188).

and elbowing of rivals, jostling to claim priority for each new idea or research finding in a merry-go-round of epistolary exchanges, was not Hobbes's way of doing things. And this is not just because he had either a finer moral sense or a thicker skin: it is a matter of his intellectual character at its deepest level.

Hobbes was a system-builder. This does not mean that he thought everything should be deduced from first principles, merely that everything should find its place in a general explanatory scheme of things. It was the large-scale construction, and the resulting interrelation of its parts, that was of consuming interest to him. He was not engaged in the kind of 'research' that could throw up discrete discoveries and propositions—here a new observation of the rings of Saturn, there a new formulation of the laws of impact, there a new design of clock. Whenever he assembles in one of his books (*Decameron physiologicum*, for example) a number of suggested explanations of separate physical phenomena—winds, tides, magnetism, spontaneous generation—one senses an air of diffidence in his performance, as if his heart were not really in it. The problem is not merely that these explanations are dependent on supposition (they propose, that is, 'possible generations' of effects, and are thus, according to one of his two conflicting theories of science, not examples of true science at all);[25] it is that even were such explanations to count as scientific, there would still be something unsatisfactorily contingent about selecting these items in particular from the sheer range of things that could be explained. It is the guiding principles, not their specific applications, that matter. As one of the speakers in *Decameron physiologicum* puts it on the final page of the text: 'The Questions of Nature which I could yet propound are innumerable. And since I cannot go through them, I must give over somewhere, and why not here?'[26] This is not the attitude of a man whose work advanced by means of an accumulation of research breakthroughs on specific points. The only specific breakthroughs that Hobbes was keen to claim and promulgate were his mathematical ones, especially his frequent squarings of the circle and duplications of the cube: and these were matters on which, alas, few rivals were likely to claim his discoveries as their own.

[25] See my 'Hobbes's Science of Politics', pp. 154–5.
[26] p. 131 (*EW* vii, p. 137).

A picture of Hobbes's working methods, at least in the latter part of his life, is supplied by Aubrey:

> he sayd that he sometimes would sett his thoughts upon researching and contemplating, always with this rule that he very much and deeply considered one thing at a time (scilicet, a weeke or sometimes a fortnight). [. . .] He rose about seaven, had his breakefast of bread and butter; and tooke his walke, meditating till ten; then he did putt down the minutes of his thoughts, which he penned in the afternoon.[27]

The advantages of this type of contemplative life, in the peace and intellectual solitude of Chatsworth or Hardwick, are obvious. But the disadvantage was recognized by Hobbes himself: 'he sayd, the want of learned conversation was a very great inconvenience, and that though he conceived he could order his thinking as well perhaps as another man, yet he found a great defect'.[28] The defect was noticed by his critics too. John Wallis observed that, '(as a great Person was pleased to phrase it) *He Thinks too much, and Converses too little*, either with Books, or Men'.[29] Wallis was the first to remark on Hobbes's tendency in his later works (beginning with *Examinatio et emendatio*, the object of Wallis's criticism here) to expound his arguments in dialogue form. Maliciously, but perceptively, Wallis described it as

> a Dialogue, between A and B (*Thomas* and *Hobs*;) Wherein *Thomas* commends *Hobs*, and *Hobs* commends *Thomas*, and both commend *Thomas Hobs* as a third Person; without being guilty of self-commendation. For this reason; and, because he hath found it difficult to converse with *others* without being Contradicted, and (so) Provoked; he might think it most convenient to *talk to himself*.[30]

Wallis may have identified a kind of process of sublimation here, by which Hobbes's desires for intellectual companionship found surrogate expression in a literary form. But of course Wallis could not resist combining this observation with the popular caricature of Hobbes as an irascible, intolerant, and dogmatic man. This caricature had wide currency, and was based on a genuine but partial truth: Hobbes could indeed be intolerant of contradiction, but only in company which he

---

[27] *ABL* i, pp. 338–9, 350–1.
[28] Ibid., i, p. 338.
[29] *Hobbius heauton-timorumenos*, p. 8.
[30] Ibid., p. 15.

felt was predisposed to hostility towards him.[31] If we had only the testimony of Wallis, Ward, Hooke, Boyle, and their friends to go by, we should have to conclude that Hobbes was by his very nature a solitary dogmatist, incapable of engaging in discussion or responding to criticism. Fortunately, however, we have the testimony of Hobbes's correspondence, which tells a rather different story.

Two limitations of the correspondence in this regard must of course be recognized. The first is the one-sidedness of what survives: Hobbes's replies to criticisms can usually be reconstructed only sketchily from the replies to his replies. And the second is the acknowledged disparity in intellectual stature between him and his most regular correspondents: in answering queries from du Verdus or Sorbière, Hobbes was not engaging with an intellectual equal in the way that he might have done with, say, Gassendi. (Though it must be said that Hobbes's two letters to Gassendi—Letters 62 and 66—are curiously slight, and that in the earlier of them Hobbes seems studiously to have avoided having to express an opinion on a technical matter which belonged rather to Gassendi's area of expertise than to his own.)

Within these limitations, nevertheless, the correspondence does yield important evidence of Hobbes's willingness to engage in debate, to consider criticisms, and sometimes as a result to revise or add to his works in subsequent editions. There is plenty of confirmation here of Aubrey's testimony about 'His Goodness of Nature, and Willingnes to instruct any one that was willing to be informed, and modestly desired it. wch I am a witnesse of, both as to my owne part, & also to others'.[32] Hobbes's long and punctual reply (Letter 117) to Sorbière's arguments about the vacuum (Letter 114) is not the work of a man intolerant of contradiction; and when he tells Sorbière, 'I eagerly await your opinion of those things which I wrote to you recently about the experiments at Gresham College', one feels that this is not a mere flourish of courtesy.[33] Du Verdus's heroic attempts to grapple with the English text of *Leviathan* prompted Hobbes to supply several further explanations and amplifications of the arguments of the second half of the book, one of which was incorporated into his Latin revision of the

---

[31] See my discussion of this point in 'Hobbes and the Royal Society', pp. 48–50.

[32] Bodl. MS Aubrey 9, fo. 46ᵛ.

[33] 'sententiam tuam auidé expecto de ijs quae nuper tibi scripsi circa experimenta Londini nuper exhibita in Collegio Greshamensi' (Letter 146).

text.[34] And perhaps the shrewdest criticisms of Hobbes's political philosophy came from du Verdus's young friend François Peleau, whose objections Hobbes dutifully answered, but not always to Peleau's satisfaction.[35] Although Hobbes's 'skirmish' with de Sluse (Letters 156, 161, 165) showed an undeniable streak of mulish stubbornness, we should not forget his earlier graceful acceptance of criticisms of the geometrical sections of De corpore by Mylon, two of which Hobbes himself quoted in print.[36]

Hobbes's French friends were to play an important part in the textual history of several of his works. Proofs of De homine were apparently sent to du Verdus several years before its publication;[37] the text of Problemata physica was corrected in the light of comments made by du Verdus and the astronomer Jean Picard in 1664;[38] and the entire project of publishing Hobbes's works in Latin (the Opera omnia of 1668), including his new translation of Leviathan, would probably never have come about were it not for Sorbière in particular and, in general, the constant pleas of Hobbes's French friends for a translation of Leviathan into a language they could understand. In return, Hobbes was kept in touch with some of the latest developments in French intellectual life, with reports of new publications by Cureau de la Chambre or Maignan, a lecture by Roberval, discussions at the house of de Montmor, and new researches or forthcoming publications by Pascal, Fermat, Pecquet, Boulliau, Vatier, and others. The letters Hobbes received from Sorbière about the de Montmor 'academy' (most of them hitherto unpublished) constitute the fullest description of the atmosphere and workings of that important scientific gathering; and other letters from Sorbière also enable us to identify two hitherto unrecognized works by Gassendi.[39]

To Hobbes, the psychological value of this attention and admiration was considerable. He referred proudly in one of his works to Sorbière's

---

[34] See Letter 108 n. 13.

[35] Letter 110.

[36] See Letter 76 n. 19.

[37] See Letter 68 n. 7.

[38] See Letter 163 n. 20. This letter casts interesting light on a hitherto unknown episode of Picard's life.

[39] On the de Montmor 'academy' see Letters 133, 150–2. The two works which Sorbière confidently attributed to Gassendi are the two polemical replies to Morin published under the name of Sorbière's fellow disciple of Gassendi, François Bernier (see Letter 105 n. 6).

translation of *De cive*, for example ('The Book it self translated into French hath not onely a great Testimony from the Translator *Serberius*, but also from *Gassendus*, and *Mersennus*'),[40] and when he wrote in 1674 that 'my reputation, such as it is, took wing a long time ago and has soared so far that it cannot be called back', he was surely envisaging a trajectory that headed south, across the Channel.[41] The asymmetry between the attitudes taken to Hobbes by his contemporaries at home and abroad must have been painfully obvious to Hobbes himself. Few Hobbes scholars seem to have commented on it, however, until Quentin Skinner published these acute remarks:

> There are grounds for suggesting [...] not merely that the conventional account of Hobbes's total rejection is false, but that it has arisen from a partial view of the evidence, from excessive concentration on a parochial English reaction. Hobbes was widely denounced in England, but he seems to have been widely accepted abroad. We have to square his unthinking rejection by many English critics with the equally unthinking discipleship implied by many of his foreign correspondents.[42]

That Hobbes was commonly described in England as a promoter of atheism, a defender of arbitrary and iniquitous rule, a repudiator of the basis of morality, etc. is well attested. That these conclusions were inescapable for any contemporary reader of his works, even only in England, is far less obvious: the intriguing letter to Hobbes from Edward Bagshaw (Letter 134), treating him with respect as a valuable ally in the defence of Calvinist theology, is sufficient counter-evidence. To give a full explanation of the hostile reaction to Hobbes in English intellectual circles would involve weaving together many different strands from the political history, ecclesiology, and theology of the period.[43] It is hard to believe that John Wallis, for example, would have devoted so much of his time and energy to his vendetta with Hobbes, had he not had more important underlying motives than the mere conviction of geometrical error. As Hobbes himself explained to Sorbière, 'My quarrel with him is not like the quarrel between

---

[40] *Six Lessons*, p. 56 (*EW* vii, p. 333).

[41] 'fama enim mea qualicunq; est jamdudum pennata evolavit irrevocabilis' (Letter 197).

[42] 'Thomas Hobbes and his Disciples', p. 163.

[43] I have discussed one strand, Hobbes's uncomfortable closeness to the proponents of 'rational religion' in Restoration England, in 'Hobbes and the Royal Society', pp. 60–6.

Gassendi and Morin or Descartes. I was dealing at the same time with all the ecclesiastics of England, on whose behalf Wallis wrote against me.'[44] Henry Stubbe's long series of letters to Hobbes from Oxford supplies valuable evidence of the real nature of the contest against Wallis, with both geometry and grammar serving as stalking-horses for ecclesiology. In Interregnum Oxford Wallis was regarded as a leader of the Presbyterians, a defender of the 'Kyrke'—in other words, a prime representative of those claims to spiritual jurisdiction in temporal affairs which Hobbes was determined to refute.

The contrast here between Hobbes's English critics and his French friends is remarkable, not least because so many of his French friends and admirers were in fact Presbyterians themselves—that is, members of the French Protestant Church. Out of all the varieties of organized Christianity, the two forms that Hobbes criticized most fiercely were Roman Catholicism and Presbyterianism; and yet, extraordinarily, when we list his closest French friends we find that they were nearly all of them either Presbyterians or Roman Catholic priests. Mersenne was a Minim friar; Gassendi was a priest; even du Verdus was a subdeacon. (Other more distant admirers included the abbé Bourdelot, the abbé Picard, and Michel de Marolles, abbé de Villeloin.) On the Huguenot side we have the brother and the son of a minister (Abraham and François du Prat), the cousin of a well-known minister and the representative of a leading family from the Huguenot stronghold of Montauban (de Martel), and the nephew of a famous minister (Sorbière) who was for several years the director of a Huguenot academy before, for good measure, publicly announcing his conversion to Catholicism. We even have a friendly letter (Letter 173) to Hobbes from one of the most famous Huguenot preachers of his age, Alexandre Morus, whose Hobbesian connection has hitherto been unknown.

How important the Protestant background of so many of these people was to Hobbes is difficult to estimate. Partly, no doubt, it is just a reflection of the extent to which the English community of visitors and *émigrés* in France tended to associate with Huguenots—who could be employed, for example (like François du Prat), as tutors to their children without danger of perverting them to Rome. It also reflects the general intellectual vitality of the Huguenots in this period, stimulated

---

[44] 'Controuersia inter me et illum non est similis controuersiae inter Gassendum, et Morinum vel Cartesium mihi res erat cum omnibus simul Ecclesiasticis totius Angliae in quorum gratiam scripsit contra me Wallis' (Letter 112).

as they were by their connections with Holland, the intellectual entrepôt of Europe. Whether Hobbes ever argued with these friends about their Presbyterianism we do not know; but he must have been aware of the debates over whether or not to attend the Huguenot Church at Charenton which agitated Anglicans in Paris such as his patron Lord Scudamore or his old acquaintance George Morley. Perhaps it was sufficient for Hobbes's purposes that the Huguenot Church was not a national Church endowed with temporal power, and existed only on sufferance from the French King.

As for the priestly status of Mersenne and Gassendi, this reflects one of the special features of intellectual life in the seventeenth-century Catholic world, the role of the Church (and especially of orders such as the Minims and the Jesuits) in the teaching and publication of mathematics and science. We know that Hobbes and Mersenne amicably agreed to disagree on matters relating to Catholicism (though Mersenne did ensure the publication of the whole of *De cive*, including its final section on religion, which du Verdus had to omit from his French translation of the work). And Gassendi, in his letter of commendation printed in the third edition of *De cive*, simply excepted from his praises Hobbes's treatment of religious matters, 'in which we are of different opinions'.[45] Most interesting of all is the case of du Verdus, who, although his subdiaconate was a mere formality, was nevertheless a devout Catholic with an increasingly messianic tinge to his faith. His letters to Hobbes display both a hearty enthusiasm for the attack in part 4 of *Leviathan* on the scholastic and Catholic 'Kingdome of Darknesse', and a capacity to talk about God's judgements or blessings which shows no sign of fear on du Verdus's part that in writing like this he may thereby be exposing himself to Hobbes's ridicule. If, on reading these letters, one tries to sum up what it is that so marks the distinction between France and England, one has surely to say that in Catholic France anticlericalism was still an understood and accepted part of people's mental world. Anticlericalism was not only alive and well, but it was also recognized as something quite different from atheism. (Du Verdus was accused of 'atheism' by the Jesuits in Bordeaux; but they, as he explains, had special reasons for hostility towards him.) In England, on the other hand, whether because of the effects of Puritanism, or of the Laudian campaign in the Church, or because of more deep-rooted reasons to do with the different social

---

[45] 'in quâ sumus ἑτερόδοξοι (*HW* ii, p. 85).

conditions of the priesthood, this valuable distinction had been obscured—as Hobbes, an archetypal anticlericalist, was to discover to his cost. 'Do you think I can be an Atheist and not know it?' he asked John Wallis, unanswerably, 'Or knowing it durst have offered my Atheism to the Press?'[46] Whether, knowing it, he offered it to the post, may also be doubted; and certainly the surviving evidence of the correspondence offers no levers by which the evidence of his published works could be overturned. The closest we ever come to a discussion of this issue is in an extraordinary little letter from François Peleau, touching on 'a rather ticklish subject, namely the non-existence of a God distinct and different from the world'.[47] But Hobbes's answer to that letter does not survive. Whether a draft of his reply was later consigned to a bonfire or a stove at Chatsworth, Hardwick, or Little Salisbury House in the Strand can never now be known.

II

As I have suggested, Hobbes did not usually write letters with the prospect of publishing them uppermost in his mind—or even present in his mind at all. He does not seem to have been offended when Sorbière published part of one of Hobbes's letters in his *Relations, lettres et discours* in 1660.[48] But even after this, he apparently had no idea of the way in which every letter that reached Sorbière or passed through his hands was liable to be copied and filed away, for possible future publication: answering de Sluse's criticisms in 1663 (which he had received from Sorbière), Hobbes ingenuously returned de Sluse's letter with his reply (Letter 161), thinking that without the original letter Sorbière would be unable to follow the argument. In a handful of cases Hobbes was evidently writing either directly for publication (Letter 197) or with the idea that his letter could be made use of in some form or other (Letters 145, 184). But most of his surviving letters seem to be genuinely private documents. And this in turn has some consequences—but not purely negative ones—for the stylistic character of these writings.

---

[46] *Six Lessons*, p. 62 (*EW* vii, p. 350).
[47] 'vne Matiere vn peu chatouilleuse, telle que la Nullité de l'existence d'vn Dieu, distinct, et different, du Monde' (Letter 120).
[48] See Letter 140, general note.

No form of writing, however private or informal, can be altogether free of literary conventions. Ordinary personal correspondence, otherwise known as 'familiar letters', became a published literary genre during Hobbes's lifetime—first with the immensely popular *Epistolae Ho-elianae* of James Howell (1645), then with two minor collections of letters by Robert Loveday (1659) and Thomas Forde (1660), and then with the *Sociable Letters* of Hobbes's patroness the Marchioness of Newcastle (1664). But long before such works were published, the standard English textbook on letter-writing, Angel Day's *The English Secretary*, had given serious attention to the stylistics of familiar correspondence. Day's book ran through at least nine editions; it was first published in 1586, two years before Hobbes's birth, and the last edition was in 1626, two years before the end of Hobbes's employment as 'Secretary' to the second Earl of Devonshire.[49] *The English Secretary* had a significantly double-edged argument: on the one hand, Day regarded a plain style as the natural manner for letter-writing, while on the other hand he was also keen to demonstrate that every variety of 'Tropes, Figures, and Schemes' (as he put it in the long title of his book) could also be put to epistolary use.

Seeing an Epistle hath chieflie his definition herof, in that it is tearmed the familiar and mutuall talke of one absent friende to another: it seemeth the Character thereof, should according thereunto be simple, plaine, and of the lowest and meanest stile, vtterlie deuoid of anie shadow of hie and lofty speaches: yet neuerthelesse [. . .] in the argument of a great many of them [. . .] is required (as I said before) a more high and loftie deliuerance, partaking manie waies with that kinde accustomed in Orations.[50]

'Breuitie of matter', he suggested, was intrinsic to the nature of a letter:

For which cause some haue beene of opinion, that continuance of matter ought not to be vsed in an *Epistle*, for that it thereby looseth the shew of an *Epistle*, and taketh vpon it the habit of an *Oration*: Yet of such sort are in this *method* sundry *Epistles*, the titles whereof are; *Hortatorie, Dehortatorie, Laudatorie, Vituperatorie, Suasorie, Petitorie, Monitorie, Accusatorie, Excusatorie, Consolatorie, Inuectiue* and such like, whose speciall vses do of necessitie admit such scope as in everie

---

[49] Hobbes is described as 'Secretary' to the late Earl both on the title-page of his translation of Thucydides, and in the legal document drawn up by him and the third Earl in 1639 (Chatsworth, MS Hobbes D. 6, fo. 2ʳ).

[50] *The English Secretary*, part 1, p. 8.

ordinarie Epistle is not found, and though they beare in them many *Oratorie* parts, yet lose they not at all for all that, neither name nor habit of an *Epistle*.[51]

Day's claim that even the most simple familiar letter about 'common and ordinarie matter' must have the structure of a classical oration (exordium, propositio, confirmatio, confutatio, peroratio) was far-fetched, of course. One widely circulating type of letter, the news-letter from Court to country or from foreign land to England, naturally developed a simpler narrative-episodic structure of its own: Hobbes was certainly well acquainted with this type, having translated the entire series of news-letters sent by Fulgenzio Micanzio from Venice to the second Earl of Devonshire between 1615 and 1625.[52] The long letter to Hobbes from Robert Mason (Letter 1), albeit written 'here amongst yᵉ Clerks in Cambr.', also belongs to this genre, and helps to illustrate the nature of the stylistic pressures on even such a simple form of communication as this. Mason (like George Aglionby in Letter 3) can hardly touch on a topic without turning it round in a witty conceit, adding a jest or a pun, drawing a moral, applying a fable, or weaving in a classical quotation. And this ornate performance, we should remember, was written on terms of approximate social equality, by a don gossiping with a tutor; we should then try to imagine what elaborate flourishes Mason would have performed had he been writing to the Earl of Devonshire or the Duke of Buckingham.

If we bear these two kinds of stylistic pressure—artistic and social—in mind, we can notice the distinctive character of Hobbes's epistolary style (or styles) almost from the earliest examples of it. His attempts at news-letters are perfunctory; the recitation of public facts does not interest him, and since he is even more uninterested in dressing up such recitations in the finery of fables and quotations, he keeps these matters to a minimum. 'This towne [i.e. Orléans] is without newes' (Letter 7); 'There is no newes at Court but of Maskes' (Letter 10); 'you may with more reason looke for letters from me thence [i.e. from France], where euery thing will be newes, then from this place, where nothing has bene newes to me a great while' (Letter 11); 'All that passeth in these parts is equally Newes, & therefore no Newes' (Letter 17). Where the etiquette of address to a social superior or patron is concerned, Hobbes employs a style which is seldom effusive; but that

---

[51] *The English Secretary*, part 1, pp. 2–3.

[52] Chatsworth, Hobbes MSS, 'translations of Italian letters'; a transcript is BL MS Add. 11309. See my *De Dominis*, pp. 49–50, and Gabrieli, 'Bacone, la riforma, e Roma'.

does not mean that he is perfunctory. The very neatness, the artful economy, of his flourishes implies a kind of stylistic self-consciousness which itself expresses Hobbes's sense of his position, largely obviating the need to state it: 'I haue receaued yor Lo^{ps} guift, proportioned to your owne goodnesse, not to my seruice' (Letter 16); or again, 'your letters [. . .] haue bene [. . .] great spurres to my endeauor, but it seemes yor Lo^p thinkes siluer spurres haue a greater effect, wch is an errour, but such a one as I see more reason to thanke you for, then to confute, and therefore wth my most humble thankes I end this point' (ibid.). Only in some of his letters to Sir Gervase Clifton do we sometimes find Hobbes putting together little more than airy confections of compliments— and, characteristically, saying so at the same time: 'In such sterility of matter, and infelicity of brayne, it resteth that out of the bowells of my affection I spinne out a line or two to assure you that I [>am] sensible of your fauors',[53] and so on (Letter 14). Even in these letters, however, there is usually a single focus on a not-too-elaborate metaphor or conceit: one striking example is the 'perspectiue glasse' which Hobbes uses in Letter 13 both to construct a simile and to remind his patron (in a gentle in-joke) of Hobbes's own scientific preoccupations.

If one or two of these letters strike the reader as over-elaborate, he should bear in mind the far more formal, mainly French-influenced, pseudo-courtly style which Hobbes was reacting against.[54] Jaded by the experience of reading a volume of letters by Jean-Louis Guez de Balzac, James Howell wrote:

Others there are among our next transmarine Neighbours Eastward, who write in their own Language, but their Style is soft and easy, that their Letters may be said to be like Bodies of loose Flesh without Sinews, they have neither Joints of *Art* nor *Arteries* in them; they have a kind of simpering and lank hectic Expressions made up of a Bombast of Words, and finical affected Compliments only: I cannot well away with such sleazy Stuff, with such Cobweb-compositions, where there is no Strength of Matter, nothing for the Reader to carry away with him, that may enlarge the Notions of his Soul.[55]

Fine specimens of such cobweb-compositions will be found in the present edition in the letters of Thomas de Martel, some of which, if

---

[53] '[>am]' is an interlineation: see the section below, 'Principles of transcription'.

[54] Day gives a fine example of the 'ridiculous maner of writing' (*The English Secretary*, part 1, p. 6).

[55] *Epistolae Ho-elianae*, i, p. 19.

boiled down for their factual content, would yield no residue at all. When Hobbes, on the other hand, has to write formal letters of compliment (such as Letter 145), his style becomes more pithy and Senecan, not less. There is a tendency here towards the sententious, in the strict sense of the term: that is, towards the employment or development of *sententiae*. Letter 28 is an especially good example of this style, a letter of reproof which is comparable to (and, incidentally, far better than) the model of a 'dehortatory' or 'disswasorie' epistle in Day's book.[56] Addressed to the Hon. Charles Cavendish, a headstrong student at Paris, it has something of the character of a formal, public performance (we can imagine that the most demanding reader Hobbes had in mind while writing it was not the student himself but his mother, who would scrutinize the final draft); yet the balance between universal *sententiae* and Hobbes's special kind of psychological analysis is maintained throughout. 'And of the two quipping & reviling the former is ye worse, because being the same iniury, it seemes to hide itself under a double construction, as if a man had a good will to abuse another but were afraid to stand to it. Whereas ye words of a Gentleman should be perspicuous & justifiable & such as shew greatnesse of couradge not spleene.'

This is a splendid but an untypical performance. Hobbes is at his most characteristic when he is most at his ease, writing purely private correspondence which explains an idea, pursues an argument, or punctually replies to a query. Sometimes the writing slackens stylistically as a result, with Hobbes's easy, speaking tone (for example, in Letter 58) turning the sequence of the phrasing into something almost too casual. That is a fault which the Latin language, with its natural effects of syntactical stiffening, helps to correct—though Hobbes's Latin epistolary style still contrasts strongly with the self-conscious, quotation-riddled, over-elaborate performances of writers such as Sorbière. Hobbes was evidently at ease writing in Latin (though, oddly enough, not at ease speaking it);[57] but one thing which shines through less clearly in his Latin letters is his surprisingly gentle and self-deprecatory sense of humour. Du Verdus preserved one example of it when he told Hobbes he was charmed by 'your comment that I should have two teachers, a writing master to read your letters,

---

[56] Day's model letter is also aimed at the moral improvement of a student (*The English Secretary*, part 1, pp. 76–9).

[57] See L. Huygens, *The English Journal*, p. 75.

and an English master to understand your French'.[58] In a similar vein, we have Hobbes's remark to the Earl of Newcastle that 'I haue a cold that makes me keepe my chamber, and a chamber, (in this thronge of Companye that stay Christmas here) that makes me keepe my Cold' (Letter 24). That strikes the authentic Hobbesian note.

It is not, I think, mere courtesy on the part of Hobbes's friends that they tell him so often that his letters have given them delight. 'You are a good friend, a good courtier, and of the best temperament in the world', wrote Sorbière to Hobbes in 1664; 'I remember [. . .] the gaiety of all your conversations last year, which I shall always remember as one of the happiest times of my life.'[59] Of Hobbes's conversations we have only a few precious fragments, preserved by John Aubrey. But in the letters which have come down to us we may also catch an echo here and there of 'the familiar and mutuall talke of one absent friende to another'.

---

[58] 'Ce que vous me dites [. . .] qu'il me faudra deux maistres: l'ecriuain pour lire uos lettres; et celuy de la langue Angloise pour aprendre vostre françois' (Letter 84).

[59] 'Vous estes bon ami, bon Courtisan, & de la meilleure humeur du monde. Je m'en rapporte [. . .] à la gayeté de toutes uos conuersations de l'annee passee, dont je me souuiendray tousjours, comme d'un des plus beaux endroits de ma uie' (Letter 166).

TEXTUAL INTRODUCTION

A DESCRIPTION OF THE MAIN MANUSCRIPTS

The principal manuscripts and/or groups of manuscripts (excluding individual letters in separate volumes) are as follows.

Bibliothèque nationale, Paris

MS f.fr. n.a. 6206: one of three bound volumes of Mersenne's correspondence (the others being MSS f.fr. n.a. 6204, 6205) assembled from his papers after his death by his friend and biographer, Hilarion de Coste. (For a fourth volume in the set, see the section 'Missing letters', below.) One other Hobbes letter, formerly contained in this volume, is now at Harvard (Letter 59).

MS f.l. 10352: this large folio volume is a collection of Sorbière's correspondence, transcribed from Sorbière's copies of the letters he sent and the originals of the letters he received, by his son, Henri (see the entry for Sorbière in the Biographical Register). It is in two parts, each foliated separately: part 1 contains letters from Sorbière, and part 2 letters to him. Henri Sorbière seems to have been a faithful transcriber, though there are signs that he had trouble sometimes in reading Hobbes's hand.

Bodleian Library, Oxford

MSS Aubrey 9, 12: collections of notes, memoirs, and materials assembled by John Aubrey. MS Aubrey 9 contains the main text of his draft biography of Hobbes. Material from these Aubrey MSS is also transcribed in BL MS Egerton 2231; but that is clearly a much later transcript with no textual authority.

MS Rawlinson D 1104: this manuscript is inscribed 'Rich. Holdsworth, Archdeacon of Huntingdon, & Maʳ of Emanuel Coll.', and it also contains some letters by him. Holdsworth (1590–1649) was first a Fellow of St John's College, Cambridge (like Hobbes's correspondent Robert Mason, whose letter is contained in this manuscript), then Master of Emanuel College (1637). His large personal library included nearly 200 manuscripts. The transcripts of Hobbes's letters in this manuscript appear to follow his original spelling, and the transcripts from Digby reproduce his idiosyncratic use of 'j' for first person 'I'—which suggests that the copyist had the originals in front of him. An associated set of transcripts, in Bodl. MS Rawlinson C 232 (retrograde), appears to be copied from MS Rawlinson D 1104: the main text of MS Rawlinson C 232 is in the same hand as MS Rawlinson D 1104, but the retrograde section is in a different, hastier hand. (Evidence that it was copied from MS Rawlinson D 1104 can be found in Letter 28, where MS Rawlinson D 1104 has a word which looks at first sight like 'Chattisworth' but is in fact 'Chattesworth': MS Rawlinson C 232 has 'Chattisworth'.)

British Library, London

MS Add. 32553: a bound volume containing a group of letters to Hobbes, mainly from Henry Stubbe, but also including letters from Aubrey, Barlow, Mylon, Pullen, and Tanny. It was previously in the collection of the antiquary James Crossley (1800–83): a note at the beginning of the volume records that it was acquired 'at Sotheby's (Crossley sale) 20 June 1883'. Since these letters bear precisely the same style of endorsement (by James Wheldon) as the group of 'letters from foreign correspondents' at Chatsworth, and since that group also contains letters from Stubbe, Mylon, and Tanny, it seems likely that the letters now in BL MS Add. 32553 were originally extracted from the Chatsworth group and given or lent to Crossley by the Duke of Devonshire.

MS Add. 70499: this volume, formerly MS Loan 29 (Portland)/235, is a collection of the correspondence of the first Duke of Newcastle, previously preserved at Welbeck Abbey.

Chatsworth, Derbyshire

Hobbes MSS, 'Letters from foreign correspondents': this collection of letters has remained at Chatsworth since Hobbes's death. White Kennett recorded, in a memorandum added to the entry on Hobbes in Wood's *Athenae*: 'When I was at Chatsworth, after the funeral of the duke of Devonshire in Sept. 1707, [. . .] Mons. Huet told me, there was an old trunk of his [sc. Hobbes's] papers in the house, containing chiefly the correspondence between him and foreigners.'[1] What

---

[1] iii, col. 1217.

remains is hardly a trunkful, and it may be suspected that some letters have subsequently been detached from this collection (see the entry for BL MS Add. 32553, above). The numbering of these letters is modern; it attempts to place them in chronological order, though my redating of some of the letters disrupts the sequence.

Hobbes MSS: the classification of the Hobbes MSS at Chatsworth is modern, and it is possible that some items unconnected with Hobbes have ended up in this group. Letters 139 and 148 should probably both have been classified with the 'letters from foreign correspondents' (above); 139 was probably excluded from that group because its nature as part of the Sorbière correspondence was not recognized, and 148 was excluded because it was mistakenly believed to be a letter in Hobbes's own hand.

Nottingham University Library, Nottingham

Clifton MSS: the Clifton correspondence, consisting mainly of the correspondence of Hobbes's employer, Sir Gervase Clifton, is deposited (with other Clifton papers) at Nottingham University Library, having previously been at Clifton Hall, Clifton (Notts.).

Royal Society, London

MS H. 1: one of the collections of letters received at the Royal Society, arranged in volumes by Henry Oldenburg.

PRINCIPLES OF INCLUSION

This is an edition of letters to and from Hobbes. I have not attempted to include letters between third parties which happen to mention Hobbes (some of which are listed in E. G. Jacoby's 'Epistolarium Hobbesianum').[2] An edition including such material is an unsatisfyingly open-ended thing, and the fact that these other people's references to Hobbes occur in letters can only be contingently related to the principal purpose of an edition of Hobbes's own correspondence. (What matters in these third-party cases is not that the material is in letter form, but that it mentions Hobbes; in which case, why not include mentions of Hobbes in diaries, journals, notebooks, news-sheets, and so on?)

[2] In Tönnies, *Studien*, p. 363–75.

What counts as a letter is more easily recognized than defined. Not everything that begins with a salutation and ends with a valediction is a letter; nor is everything that is sent from one individual to another by post or hand. Criteria for inclusion can be derived from the concept of *correspondence* more readily than from the idea of a letter. Thus the dedicatory epistles to Hobbes's works, although in letter form, are not part of Hobbes's correspondence, and are not included here: they will be printed in their proper places in the Clarendon edition, with the works to which they belong.[3] Similarly, the fact that a printed work is in letter form does not automatically qualify it for inclusion here; if it did, this edition would have to contain not only Hobbes's 'Answer' to Davenant's Preface to *Gondibert*, but also the Preface itself, formally a letter from Davenant to Hobbes (which occupies forty-four pages in its modern edition). Other such candidates would include the whole text of *Of Libertie and Necessitie* (written in the form of a letter to the Marquess of Newcastle), the 'Extract of a Letter' from Stubbe printed in *Markes*, the entire text (excluding the section by André Tacquet) of Moranus' *Animadversiones*, and perhaps even the text of *Mr Hobbes Considered*, which, though in the form of a letter to Wallis, is unsigned and refers to Hobbes in the third person. All the works by Hobbes just mentioned (including Stubbe's 'Extract of a Letter', which is an intrinsic part of Hobbes's text) will have their proper places elsewhere in the Clarendon edition; so too will Hobbes's printed addresses to the Royal Society. I have admitted here only those printed letters which, in my judgement, have something of the character of correspondence: in other words, letters which are not just short treatises that happen to be in letter form, but which are rooted in circumstance and specific to the individuals to whom they are addressed. (Inevitably, there are borderline cases. Letter 201 *is* a short treatise, but it comes clothed in a sufficient minimum of circumstantial details; and it would not otherwise find a place in the Clarendon edition. Letter 197 was evidently intended for publication. But despite its public nature, this work has the character of a letter rather than of a treatise.)

Conversely, there may be short unprinted pieces of writing by Hobbes, sent through the post, which do not count as letters: for

---

[3] I agree here with Jean Mesnard, who argues persuasively against the inclusion of dedicatory epistles in editions of correspondence ('A propos de la correspondance de Pascal', p. 85). I have excluded even the dedicatory epistle to *Behemoth*, which, though highly untypical of the genre, is part of the MS fair copy (St John's College, Oxford, MS 13), and is surely more of a public performance than it claims to be.

example, the geometrical proposition in Hobbes's hand which was enclosed in a letter from Sir Charles Cavendish to John Pell in 1645.[4] Strictly speaking, Hobbes's petition to Charles II (Letter 210) is not a letter either; but whereas Hobbes's occasional mathematical writings will find a natural home in the volumes of his mathematical works in this edition, there is no more natural place for a personal petition to the King than in this volume. Where all excluded writings by Hobbes are concerned, the reader has the consolation of knowing that they will eventually appear elsewhere in the Clarendon edition. Where writings sent to Hobbes are concerned, this consolation will not apply; I am therefore inclined to be more liberal in my admission of such material. But my guiding principle has been that the material must be either a letter to Hobbes or an enclosure which belongs to a surviving letter to Hobbes. In one case I have drawn this rule even more tightly, excluding the enclosure to one letter (Letter 81) on the grounds that it is merely a manuscript copy of a printed work, the text of which is easily available elsewhere. I have relaxed the rule in only one instance: the manuscript by M. de la Moulinière, printed here as Letter 139, which was enclosed in a letter (itself now lost) from Sorbière to Hobbes. I have included this item because of its intrinsic interest as a discussion of a passage in *Leviathan*; because the letter in which it was sent can be precisely dated; and because it is referred to by Hobbes in his next letter to Sorbière. (Had I not printed it as Letter 139, I should have had to reproduce most of it in any case as a note to Hobbes's letter, in order to explain his comments there.) Otherwise, to start including things which were once enclosed in no-longer-extant letters would be to open wide the floodgates: various manuscript treatises by other authors which survive among Hobbes's papers at Chatsworth may well have been sent to him by post under covering letters, but it would be absurd to print them here as enclosures to letters which no longer exist. Also excluded, therefore, are letters which survive among Hobbes's papers and were presumably forwarded to him at some stage, but which are neither by him nor to him: a letter from François du Verdus to Andrew Crooke, and a letter from John Wallis to an unnamed nobleman.[5] Such

---

[4] BL MS Add. 4278, fo. 200.

[5] Chatsworth, Hobbes MSS, letters 23, 51. The letter from Wallis, which refers to Hobbes in the third person, ends 'Dominationis vestrae observantissimus' (roughly, 'Your Lordship's most dutiful servant'): the most likely recipient was Lord Brouncker. This letter is omitted from the calendar of Wallis correspondence published by Christoph Scriba ('A Tentative Index').

material would only be included here if it had been enclosed in a letter to Hobbes which also survives. It is under this rule that I have included such items as Sir Kenelm Digby's account of the possessed nuns of Loudun, du Verdus's French translation of chapter 4 of *Leviathan*, and his bizarre lesbian love-poem in Italian blank verse.

One other category must also be mentioned: letters to a third party for Hobbes. This includes the two letters from Huygens, of which the former at least was sent explicitly for Hobbes; and it would include the two letters from de Sluse, except that they both take their places anyway as enclosures in letters from Sorbière. Otherwise the only letters to third parties for Hobbes are those sent by Descartes to Mersenne. Here Descartes has fortunately made an editor's task very easy: he distinguishes the sections that he wishes to be forwarded to Hobbes by writing them in Latin. These sections alone, therefore, are included in this edition.

NON-LETTERS

The following items, described as letters by other scholars, are not included in this edition, either because they are not letters to or from Hobbes, or because they are not letters, or because they do not exist.

Jean de Beaugrand to Hobbes: a manuscript copy of a work by de Beaugrand, 'De la manière de trouver des tangentes des lignes courbes par l'algèbre et des imperfections de celle du S. des C.', surviving in a group of Sir Charles Cavendish's papers (BL MS Harl. 6796, fos. 155–61), is incorrectly described by Michael Mahoney as a letter to Hobbes.[6]

William Brouncker, Viscount Brouncker, to Hobbes: Jacoby lists this in his 'Epistolarium';[7] it is printed in *HOC* iii, pp. 342–3, where it is also presented as a letter from Brouncker to Hobbes. It is a refutation (beginning: 'The Authors first mistake') of the geometrical proposition which Hobbes had presented to the Royal Society in September 1661.[8] Brouncker wrote this refutation at the Royal Society and sent it, via Sir Robert Moray, to Huygens.[9] He may well have sent a copy to Hobbes

---

[6] *The Mathematical Career of Fermat*, p. 50.
[7] Tönnies, *Studien*, p. 372.
[8] See the entry 'Hobbes to Charles II', and the MS references given there.
[9] See HOC iii, p. 336; the MS, in Brouncker's hand, is LUL MS Hug. 45, fos. 895–6.

too; but even if such a copy survived among Hobbes's papers, it could not be properly described as a letter.

Christian Cavendish, Countess of Devonshire, to Hobbes: Jacoby lists this in his 'Epistolarium',[10] but the document he refers to (now classified as Chatsworth, MS Hobbes D. 6) is a legal statement, not a letter.

William Cavendish, Marquess of Newcastle, to Hobbes: this is described by Kathleen Jones as follows: 'A letter still survives from Newcastle to Hobbes, written in 1648 in Paris, concerning "perspective glasses" which Hobbes had bought for him.'[11] This refers, I believe, to NUL MS Pw 1. 406 (Cavendish Misc. 43), which is not a letter but a 'Memorandum' by Newcastle, dated 'Paris the 21ᵗʰ off Julye 1648', recording his indebtedness to Hobbes for a loan of 106 pistoles, and endorsed by his son, Lord Mansfield, to the effect that Hobbes may dispose of 'the prospective glasses' in lieu of repayment.

Hobbes to William Cavendish, third Earl of Devonshire: Jacoby lists this in his 'Epistolarium' as an unpublished letter dating from 1679, and describes it as 'undated'.[12] He refers to Tönnies, *Thomas Hobbes: Leben und Lehre*, p. 62, where Tönnies mentions the dedicatory epistle to a manuscript treatise by Hobbes on cyclometry (now classified as Chatsworth, MS Hobbes A. 9). As I have explained above, I do not regard dedicatory epistles as correspondence.

Hobbes to Charles II: Jacoby lists this as a letter in his 'Epistolarium'.[13] It is the geometrical proposition, entitled 'To find two mean Proportionals between two streight lines giuen', which Hobbes submitted to the Royal Society in September 1662, having secured a request from the King that the Fellows of the Society give it their consideration; it was answered by Brouncker (see the entry for Brouncker's non-letter to Hobbes, above). It is printed as a letter to Charles II (from Brouncker's transcript) in *HOC* iii, pp. 339–41. Other transcripts of this item are in BL MS Sloane 243, fos. 68–72; R.Soc. Register Book 1, pp. 99–100; R.Soc. Register Book Copy 1, pp. 101–3; and PRO SP 9/7/19, pp. 158–61.

Hobbes to Mr Finny: although this manuscript (Chatsworth, MS Hobbes D. 7) is listed by Peter Beal as a letter to '? Mr Finny or Hinny', I am

---

[10] Tönnies, *Studien*, p. 363.

[11] *A Glorious Fame*, p. 118.

[12] Tönnies, *Studien*, p. 375.

[13] Ibid., p. 372.

confident that it is neither to Mr Finny, nor from Hobbes.[14] It is a small scrap of paper with, on one side, an instruction in the hand of the third Earl of Devonshire, beginning 'Write to M.r ffinny that he has hindred me in Gringley and South Leverton, and that he must throw open his inclosures.' On the other side, in a different hand, is the rough draft of a letter. However, it is clear from the contents of this draft that it has nothing to do with the instruction on the recto. The handwriting of the draft resembles, at a first glance, a small but quite regular version of Hobbes's hand. However, I believe that it is in fact the hand of James Wheldon. There are two reasons for reaching this conclusion: first the hand itself, and secondly the contents, which show that it must date from 1679. The hand is that of the endorsements on most of the letters to Hobbes from foreign correspondents at Chatsworth, which is distinguishable from Hobbes's hand: these endorsements were probably made after Hobbes's death by his executor, James Wheldon. Being cramped and tiny in this instance, it does not obviously resemble the main surviving specimens of Wheldon's hand, all of which are very fair copies. But certain letters, notably 'w' and most of the majuscules, reveal Wheldon's hand; and as he discovers towards the end of the draft that he has paper to spare, the writing becomes larger and more regular, and more obviously his own. Although less even than his fair hand, it lacks that jaggedness and what might be called angular momentum which always characterized Hobbes's own rough hand.

As for the dating of this manuscript, the evidence can most easily be presented by printing it in full. (For an explanation of the conventions used here, see the section 'Principles of transcription', below.)

S.r

My hon:ble Lord [the Earle *deleted*] was yesterday at Welbeck, and his grace ye Duke of Newcastle desired my Lords [Velds?] in Nottinghamshire for M.r Jervas Pierpont beleeving he [was *deleted* >is] a fit p[er]son[15] to be chosen Knight of ye Shire for y[on]d.r[16] County this next Parliament to serue both the King & yt County. and Mr Ballock[17] not being here [>my Lord] commanded me to [write vnto *deleted* >desire] you to acquaint his frends and tenants [>at

---

[14] *Index of English Literary Manuscripts*, ii, part 2, p. 569. Since I checked Dr Beal's section on Hobbes before publication, I must fully share the responsibility for his error.

[15] Contraction expanded.

[16] Contraction expanded.

[17] Unidentified, but evidently a clerk or servant of the third Earl of Devonshire.

Turton & bea[sto]n Velds][18] with this matter, and I make no doubt but you [>they herein] will readily [doe it, *deleted*] comply with his Lo.ps desire, which he will take well at their hands.

Gervase Pierrepont (*c.*1656–1715), youngest son of the Hon. William Pierrepont, was proposed as a candidate for Nottinghamshire in the general election of March 1679, and stood (unsuccessfully) in the election of October 1679.[19] This draft can be no earlier than late January or early February 1679. On 24 January [/3 February] 1679 the Earl of Danby wrote to the Duke of Newcastle, informing him that Parliament had been dissolved and a new Parliament called for 6 [/16] March; he said the King had commanded him 'to lett y^r Grace know from him, that hee desires you will promote as much as you can the choice of good members in those places wch are influenced by yor Grace'.[20] Hobbes was 90 or 91 when this draft was written, and had suffered from the progressive onslaught of the 'shaking palsy' since the 1650s; it is highly unlikely that he could have written such a tiny and, for him, regular hand at this time, or indeed that his patron would have thought of employing him on such business.

Hobbes to John Pell: Jacoby lists this as an unpublished letter, dated 22 April 1645, in his 'Epistolarium'.[21] He refers, however, to Hervey, 'Hobbes and Descartes', p. 74, where it is correctly stated that this letter, although mentioned in another letter by Pell, is not extant.

Edward Hyde to Hobbes: Hyde's notes on *De cive* (Bodl. MS Clarendon 126, fos. 8–18^r) occasionally appear to address Hobbes in the second person; this has led Colum Hayward to suggest that they may constitute the draft of a letter to Hobbes.[22] Hyde in fact writes in the third person here, using the second person only once or twice for rhetorical questions. These jottings may have later supplied some of the material

---

[18] 'beaston' is a conjectural expansion. These references are possibly to Toton and Beeston Fields. Toton (also spelt 'Towton', 'Touton', 'Toveton') and Beeston (pronounced locally without the 't') were villages south-west of Nottingham; Toton Fields and Beeston Fields are both local place-names, and 'Feld' was a common termination for 'Field' in Notts. (see Gover *et al.*, *Place-Names of Nottinghamshire*, pp. 139, 152, 281).

[19] Henning, *House of Commons 1660–1690*, i, p. 350.

[20] BL MS Add. 70500, fo. 120^r.

[21] Tönnies, *Studien*, p. 366.

[22] Hayward, 'The *Mores* of Great Tew', p. 196.

1

for a letter to Hobbes, but they are several steps away from being even a rough draft of a letter.

Other items in Jacoby's list which do not correspond to letters printed in this edition are either dedicatory epistles to Hobbes's works, or the results of misdatings or misidentifications.

MISSING LETTERS

How can an editor of an author's complete correspondence know that his edition is complete? The short answer is that he cannot. Although I am hopeful that I have included all letters ever mentioned in scholarly works on Hobbes, I also think it likely that other letters, not known either to me or to other Hobbes scholars, will eventually turn up. At an early stage in my work I sent questionnaires to approximately 350 libraries and archives in Europe and America; I am very grateful to all the librarians who answered my queries, but have to confess that not a single new Hobbes letter was discovered by this method. One archivist reassuringly told me: 'with a figure as important as Hobbes, if a library has something by him, it knows about it, and the world will know about it too'. This is roughly true of Hobbes,[23] but it does not of course apply to obscure figures such as du Verdus and de Martel; and many collections catalogue letters under the name of the writer only, not the recipient. The letter from Adrian May to Hobbes, for example (Letter 49), was correctly listed as a letter to Hobbes in the catalogue of the Harleian manuscripts, published nearly 200 years ago; but since this letter is itself the only piece of evidence of any connection between May and Hobbes, no Hobbes scholar has ever had occasion to look May up in the catalogue, and the letter has remained unknown—until I chanced upon it. In my questionnaire to French and Belgian libraries I enquired also about any letters by Hobbes's known French and Belgian correspondents (drawing a blank there too). The intensive researches conducted by the editors of the Mersenne correspondence have not uncovered any new Hobbes material, and this encourages me to think that any hidden Hobbes letters in French archives must be very well hidden indeed. (However, since France has nothing equivalent to the publications of the Historical Manuscripts Commission for the

---

[23] Very roughly, as my references elsewhere in this edition to MSS in Copenhagen and Leipzig (correctly identified in the catalogues of those libraries, but hitherto unknown to Hobbes scholars) will suggest.

coverage of private archives, the scope for new discoveries in that country is certainly not exhausted.) But the most likely resting-places of unknown Hobbes letters are, I suspect, inadequately calendared family archives and small private collections in the United Kingdom.

There can be little point in trying to compile a list of all the letters, now apparently lost, which happen to be mentioned either in Hobbes's correspondence or in correspondence between third parties. Whether specific letters get mentioned or not is largely contingent; some references to correspondence are quite unspecific; and in addition we have Hobbes's general assurance in Letter 112 that he replied to every letter he received from his French friends. Of the various entire collections of letters from Hobbes which appear not to have survived, the most desirable would perhaps be those he sent to François du Verdus from England from the 1650s to the 1670s, and those he sent to Robert Payne from France in the 1640s and up till the latter's death in 1651. But du Verdus's papers passed into the hands of a devout Roman Catholic priest (see the Biographical Register, 'du Verdus'), and there is no record of any Hobbes items being preserved thereafter. Hobbes's letters to Payne may even have been returned eventually, with other Payne papers, to Hobbes (see the Biographical Register, 'Payne'): in which case the chances of discovering them now must be judged slim, since the one place where scholars have searched rather thoroughly for Hobbes correspondence is among Hobbes's own papers.

When listing manuscripts in the head-notes to the letters, I have distinguished between 'unknown' and 'unlocated' manuscripts: the former means what it says, while the latter implies that the manuscript is known to have been intentionally preserved for some time after Hobbes's death—in some cases, up until the nineteenth century (Letters 37, 63) or even the twentieth (Letter 184)—but cannot now be traced. Fortunately, the complete or partial texts of these letters do survive in some form or other. But there are other letters, known to have been intentionally preserved for some time after Hobbes's death, of which the text has never been recorded. Of these, the following four can be described in some detail.

Hobbes to Marin Mersenne, 5 [/15] November 1640: this is the long letter, criticizing Descartes's optical theories and putting forward Hobbes's own explanation of refraction, to which Descartes replied so acerbic-ally in Letters 29 and 32. Although the date of it is not mentioned there, it is known to have been preserved in a bound volume of Mersenne correspondence after Mersenne's death (the fourth such volume: see above, under 'A description of the main manuscripts', the entry for BN MS f.fr. n.a. 6206). This volume, consisting mainly of letters from Pierre Fermat to Mersenne, disappeared some time in the late eighteenth or early nineteenth centuries, but not before the mathematician Louis-François Arbogast (1759–1803) had listed its contents, including 'a long letter from Thomas Hobbes, addressed to Mersenne, dated 5 November 1640, 56 folio pages'.[24] The disappearance of this letter (and of the rest of the volume) has been blamed in the past on the bibliophile, French government surveyor of manuscript collections, and unparalleled kleptomaniac Guillaume Libri (1803–69). But Armand Beaulieu has demonstrated that this is one crime of which Libri was innocent: when Libri himself published one of Fermat's letters to Mersenne, he relied on a transcription by Arbogast, having no access to the original.[25]

The contents of those fifty-six folio pages—evidently, more a treatise than an ordinary letter—are not entirely lost, however. As Frithiof Brandt first demonstrated, the final section of the letter, as quoted and controverted by Descartes, corresponded very closely to the short treatise on optics by Hobbes which Mersenne published in his *Universae geometriae synopsis* in 1644 (and which, to prevent confusion, is referred to in this edition as Hobbes, 'Optica').[26] What Brandt failed to observe, on the other hand, was that several of the statements quoted by Descartes from the earlier part of Hobbes's letter correspond very closely to statements in Hobbes's Latin manuscript treatise on optics (BL MS Harl. 6796, fos. 193–266, which, to prevent confusion, is referred to in this edition as Hobbes, Latin Optical MS). Brandt was led by other arguments to suppose that the Latin Optical MS was written several years later; but those arguments are inconclusive, and have been largely undermined by the discovery of another Hobbes manuscript (unknown when Brandt was writing), his criticism of Thomas White (referred to in this edition as Hobbes, *Anti-White*). The evidence against Brandt's argument, and further considerations too,

---

[24] 'une longue lettre de Tho. Hobbes adressée à Mersenne du 5 nov. 1640, en 56 pages in fol.' (see Fermat, *Œuvres*, i, p. xxviii; de Waard, 'A la recherche de la correspondance', pp. 22–3; *MC* x, p. 210).

[25] Beaulieu, 'Voies ardues pour l'édition d'une correspondance', p. 52n.

[26] Brandt, *Hobbes' Mechanical Conception of Nature*, pp. 93–7. Brandt was unaware, however, of Arbogast's reference; and he confused matters somewhat by treating the two successive instalments of the letter received by Descartes as two separate letters.

have been cogently presented by Dr Richard Tuck to show that the Latin Optical MS was written (as Tönnies originally suggested) between 1637 and 1640.[27] To this I would add one further line of argument which seems to me conclusive, showing as it does that the surviving copy of the Latin Optical MS was transcribed for Sir Charles Cavendish, in England, before Hobbes's departure from London to Paris at the end of 1640.

This transcript is one of a group of transcripts with certain common features, all of them copies of works evidently derived from Mersenne in Paris. They include de Beaugrand's treatise on tangents, Le Maire's 'Méthode pour la musique almérique', Descartes's 'Recueil du calcul qui sert à la géometrie', and de Beaune's 'Notes brièves'.[28] Of these, the Descartes piece is inscribed in Sir Charles Cavendish's hand: 'Mr Des Cartes his tract sent me by Mersennus March 1 1640'.[29] We know that this work was requested by Sir Kenelm Digby in a letter to Mersenne of 14 [/24] February 1640: 'you will greatly oblige me by letting me see it, and I shall send it back to you. If you give it to M. du Bosc, he will have it delivered to me by secure means.'[30] Whether it came via du Bosc (who was an old friend of Hobbes, having been connected with the Cavendish family since the 1620s), or whether it came directly from Mersenne, it seems very likely that this was the copy which reached Sir Charles Cavendish on 1 [/11] March.[31] The importance of this part of the evidence is that it indicates that the manuscript was meant to be returned to Mersenne, so that Sir Charles may have had it for only a short time before passing it on to Digby (or back to Mersenne). The version surviving in BL MS Harl. 6796 is very probably, therefore, a transcript made by an amanuensis working for Sir Charles at some time very close to 1 [/11] March 1640. And this is important, because the

[27] 'Hobbes and Descartes', pp. 19–27.

[28] BL MS Harl. 6796, fos. 155–61, 175–7, 178–92ʳ, 267–90.

[29] Ibid., fo. 178ʳ. A modern annotation underneath this inscription incorrectly identifies it as in Hobbes's hand.

[30] 'Vous m'obligerez beaucoup de me le faire voir, et ie vous le renuoyeray. Si vous le donnez a Monsr du Bosc, il me le fera tenir seurement' (MC ix, p. 122).

[31] See de Waard, 'Un écrit de Beaugrand', p. 168n. However, de Waard supposes that the MS was returned to Mersenne almost immediately; he bases this supposition on Digby's letter of 5 [/15] Mar. 1640, where Digby says he returned Descartes's 'introduction [...] à l'Algebre' a fortnight ago. This may refer instead to de Beaune's 'Notes brièves'; or perhaps Digby returned it via Sir Charles Cavendish, in which case Sir Charles's inscription on the transcript is a little misleading.

crucial unnoticed feature of this transcript, the transcripts of the works by de Beaugrand and de Beaune, and the Hobbes Latin Optical MS is that not only are they in the same amanuensis's hand, but they also contain geometrical or optical diagrams drawn and lettered in Hobbes's hand. (This is evident in the case of the Latin Optical MS, which also has annotations and corrections in Hobbes's hand, and it becomes evident when one compares the diagrams in that work with those in the other three.) I have not found other examples of this amanuensis's hand among Sir Charles Cavendish's papers, and therefore doubt whether he can have been anyone in his regular employ. It is not necessary to suppose that all these works were copied out in quick succession in February or March 1640; but it is necessary to conclude that they must all have been transcribed before Hobbes left England at the end of that year. He was not to see Sir Charles again until 1645, in Paris.

So, both for the reasons just stated and on internal grounds, we may suppose that the missing letter from Hobbes to Descartes of 5 [/15] November 1640 drew directly on the material which is contained in the Latin Optical MS. It is for that reason that I have used both it and Hobbes's 'Optica' as sources in my annotations to Letters 29 and 32.

François du Verdus to Hobbes, [6/] 16 May 1654: this letter was offered for sale by the Parisian dealer, Gabriel Charavay, in 1917. The entry from his catalogue was reproduced in an article by Ulysse Bigot. The letter was described as consisting of three quarto pages, and summarized as follows: 'He writes to Hobbes first about trigonometrical calculations, and tells him that during the recent troubles he had to hide his books and papers in the house of a *bourgeois* on the Rue Saint-Denis. He dwells on his relations with Gassendi, who is going to have his "Epicurus" printed. He would like to know English in order to read Hobbes's *Leviathan* fluently.'[32]

Hobbes to an unnamed colonel, and to Sir John Birkenhead, late 1669 or 1670: in 1669 Daniel Scargill, an allegedly dissolute Fellow of Corpus Christi College, Cambridge, was obliged to perform a public recantation in the

---

[32] 'Il lui parle d'abord de calculs trigonométriques et lui raconte que durant les derniers troubles il a dû cacher ses livres et ses papiers chez un bourgeois de la rue Saint-Denis. Il insiste sur ses rapports avec Gassendi, qui va faire imprimer son Épicure. Il voudrait savoir l'anglais pour lire couramment le *Léviathan* de Hobbes' (Bigot, 'Une lettre inédite', p. 273).

University Church of St Mary's for having held 'divers wicked, blasphemous, and Atheistical positions [. . .] professing that I gloried to be an *Hobbist* and an *Atheist*; and vaunting, that Hobbs should be maintained by *Daniel* that is by me'.[33] After this recantation had been published, Hobbes wrote a reply or protest, in the form of a letter, for publication. Aubrey recorded the following in his biographical notes on Hobbes (written probably in early 1680): 'Mr Hobbes wrote a letter to . . . . . . [>a Colonell, as I remember] concerning Dr Scargill's Recantation sermon preached at Cambridge, about 1670. wch he putt into S^r Jo: Birkenheads hands to be licensed, wch he refused (to collogue & flatter the Bishops) & would not returne it, nor [>give] a copie: Mr Hobbes kept no copies, for which he was sorry he told me he liked it well himselfe.'[34] To this Aubrey later added a further note: 'Dr Birket (my old acquaintance) hath the ordering of S^r Jo: Birkenheads Bookes and Papers; he hath not found it yet, but hath found a letter of Mr Hobbes to him about [it] & hath promised me if he finds it to let me have it. M[emorandu]m S^r Ch: Scarborough told me y^t he hath a Copie of it, but I could not obtain it of him: but I will try again, if Dr Birket cannot [find it. *page torn*].'[35] There are thus two texts which had apparently been preserved: one of Hobbes's letter to 'a Colonell' for publication, and the other of his letter to Sir John Birkenhead. But there is no trace of either of these elsewhere in Aubrey's papers. The mystery is rendered more mysterious by the fact that Aubrey had apparently already tracked down a copy of Hobbes's letter to the colonel several years earlier. On 29 August [/8 September] 1676, he wrote to Anthony Wood: 'I am to write to him [sc. Hobbes] tomorrow & after neer a yeares search have found out his l[ette]re concerning Dr Scargills recantation sermon, a copie wherof he had not, & much desired it, & if you please you shall have a Copie.'[36] Wood mentioned

---

[33] Scargill, *The Recantation*, p. 4. See the discussions of this episode in Krook, 'Recantation of Scargill', and Mintz, *Hunting of Leviathan*, pp. 50–2.

[34] Bodl. MS Aubrey 9, fo. 54^v. The passages presented in square brackets here are interlineations: see the section below, 'Principles of transcription'.

[35] Ibid., fo. 55^r. The word 'it', placed in square brackets here, is omitted in the MS; 'Memorandum' is an expanded contraction; for other conventions used here, see the section below, 'Principles of transcription'. Aubrey's friend Dr Henry Birket or Birkhead (1617 or 1618–96) would have known the courtier and littérateur Sir John Birkenhead (1616–79) when they were both Fellows of All Souls in the early 1640s. For Sir Charles Scarborough, see Letter 199 n. 14.

[36] Bodl. MS Ballard 14, fo. 119^r: 'lettere' is an expanded contraction.

the work in his entry on Hobbes in *Athenae*, giving one or two more circumstantial details: '*Defence in the Matter relating to Dan. Scargil Bach. of Arts of C. C. Coll. in Cambridge*, written in one sheet; a copy of which sir John Birkenhead had in his possession; which, after his death, came into the hands of Hen. Birkhead.'[37] No copy has been found among Wood's papers either.

PRINCIPLES OF TRANSCRIPTION

With four exceptions, all transcriptions of manuscript letters have been either made directly from the originals, or made in the first instance from photocopies or photographs and then taken back to the originals and checked against them. The exceptions are the three letters in American archives (Letters 59, 66, 88), which have been transcribed from photographs, and the letter at Bowood House (Letter 198), which has been transcribed from the microfilm in the Bodleian Library. In these cases it is possible that the odd comma or accent is a speck of dust on the negative.

My aim has been to reproduce as accurately as possible the original text, altering or omitting only those kinds of detail which are of no importance to the study of its meaning. Thus the original lineation of the text is not preserved;[38] from printed sources, catchwords and running-titles are omitted; but the original spelling, capitalization, and punctuation have been adhered to. The only exceptions to this rule are that long 's' has been normalized, the ligatures æ and œ are presented as 'ae' and 'oe', and simple, unambiguous contractions (for example, 'bonū', 'comunis') have been silently expanded. The capitalization of texts from manuscript sources is occasionally, nevertheless, a matter of editorial judgement: in some hands there is no distinction in shape between the capital and lower-case forms of some letters, merely indeterminate gradations of size. ('M' and 'C' are particularly troublesome in this respect.) Some writers of this period employ an initial form of a letter which differs in shape from its medial form; this may

---

[37] iii, col. 1215.

[38] There is one exception to this rule: the French formula used in addressing the cover of a letter, which begins:

A Monsieur
  Monsieur Hobbes.

Here the lineation is retained, being treated as a paragraph break.

resemble a capital letter, but in cases where it is applied indiscriminately to all words beginning with that letter, it does not perform the function of a capital, and has been disregarded accordingly. The accentuation found in French and Latin texts, though sometimes erratic (especially in the French), has been reproduced as accurately as possible; so too has the use of superscripts. In punctuation, only gross offences against logic have been corrected in the text, with the uncorrected reading given in the apparatus: this is usually a matter of restoring the missing second half of a pair of parentheses or inverted commas. In some instances, a full stop is followed by a new clause beginning with a lower-case letter. This is not an offence against logic, but a recognized convention of seventeenth-century punctuation. As late as 1687 one standard English textbook could state: 'A *Period* [. . .] is placed at the bottom of the Line, and is markt thus, (.) A *Semiperiod* may have the same mark, but distinguisht from the former by a less breach in the line, and the word following beginning with a small Letter.'[39]

Some readers may wish that I had presented a modernized version of the texts, doubting whether anything of significance can be learned from the preservation of original punctuation, spelling, etc. If so, they should consider the following extract from Letter 16, as partially modernized by the editors of HMC, *Portland*. Hobbes is commenting here on the work of Walter Warner:

I would he could give good reasons for the facultyes and passions of the soule, such as may be expressed in playne English, *if* he can; he is the first—that I ever heard of—could speake sense in that subject. If he cannot I hope to be the first.[40]

In this version of the text, Hobbes appears to acclaim Warner as the first person ever to have spoken sense about the faculties and passions of the soul; he seems to imply that if anyone can discuss these matters in plain English, it is Warner. Yet what Hobbes actually wrote was as follows:

I would he could giue [a *deleted*] good reasons for ye facultyes & passions of ye soule, such as may be expressed in playne English. [I do *deleted*] if he can, he is

---

[39] Cooper, *English Teacher*, pp. 114–15. Cooper noted that the semicolon 'dayly comes more into use' as the sign for a semiperiod. By the time Cooper wrote, it had in fact almost entirely supplanted the full stop for this purpose in printed texts; but handwriting lagged decades behind the printed word.

[40] p. 126.

the first (that I euer heard [>of) could] speake sense in that subiect. if he can not I hope to be ye first.

As will be explained below, the first two sets of square brackets represent deletions, and the third an interlineation. If the reader omits the material in the first two, and includes the material in the third, he will obtain the version of the passage that represents Hobbes's final intentions—which turns out to be saying almost the opposite of the modernized version. Hobbes is not hailing Warner as the first to speak sense in that subject: he is lumping him with all the other writers who have been unable to discuss such things in plain English. Seeing the two deletions and the interlineation here also gives us some sense of how Hobbes's pen wavered at this point, as he struggled to make his true feelings plain without seeming over-scornful or immodest; and the shift from 'heard' to, on second thoughts, 'heard of' nicely upgrades the magnitude of the philosophical task which Hobbes was now setting himself to perform.

Conventions used in the transcriptions and notes

One purely editorial convention has been used in the presentation of each letter: the salutation, valediction, signature, place and date of writing, postscript, address, and endorsement are presented in that order, according to a uniform format. In most cases this is not at variance with the organization of the original, but occasionally it means transposing the place and date of writing, or the postscript, from the head of the letter to its foot. Another convention used throughout this edition is that words presented in italics here represent words underlined in the original. (Other forms of emphasis, such as over-lining, may also be presented in italics, but these cases are specified in the notes.)

A simplified method of formulaic transcription has been used, in order to present information about the text as conveniently as possible within the text itself. Had the bulk of the correspondence consisted of very rough drafts, a different method of transcription would have been chosen; but in most cases the method used here does not, I believe, clutter the page intolerably. Only in one instance (Letter 192, a much-altered draft) will it seriously impede the reader: there I have also supplied a clear-text reading version of the letter in the general note.

The following rules of transcription apply.

Uncertain readings

The word or passage is enclosed in square brackets, and followed by an italicized question mark (or unitalicized, if the text itself is in italics at that point). Thus:

I have [delivered *?*] your letters

Deletions

Where the deleted words are legible, they are presented in square brackets, followed by the italicized word '*deleted*' (or unitalicized, if the text itself is in italics at that point). Thus:

I have [sent *deleted*] delivered your letters

I have tried to present in this way all legible deletions that amount to a whole word or more; in a few cases I have also presented deleted beginnings of words, where they seem significant. But I have not usually bothered to present deleted words if those same words were merely being held over by the writer to a later point in the same sentence: thus I do not present deletions of the form

I have [quickly *deleted*] delivered your letters quickly

Where the word or passage is not legible, I state in square brackets the extent of the deletion. Thus:

I have [*two words deleted*] delivered your letters

Interlineation

Interlined material is presented in square brackets, preceded by a '>' sign, which is meant to be reminiscent of a caret mark. Thus:

I have [>not yet] delivered your letters

Such material is placed at the point where the original caret mark stands (if present) or should stand; but the original caret mark itself is not reproduced. Where an interlineation replaces material originally written on the line and then deleted, the deletion is presented first, and the two sets of square brackets are fused into one. Thus:

I have [already *deleted* >not yet] delivered your letters

Other information in the text

Other information is presented in self-explanatory formulas (always within square brackets), such as [*page torn*] or [*word blotted*]. (Blotting, as opposed to deletion, is presumed to be unintentional.) These formulas may be combined with conjectural restitutions of the text. Thus:

I have [*page torn* deli]vered your letters.

Textual information in the notes

Not everything can be presented in the text itself. A variant reading from another manuscript or printed source will be either presented in the notes, or (if it is judged to be a superior reading) promoted to the text and the inferior variant of the copy-text presented in the notes. In all such cases, the note is keyed to the text with a superscript reference number, and square brackets are not used in the text. If the version recorded in the note substitutes several words, these will begin with the last word which both versions of the text had in common: to perform the substitution, the reader should work backwards from the superscript number in the text until he reaches the initial word of the passage in the note.

If, however, a word or passage is presented in square brackets in the text and keyed to a different reading in the note, this means that the material in the square brackets is an editorial emendation, replacing an obvious error in the copy-text or supplying an evident omission. In such cases, the note records the original reading. The square brackets mark the fact that the word itself has been supplied or corrected by me, not simply transferred from an alternative version of the text.

Other textual notes will be self-explanatory. Two useful conventions are taken from Warrender: the use of the swung dash, '~', as a handle by which to hold solitary punctuation marks in the textual apparatus, and the use of the equals sign to introduce notes explaining the meaning of a word. As mentioned above, small and unambiguous contractions are silently expanded in the text; but in cases involving any possible room for doubt, the expansion is presented in square brackets in the text, and the word is keyed to a note: 'Contraction expanded'.

THE ARRANGEMENT OF THE NOTES

The head-note

After the date, name of correspondent, and place of writing, I give the source of the text. In the case of manuscripts I have tried to list here all the known copies of the letter; but the copy-text is always the first manuscript listed (unless I state otherwise in the notes to the letter). Usually, where there are several manuscripts, the first one listed is the original letter and the other copies are transcripts derived from it: in these cases I have checked the transcripts, but have not normally admitted any variants from them. When listing the manuscripts, I try to distinguish between original letters in Hobbes's hand, original letters in the hand of an amanuensis, original letters in the hand of an amanuensis but signed and/or corrected by Hobbes, drafts, autograph copies (i.e. not drafts but copies made and usually retained by the author), and transcripts.

I then list previous printings of the text. In the case of Hobbes's correspondence with Descartes and the two letters from Leibniz, I have included here only first printings and major editions; in all other cases I have tried to give a comprehensive list (excluding only reprintings and subsequent editions of the publications listed).

The unified sequence of notes to the text

Most editions of this kind of material use two sequences of notes: textual notes (recording variants, etc.), keyed to superscript letters or listed by line number, and explanatory notes, keyed to superscript numbers. I have combined both kinds of note in a single system, for three reasons.

The first is typographical. Superscript letters are already present as part of the text; to have additional superscript letters tacked on to them would be confusing. The traditional series of asterisk, dagger, double dagger, etc. would be insufficient for those letters (not too many, fortunately) which carry a large number of textual notes. And line-numbering would need to be applied to some pages but not to others, producing a visually uncomfortable effect.

The second reason is organizational. For letters in French or Latin, the sequence followed in this edition is: text—translation—notes. If two distinct sets of notes are used, of which one applies only to the text, not to the translation, the sequence must then be: text—textual notes—

translation—explanatory notes. Readers subjected to such a sequence quickly run out of patience and thumbs.

The third reason is that although many readers will work mainly from the translation, this will not be because they are Frenchless or Latinless: they may like to be alerted to the presence of textual notes, even though those notes demand recourse to the original text as well. In a unified sequence of notes, the reader of the translation is made aware of the existence of all the notes. However, for the sake of those readers of the translation who are not concerned with the textual variants of the original, I have distinguished the superscript numerals of textual notes in the translation by enclosing them in brackets. Readers uninterested in textual matters may disregard these notes. Where a textual note and an explanatory note coincide at the same point, I have used a single superscript and not bracketed it.

The general note and numbered notes

In many cases I have placed before the end-notes (the numbered notes at the end of each letter) a general note: this explains the sigla used in the end-notes, and specifies which copies of printed sources have been used. The general note may also discuss the circumstances of the writing of the letter, or what is known about any reply to it, if the reply itself now appears to be lost. Questions of attribution and dating are also discussed in the general note. With some of the mathematical letters, the general note also includes Dr Graeme Mitchison's summary of the argument of the letter in modern notation (over the initials G.M.).

The numbered end-notes are, as I have said, both textual and explanatory. In the latter category I have tried to identify names, book titles, quotations, etc. Where biographical information is given without reference to specific sources, the reader can assume that it will be found in standard reference works such as the *Dictionary of National Biography*, the *Dictionary of Scientific Biography*, the Belgian *Biographie nationale*, the *Dictionnaire de biographie française* (for names up to G), the *Nieuw nederlandsch biografisch woordenboek*, and the still valuable *Nouvelle biographie générale*. I am especially indebted to the first two of these, though I have sometimes had to correct matters of chronology or publishing history in the *DSB*. A few names are left unidentified, for fear of insulting the reader: thus I have not thought it necessary to have notes identifying Euclid, Galileo, Pascal, Cromwell, or Louis XIV. Otherwise, the following rule is strictly adhered to: the only names which receive no annotation in the end-notes are those names for which entries can be found in the Biographical Register at the end of the book. (But where the reference in the letter is ambiguous—for example, 'M. du Prat', which could refer to either of the two du Prats in the Biographical Register—I do attempt to assign a Christian name in a note.) All other names are annotated at their first mention in each letter. In a few cases (John Wallis being the most obvious), the reader may tire of being directed to an explanatory note in letter after letter. But when editing a book of this kind one has to recognize that most readers will not start at the beginning and read to the end; a book of letters can be opened and read at any point. This means that the annotation of each letter must be self-sufficient—not presuming cumulative knowledge in the reader, but either supplying what he needs to know, or directing him to other notes which will supply it.[41]

One other form of potentially tiresome note must also be acknowledged here. Whenever a letter to or from Hobbes is mentioned, this receives a note. If the letter survives, its place in this edition is referred to by letter number. Otherwise I record the fact that it has not apparently survived. I say 'apparently', because it is always possible that some of these letters will turn up one day. If that happens, they can be printed in a later volume of the Clarendon edition; and it will then be convenient to be able to cross-reference them to specific notes here, however redundant such notes may seem to be at present.

Despite the proliferation of notes in some cases, I should like to claim that my approach to annotation has been reasonably minimalist. In adding references to Hobbes's works, I have usually followed the rule that the note should tell the reader what Hobbes's letter is referring to, not what it reminds me of. In other words, I have usually avoided the kind of note which says: 'Hobbes also discusses this topic in the following places in his published works . . .'. Such notes, though possibly stimulating to the reader, are not elucidations of the letter itself. (For an apparent exception to this rule, see my comments on Hobbes's lost letter to Descartes and his Latin Optical MS and 'Optica', in the section 'Missing Letters', above.) I have also avoided the type of note which says: 'For an interesting discussion of this aspect of Hobbes's thought, see the following recent article . . .': such notes

---

[41] There is one small exception to this rule: the names of places from which letters are regularly written (e.g. Hardwick) are not explicated every time. The reader's patience and my dutifulness must both have their limits, and I can only hope that they roughly coincide.

are too quickly outdated. And I have a particular antipathy to the kind of anachronistically subjective note which, say, compares Hobbes to Kant.

However, the notes which identify individuals are sometimes fuller than is strictly required for an understanding of the mention of that person in the letter; it is my hope that in this way a little of the texture of Hobbes's intellectual milieu will be filled in, though without such details becoming too obtrusive. The degree of detail is influenced partly by the person's proximity to Hobbes, so that his old friends receive more attention than his casual acquaintances. But the general principle governing such notes as these is an inverse law of historical importance: well-known figures who are listed in standard reference works are dealt with more summarily than minor figures for whom the reader would otherwise have no easily available source of information. The pursuit of minor details about minor figures may sometimes be distracting, but from time to time it has thrown up valuable information which would otherwise have remained obscure. (To give just one example: a 'Mr Benoist' is mentioned only once in the correspondence, as the man who performed the errand of delivering a book to Hobbes in 1662. It might seem an excess of zeal on the part of an editor to try to put together a biographical sketch of such a person; but had I not attempted to do so, I should never have discovered the nature of his connection with Hobbes's old friend and disciple Thomas de Martel.) For some names I have considered several possible identifications without being able to clinch the matter: in these cases I have presented my findings, incomplete though they are, in the hope that some future researcher may be able to carry the matter further from there. And from time to time the word 'unidentified' is used, like a gravestone, to mark the final resting-place of many hours of wasted effort.

THE BIOGRAPHICAL REGISTER

The Biographical Register includes entries for all the people whose letters to or from Hobbes are printed in this edition. Here again, the inverse law of historical importance predominates. There are several correspondents whose names cannot be found in any major biographical reference work: people such as George Aglionby, Charles du Bosc, Pierre Guisony, Robert Leeke, Adrian May, François Peleau, Abraham and François du Prat, and Philip Tanny. Also in this category are some of Hobbes's closest friends: François du Verdus, Thomas de

Martel, and Robert Payne. In these cases I have tried to piece together almost all the available evidence of their lives and activities, much of which is assembled and presented here for the first time. I say 'almost all', however, because one thing I have tried not to do in the Biographical Register is to repeat at any length information which is already contained in the letters themselves. (Thus in the case of du Verdus, for example, I refer to, rather than recapitulate, his long auto-biographical letters, which are themselves the fullest surviving sources for the story of his life.)

With major historical figures such as Descartes or Charles II, on the other hand, the reader can easily obtain biographical information elsewhere. Here I have attempted something different: within the framework of a mini-biography, supplying a skeleton of dates and publications (especially those works mentioned in the correspond-ence), I have also tried to give an account of the nature of these people's relations with Hobbes—how they knew him, how he influenced them, what he thought of them, and they of him. These mini-biographies give special attention to the period of the subject's life when he was in contact with Hobbes; thus Leibniz's mature achievements, for example, are dealt with very summarily, and the entry concentrates on the background to his letters to Hobbes. A subsidiary purpose of these biographies is also to point out some of the connections between Hobbes's various correspondents themselves. Often a web of mutual acquaintance can be woven together: anyone who reads in succession the entries for Mersenne, Gassendi, Sorbière, Abraham du Prat, de Martel, and du Verdus will be able to build up a composite picture which interlocks at many points. Sometimes, indeed, the connections are so strong (as, for instance, between Robert Payne and Sir Charles Cavendish) that some duplication of material between the entres is unavoidable. But in general I hope that the material presented in the Biographical Register ramifies in enough different directions to give the reader a sense of the sheer range of Hobbes's various intellectual and social milieux.

REFERENCES

All references to publications are given in short-title form, with full titles in the bibliography. However, dates and places of publication, and/or full titles, may also be given when such information is relevant to the purposes of the note. Where a work consists of a series of entries in alphabetical order, I have dispensed with superfluous page references. For the convenience of the reader, I have generally tried to avoid consolidating whole strings of references in single notes.

For references to Hobbes's works, the following rules apply (modifying the principles set out by Howard Warrender in his preface to *HW* ii, pp. 35, 53–4). Where a work by Hobbes is, in its original editions, divided into both chapters and numbered sections or 'articles', the reference is given in that form, with capital roman numerals for the chapter, and an arabic numeral for the section. Such a reference is sufficient, and equally valid for all editions; occasionally a section will be longer than a page, but frequently it will be shorter. Where section-numbering is not present in the original edition, however, I have not attempted to supply it. References to such works are normally given in double form: first, to the page number of the first edition, and then to the volume and page number of Molesworth's edition (*EW* and *OL*). The reference to Molesworth's edition is purely for the convenience of the reader; in all these cases, any quotation that I make derives from the original edition, and will therefore differ in spelling, punctuation, and capitalization from Molesworth's version. For references to volumes in the Clarendon edition, the abbreviation *HW* is used: this stands for 'Hobbes's Works', and by a happy coincidence it also perpetuates the initials of Howard Warrender. In future volumes of this edition, texts which lack original section-numbering will be cited, when they have appeared in the edition, by *HW* volume and page numbers; but since the only text to have appeared in *HW* up till now, *De cive*, is numbered by sections, I have not needed to give page references to it.

References to the English text of *Leviathan* are to page numbers of the first edition only. These can also be found in the margins of the editions by W. G. Pogson Smith and R. Tuck, and in the text of C. B. Macpherson's edition. They will also be presented in the text of the edition in *HW*.

DATES

The Julian calendar (Old Style: 'OS') used in England in the seventeenth century was ten days behind the Gregorian calendar (New Style: 'NS') used on the Continent. In addition, the year was generally treated in England as beginning from 25 March; in France and Holland (but not in Tuscany) it was taken to begin on 1 January. These two facts pose many problems for an edition of correspondence which includes letters sent between England and the Continent, letters written by Englishmen on the Continent to England, letters written by Englishmen on the Continent to other Englishmen on the Continent, a letter written by a Frenchman in England, and so on.

Hobbes's general practice when writing to England from the Continent was to use NS and say so; his general (but not universal) practice when writing to the Continent from England was to use OS. In many cases, the original date given is ambiguous, and an editorial judgement has to be made; this judgement may be based on the writer's general practice, on the letter's place in a sequence of correspondence, or on datable internal evidence. Where no such guidance is available, I assume that writers used OS on English soil and NS on the Continent. In all cases I present the date in double form, with square brackets enclosing that version of the date which is the product of my editorial judgement. Thus if a document is dated 20 June, and I judge that this is OS, I give it as '20 [/30] June'. If I judge that it is NS, I give it as: '[10/] 20 June'. (This rule is applied to the presentation of dates in all editorial material, but not in the texts themselves.) Sometimes a letter-writer will remove all ambiguity by stating that he is using OS or NS; in these cases I present both forms of the date without square brackets. Thus if the document states '20 June NS', I refer to it thus: '10 /20 June'. The dates of known historical events (where such problems of judgement do not arise) are also presented in this form.

The dating of the year causes fewer problems in practice, partly because many English writers habitually used the form 1656/7 when writing after the beginning of the continental 1657 but before the end of the English 1656. I always treat the year as beginning on 1 January; if I judge that a writer has used the English date between 1 January and 24 March, I say so in a note.

TRANSLATIONS

I have tried to translate all the French, Latin, Greek, and Italian material in this edition into clear modern English. The only exception is that where a letter quotes passages from a Latin work by Hobbes, I have used the original published translation for those passages (except in cases where it obscures the point of the quotation) in my translation of the letter. My aim in my own translations has been to produce versions which are accurate, but not slavish to the point of discomfort: I have often broken long sentences into smaller ones, or otherwise rejigged the syntax of a sentence to produce something which will be tolerable to an English ear. I have also introduced paragraphing in the translations where it is lacking in the originals. However, I have tried not to remove original stylistic blemishes unnecessarily: if a writer uses the same word three times in a sentence in French, it is not the translator's job to vary the monotony with synonyms. Sometimes the English cannot fail to seem slightly stilted: we have no equivalents of the elaborate valedictions of French epistolary style, we have lost the use of the vocative in ordinary speech and writing ('tell me, distinguished Sir'), and even the simple construction which begins a sentence with 'For' (the ubiquitous French 'Car' and Latin 'Nam') now sounds uncomfortably bookish in spoken English.

It must be emphasized that these translations do not in any way claim equal standing with the original texts of the letters. An element of editorial smoothing-over is incorporated in the translations: they present only a version of the text in its final form (ignoring deletions), and if a name has been misspelt in the original, it is silently corrected in the translation.

All these translations are my own, though I must record a special debt of gratitude to Mr Nigel Hope, who checked my translations from the Latin and Greek and made some valuable corrections and suggestions. When Professor Warrender began work on the correspondence in the 1960s, he commissioned transcriptions and translations of many of these letters from his research assistants, Mary Faris and Carol Needham. Some of this work was presented in his edition of *De cive* (*HW* ii, pp. 300–15). At an early stage in my own work on the correspondence, I decided that it was necessary to make my own transcriptions and translations. However, I was able to consult the draft translations by Professor Warrender's assistants, and although I have disagreed with them on many points, I have also been influenced by felicitous phrasings from them here and there. Knowing how much hard work they had to do, I hope that it will give them some satisfaction to see this edition in print at long last, even though their own wordings of the letters are not contained in it.

ACKNOWLEDGEMENTS

For permission to publish the texts of these letters, I am grateful to the following individuals and institutions:

The Controller of HM Stationery Office (representing the Crown)

(Letters 178, 181); His Grace the Duke of Devonshire and the Trustees of the Chatsworth Settlement (Letters 64–5, 67–72, 74–82, 84–5, 89–90, 92–5, 99–100, 103, 105–6, 108, 110, 115, 120–1, 124, 126–30, 132, 134, 136–9, 144, 147, 154–5, 157–9, 162–3, 165–6, 168, 170–7, 179–80, 182, 186, 190, 196, and the draft letter printed under the heading 'Hobbes to Mr Finny', above); the Earl of Shelburne (Letter 198); Col. P. T. Clifton and Nottingham University Library (Letters 4–9, 11, 13–14); Mr Richard Waller (Letter 39); the Biblioteca nazionale centrale, Florence (Letters 187–8); the Bibliothèque nationale, Paris (Letters 29, 33–4, 38, 40–8, 50–5, 57, 60–2, 112, 114, 117–18, 135, 140–2, 146, 150–2, 156, 160–1, 164, 169, 185); the Bodleian Library, Oxford (Letters 1–3, 20, 23, 25–8, 153, 167, 193, 202, 204–5, 208, and the letter from Crooke to Wood printed in the general note to Letter 197); the Trustees of the British Library (Letters 10, 15–16, 18–19, 21–2, 24, 31, 35, 49, 83, 86–7, 91, 96–8, 101–2, 104, 107, 109, 111, 113, 116, 119, 122–3, 125, 131, 189, 194, 200, 210); the Historical Society of Pennsylvania, Philadelphia (Letter 66); the Houghton Library, Harvard College, Cambridge, Mass. (Letter 59); the Huntington Library, San Marino (Letter 88); the Niedersächsische Landesbibliothek, Hanover (Letter 195); and the President and Council of the Royal Society, London (Letters 73, 143, 149, 183, 191–2).

I am very grateful to those members of the staff of all the institutions listed above who have helped me with my work. Above all, I should like to record my indebtedness to the three exceptionally friendly, helpful, and well-informed guardians of the Hobbes materials at Chatsworth: Mr Peter Day, Keeper of Collections, Mr Michael Pearman, Librarian, and Mr Tom Askey, Archivist. I should also like to thank the staff of the Cambridge University Library, and especially the ever-patient and super-efficient staff of the Rare Books Room, where much of the research for this edition was carried out. I have also made frequent use of the British Library; those who have worked there in recent years will understand me when I say that I am particularly indebted to the staff of the Book Delivery Enquiries desk. Apart from the libraries and archives already mentioned, I should also like to thank the following:

Aberystwyth: the National Library of Wales. Albi: the Archives départementales du Tarn. Bordeaux: the Archives départementales de la Gironde; the Archives municipales. Cambridge: Gonville and Caius College Library; the Pepys Library, Magdalene College; Trinity College Library. Castres: the Bibliothèque municipale (with special thanks to the librarian, M. Lévy, who, after I had arrived with my customary good fortune on the one weekday when the library is closed until the afternoon, opened the whole library for me). Copenhagen: the Royal Library. Durham: the University Library. Florence: the Archivio di stato. Geneva: the Bibliothèque publique et universitaire. The Hague: the Royal Library. Leiden: the University Library. Leipzig: the University Library. London: the Athenaeum; the College of Arms; Dulwich College; Dr Williams's Library; the Historical Manuscripts Commission; the Royal College of Physicians; the University Library. Montauban: the Archives départementales de Tarn-et-Garonne; the Bibliothèque municipale. Munich: the Bayerische Staatsbibliothek. Nottingham: the Nottinghamshire Record Office. Paris: the Archives de l'Académie des sciences; the Archives nationales; the Bibliothèque de l'Institut; the Bibliothèque Mazarine; the Bibliothèque de la Société de l'histoire du protestantisme français. Oxford: the libraries of Christ Church, Corpus Christi College, Hertford College, Magdalen College, Queen's College, St Hugh's College, St John's College, Trinity College, Worcester College. Reading: the Berkshire Record Office. Sheffield: the University Library. Toronto: the University Library. Toulouse: the Archives départementales de Midi-Pyrénées et de la Haute-Garonne; the Bibliothèque communale. Worcester: the Hereford and Worcester Record Office.

I am very grateful to Dr Graeme Mitchison for his help in interpreting Hobbes's mathematical correspondence, and especially for the analyses in modern notation which I have appended to some of these letters; to Mr Nigel Hope, for his scrutiny of my translations from the Latin, and his help in unscrambling Henry Stubbe's pseudo-Homeric poetry; and to Dr Jan Moore, for her painstaking collation of most of the texts of Letter 197. I should also like to thank Professor Onofrio Nicastro, not only for his friendly encouragement, but also for the magnificently detailed notes to his edition of Stubbe's letters to Hobbes, from which I have benefited greatly. For help on specific points I am grateful to Dr Peter Beal, Dr Paul Hopkins, Dr Richard Luckett, Professor Henry Roseveare, and Sir Keith Thomas. For technological assistance I am indebted to Dr John Robson and Mr Andrew Gwatkin.

Grants covering some of the expenses incurred in this project came from the Economic and Social Research Council and the British Academy: the latter institution has given its support to the Editorial Board of the Clarendon edition via one of our board members, Professor Quentin Skinner, to whom I am especially grateful.

The preparation of this edition has dominated my life over the last five years to an unnatural degree. Lame or quaint though it may sound, I should like to take this opportunity to apologize for letters unanswered and friendships neglected.

Finally, I should like to thank two of the most civilized and congenial institutions in the country: Gonville and Caius College, Cambridge (for enabling me to start work on this project) and *The Spectator* (for enabling me to finish it).

ABBREVIATIONS USED
IN THIS EDITION

The siglum 'MS', used in the end-notes to a letter, stands for the manuscript source listed in the head-note; if more than one manuscript source is given there, it stands for the first one so listed. Other sigla used in the end-notes to the letters are not presented in this general list of abbreviations: they are specific to each letter, and will be explained in the letter's general note.

A&T   R. Descartes, *Œuvres*, ed. C. Adam and P. Tannery, rev. edn., 11 vols. (Paris, 1974)

ABL   J. Aubrey, *'Brief Lives', chiefly of Contemporaries, set down by John Aubrey, between the Years 1669 and 1696*, ed. A. Clark, 2 vols. (Oxford, 1898)

Add.   Additional

ADG   Archives départementales de la Gironde, Bordeaux

ADT   Archives départementales du Tarn, Albi

ADTG   Archives départementales de Tarn-et-Garonne, Montauban

AMB   Archives municipales, Bordeaux

AN   Archives nationales, Paris

Athenae   A. Wood, *Athenae oxonienses*, ed. P. Bliss, 4 vols. (London, 1813–20)

BL   British Library, London

BN   Bibliothèque nationale, Paris

BNC   Biblioteca nazionale centrale, Florence

Bodl.   Bodleian Library, Oxford

BSHPF   Bibliothèque de la Société de l'histoire du protestantisme français, Paris

CSPD   *Calendar of State Papers, Domestic Series* (London, 1856–)

CUL   Cambridge University Library

DNB   *Dictionary of National Biography*, 63 vols. (London, 1885–1900)

DSB   *Dictionary of Scientific Biography*, 18 vols. (New York, 1970–90)

EW   Hobbes, *The English Works*, ed. W. Molesworth, 11 vols. (London, 1839–45)

Fasti	A. Wood, *Fasti oxonienses; or, Annals of the University of Oxford*, 2 vols., appended to vols. iii and iv of Wood, *Athenae oxonienses*, ed. P. Bliss (London, 1813–20)
f.fr.	fonds français
f.l.	fonds latin
Foster	J. Foster, *Alumni oxonienses: The Members of the University of Oxford, 1500–1714*, early series, 2 vols. (Oxford, 1892)
G.M.	Commentary supplied by Dr Graeme Mitchison
Harl.	Harleian
HMC	Historical Manuscripts Commission
HOC	C. Huygens, *Œuvres complètes*, 22 vols. (The Hague, 1888–1950)
HW	*The Clarendon Edition of the Works of Thomas Hobbes*, ed. H. Warrender *et al.* (Oxford, 1983–)
KBK	Royal Library, Copenhagen
LUL	Leiden University Library
MC	M. Mersenne, *Correspondance*, ed. C. de Waard, B. Rochot, and A. Beaulieu, 17 vols. (Paris, 1932–88)
MS	manuscript
n.a.	nouvelle acquisition
n.d.	no date of publication
NLH	Niedersächsische Landesbibliothek, Hanover
n.p.	no place of publication
NRO	Nottinghamshire Record Office, Nottingham
NUL	Nottingham University Library
OC	H. Oldenburg, *Correspondence*, ed. and tr. A. R. and M. B. Hall, 13 vols. (Madison, Wis., and London, 1965–86)
OCC	Christ Church, Oxford
OED	*The Oxford English Dictionary*, 12 vols. (Oxford, 1933)
OL	Hobbes, *Opera philosophica quae latine scripsit omnia*, ed. W. Molesworth, 5 vols. (London, 1839–45)
OQC	Queen's College, Oxford
OTC	Trinity College, Oxford
OWC	Worcester College, Oxford
PRO	Public Record Office, London
R.Soc.	Royal Society, London
SP	State Papers

VCH	*Victoria County History*
Venn & Venn	J. Venn and J. A. Venn (eds.), *Alumni cantabrigienses: A Biographical List of All Known Students, Graduates, and Holders of Office at the University of Cambridge, from the Earliest Times to 1900*, part 1, 2 vols. (Cambridge, 1922)

Robert Mason to Hobbes, from Cambridge

Bodl. MS Rawlinson D 1104, fos. 18–20 (transcript).
Printed in Tönnies, 'Lettres inédites', pp. 81–4.

Good m^r H.

You haue I thank you satisfyed my expectation to ye full, for upon my returne to Cambr.[1] I found a most frendly letter from you, Let not I pray ye varietie of reports, the sudden contradiction in newes, or ye feare of prevention in it, henceforth keep your pen from communicating with your friend such occurrences of these actiue times, as your vacant houres, from your more serious affaires shall permit you. For were your news as uncertain as ye match you write of, or as stale as ye oysters use to be at Northampton, where ye Major of ye Town may open with his dagger sheath,[2] yet it could not be but welcome to a hungry scholler, being serv'd in wth such cleane language, such remarkable circumstances as your letter exprest itself in. I am glad to heare Sr Horace Veere is past danger of intercepting,[3] I hope he hath likewise past ye danger of his Majesties displeasure. If he hath not he hath ill luck to come from ye hazard & ye defence of his life, to ye hazard or ye defence of his Honour, Something I heare is obiected concerning his delivering up of Manhem, but I doubt not but Sr Horace Veere out of his own sufficiency in that decayed English discipline, will giue such an account of his service, & such satisfaction to his Majesty, as his M.^{tie} may wish of him as a great King somtimes did of a discreet & valiant General, viz. that he had decem tales.[4] It is a hard matter for a man to fight against an Enemy with one hand tyed behind him. It were to be wisht those men had as much Providence in them as Charitie, who think if ye Emp^r[5] were once possest of every part in the Palatinate, his Imperial Majesty would then render the whole; for I haue heard some men say, that ye Palatinate lyes as conveniently for ye Emp^r, as Bohemia did for ye Palsgraue,[6] or as Portugall sometimes did for the K. of Spain, & that in the meane time he had a farmer that knew well enough how to make the most of it. As for promises & oaths and such like engagements, they are now adajes accounted of but as weake obligations betwixt a Catholicke Prince & a Heretick, wch are commonly Spurned aside when they ly in their way either to greatnes or commodity; besides promises which are made upon a kind of necessity, are seldom

I

times kept, but upon necessity. But let us hope for a restitution, & grant that to be intended indeed wch is pretended in shew, yet when a Prince comes to receiue his own as a gift from ye hands of a Conquerour, that shall ever be jealous both of his power & will; he cannot but at ye least expect a proffer of dishonourable conditions, and questionles a Countrey lost & purchas't with ye blood [of so *blotted*] many braue men, where a iust war is pretended on both sides, can neither willingly be restored nor thankfully accepted. That man⁷ was master of his Art, who when the tempest grew big beyond his Majesties expectation in ye Palatinate, & the storme was at ye very height in Bohemia, had in ye midst of all those whirlewinds, rak't up as it were in ashes here ye hope of a match,⁸ which should serue at a pinch, to kindle & warme his Majesties affection to ye Spaniard, if at any time it had grown cold, through ye unsufferable iniuries acted upon his son in law; he is now at Rome,⁹ but whilst he continued in England using much upon ye Thames, he learnt one trick of our English watermen which he will carry with him to his graue & y^t is to look one way & pull another; A man otherwise infinitely deserving of ye State he liues in, whose good service done to his Master & Countrey, cannot but wrest a iust commendation even from his enemies, & it were to be wisht we could parallel him; my Lord Digby¹⁰ is thought to come the nearest unto him of any that are now imployed, & yet his L^dship hath hitherto had ye luck of other Alchymists of State, that with all their labour & travaile many times purchase only a part of their proiect, This interest is Gold, but Gold they find none, yet by much labour they find out some conclusions, some experiments which yeild some profit to themselves & Countrey: So hath it bin as yet wth ye best of his L^ps proceedings, his intent has bin Gold & a dowrey, but his proiects & his ends haue bin farr richer then his purchase. It is worth the observation; to remember when the Spanish match was first whispered, with what a universal distaste it was received, & now I haue heard many good Protestants desire it. Whether it be that our Nation cannot brook ye contempt of a refusall from ye Spaniard, or that every good subiect wooes likewise with ye affection of his Prince, or that in a case of necessity where Loue & Hatred are to be weighed one against ye other, Loue to ye Palsgraue doth quite weigh down our dislike to ye Spaniard, by whose meanes he is likest to come by his own again, I pray [send *blotted*] me your opinion. The Archb.p of Spaletto¹¹ it seems [was *blotted*] welcom to Rome, contrary to many mens expectation here, who thought he should haue bin entertain'd there as ye Chough was by its fellowes in ye Fable. The

Chough contemning his own diett in respect of yᵉ Doues, whited himself all over, & by this fallacy was admitted into the Doue-cote, where he lived for a time & went for a Doue, till he discovered his kind by his voyce, & then he was shamefully driven out by them, then thinking afterwards to haue returned to his fellowes, & haue fed amongst yᵉ Choughs, he was likewise beaten from amongst them because of his colour. But it fell out better with the Archbishop, for he was welcom to yᵉ Protestants for his colour, & to yᵉ Romanists for his Language being able to tell a good tale for himself. Yet I know some Catholicks, who to this houre suspect him for some opinions & think he has long since dyed himself in such a colour of Reformation as all the holy water in Rome cannot wash out of him. But let his Religion be capable of wᵗ colour it will, & let him be never so profest & skillfull a dier himself, yet I hope he hath not dipt in grain¹² any of yᵉ consciences of our nobilitie. I must needs confess I wondred when you wrote me word he was at Rome,¹³ since himself in his own books says of it Roma est Babylon illa Apocalyptica de qua Deus clamat vel clamaturus est illud Exite ex illa popule mi, ne communicetis de plagis eius.¹⁴ But Bᵖ Morton guesst aright of him scilicet ingentem carnis eius molem spiritum obruisse.¹⁵ As for yᵉ Assembly of Cardinals at Rome, I think their care be already taken for England, for it is at this instant full of their Emissaries, & I feare it may be as truly obiected to this nation concerning Seminaries & Jesuits, as it was somtimes to Rome of yᵉ Mathematicians. Hoc genus hominum in Anglia & vetabitur semper & retinebitur, genus hominum potentibus infidum sperantibus fallax.¹⁶ I pray hereafter be as free with me as you see I am wᵗʰ you, for you may with the same security impart your news to me, as, I hope, I haue now writt my mind to you, & I trust we shall neither of us be thought immodestly to abuse the libertie of true & loyall subiects, for mine own part as I am not of their curiositie who would seeme to be [ignorant *blotted*] of nothing that shall occurre remarkable[; for *blotted*] there are many things, as your letter discreetly intimates, whereof it becomes us to be ignorant, so I would be loath to be thought so great a stranger to yᵉ Commonwealth I liue in as not to know what yᵉ greater sort of men do, that wish a prosperous successe to yᵉ designes both of their Prince & Countrey, which I hope henceforth to haue from you, tis no matter though it be at yᵉ sixt, seventh, or 50ᵗʰ hand. The proceedings in Commonwealths as they come unto yᵉ knowledg of yᵉ subiect are not unfitly compared to yᵉ currents of rivers, for as all rivers run into yᵉ Sea, & yet some are carryed with a more slow & swift torrent as their chanels are more or lesse indented, & some there are we read of, that haue secret passages vnder ye earth into the sea, So all affairs of State at length fall into ye discours of ye multitude, yet some sooner according to the rectitude of their relations, others later, as their truth is empesht[17] by ye turnings & twinings it finds in the braines of some partiall & affected Relations. Other affairs again of deeper consequence are (as they ought to be) more closely & secretly managed & not so much as whispered of, nay they are kept even from ye guesses of ye subtlest Politicians, till of a sudden they let themselves out both into rumor & admiration. Arcana imperij nihil moror. periculum intelligere.[18] My ambition reaches no furder then ye Exchange,[19] W. Barrets shop,[20] or ye middle Isle in Pauls,[21] where when old Wymarkes[22] mint goes, I would desire you would but send me now & then of his coyne, it will passe for currant here amongst ye Clerks in Cambr. & so I take my leaue of you desiring you to measure my affection by my lines, & to pardon this prolixitie, wherein if I offend ye second time, the punishment of making a long letter light vpon me. A Dio. I haue sent my Lord Cavendishe Butlers picture,[23] I pray present it with my most humble service [unto *blotted*] his Lordship. if ye painter had had time he shold [haue *blotted*] written vpon it, those few lines which I haue sent you inclosed, which might briefly express the quality of the person whom it represents, which if you can gett done before my Lord see it, you shall knitt one knot more upon the tye of his affection who is

Your true & loving friend
Robert Mason

Camb. Dec. 10. 1622.

A few words in the MS were accidentally blotted in 1903 by A. J. Jenkinson, who supplied the blotted words on interleaved slips.

[1] Mason was a Fellow of St John's College, Cambridge: see the Biographical Register.

[2] 'The Mayor of Northampton opens oysters with his dagger' was a proverbial phrase, explained by Thomas Fuller as follows: 'This Town being eighty miles from the Sea, Sea-fish may be presumed stale therein' (*Oxford Dictionary of English Proverbs*, p. 519).

[3] Sir Horace Vere (1565–1635), a distinguished soldier, commanded the English volunteer forces which went to the Palatinate in 1620 to fight on behalf of James I's son-in-law, the Elector Palatine, against the Imperial army. Besieged in Mannheim in Sept. 1622, he was obliged to capitulate on 18/28 Oct. but was permitted to leave with the honours of war and march to The Hague.

[4] 'ten such men' (source unidentified).

⁵ Ferdinand II (1578–1637), Holy Roman Emperor since 1619.

⁶ The Palsgrave (Frederick V, Elector Palatine) had accepted an invitation by the rebellious Protestants of Bohemia to become ruler of that country in 1619.

⁷ Diego Sarmiento de Acuña, Count of Gondomar (1567–1626), Spanish Ambassador to James I.

⁸ The projected marriage between Prince Charles and the Infanta of Spain.

⁹ Gondomar was not at Rome. Mason was possibly misled by the fact that Gondomar and de Dominis (see n. 11) had left England together; but while de Dominis proceeded to Rome, Gondomar returned to Spain.

¹⁰ John Digby, first Earl of Bristol (1580–1653), the diplomat who undertook an embassy to the Emperor Ferdinand II in 1621 and was Ambassador to Spain in 1610–16, 1617–18, and 1622–4.

¹¹ Marcantonio de Dominis (1560–1624), Roman Catholic Archbishop of Spalato (Split, in Dalmatia), had travelled secretly to England in 1616, joined the Church of England, published several attacks on the papacy, and become Dean of Windsor. Dissatisfied both by his lack of further preferment and by King James's lack of interest in his ecumenist projects, he left England in Apr./May 1622, rejoined the Roman Catholic Church, and travelled to Rome, arriving at the end of Oct. After a period of reconciliation there, during which he was obliged to write retractions of his earlier works, he died a prisoner of the Inquisition. See Malcolm, *De Dominis*.

¹² = dyed thoroughly, dyed fast (from the use of kermes, a dye-yielding insect, popularly believed to be a grain: *OED* grain *sb.* 10b).

¹³ Hobbes would have learned this from the letter of [23 Oct./] 2 Nov. 1622 from Fulgenzio Micanzio to the second Earl of Devonshire, which he had translated: see the transcript in BL MS Add. 11309, fo. 56.

¹⁴ 'Rome is that Babylon of the Book of Revelation, about which God cries out or will cry out: "Come out of her, my people, that ye receive not of her plagues"' (quoting Rev. 18: 4). This is a slightly condensed quotation from de Dominis, *De republica ecclesiastica*, i, p. 566.

¹⁵ 'Namely, that the vast mass of his body overwhelmed his spirit': de Dominis was famously fat, and was accused by Protestant writers both of gluttony and of greed for temporal rewards. Thomas Morton (1564–1659), Bishop of Lichfield and Coventry (later Bishop of Durham), had interviewed de Dominis before his departure (see Neile, *De Dominis*, p. 49).

¹⁶ 'This type of people will always be forbidden and repressed in England, a type which cannot be trusted by the powerful, and deceives the trustful' (adapting Tacitus, *Historia*, 1. 22). 'Mathematicus' was used by Tacitus to mean 'astrologer' or 'necromancer'.

¹⁷ = impeached, hindered (*OED* impeach *v.*).

¹⁸ 'I do not object to the existence of state secrets; one must understand the danger.'

¹⁹ The London bourse, built by Sir Thomas Gresham, at the corner of Threadneedle St. and Cornhill. The central courtyard, surrounded by a covered walk, was the main place of business in the merchant community and one of the two main centres of news-gathering and gossip in London.

²⁰ William Barrett, a prominent bookseller in St Paul's Churchyard from 1607 to 1624, specializing in books of travel (McKerrow (ed.), *Dictionary of Printers 1557–1640*).

²¹ St Paul's Cathedral was the other main centre of news-gathering, gossip, and rendezvous in London (see n. 19).

[22] Edward Wymark, 'a wealthy man, great novellant, and constant Paul's-walker' (Fuller, *Worthies*, iii, p. 175). He is frequently mentioned, between 1606 and 1620, as a source of humorous and salacious stories in the correspondence of Dudley Carleton and John Chamberlain (Lee (ed.), *Carleton to Chamberlain*, e.g. pp. 76, 88, 113).

[23] Unidentified; possibly a portrait of William Cavendish, the future second Earl of Devonshire ('Lord Cavendish') by a painter called Butler, though no portraitist of that name is known for this period. If so, it may perhaps be identified with the portrait of the second Earl which now hangs in the Long Gallery at Hardwick Hall, Derby.; but no lines have been added to that picture other than the family motto, 'Cavendo tutus'.

LETTER 2   6 [/16] NOVEMBER 1628

Hobbes to Christian Cavendish, Countess of Devonshire, from London

Bodl. MS Rawlinson D 1104, fo. 15^v (transcript); Bodl. MS Rawlinson C 232, fos. 79–78^v retrograde (transcript).
Printed in Tönnies, 'Analekten', pp. 291–2.

To my Lady Devonshire

May it please your Ladiship

I haue made an Epistle dedicatorie to my Lord,[1] according to y^t forme wch your Ladiship gaue me leaue to use. Wherein I haue intended to do his L.^{p} honor, as far as my discretion & ye nature of an epistle will permitte. But because I may faile, through ignorance to do what I entend, & it is my duty to acquaint yor Ladiship with my doinges, in thinges that concerne my Lord, I haue sent it to you to correct or alter as shall seeme necessary to yor Ladiships better judgment. Humbly desiring it may be sent vp againe, as soone as conveniently may be, because the Presse will shortly be ready for it. So I humbly take leaue, beseeching your Ladiship to hold a good opinion of me (esp. touching my dutifull respect to you & iust estimation of your noble Vertues) without which no benefit bestowed vpon me can be comfortable

Yo^r Ladiships most dutifull & obedient servant
Tho Hobbes

London. From yor La.^{ps} house[2] Nov. 6. 1628.

[1] The dedicatory epistle to Hobbes's translation of Thucydides, *Eight Bookes of the Peloponnesian Warre* (sigs. A1–2): this epistle, addressed to Christian Cavendish's son,

the third Earl of Devonshire, is a eulogy of her husband, the second Earl, who died on 20/30 June 1628.

² Devonshire House, in Bishopsgate.

LETTER 3   8/18 NOVEMBER 1629

George Aglionby to Hobbes, from Leicester Abbey, Leics.

Bodl. MS D 1104, fo. 17 (transcript).
Printed in Tönnies, 'Lettres inédites', pp. 84–6.

Mr Hobbes

I receiued your kind letter at Leicester where we yet continue, and as I think shall do this fortenight, for which I am sorrie, because I desire to be as neer you as my Lady hath any house.¹ Now for your Interrogatories, my Lady Anne² (who doth most very kindly commend herself to you & wishes you a safe & speedy returne) is (you know) faire & ripe, & tis pitty she is so long a forbidden fruit. I am sure she could be willing to be gathered by my Lord Craven,³ but because I heare nothing of him having bin in England this moneth, I feare his hands are full already: my Lᵈ Bruce⁴ is here with my Lady, & my Lady of Oxford⁵ at Leicester with her sister, they meet every day & I am vpon good grounds persuaded it will be a match. I heare many of his friends are unwilling, yet I belieue he is so forward in it that they must be contented if not pleased: He is a noble Gentleman; & I wish him as good daies as he will haue nights. Though there be at this time no Parliament yet there is a Committie of Lords, namely my Lᵈ of Bedford⁶ my Lord of Clare,⁷ & my Lᵈ of Somersett,⁸ remember they are rich men all. The cause as I heare is a manuscript found with them, intituled, The present policie & government of the State & Church of England.⁹ I haue not read of any times so good of wᶜʰ to write at yᵉ present hath not been a crime. The Scope of this writing, as is said, is to advance yᵉ libertie & defeat yᵉ prerogatiue. My L.ᵈ of Clare hath followed his Sons example both in his attempt & punishment.¹⁰ But my Lᵈ of Somerset, as it seemes to me hath ingaged himself in a busines wᶜʰ nothing concernes him, namely yᵉ Liberty of yᵉ Subject. My L.ᵈ of Bedford being examined of whom he receiued this writing, answered (as they say) that if it were a crime, revealing his author would make him no lesse guilty, therfore he would discover none, & being further examined touching his searching of some records concerning yᵉ Liberty, replied that yᵉ records as he thought, were the subiects, & that he judged it no offence, if out of them he desired to know yᵉ utmost both of his right & duty. Yet one thing you must not omitt to obserue, that because his offence was touching yᵉ records, they haue most wittily committed him to the Rolles.[11] I told you it was a M.S. therfore Sʳ Rob. Cotton must haue his share,[12] & they say he also is committed. He may now learn that Imprisonmᵗ is almost as old as Liberty, of which himself may become a very ancient president.[13] There is a report that others also are sent for whether by decree of the Councell, or the People only I know not. At first my Lᵈ of Essex[14] a man of the sword, that is to say one of whom there is no use in peace, but he may like old armour be layd up safe. Then the Bᵖ of Lincoln, [*marginal note:* Williams][15] who since his falling from grace hath bin a State Puritan, & certainly accounts it very Arminian dealing for an Orthodox Bp to be abridged of his Christian liberty. Lastly a certain seditious Physician called Dr. Turner,[16] one who disputes of all rule, but obeyes none; no not so much as the rule of civilitie for good manners, nor that of Physick for good diett. Let yᵉ Dʳ look how he can purge himself; if he bee layd vp, all his Physick will hardly make him soluble for there is no such binder as yᵉ Kings displeasure. It is reported & belieued that the Ld Keeper[17] shall resigne his place to yᵉ Archbishop of York.[18] [*marginal note:* Neyle][19] I doubt not but yᵉ Puritans, id est, yᵉ common Lawyers will call this Spirituall wickednes in high places. Yet methinkes if yᵉ Clergy cannot keep yᵉ office wholly as they were wont, yet it is equall that at yᵉ leste it should be divided between yᵉ Law & yᵉ Gosple. This is all yᵉ news I remember. It is a duty in my letter to remember my Lords loue to you. Mʳ Ramsden[20] doth the same & Mʳⁱˢ Stradling[21] hath affection but not french enough to write to you, which she intends to do. My paper grows to an end, & with it my Letter. I do therefore say over yᵉ close of your Letter to you againe, & rest

Your assured friend
Aglionby.

Leicester Abbie. Nov. 18. or. 8. 1629.

[*postscript:*] Mʳ Gale[22] remembers his loue to you.

[*addressed:*] To Mʳ Tho. Hobbes at Geneva[23]

---

[1] Leicester Abbey, the house bought by the first Earl of Devonshire from Sir Henry Hastings in 1613 (Chatsworth MS Hardwick 29, p. 320), was the favourite residence of

Christian, Countess of Devonshire ('my Lady'); it was largely destroyed in 1645 (*VCH Leics.*, iv, p. 451).

[2] Anne, daughter of the second Earl of Devonshire, who married Lord Rich, elder son of the second Earl of Warwick, in 1632, and died in 1638.

[3] William Craven (1606–97), created Baron Craven of Hampsted Marshall in 1627, the distinguished military commander who spent most of his subsequent career in the service of James I's daughter, Elizabeth, Queen of Bohemia.

[4] Thomas Bruce (1599–1663), Lord Kinloss, later created first Earl of Elgin, was the brother of Christian, Countess of Devonshire ('my Lady').

[5] Diana, Countess of Oxford (widow of Henry, eighteenth Earl of Oxford), who married Thomas Bruce on 12/22 November 1629.

[6] Francis Russell (1593–1641), fourth Earl of Bedford; he had supported the Commons during the debates on the Petition of Right in 1628.

[7] John Holles (1564?–1637), first Earl of Clare, a close friend of the Earl of Somerset; he had long been out of favour at Court.

[8] Robert Carr (d. 1645), first Earl of Somerset, the Scottish courtier who had been promoted by, and had then fallen out of favour with, James I; having been tried for the murder of Sir Thomas Overbury, he was imprisoned from 1615 to 1622, and had led a restricted and politically inactive life since then.

[9] This MS (PRO SP 14/77/65) is printed in Rushworth, *Historical Collections*, ii, pp. 39–44. Written originally by Sir Robert Dudley (illegitimate son of the Earl of Leicester) in 1614 to curry favour with King James, it advocated placing the country under martial rule and imposing new taxes by the sole authority of the Crown. A copy from the collection of the antiquary Sir Robert Cotton was lent out by Cotton's librarian to the MP Oliver St John, from whom copies passed to the Earls of Bedford, Somerset, and Clare. When a copy reached Sir Thomas Wentworth he regarded it indignantly as a caricature of his own advice to King Charles, and on 5/15 Nov. took it to the King, who ordered an inquiry to be made. St John, Cotton, and the three earls were arrested and prosecuted in the Star Chamber. See Gardiner, *History of England 1603–1642*, vii, pp. 138–41, and Sharpe, *Cotton*, pp. 143–5.

[10] The Earl of Clare was the father of the MP Denzil Holles (1599–1680), whose actions at the adjournment of Parliament in Mar. (when he had helped to restrain the Speaker in his chair) had led to his arrest and imprisonment in the Tower.

[11] A house on Chancery Lane, next to Serjeants' Inn; so called because the records or 'rolls' of Chancery were kept there.

[12] Sir Robert Cotton (1586–1631), the prominent lawyer and antiquarian, whose library contained more than 400 MSS (see Sharpe, *Cotton*, p. 69 and *passim*).

[13] = precedent (*OED* precedent *sb.*).

[14] Robert Devereux (1591–1646), third Earl of Essex, the future parliamentary general who had sided with the critics of the Crown during the debates on the Petition of Right in 1628.

[15] John Williams (1582–1650), appointed Bishop of Lincoln in 1621, had supported some of the criticisms of the Crown in the Petition of Right. He was not a puritan, but was an opponent of Bishop Laud, with whom 'Arminianism' was popularly identified.

[16] Samuel Turner (d. *c*.1647), who had qualified MD at Padua in 1611, and who as MP for Shaftesbury in 1626 had launched the attack on the Duke of Buckingham which led to Buckingham's impeachment.

[17] Thomas Coventry (1578–1640), first Baron Coventry, who had succeeded John Williams as Lord Keeper in 1625. He had taken a conciliatory attitude to the Petition of Right, and in Sept. 1629 had tried to find a compromise over the bailing of the seven MPs imprisoned by the King.

[18] Samuel Harsnett (1561–1631), a fierce anti-puritan, was elected Archbishop of York in 1628. He did not become Lord Keeper, but he was made a member of the Privy Council on 10/20 Nov. 1629.

[19] This is an error: Richard Neile (1562–1640) did not become Archbishop of York until 1631.

[20] Unidentified; presumably an employee of the Devonshire household.

[21] In the summaries of accounts for the Devonshire household for 1636–8 loosely inserted in Chatsworth MS Hardwick 28, 'Mrs Stradling' is listed as receiving a half-yearly wage of £5 at Christmas 1636.

[22] Robert Gale (d. 1660) matriculated at Christ's College, Cambridge (1609; BA 1613, MA 1616), was ordained in 1616, and some time thereafter became chaplain to Christian, Countess of Devonshire. In the Devonshire household accounts loosely inserted in Chatsworth MS Hardwick 28, he receives a half-yearly wage of £20. He was rector of Brindle, Lancs. (1637–40), and rector of Epworth, Lincs. (1641–60). In the 1650s, at Roehampton, he helped the Countess to conduct a secret correspondence with the Duke of Hamilton and the Earls of Holland and Norwich on the restoration of the monarchy (Pomfret, *Life of Lady Christian*, p. 73).

[23] The addressing of this letter to Geneva is puzzling, since Letter 4 makes clear that Hobbes and his pupil arrived in Geneva in April 1630. The most likely explanation is that Hobbes had previously told Aglionby to send his next letter to Geneva, expecting to be there by late 1629, and that the journey had then been delayed.

LETTER 4   19/29 APRIL 1630

Hobbes to Sir Gervase Clifton, from Geneva

NUL MS Clifton C 561 (original).
Printed in de Beer, 'Some Letters', pp. 200–1.

Hon:^{ble} sir.

Mr Clifton[1] wth his companie and followers,[2] are safely arriued here in Geneua, and euery man I thanke God in perfect health. we set forth from Paris the .5.th of Aprill stilo nouo. in .13. dayes we came to Lyons in a Coach, wth more tediousnesse of mind then payne of body, from lions after .4. dayes stay there, we went on horsebacke to Geneua where we arriued the 23th of the same moneth. Wee lodge in the house of one Mr Preuost[3] a minister of the most estimation of any man in the cittie. a very wise and honest man [*word deleted*] and not of [>the] Geneua print,[4] more then is necessary for an inhabitant and minister of the place. The towne is free from noyse, company, and ill example, free from contagion, and warre, and fitte for study and retirednesse, hauing also good ayre and walkes wch in other great townes are wantinge. Wee intend to stay here till the beginning of September, that if it be possible wee may get an opportunity to Winter in Italy. But I haue no hope of it; the warres[5] haue made all the wayes so dangerous, and difficult, that not a man here, or any where by the way to whom we discouered our purpose but dissuades vs from it. Peace is not expected till one or both parties be wearied, wch will not be this summer; Therefore I thinke we shall spend a winter more in France, and so come home by the low contries. This day I shall by vertue of our Letters of Credit take .60.^li of our new allowance, our old stocke ending now. if your letters of credit had bene for .25.^li more then they are I would [*word deleted*] at mid-sommer next haue taken so much here, and caused it to be repayd you by Mr Purslow,[6] so much being then due to mee from my Lady.[7] I pray you therefor let me haue a letter of credit for .25.^li apart by the next, for I know no other way to haue my mony here at that time, and I will send Mr Purslow an acquittance assoone as midsommer day is past by wch that some shall be payd w^thout scruple. In this time of our stay here Mr Clifton hath taken an Italian Master who hath promised to make him speake good Italian in .3. monethes, which he is apt to learne, and w^thin few dayes there will come to him a master of writing for the Italian hand, wth wch two exercises I doubt not but he will spend his time profitably and to your Content.

There went from Lions while we were there two Englishmen into Italy, whereof one perhaps you know, his name is Mr Smithy,[8] the other is one Captayne Say or Sale.[9] They go down the Rhosne a good way, and then by Land through Prouence to Tolon, a iourny of seuen or eight dayes in wch they can ly in no towne that hath not the plague, and most of the townes in Prouence haue it in vigor. from Tolon they make the rest of their way by water, wch will be .4. dayes at least, and comminge so into Italy are sure to be receaued into no towne there till they have bene .40. dayes ayred in the fieldes, on these termes we might haue gone wth them, but I refused. Wee are I thanke God safe from all dangers of [>that] kind here in Geneua. and it were not discretion to passe through the plague on no greater an errand then [>ye] curiosity of trauellers. Thus wth my humble seruice remembred to my Lady[10] & M^ris Abbots[11] I remayne

your most humble seruant Tho: Hobbes

from Geneua Apr. 19/29 1630

This letter is neither addressed nor endorsed; it was probably sent enclosed in another letter, perhaps NUL MS Clifton C 481, an undated letter from Walter Waring to Sir Gervase Clifton, which describes their arrival in Geneva and is endorsed in another hand 'Y^g M^r [Young Master] & Mr Hobbs'.

[1] Hobbes's pupil, Gervase Clifton (born 1611–13, d. 1676), elder son of Sir Gervase Clifton. Thoroton described him as 'the wretched unfortunate Sir Gervas his Father's greatest foil' (*Antiquities of Nottinghamshire*, ed. Throsby, i, p. 108): his subsequent life was so dissolute that he was disinherited, the title and estate passing to his younger brother, Clifford. In Mar. [/June] 1639 Sir Gervase wrote despairingly to the Earl of Newcastle: 'it is true my Wife lyes att this present gaspinge, & my Sonne gapinge not for what I leaue dyinge, but what I haue liuinge my backe being turned, to make a prey of all my convertible goodes within dores & without' (NUL MS Clifton C 348). Later that year the young Gervase Clifton was arrested for 'many Robberies' (NUL MS Clifton C 535).

[2] Gervase Clifton had left England with three servants (*CSPD* 1629–31, p. 68). His party also included a travelling companion and fellow student of foreign languages, Walter Waring, probably the son of Sir Gervase's friend and agent, Gervase Waring (see Letter 9 n. 5). Describing their journey from Paris in a letter to Sir Gervase, Walter Waring wrote: 'o^r company for variety, answearable, Protestants Papists & Turkes, whom we delighted much, when they vnderstood our differences' (NUL MS Clifton C 481).

[3] Pierre Prevost (1549–1639): his father, Claude, had been Principal of the College of Geneva, and Pierre had served as pastor of Russin (1597), Vitry-le-François (1598), and Russin again (1600), being admitted *bourgeois* of Geneva in 1601 (Stelling-Michaud (ed.), *Le Livre du Recteur*, v; I am grateful to Philippe Monnier of the Bibliothèque publique et universitaire, Geneva, for this reference).

[4] A colloquial term (derived from the distinctive typeface of the Geneva bibles) meaning of Calvinist opinions.

[5] The war of the Mantuan succession (1629–30). Spanish troops were besieging the fortress of Casale (south-west of Milan), and French troops had invaded Savoy.

[6] Thomas Purslow was the steward of the Cavendish household in London from at least 1618 (Chatsworth, MS Hardwick 29, pp. 536 ff.) until his death in April 1632 (Chatsworth, MS Hardwick 27, entry for that date).

[7] Christian Cavendish, Countess of Devonshire.

[8] Unidentified.

[9] Unidentified.

[10] Mary, Lady Clifton (Sir Gervase's third wife), daughter of John Egioke and widow of Sir Francis Leeke of Sutton Scarsdale; she died on 19/29 Jan. 1631.

[11] Bridget Abbot, sister of Mary, Lady Clifton (see NUL MS Clifton C 2). She was the widow of Robert Abbot (1560–1617), the Bishop of Salisbury and brother of George, Archbishop of Canterbury; her first husband was John Cheynell, Fellow of Corpus Christi College, Oxford, and her son by that marriage was Francis Cheynell, the future persecutor of William Chillingworth.

Hobbes to Sir Gervase Clifton, from Geneva

NUL MS Clifton C 560 (original).
Printed in de Beer, 'Some Letters', pp. 202–3.

Hon:^ble Sir.

   This day fortnight, Mr Clifton and I sent letters to you,[1] whereby you
might know of our safe arriuall at Geneua. In mine, you might find I
haue taken vp threescore pound of our allowance for this halfe yere wee
now are in. about .2. monethes hence I entend to take vp the rest. I long
much to know his name, and abiding place, whom you haue left in
London, during your absence, to receaue our letters, and to do such
thinges for vs there, as wee shall haue need to be done. For not being
able yet to resolue to what place to go next, I shall haue but little time,
for the procuringe from you of new letters of credit for the next halfe
yere. and yor being in the contry [>will] cause our letters to be very old
ere they arriue, and perhaps sometimes miscarry. Therefore I beseech
you assoone as you can, let me know who it is in London that I should
write to for those letters of credit, that I may receaue them at such time
and in such place as I shall require them. There is no possibility for the
present nor hope for the future of going into Italy, in respect of the
warres,[2] and going vp and downe of troupes in all partes betweene vs,
and it. And though I know you would gladly haue your sonne see that
contry, yet I presume you would [>not] haue him venture vpon a
iourney, [of *deleted*] where the danger so farre exceedes the profit. Wee
are in a place where Mr Clifton liues contentedly, [>&] to the benefit-
ting of his minde, as much as any place in the world can afford. He
studies as much, if not more [>then] I desire exercises his body
enough, and learnes Italian so fast that I doubt not but he will be able to
speake the languadge though we be denyed to see the contry. Seeing we
begin to lay by the hope of Italy we begin [>also] to aduise of our next
wintering place. There are but .3. places to be thought on. Eyther we
must returne into France, and spend the winter at Orleans, or some
other towne on the Riuer of Loyre, wch iourney will be not difficult, nor
the place when we come to it vnprofitable. Or else we must go into y^e
Low Contries, wch wee may well do next September, by Basil,[3] and so
downe the riuer of Rhine; But wee must haue a passeport from the
Archduchesse,[4] or Spaniards, w^ch [>we must haue *deleted*] (whensoeuer

we go into Holland, whether [>it] be before or after the winter,) will be necessary, and [will *deleted*] must be done by your meanes. Or lastly wee must stay the winter in this towne, wch I like least of the .3. but leaue all to your direction and Commandement, wch I desire to receaue wth as much speed as can be, and particularly who it is to whom I may addresse my letters, (wch I shall write in August next) for the procuringe of our next letters of credit. The Duke of Sauoy hath euilly entreated the French that liued in his court, aswell the seruants of his daughter in law the k: of France his sister,[5] as others, sending them away stripped of all they had and wth no security of their passage, so that many of them were murdered by the way. This asperity of his hath so exasperated the k. that he thinkes of [nothing but *deleted* >no lesse then] putting the Duke out of all both Sauoy and Piemont. Chambery he [the *deleted*] hath already if the report be true that came hither this morninge;[6] but howsoeuer, it is impossible for that towne to endure an assault of so great an army as is wth the king. This newes is enough [>to] let you see we [can *deleted* >are] not likely to haue good passage through Sauoy. and this is all the newes I yet haue. So I humbly take leaue and remayne

your most humble servant
Tho: Hobbes

Geneua May .10. stilo veteri 1630

[*addressed:*] To the Honorable Sir Geruas Clifton knight and Baronet present these.

[*endorsed:*] Mr Hobbs.s Letter 10th of May Old Stile 1630

---

[1] On Gervase Clifton see Letter 4 n. 1; Hobbes's letter, referred to here, is Letter 4 (dated three weeks earlier, rather than a fortnight).

[2] See Letter 4 n. 5.

[3] = Basel.

[4] Isabella Clara Eugenia (1566–1633), daughter of Philip II of Spain, widow of Archduke Albert of Austria, and regent of the Spanish Netherlands.

[5] In order to prosecute the war of the Mantuan succession, France had requested passage for its troops through Savoy. This was denied at first by the Duke of Savoy, Charles Emmanuel I (1562–1630), whose son Victor Amedeus had married Chrétienne, sister of Louis XIII of France; but after a French invasion he was forced to sign the Treaty of Susa in March 1629, allowing the French to pass through Savoy and occupy territory there. During March 1630 the French had seized other positions in Savoy and had attempted to capture the Duke. Hobbes's comments seem to reflect the reasons given for these actions in official French propaganda.

[6] Chambéry fell to French troops on 6/16 May 1630 (de Beer, 'Some Letters', p. 203 n.).

LETTER 6   30 JUNE/10 JULY 1630

Hobbes to Robert Leeke, from Orléans

NUL MS Clifton C 562 (original).
Printed in de Beer, 'Some Letters', pp. 203–4.

Sir

I thanke you for yor letter of the 30.th of May wch I haue receaued here the 8th of July, Sir Geruas[1] should not haue giuen his bond to s.^{r} w. Curten[2] for y^{or} paym^t of ye whole somme vpon my receipt of the letter of Credit, but for the sommes particularly as I tooke them. but the matter is not great. I haue now, (seeing nothing is saued by leauing it in the Merchants hands,) taken vp the rest of this halfe yeres allowance. My other .2. billes of 65.^{li} and of 25^{li} I meane not to take vp till the beginning of our next halfe yere, at wch time I make account to be againe in Paris, wch I take to be the best place to stay in all winter, for vs that haue allready vewed so much of the Contry. There is no newes from the army, it seemes they do no wonders on neyther side. The french vse to do most at first, and according to that, has bene their proceeding in Piemont & Sauoy.[3] God keepe you in health for our merry meeting in England wch I hope will be next spring at farthest. Commend me kindly to Mr Babington[4] & Mr Foukes.[5] So I rest

yor most assured frend
T Hobbes

Orleans July 10. stilo nouo 1630

[*addressed:*] To my [>very] louing frend Mr Robert Leeke giue these at Clifton.[6]

[*endorsed:*] M^r: Hobbs.s Letter To M^r: Leek 1630

[1] Sir Gervase Clifton.
[2] Sir William Courten or Corteene (1576–1636), a prominent London merchant of Huguenot origin.
[3] See Letter 5 n. 5.
[4] A member of Sir Gervase Clifton's household; a letter to Sir Gervase from the Earl of Kingston of 8 [/18] July 1630 refers to 'y^r serv^t Mr Babington' (NUL MS Clifton C

282). Perhaps the 'Fernando Babbington of Nottingham, gent.' who married Anne Alvie of Nottingham in 1640 (Blagg and Wadsworth, *Nottinghamshire Marriage Licenses*, i, p. 180).

⁵ Ralph Fowcks, Fowke, or Foucke, a member of Sir Gervase Clifton's household. The signature 'Raphe Fowcks' appears on an indenture made by Sir Gervase in Dec. 1649 (NUL MS Clifton A 305), and Sir Gervase's will, of Oct. 1662, refers to lands recently purchased 'in the names of Robert Milford and Ralph Foucke' (NUL MS Clifton D 1503). He was a man of some literary tastes: a list of books lent out of Sir Gervase's study in the early 1630s records the loan 'to Ralph' of translations of Ovid and Pindar (NUL MS Clifton A 301).

⁶ Clifton Hall, Notts., the seat of Sir Gervase Clifton.

LETTER 7   25 JULY/4 AUGUST 1630

Hobbes to Robert Leeke, from Orléans

NUL MS Clifton C 563 (original).
Printed in HMC, *Various*, p. 396; de Beer, 'Some Letters', pp. 204–5.

Good Mʳ Leeke,

I have receaued your letter of the .5. of July. the other packets you mention, I know not whether I have receaued them or not. But I haue receaued [one *deleted* > a] packet wherein I had letters of credit, one for .65.ˡⁱ (part of our next halfe yeres allowance) and another for .25.ˡⁱ for Mʳ Cliftons[1] priuate expence. If any other letters of credit besides these haue bene sent, I haue neyther receaued nor expected them. This towne is without newes, but for other passe-time here is enough. So praying for yoʳ health & our merry meeting I rest

   your most assured frend
   Tho: Hobbes

Orleans Aug .4. stilo nouo. 1630

[*postscript:*] I pray you commend my loue to Mʳ Babington[2]

[*addressed:*] To my very louing frend Mʳ Robert Leeke giue these

---

¹ See Letter 4 n. 1.
² See Letter 6 n. 4.

LETTER 8   2 [/12] NOVEMBER 1630

Hobbes to Sir Gervase Clifton, from Hardwick

NUL MS Clifton C 566 (original).
Printed in HMC, *Various*, p. 399; de Beer, 'Some Letters', p. 205.

Honorable Sir.

That I am welcome home, I must attribute to yo[r] fauorable letter, by w[ch] my lady[1] vnderstandes yo[r] good acceptance of my seruice to M[r] Clifton.[2] This fauo[r] of yours I esteeme no small part of your liberality, and shall hate my owne nature, when I shall cease to acknowledge both that, and the rest of your benefits, by w[ch] I am obliged to striue all I can to approue my selfe (when you shall be pleased to command me)

your most humble & obedient seruant
Tho: Hobbes

from Hardwicke[3]
this .2. of Nouemb. 1630

[*postscript:*] I made your man stay [>here] till .12. a clocke, because I [was ignorant of *deleted*] knew not whether she would write to you or not. but it seemes there is nothing in the letter that requires a present answer. I beseech you S[r] to remember my humble seruice to my Lady[4] and M[rs] Abbots[5] & M[ris] Leeke.[6]

[*addressed:*] To the Hon:[ble] Sir Geruas Clifton knight and Baronet giue these

---

[1] Christian, Countess of Devonshire.
[2] See Letter 4 n. 1.
[3] Hardwick Hall, one of the two Derby. seats of the Earls of Devonshire.
[4] Mary, Lady Clifton (see Letter 4 n. 10).
[5] See Letter 4 n. 11.
[6] Probably Elizabeth, daughter of Sir Guy Palmes and wife of William Leeke, the son of Sir Gervase Clifton's third wife, Mary, by her previous marriage to Sir Francis Leeke of Sutton Scarsdale.

LETTER 9   23 NOVEMBER [/3 DECEMBER] 1632

Hobbes to Sir Gervase Clifton, from Loughborough

NUL MS Clifton C 198 (original).
Printed in HMC, *Various*, p. 401.

Honble Sir

The letter I am writinge is yet in Competition wth me whether it or I shall haue the hono^r to kisse your hands. If it get the victory it is for [these Reasons *altered to* this Reason]. I haue but one night to dispose of, in wch I should come to Clifton so ill dressed from the way, as I should not haue the face to come into yor presence, besides It is not certayne you will be come home. This letter therefore that can stay better then I [shall *deleted*] may for this present supply all the service I could do you there, wch is to tell you that wee go to London about Tuesday come fortnight, and that a messenger expresse from the Queene came to my Lady of Oxford[1] and my Lady[2] for that purpose. I am sorry to heare from Mr Clifton[3] that you entend to stay in the Contry, pretending the proclamation,[4] wch is [not *deleted*] a barre to you no longer then yo^rselfe please. There is no newes from abroad, nor from any place, so that I may here put an end to the trouble I haue put you to of reading nothing in effect but my desire to expresse my selfe

your most humble and most obliged seruant
Tho: Hobbes

Loughborowgh.[5] ye 23th of Nouemb. 1632

[*addressed:*] To the Hon:^{ble} Sr Geruas Clifton Knight and Baronet present this at Clifton

[*endorsed:*] from Mr Hobbs Novr 23 1632

---

¹ See Letter 3 n. 5.
² Christian Cavendish, Countess of Devonshire.
³ See Letter 4 n. 1.
⁴ A royal proclamation of 20/30 June had ordered all gentlemen to leave London and return to their houses in the country, both in order to strengthen the defence of the realm and to rid London and Westminster of 'the great Number of loose and idle People, that follow them and live in and about the said Citties'. They were also warned

not to 'put themselves to unnecessary charge in providing themselves to returne in Wynter to the said Citties' (Rymer, *Foedera*, xix, pp. 374–6).

[5] Loughborough (Leics.), the home of Sir Gervase Clifton's friend and agent Gervase Waring, probably the father of the Walter Waring who had accompanied the younger Gervase Clifton on his foreign tour with Hobbes. See NUL MS Clifton D 1468, which refers to 'Gervase Waring of Loughborowe [. . .], gent', and Walter Waring's letter to Sir Gervase, NUL MS Clifton C 481.

LETTER 10   26 JANUARY [/5 FEBRUARY] 1634

Hobbes to William Cavendish, Earl of Newcastle, from London

BL MS Add. 70499, fos. 172–3 (original).
Printed in HMC, *Portland*, p. 124; Bickley (ed.), *Letter Book*, pp. 18–19.

Right Hon:[ble] and my Singular good Lord.

My Lady[1] and her family Came to London in good health on Thursday last. There mette her on the way at Stony-Stratford[2] my Lord of Warwicke.[3] at Brickhill,[4] the Queenes Litter, wth the Littermen in their coates, attendinge the comminge of my Lady Rich,[5] who went in it to Dunstable and thence sent it before her againe to Barnet. At Barnet my Lord Rich[6] met her, and betweene Highgate and Islington, my Lord of Holland,[7] and my Lord of Elgen.[8] So that she was very honorably conducted to her house. My first businesse in London, was to seeke for Galileos dialogues;[9] I thought it a very good bargaine, when at taking my leaue of your Lordship I vndertooke to buy it for you, but if yo[r] Lo[p] should bind me to performance it would be hard enough, for it is not possible to get it for mony; There were but few brought ouer at first, and they that buy such bookes, are not such men as to part wth them againe. I heare say it is called in, in Italy, as a booke that will do more hurt to their Religion then all the bookes haue done of Luther and Caluin, such opposition they thinke is betweene their Religion, and naturall reason. I doubt not but the Translation of it will here be publiquely embraced, and therefore wish extreamely that D[r] Webbe[10] would hasten it. There is no newes at Court but of Maskes, which is a stay to my Lords going to Oxford, because he is one of the Maskers.[11] w[ch] I am glad of for this cause, that I shall haue the more time for the businesse I haue so long owed to your Lo[p], whose continuall fauors make me ashamed of my dull proceedinge, sauinge that into ye number of those fauors I put yor Lo^ps patience and forbearance of me,

yor Lo^ps most obliged and most humble seruant
Tho: Hobbes

London Jan. 26. 1633

[*addressed:*] To the Right Honorable my very good Lord The Earle of Newcastle present these at Welbecke[12]

The year of this letter is determined both by Hobbes's usual practice and by the reference to the masque at Court (see n. 11).

[1] Christian Cavendish, Countess of Devonshire.

[2] A small town in Bucks., on the main road from the Midlands to London (Watling St., the modern A5).

[3] Robert Rich (1587–1658), second Earl of Warwick, the future parliamentary admiral during the Civil War.

[4] A village in Bucks., also on Watling St., ten miles south-east of Stony Stratford (see n. 2).

[5] Christian Cavendish's daughter (see Letter 3 n. 2).

[6] Robert Rich (1611–59), later third Earl of Warwick.

[7] Henry Rich (1590–1649), first Earl of Holland, second son of the first Earl of Warwick, courtier and Chancellor of Cambridge University.

[8] Christian Cavendish's brother (see Letter 3 n. 4).

[9] *Dialogo dove si discorre sopra i due massimi sistemi del mondo* (Florence, 1632).

[10] Dr Joseph Webbe graduated MD from Padua University in 1603 or 1604 and applied for admission to the Royal College of Physicians in 1616 (Munk *et al.* (eds.), *Roll*, i, p. 159). In the 1620s he was a private schoolmaster, specializing in the teaching of languages; in his treatise *An Appeale to Truth* (1622) he argued that grammar should be acquired by practice, not by the study of grammar books (Vincent, *The State and Education 1640–1660*, p. 14; Salmon, *Works of Lodwick*, pp. 59–60). In 1631 Webbe was sent to the Earl of Pembroke with a recommendation from the Earl of Newcastle (BL MS Add. 70499, fo. 143^r), and from another letter of that year it appears that Webbe was employed by Newcastle in developing telescopes, or some other kind of optical instruments ('the D^rs glasses' (ibid., fo. 145^r)). An early 17th-cent. MS translation of Galileo's *Dialogo* in the British Library (MS Harl. 6320) may perhaps be the translation by Webbe referred to here, which was probably commissioned by Newcastle and his brother (see Hall, 'Galileo's Influence on English Scientists', p. 407). No translation was published, however, until that of Sir Thomas Salusbury in his *Mathematical Collections* (1661).

11 The third Earl of Devonshire ('my Lord') took part in a performance of Thomas Carew's masque *Coelum Britannicum* at Court on 18/28 Feb. 1634 (Carew, *Poems*, pp. 185, 273–4).

12 Welbeck Abbey, Notts., one of the seats of the Earl of Newcastle.

Hobbes to Sir Gervase Clifton, from London

NUL MS Clifton C 199 (original).

Hon:^{ble} Sir,

My Lord[1] is now so neere his time of trauaylinge, as I feared I should want the opportunity of taking my leaue of you. for if the resolution that now is hold, wee shall be gone towards France eyther in Easter weeke or the next weeke after. It was intended once, he should haue spent this sommer in Oxford, and not haue gone ouer till Autumne, but in respect of the diseases that time is subiect to, it has bene thought fitt to send him now.[2] I am almost ashamed to aske you what seruice you will Command me in France, because I haue done you so little here as that I haue not so much as written to you since my beeing at Hodsocke.[3] Neuerthelesse you may with more reason looke for letters from me thence, where euery thing will be newes, then from this place, where nothing has bene newes to me a great while. If there be any newes beyond sea stirring so as to come to my knowledge, I will not be backeward to write them to you, not that you care [much *deleted*] for them, but because I will seeke all occasions to hold fast my relation to you, wch I set at a higher rate, then my seruice can make shew of. Wee intend to liue this sommer, in some towne nere the Loyre, and not to come to Paris till toward winter, and then to stay all winter there; if [there be *deleted*] you haue any particular employm^t for me, wch you thinke I can performe, I beseech you let me know it, and I will do my best to serue you to yor Contentment. In the meane time I take my leaue and remayne

your most humble and obliged seruant
Tho: Hobbes

London Deuonsh. house. March. 27. 1634

[*addressed:*] To the Honorable Sr Geruas Clifton Knight and Baronet present these at Hodsocke

[*endorsed:*] Mr Hobbis When Going abroad W^t: the Earl of Devonshire March 27th 1634

[1] William Cavendish, third Earl of Devonshire.

[2] There is some evidence, however, that the original plan was adhered to: John Aubrey recorded that in July or Aug. 1634 Hobbes visited friends in Wilts. for 'a weeke or better' (*ABL* i, pp. 331–2). It is possible, therefore, that Hobbes and his pupil were in Oxford (a suitable base for a short excursion into north Wilts.) at that time.

[3] One of the seats of Sir Gervase Clifton, near Worksop, in north Notts.

LETTER 12   21/31 OCTOBER 1634

Hobbes to ?, from Paris

MS unlocated.

Printed (from the original MS) in Peck (ed.), *Desiderata curiosa*, i, bk. 6, no. 10, p. 23; Hobbes, *Works*, pp. 668–9; *EW* vii, pp. 452–3.

Worthy Sir,

I HAVE bene behind hand with you a long Time for a Letter which I received of yours at *Angers*, that Place affording nothing wherewith to pay a Debt of that Kind. All Matter of Newes being sooner knowne in *England* then there. And the Newes you writ me was of that Kind, that none, from *England*, could be more wellcome. Because it concerned the Honor of *Welbecke* & *Clifton*, two Houses to which I am very much obliged.

Monsieur, having given the Slip to the *Spaniards* at *Bruxelles*, came to the King about ten Dayes agoe at S. *Germains*, where he was receaved with great Joy.[1] The next Day the Cardinall entertayned him at *Ruelle*.[2] And the Day after that he went to *Limours*, where he is now; and from whence he goes very shortly to *Bloys*, to stay there this Winter. The Cardinall of *Lyons* is going to *Rome* to treate about the Annulling of Mounsieurs Marriage, which is here by Parliament declared voyd; but yet they require the Sentence of the Pope.[3] There goes somebody thither, on the Part of his Wife, to get the Marriage approved. But who that is I know not. The *Swedish* Party in *Germany* is in low Estate;[4] but the *French* prepare a great Army for those Parts, pretending to defend the Places which the *Swedes* have put into the King of *France* his Protection; whereof *Philipsbourgh* is one,[5] a Place of great Importance for the lower *Palatinate*. This is all the *French* News.

For your Question—*Why a Man remembers lesse his owne Face, which he sees often in a Glasse, then the Face of a Friend, that he has not seene of a great Time?* My Opinion in generall is, that a Man remembers best those Faces whereof he has had the greatest Impressions; & that the Impressions are the greater for the oftner seeing them, & the longer Staying upon the Sight of them. Now, you know, Men looke upon their owne Faces, but for short Fits; but, upon their Friends Faces, long Time together, whilest they discourse or converse together; so that a Man may receave a greater Impression from his Friends Face in a Day, then from his own in a Yere: And, according to this Impression, the Image will be fresher in his Mind. Besides, the Sight of ones Frends Face two Howres together, is of greater Force to imprinte the Image of it, then the same Quantity of Time by Intermissions. For the Intermissions do easily deface that which is but lightly imprinted. In generall, I thinke, that, That lasteth longer in the Memory, which hath been stronglier receaved by the Sense.

This is my Opinion of the Question you propounded in your Letter. Other new Trueths I have none, at least they appere not new to me. Therefore, if this Resolution of your first Question, seeme probable; you may propound another, wherein I will endeavor to satisfie you, as also in any Thing of any other Nature you shall command me, to my utmost Power: taking it for an Honor to be esteemed by you, as I am in Effect,

Your humble & faythfull Servant,
Tho. Hobbes.

Paris, Oct. 21/31. [1634][6]

[*postscript:*] My Lord Fielding & his Lady[7] came to Paris on Saturday Night last.

Another version of this letter, retaining the discussion of a man's memory of his face, but with a different introduction and a different conclusion, was printed in Grose and Astle (eds.), *The Antiquarian Repertory* (2nd edn., rev. Jeffery), i, pp. 388–9 (text here from CUL Mm. 34. 1), as follows:

Mr. Thomas Hobbes to his Friend the Earl of Devonshire.
Paris, January 10, 1649

MY NOBLE LORD,

I HAVE long owed your Lordship for a letter which I received at Tours; but, that place affording no news. I delayed answering it till I arrived here.—For your question [. . . *etc.*] [. . .] receaved by the sense.

For the news. The king has been compelled by the Frondeurs to quit his capital, at the very time when the treaty of Munster renders his power respectable all over Europe. He withdrew to St. Germans, the sixth instant at night; and on the 7th, the Prince of Condè, accompanied by the Duke of Orleans, formed the blockade of Paris. Alas! my worthy Lord, how little is my situation improved:— I quitted England, tired of its troubles; and here I find myself as badly off as I was when in mine owne country!—I remain, my noble Lord,

Your Lordship's most fayfhfull and most humble servant,

THOMAS HOBBES

I assume that these passages are forgeries, added by Edward Jeffery, the reviser of the edition, to give the impression that he was reproducing an original MS, rather than copying a text from a similar but earlier collection. Peck gave details of provenance for his MS (see below); Jeffery gives none. The introductory passage here is obviously a reworking of the opening sentence in Peck's version, and the final passage here is in a style which is neither Hobbesian ('the sixth instant') nor even 17th-cent. ('as badly off'). Hobbes did not leave England because of any 'troubles' comparable to the Fronde; he left in 1640, nearly two years before the outbreak of the Civil War.

The text of Letter 12 is taken from CUL S540. a. 73. 1 (siglum: 'Peck'), collated with BL 505. ff. 8. The formal features of Peck's text are reproduced here, except that his paragraph-numbering is omitted and his italics and black letter are both rendered as italics (it can be presumed that neither form of emphasis derives from the original MS); and one evident misprint is corrected at n. 6.

A marginal note printed by Peck gives the provenance of the MS, as follows: '21 Oct. 1634, the tenth year of Charles I's reign. From the autograph itself, in my possession. It was given to me by that learned and reverend man, William Standfast MD, rector of Clifton, Notts.' ('Oct. 21 1634. 10 C. 1. Ex ipso Autographo penes me. D.D. Vir doctus, reverendusque *Guliel. Standfast*, M.D. Rector de *Clifton* in Comit. *Nott.*') William Standfast, born in 1682 or 1683, became vicar of Clifton in 1721. His will is dated 1754 (NRO DD SX 8/1): most of his estate passed to his daughter-in-law, Elizabeth Eyre, but the present location of his MSS (if they survive) is unknown. From the fact that Standfast was rector of Clifton, one might presume that the original recipient of this letter was someone connected with Sir Gervase Clifton's family; Hobbes's reference to the houses of Welbeck and Clifton seems to confirm this, though the recipient might equally have been an employee of the Newcastle Cavendishes (the house of Welbeck) who happened to have news of the Cliftons. Yet the other MS which Peck received from Standfast (Letter 17) is addressed to Mr Glen, who may be identified with someone who was an employee not of either of those families but of the Countess of Devonshire (see the Biographical Register). Peck supposed that Glen was 'the Person whom both these Letters of Mr. *Hobbes* were addressed to' (*Desiderata curiosa*, i, bk. 6, p. 24), although the valedictory formulas of the two letters differ, suggesting two recipients enjoying different degrees of acquaintance with Hobbes. Nevertheless, from the style of the salutation and valediction here we may assume that this letter was written to someone of roughly equal status to Hobbes—if at Welbeck, then perhaps Robert Payne, and if at Leicester Abbey, Chatsworth, or Hardwick, then perhaps Mr Glen or Robert Gale.

[1] Gaston d'Orléans (1608–60), 'Monsieur', the younger brother of Louis XIII, had previously taken refuge at the Spanish Court in Brussels after fomenting the unsuccessful rebellion against his brother by the duc de Montmorency in 1632. Saint-Germain was the royal residence to the west of Paris.

[2] Rueil, near Saint-Germain, was the residence of Armand-Jean du Plessis, Cardinal Richelieu (1585–1642), chief minister of Louis XIII.

³ Gaston d'Orléans had secretly married Princess Marguerite of Lorraine in 1632. Louis XIII and Richelieu argued that the marriage was invalid because it was contracted without royal consent. The Parlement of Paris declared it invalid on 26 Aug./5 Sept. 1634. Richelieu's brother, Alphonse-Louis du Plessis (1582–1663), Cardinal and Archbishop of Lyon, was sent as a special envoy to Pope Urban VIII in early 1635.

⁴ Sweden, in alliance with the league of German Protestants, had occupied Bavaria in 1633; but it suffered a severe defeat when the Swedish garrison at Nördlingen was overwhelmed by the Imperial army on 23 Aug./2 Sept. 1634.

⁵ During 1634 Richelieu had been negotiating with the Swedish minister Oxenstierna over Philipsburg and other Rhineland fortresses which had been captured by Sweden and were claimed by France. In Nov. 1634 Richelieu offered the German Protestants a treaty under which France would provide 12,000 soldiers and subsidies to those who continued to fight against the Habsburgs.

⁶ 1694 *Peck*.

⁷ Basil Feilding (*c*.1608–74), later second Earl of Denbigh (and husband of Anne, daughter of Sir Richard Weston, first Earl of Portland), was on his way to the republic of Venice, to which he had been appointed Ambassador Extraordinary in Sept. 1634.

LETTER 13   20/30 JANUARY 1635

Hobbes to Sir Gervase Clifton, from Paris

NUL MS Clifton C 564 (original).

Honorable Sir,

No newes, nor seruice I can do you, but the ambition to remayne in your memory hath produced this Letter, wch is, an acknowledgm^t of your fauo^rs, a confession vnder my hand of my great obligation to you, of which though I be sensible, I am not in the way (wch is a quality, generous men require where they shew fauor) to be able to disoblige my selfe, nor would, if I were able, that my seruice should ayme at that end. If you beleeue this, my letter will haue the effect of a perspectiue glasse, wch shewes you not onely a towre afarre of in grosse, but also the battlements and windowes and other principall partes distinctly, as this shewes you my principall quality, gratitude, by wch onely I pretend to your good opinion, and the hono^r to be esteemed

your most humble and obedient seruant
Tho: Hobbes

Paris Jan: 20/30 1634

[*addressed:*] To the Right Honorable Sir Geruas Clifton at Clifton

[*endorsed:*] Mr Hobbs. January 1634

LETTER 14   21 APRIL/1 MAY 1635

Hobbes to Sir Gervase Clifton, from Paris

NUL MS Clifton C 565 (original).

Honorable Sir.

When I receaued yor letter with mine owne backe againe, me thought it look't, as I had bene fishing and catch't yours with mine. But I beseech you beleeue that though I find infinite contentment in ye honor you do me by answering mine, yet I consider my obligation to you, better then to exact your trouble on euery occasion that I do my duty, or [> to] thinke it a sinne in you not to giue me letter for letter. you should haue mine often, if I had any curiosity towards newes, or lucke in writing them, For I seldome attempt that subiect, but all proues cleane contrary to my intelligence. In such sterility of matter, and infelicity of brayne, it resteth that out of the bowells of my affection I spinne out a line or two to assure you that I [> am] sensible of your fauors, and take greater Content in nothing in the world then in your good opinion, and the hono^r of being esteemed

your most humble and obedient seruant
T: Hobbes

Paris Apr. 21/May. 1 1635

[*postscript:*] My Lord[1] thankes you for your remembrance of him and commanded me to present his humble seruice to you.

[*addressed:*] To the Honourable Sir Geruas Clifton night and Baronet at Clifton

[*endorsed:*] Mr Hobs. May. 1635

---

[1] William Cavendish, third Earl of Devonshire.

[early AUGUST 1635]

Hobbes to Sir Gervase Clifton, from Paris

BL MS Lansdowne 238, fo. 151ᵛ (transcript).
Printed in *EW* vii, p. 451; de Beer, 'Some Letters', pp. 199–200.

A L[ette]re[1] from Mʳ: Hobbs to my M[aste]ʳ²

Honorable Sʳ

   Though I may goe whither and when I will for anie necessity you have of my service, yet there is a necessity of good manners that obliges me as yoʳ servant to lett you knowe att all times where to find me, Wee goe out of Paris 3. weekes hence or sooner towards Venice, but by what way I knowe not because the ordinary high way through the territory of Milan is encumbred with the warre betweene the French and the Spaniards.[3] Howsoeuʳ wee hope to be there in October next. If you require anie service that I can doe there it may please you to convey yoʳ command by Devonshire howse. But if you command me nothing I haue forbidden my L[ette]res[4] to looke for Answer their busines being only to informe and to lett you knowe that the image of yoʳ noblenes decayes not in my memory, but abides fresh to keepe me eternally

   yoʳs Tho: Hobbs.

This is one of several letters to Sir Gervase Clifton in an early transcription, in a secretary hand. Because this letter is addressed to Sir Gervase, previous editors have assumed that it was written while Hobbes was in Clifton's service: Molesworth dated it 1629–30, and de Beer *c.*5/15 March 1630. But the contents of the letter make it clear that Hobbes was now in the service of the Cavendish family again. It is dated here by comparison with Letter 16, which refers to departure from Paris in the following week.

   [1] Contraction expanded.
   [2] Contraction expanded: 'my Master' is identifiable as Sir Gervase Clifton from the internal evidence of several other letters to him in the same group of transcripts in BL MS Lansdowne 238.
   [3] Having declared war on Spain in May 1635, France had sent troops to harass Spanish forces in northern Italy, and had encouraged Savoy and Venice to attack Milan.
   [4] Contraction expanded.

Hobbes to William Cavendish, Earl of Newcastle,
from Paris

BL MS Add. 70499, fos. 184–5 (original).
Printed in HMC, *Portland*, pp. 125–6.

Right Hon:^ble and my singular good Lord.

I haue receaued yor Lo^ps guift, proportioned to your owne goodnesse, not to my seruice. If the world saw my little desert, so plainely as
they see yor great rewards, they might thinke me a mountibancke and
that all that I do or would do, were in ye hope of what I receaue. I hope
yor Lo^p does not thinke so, at least let me tell yor Lo^p once for all, that
though I hono^r you as my Lord, yet my Loue to you is iust of ye same
nature that it is to m^r Payne, bred out of priuate talke, without respect
to yor purse; your letters since comming abroad haue bene great testi-
monies of your fauor, and great spurres of my endeauor, but it seemes
yor Lo^p thinkes siluer spurres haue a greater effect, wch is an errour, but
such a one as I see more reason to thanke you for, then to confute, and
therefore wth my most humble thankes I end this point. I told M^r
Benjamin[1] and mons^r de Pre (who is Monsr Beniamins eldest sonne,
and teaches vnder his Father) of the faults yor Lo^p found in ye Horse.
For ye opening his mouth, they confesse it, and say that when he was
young and first began to be dressed he put out his head too much, w^ch
they that dressed him, endeauoring to amend, for want of skill, did by a
great bitte conuert into this other fault of gaping, For his feete they
obstinately deny that he has any fault in them at all, and do suppose
that the iourny may haue hurt him, or his wearinesse made it seeme so.
That he has no other ayre but coruettes,[2] is a thing yor Lo^p was made
acquainted with before. The greatest fault is his price. wch price adding
the 40 pound you gaue me, is a very good reason why he should hence-
forward be called Le Superbe. I vnderstand not how m^r Warner[3] will
demonstrate those inuentions of the multiplyinge glasse and burning
glasse so infinite in vertue as he pretends;[4] if he [>can] know the art
already, a little time will serue to make ye demonstration, especially to
Sr Charles, and m^r Payne, who are not scrupulous to grant him any
reasonable suppositions, and vnderstand as much as he in any thing
demonstrable; if he know it not yet, it is a bold promise. Besides when it

is demonstrated, if it cannot also be practised tis worth nothinge, but like yᵉ probleme How to make a bridge ouer ye sea. wᶜʰ is no more but to make the height of his arch in the same proportion to yᵉ breadth of the sea, that an arch of a roome is to yᵉ breadth of a roome. But such an arch cannot be made. so when it is demonstrated how yᵉ glasse must be made to burne a mile of, if the glasse must be so bigge as cannot be made, the art will be no more worth, then the art of making ordinary burning glasses. For my part I thinke mʳ Payne will do more that way then mʳ Warner. I hope yoʳ Loᴾ will not bestow much vpon yᵉ hopes; but suffer the liberall sciences to be liberall, and after some worthy effect, yoʳ Loᴾ then may be liberall also, as I doubt not but you will. For yᵉ soule I know he has nothinge to giue yoʳ Loᴾ any satisfaction. I would he could giue [a *deleted*] good reasons for yᵉ facultyes & passions of yᵉ soule, such as may be expressed in playne English. [I do *deleted*] if he can, he is the first (that I euer heard [>of) could] speake sense in that subiect. if he can not I hope to be yᵉ first. On wednesday next we go towards Lions, and there we shall consider of our way into Italy. If yoʳ Loᴾ be pleased to continue me the honoʳ of your Letters, you must send them to my Lady,⁵ or to Deuonshire house till such times as I can giue you a better addresse, if a better can be. S.ʳ Wᵐ Corteene⁶ sends my Ladies letters, yoʳ Loᴾ may send them in his couer, immediately, without sending them to Deuonshire house. I thinke I shall write no more to yoʳ Loᴾ till I come to Venice because we shall be perpetually in motion. I pray God to Continue yoʳ Loᴾ in health.

  yoʳ Loᴾs most humble and most obedient seruant
  Tho: Hobbes

Paris Aug 15/25 1635

¹ M. Benjamin was the manager of the famous de Pluvinel riding school in the rue Saint-Honoré in Paris (Stoye, *English Travellers*, p. 36). He took charge of the school on the death of Antoine de Pluvinel in 1621 (Kaufman, *Conscientious Cavalier*, p. 243).
² Basic dressage consisted of mastery of the 'courbette' and the 'terre à terre': a horse was regarded as trained if it could do these. (Other movements, such as the 'capréole', were more advanced.) On the courbette or corvette, see de Pluvinel, *L'Instruction du Roy*, pp. 38–40, 90.
³ Walter Warner (b. 1557–60, d. 1642–4) proceeded BA at Oxford in 1579, was a member of the circle of Sir Walter Raleigh and Richard Hakluyt in the 1580s, and had entered the service of the ninth Earl of Northumberland by 1590, working for him as secretary, literary assistant, and librarian (Shirley, *Thomas Harriot*, pp. 372, 66, 365–7). From 1616 he was paid a pension by the Earl, and seems to have lived more independently as a mathematician and scientific researcher (ibid., p. 372). By 1627 he was

working on refraction with Sir Thomas Aylesbury, who had become his patron (Jacquot, 'Harriot, Hughes, Warner', p. 117). In 1631 he edited a mathematical work by his old friend Thomas Hariot, *Artis analyticae praxis*; his role as editor is not stated there, but Robert Payne annotated the title-page of his copy 'Per Walterum Warnerum, Mathematicum et Philosophicum' (Bodl. Savile O 9). He compiled tables of logarithms with John Pell, corresponded with Payne and Sir Charles Cavendish on optics, prepared a metaphysical treatise, 'Of states, alterations, causes' (BL MS Add. 4394, fos. 129–271, 382–91), and was rumoured to have given Harvey the idea of the circulation of the blood (*ABL* ii, p. 291). He probably died some time between 1642 and 1644 (Kargon, *Atomism*, p. 35), though Anthony Wood placed his death in late 1640 (*Athenae*, ii, cols. 302–3).

⁴ Warner was preparing a treatise on the construction of telescopes, which he sent to Sir Charles Cavendish in early 1636. See Sir Charles's letters to Warner of 2 [/12] May and 2 [/12] Sept. 1636: BL MSS Add. 4407, fo. 186, and Add. 4444, fo. 93 (printed in Halliwell (ed.), *Collection of Letters*, pp. 66–7).

⁵ Christian Cavendish, Countess of Devonshire.

⁶ See Letter 6 n. 2.

LETTER 17   6/16 APRIL 1636

Hobbes to Mr Glen, from Florence

MS unlocated.

Printed (from the original MS) in Peck (ed.), *Desiderata curiosa*, i, bk. 6, no. 11, p. 24; Hobbes, *Works*, p. 669; *EW* vii, pp. 454–5.

Worthy Sir,

I Received here in *Florence*, two Dayes since, a Letter from you of the 19th of January. It was long by the Way; but, when it came, it did thoroughly recompence that Delay. For it was worth all the Pacquets I had received a great while together. All that passeth in these parts is equally Newes, & therefore no Newes. Else I would labour to requite your Letter in that Point, though in the handsome setting downe of it, I should still be inferior.

I long infinitely to see those Bookes of the Sabbaoth;¹ & am of your Mind, they will put such Thoughts into the Heads of vulgar People, as will conferre little to their good Life. For, when they see one of the ten Commandments to be *Jus humanum*² merely (as it must be, if the Church can alter it) they will hope also, that the other nine may be so too. For every Man hitherto did believe that the ten Commandments were the Morall, that is, an Eternal Law.³

I desire also to see *Seldens Mare clausum*,⁴ having already a great Opinion of it.

You may perhaps, by some that go to *Paris*, send me those of the Sabaoth. For the other, being in Latin, I doubt not but to find it in the *Rüe S. Jaques*.[5]

We are now come hither from *Rome*, & hope to be in *Paris* before the End of *June*. I thanke you againe for your Letter, & desire you to beleeve that I can never grow strange to one, the Goodnesse of whose Acquaintance I have found by so much Experience. But I have to write to so many, that I write to you seldomer then I desire, which I pray pardon, & esteem me

Your most affectionate Frend & humble Servant,
Tho. Hobbes.

Florence, Apr. 6/16. 1636.

[*postscript:*] My Lord, & Mr. *Nichols* & all our Company,[6] commend them to you.

[*addressed:*] *To my very worthy Frend Mr.* Glen

The details of the copy-text and transcription for this letter are the same as those for Letter 12; this letter also bears a marginal annotation by Peck giving the same provenance for the MS as for that letter (see Letter 12, general note).

[1] This probably refers to a single work, Heylyn's *The History of the Sabbath. In Two Bookes* (1636). However, if Hobbes was referring to other works as well, he may have meant any of the following anti-sabbatarian treatises published in the renewed controversy over observance of the Sabbath which had followed the Declaration of Sports of 1633: F. White, *Treatise of the Sabbath-Day*; Dow, *Discourse of the Sabbath*; Pocklington, *Sunday no Sabbath*; anon. [Sanderson], *Sovereign Antidote against Sabbatarian Errors*.

[2] 'Human law'.

[3] Heylyn argued that Sabbath observance 'was no part of the *Morall Law*, or *Law of Nature*', and that 'the Emperour Constantine [. . .] was the first also that made any law about the keeping of the *Lords day* or *Sunday*' (*History of the Sabbath*, bk. 2, p. 66).

[4] John Selden's *Mare clausum*, written originally in 1618 in reply to Grotius' *Mare liberum*, and published in 1635. It used a combination of natural law theories and historical evidence to argue in defence of English claims to sovereignty over the North Sea and North Atlantic.

[5] The street where many of the Parisian booksellers had their shops.

[6] A Mr 'Nicols' is listed in the Pilgrim Book of the Jesuits' English College in Rome as dining with the Earl of Devonshire, Hobbes and a Mr 'Magdonel' (Macdonnel) at the College on [16/] 26 Dec. 1635 (see Chaney, *Grand Tour*, p. 301, correcting the entry in Foley (ed.), *Records of the English Province*, vi, p. 612). I am grateful to Dr Chaney for this reference.

LETTER 18   13/23 JUNE 1636

Hobbes to William Cavendish, Earl of Newcastle, from Paris

BL MS Add. 70499, fos. 202–3 (original).
Printed in HMC, *Portland*, p. 128; *MC* vi, p. 101 (extract).

Right Hon:^{ble} and my Singular good Lord.

I writte to your Lo^p my last letters from Lyons, where we stayed .3. dayes, wch leasure was the cause my letter was so tedious. I haue nothinge to write from hence but that we are here, and arriued, June. 1/11. Wee are vnsettled, I haue no time (for going vp and downe wth my Lord)[1] neyther for my selfe, nor for Mydorgius,[2] nor for bookes. All I study is a nights, and that for a little while is ye reading of Certayne new bookes, especially m^r Seldens Mare Clausum,[3] and a booke of my Lord of Castle Ilands Concerning truth.[4] wch is a high point, and both these bookes are new set forth since I came abroad. Mydorgius tels me he has sent to Sr Charles his treatise of refraction perfected.[5] I hope Mr Payne will tell me in his next what satisfaction it giues you all, he has no Copie in his hands but scattred and blotted papers, so that I must haue patience till I come to Welbecke. My Lord is now writing to your Lo^p, if he make an end before the post go his letter will go wth this, if not it will come a weeke after I beeseech yor Lo^p to pardon this shortnesse, and also obteyne pardon for me from Sr Charles that I write not to him this [weeke *deleted*] time. For Mr Payne I will make my peace my selfe. so wth my humble seruice and acknowledgm^t of all yor Lo^ps fauors I take my leaue and rest

your Lo^ps most humble and most obedient seruant
Tho: Hobbes

Paris June 13/23 1636

[*postscript:*] mons^r Toras is newly killed in Piemont as I heare.[6]

[*addressed:*] To the Right Honorable The Earle of Newcastle at Welbecke

---

[1] William Cavendish, third Earl of Devonshire.

[2] Claude Mydorge, sieur de la Maillarde (1585–1647), mathematician and writer on optics. The son of a senior judge, he trained as a lawyer and became treasurer of

Amiens. In 1625 he befriended Descartes, spending large sums on lenses for his researches in optics; in 1638 he was an intermediary between Descartes and Fermat when the latter criticized Descartes's 'Dioptrique', and reconciled them. He published a work on conic sections in relation to the reflection and refraction of light, *Prodromi catoptricorum et dioptricorum libri duo* (1631), which he later expanded into *Conicorum operis* [...] *libri quatuor* (1639). He also wrote a criticism of a popular mathematical book, *Examen du livre des recreations mathématiques* (1638), and a comprehensive treatise on geometry, 'La Théorie et la pratique de la géometrie' (BN MS f.fr. 656), which was apparently never published.

³ See above, Letter 16 n. 4.

⁴ *De veritate* (1624), a treatise on metaphysics and epistemology by Sir Edward Herbert, who was created Lord Castleisland in the Irish peerage in 1624 and Lord Herbert of Cherbury in the English peerage in 1629.

⁵ De Waard has conjectured that this may have been a MS of bks. 3 and 4 of *Conicorum operis libri quatuor* (see n. 2) (*MC* vi, p. 102). Sir Charles Cavendish had been in contact with Mydorge since at least as early as June 1631 (BL MS Add. 70499, fo. 145ʳ), and when bks. 3 and 4 were printed in 1639 Mydorge sent Sir Charles a copy (Bodl. Savile Q 9).

⁶ Jean de Saint-Bonnet, seigneur de Toiras (1585–1636), a distinguished commander, best known to the English for his successful defence of the Isle of Rhé against the Duke of Buckingham in 1627. Having become commander of the Duke of Savoy's army in 1636, he was killed by a musket-shot at Fontanetto d'Agogna (on the border between Savoy and Milan) on 4/14 June.

LETTER 19   29 JULY/8 AUGUST 1636

Hobbes to William Cavendish, Earl of Newcastle, from Paris

BL MS Add. 70499, fos. 210–11 (original).
Printed in HMC, *Portland*, pp. 128–9.

Right Honorable and my singular good Lord.

In thinges that are not demonstrable, of wᶜʰ kind is yᵉ greatest part of Naturall Philosophy, as dependinge vpon the motion of bodies so subtile as they are inuisible, such as are ayre and spirits, the most that can be atteyned vnto is to haue such opinions, as no certayne experience can confute, and from wᶜʰ can be deduced by lawfull argumentation, no absurdity, and such are your Loᵖˢ opinions in your letter of the .3ᵈ of July wᶜʰ I had the honor to receaue yᵉ last weeke; namely, That the variety of thinges is but variety of locall motion in yᵉ spirits or inuisible partes of bodies. And That such motion is heate. For the optiques I know Mʳ Warner¹ and Mʳ Mydorge² are as able men as

any in Europe, but they do not well to call their writings demonstrations, for the grounds and suppositions they vse, so many of them as
[are of *deleted*] concerne light, are vncertayne and many of them not
true. M^r warner has sent a tract to Sr Charles^3 concerninge the place of
the Image in conuexe and concaue glasses. I pray yor Lo^p let him see
that peece of ye conuexe glasse wherein appeare the Images of the firre
trees, and see if he can applye his reasons to it, and demonstrate why
the Images of those trees wch are long since perhaps burnt a thousand
mile hence should be in that place where they are.^{4} If the experiment of
ye mans image in ye glasse of bloud^5 might be made againe, and shewed
him I would haue him answer to that also. For my part my opinion of
the firre trees is that the same [vertue *deleted*] motion by wch the tree it
selfe was able to produce the image of a tall tree in ye ey of a man that
looked on it, remayning in ye rosin and by it mouing in the glasse,
workes the little image of a tree in the ey of him that lookes upon y^e
glasse, and therefore a little [>image of a] tree, because now a little or
feynt motion. This reason is not cleare enough to make one see how
nature workes it, but the old way by beames and reflection, and
refraction leaues a man destitute of any thing to say to it I pray you my
Lord if you can conueniently let that experiment of the bloud, eyther of
a man or horse be tryed againe. for it deserues to be knowne for y^e
wonder. I am sorry yor Lo^p finds not so good dealing in ye world as you
deserue. but my Lord, he that will venture to sea must resolue to
endure all weather, but for my part I loue to keepe aland.^{6} And it may be
yor Lo^p will do so to. whereby I may haue the happinesse wch yor Lo^p
partly promises me in ye end of your letter to [lay our *deleted* >conferre]
meditations for a good time together, wch will be not onely honor to me,
but that happinesse which I and all that are in loue wth knowledge vse to
fancy to them [self *deleted*] selues for the true happinesse in this life. In
wch hope I remayne

  your Lo^{p}s most humble and most obliged seruant
  Tho: Hobbes

Paris July. 29/Aug. 8 1636

[*postscript:*] Prince Thomas,^{7} Piccolomini,^{8} & Jean de Wert,^{9} hauing
wasted Picardy, are now wthin a dayes iourney of Paris. The common
people feare [famine *deleted*] a siege, and there are soldiers leuying in
tumult to go meet them. The lacquayes are all commanded to the
warre; but I feare they are too much rogues to go.

¹ See Letter 16 n. 3.

² See Letter 18 n. 2.

³ Sir Charles Cavendish; the tract, entitled 'De loco imaginis', is BL MS Harl. 6756.

⁴ More than forty years later Hobbes described this phenomenon as follows: 'I have seen in the hands of a Chymist of my acquaintance at *Paris*, a broken Glass, part of a Retort, in which had been the Rozin of Turpentine, wherein though there were left no Rozin, yet there appeared in the piece of Glass many Trees; and Plants in the ground about them; such as grow in Woods; and better designed than they could be done by any Painter' (*Decameron physiologicum*, p. 77: *EW* vii, p. 133). Another account was supplied by Sir Kenelm Digby: 'I remember another pretty experiment that Doctor *Davisson* shewed me in his Laboratory at *Paris*. He had been drawing the Oyle and Spirit of a certain kind of resinous Gumme: And it so happened that the Glasse along which it rose; was all covered over in the inside with Portraitures of Firre-Trees (from whence that resin distilled) so exactly done that no Painter in the World could have drawn their shapes more compleatly' (*Discourse concerning the Vegetation of Plants*, pp. 82–3). William Davisson himself described the phenomenon in his *Philosophia pyrotechnica*, pp. 73–4, adding that the truth of his account could be confirmed by more than fifty men 'who either saw the glass vessel at my house, or were present at my lectures when I performed that experiment' ('qui aut apud me vasculum viderunt, aut lectionibus meis (tunc quum istam operationem perficiebam) assistebant' (ibid., p. 73)). William Davisson (originally, Davidson) was a Scottish Paracelsian chemist and astrologer who settled in France in 1614, practised medicine among the Scottish and English community in Paris, lectured on chemistry, became a physician to Louis XIII in 1644, occupied a similar post in Poland from 1651 to 1669, and died shortly after his return to France (see Constant, *L'Enseignement de la chimie au Jardin royal*, pp. 83–8).

⁵ This probably refers to the startling phenomenon described by Pierre Borel: 'According to M. de Gerzan and others, when N. de Richier, a soap-maker, and Bernard Germain were distilling human blood at Paris, they observed in the retort a human image, from which bloody rays seemed to shoot out, and when they broke open the vessel they found something just like a human skull in the residues' ('N. de Richier saponarius & Bernardus Germanus ex relatu D. de Gerzan & aliorum, sanguinem humanum Lutetiae distillantes [. . .] Viderunt in cucurbita phantasma humanum è quo sanguiniei radij prosilire videbantur & rupto vase inuenerunt tanquam cranium humanum in foecibus' (*Historiarum et observationum centuriae IV*, cent. 4, obs. 62, p. 325)). M. de Gerzan was François du Soucy, sieur de Gerzan, a minor French alchemical writer; however, I have not found any account of this phenomenon in his *Sommaire de la medecine chymique*, *Le Grand et Vray Or potable*, or *Le Projet du plan de la creation du monde*.

⁶ = on land.

⁷ Prince Thomas of Carignano (1596–1656), younger brother of the Duke of Savoy, Victor Amedeus I: in 1634 he had refused to support his brother's pro-French policies and had fled to the Spanish Netherlands, entering the service of the Habsburgs as a military commander.

⁸ Ottavio Piccolomini (1599–1656), the Austrian general who had been sent to The Netherlands in 1635 with an army of 20,000 men to assist the Spanish forces there against the French.

⁹ Jean de Werth (1594–1652), the German general who had been made commander of the Bavarian army in 1634. In 1636 de Werth, Piccolomini, and Prince Thomas joined

forces at the siege of Liège and then invaded Picardy, seizing La Capelle (30 June/10 July) and Roye. The French army withdrew to Compiègne; but de Werth then lost time besieging Corbie (which capitulated on 5/15 Aug.), and the reorganization of the French army, together with the threat of a Dutch attack from the rear, obliged him to retreat.

LETTER 20   1 [/11] OCTOBER 1636

Sir Kenelm Digby to Hobbes, from Paris

Bodl. MS Rawlinson D 1104, fos. 13ᵛ–14ʳ (transcript).
Printed in Tönnies, 'Lettres inédites', p. 86.

Sir,

I stayed little with my L^{d1} this morning because j^2 would not hinder his making ready, and for yᵉ same reason returned not vp to you. But went presently to speak with my Cousin Fortescu^3 whom j acquainted with what passed, and make account he hath giuen you satisfaction for the other fifty francs ere this. So now you will not say j hold you too hard to yᵉ bargain. My Lord telleth me he shall dine at home to morrow, therefore I will then come to wait upon his Lo. & giue myself the contentment of your sweet & learned conversation which I grieue to think I am thus at the Eeue of loosing, for a while at the least. In yᵉ meane time I send you my packet that you may putt it up in a Trunk, it being too bigg for a valise. I confesse it is too unmannerly to charge you with such a burthen, but my desire to have it come safe, maketh me presumptuously lay hold on your favour; wᶜʰ yet if it be incommodious to you, leaue behind. I kisse your hands Sir, & reste

Your affectionate & humble Servant
Kenelme Digby.

1. Oct. 1636.

From the reference to Hobbes's imminent departure from Paris in this letter, and the date of Letter 21, it seems probable that Digby was using Old Style in this letter.

[1] William Cavendish, third Earl of Devonshire.

[2] The use of 'j' for 'I' was a peculiarity of Digby's handwriting; its presence here suggests therefore that the copyist of this MS was transcribing directly from original letters (cf. Letter 26).

[3] 'Cousin' being an elastic term in the 17th cent., this probably refers to John Fortescue (son of Sir Francis Fortescue), whose wife, Frances, was a sister of Digby's wife, Venetia Stanley. John Fortescue (1592–1656) was created a Baronet of Nova Scotia

in 1636 (T. Fortescue, *History of the Family of Fortescue*, p. 419). Otherwise it could refer to John Fortescue's brother, Adrian (1601–53), who is known to have travelled widely in Europe, studying philosophy and foreign languages (ibid., p. 418). But there is other evidence that Digby had friendly relations with John Fortescue: Digby's recipe book includes a 'recipe for white Metheglin from Sir J. Fortescue' (*The Closet of Sir Kenelme Digby*, p. 46).

LETTER 21   16 [/26] OCTOBER 1636

Hobbes to William Cavendish, Earl of Newcastle, from Byfleet (Surrey)

BL MS Add. 70499, fos. 212–13ʳ (original).
Printed in HMC, *Portland*, pp. 129–30.

Right Honorable and my singular good Lord.

Before yoʳ Loᵖ come to mine you will know by other letters, that wee are come from beyond sea so farre as Byflet,[1] which is the period of my Lords trauels, but not of mine. For though my Lady and my Lord[2] do both accept so wel of my seruice as I could almost engage my selfe to serue [>them] as a domestique all my life, yet [my *deleted*] the extreame pleasure I take in study ouercomes in me all other appetites. I am not willing to leaue my Lord so, as not to do him any seruice that he [>thinkes] may not [otherwise *deleted* >so well] be done by another; but I must not deny my selfe the content to study in yᵉ way I haue begun, [>&] that I cannot conceaue I shall do any where so well as at Welbecke, and therefore I meane if yoʳ Loᵖ forbid me not, to come thither as soone as I can, and stay as long as I can without inconuenience to yoʳ Loᵖ.

For the reason of the species passing through a hole to a white paper, my opinion is this. The lucide body, as for example, the sunne, lighting on an obiect, as for example, the side of a house doth illuminate it, that is, to say giue it the same vertue, though not in the same degree, of diffusing light euery way, and illuminating other obiects wᵗʰ a lesse light, but the light that commeth from the house [sight *deleted*] side, is not pure light, but light mingled, that is to say, color, This light mingled, or colour, passing through the hole [is it *deleted*] there crosses, and goes wᵗʰ yᵉ figure inuerted to the white paper, and giues the paper in that part where it falles a power to diffuse light euery way, and so it comes to yᵉ eye wheresoeuer they stand (if a direct line may thence come to ye eye) And it is not as Galileo sayes; that illumination is made by reflexion, and that the asperity of the obiect makes it be seene euery way wch otherwise would be seene onely in one point, where angles of incidence and refraction were equall.[3] But whereas I vse the phrases, the light passes, or the coulor passes or diffuseth it selfe, my meaning is that the motion is onely in ye medium, and light and coulor are but the effects of that motion in ye brayne. But if one should aske me what kind of motion I can imagine in the medium [> or ayre] that touches the wall, wch should beget such motion in ye wall or parts of it, as should moue the ayre againe, euery way, that I can not answer. This proposition so true, and so well receaued, simile generat sibi simile,[4] is too hard to be demonstrated, and too manifest to be denyed. For the little man in the glasse,[5] I beleeue it may proue right, for me thinkes it is no greater a wonder then the Trees.[6] and for making of ice it is easy, for fill a glasse bottle or I thinke any bottle wth watter and couer it ouer head and eares in snow and bay salt[7] equaly mixt, or somewhat more snow then salt, and in an houres time, the watter in ye bottle shall become one lumpe of Ice. this I haue seene. I trouble yor Lo^p no further at this time, but take leaue remayning

   your Lo^ps humble and most obliged seruant
   Tho Hobbes

Byflet octob. 16 1636

[*addressed:*] To the Right Honorable the Earle of Newcastle

---

   [1] Thomas Bruce, first Earl of Elgin and brother of Christian Cavendish, Countess of Devonshire, was later Keeper of the King's Park of Byfleet in Surrey.
   [2] Christian Cavendish, Countess of Devonshire ('my Lady') and William Cavendish, third Earl of Devonshire ('my Lord').
   [3] In his discussion of the moon's surface in the 'first day' of the *Dialogo*, Galileo argues that because light from a single source is reflected in all directions from a rough surface but in only one direction from a smooth surface, a rough surface will seem brighter, when viewed from most directions, than a smooth one (*Opere*, vii, pp. 102–5).
   [4] 'one thing gives rise to another similar thing'.
   [5] See Letter 19 n. 5.
   [6] See Letter 19 n. 4.
   [7] Salt in large crystals, obtained from sea-water by slow evaporation.

LETTER 22   26 OCTOBER [/5 NOVEMBER] 1636

Hobbes to William Cavendish, Earl of Newcastle, from Byfleet (Surrey)

BL MS Add. 70499, fos. 214–15 (original).
Printed in HMC, *Portland*, p. 130.

Right Honorable and my singular good Lord.

I giue yor Lo^p most humble thankes for yor letter by Mr Tomkins,[1] and for yor Lo^{ps} fauor wch I haue continually experience of to my great comfort. I expect now onely a safe time of trauelling to come to wayte vpon yor Lo^p at Welbecke, w^{ch} (the sicknesse now decreasinge) I hope may be wthin little more then a moneth. wherein I apprehend not so much the infection for my selfe, as the feare [and *deleted* >or] danger might come to your family, by receauing such as must lodge by the waye in common Innes. The hope of not being long from yor Lo^p, makes me let Philosophy alone till then; and then if I haue any thinge you shall fetch it out, by discourse for by that meanes I shall take in as much more, and so be no looser. So wth my most feruent prayers for ye Continuance of yor Lo^{ps} health and prosperity I remayne

  yor Lops humble and most obliged seruant
  Tho: Hobbes

Byflet. Octob. 26 1636

[*addressed:*] To the Right Honorable The Earle of Newcastle

---

[1] Unidentified: presumably a servant of the Earl of Newcastle, or possibly Nathaniel Tomkins, brother-in-law of Edmund Waller.

LETTER 23   26 OCTOBER [/5 NOVEMBER] 1636

Robert Payne to Hobbes, from Welbeck Abbey

Bodl. MS Rawlinson D 1104, fo. 18 (transcript).
Printed in Tönnies, 'Lettres inédites', pp. 86–7.

Sir,

Mr Handson[1] being at Welbeck & Mr Hobbes at Byflett I could not but sett penne to paper once againe, though I haue little more to write, then what my two former letters contein'd. If you see Mr Warner[2] (as I presume you will; Cranborne lodg[3] being but 8 or 10 miles from Byflett in ye Forest of Windsore) you may take notice of ye Tracts he sent Sr Charles (Cauendishe) but not of ye exceptions I haue taken to them.[4] I remember in one letter of yours you mentioned my Lord Herberts book De Veritate,[5] Before I request your opinion of it, let me first aske you whether you vnderstand it; for I professe I doe not, though I haue seen it, & perhaps it would pose the writer. But I am content to think it my weaknesse of Vnderstanding that makes me uncapable of his sublime conceptions, yet lett me tell you, there are some who are accounted no dolts that for this book are in my case. The title of it drew me on, as perhaps it did others to reade it, but I am not wiser, in that subiect, for all it could yet teach me. If I had as great an opinion of it, as they say the Author hath of himself, it were a rare book. Indeed ye Subiect is good, & requires a profound & cleare witt to handle it. & if it had bin well performed, would haue sett us in a faire way to find out truth, or saue us much labour by discovering it to be [uninvestigable][6] by humane witt * * * But I forget I tire you, I rest

Your most assured friend & serv.t
Rob. Payne.

Welbeck. Octob. 26. 1636.

---

[1] John Hanson was an employee of the Countess and third Earl of Devonshire: in 1632 he became steward of the household at Devonshire House in London (Chatsworth MS Hardwick 27: entry for Apr. 1632), a post he continued to hold in the 1650s and 1660s (Chatsworth, MSS Hardwick 14 and 42A). A draft of Hobbes's will of 1674 includes a bequest of £20 to 'J. Hanson' (Chatsworth, MS Hardwick 19, final page).

[2] See Letter 16 n. 3.

[3] The country residence of Warner's patron, Sir Thomas Aylesbury: 'Warner had [. . .] som alowance from Sir Tho. Alesbury with whome he vsually spent his sumer in Windesor park, and was welcom, for he was harmless and quet' (*ABL* ii, p. 16).

40

[4] For the two tracts, see Letters 16 n. 4, and 19 n. 3. Payne had already expressed some objections in a letter to Warner of 3 [/13] Oct. 1636: BL MS Add. 4458, fos. 26–7.
[5] See Letter 18 n. 4.
[6] investigable *MS*.

LETTER 24   25 DECEMBER 1636 [/4 JANUARY 1637]

Hobbes to William Cavendish, Earl of Newcastle, from Byfleet (Surrey)

BL MS Add. 70499, fos. 216–17 (original).
Printed in HMC, *Portland*, p. 130.

Right Honorable and my very good Lord.

I would not haue your Lordship thinke any cause of my not writinge, worthy the hunting after if it were any other, but ye slipping away of a messenger ere I was aware, at one time, and want of what to say, at least pertinently, another time, I [cannot *deleted*] could not excuse it; for it would be a great crime in me to forbeare my respects, and my duty to yor Lordship vpon any reason but such playne [one *page torn*] as I haue alledged, or vpon sicknesse whereof I am not free at this present. If two thinges had bene, that is, fayre weather, or tolerable wayes, and free accesse to London I had bene at Welbecke ere this time. but assoone as I haue beene but a weeke in London wch I hope will be about three weekes hence I meane to goe thence immediately after to yor Lo^p. Mr Payne willed me to go to M^r warner who liues but 8 miles of to get his answer to certayne letters of his,[1] but one while the frost and at other times the flouds made the wayes impassable for any but very ranke riders, of wch I was neuer any. I have a cold that makes me keepe my chamber, and a chamber, (in this thronge of Company that stay christmas here) that makes me keepe my Cold. Here are besides my Lady and her mother and sonnes,[2] my Lord of Elgen[3] and my Lady Oxford,[4] and my Lady Rich.[5] After Christmas my Lady meanes I heare to go to Amptill[6] wth her Brother, and thence it is that I hauing bene first at London, meane to take my iourney into Nottinghamshire Here is no newes that I know of. so I humbly take leaue and remayne

yor Lo^ps humble and most obliged seruant
Tho: Hobbes

Byflet Dec. 25. 1636

[*postscript:*] I humbly pray yor Lo^p to excuse my not writing to Sr Charles.[7] For it is late, and I not well, but if your man go to towne before I haue done, this will come to late wch is the mayne excuse.

[*addressed:*] To the Right Honorable Earle of Newcastle at Welbecke

¹ See Letter 23.
² 'My Lady' was Christian Cavendish, Countess of Devonshire; her mother was Magdalen, daughter of Sir Alexander Clerk of Balbirnie, Fife, who, after the death of her first husband, Lord Bruce, in 1611, had married Sir James Fullerton in 1616; the two sons were William, third Earl of Devonshire, and the Hon. Charles Cavendish (see the Biographical Register).
³ See Letter 3 n. 4.
⁴ See Letter 3 n. 5.
⁵ See Letter 3 n. 2.
⁶ Ampthill, Beds., the English seat of the Earl of Elgin.
⁷ Sir Charles Cavendish.

LETTER 25   17 [/27] JANUARY 1637

Sir Kenelm Digby to Hobbes, from Paris

Bodl. MS Rawlinson D 1104, fos. 12ᵛ–13 (transcript).
Printed in Tönnies, 'Lettres inédites', pp. 87–8.

Enclosure: Bodl. MS Rawlinson D 1104, fos. 22–3 (transcript); Bodl. MS Smith 21, pp. 57–62 (transcript).

Worthy and honoured Sir,
   [*Four lines deleted*]
Your most frendly Letter of the 26. Nov: [coming *altered to* came] [> not] to my hands untill a few dayes agone, that at my returne from Tours and the Divels of Loudun,¹ it was delivered me by Monsr de Bosc. I humbly thank you for it: and acknowledg more to be due from me to you, then yor courtesie would fasten vpon me. I am exceeding glad to heare you haue so perfect freedome both of minde and time to study; and do expect proportionable effects of them: which produced, (j know) must make all men admire and discourage the boldest from ayming to imitate. In your Logike,² before you can manage men's conceptions, you must shew a way how to apprehend them rightly: and herein j would gladly know whither you work vpon the generall notions and apprehensions that all men (the vulgar as well as the learned) frame of all things that occurre unto them; or whither you make your ground to

be definitions collected out of a deep insight into the things themselues. Methought you bent this way when we talked hereof; & still j am
of opinion it is too learned a one for that which ought to be the
instrument of other scjences. As you write any thing, j pray you
communicate it with me. I humbly thanke you for your care in the con-
veyance of my packets; and beg your pardon for my so unmannerly
trobling you. For news lett me tell you; this state is now upon more
uncertainties & dependeth more of ye future then when you were here
and that the Spanish army was at their gates.³ They are oppressed with
poverty & want at home, threatned by the Enemy abroad, & in distresse
of whom to trust within; so that all is distraction.⁴ It is surmised
Monsieurs⁵ party is stronger & his designes more steddy then at the
first was conceiued. It is whispered the King will go towards him, & he
as fast into Gascony, where Monsr d'Espernon⁶ will be for him. Their
affaires in Italy are ruined: Modena hath receiued a garrison of
Spaniards; & so must Parma and Piacenza, if the league of ye Italian
Princes hinder not.⁷ My Paper will let me say no more, but w^t j must
ever find roome to sett downe; wch is Sir that j am

  Your most affectionate and humble servant
  Kenelme Digby.

Paris. 17. Jan. 1637.

[*postscript:*] I haue entreated Monsr de Bosc to send you a coppy of a
letter j wrote to the Prince of Guemene⁸ concerning the possession at
Loudun; whereby you will perceiue my opinion in that affaire. I
presume to send it you because at my returne hither j found it had a
faire passage through better hands then j designed it for.

[*enclosed:*]
Copie de la Lettre de Sr Kenelme Digby a Monsieur le Prince de
Guemené touchant les possedeés de Loudun.

Monseigneur
  Pour obeir a vostre Commandement et accomplir ma promesse Je
prends la hardiesse de vous addresser la presente, pour vous informer
de ce que nous avons veu a Loudun ou Monsr de Montagu⁹ a esté receu
avec tout l'honneur que peuvent faire les hommes & tout le respect que
peuuent rendre les Diables, Ils se sont montrez tres obeyssants a faire
touttes les actions exterieures qui leur ont esté commandeez pour nous
satisfaire. Mais pour ce qui est des commandements qui se forment

dans L'Imagination seulement, ou de descouurir les pensees (Je parle des miennes) Ils ont rebelles au dernier point.[10] Quand a leurs contorsions et grimaces, elles nous ont apparu (selon la relation de ceux du lieu) a la facon ordinaire; qui sont assez estranges pour tenir en suspens mon Jugement, mais non pas pour m'asseurer quelles soient impossibles a la nature. Les plus fortes raisons que je trouue pour la possession, sont les morales, non les naturelles, Jugeant sur ce que Jay veu non sur ce qu'on men dit: Et je ne scaurois comprendre comment tant de diverses personnes (hommes et femmes) qui n'ont rien de commun en leurs Interests particuliers, fortuittement assemblez de tant de divers lieux, Plusieurs d'entre elles estimeez d'une grande probité & preudhomie, & nulles noteez au contraire (ny des Religieuses ny des Exorcistes) puissent si dextrement et unanimement conspirer sans se lasser a maintenir par tant d'anneez vne telle fourbe qui ne leur apporte aucun profitt, et ou il faut tous les iours endurer tant de travail et d'incommodité. Cecy me semble surmonter la patience et obstina-tion humaine; comme aussi de surpasser la conduite d'aucun esprit pour fin qu'il soit, de tenir tousjours tant de diverses roües en con-tinuelle motion en vne si chatouilleuse affaire, sans qu'aucune face vn faux pas qui puisse descrier les autres, ou il y a perpetuellement vn si grand nombre de spectateurs de touttes sortes d'affections pour remarquer et rehausser chaque defectuosité. Dautre costé ie suis d'accord que la haine et la malice peuuent induire quelques naturels a des resolutions quasi incroiables, et la vanité de sembler au monde davoir quelque chose de singulier par dessus les autres en matiere surnaturelle et une complesance interieure de bien jouer son role en un jeu si extraordinaire et difficille, Et dautre part vne facile credulité en quelques ames douces et pieusement foibles, qui les peut induire a conspirer a tromper non seullement autruy, mais elles mesmes aussy, Et vn contentement de se voir monstres du Diable et davoir le pouuoir de le gourmander et tourmenter et humilier a leurs pieds, qui les fait mespriser les autres humains et estimer leur condition par dessus les Roys & le Pape mesme. Touttes ces considerations, disje pourrojent gagner tel pied sur quelques ames que destre cause de quelques effects & actions qui puissent sembler surnaturelles & touttes fois ne le fussent pas, Et aussy a laventure comme dans le train dune vie excellente et spirituelle, Dieu se mesle quelques fois imperceptiblement et donne vne teinture de sa divine bonté a plusieurs des actions d'une telle sainte personne pour les rendre meritoirement admirables, mesmes sans son sceu. Tout de mesme il pourra arriver quentre des creatures perdues ou la fraude et la malice abondent, le Diable (qui ne perd pas les occasions d'avancer ses interests) se pourra ingerer entre des sujets si proprement disposez pour luy, et secrettement cooperer a leur art & industrie pour eslever & raffiner leur actions au plus haut point de la nature, sans toutte fois exceder tout a fait ceste sphere.

Voicy Monseig.^r la reflection que je fais sur ce que iay veu, dont la conclusion en moy est, qu'encoreque je naje esté present a aucune action pour me convaincre evidemment d'un agent surnaturel en ces possedeez, toutesfois le corps de touttes circomstances en gros me le persuadent grandement; et ce m'est quelque satisfaction, que je ne men reviens pas delles entierement mal satisfait. Et sur ce que Jay eu de la relation dautruy Je fais cette reflection: que la nature de la plus part des hommes est entierement encline a desirer que choses fort estrangez reusissent entierement veritables quand elles s'approchent tant soit peu de la verite, & principallement si eux mesmes, pretendent a un bonheur particulier de les avoir veu, et ainsi ils s'eschauffent en la poursuitte jusques a se persuader quelles le sont; ou au moins jusques a tascher de le persuader a autruy, si eux mesmes sont en doute: Car on ne se contente pas de raconter vne frede & simple narration a qui est en expectation d'une histoire extraordinaire. Et en quelques vns la pieté se mesle parmy cette humeur naturelle. Et quand vne fois la croiance dune telle chose est establie il leur sembleroit quasi vne impieté de ne contribuer du leur pour la maintenir, et beaucoup plus, d'esplucher de trop pres ou de le contredire. J'espere que Madame de Guemené[11] en allant cet Este au Verger[12] donnera le tourment a ces Princes des Tenebres de voir la plus belle, & la plus vertueuse Princesse du monde (car ce qui leur est si contraire ne peut failler de les affliger) et je ne doute point que son clair et net esprit n'esclarcisse ceste affaire plus que jusques a ceste heure elle n'a este: Et a son iugement en cecy (comme en touttes autres choses) je me suis resolu de me rapporter; Car ainsy je ne scaurois errer, Et pourtant je me suspendray le mien ne me laissant pancher ny dun costé ne dautre; quelles raisons persuasiues que se puissent presenter, Voila l'Estat de mon entendement, et pour celuy la de mon Coeur, tout est comprins en me signant

Monseigneur
Vostre tres humble et tres affectionne serviteur
Digby

De Loudun, ce 27 X^{bre} 1636. estant Samedy.

45

[*postscript:*] Auquel iour nous avons veu renouveller selon la coustume, les caracteres sur la main de la mere prieure,[13] mais pour dire la verité ce miracle ma donné aussi peu de contente quaucune chose que nous avons encor veu icy.

Je vous supplie Monseig.r ne divulger ce que je vous dis sur laffaire de ces possedes, Car peut estre quelques personnes pourroient interpreter mon discours autrement que ie ne lentens, et ie ne voudrois pas estre daucun party en vne affaire tant controversee ou je voie tant de ferveur et asprete du chasque costé et qui me touche si peu.

Translation of enclosure to Letter 25

Copy of Sir Kenelm Digby's letter to the prince de Guémené, concerning the possessed people at Loudun.

My Lord,

To obey your command and fulfil my promise, I am taking the liberty of sending you this letter to tell you what we saw at Loudun, where Mr Mountagu[9] was welcomed with all the honour that men can show and all the respect that Devils can give. They were very compliant, performing all the external actions which they were ordered to perform for our satisfaction. But as for orders given only in the imagination, or commands that they should reveal the contents of thoughts (I mean my own), they were disobedient from start to finish.[10] So far as their grimaces and contortions are concerned, they appeared in their usual style (according to what we were told by the people of that place); they were strange enough to make me suspend judgement, though not so strange as to make me feel certain that they could not be produced by nature.

Judging by what I saw, not by what I was told, the strongest evidence I can find for possession is moral, not physical. I can see no reason why so many different people, men and women, having no particular interest in common, gathered by chance from so many different places, and many of them highly regarded for their honesty and integrity, without a single exception (either among the nuns or among the exorcists), should keep up such an unflagging conspiracy so cleverly and so unanimously, in order to sustain for so many years a fraud which brings them no advantage and which requires them to endure so much labour and discomfort every day. This seems more than human patience and determination could sustain. And it also surpasses the powers of human wit, however astute, to keep so many wheels in continual motion in such a delicate matter, without any of them putting a foot wrong and giving away the others, when there are so many observers constantly present, motivated in all sorts of ways, and able to notice and pick out every inconsistency.

On the other hand I agree that hatred and malice can sometimes lead simple people to resolve to do almost unbelievable things—together with a pride in making everyone think that one has some extraordinary supernatural ability, and the private satisfaction of playing one's part well in such an unusual and difficult game. And on the other side there is the gullibility of some gentle and piously weak-natured souls, which can make them conspire to deceive themselves as well as others. There is also the satisfaction people may have of thinking themselves monstrous creatures of the Devil, and the pleasure of having the power to rebuke, torment, and humiliate him at their feet, which makes them feel contempt for the rest of mankind and think of themselves as greater than kings or the Pope himself.

All these motives, I am suggesting, could take enough of a hold over some souls to produce some actions and effects which might seem supernatural without actually being so. And just as, adventitiously, God may imperceptibly mingle his activity with that of an excellent, holy life, giving a tincture of his divine goodness to several of the actions of such a holy person in order to make them admirable and meritorious, even without that person being aware of it: so too with some lost creatures whose souls are full of fraud and malice, the Devil (who loses no opportunity to promote his interests) may worm his way into subjects who are so well fitted for his use, and may secretly co-operate with their skill and determination, raising and refining their actions to the utmost limit of what is naturally possible, but without ever quite exceeding the natural realm.

This, my Lord, is the meditation I have made on what I saw. My own conclusion is that although I have not witnessed any action which would clearly convince me that a supernatural power was at work in these possessed people, nevertheless when all the details are put together I find the overall body of evidence very persuasive. And it is some satisfaction to me that I have not returned from the nuns of Loudun entirely disappointed. As for what I gathered from other people's accounts, I bear this in mind: that most men are by nature overwhelmingly inclined to wish that very strange things will turn out to be true when they resemble truth in the least degree. This is especially so if they themselves claim the particular good fortune of having seen those things; in this way they become so excited by the chase that they convince themselves the things are true—or, at least, they try to convince others if they themselves are still in doubt. No one is content, after all, to tell a cold, simple narrative of facts to someone who is expecting to hear a tale of the extraordinary. And in some people this natural disposition is intermingled with piety, so that once belief in such a thing has become established, they think it would be more or less impious of them to fail to play their part in keeping it up—or, still worse, to examine it too closely or deny it.

I hope that when Mme de Guémené[11] goes to Le Verger[12] this summer it will torment those Princes of Darkness to see the most beautiful and most virtuous princess in the world (for they cannot fail to be pained by whatever is the opposite of their own nature). I do not doubt that her fine and lucid intellect will do more to clear up this matter than has been done up till now, and I am determined to follow her judgement in this, as in all other things. In this way I shall be unable to err; however, I shall suspend my own judgement, not allowing myself to incline to one side or the other, whatever the persuasive reasons which may be put forward.

There you have the state of my understanding; as for the state of my heart, it can be summed up completely by signing myself,

My Lord,
Your most humble and affectionate servant,
Digby

Loudun, 27 December 1636, which is a Saturday.

[*postscript:*] On which day, as is usual, we saw the marks on the Prioress's hand renew themselves.[13] But to tell the truth this miracle gave me as little satisfaction as anything we have seen here.

I beg you, my Lord, not to divulge what I tell you about the affair of these possessed people; it is possible that some people might interpret my account differently from how it is intended, and I do not wish to be on either side of such a disputed issue, in which so much zeal and bitterness is displayed on each side, and which has so little to do with me.

The date of Letter 25 could be Old Style or New Style; the evidence of Letter 20 suggests that Digby used Old Style when writing to England from the Continent. The enclosure, however, written in France to a Frenchman, uses New Style.

It is quite likely that Letter 25 was sent via du Bosc; both for that reason and because the text of the letter to the prince de Guémené is preserved in the same MS transcript as Letter 25, it is treated here as an enclosure to that letter. Other copies of the letter to the prince de Guémené seem to have circulated among Digby's friends: one is recorded in a list of 'Originall Letters to & from M:ʳ Selden' (BL MS Harl. 7526, fo. 36ᵛ). Bodl. MS Smith 21 is probably a transcript of that collection of Selden correspondence.

¹ In 1632 the nuns of the Ursuline convent at Loudun (a town south of the Loire, between Saumur and Poitiers) claimed to be suffering from demonic possession, and accused a local priest, Urbain Grandier, of sorcery. Grandier was burnt at the stake in 1634, but the signs of possession (convulsions, hysteria, and blasphemy) continued, and public exorcisms of the demons became a weekly spectacle, attracting visitors from all over France.

² Probably an early version of the first part of *De corpore*; possibly to be identified with the notes 'De principiis' (National Library of Wales MS 5297, printed in Hobbes, *Anti-White*, pp. 449–60).

³ See Letter 19 n. 9.

⁴ France was still at war with Spain, and throughout 1636–7 there were peasant uprisings in many parts of France.

⁵ Gaston d'Orléans (see Letter 12 n. 1).

⁶ Jean-Louis de Nogent, duc d'Espernon (1554–1642), the unpopular governor of Guyenne under Louis XIII.

⁷ The French war effort in central Italy had petered out in the late summer of 1636; the former French ally the Duke of Modena had come to an agreement with Spain, and the Duke of Parma, who had been besieging Piacenza, was rumoured to be negotiating with Spain as well.

⁸ Louis de Rohan, prince de Guémené, duc de Montbazon (1598–1667), courtier and military commander.

⁹ Walter Mountagu or Montagu (*c*.1603–77), younger son of the first Earl of Manchester, a frequent visitor to France and an unofficial envoy of Henrietta Maria to the French Court (see Stoye, *English Travellers*, pp. 312–13, and Kaufman, *Conscientious Cavalier*, pp. 99–100). Mountagu had already visited Loudun in Nov. 1635, in the company of Thomas Killigrew (whose description of the visit is in Bodl. MS Ashmole 800, fos. 21–7). That visit had made a deep impression on Mountagu, who immediately thereafter had written a letter to his father announcing his conversion to Catholicism (later published as *A Coppy of a Letter*, 1641).

¹⁰ Thomas Killigrew had encountered similar difficulties in 1635: 'One Miracle I had mist if M:ʳ Mountague had not sent for me, wᶜʰ was to obey what the Preist commaunded him Mentally without speaking it to him, to confirme me it was yᵉ Diuill by the knowledge of his thoughts wᶜʰ I confesse had bin Strange if I could haue bine satisfied by his telling me mine, but I was refused' (Bodl. MS Ashmole 800, fo. 23ʳ).

¹¹ The prince de Guémené's wife was his first cousin, Anne de Rohan, princesse de Guémené (1603–85).

¹² The château of the de Guémené family, near Seiches, fifteen miles north-east of Angers: it was built in the 15th cent. and destroyed in the 18th.

¹³ The prioress of the convent, sœur Jeanne des Anges, would pronounce a holy name, and then show her hand to those present: it had 'a greate many Redd specks, & they contracted into Letters', spelling the name (Bodl. MS Ashmole 800, fo. 26ᵛ).

Sir Kenelm Digby to Hobbes, from London

Bodl. MS Rawlinson D 1104, fos. 11ᵛ–12 (transcript).
Printed in Tönnies, 'Lettres inédites', pp. 88–9; Bligh, *Sir Kenelm Digby*, p. 236.

Most honored Sir,

Nothing but impossibility of payment could haue cast me into so great an arreare with you. This is the first time j haue bin able to govern a penne these 6 weekes: And very badly now, as you will perceiue by my scribling: for it is so long since a fall from my horse rendered my arme uselesse. It was out of ioynt; & so long before j could haue it sett, that a gelly growing in the panne[1] hath made it apt to slippe out againe euer since: so that it hath bin sett 4 or 5 times. But j hold you too long upon so dull a theame, Yet it may serue to filosofize vpon. A great Lady at Paris wrote me a letter dated about the time of my fall, that she had a strong apprehension some such misadventure had hapned to me, & therefore sent me a scarfe of her owne making, as conceiuing j might haue use of it. This scarfe & letter came to me about 6 daies after my fall, by the Post. What may be the reason of this foreknowledg, or present knowledg at a distance? Is it that the soule being a spiritt hath within itself the knowledg of all things, & so delivereth ouer to the fantasie a misty notion of wᵗ occurreth to some particular that it (the fansy) is continually beating upon? Or hath the soul a power to deduce all knowledg concerning any particular obiect, out of the species that are administred to it by the senses, when she speculateth intensely vpon them?[2] Which latter j should conceiue to be the way that seperated soules know all that is done in yⁱˢ world by ioining & diuing into the species they carry from hence. You that know more then all men liuing, take occasion from hence to instruct me. I summon you of your promise; which is that as soon as you haue done any peice of your Logike,[3] you will lett me see it. I confesse I exceedingly value all that cometh from you; for you ioyne nature and solide reason together; whereas many others that are accounted learned, begett Chymeras and build castles in the ayre. My aking arme will let me be no longer. Therefore remembring my humblest seruice to my noble Lord[4] j rest

Your most affectionate & humble servant
Kenelme Digby.

London. 11. 7.ᵇᵉʳ 1637.

[*addressed:*] To my worthy frend Mr. Hobbes at My Lord of Devonshire his house.

---

[1] = socket (*OED* pan *sb*. 4b).

[2] In a letter to the lady at Paris (unnamed in that letter also), written six days earlier, Digby had already made use of both of these explanations, and of a third, which was that each person emits 'a ceaseless emanation of little corpuscles or atoms' ('vne perpetuelle emanation de petits corpuscules ou atomes'), to which a sensitive person can react at a great distance (BL MS Add. 41846, fos. 96–101, here fo. 98ᵛ).

[3] See Letter 25 n. 2.

[4] William Cavendish, third Earl of Devonshire.

LETTER 27   4 [/14] OCTOBER 1637

Sir Kenelm Digby to Hobbes, from London

Bodl. MS Rawlinson D 1104, fo. 12ᵛ (transcript).
Printed in Tönnies, 'Lettres inédites', p. 89; Nicolson, 'Early Stages of Cartesianism', p. 358; Bligh, *Sir Kenelm Digby*, pp. 236–7; *MC* vi, p. 312.

Sir,

I come now with this to make good wᵗ j promised you in my last: which is to putt Monsieur des Cartes (whom Mydorge[1] so much admireth) his book[2] into your hands. I doubt not but you will say this is a production of a most vigorous and strong braine; and that if he were as accurate in his metaphysicall part as he is in his experience, he had carryed the palme from all men liuing: wᶜʰ yet neverthelesse he peradventure hath done. I shall be very glad to heare your opinion of him; and so in hast j take my leaue & rest

Your true frend & Servant
Kenelme Digby.

London. 4. 8.ᵇᵉʳ 1637.

---

[1] See Letter 18 n. 2.

[2] *Discours de la méthode*.

LETTER 28   22 AUGUST [/1 SEPTEMBER] 1638

Hobbes to the Hon. Charles Cavendish, from Chatsworth

Bodl. MS Rawlinson D 1104, fos. 14–15 (transcript); Bodl. MS Rawlinson C 232, fos. 82ᵛ–79ᵛ retrograde (transcript).

Printed in Tönnies, 'Analekten', pp. 294–6; Reik, *Golden Lands of Hobbes*, pp. 197–8.

Most Noble Sir.

I am farr from beleiuing yᵉ reports yᵗ come hither concerning yoʳ conversation[1] at Paris. Neverthelesse for the satisfaction of my particular affection to yourself, & of my long obligation to your house, I have taken occasion thereby to use the priuiledge of my study to write unto you a word or two touching the nature of those faults that are reported of you. And seeing I belieue you are no more guilty of them then all other men of your age, I hope how seuerely soeuer I shall censure the crime you shall haue no cause to think I censure you, but that I say is rather counsayle for the future then reprehension of any thinge past. Which I shall leaue to your choyce to weigh as the humble aduice of a servant, or to laugh at it, or call me foole or Thucidides for my presumption. First therefore I must humbly beseech you to avoyd all offensiue speech, not only open reviling but also that Satyricall way of nipping[2] that some use. The effect of it is the cooling of the affection of your servants, & yᵉ prouoking of the hatred of your equalls. So that he which useth harsh languadge whether downeright or obliquely shall be sure to haue many haters, & he that hath so, it will be a wonder if he haue not many iust occasions of Duell. Of which though the immediate cause be in them that giue such occasion, yet is he originally to blame that deserued their hatred; And of the two quipping & reviling the former is yᵉ worse, because being the same iniury, it seemes to hide itself under a double construction, as if a man had a good will to abuse another but were afraid to stand to it. Whereas yᵉ words of a Gentleman should be perspicuous & justifiable & such as shew greatnesse of couradge not spleene. To encouradge inferiours, to be cheerefull with ones equalls & superiors, to pardon the follies of them one converseth withall, & to help men of, that are fallen into yᵉ danger of being laught at, these are signes of noblenesse & of the master spirit. Whereas to fall in loue with ones selfe vpon the sight of other mens infirmities, as they doe that mock & laugh at them, is the property of one that stands in competition with such a ridiculous man for honor. They are much deceiued that think mocking Witte. for those be few y^t cannot do it. And what witte is it to loose a frend though the meanest in the world for the applause of a jest. This fault I know is no more yours then every ones that adversity or age hath not driuen from it, & therefore I think I may without offence represent it to you in its owne nature, that is as the most unnoble thing in ye world. If a man could value himself moderately, & at the rate that other men hold him currant, examyning what true and iust title he hath to pretend to more respect & priviledge then others, and that done would not (as Children that crye for euery thing that is denyed them) expect more then is due, & when he cannot haue it fall into choller, I think it were not possible for that man either out of passion or in passion to be offensiue. Secondly I beseech you take no occasions of quarrell but such as are necessary & from such men only as are of reputation. For neither words uttered in heate of Anger, nor ye wordes of youthes unknowne in the world, or not knowne for Vertue are of scandall sufficient to ground an honourable duell on. When two boyes go out of the Academie to Pré aux clercs^3 no man but thinkes them boyes as before. Nor is their Act Valour. For hauing engaged themselues rashly they are forced to the feild wth shame, & expect their aduersary with cold hartes, & prayers that he may be preuented. does the world call this valour.

Lastly, I think it no ill Counsell, that you professe no loue to any woman which you hope not to marry or otherwise to enioy. For an action without designe is that which all the world calles Vanity. And now I haue done my taedious discourse which I would not haue written without a great opinion that you can heare reason patiently, and that your nature is so good as to pardon the boldnesse and indiscretions that proceed from true affection & duty as this does from me who am

your most obedient and most humble servant
Tho. Hobbes.

Chattesworth Aug. 22. 1638.

[*addressed:*] To Mr Cavendish.

Both Tönnies and Reik have assumed that this letter was addressed to the third Earl of Devonshire; but he was not in Paris in 1638, and would not have been addressed as 'Mr Cavendish'. See the entry for the Hon. Charles Cavendish in the Biographical Register.

^{1} = behaviour (*OED* conversation 6).
^{2} = making sharp censures (*OED* nip *v*. 7).

³ The fields north of the abbey of Saint-Germain-des-Prés, Paris. It is not clear which 'académie' is intended here; as James Howell explained in 1642, 'For private Gentlemen and Cadets, there be diverse *Academies* in *Paris*, colledge-like, where [. . .] one may be very well accommodated [. . .] and be taught to manage Arms, to Dance, Vault, and ply the Mathematiques' (*Instructions for Forreine Travell*, p. 27). The closest 'académie' to the Pré aux Clercs would have been M. du Vaux's, in the faubourg Saint-Germain.

LETTER 29   [11/] 21 JANUARY 1641

René Descartes to Marin Mersenne for Hobbes, from Leiden

BN MS f.fr. n.a. 10556, fo. 34 (transcript).
Draft printed in Descartes, *Lettres*, ed. Clerselier, iii, pp. 119–22; *Epistolae*, iii, pp. 68–71; *OL* v, pp. 278–82; text derived from both draft and MS printed in A&T iii, pp. 287–92; Descartes, *Correspondance*, iv, pp. 257–64; *MC* x, pp. 426–31.

Reuerendissimé Pater

Legj partem epistolae ad V. Rᵃᵐ ex Angliâ missae,¹ hicque à d. de Zuylichem² mihj concessae, et valde miratus sum quod cum ex modo scribendj eius author Ingeniosus et doctus appareat, in nulla tamen re quam vt suam proponat³ à veritate non aberrare videatur. Omittam Initium de anima et deo corporeis,⁴ de spiritu Interno, et reliquis quae me non tangunt, etsj enim dicat materiam meam subtilem⁵ eamdem esse cum suo spiritu Interno non possum tamen id agnoscere, primo quia illum facit causam duritiej, cum mea potius à contrà mollitiej sit causa; deinde quia non video quâ ratione iste spiritus valdé mobilis corporibus duris Ità includj possit, vt numquam ex iis egrediatur, nec quomodò ingrediatur mollia cum durescunt. sed venio ad ea quae scribit contra dioptricam. Inprimis ait me clariùs loquuturum fuisse sj pro determinatione motum determinatum dixissem,⁶ quâ In re ipsj non assentior, etsi enim dicj possit velocitatem pilae ab *a* ad *b* componj ex duabus aliis,⁷ ab *a* ad *h* et ab *a* ad *c*, abstinendum tamen esse putauj ab isto modo loquendj, ne fortè ità Intelligeretur vt istarum velocitatum in motu sic⁸ composito quantitas et vnius ad alteram⁹ proportio remaneret, quod nullo modo est verum: nam sj exemplj causa ponamus pilam ab *a* ferrj dextrorsum vno gradu¹⁰ celeritatis, et deorsum vno etiam gradu, perueniet ad *b* cum duobus gradibus celeritatis, eodem tempore quo alia, quae feretur etiam ab *a* dextrorsum vno gradu celeritatis, et deorsum duobus, perveniet ad *g* cum tribus gradibus

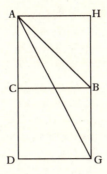

celeritatis: vnde sequeretur lineam ab esse ad ag vt 2 ad 3 quae tamen
est vt 2 ad √10 et caet.

Quod ait postea terram tollere celeritatem deorsum, est contra
hypothesim, supposuj enim nihil planè de celeritate detrahj; et contra
omnem experientiam, alioqui enim pila perpendiculariter in terram
incidens nunquam resileret. nullâ Igitur in parte laborat mea
demonstratio, sed ille seipsum valde fefellit quia motum à determinatione non distinxit, motus enim ipse nullo modo minuj debet vt
reflexio fiat ad angulos accuratè aequales. praeterea id quod assumpsit,
nulla vj amouerj quod non cedit leuissimae,[11] nullam habet speciem veritatis,
quis enim credat exempli gratiâ In bilance pondus centum librarum
aliquantulum cedere ponderj vnius librae in aliâ lancis parte [positj
altered to positae], quoniam cedit ponderj 200 librarum: concedo tamen
libenter partem terrae in quam pila Impingit aliquantulum ej cedere, vt
etiam partem pilae in terram Impingentem nonnihil Introrsum
recuruarj, ac deinde quia terra et pila restituunt se post ictum ex hoc
Iuuarj resultum pilae: sed affirmo[12] hunc resultum magis semper
Impedirj ab istâ incuruatione pilae et terrae, quàm ab ejus restitutione
iuuetur; atque ex eo posse demonstrarj reflexionem pilae aliorumque
ejusmodj corporum non extremè durorum numquam fieri ad angulos
accuratè aequales, sed absque demonstratione facilè est experirj pilas
molliores non tam altè resilire nec ad tam magnos angulos quàm
duriores. Vndè patet quam perperam adducat istam terrae mollitiem ad
aequalitatem angulorum demonstrandam, praesertim cùm ex ea
sequatur si terra et pila tam durae essent vt nullo modo cederent
nullam fore reflexionem quod est Incredibile; patet etiam quàm meritò
ego et terram et pilam perfectè duras assumpserim vt res sub examen
mathematicum cadere possit. Non foelicior est circa refractionem, cùm
distinguit eam quae fit quando corpus motum permeat media
ipsummet[13], ab eâ quae fit quando non permeat,[14] vtraque enim fit

versus eamdem partem à corpore eiusdem generis, nec satis Intellexit
id quod scripsi eâ de re, non enim dico lumen facilius propagarj In
denso quam in raro; sed in duro (in quo scilicet materia subtilis non
communicat motum suum parietibus meatuum quibus inest) quàm in
mollj, siue hoc sit rarius siue densius, habeoque eius rej et
experientiam et demonstrationem, tam de ipso lumine quam de
Corporibus quae tactu sentiuntur, nec valet exceptio ex tapetis asperit-
ate desumpta; in tapete enim ex serico vel corio nullo modo aspero
Idem continget.[15] Quod ait ab amico suo esse demonstratum non vidj,[16]
nec ideo possum de eo judicare. Miror vero quod subiungat meam
demonstrationem non esse legitimam cum tamen nihil planè afferat ad
eam Impugnandam, nisj quod dicat quaedam repugnare experientiae,
quae cum experientia consentiunt et sunt verissima. Sed non videtur
aduertisse differentiam quae est Inter refractionem pilae, aliorumue
corporum In aquam Incidentium ac refractionem luminis, cum tamen
sit duplex et maxima, primo, quia vna refractio fit versus perpendicularem, alia modo contrario, et cum radij luminis tertiâ suj Impetus parte
aut circiter facilius per aquam transeant quàm per aerem, non tamen
ideo pila mulctarj debet ab eadem aqua, tertiâ parte suae velocitatis,
nullaque est inter ista duo connexio. Deinde quia lumen quidem
debile, non ad alios angulos quàm forte ab eadem aqua refringitur, sed
planè aliud est de pilâ, quae magnâ vj in aquam impulsa[17] non tantâ
parte suae velocitatis ab ea potest mulctarj quàm sj lentius procedat.
Ideoque non mirum est quod expertus sit globum plumbeum, maximâ
vj sclopeto emissum aquam Ingredj in eleuatione 5 graduum[18] quia
tunc forte non millesimâ suae velocitatis parte mulctabitur.[19] Affingit
mihj postea quod supposuerim omnem jacturam velocitatis computandam esse in motu deorsum, dixj enim constantissimè computandam
esse in toto motu simpliciter sumpto. Modus vero quo ipse vtitur ad
refractionis causam explicandam vel ex eo apparet non esse accuratus
quod aperte pugnet cum eo quod ante admisit vt ab amico suo demonstratum nempe esse in refractione, vt sinus angulj inclinationis vnius ad
sinum angulj inclinationis alterius, ita sinum angulj refractj in vna
inclinatione ad sinum angulj refractj in alterâ,[20] exsurgit enim ex ejus
parallelogrammo, plane alia, et quidem maximè Irrationalis, inter istos
sinus proportio. reliquum epistolae nondum vidj, nec ideo possum
respondere. Sum

Vae. Rae. addictissimus[21] famulus
descartes

Translation of Letter 29

Most reverend Father,

I have read part of the letter which was sent to your Reverence from England,[1] and forwarded to me here by M. Huygens;[2] and I was very surprised by the fact that, although the style in which it is written makes its author look clever and learned, he seems to stray from the truth in every single claim which he advances[(3)] as his own. I shall leave aside the initial section on his 'internal spirit', and on his corporeal soul and corporeal God,[4] and other things which do not concern me. For even though he says that my subtle matter[5] is the same as his internal spirit, I cannot agree: first, because he makes his spirit the cause of hardness, whereas my subtle matter is, on the contrary, the cause of softness; and secondly because I cannot see how that very mobile spirit can be so enclosed in hard bodies that it never escapes from them—nor how it can enter into soft bodies, when they grow hard. But I proceed to his objections to my 'Dioptrique'.

First, he says that I would have expressed myself more clearly if I had said 'determined motion' instead of 'determination'.[6] On which point I do not agree; for even if the velocity of the ball moving from A to B can be said to be composed of two other velocities,[(7)] from A to H and from A to C, nevertheless I decided not to describe it in that way, in case I gave the impression that the quantity of those velocities, and their proportion to each other,[(8)] continued to exist in the motion which was thus[(9)] composed of them—which is completely false. For if we suppose, for example, that the ball at A is moved to the right with one degree[(10)] of speed, and downwards also with one degree of speed, it will reach B with two degrees of speed, in the same time that it takes another ball, moved to the right from A with one degree of speed and downwards with two degrees, to reach G with three degrees of speed;

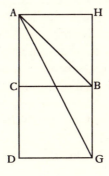

from which it would follow that the line AB was to AG as 2 is to 3, whereas in fact it is as 2 is to $\sqrt{10}$, and so on.

His next claim, that 'the ground takes away the downwards speed', is contrary to my hypothesis, since I supposed that absolutely nothing was removed from the speed. It is also contrary to all experience: otherwise a ball striking the ground vertically would never rebound. My demonstration, therefore, does not get into difficulties at any point. But he has thoroughly deceived himself, by failing to distinguish the motion from the determination; for the motion itself must not be diminished at all, if reflection is to take place at exactly equal angles.

Further, his assumption that 'that which does not yield to the slightest force cannot be moved by any force at all'[11] has no semblance of truth. For who can believe, for example, that a weight of 100 pounds on a pair of scales yields ever so slightly to a weight of one pound placed on the other arm of the scales, because it does yield to a weight of 200 pounds? I freely concede that the part of the ground which is struck by the ball does yield just a little to its force, and that the part of the ball which strikes the ground does bend inwards a little; and that because both of them, the ball and the ground, return to their original shapes, this helps the rebound of the ball. But I maintain[12] that this rebound will always be more hindered by that bending inwards of the ball and the ground, than helped by their return to their original shapes. It is from that fact that I can demonstrate that the reflection of balls, and of other bodies of that kind which are not extremely hard, never takes place in exactly equal angles. But without a demonstration, one can easily observe from experience that softer balls do not rebound as high, or at such large angles, as harder ones. From which it is clear how wrong he is to put forward this softness of the ground as part of his demonstration of the equality of the angles, especially since it follows that if the ground and the ball were so hard that they did not yield at all, there would be no reflection—which is impossible to believe. It is also obvious how right I was to assume that both ground and ball were perfectly hard, so that the problem could be examined mathematically.

He is no more felicitous on the subject of refraction, when he distinguishes between the refraction which takes place when the moved body itself[13] passes through media, and the refraction which takes place when it does not;[14] for in both cases, if the bodies are of the same kind, they will be refracted in the same direction. Nor has he sufficiently understood what I wrote on the subject. For I do not say that light is propagated more easily in a dense medium than in a rare one; rather, I say it is propagated more easily in a hard medium (that is, one in which the subtle matter does not communicate its own motion to the walls of the channels in which it is contained) than in a soft one—whether it is denser or rarer. And I can support that statement from both experience and demonstration, concerning light itself as well as tangible bodies. That objection, involving the roughness of a carpet, is not valid; for on a carpet made of silk or hide, which is not at all rough, the same thing happens.[15] I have not seen the demonstration which he says his friend has made,[16] and so I cannot make any judgement on it.

I am surprised that he should add that my demonstration is invalid, since he puts forward absolutely no reason for rejecting it, except to say that some things in it are contrary to experience, when in fact they agree with experience and are perfectly true. But he seems not to have noticed the difference between the refraction of a ball, or of some other bodies entering water, and the refraction of light—although they are extremely different, and different on two counts. First, because one refraction takes place towards the perpendicular, and the other in the opposite direction; and although the rays of light pass more easily through water (by about a third of their speed) than they do through air, nevertheless that does not mean that a ball must also be deprived of a third of its velocity by water: there is no connection between the two cases. Secondly, because a weak light is not refracted in the same angles as a strong one by the same water; whereas it is quite different in the case of a ball, which, projected[(17)] into the water by a strong force, cannot have as much of its velocity taken away by the water as it would if it travelled more slowly. So it is not surprising that a ball of lead, fired with very great force from a gun, should have been seen to enter the water at an elevation of five degrees:[18] for in those conditions it may not lose[(19)] so much as one-thousandth of its velocity.

Next, he falsely accused me of having supposed that all the loss of speed should be reckoned as belonging to the downwards motion; whereas I constantly affirmed that it should be reckoned as belonging to the whole motion, taken as a single motion. In fact his own way of explaining the cause of refraction is evidently incorrect, in so far as it clearly contradicts that which he previously allowed as having been demonstrated by his friend: namely that in refraction, the sine of the angle refracted in one inclination is to the sine of the angle refracted in another, as the sine of one angle of inclination is to the sine of the other.[20] For the proportion between those sines which results from his parallelogram is completely different—and, indeed, extremely irrational. I have not yet seen the rest of his letter, and so cannot reply to it. I am

> Your Reverence's most devoted[21] servant,
> Descartes

The MS is a copy of the letter as sent, preserved in a collection of letters to Mersenne (mainly by Pierre Fermat) in a 17th-cent. copyist's hand. The version printed by Clerselier is the text of Descartes's draft. I give here the text of the MS (reproducing its formal features, unlike A&T, which takes it as the copy-text but alters punctuation, accentuation, and orthography); however, a small number of evident errors in the MS are replaced here by correct readings from Clerselier in the text, and the erroneous readings of the MS recorded in the notes. Otherwise the notes also record the material variants in Clerselier's version (from CUL M. 3. 44, collated with BL 535. f. 13; siglum: 'Cler').

This letter was enclosed in another letter to Mersenne, with the following words of explanation: 'Yesterday M. Huygens sent me the book by Morin [*Quod Deus sit*], with the three sheets by the Englishman. I have not read the former yet; but as for the latter, you will see what my reply is. I have written it on a separate sheet, so that you can show it to him, if you see fit' ('M.ʳ de Zuytlichem, m'envoya hier le livre de M. Morin, avec les trois feuilles de l'Anglois. Je n'ay pas encore lû le premier; mais pour les dernieres, vous verrez ce que j'y répons. Je l'ay mis en un feuillet à part, afin que vous luy puissiez faire voir, si vous le trouvez à propos' (*MC* x, p. 422)). Thus Descartes began his procedure of sending separate sheets, or separate sections of his letters, in Latin, for Hobbes (as opposed to the French in which he normally corresponded with Mersenne).

The letter just quoted, in which this letter for Hobbes was enclosed, is not itself dated, but on internal evidence it has been dated probably to [11/] 21 Jan. 1641, and certainly to the period between [7/] 17 and [11/] 21 Jan. 1641 (see *MC* x, p. 420).

¹ Hobbes's letter has not survived (see the Introduction, pp. lii–liii).

² Constantijn Huygens, Heer van Zuylichem (1596–1687), scholar, diplomat, prolific neo-Latin poet, and father of Christiaan.

³ proponit *Cler*.

⁴ In the Latin Optical MS, completed probably in 1640 (see the Introduction, pp. liii–liv), Hobbes criticized Descartes's statement in the 'Dioptrique' that sensation is experienced by the soul, not the body. 'For since vision is nothing other than motion, it follows also that the thing which sees is nothing other than that which is moved, namely some body or other' ('Cùm autem *visio* [. . .] nihil aliud sit praeter motum, sequitur etiam *videns* [. . .] aliud non esse praeter id quod mouetur, nempe corpus aliquod' (IV. 14, BL MS Harl. 6796, fo. 248ʳ)). However, the extension of this argument to God is probably Descartes's, not Hobbes's; the following paragraph of the Latin Optical MS adds the qualification 'excluding God, who is inconceivable' ('excepto [. . .] Deo inconceptibili' (IV. 15, BL MS Harl. 6796, fo. 248ᵛ).

⁵ Descartes introduced his theory of subtle matter in the first discourse of the 'Dioptrique' (A&T vi, p. 87).

⁶ For Descartes's concept of the determination of motion see the second discourse of the 'Dioptrique', A&T vi, pp. 94–5. Hobbes criticized this in the Latin Optical MS,

arguing that Descartes's use of the term 'determinatio' was ambiguous and that one possible meaning of it was 'determined motion' (II. 4, 8, BL MS Harl. 6796, fos. 205ᵛ– 206ʳ, 208).

⁷ aliis, scilicet *Cler*.

⁸ sit *MS*.

⁹ alterum *MS*.

¹⁰ gratu *MS*.

¹¹ The Latin Optical MS argues: 'So that part of the body which is opposed to the incoming body either yields to the slightest motion, or cannot be moved by any motion whatsoever' ('Ergo pars corporis quae incurrenti opponitur, vel leuissimo motui cedit, vel nullo omnino motu commoueri potest' (I. 13, BL MS Harl. 6796, fo. 200ᵛ)). Hobbes was arguing that the rebound of a projectile off a hard surface was due to the surface bending inwards and then springing back into shape.

¹² affirimo *MS*.

¹³ ipsummet *omitted Cler*.

¹⁴ Cf. Hobbes's account in Letter 31, p. 84: 'in the motion of a bullet, the bullet it selfe passeth through the seuerall media, whereas in the motion of light the body moued wch is the medium, entreth not into the other medium but thrusteth it on'.

¹⁵ In the second discourse of the 'Dioptrique', Descartes argued that light, being a motion in the subtle matter within the pores of a body, would lose less of its speed in a hard medium than in a soft one (A&T vi, p. 103). The analogy he offered was of a ball which rolls less easily on a soft carpet than on a bare table. Hobbes had evidently objected that it was the roughness, not the softness, of the carpet which produced this effect.

¹⁶ See n. 20.

¹⁷ impulsâ *Cler*.

¹⁸ In the Latin Optical MS Hobbes argued that it was a consequence of Descartes's argument that a projectile passing from air to water at thirty degrees or less would be reflected from the surface of the water; he reported that, according to his own experiments with a gun, a lead bullet would enter water at an angle of five degrees, and would be reflected at two degrees or less (II. 8, BL MS Harl. 6796, fo. 208ʳ).

¹⁹ mulctabatur *Cler*.

²⁰ This probably refers to the eighth theorem of the treatise on refraction by Walter Warner (see Letter 16 n. 3), later printed as bk. 6 of Mersenne, *Universae geometriae synopsis*: 'In refracted vision the sines of the angles of incidence are proportional to the sines of the refracted angles which correspond to those incident angles' ('In visione refractâ sinus angulorum incidentiae, sinibus angulorum refractorum incidentis respondentium proportionales sunt' (p. 564)).

²¹ Sum

    R. PATER

    V. R. Deuotissimus *Cler*.

LETTER 30   [28 JANUARY/] 7 FEBRUARY 1641

Hobbes to Marin Mersenne, from Paris

MS unknown.

Printed in Descartes, *Lettres*, ed. Clerselier, iii, pp. 127–36; Descartes, *Epistolae*, iii, pp. 71–8; *OL* v, pp. 282–94; A&T iii, pp. 300–13; Descartes, *Correspondance*, iv, pp. 270–89; *MC* x, pp. 487–99.

REVERENDISSIME PATER,

Quod ea quae superiori Epistolâ tuo iussu tibi scripsi,[1] Domino Descartes minùs arrideant, plurimùm doleo, tùm quod ingenium eius plurimi aestimo, tùm quod nullam rationem adhuc inuenio propter quam ea quae reprehendit debeam mutare; Libentissimè enim mutarem (si Paralogismos meos possem detegere) quae minus rectè dicta sunt; quippe qui nihil edidi in publicum, quo tenear, vnâ cum honore, errores meos pertinaciter defendere; Ne tamen tanti viri authoritate existimatio mea apud te opprimatur, visum est mihi, Epistolâ hâc, objectionibus eius, eo ordine quo à te relatae sunt, paucis quantum possum & quâ possum perspicuitate respondere.

Dicis primo loco, Dominum Descartes, non agnoscere spiritum illum Internum, quem ego ibi suppono, eundem esse cum materia subtili quam supponit ille.[2]

Respondeo, certè ego per spiritum intelligere me dixi corpus subtile & fluidum; quid autem intersit inter corpus subtile & materiam subtilem, equidem non intelligo.

Adducis proximo loco, causas quare hoc non agnoscit, quas dicis esse duas; primam, quia ego statuo spiritus Internos causam esse duritiei, ille materiam subtilem causam esse mollitiei; Secundam, quia non videt ille, quâ ratione iste spiritus valde mobilis corporibus duris ita includi possit, vt nunquam ex iis egrediatur; nec quomodo ingrediatur quando mollia durescunt.[3]

Quaeso te Reuerendissime Pater (tibi nunc soli satisfacere satago) nunquid tibi capere impossibile est, spiritum fluidum & subtilem talem & tam velocem motum habere posse, vt partes eius minùs cedant tactui & impulsui nostro, quam si eaedem, alio motu, & minùs veloci concitarentur. Quid autem est durum, praeter id cuius partes, stante toto, minùs; molle, praeter id cuius partes magis, corporis incurrentis impulsui cedunt? Quod si sit verum (nam supposui tantùm huiusmodi motuum in spiritibus diuersitatem, vt rem possibilem), sequetur idem corpus tenue, siue materiam subtilem, causam fore & mollitiei & duritiei, prout diuersa velocitate, & diuerso modo mouebitur; Prima ergo causa propter quam negat eandem esse rem, spiritum & materiam subtilem, ostendit potius voluntatem, quam rationem dissentiendi. Quod attinet ad secundam causam dissentiendi, nempe quod non vidit qua ratione &c. Dico eam non esse sufficientem causam quare dissentiret, sed potius quare diligentius consideraret. Neque enim ego dixi durescere corpora per ingressum spirituum, neque mollescere per exitum eorundem; Sed spiritus subtiles & liquidos, vehementiâ motûs sui, posse constituere corpora dura, vt adamantem; & lentitudine, alia corpora mollia, vt aquam vel aërem. Hypothesis autem illa vehementiae motûs spirituum in vno corpore, majoris quam in alio, ad saluandum Phaenomenon duritiei, mihi quidem non videtur inferior illâ Domini Descartes, qui ponit atomorum suarum nodos & implicationes quasdam, quibus partes corporum durorum debeant cohaerere.[4] Si quis enim interrogaret illum, quibus vinculis & quibus nodis particulae illarum partium crassiorum, quas in duris supponit, inter se cohaereant, credo haereret; neque se sciret vllo modo meliùs extricare, quàm supponendo motum aliquem materiae subtilis in illis ipsis atomis, quas ponit pro minimis.

Dicis tertio, quod vbi dixerim illum clariùs locuturum fuisse, si pro determinatione, posuisset motum determinatum, eum mihi non assentiri, sed respondere, his verbis. Etsi enim dici possit velocitatem pilae ab A ad B componi ex duabus aliis, ab A ad H, & ab A ad C, abstinendum tamen esse putaui ab isto modo loquendi ne fortè ita intelligeretur, vt ipsarum velocitatum, in motu sic composito, quantitas, & vnius ad alteram proportio, remaneret; quod nullomodo est verum. Nam si exempli gratiâ ponamus pilam ab A ferri dextrorsum vno gradu celeritatis, & deorsum vno etiam gradu, perueniet ad B cum

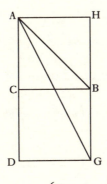

duobus gradibus celeritatis, eodem tempore quo alia quae ferretur etiam dextrorsum vno gradu celeritatis, & deorsum duobus, perueniet ad G cum tribus gradibus celeritatis, vnde sequeretur lineam AB esse ad AG vt 2. ad 3. quod tamen est, vt 2. ad r. 10.[5]

Resp. Quoniam confitetur Dominus Descartes, dici posse velocitatem pilae ab A ad B componi posse ex duabus aliis ab A ad H et ab A ad C, debebat confiteri quoque, id verum esse; nam existimat is, à Philosopho, in Philosophiâ, nihil dici posse, quod non sit verum. Sed abstinuit ab isto loquendi modo, quoniam inde colligi videtur posse id quod falsum est, nempe rationem lineae AB, non esse ad lineam AG vt 2. ad r. 10. sed vt 2. ad 3. quae ratio abstinendi non est iusta. Nam si non rectè infertur ab isto modo loquendi falsitas illa, non debebat timere à Paralogismis quos alij postea sibimetipsis possent facere; Sed ipse putauit illationem illam veram esse, quam ideò ipse quoque colligit, sed fallaci ratiocinatione. Nam & si pilam ponamus ferri ab A dextrorsum vno gradu celeritatis, & deorsum vno etiam gradu, non tamen perueniet ad B duobus gradibus celeritatis; similiter si A feratur dextrorsum vno gradu, deorsum duobus, non tamen perueniet ad G tribus gradibus, vt ille supponit. Supponamus enim duas rectas constitutas ad angulum rectum, AB, AC, sitque velocitas ab A versùs B in ratione ad velocitatem ab A versùs C, quam habet ipsa AB ad ipsam AC, hae duae velocitates componunt velocitatem quae est à B versùs C. Dico velocitatem à B versùs C, esse ad velocitatem ab A versùs C, vel ab A versùs B, vt recta BC ad rectam AC vel AB. Ducatur ab A recta

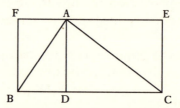

AD, perpendicularis ad BC, & per A, recta FAE eidem BC Parallela; item BF, CE, perpendiculares ad FE. Quoniam igitur motus ab A ad B componitur ex motibus ab F ad A et ab F ad B, non contribuet motus compositus AB plus celeritatis ad motum à B versùs C, quam possunt contribuere componentes FA, FB; sed motus FB nihil contribuit motui à B versus C, motus enim ille determinatur deorsum, nec omnino tendit à B versùs C. Solus igitur motus FA dat motum à B versus C. Similiter probatur AC dare motum à D versùs C in virtute solius AE; sed celeritas quam participat AB, ab FA, et quâ operatur à B versus C, est ad celeritatem totam AB, in proportione FA vel BD ad AB. Item celeritas quam habet AC, virtute AE, est ad celeritatem totam AC, vt AE, vel DC, ad AC. Sunt ergo ambae celeritates junctae, quibus fit motus à B versùs C, ad celeritatem simpliciter sumptam in AC, vel in AB, vt tota BC, ad AC vel AB. Quare sumptâ praecedenti figurâ erunt

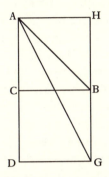

celeritates per AB, AG, vt ipsae AB, AG, hoc est vt r. 2. ad r. 5. hoc est vt r. 4. ad r. 10. hoc est vt 2. ad r. 10. & non vt 2. ad 3. Non igitur sequitur absurdum illud ab isto modo loquendi, quod putabat D. Descartes. Vides Pater quàm pronum sit etiam doctissimis viris per nimiam securitatem quandoque παραλογίζεσθαι.

Quarto, scribis dicere illum, non debuisse me dicere, celeritatem sublatam esse à terra, propterea quòd ille contrarium supposuerat, & propterea quòd contra experientiam est; alioqui enim pila per-pendiculariter in terram incidens nunquam resiliret.[6]

Respondeo, certè ego in Epistolâ meâ hypothesim illius non sustuli, sed dixi ipsum eam sustulisse, ideoque eâ vti non debuisse (nam quantum ad meam de ea re opinionem attinet, puto sanè dari motum qui neque tolli neque ideo minui vnquam possit) sed vt iudices vtrùm suam ipsius abstulerit hypothesim, nec ne, repetamus figuram. Supponit ille, moueri A versùs B, motu quidem nunquam cessaturo, sed tamen qui non semper erit in eâ determinatione vt ille loquitur; hoc est, ibit semper aequaliter quod mouetur, sed non ibit semper per eandem viam, siue lineam directam; Concedo. Praetereà componitur

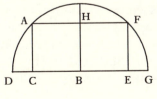

determinatio (siue via) ab A versùs B, à duabus aliis viis (siue determinationibus) quarum vna est deorsum ab A versùs C, altera lateralis ab A versùs H. Concedo quoque. Ex his probare se putat motum ab A in B procedere à B in F per angulum FBE aequalem angulo ABC, sine destructione hypothesis suae; quod negaui. Quando enim pila quae mouetur ab A versùs B peruenerit ad B, perdit determinationem (siue viam) quam habebat deorsum ab AH versùs CB, restat ergo determinatio quae dextrorsum erat ab AC versùs HB; retinetur autem gradus velocitatis quem habebat ab initio; ibit igitur ad circumferentiam circuli in G. Oportuit igitur illum demonstrasse quòd retentâ velocitate integrâ quam habebat ab A versùs B, impossibile esset pilam promoueri longiùs in eâdem determinatione, quam ad E, quod facere non potuit, nisi determinatio illa ab A versùs H sumeretur pro motu. Sed et ipse videtur determinationem illam intelligere pro motu, quoniam, in demonstratione eius, attribuit ei quantitatem; determinatio enim, siue via pilae, non habet quantitatem, nisi quatenus, secundum eam, pila lineam describit tantâ vel tantâ longitudine. Iam verò si determinationes illae duae perpendicularis & lateralis sint motus, manifestum est pilam, quando venit ad B, perdere partem illam motûs sui quam habebat ab A versùs C. Ideoque post impactum in B, minùs velociter fertur quam ante; quae est propriae hypothesis suae destructio. Quod addit talem motus diminutionem esse contra experientiam, quia videmus ea quae incidunt in terram perpendiculariter, ad perpendiculum resurgere, miror quomodo ab experientiâ sciri potest vtrum reflexio haec ad perpendiculum fiat, ab eo quod nulla fit motûs jactura, an vero à motûs restitutione; nam idem effectus fieri potest vtrouis modo. Verum est, quod experientia docet fieri reflexionem per angulos aequales, sed non à quâ causâ.

Scribis quinto, Dominum Descartes libenter concedere partem terrae incurrenti pilae aliquantulum cedere, ipsiusque pilae partem incurrentem non nihil introrsum incuruari, & vtrumque, scilicet pilam & terram, se restituere, *Et nullâ vi amoueri quod non cedit leuissimae*, videri ipsi nullam habere veritatis speciem.[7]

Resp. ostenderam tamen, si vis leuissima non faciet cedere id cui impingit, saltem aliquantulum, dupla vis non sufficit, quia bis nihil, nihil est, & sic quotiescunque multiplicaueris vim illam, fiet nihil. Quae sanè demonstratio est, cuius vitium ille non detegit; sed ait pugnare cum experientia; quia in bilance, appensum pondus 100. librarum mouebitur à 200. libris ex altera parte iugi appensis, ab vna libra non mouebitur; quasi ego dixerim vim leuissimam sufficere ad mouendum à loco suo non modo partem in quam impingit & quam tangit, sed etiam totum quod illi parti adhaeret. Quando is concedit partem terrae cui incurrit pila, aliquantulum cedere, intelligitne totum telluris orbem loco cedere? Puto non. Quare igitur non sufficit ad confirmationem propositionis meae, quod, sicut terra premitur, & parte sua aliqua recedit, propter pilam impactam, ita iugum bilancis aliquantulum premitur, & pars eius deprimitur, propter pilam suspensam. Et sicut multiplicata vis impactae pilae, sufficit ad mouendam totam tellurem, ita multiplicata vis suspensae librae, vel pilae, vel si placet plumae, sufficit ad tollendum pondus 100. librarum.

Sexto, quod dicis eum affirmare resultum pilae magis impediri ab ista incuruatione pilae & terrae, quam ab eius restitutione iuuetur, atque ex eo posse demonstrari reflexionem pilae, & aliorum eiusmodi corporum non extremè durorum, nunquam fieri ad angulos accuratè aequales.[8]

Respondeo, verum hoc est de pila & eiusmodi corporibus, propterea quod non modo velocitas in iis continuò minuitur vel augetur à grauitate, sed etiam corpora in quae incidunt, non perfectè compensant jacturam illam velocitatis; ideoque quatenus loquutus sum de pila, in exemplum reflexionis luminis, supponebam motum eius neque minui eundo, & perfectè restitui quod perdiderat in occursu corporis resistentis. Sed in lumine, cuius neque motus neque à grauitate neque à leuitate diuertitur, & cuius materia facillimè mobilis est, ideoque motus eius restitui à resistente integrè potest, angulorum aequalitas rectè ex tali restitutione saluari potest.

Septimo ais, dicere illum, perperam à me adduci istam terrae mollitiem ad aequalitatem angulorum demonstrandam, praesertim cum ab eâ sequatur, si terra & pila tam durae essent, vt nullo modo cederent, nullam fore reflexionem, quod est incredibile.[9]

Resp. primùm me non adscribere reflexionem mollitiei terrae, sicut neque vitri vel chalybis; Sed scire me, docente experientiâ, fortiorem esse reflexionem, quo durius est corpus in quod impingitur, & quod impingit, modò non sit durities ea actu infinita[10] (quod est impossibile). Nam si non sit ea durities actu infinita, cedet vi alicui, & proinde etiam

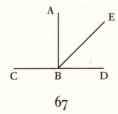

vt ante ostensum est leuissimae. Dura autem quo magis sunt dura, tanto magis se restituunt, ideoque tantò fortiorem faciunt reflexionem. Quod si supponeret quis duritiem illam actu infinitam & impossibilem, tam in impingente, quam in eo in quod impingitur, nemo vnquam experientiâ cognoscet, vtrum reflexio fieret nec ne; Sit enim durum actu in infinitum, tam quod descendit per AB, quam quod substernitur in CD. Quae ratio reddi potest quare non vel quiescat in B id quod ibi impingit, vel, si frangi potest quare non pars altera moueatur per BC altera per BD, vel si descenderit obliquè per EB, quid impedit (si frangatur) quo minus pars moueatur, fortasse pars major, per BC, altera pars minor, per BD. Nam quod aliter fieri videmus, id prouenire potest ex eo quod non dentur corpora infinitae duritiei.

Octauo quod dicis, distinctionem quam attuli inter refractionem eorum quae media permeant (vt quando pila permeat aërem & aquam) & eorum quae non permeant, ab eo non approbari, propterea quod vtroque modo, si corpora sint eiusdem generis, refringuntur versùs easdem partes.[11]

Respondeo, me non satis intelligere quae corpora ille sub eodem, & quae sub diuerso genere collocat. Ego sanè duo genera propagationis motûs posui, quamquam in eodem genere corporis; Potest enim pila corpus durum perfringere, in quo casu dico viam pilae refringi intra durum, in partes à perpendiculo auersas; potest etiam eadem pila à duritie corporis repelli, ita tamen vt motus propagetur successiuè per totam corporis crassitiem, vt quando campana percutitur malleo, (vel, quando, vt ego censeo, lumen propagatur per medium durius eo ex quo [veneret][12]) & dixi in hoc casu, fieri refractionem versùs perpendiculum, quam ille distinctionem non confutauit, neque ego mutare debeo, nisi Dominus Descartes demonstret aliquid in contrarium. Nam suppositiones illae de pororum parietibus, & de velociori motu luminis in duro quam in molli, vel in denso quam in raro, (vtro enim modo loquendum sit nescio, donec mihi definitiones suas duri, mollis, densi, & rari communicauerit, quod in libris suis non fecit) aberrant, meâ quidem sententiâ, à verâ methodo demonstrandi.

Nono scribis, Domino Descartes videri, me nihil attulisse contra demonstrationem eius refractionis, quam tamen damnaueram; neque aduertisse differentiam quae est inter refractionem pilae aliorumque corporum in aquam incidentium, & refractionem luminis.[13]

Respondeo me illam distinctionem & animaduertisse, & attulisse, nempe illam ipsam quam ille proximè suprà damnauit, & ego defendi. Vtrum autem nihil attulerim contra eius explicationem refractionis, iudicabis tu Reuerendissime Pater, qui ipsam meam Epistolam apud te habes; Confitetur tamen obiecisse me repugnantiam quandam cum experientiâ in hypothesi eius, quod certè ipsum non est parum, cui tamen obiectioni non respondet. Obseruaui quidem in fluminibus, velociùs ferri aquam inter nauigia quàm liberam, & vbi non impeditur; Applicari autem hoc praesenti dubio non potest, quia id accidit ex eleuatione aquae, vnde sequitur motus velocior a grauitate, quod fieri non potest in materia subtili dum permeat poros corporum durorum, quia nulla ibi fit eleuatio, neque est vlla grauitas materiae eius subtilis; Similiter quando corpus graue mouetur tardiùs super tapetem sericum quam super mensam marmoream, ratio eius rei est quod insurgentes tapetis partes anteriores, opponunt se prementi graui, & impediunt motum totius, propter consistentiam eius; Id tamen accidere non potest materiae subtili, quae & fluida est maximè, & minimè grauis; Adde quod corpus planum faciliùs mouetur super tapetem sericum, sequendo inclinationem pilorum, modò extremitas corporis moti, promineat vltra extremitatem tapetis, & supposito quod tapes pressus non conetur se restituere.[14] Quae omnia impedimenta absunt à motu materiae subtilis per duri poros.

Scribis decimo loco quod queritur Dominus Descartes me affinxisse ei, quod computauerit omnem jacturam velocitatis in motu deorsum; dixisse autem illum constantissimè computandum esse in motu toto simpliciter sumpto.[15]

Respondeo, fateor dixisse illum directè, computandam esse illam jacturam in motu toto; Sed cum dixit determinationem perpendicularem tantum & non lateralem, minui in primâ duri penetratione, dixit per consequens motum totum perpendicularem minui; nam determinatio minui non potest, nisi per determinationem intelligat motum. Non ergo constantissimè dixit jacturam motus computandam esse in toto motu simpliciter. Si igitur ille vtrumque contradictoriorum dixit, ego autem alterum eorum ei adscribo, non est hoc ei aliquid affingere. Praetereà, si ille jacturam velocitatis totam computat in toto motu, nullam autem computat in motu laterali, necesse est vt totam computet in solo perpendiculari.

Vides Reuerendissime Pater, quam clarè & perspicuè illius obiectionibus, breuiter tamen, respondi. Ex quo patet doctissimum & ingeniosissimum virum, vel incuriâ vel praeiudicio, non satis intendisse animum ad ea quae scripseram; nihilominus liberum tibi sit, communicare ei reliqua quae in eâdem Epistolâ continentur circa refractionem; videbit enim Parallelogrammum illud quo vsus sum, ad explicandam refractionem pilae, minimè pertinere ad refractionem luminis, prout ille suspicatur. Quod attinet ad demonstrationem amici mei, eam, nisi periit eo quem nosti casu, credo me habiturum proximâ septimana, si habuero, tibi eam communicabo, neque Domino Descartes eandem inuidebo in quo iudicandi facultatem summè admiror, diligentiam desidero, quam si auctore te in legendis meis adhibere velit, nemo est cui ego censuram eorum libentiùs deferrem. Plurimum vale, et faue

Tui obsequentissimo
HOBBES

Parisiis Feb. 7. 1641.

Translation of Letter 30

Most reverend Father,

I am very sorry that M. Descartes is rather dissatisfied with the contents of the letter which I wrote to you at your request[1]—both because I have a high opinion of his intellect, and because I still find no reason to change the things to which he objects. For I should very willingly change those things which are incorrectly stated, if I could detect my paralogisms; it is not as if I had published anything, which would make me feel bound to defend my errors stubbornly as a point of honour. However, to prevent your opinion of me being lowered by the authority of such a great man, I have decided to reply to his objections in this letter, answering them as concisely and as clearly as I can, in the order in which you passed them on to me.

First, you say that M. Descartes does not agree that that internal spirit which I suppose to exist is the same as the subtle matter which he supposes.[2]

I reply as follows. I definitely said that what I mean by 'spirit' is 'a subtle and fluid body': I really do not see, however, what the difference is between a 'subtle body' and 'subtle matter'.

Secondly, you give the reasons why he does not agree to this, of which you say there are two: first, because I posit those internal spirits as the cause of hardness, while he posits subtle matter as the cause of softness; and secondly, because he does not see how that very mobile spirit can be so enclosed in hard bodies that it never escapes from them—nor how it can enter into them, when soft bodies become hard.[3]

I beg you, most reverend Father (and at this point I have enough work to do just trying to satisfy you), is it really impossible for you to understand that a fluid and subtle spirit can have such, and so rapid, a motion that its parts yield less on being touched or hit by us than they would if they had a different, less rapid motion? What, after all, is a hard thing, if not something whose parts (when the whole thing holds together) yield *less* to the blow of some body that strikes it, and what is a soft thing, if not something whose parts yield *more*? And if that is true (for I have only supposed this kind of difference in the motions of spirits as something possible), it will follow that the same fine body, or subtle matter, will be the cause of both softness and hardness, according to the different speeds and manners in which it moves. So the first explanation he gives for his denial that my spirit and his subtle matter are the same thing indicates a desire to disagree with me rather than a reason for doing so.

As for his second explanation, namely that he 'does not see how', etc., I reply that that is not a sufficient reason for disagreeing with me, but rather a reason why he should consider the matter more carefully. For I did not say that bodies are made hard by spirits entering them, or soft by spirits going out of them. What I said was that subtle and fluid spirits can make some bodies, such as steel, hard, by the violence of their motion, and other bodies, such as water or air, soft, by the slowness of their motion. This hypothesis, which supposes that the motion of the spirits is more violent in one body than in another, strikes me as no less suitable for explaining the phenomenon of hardness than M. Descartes's hypothesis, which posits certain knots and entanglements of his atoms, which are meant to make the parts of hard bodies stick together.[4] For if one were to ask him by what chains and knots the particles of those denser parts which he posits in hard bodies stick together, I think he himself would be stuck, and would not be able to find any better way out than to suppose that there is some motion of subtle matter inside those very atoms, which he posits as the smallest possible things.

Thirdly, you say that he does not agree with my claim that if he had said 'determined motion' instead of 'determination', he would have expressed himself more clearly. He replies, you say, as follows. 'Even if the velocity of the ball moving from A to B can be said to be composed of two other velocities, from A to H and from A to C, nevertheless I decided not to describe it in that way, in case I gave the impression that the quantity of those velocities, and their proportion to each other, continued to exist in the motion which was thus composed of them—which is

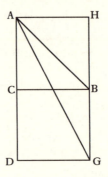

completely false. For if we suppose, for example, that the ball at A is moved to the right with one degree of speed, and downwards also with one degree of speed, it will reach B with two degrees of speed, in the same time that it takes another ball, moved to the right with one degree of speed and downwards with two degrees, to reach G with three degrees of speed; from which it would follow that the line AB was to AG as 2 is to 3, whereas in fact it is as 2 is to the square root of 10.'[5]

I reply as follows. As M. Descartes admits that it can be said that the speed of the ball from A to B can be composed of two other speeds, from A to H and from A to C, he should also have admitted that it is true. For according to his own opinion nothing can be said, by a philosopher in philosophy, which is not true. But he 'decided not to describe it in that way', because he thought that a false conclusion might be drawn as a result, namely that the ratio of the line AB to AG was not that of 2 to the square root of 10, but that of 2 to 3. That, however, is no justification for his decision. For if that false statement is not correctly derived from that method of description, he need not worry about the paralogisms which other people, for their part, might later make. But he thought that conclusion was true, since he reached it himself—though by false reasoning. For, if we suppose a ball at A to be moved to the right with one degree of speed, and downwards also with one degree, it will not in fact reach B with two degrees of speed; similarly, if A is moved to the right with one degree, and downwards with two, it will not in fact reach G with three degrees, as he supposes. Let us suppose two straight lines, AB and AC, forming a right-angle, and let the velocity from A to B have the same ratio to the velocity from A to C as the ratio between AB and AC themselves; these two velocities compose the velocity from B to C. I say that the ratio between the velocity from B to C and the velocity from A to C (or from A to B) will

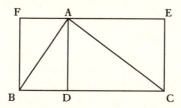

be the same as the ratio between the straight lines BC and AC (or AB). Let the straight line AD be drawn from A, perpendicular to BC, and let the straight line FAE be drawn through A, parallel to BC; and also let BF and CE be drawn, perpendicular to FE. Then, since the motion from A to B is composed of the motions from F to A and from F to B, the composed motion AB will not contribute more speed to the motion from B to C than can be contributed by the components FA and FB. But the motion FB contributes nothing to the motion from B to C, since that motion is determined downwards, and does not in the least tend from B towards C. So only the motion FA supplies the motion from B to C. Similarly it can be shown that AC supplies the motion from D towards C by virtue of AE only; but the speed which AB shares from FA, and by which it is taken from B to C, is to the total speed AB in the ratio of FA or BD to AB. Again, the speed which AC has, by virtue of AE, is to the total speed AB in the ratio of AE or DC to AC. So the two speeds joined together, by which the motion from B to C takes place, are to the speed taken on its own in AC or AB in the ratio of the whole line BC to AC or AB. Which is why, taking the previous diagram again, the speeds along AB and AG will be in the same ratio as the lines AB and AG themselves, i.e. the ratio of the square root of 2 to the square root of 5, i.e. the ratio of the square root of 4 to the square root of 10, i.e. the ratio of 2 to the square root of 10, and not 2 to 3. So the absurd consequence which M. Descartes thought would arise from that

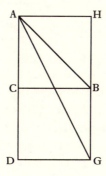

method of description does not arise. You see, Father, how inclined even the most learned men are to commit paralogisms, sometimes, through excessive carelessness.

Fourthly, you write that he says I should not have said that speed is taken away from the ball by the ground, for two reasons: first because he supposed the opposite, and secondly because it is contrary to experience. For otherwise, he says, a ball falling vertically on the ground would never rebound.[6]

I reply as follows. I did not in fact destroy that hypothesis of his, but rather I said that he himself had destroyed it, and that therefore he should not have used it. (For, as for my own opinion on that matter, I think that motion, once imparted, can never be either taken away or, by the same token, diminished.) But to let you decide whether he over-turned his own hypothesis or not, let us go back to the diagram. He

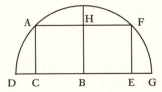

supposes that A is moved towards B, by a motion which indeed will never cease, but which will not, however, always have the same deter-mination (as he puts it). That is, it will always go at the same rate, but not always by the same path or straight line. I agree. Further, the deter-mination (or path) from A to B is composed of two other paths (or determinations), of which one is downwards from A to C, and the other is sideways from A to H. There too I agree. From this he thinks he can show that the motion from A to B proceeds from B to F by an angle FBE equal to the angle ABC, without destroying his hypothesis. That is what I denied. For when the ball, which is moved from A towards B, reaches B, it loses the determination (or path) which it had downwards from AH to CB; so there remains the determination to the right which it had from AC to HB. However, it keeps the degree of velocity which it had from the beginning; therefore it will go to the circumference of the circle at G. So he should have demonstrated that, if the entire velocity which it had from A to B was retained, it was impossible for the ball to continue in motion further, in that determination, than to E; which could not be done, unless that determination from A to H were taken to be a motion. But he too seems to take that determination in the sense of a motion, since, in his demonstration, he attributed quantity to it; and the determination or path of a ball does not have quantity, except in so far as the ball describes a line of such and such a length when it follows that path. So in fact, if those two perpendicular and lateral determinations are motions, it is obvious that when the ball reaches B, it loses that part of its motion which it had from A towards C. Accordingly, after striking B, it will move less rapidly than before; and that destroys his own hypothesis. As for his additional remark that such a diminution of motion is contrary to experience, because we see that things which fall vertically onto the ground rebound vertically, I wonder how we can know from experience which of two possible explanations for this vertical rebound is correct: either that no motion is lost, or that there is a restitution of motion. For the same effect can come about in either way. It is true that experience teaches us the fact that reflection takes place in equal angles; but it does not teach us what the cause is.

Fifthly, you write that M. Descartes freely concedes that the part of the ground which is struck by the ball does yield just a little, and that the part of the ball which strikes the ground does bend inwards a little; and that both of them, the ball and the ground, return to their original shapes. You add that he thinks there is no semblance of truth in the claim that 'that which does not yield to the slightest force cannot be moved by any force at all'.[7]

I reply as follows. My aim was to show that if the slightest force does not cause the thing struck by it to yield, at least by a tiny amount, then twice that force will not suffice to do so; for twice nothing is nothing, and will remain nothing however many times you multiply the force. That is indeed the demonstration which, although he exposes no error in it, he says is contrary to experience. For, he says, in a pair of scales a weight of 100 pounds will be moved by 200 pounds hanging on the other side, but will not be moved by one pound—as if I had said that the slightest force is sufficient to displace not only the part which is struck and touched by it, but also the entire body to which that part belongs. When he agrees that the part of the ground which is struck by the ball yields slightly, does he think that the entire sphere of the earth is displaced? I think not. So why is it not sufficient, in order to confirm my proposition, to say this: that just as the ground is pressed down, and yields in some part, because of the impact of the ball, so the arm of the scales is pressed down slightly, and a part of it is lowered because of the ball which hangs from it. And, just as the force of the ball's impact would be enough to move the whole earth if it were multiplied enough times, so the multiplied force of a suspended weight, or ball—or feather, if you like—will be enough to lift a weight of 100 pounds.

Sixthly, you say he states that the rebound of a ball is always hindered by that bending inwards of both ball and ground, more than it is helped by their returning to their original shapes. And hence he says it can be demonstrated that the reflection of a ball, and of other bodies of that kind which are not extremely hard, never takes place in exactly equal angles.[8]

I reply as follows. This is true about balls, and other bodies of that kind, not only because their velocity is continually reduced or increased by their heaviness, but also because the bodies which they strike do not entirely compensate that loss of velocity. So, when I discussed the ball, as an example of the reflection of light, I was supposing that its motion was not reduced as it went along, and that the motion which it lost when it hit a resisting body was entirely restored to it. But in the case of light, the motion of which is affected neither by heaviness nor by lightness, and the matter of which is extremely mobile, its motion can be entirely restored to it by the resisting body, and the equality of the angles can be accounted for correctly by such a process of restitution.

Seventhly, you say that he claims I was wrong to put forward this softness of the ground as part of my demonstration of the equality of the angles: especially since it follows that if the ground and the ball were so hard that they did not yield at all, there would be no reflection—which is impossible to believe.[9]

I reply as follows. Firstly, I did not attribute reflection to the softness of the earth, any more than I did to the softness of glass or steel. I said that I know, by experience, that reflection is stronger, the harder the struck and striking bodies are—provided that that hardness is not actually infinite[10] (which is impossible). For if the hardness is not actually infinite, it will yield to some force, and therefore it will also yield, as I have demonstrated above, to the slightest force. Hard things, though, restore themselves more strongly to their original shape, the harder they are; and so the reflection they cause is that much stronger too. If one supposed that both the striking and the struck objects were of that actually infinite hardness, no one would ever be able to know by experience whether reflection would take place or not. For let both the body which descends from A to B, and the body which lies at CD, have an actually infinite hardness. What reason can one give why the body which strikes B should not either rest there, or, if it can be broken, why

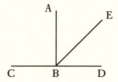

one part should not move from B to C, and the other from B to D? Or, if it descends at an angle from E to B, and if it breaks, what is there to prevent one part, perhaps the larger one, from moving from B to C, and the other from B to D? For the fact that we observe a different result may be due to the fact that infinitely hard bodies do not exist.

Eighthly, you say that he disapproves of the distinction I made between the refraction of those bodies which pass through media (as when a ball passes through air and water) and the refraction of those which do not. The reason why he disapproves is that in both cases, if the bodies are of the same kind, they will be refracted in the same direction.[11]

I reply as follows. I do not understand clearly enough which bodies he classifies as being of the same kind, and which as being of a different kind. For my own part, I posited two kinds of propagation of motion, albeit in the same kind of body: for a ball can either break through a hard body, in which case I say that the path taken by the ball is refracted within the hard body in a direction away from the perpendicular; or else the same ball can be driven back by the hardness of the body, with the result, however, that its motion is propagated successively through the entire thickness of the body, as when a bell is struck by a hammer (or as when, in my opinion, light is propagated through a harder medium than the one from which it came[12])—and in that case, I said, the refraction will be towards the perpendicular. That is a distinction which he did not refute; nor do I need to alter it, unless M. Descartes demonstrates something to the contrary. As for his suppositions about the walls of pores, and about the motion of light being faster in hard bodies than in soft ones, or in dense bodies rather than in rare ones (for I do not know which of these pairs of terms to use, until he lets me know his definitions of 'hard', 'soft', 'dense', and 'rare', which he has not given in his books), they stray, in my opinion, from the true method of demonstration.

Ninthly, you say that M. Descartes thinks I have not put forward any disproof of his demonstration of refraction, although I condemned it.

Nor does he think I have noticed the difference between the refraction of a ball, or of other bodies, entering water, and the refraction of light.[13]

I reply as follows. I both noticed that distinction, and put it forward in my argument: for it is the very distinction which he was condemning in the previous section, and I was defending. But as to whether I put forward no disproof of his explanation of refraction, you will be the judge of that, most reverend Father, since you have my letter with you. He admits, however, that I objected that his hypothesis involved something contrary to experience—not an insignificant objection, although he does not reply to it. The observation I made was that in rivers the water moves more quickly between two boats than it does where it is free and unimpeded. However, this cannot be applied to the present problem, because it happens by reason of the water being raised up, which means that the water gains greater speed from its weight; and that cannot happen in the case of subtle matter, while it passes through the pores of hard objects, because there is no increase in height there, and the subtle matter is not at all heavy. Similarly, the reason why a heavy object moves more slowly on a silk carpet than it does on a marble table-top is that the parts of the carpet which stick up in front of the object resist the pressure of the heavy object, and impede the motion of the whole object, because of its solidity; but that cannot happen in the case of subtle matter, which is extremely fluid and extremely light. Note too that a flat body will move more easily over a silk carpet, following the way the pile of the carpet lies, provided that the end of the body extends beyond the edge of the carpet, and supposing that the surface of the carpet, once pressed down, does not try to spring back.[14] All those impediments are lacking in the case of the motion of subtle matter through the pores of a hard body.

Tenthly, you say that M. Descartes complains that I have falsely accused him of reckoning all the loss of velocity as belonging to the downwards motion; whereas he constantly affirmed that it should be reckoned as belonging to the whole motion, taken as a single motion.[15]

I reply as follows. I agree that he did explicitly say that that loss of velocity should be reckoned as belonging to the whole motion. But since he said that only the perpendicular determination, not the lateral one, was diminished on first entering the hard object, he implied that the whole perpendicular motion was diminished; for a determination cannot be diminished, unless by 'determination' he means 'motion'. It follows that he did not constantly say that the loss of motion should be reckoned as belonging to the whole motion, taken as a single motion.

So if he has said two contradictory things, and I am ascribing the second one to him, I am not thereby laying a false accusation against him. Besides, if he reckons the whole loss of velocity as belonging to the whole motion, and reckons that there is no loss in the lateral motion, he must necessarily be reckoning the whole loss as belonging to the perpendicular motion only.

You see, most reverend Father, how clearly and closely—and yet briefly—I have replied to his objections. From which it can clearly be seen that, whether through carelessness or through prejudice, that extremely learned and intelligent man did not attend closely enough to what I had written. Nevertheless, feel free to let him know the other things which are contained in the same letter on the subject of refraction: that will enable him to see that the parallelogram which I used to explain the refraction of a ball has very little to do with the refraction of light, just as he suspects.

As for the demonstration by my friend, I think I shall have it next week, unless it has been destroyed (for reasons which you know).[16] If I get it I shall send it to you, nor shall I mind M. Descartes seeing it too. For I have the highest admiration for his powers of judgement. I just wish that he would read more carefully what I have written; and if you could make him do that, there is no one to whose criticism I would rather submit. I hope you are very well, and that you will look kindly upon

Your most obedient servant,
Thomas Hobbes

Paris, 7 February 1641

One evident misprint in Clerselier's text (CUL M. 3. 44, collated with BL 535. f. 13; siglum: 'Cler') is recorded at n. 12.

[1] See Letter 29 n. 1.

[2] Letter 29, pp. 54, 57.

[3] Ibid., pp. 54, 57.

[4] In the first discourse of the 'Météores', Descartes argued that the smallest particles of most bodies are very irregularly shaped, so that they cohere with one another when they are entangled together ('entrelacées'): A&T vi, p. 233.

[5] Letter 29, pp. 54–5, 57–8.

[6] Ibid., pp. 55, 58.

[7] Ibid.

[8] Ibid.

[9] Ibid.

[10] Uncharacteristically, Hobbes is using scholastic terminology here: 'actually' here means that a potentiality is realized 'in act' ('in actu' as opposed to 'in potentia').

[11] Letter 29, pp. 55–6, 58.

[12] venerat *Cler*.

[13] Letter 29, pp. 56, 59.

[14] See ibid., n. 16.

[15] Ibid., pp. 56, 59.

[16] See ibid., n. 20. The reason for the delay and uncertainty is given in Letter 31 (p. 81), where Hobbes explains that he is still waiting for the recovery of his trunk.

LETTER 31   [29 JANUARY/] 8 FEBRUARY 1641

Hobbes to Sir Charles Cavendish, from Paris

BL MS Harl. 6796, fos. 291–5 (original).

Printed in *EW* vii, pp. 455–62; *MC* x, pp. 501–6 (extracts). Facsimiles printed of fo. 291 in *Isographie des hommes célèbres*, ii, and of fo. 293ᵛ, with transcription, in Greg, *English Literary Autographs*, pl. 86.

Honorable Sir

The Last weeke I had the honor to receaue two letters from you at once one of the 30 of Dec. the other of the 7ᵗʰ of Jan. wᶜʰ I acknowledged but could not answer in my last. In the first you begin with a difficulty on the principle of monsʳ de Cartes, That it is all one to moue a weight two spaces or the double of that waight one space, and so in other proportions.[1] to wᶜʰ you obiect the difference of swiftnesse wᶜʰ is greater when a waight is moued two spaces, then when double waight is moued one space. Certenly De Cartes his meaning was [> by force] the same that mine, namely a [Composition of the proportion *deleted*] multiplication of [> the] weight of a body, in to the swiftnesse wherewᵗʰ it is moued so that when I moue [one *deleted*] a pound two foote at the rate of a mile an howre, I do the same as if [I moued *deleted* > of] 2 poundes I moued one [foote *deleted* > pound a foote] at yᵉ rate of a mile an hower, the other [foote *deleted*] pound another foote at the same rate, not in direction but parallell to the first pound. as if the wayt AB were moued to, CD, at the rate of a mile an howre. Tis all one as if the waight AE were moued to FH at the same rate; here is all the difference. this swiftnesse [of *deleted*] or rate of a mile an howre is in the first case layd out in the 2 spaces [AD *deleted*] AG. GC. the later in the 2 spaces AG. EG. The first case is like as if a footman should run wᵗʰ double swiftnesse endwayes wᶜʰ [> is] the doubling of swiftnesse in one man,

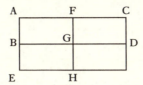

[>in] the other, it is as if you doubled the Swiftnesse by doubling the man. for euery man has his owne swiftnesse and so AH, is the swiftnesse AG doubled, as well as AD. for that, that mons[r] de Cartes will not haue iust [the for *deleted*] twice the force requisite to moue the same weight twice as fast I can say nothing, the papers I haue of his touching that[2] are in my trunke, w[ch] hath bene taken by Dunkerkers, and taken againe from them by french, and at length recouered by frends I made, but I shall not haue it yet this fortnight In the meane time I am not of that opinion. but do assure my selfe, the patient being the same, double force in the Agent shall worke vpon it double effect. In the same letter you require a better explication of y[e] proportion I gather betweene wayght and swiftnesse. wherein because you haue not my figure, I imagine you haue mistaken me very much, and first you thinke I suppose DE equall to AB w[ch] I am sure is a mistake, for I put AB for any line you will to expresse a minutum secundum.[3] I will therefore go ouer againe the demonstration I sent you before and see if I can do it cleerer. Let AB stand for the time knowne wherein the waight D, descendeth to E, And let there bee a Cylinder of the same matter the waight D consisteth of and let the altitude of that Cylinder be DC, w[ch] I did show before was the swiftnesse wherew[th] that Cylinder presseth, not wherew[th] it falleth, and wee are now to enquire how farre such matter as the Cylinder is made of must descend from D, before it atteyne a swiftnesse equall to this pressing swiftnesse DC. And I say it

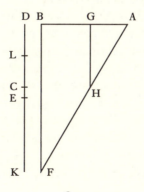

must fall to L. For in the time AB it is knowne that the waight in D will fall to E, and it is demonstrated by Gallileo,[4] that when such waight comes to E it shall be able to go twice the space it hath fallen, in y^e same time therefore the waight D being in E, hath velocity to carry him the space DK (wch I put double to DE) in the same time AB. but I put BF equall to DK, therefore in the time AB, [the velocity *deleted*] the waights velocity acquired in E shall be such as to go from B to F, without encrease [>of velocity] by the way. Hence I [*word deleted*] go on to finde [>in] what point [*word deleted*] the waight in D [*words deleted*] comes to [*line deleted* >when it getteth a velocity equall to CD.][5] therefore I [*word deleted*] apply DC in GH parallell to BF. and then it is, as the time AB to the time AG, so the velocity acquired at the end of the time AB, to the velocity acquired at the end of the time AG, for the swifnesses acquired from time to time (I say not from place to place but) from time to time, are proportionable to the times wherein they are acquired, wch is the postulate on wch Galileo builds all his doctrine. And as AB to AG so the line BF to the line GH. therefore the velocity acquired at the end of the time AB is to the velocity acquired at the end of the time AG, as is the line BF to the line GH. but at the end of the time AB, the waight D is by supposition in E, in that degree of velocity as to go BF or DK in the same time AB, [therefore the [>degree of] velocity *deleted*] the question therefore is, where the waight D shall be, at the end of the time AG, for there it hath the velocity of going GH [>or DC] in the same time, because the Velocity GH is to the velocity BF as the line GH to the line BF or as the time of descent AG to the time AB. But because the spaces of the descent are in double the proportion of the times of descent, make it as BF to GH that is DK to DC, so DC to another, DL. the velocity therefore acquired in the point of descent E, namely the velocity DK or BF, is to the velocity acquired in the point L. namely the velocity GH or DC (wch is the velocity of the Cylinders waight) as DK to DL. and therefore in L. the waight D has acquired a Velocity equal to the velocity of the waight of the Cylinder.

In the same letter you desire to know how any medium, as water, retardeth the motion of a stone that falles into it. to wch I answer out of what you say afterwards, That nothing can hinder motion but contrary motion, That the motion of the water when a stone falles into it, is point blancke contrary to the motion of the stone, for the stone by descent causeth so much water to ascend as the bignesse of the stone comes to. for imagine so much water taken out of the place w^{ch} [>the] stone occupies and layd vpon the superficies of the water, it presseth downe-ward as the stone does, and maketh the water that is below to rise vpwards, and this rising vpwards is contrary to the descent; and is no other operation then wee see in scales, where, of two equall bullets in magnitude, that wch is of heauier metall maketh the other to rise. And thus farre goes your letter of Dec. 30.

For the first Quaere in your second letter Concerning how we see in the time the lucide body contracts it selfe, I haue no other solution but that wch your selfe hath giuen, wch is that the reciprocation is so quicke that the effect of the first motion lasteth till the next comes; and longer, for by experience we obserue that the end of a firebrand swiftely moued about in a circle, maketh a circle of fire, wch could not be, if the impression made at the beginning of the circulation did not last till the end of it, for if the same fire brand be moued slower there will appeare but a peece of a circle [> bigger or lesser] according to the swiftnesse or slownesse of ye motion. For the cause of such reciprocation it is hard to guesse what it is, it may well be the reaction of the medium, for though the medium yeld, yet it resisteth to, for there can be no passion wthout reaction. And if a man could make an Hypothesis to salue that contraction of ye sun yet such is the nature of naturall thinges, as a cause may be againe demanded of such Hypothesis, and neuer should one come to an end, wthout assigning the Immediate hand of God. whereas in mathematicall sciences wee come at last to a definition wch is a beginning or Principle, made true by pact and consent amongst our selues. Further you conceaue a difficulty how the medium can be continually driuen on if there be such an alternate contraction, to wch first I answer that the motion forward is propagated to the vtmost distance in an instant, and the first push is therefore enough. and [next *deleted*] in another instant is made the [*word deleted*] returne backe in ye like manner. And though it were not done in an instant yet wee see by experience in riuers, as in ye Thames, that the tide goes vpward towards London pushed by the water below, and yet at the same instant the water below is going backe to the sea. for seeing it is high water at Blackwall[6] before tis so at Greenwich, the water goes backe from Blackwall, when it goes on at Greenwich, and so it would happen though Blacwall and Greenewich were neuer together, then that any quantity could come betweene.

In my letter from London speaking of the refraction of a bullet I thinke I deliuered my opinion to be, that a bullet, falling out of the thinner medium into the thicker, looseth in the Entring nothing but motion perpendicular, but being entred he looseth proportionally both

83

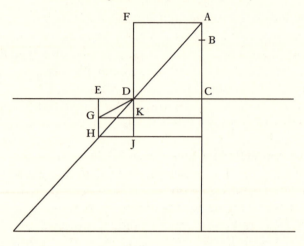

of the one and the other. for suppose a bullet whose diameter is AB be in the thinner medium and enter at C into the thicker medium, the thicker medium, at the first [▷touch] of of B in the point C worketh nothing vpon the line AB, and when the diameter AB is enterd suppose halfe way, yet the thicker medium operates [▷laterally] but on one halfe of it, so that in the somme, there is a losse of velocity perpendicular (to the quantity that the diameter AB requires) without any offence to the motion laterall, but so much of the diameter as is within the thicker medium is retarded both wayes, and looses of his absolute motion, wch is compounded of perpendicular and laterall, and that proportionally. suppose now, that a bullet passe from A to D, and receaue a peculiar losse of his perpendicular motion by entring at D, so great, that he proceed in the Perpendicular but halfe so farre, as for example from D to J, and then being [quite *deleted*] in, the thickenesse of the medium take away more of his velocity both perpendicular and laterall suppose halfe that wch was left of the perpendicular motion and halfe of his first lateral motion, so that the perpendicular motion, is but DK, and the laterall motion DE, then will the line of refraction be DG. As for that argumentation of Des Cartes, it is in my opinion, as I haue heretofore endeauored to shew you a mere paralogism[7] Lastly you make this Quaere, why, light hath not at seuerall inclinations, seuerall swifnesses, as well as a bullet. Wherein we are first to consider that in the motion of a bullet, the bullet it selfe passeth through the seuerall media, whereas in the motion of light the body moued wch is the medium, entreth not into the other medium but thrusteth it on, and so the parts of that medium thrust on one another, whereby the laterall motion of the thicker medium, hath no thing to worke vpon, because nothing enters, but stoppes onely and retards, in oblique incidence that end wch comes first to it, and there by causes a refraction the contrary way to that of a bullet, in such manner as I set forthe to you in one of my letters from hence concerning the cause of refraction. And this is all I can say for the present to the quaeres of yor two last letters. I haue enquired concerning perspectiues after ye manner of de Cartes,[8] Mydorgius[9] tells me there is none that goes about them, as a thing too hard to do. And I beleeue it, For here is one mons^r de Bosne[10] in towne, that dwells at Bloys, an excellent workeman, but by profession a lawier, and is counsellor of Bloys, and a better philosopher in my opinion then de Cartes, and not inferior to him in the Analytiques, I haue his acuaintance by Pere Mersenne, he telles me he hath tryed De Cartes his way but cannot do it, and now he workes vpon a crooked line of his owne inuention. He sayes he shall haue made one w^thin a moneth after he shall returne to Bloys, after that, he will see what he can discouer in the heauens himselfe, and then if he discouer any new thing he will let his way be publique together wth the effects. This is all the hope I can giue you yet. So wth my prayers to God to keepe you in prosperity this troublesome time I rest

your most humble and obedient seruant
Tho: Hobbes

paris feb. 8 stilo no. 1641

[*addressed:*] To the Right Honorable Sr Charles Cavendysshe present these at Wellingor[11]

---

[1] Descartes used this principle, which he described as the general foundation of statics, in the 'Examen' which he sent to Mersenne (see n. 2).

[2] Hobbes was probably thinking of the 'Examen' sent by Descartes to Mersenne on [3/] 13 July 1638 (A&T ii, pp. 222–45: *MC* vii, pp. 347–68), of which Hobbes had received a copy from Mersenne in 1640 (Chatsworth, MS Hobbes C. i. 6).

[3] = second. Properly, 'pars minuta secunda': in the old (medieval Latin) terminology for the system of sexagesimal fractions, the unit of the first division into sixty was 'pars minuta prima', and the unit of the next division was 'pars minuta secunda'.

[4] *Discorsi e dimostrazioni*, day 3, prop. 2 (*Opere* viii, pp. 209–10).

[5] The deleted words cannot be read with certainty, but what Hobbes appears to have written first was as follows: 'Hence I go on to finde what velocity the waight in L acquireth when it comes to C (that is where it hath gone the length of the standing

cylinder of the same matter) therefore [. . .]'; 'point' was added at the end of a line, 'L' changed to 'D', and the other changes made by deletion and interlineation, as recorded in the text.

⁶ A village east of London, on the north bank of the Thames, two miles downstream from Greenwich.

⁷ See the final section of Letter 30.

⁸ Telescopes with elliptical or hyperbolic lenses, as recommended by Descartes in the eighth discourse of the 'Dioptrique' (A&T vi, pp. 185–96).

⁹ See Letter 18 n. 2.

¹⁰ Florimond de Beaune (1601–52), lawyer (*conseiller*) at the 'Présidial' court at Blois, mathematician, lens-grinder, and astronomer. He formed a favourable impression of Hobbes on this visit to Paris in 1641 (see *MC* x, p. 529). His only published work in his lifetime was the 'Notes brièves' on Descartes's *Géométrie*, which was translated and appended to the first Latin edition of that work edited by van Schooten (*Geometria cum notis Florimundi de Beaune*, 1649). Hobbes had probably already seen a copy of the 'Notes brièves' which was sent to Sir Charles Cavendish by Mersenne; but he may not have known that it was by de Beaune, since Sir Charles annotated it 'Fermat' (BL MS Harl. 6796, fos. 267–90, here fo. 267ʳ). Of other MSS by de Beaune the 'Méchaniques' and 'Dioptrique' have not survived, but a proposition on tangents was discovered among Boulliau's papers by Paul Tannery (*Mémoires scientifiques*, x, pp. 382–3), and a complete MS treatise, *Doctrine de l'angle solide*, was discovered in 1963 and published by Pierre Costabel in 1975.

¹¹ Wellingor, Lincs., one of the estates of Sir Charles Cavendish.

LETTER 32   [8/] 18 FEBRUARY 1641

René Descartes to Marin Mersenne for Hobbes, from Leiden

MS unlocated.

Draft printed in Descartes, *Lettres*, ed. Clerselier, iii, pp. 149–52; Descartes, *Epistolae*, iii, pp. 79–81; A&T iii, pp. 313–18; Descartes, *Correspondance*, iv, pp. 290–7; *MC* x, pp. 511–16.

Reverendissime Pater,

Etsi sperassem ea quae in superioribus meis Litteris¹ responderam ad initium scripti à doctissimo quodam Anglo ad Reuerentiam vestram missi, me liberatura esse onere ad reliqua respondendi; quia tamen nihilominus vltima octo folia² scripti ejusdem³ à vestra Reuerentia hodie accepi, simulque admoneor aliquos esse ex doctis vestris⁴, qui ea quae ibi de refractionibus, aliter quam in meâ Dioptricâ traduntur, pro veris & rectè demonstratis admittant, officij mei esse existimo, breuiter hîc ostendere⁵ quibus ex notis aurum ab orichalco dignosci possit.

In fine 3. folij vtitur valde inani ratione, vt refutet id quod scripsi[6] Diop.[7] pag. 19. *quia* inquit, *sequeretur pilae inesse intellectum rerum Geometricarum*[8]; tanquam si ex eo quod aliquid fiat in natura juxta leges Geometriae, sequatur idcircò in corporibus in quibus id fit esse intellectum. Ego vero satis esse putaui ad demonstrandum aliquid fieri[9], quod Geometriae leges docerent ita fieri opportere; Nec ille quicquam noui hîc affert, sed tantum rem à me traditam magis explicat, dicendo *in magna inclinatione resistentiam aquae superare impulsum deorsum*[10], quod, vt intellectu facillimum, explicare neglexeram; Sed hoc explicando in magnam difficultatem à suis principiis adducitur; Quomodo scilicet pila resiliat[11]; an enim dicet aquae superficiem incuruari etiam instar arcus, & dum se restituit pilam sursum repellere.

In reliquis omnibus agit de[12] refractione, & in prima sua hypothesi falsum assumit, *quod nempe omnis actio sit motus localis*[13]. Cum enim, exempli causa, baculo innixus terram premo, actio meae manus communicatur toti isti baculo, & transit vsque ad terram, quamuis nullo planè modo baculum illud, nec quidem insensibiliter vt infra assumit, moueri supponamus.

Quintam etiam hypothesim, *quod aër sit minus contumax aduersus motum luminis, quam aqua vel vitrum*[14], non probat; cumque eius contrarium in Dioptricâ demonstrarim, ille vero nullam dicti sui afferat rationem, quaero vtri magis sit credendum: Neque enim verisimilitudinem aliquam in eo esse putandum est, quod aër facilius cedat motui manuum, quam aqua vel vitrum quoniam actio luminis non est[15] in ipsis corporibus aëris & aquae, sed in materia subtili eorum poris contenta.

Hîc autem ex occasione animaduerto[16], me in praecedenti Epistola scripsisse *lumen faciliùs propagari in duro, quam in molli*[17]; quod ita est intelligendum, vt durities ista non referatur ad tactum manuum nostrarum, sed ad motum materiae subtilis tantùm; ne fortè quis putet inde sequi, refractionem esse debere multo majorem in vitro quam in aquâ; etsi enim vitrum sit multo durius respectu tactûs nostri[18], non tamen multo minus[19] resistit motui materiae subtilis.

Prima propositio[20] planè est imaginaria, destruiturque eius probatio ex eo quod vtatur ad ipsam[21] primâ suâ hypothesi iam refutatâ.

Secunda propositio,[22] si in ipsâ, pro *rejectione* ponatur *repulsio*, vt etiam de[23] impulsione sine motu possit intellegi, vera est, & mea.

Quae in tertiâ[24] habet de Systole etc.[25] planè destruuntur ex iam dictis; vt & ea quae dicit in corollario de inclinatione,[26] quam vult esse motum, idque ob valdè levem[27] rationem: *quia*, inquit, *principium motus est motus*[28]; quis enim illi concessit inclinationem esse principium siue partem motus.

In propositione quartâ malè dicit *radium esse spatium solidum*[29], meliùs fortè dixisset, esse vim per spatium solidum diffusam; Sed adhuc meliùs, si cum omnibus Opticis radium vt lineam tantum[30] consideraret: non enim vtitur postea ejus latitudine, suâque lineâ lucis, nisi ad[31] imaginarias rationes adornandas.

Sed praecipuus eius error est in causâ Physicâ refractionis radiorum explicandâ:[32] tota enim fictitia est, & à mechanicae principiis aliena. Fictitia, quia nititur latitudine quam radiis gratis affingit, quamque in decimâ quartâ propositione iisdem detrahit,[33] & nihilominus eodem modo refringi fatetur; Et quia si vera esset, multo magis haberet locum in motu pilae quam in radiis luminis, quod tamen ipse suprà negauit, atque experientiae repugnat; Vt & ratio propter quam suprà voluit pilam in aquâ refrangi·à perpendiculari, radiis luminis meliùs, vel saltem aeque benè ac motui pilae, potest applicari; In ipsâ enim nulla fit mentio motus successiui; In alterâ autem quam affert pro radiis, fictitij cujusdam Parallelogrammi considerat motum successiuum, estque à legibus mechanicae aliena; tum quia supponit motum partis

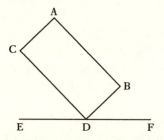

D, Parallelogrammi ABCD, tantundum tardari a superficiè aquae EDF, cum primum illam ingreditur, quam paulò post, cum plures partes lineae CD in aquam demersae sunt, tum quia in transitu radij à medio densiori in rarius vult augeri celeritatem motus, nec tamen dare potest vllam causam istius augmenti; facilè enim intelligitur motum tardari à densitate medij; non autem[34] inde sequitur, vbi non est [tanta][35] densitas, illum augeri, sed tantum minus imminui; tum propter alias causas quas omnes recensere esset longum.

Quinta propositio, quod radius obliquè incidens sit considerandus vt habens latitudinem,[36] jam est refutata, & pugnat cum decimâ quartâ; nec valet eius probatio, ad quam gratis assumit *considerari radium vno termino longiùs operari quam altero.*[37] Quod nemo ipsi concedet qui radium absque latitudine considerabit.

Sequentia, vsque ad decimam quartem propositionem, satis vt puto sequuntur ex eius principiis, dico, vt puto, quia satis attente non legi, vt ausim affirmare. Caeterùm non mirum est quod ex falsis hypothesibus sequatur verum, quia illas[38] ad veritatem sibi ante cognitam accommodauit.

In fine de Coloribus[39] nihil habet quod non antè scripserim, nisi quod rem sufficienter non explicet; Et malè ait me globulos supponendo,[40] priorem meam hypothesim destruxisse; quia illos globulos describendo, non affirmaui nihil esse in spatiolis quae ab ipsis non implentur[41]; nec opus habui plura explicare, quam quae ad institutum meum faciebant; Denique vt verbo absoluam, ne minimam quidem rationem in toto hoc scripto reperi à meis diuersam, quae vera & legitima esse videatur. Sum,

Reverendissime Pater,
V.^ae R.^ae devotissimus famulus
Descartes[42]

Translation of Letter 32

Most reverend Father,

I had hoped that the reply I made in my previous letter[1] to the first part of the paper which you had received from a certain very learned Englishman would have freed me from the burden of having to reply to the rest of it. Yet today I nevertheless received the last eight pages[2] of that same[(3)] paper from your reverence, and at the same time I have been warned that some of your learned men[(4)] accept as true and correctly demonstrated his arguments about refraction, which differ from the ones I use in my 'Dioptrique'. So I think it is my duty to show[(5)] here, briefly, how to tell gold from brass.

At the end of the third page he uses an utterly worthless argument to refute what I wrote[6] on p. 19 of my 'Dioptrique'[(7)]: 'because', he says, 'it would follow that the bullet has an understanding of geometry'[(8)]. As if it follows, from the fact that something happens in the physical world in accordance with the laws of geometry, that the bodies in which that happens have understanding! For my part, I thought it sufficient, in order to demonstrate that something happened[(9)], that the laws of geometry taught that it should happen. And when he says that 'at a very inclined angle, the resistance of the water overcomes the downwards impetus'[10], he is not saying anything new, but merely giving a fuller explanation of my own teaching, on a point which I had neglected to explain because I thought it extremely easy to understand. But in explaining this, he is led into great difficulty by his own principles: for how does the bullet rebound[11]? Will he say that the surface of the water bends inwards like a bow, and, in restoring itself to its original shape, pushes the ball upwards?

In all the rest the subject is[12] refraction; and in his first hypothesis he makes a false assumption when he says that 'all action is local motion'[13]. For when I press, for example, with a stick against the ground, the action of my hand is communicated to the whole of that stick, and is transmitted as far as the ground, even though we do not suppose in the slightest that the stick is moved—not even indiscernibly, as he goes on to assume.

He does not prove the truth of his fifth hypothesis, that 'air is less resistant to the movement of light than water or glass'[14]. Given that I demonstrated the opposite in my 'Dioptrique', and that he puts forward no reason whatever for his claim, I ask you: which of us should you rather believe? For one should not think that his argument gains any plausibility from the fact that air yields more easily than water or glass to the motion of our hands; since the action of light takes place not[15] in the actual bodies of air or water, but in the subtle matter contained in their pores.

This is a suitable place to comment[16] on the fact that I wrote in my earlier letter that 'light is propagated more easily in a hard body than a soft one':[17] it should be understood that hardness there means not hardness to the touch of our hands, but hardness to the motion of subtle matter only. Otherwise one might think it followed from that that refraction should be much greater in glass than in water; for even though glass is much harder to our touch[18], it is not much less[19] resistant to the motion of subtle matter.

His first proposition[20] is obviously pure fantasy; and the proof he gives of it is destroyed by the fact that in order to make the proof[21], he uses his first hypothesis, which I have already refuted.

In his second proposition,[22] if one replaces 'throwing off' with 'pushing off', so that it can be understood as[23] meaning pushing without motion, the argument is correct—and my own.

In his third proposition,[24] the things he says about the systole, etc.[25], are obviously destroyed by what I have already said. So too are the things he says in the corollary about inclination, which he claims to be motion.[26] The reason he gives for that claim is extremely feeble[27]: 'for', he says, 'the beginning of motion is motion'[28]. But who granted him that inclination was the beginning or a part of motion?

In his fourth proposition he is wrong to say that 'a ray is a solid space'.[29] It would be better if he had said it was a force diffused through a solid space; but it would be even better if, in accordance with all the writers on optics, he had considered a ray as a line only[30]. For in what he goes on to say, he does not make use of its breadth, nor of his 'line of light', except in[31] fitting out his imaginary arguments.

But his main error lies in his explanation of the physical cause of the refraction of rays:[32] it is completely illusory, and contrary to the principles of mechanics. Illusory, because it is based on the breadth which he gratuitously attributes to rays (and which, in his fourteenth proposition, he takes away from them,[33] while saying nevertheless that they are refracted in the same way); and also because if that explanation were true, it would take place much more in the motion of a bullet than in rays of light—which he himself previously denied, and which is contrary to experience. So too the argument which he previously used to explain a bullet being refracted away from the perpendicular in water can be applied better to rays of light, or at least just as well to them as to the motion of a bullet. For in that argument there is no mention of successive motion; whereas in the other argument which he uses for rays of light, he considers the successive motion of a sort of imaginary parallelogram. That argument is contrary to the laws of mechanics. First, because he supposes that when part D of the parallelogram ABCD first crosses the surface of the water EDF, its motion is thereby slowed down by the same amount as it is slowed down a little later when several parts of the line CD have entered the water. Secondly, because he claims that the speed of the motion is increased when the ray passes from a denser medium into a rarer one, yet cannot give any reason for making that claim. For one can easily

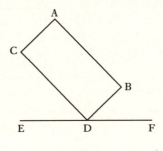

understand that the motion is slowed down by the density of the medium; but[34] it does not follow that the motion is increased in a less[35] dense medium, merely that it is less diminished. And there are other objections to his argument, which it would take a long time to list.

His fifth proposition, that 'a ray which falls obliquely should be considered as having breadth',[36] has already been refuted, and conflicts with his fourteenth. Nor is his proof of it valid, for which he makes the gratuitous assumption that 'the ray is considered as operating to a greater distance on one of its edges than on the other'.[37] No one who considers the ray as having no breadth will grant him that.

All the rest, up to the fourteenth proposition, follows reasonably enough, I think, from his own principles; I say 'I think', because I have not read it carefully enough to dare to make a definite claim. Besides, it is not surprising that a true consequence can be drawn from false hypotheses, since he has adapted his hypotheses[38] to a truth which he already knew.

The section on colours at the end[39] contains nothing that I had not already written, except in so far as his explanations are inadequate. And he is wrong to say that when I supposed the existence of small spheres,[40] I destroyed my previous hypothesis. For, when I described those small spheres, I did not claim that there was nothing in the little spaces which were not occupied[41] by those spheres; nor was there any need for me to explain more things than I had set out to explain. Finally, to sum up, I have not found the slightest argument in this entire paper which both differs from my own arguments and appears to be valid and true. I am, reverend Father,

Your reverence's most devoted servant,
Descartes[42]

A copy of Descartes, *Lettres*, ed. Clerselier, iii, in the Bibliothèque de l'Institut, Paris, (MS 4471) has MS annotations supplying material from the text of the letter as sent, with a marginal note, 'collated with the original, which belongs to M. de La Hire' ('Collationnée sur l'original de M. de la Hire': i.e. the mathematician Philippe de La Hire, 1640–1718). These annotations are incorporated in the text here, and the material variants from the printed version are recorded in the notes (siglum: 'Cler'). One type of formal variant, the underlining of passages in MS (italics here), is also incorporated and recorded: these underlinings indicate passages quoted by Descartes from Hobbes's text. One evident error in Cler, not corrected in MS, is corrected here at n. 35.

[1] Letter 29

[2] From the passages quoted in this letter, it is clear that the latter part of these eight pages corresponded closely to the short Latin treatise on optics by Hobbes later printed

as bk. 7 of the 'Optica' in Mersenne, *Universae geometriae synopsis* (pp. 567–89), which will be referred to here as Hobbes, 'Optica'. See the Introduction, p. liii, and Brandt, *Hobbes' Mechanical Conception*, pp. 94–6.

³ ejusdem *omitted Cler.*

⁴ viris *Cler.*

⁵ monere *Cler.*

⁶ A&T vi, pp. 99–100.

⁷ Diop. *omitted Cler.*

⁸ *Not italic Cler.*

⁹ demonstrandum quid fieret *Cler.*

¹⁰ *Not italic Cler.*

¹¹ pila sursum resiliat *Cler.*

¹² agit tantum de *Cler.*

¹³ *Not italic Cler.* Cf. Hobbes, 'Optica', hyp. 1: 'Every action is local motion in that which acts' ('Omnis Actio est motus localis in agente').

¹⁴ *Not italic Cler.* Cf. Hobbes, 'Optica', hyp. 5: 'I call a rarer medium that which is less resistant to the reception of motion, and a denser medium that which is more resistant. But I suppose that air is rarer than water, glass, or crystal' ('Medium rarius voco quod minus contumax est aduersus motum recipiendum. Densius quod magis. Aerem autem rariorem suppono quàm aquam, quàm vitrum, quàm cristallum').

¹⁵ vitrum neque enim actio luminis est *Cler.*

¹⁶ aduerto *Cler.*

¹⁷ *Not italic Cler.* See Letter 29, pp. 56, 59.

¹⁸ respectu manuum nostrarum *Cler.*

¹⁹ multo magis *Cler.*

²⁰ Cf. Hobbes, 'Optica', prop. 1: 'Every lucid body expands and swells into a greater mass, and then contracts again, having a ceaseless systolic and diastolic motion' ('Omne lucidum dilatat se, tumescitque in molem maiorem, iterumque contrahit se, perpetuam habens systolem & diastolem').

²¹ ipsam probandam *Cler.*

²² Cf. Hobbes, 'Optica', prop. 2: 'Motion is propagated from the lucid body to the eye by a continual throwing off of the contiguous part of the medium' ('Motus à lucido ad oculum propagatur per continuam reiectionem partis medij contiguae').

²³ vt de solâ impulsione, non de *Cler.*

²⁴ Cf. Hobbes, 'Optica', prop. 3, entitled 'To consider how light happens, and what it is' ('Considerare quomodo fiat lumen, & quid sit?').

²⁵ etc. *omitted Cler.*

²⁶ The corollary to Hobbes, 'Optica', prop. 3 does not mention inclination; Hobbes rejects Descartes's distinction between inclination and motion in the Latin Optical MS, I.10 (BL MS Harl. 6796, fo. 198ʳ).

²⁷ motum, hocque ob egregiam *Cler.*

²⁸ *Not italic Cler.*

²⁹ *Not italic Cler.* Cf. Hobbes, 'Optica', prop. 4: 'A ray is a solid space' ('Radius est spatium solidum'). 'Solid' here means three-dimensional.

³⁰ Opticis illum tantum ut lineam *Cler.*

³¹ consideraret: vtitur enim tantum posteà radij latitudine, vt & suâ lineâ lucis, ad *Cler.*

³² Cf. Hobbes, 'Optica', prop. 4, the section entitled 'Causa physica'.

³³ Cf. ibid., prop. 14, where, discussing refraction at curved surfaces, Hobbes treats the ray as a mathematical line.

³⁴ medij; Sed non *Cler*.

³⁵ tantâ *Cler and MS*.

³⁶ Cf. Hobbes, 'Optica', prop. 5: 'A ray which falls perpendicularly on a plane surface can be considered as a mathematical line, but one which falls obliquely should be considered as having breadth' ('Radius incidens perpendiculariter in superficiem planam considerari potest tanquam linea Mathematica, sed incidens in eandem obliquè considerandum est vt habens latitudinem').

³⁷ Cf. ibid., prop. 5: 'which, however, is considered as operating to a greater distance on one of its edges than on the other' ('quod tamen consideratur vno termino operari longius quam altero').

³⁸ illas hypotheses *Cler*.

³⁹ Cf. the discussion of the prism in the last paragraph of Hobbes, 'Optica', prop. 14.

⁴⁰ See discourse 8 of the 'Météores', A&T vi, p. 331.

⁴¹ quae ipsi non replent *Cler*.

⁴² Sum [. . .] Descartes *omitted Cler*.

LETTER 33   [22 FEBRUARY/] 4 MARCH 1641

René Descartes to Marin Mersenne for Hobbes, from Leiden

BN MS f.fr. n.a. 5160, fos. 23–26^r (original).

Text of MS printed in A&T iii, pp. 321–6; Descartes, *Correspondance*, iv, pp. 299–305; *MC* x, pp. 524–9.

Draft printed in Descartes, *Lettres*, ed. Clerselier, iii, pp. 158–61; Descartes, *Epistolae*, iii, pp. 82–4.

Ad 1um.[1] *Per spiritum* inquit *intelligere me dixit corpus subtile et fluidum, ergo idem est cum ejus materiâ subtili*.[2] Tanquam si omnia quibus eadem aliqua generalis descriptio conuenit eadem idcirco sint dicenda. equus est animal quadrupes et lacerta etiam animal quadrupes[3] ergo equus et lacerta idem sunt. egregie.[4]

Ad 2.[5] Quandoquidem vult sustinere suum spiritum internum et meam materiam subtilem esse vnum et idem habet hic duo contradictoria[6] probanda nempe idem corpus subtile vi suae agitationis esse causam duritiei, quod ille opinatur, et simul etiam vi[7] suae agitationis esse causam mollitiei quod ego existimo. Sed mutat quaestionem et postquam finxit duritiem esse a motu maxime[8] veloci mollitiem verò a motu minus veloci vult hoc sufficere ad suum institutum, etsi ego e contra[9] putem motum magis velocem efficere mollitiem et duritiem esse a quiete. Additque *me hic ostendere potius voluntatem quam rationem dissentiendi*,[10] nempe quia nolo admittere duo contraria[11] esse vnum et idem. Nunquid ille potius ostendit sibi perinde esse quid sustineat modo tantùm altercetur.[12] Nam quid ad rem si eius corpus subtile idem sit quod mea materia subtilis vel non sit, cum praesertim si esset idem possem[13] dicere illum a me esse mutuatum quia prior scripsi. Quidque magis ridiculum et impudens[14] quam quod velit vt fatear me sentire plane contrarium eius quod revera sentio, et mille in locis testatus sum me sentire, vt scilicet illi[15] assentiar. Caetera quae hîc addit sunt adhuc ineptiora[16] et mihi affingit opinionem de causa duritiei quam nunquam habui vt nosti, sed rogo ne plura ex te discat de meis principijs quam jam nouit, nam indignus est.

Ad .3. Credidi illud, quod fassus sum dici posse, aliquo sensu posse intelligi in quo sit verum, sed et alio etiam sensu eoque magis obuio posse intelligi in quo sit[17] falsum, ideoque ab isto loquendi modo abstinui vt minus apto et qui lectoribus errandi occasionem praebuisset, quae causa fuit iustissima, ille vero valde iniustus est quod pro justâ non admittat, et plane importunus et absurdus[18] quod inde velit inferre me rem non recte intellexisse cum ipse illam ne nunc quidem intelligat vt mox patebit. proponitque hîc inanissimam demonstrationis laruam vt non satis attendentibus illudat. Nam in primis[19] vellem scire quid supponat cum ait. *Sit*[20] *velocitas ab A versus B in ratione ad velocitatem ab A versus C quam habet ipsa AB ad ipsam AC hae duae velocitates componunt velocitatem quae est à B versus C*[21]. Non enim potest supponere pilam ab A moueri eodem tempore versus B et versus[22] C, hoc enim fieri nequit. Sed proculdubio voluit dicere *a B versus A* vbi dixit ab A versus B. ita scilicet vt intelligamus pilam moueri a B versus A supra lineam BA dum interim haec linea BA mouetur[23] versus NC, ita vt eodem tempore pila perueniat a B ad A et linea BA ad lineam NC, sic enim motus pilae describet lineam BC. Sed forte ista de industria

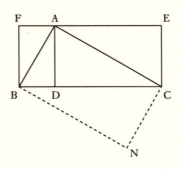

turbauit vt aliquid dicere videretur in sequentibus vbi tamen reuera nihil dicit[24] quod non sit plane nugatorium. Vt enim probet velocitatem a B ad C componi ex velocitatibus a B ad A et ab A ad C diuidit utramque dicendo. *Quoniam motus ab A ad B* (hoc est a B ad A) *componitur ex motibus ab F ad A et* [*ab*][25] *F ad B, non contribuet motus compositus AB plus celeritatis ad motum a B versus C quam contribuit FA, nec AC quam contribuit AE*[26] etc. Vnde inferre debuisset BC componi ex FA et AE, non autem ex BA et AC, atque sic apparuisset eius nugatio nam FA et AE idem est quod BC. Dicere autem celeritatem BC componi ex BA et AC quia in BA et AC continentur FA et AE idem est ac si diceret[27] securim componi ex silua et ex monte, quia silua lignum contribuit[28] ad manubrium et mons ferrum ex ipso effossum. Postque has ineptias[29] homo scilicet vrbanissimus me incusat[30] tanquam si quem paralogismum admisissem, sed[31] qua in re quaeso, Nempe vbi dixi me isto[32] tam improprio loquendi modo uti noluisse.

Ad 4.[33] Hic ostendit se in eo ipso errare in quo paulo ante dixit *me non timere debuisse*[34] *a paralogismis quos alii postea sibimet ipsis facerent,*[35] nam per hoc ipsum sibi paralogismum facit[36], quod motum determinatum loco determinationis quae est in motu consideret. Ad quod intelligendum notandum[37] est motum determinatum esse ad ipsam determinationem motus, vt corpus planum est ad planiciem[38] siue superficiem eiusdem corporis. nam quemadmodum mutatâ una superficie non sequitur reliquas mutari, vel plus minusue corporis illis adiungi etiamsi omnes in eodem sint corpore, ac sine ipso esse non possint[39]. ita mutatâ unâ determinatione non sequitur aliam mutari, vel plus minusue motûs[40] illi adiungi, quamuis neutra possit esse sine motu. Quam rem[41] si noster intellexisset non diceret *oportuisse me demonstrasse quod retentâ*[42] *integrâ velocitate ab A versus B impossibile esset pilam promoueri longius in eâdem determinatione quam ad E.*[43] vidisset enim id ex hoc ipso esse demonstratum, quod demonstrarim determinationem dextrorsum non esse mutatam quia non potest augeri nec[44] minui motus in illam partem quin tantundem illi determinationi accedat vel recedat, vt neque potest corpus in superficie mutari quin etiam superficies mutetur[45]. Nec postea dixisset. Jam verò si determinationes illae sint motus etc.[46]

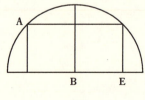

Neque enim magis sunt[47] motus quam superficies sunt corpora, sed in hoc errauit et paralogismum sibi fecit[48], quod motum determinatum considerauit loco determinationis motus. vt promiseram me probaturum.[49]

Translation of Letter 33

On his first point:[1] 'I said', he writes, 'that what I mean by "spirit" is "a subtle and fluid body": therefore it is the same as his "subtle matter"'.[2] As if all things that come under the same general description should therefore be called the same. Horses are quadrupeds; and lizards are quadrupeds[3]; therefore horses and lizards are the same thing. A fine argument.[4]

On his second point:[5] since he does wish to maintain that his internal spirit and my subtle matter are one and the same thing, he takes it upon himself to prove two contradictory[6] things here. First, that that same subtle body causes hardness by the force with which it moves around, which is what he thinks; and then at the same time that it causes softness by the force[7] with which it moves around, which is what I think. But he alters the question, and having imagined that hardness is the result of extremely[8] rapid motion and softness the result of less rapid motion, he claims that that is sufficient for what he set out to argue—even though I, on the contrary,[9] think that the more rapid motion causes softness, and hardness is caused by rest. He also adds that I 'indicate rather a desire to disagree than a reason for doing so',[10] doubtless because I do not wish to agree that two opposites[11] are one and the same thing. Is it not rather he who shows that he does not mind what argument he defends, so long as he can keep up a quarrel?[12] For what does it matter whether his subtle body is the same as my subtle matter or not, especially since, if it were the same, I could[13] say that he had borrowed it from me, given that I wrote about it first? And what could be more ridiculous or more impudent[14] than his claim that I hold an opinion which is the complete opposite of what I really think— and have affirmed in a thousand places that I think—so that he can claim that I agree with him?[15] The other things he adds here are even more feeble;[16] and he attributes to me an opinion about the cause of hardness which I have never held, as you know. But I beg you not to teach him any more of my principles than he already knows, for he is not worthy of them.

On his third point: that which I said 'one can say', I thought could be understood in one sense in which it was true, but could also be understood in another, more obvious, sense, in which it was[17] false. That is why I refrained from using that manner of speaking, because it was less suitable, and might have given rise to misunderstandings on the readers' part. And it was a perfectly fair reason for doing so. In not admitting it as a fair reason, he is in fact being completely unfair; and it is utterly tiresome and absurd[18] of him to try to argue from that that I did not understand the matter correctly—since he himself does not understand it even now, as will become clear in a moment. And he puts forward here the most worthless ghost of a demonstration, in order to deceive the insufficiently attentive reader. To begin with,[19] I should like to know what he supposes when he says: 'let[20] the velocity from A to B have the same ratio to the velocity from A to C as the ratio between AB and AC themselves; these two velocities compose the velocity from B to C'.[21] For he cannot suppose that the ball moves from A towards B

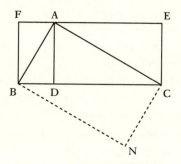

and towards[22] C in the same time: that is impossible. Doubtless he meant 'from B towards A', when he said 'from A towards B'; meaning that we should understand the ball to move from B towards A on the line BA, while during the same time this line BA moves[23] towards NC, so that in the same time the ball passes from B to A and the line BA passes to the line NC—for that is how the motion of the ball describes the line BC. But perhaps he confused the matter deliberately, to give himself the air of saying something in what followed: where, however, he actually said nothing[24] that was not complete piffle. For in order to prove that the velocity from B to C is composed of the velocities from B to A and from A to C, he divides both of them, saying: 'since the motion from A to B' (that is, from B to A) 'is composed of the motions from F to A and from[25] F to B, the compound motion AB will not contribute more speed to the motion from B to C than is contributed by FA, nor will AC contribute more than is contributed by AE . . .'.[26] From which he should have inferred that BC is composed of FA and AE, not of BA and AC. If he had done that, his trifling would have become plain: for FA and AE together are the same as BC. But to say that the speed BC is composed of BA and AC, because FA and AE are contained in BA and AC, is like saying that[27] an axe is composed of a forest and a mountain, because the forest contributed the wood[28] for the handle and the mountain contributed the iron which was dug out of it. And after these feeble arguments,[29] he finds fault with me,[30] with such perfect politeness, as if I had committed some paralogism! But[31] on what subject, I ask? No doubt it was when I said that I did not wish to use such[32] an improper manner of speaking.

On his fourth point:[33] here he shows that he makes precisely the sort of mistake which he had just referred to, when he said that I 'need not have worried[34] about the paralogisms which other people, for their part, might later make'.[35] For he here makes, for his own part, a paralogism,[36] when he takes the determined motion instead of the determination which is in the motion. In order to understand this, we should observe[37] that determined motion is to the determination of motion as a flat body is to the flatness[38] or surface of that body. If one surface is changed, it will not follow that the others are changed too, nor will it follow that more or less of the body is joined to them, even if they are all surfaces of the same body and cannot exist without it.[39] So too, if one determination is changed, it does not follow that the other is changed too, nor that it gains more or less of motion,[40] even though neither of them can exist without motion. If our fellow had understood this,[41] he would not have said that I 'should have demonstrated that, if the entire velocity which it had from A to B was retained,[42] it was impossible for the ball to continue in motion further, in that determination, than to E'.[43] For he would have seen that this was demonstrated by my demonstration of the fact that the downwards determination is not changed, because the motion in that direction cannot be increased or[44] reduced without adding to or subtracting from that determination by the same amount: just as a body cannot be changed with regard to its surface, without its surface being changed.[45] Nor would he have gone on to say,

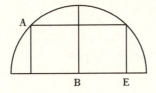

'So in fact, if those determinations are motions . . .'.[46] For they are no more[47] motions than surfaces are bodies. But his mistake (in which he committed, for his own part, a paralogism)[48] was to take the determined motion instead of the determination of the motion—which is what I promised to show.[49]

The text given here is that of the section of this letter to Mersenne which was a reply to Hobbes and was written in Latin. Descartes introduced this section as follows: 'Otherwise, having read at leisure that last paper by the Englishman, I have become completely convinced of the truth of the judgement which I expressed about him in my letter to you a fortnight ago; and I think it best if I have nothing to do with him and therefore refrain from replying to him. For if his character is as I suspect, we could scarcely communicate without becoming enemies. So it is better for us, him and me, to leave it there. I also beg you to communicate as little as possible to him of those of my opinions which you know, and which have not appeared in print. For, unless I am very much mistaken, he is aiming to make his reputation at my expense, and by devious means. So if you have promised him that you would get me to reply to his latest paper, please excuse me, telling him that I am certain that you will defend me much better than I could defend myself. And so that you can do that with less trouble, I shall give you my opinion here of his ten points.' ('Au reste, ayant leu à loisir le dernier escrit de l'Anglois, je me suis entierement confirmé en l'opinion que je vous manday il y a 15 jours, que j'avois de luy, et je croy que le meilleur est que je n'aye point du tout de commerce avec luy, et pour cete fin, que je m'abstiene de luy respondre; car, s'il est de l'humeur que je le juge, nous ne sçaurions gueres conferer ensemble sans devenir ennemis; il vaut bien mieux que nous en demeurions, luy et moy, où nous sommes. Je vous prie aussy de ne luy communiquer que le moins que vous pourrez de ce que vous sçavez de mes opinions et qui n'est point imprimé; car je me trompe fort, si ce n'est un homme qui cherche d'acquerir de la reputation à mes despens, et par de mauvaises pratiques. Que si vous luy avez promis de me faire faire response à ce dernier escrit, vous m'en excuserez, s'il vous plaist, envers luy, sur ce que je m'assure que vous me deffendrez beaucoup mieux que je ne me pourrois deffendre moy mesme. Et affin que vous y ayez moins de peine, je m'en vais mettre icy mon sentiment de ses 10 points.') Despite these disclaimers, the fact that Descartes wrote the following section in Latin suggests that he intended it to be passed on, more or less unaltered, to Hobbes.

The text of the original MS is given here, with the material variants of the printed draft in Descartes, *Lettres*, ed. Clerselier (from CUL M. 3. 44, collated with BL 535. f. 13; siglum: 'Cler') recorded in the notes; one formal variant from Cler is incorporated in the text at n. 42, and one error in both Cler and the MS is corrected and the correct reading incorporated in the text at n. 25.

¹ Primò. *Cler.*
² See Letter 30, pp. 62, 70.
³ omnia quae sub eâdem aliquâ generali descriptione conueniunt, eadem idcirco absolutè dicenda sint; vt equus est animal quadrupes, caudatum, & lacerta etiam est animal quadrupes, caudatum *Cler.*
⁴ Secundò. *Cler.*
⁵ Egregie. *omitted in Cler.*

⁶ idem, duo hîc contradictoria habet *Cler.*

⁷ quod ut ille opinatur, et simul vi etiam *Cler.*

⁸ motu magis *Cler.*

⁹ institutum; quamuis ego contra *Cler.*

¹⁰ See Letter 30, pp. 63, 71.

¹¹ nolo admittere ea, quae planè contraria sunt *Cler.*

¹² modo tantum possit disputare; *Cler.*

¹³ materia subtili, vel non sit, cùm praesertim, si idem sit, possim *Cler.*

¹⁴ magis absonum *Cler.*

¹⁵ scilicet ipsi *Cler.*

¹⁶ addit non sunt minus absona *Cler.*

¹⁷ novit. Ad tertium, quod fassus sum dici posse, credidi aliquo sensu posse intelligi, quo verum esset, sed et alio etiam sensu, eoque communiori, posse intelligi quo erit falsum; ideoque ab isto loquendi modo *Cler.*

¹⁸ et importunus *omitted in Cler.*

¹⁹ patebit; audetque hîc speciem quandam demonstrationis proponere, vt non intelligentibus illudat. Nam primo *Cler.*

²⁰ ait: Sitque *Cler.*

²¹ See Letter 30, pp. 64, 72.

²² versus *omitted in Cler.*

²³ dicere velocitatem à B versùs A & C; ita scilicet vt intelligatur pila moueri à B versùs A supra lineam BA et tota haec linea BA moueri *Cler.*

²⁴ videretur cum tamen reverâ nihil dicat *Cler.*

²⁵ ab *omitted in MS and Cler.* It is supplied by the original text from which Descartes is quoting (see n. 26).

²⁶ See Letter 30, pp. 64, 73.

²⁷ atque hic apparuit nugatio: nam FA et AE est ipsa BC. Idemque egit ac si probare vellet *Cler.*

²⁸ silva contribuit lignum *Cler.*

²⁹ ferrum ex ejus fodinis erutum. Post haec verò homo *Cler.*

³⁰ me arguit *Cler.*

³¹ sed *omitted in Cler.*

³² isto *omitted in Cler.*

³³ Ad quartum. *Cler.*

³⁴ *non debuisse timere* Cler.

³⁵ See Letter 30, pp. 64, 72.

³⁶ nam in hoc ipso paralogismum sibi fingat *Cler.*

³⁷ determinationis, consideret. Ad quod intelligendum putandum *Cler.*

³⁸ ipsam motus determinationem, ut est corpus planum ad planitiem *Cler.*

³⁹ sequitur alias mutari, vel plus corporis vel minus illis adjungi, etiamsi sint in eodem corpore, et non possint esse sine ipso *Cler.*

⁴⁰ plus motus siue celeritatis *Cler.*

⁴¹ motu. Quod *Cler.*

⁴² The underlining ceases here in the MS, because of a page-turn; the italics continue in *Cler.*

⁴³ See Letter 30, pp. 66, 74.

⁴⁴ augeri vel *Cler.*

[45] mutetur. Nec tamen determinatio est motus, vt neque superficies est corpus *Cler*.

[46] See Letter 30, pp. 66, 75.

[47] enim sunt magis *Cler*.

[48] hoc se ipsum fallit *Cler*.

[49] determinatum consideret loco determinationis; ut dixeram me probaturum. Puderet me reliqua eius verba hîc persequi tempusque in re tam inutile consumere. *Cler*. (A version of this last added sentence appears in French in the MS: 'J'aurois honte d'employer du tems à poursuivre le reste de ses fautes': 'I should be ashamed to spend my time tracking down the rest of his errors'.)

LETTER 34   [20/] 30 MARCH 1641

Hobbes to Marin Mersenne, from Paris

BN MS f.fr. n.a. 6206, fos. 1–4 (in a copyist's hand, but signed by Hobbes and with corrections in his hand).
Printed in A&T iii, pp. 341–8; Tönnies, 'Analekten', pp. 153–9; *MC* x, pp. 568–76.

Reuerende Pater.

Sic ais, *Quoniam tu facis motum Velocem tui spiritûs* [word deleted] *causam duritiei, ille verò motum suae materiae subtilis causam mollitiei, et eius quietem causam duritiei, ideo me non idem intelligere per spiritum, quod ille per materiam subtilem*.[1] Quae argumentatio similis est, ac si quis diceret, est qui putat Dominum deCartes optimum Philosophum, est qui putat contrarium, ergo illi non intelligunt eundem Dominum deCartes. Credere nullo modo possum, quod sit tua. Ego *spiritûs* nomine possum et volo intelligere *Corpus subtile*, et vocem eam *spiritus* eo modo definio. Is si vult suam *materiam* esse *Corpus*, et suum *subtile* esse *subtile*, necessario vult idem esse quod ab vtrisque diuersis nominibus significatur. si non vult, non repugno.

Quod dicis, *non fuisse opus tantâ circa hanc rem altercatione*, consentio. Sed altercatio haec ab illo, sicut ipse nosti, profecta est. [Et *deleted*] quod autem [> ais *added by Hobbes*] me potuisse [hypothesim][2] eam ab ipso *qui prior scripserat mutuasse*,[3] spero te testem mihi futurum esse, me septem abhinc annis, cum tecum in domo vestrâ dissererem primùm, de reditu arcus, praesente Domino de Beaugrand,[4] pro ratione adduxisse motum illum internum quem ibi supposui spirituum. Iam vero monitus,[5] hoc dicere apud te amplius habeo, me doctrinam illam de naturâ et productione luminis, et soni, et omnium Phantasmatum siue idearum, quam Dominus deCartes nunc respuit, explicasse Coram Dominis fratribus excellentissimis Gulielmo Comite de Newcastell [et][6] Carolo [Cauendisti *altered to* Cauendish *by Hobbes*]

Equite aurato communi nostro amico, anno 1630.[7] quod ideo dico, ne is eam doctrinam aliquando agnoscens, fundatam esse dicat principijs suis, Nae illius principia, nulla sunt, neque opus habet fundamentis qui vi ingenij in aere ipso aedificare potest quidquid vult. Quod attinet ad disputationem de differentiâ inter *motum determinatum* et *determinationem motûs*.[8] Video necessarium esse vt sententiam meam apertiùs et explicatiùs ostendam, quàm hactenus factum est.

Primùm igitur sciendum est, quod sicut omnis homo est vel Petrus vel Socrates vel aliquis jndiuiduorum, vtcunque vox haec *Homo*, vox communis sit (vna nempe quinque vocum quas declarat Porphyrius in Isagoge ad Ar[istote]lem[9]) ita quoque Motus omnis, est vel *hic*, vel *ille motus* nempe *determinatus* per terminos a quo et [ad][10] quem; vt igitur Socrates & homo non sunt duo homines, nec duae res, sed vnus homo sub duabus appellationibus (nam quae res nomine *socratis* [ad *deleted*] eadem et nomine *hominis* appellata est) Ita *motus* et *motus determinatus* vnus sunt motus, et vna res sub duobus nominibus.

Secundò, sciendum est quod causa efficiens cuiuscun[que][11] motûs propositi, est causa efficiens quoque per quam mot[us][12] ille sic determinatur, ita vt motûs determinatio actiuè sumpta sit actio mouentis per quam fertur patiens versus vnam partem potiùs quam versus aliam. Quod si aliquando vox haec *Determinatio motûs* significet passiuè, hoc est aliquid in patiente, [tam *altered to* tum *by Hobbes*] idem [>valet *added by Hobbes*] quod, *Esse sic motum*, hoc est *determinatè motum*, et in hoc sensu *motus determinatus*, et *determinatio motûs, idem sunt*.

Iam Dominus deCartes vbi dicit me decipi in eo quod motum determinatum dixerim loco determinationis quae est in motu, intelligit determinationem vt in corpore moto, et passiuè, et sic idem est *motus determinatus* et *determinatio motûs*. Quomodo autem intelligit ille *determinationem* esse in motu? num vt in subiecto? absurdum est. quia motus est accidens; sicut absurdum esset dicere [*Albedinem*][13] esse in colore quanquam[14] [*word deleted*] [albedo][15], talis determinatio sit, coloris, qualis motûs determinatio est moueri dextrorum vel sinistrorsum. Sed [quantum in *altered to* quantumvis *by Hobbes*] absurdum sit *determinationem* esse *in motu*, vt *accidens* in *subiecto*, ab eo tamen *Dominus deCartes* non abstinuit; nimirum, quia dixit *motum determinatum*, esse ad *ipsam determinationem motûs* vt *Corpus planum* est ad *planiciem* siue *superficiem* eiusdem corporis.[16] nam planities est in *corpore* vt in *subiecto*. Sed comparatio debebat esse huiusmodi, *motus determinatus* est ad *ipsam determinationem motûs*, vt *superficies determinata* (hoc est *plana* vel *rotunda* etc:) ad *determinationem superficiei* (hoc est ad *planitiem, rotunditatem* &c.)

Iam tantundem differet *superficies plana* a *planicie superficiei*, quantum *motûs determinatus* a *determinatione motûs*. Neque id quod dicis posteà, *quemadmodum mutatâ vna superficie non sequitur reliquas mutari, ita mutata vnâ determinatione non sequitur aliam mutari*,[17] [nihil *deleted* >quicquam *added by Hobbes*] valebit, nam *accidentium* in *subiecto* (quales sunt duae diuersae *superficies*) aliud perire, aliud manere potest. Sed quando *vnum* est tantum *accidens* sub *duobus nominibus*, vt vnus motus sub nominibus *motûs determinati* et *determinationis motûs*, si quod significatur ab vno nomine perit, perit id quoque quod significatur ab altero.

Tertiò animaduertendum est, *motum vnum* non posse habere *duas determinationes*; nam in fugurâ ascriptâ, sit A Corpus, quod incipiat

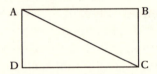

moueri versus C. viam habens rectam AC. Si quis dicat mihi moueri A per viam rectam ad C. is *determinauit* mihi motum illum; ipse enim eandem viam designare possum, vt vnam et certam; sed si dicat [mouere *altered to* moueri *by Hobbes*] A per rectam viam versus rectam DC, non mihi hujus motûs *determinationem* commonstrauit[18]; quia viae tales infinitae sunt, non sunt igitur motus ab AB versus DC, [> et *added by Hobbes*] ab AD versus BC determinationes *vnius motûs* Corporis A versus C. Sed determinationes duorum motuum, duorum corporum, quorum vnum procedit ab AB ad DC, alterum ab AD, ad [DC *altered to* BC *by Hobbes*].

Quarto ostendendum est, quo modo, *motus duo determinati* quorum vnus est corporis Longitudinem habentis AB, moti perpendiculariter ad DC. alter corporis longitudinem habentis AD, moti lateraliter ad [DC *altered to* BC *by Hobbes*], [sed perpendiculariter ad BC, *deleted*] [efficiant][19] *motum* corporis positi in A, *determinatum* ab A ad C. Supposito ergo AB ferri ad DC perpendiculariter in vno minuto temporis, item AD ferri ad BC in eodem minuto temporis, Sequetur [ergo *deleted*] ad finem illius minuti temporis dati Corpus A esse alicubi in DC, et alicubi etiam in BC, erit ergo in C vbi BC et DC concurrunt. Et quoniam AB. AD et A. faciunt eodem minuto temporis, spatia AD. AB. AC. erunt velocitates [quae *altered to* quibus *by Hobbes*] feruntur AB. AD. A, in ratione rectarum AD. AB. AC.

Quintò notandum est, quod siue moueatur A versus C ab illis duobus

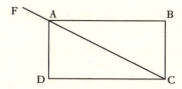

motoribus AB, AD quasi a duobus ventis, vel ab vno tantum motore, tanquam vento qui spiraret ab F, semper ipse motus effectus, ab A versus C, idem erit, et easdem semper habebit proprietates.

Postremo Considerandum est, quia duo motus corporum AB et AD conferunt suis velocitatibus, velocitatem qua fertur Corpus vnum A. quam partem celeritatis confert motus vterque seorsim. Patet autem quod motus corporis AB versus DC, non confert corpori A totam suam velocitatem, neque motus corporis AD versus BC totam suam, nam alter alterum impedit ne[20] possit proximâ viâ pergere qua coeperant, alter [alterum impedit *deleted*] ad DC alter ad BC. Quaeren[dum][21] est igitur qua proportione vtriusque AB et AD vis minuatur[.][22] Ducatur a D ad AC, perpendicularis DE. Dico *motum perpendicularem* ab AB *deorsum*,

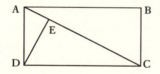

conferre motui Corporis A versus C celeritatem quanta sufficit ad mouendum ipsum versus C ad spatium quantum est AE. *motum* autem *lateralem* corporis AD conferre celeritatem motui corporis eiusdem A, quanta sufficit ad portandum ipsum ad spatium quantum est EC. Quoniam enim celeritas qua fertur AD lateraliter est ad celeritatem qua fertur AB perpendiculariter, vt recta AB ad rectam AD, vt supra ostensum est, sunt autem rectae AD et AB inter se vt A[E][23] et EC, erit celeritas *lateralis* corporis AD ad celeritatem *perpendicularem* corporis AB vt AE ad EC. Et componendo vt celeritas vtraque lateralis et perpendicularis ad celeritatem perpendicularem solam, ita vtraque recta AE et EC simul, ad vnam rectam AE. quoniam igitur vtraque [>simul *added by Hobbes*] celeritas *lateralis* et *perpendicularis* mouet corpus A per spatium AC in vno minuto, celeritas *perpendicularis* sola, sufficiet ad mouendum Corpus A eodem minuto per spatium praecisè tantum quantum est AE, eâdem ratione celeritas *lateralis* sola sufficiet ad mouendum Corpus A per spatium praecisè tantum quantum est EC, in eodem minuto secundo.[24] Atque hoc est quod volui cum dicerem celeritatem corporis A versus C Componi ex duabus celeritatibus AE et EC. nimirum diminutis in compositione, non ex celeritatibus integris AD et AB. Atque hoc, eo instituto, volui demonstrare quia Dominus deCartes inferebat ex mea sententiâ falsam consequentiam, nempe in motu sic composito euenire absurdum quod sequitur. *Ponamus pilam ab*

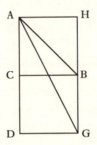

A ferri [*dextrorum* altered to *dextrorsum* by Hobbes] *vno gradu celeritatis et deorsum vno gradu celeritatis, perueniet ad B duobus gradibus celeritatis eodem tempore quo alia quae ferretur etiam dextrorsum vno gradu celeritatis et deorsum duobus, perueniet ad G tribus gradibus celeritatis, vnde sequeretur lineam AB esse ad lineam AG vt 2 ad 3. quae tamen est vt .2. ad $\sqrt{10}$.*[25] sed ex demonstratione supra proximè allatâ satis clare opinor constat, quod celeritas ab A ad B non erit ex meis principijs ad celeritatem ab A ad G v[t][26] 2. ad 3. sed vt $\sqrt{2}$. ad $\sqrt{.5}$. quae est ipsarum linearum AB a[d][27] AG proportio, atque eadem cum ratione 2. ad $\sqrt{10}$. nam celeritas ab A ad B ad celeritatem ab A ad G non est vt composita ex AH et HB ad compositam ex AH [et][28] HG, sed v[t][29] subtensae ipsae AB.AG, hoc est, vt radices quadratorum aggregatorum ex lateribus. Sed ratiocinatio qua id volebam in superiore mea ad té Epistolâ [datam altered to *datâ by* Hobbes] Parisijs, Feb. 7º.[30] non erat legitima. Fateor. Errores meos non omnino, nedum pertinaciter defendo. nisi dominus des Cartes idem faciat superior sanè ero in moralibus. sed [qui *altered to* quid *by Hobbes*] attinet ad rei veritatem inter nos disputatam, quod ego eam non satis ostenderim? Quid si sciens veritatem alicujus propositionis Element. Eucl. et tentans demonstrationem eius, non assequerer; num ideo minùs vera erit, cùm ab alijs, vel a me ipso aliò tempore demonstrata fuerit?

[Caeteras *altered to* Caeteris *by Hobbes*] illius Epistolae meae partibus, an consentit quia tacet? minimè vero id puto. sed quia nihil obiecit, nihil habeo quod huic Epistolae adijciam, nisi quod iniquior in me est, dum suspicatur me turbare de industriâ [potuisse vt videret *altered to* voluisse vt viderer *by Hobbes*] aliquid dixisse pòst.[31] si sic fecissem possem adhuc [turbore *altered to* turbare *by Hobbes*], vt error meus lateret, Sed etiam nunc istâ erroneâ meâ ratiocinatione video posse ab homine non antè occupato, eandem conclusionem verè demonstrandi via inueniri Is verò quo animo in discursu[32] secundo Dioptricorum pag. 18.[33] supponit rectam HF esse duplam AH, in Schemate tamen apposito facit eam paulò majorem quam est ipsa AH, ipse scit. tu vero mi pater id scire potes, si consideres, quod ita faciendo, linea FI extra circulum cecidisset, et per consequens pila in aquam [proceda *altered to* proiecta *by Hobbes*] in eleuatione anguli ABC, deberet reflecti, quod est contra experientiam. nunquid is turbat de jndustriâ vt videatur aliquid probare in sequentibus[34]? [mirum *altered to* nimiùm *by Hobbes*] te moror nugis alienis, finem igitur facio precatus tibi Commoda et [propterea *deleted* > prospera] omnia quae vis. Vale.

Tui studiosissimus
Tho: Hobbes

Parisijs jn vigiliâ Paschalis *1641*.

Translation of Letter 34

Reverend Father,

   You write as follows: 'since you make the rapid motion of your spirit the cause of hardness, while he indeed makes the motion of his subtle matter the cause of softness, and its lack of motion the cause of hardness, therefore I do not mean by spirit what he means by subtle matter'.[1] This form of argument is like saying: there is someone who thinks M. Descartes is the best philosopher, there is someone else who thinks the contrary, therefore they do not mean the same M. Descartes. I cannot possibly believe that you would argue like that. By the word 'spirit' I can mean, and intend to mean, 'subtle body'; and that is how I define 'spirit'. If he intends his 'matter' to be *body*; and his 'subtle' to be *subtle*, he must necessarily intend it to be the same thing, as signified by either of the two different descriptions. If that is not what he intends, then I have no further objection.

   When you say, 'there was no need to have such a quarrel on this subject', I agree. But this quarrel was started by him, as you yourself know. However, when you say that I 'could have borrowed that hypothesis[(2)] from him, as he had written about it earlier',[3] I hope you will be my witness that, seven years ago, when I first dicussed the rebound of the bow with you in your house, in the presence of M. de Beaugrand,[4] I put forward as the reason for it that internal motion which I then supposed to be a motion of spirits. Now, indeed, having received that warning,[5] I should go further and tell you this: that doctrine of the nature and production of light, sound, and all phantasms or ideas, which M. Descartes now rejects, was explained by me in the presence of those most excellent brothers William Earl of Newcastle and[(6)] Sir Charles Cavendish (who is our mutual friend) in the year 1630.[7] I say this just in case he should agree to that doctrine one day and claim that it was founded on his own principles. As for those principles of his, they are no principles at all; nor does he need any foundations, when he can build whatever he likes, by the power of his imagination, in the very air. As for our disagreement over the difference between *determined motion* and *the determination of motion*,[8] I see that I must set out my opinion more clearly and explicitly than it has been set out hitherto.

Firstly, one must know that although the name 'man' is a common name (one, in fact, of the five names that Porphyry expounds in his *Isagoge*[9]), every man is either Peter or Socrates or some other individual; and that in the same way, therefore, every motion is either this, or that motion, in other words, a motion *determined* by the limits of its start and finish[(10)]. So just as Socrates and man are not two men, nor two things, but one man described by two names (since it is the same thing which is named 'Socrates' and named 'man'), in the same way 'motion' and 'determined motion' are one motion, and one thing under two names.

Secondly, one must know that the efficient cause of any[(11)] given motion is also the efficient cause by which that motion[(12)] is determined; so that the determination of motion, taken in the active sense, is the action of the mover by which the thing that is moved is carried towards one place rather than another. And if this phrase 'the determination of motion' is sometimes taken in the passive sense, that is, as something in the thing that is moved, then it means the same as 'to be moved in such-and-such a way', that is, 'to be moved determinately', and in this sense 'determined motion' and 'the determination of motion' are the same.

Now, when M. Descartes says that I am mistaken in saying 'determined motion' instead of 'the determination which is in the motion', he means determination in the passive sense, in the body which is moved; and so 'determined motion' and 'the determination of motion' are the same. But what does he mean by the determination being 'in the motion'? He surely does not mean as in a subject? That is absurd, since motion is an accident; just as it would be absurd to say that whiteness[13] is in a colour, whereas[14] whiteness[15] is a determination of colour in the same way that being moved to the right or the left is a determination of motion. But however absurd it may be to say that determination is 'in the motion', as an accident is 'in a subject', nevertheless M. Descartes has not refrained from saying it; there can be no doubt about it, since he has said that 'a determined motion' is to 'the determination of the motion' as 'a flat body' is to the 'flatness' or the 'flat surface' of that body.[16] For *flatness* is in the body as in a *subject*. But the comparison should have been as follows: a determined motion is to the determination of the motion as *a determined surface* (that is, a flat or rounded one, etc.) is to *the determination of the surface* (that is, to flatness, roundness, etc.). Now, there is as much difference between *a flat surface* and *the flatness of the surface* as there is between *a determined motion* and *the determination of the motion*. Nor is there any validity in what you say later, that 'just as, when one surface is changed, it does not follow that the others are changed, so when one determination is changed it does not follow that the other is changed'.[17] For it is possible, with accidents in a subject (which is what two different surfaces are), that one should cease to exist while the other remains. But in the case of only one accident under two names (for example, one motion under the names 'determined motion' and 'a determination of motion'), if the thing which is meant by one name ceases to exist, the thing which is meant by the other will also cease to exist.

Thirdly, it must be observed that one motion cannot have two determinations. In the figure drawn here, let A be a body which begins to

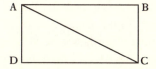

move towards C, following the straight line AC. If someone tells me that A is moved in a straight line to C, he has *determined* that motion for me; for I can indicate the path A has taken, as something single and certain. But if he says A is moved in a straight line towards the straight line DC, he has not fully indicated[18] to me the determination of this motion, since there is an infinite number of ways there. Therefore motions from AB to DC, and from AD to BC, are not determinations of one motion of the body at A towards C; rather, they are determinations of two motions, of two bodies, of which one proceeds from AB to DC, and the other from AD to BC.

Fourthly, one must show how it is that two determined motions, of which one is of a body, having the length AB, moved downwards to DC, and the other is of a body, having the length AD, moved across to BC, can bring about[19] that the motion of the body located at A should be determined from A to C. Let us suppose therefore that AB is brought down to DC in one minute, and that likewise AD is brought to BC in the same minute; it follows that at the end of that given minute the body A will be somewhere in DC, and also somewhere in BC; therefore it will be in C, where BC and DC meet. And since AB, AD, and A cover the distances AD, AB, and AC in the same minute, the velocities at which AB, AD, and A are moved will be in proportion to the straight lines AD, AB, and AC.

Fifthly, one must note that, whether A is moved to C by those two movers AB and AD, as if by two winds, or whether by only one mover, as if by a wind blowing from F, the movement which is brought about

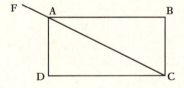

from A to C will always be the same, and will always have the same properties.

Finally, because the two motions of the bodies AB and AD contribute from their own velocities to the velocity at which the one body A is moved, one must consider what part of the speed is contributed by each motion separately. It is clear, however, that the motion of the body AB towards DC does not contribute all its velocity to the body A, and that neither does the motion of the body AD towards BC contribute all of its velocity; for each impedes the other from[20] proceeding by the most direct routes, in which they started off—the one to DC and the other to BC. So one must ask[21] in what proportion the force of each of them, AB and AD, is reduced.[22] Let the perpendicular DE be drawn from D to AC. I say that the perpendicular motion from AB downwards contributes as much velocity to the motion of the body A towards C as is sufficient to move it, on the way to C, a distance equal

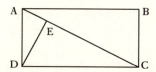

to AE. Whereas the lateral motion of the body AD contributes as much speed to the motion of the same body A as is sufficient to move it a distance equal to EC. For since the speed at which AD is moved sideways is to the speed at which AB is moved downwards as the straight line AB is to the straight line AD (as shown above), and since the straight lines AD and AB are to each other as are AE[23] and EC, the lateral speed of the body AD will be to the perpendicular speed of the body AB as AE is to EC. And, by compounding, we find that as the lateral and perpendicular speeds together are to the perpendicular speed on its own, so the two straight lines AE and EC together are to the single straight line AE. Therefore, since the speed which is at the same time both lateral and perpendicular moves the body A through the distance AC in one minute, the perpendicular speed on its own will be sufficient to move the body A in the same minute through a distance precisely equal to AE; and for the same reason the lateral speed on its own will be sufficient to move the body A through a distance precisely equal to EC, in the same minute.[24]

And that is what I meant when I said that the speed of the body A towards C is composed of the two speeds AE and EC—clearly, not from the entire speeds AD and AB, but from speeds which are reduced as they are compounded together. And the reason why I wanted to demonstrate this was that M. Descartes inferred a false conclusion from my opinion, namely that in the case of a motion so compounded the following absurdity arises: 'Let us suppose a ball to be moved from A towards the right at one degree of speed, and downwards at one degree of speed; it will arrive at B at two degrees of speed in the same time which it takes another ball, moved to the right at one degree of

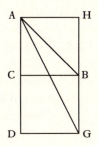

speed and downwards at two degrees, to arrive at G with three degrees of speed; from which it follows that the line AB is to the line AG as 2 is to 3; whereas it is in fact as 2 is to $\sqrt{10}$[25].' But it is, I think, sufficiently clear from the last demonstration shown above that the speed from A to B will not (according to my principles) be to the speed from A to G as[26] 2 is to 3, but as $\sqrt{2}$ is to $\sqrt{5}$, which is the proportion of the lines AB to[27] AG, and identical to the proportion of 2 to $\sqrt{10}$. For the proportion between the speed from A to B and the speed from A to G is not the same as the proportion between the speed of AH and[28] HB taken together and the speed of AH and HG taken together; rather, it is the proportion between[29] those subtended lines AB and AG, that is, the proportion between the roots of the squares constructed on the sides. But the reasoning by which I argued this in my earlier letter to you, sent from Paris on 7 February,[30] was not valid, I admit. I do not at all defend my errors; still less do I defend them obstinately. Unless M. Descartes behaves in the same way, I shall certainly be his superior in moral conduct. But how does it affect the truth of the matter under dispute if I have failed to demonstrate it sufficiently clearly? What if, knowing the truth of some proposition in Euclid's *Elements*, I tried to make a demonstration of it and failed; surely it would not be any less true on that account, if it were in fact demonstrated by others, or by me at some other time?

As for the other parts of my letter, does his silence signify agreement? I very much doubt it. But since he makes no objections, I have nothing to add to this letter, except to say that he is rather unfair towards me, when he suspects me of having wanted to cause confusion deliberately, so that I might later seem to have said something.[31] If that is what I was doing, I could still be causing confusion now, to conceal my error. But even now I see that it is possible for someone who has not previously concerned himself in the matter to reach the same conclusion, by means of my faulty reasoning, as he would reach by following the correct method of demonstration. But indeed, he himself knows what his intention was when he wrote, in the second discourse[32] of his 'Dioptrique' (on p. 18),[33] that he supposes the straight line HF to be twice AH, whereas in the accompanying diagram he makes it only slightly larger than AH itself. In fact you can know the reason, Father, if you consider that if it had been done so, the line FI would have fallen outside the circle, and consequently a ball projected into water from an elevation equal to the angle ABC should have been reflected, which is contrary to experience. It cannot be, surely, that he is causing confusion deliberately, so that he might seem to have proved something later[34]? I am delaying you too long over somebody else's trifles; so I bring this to an end, praying that all your wishes may be pleasantly and favourably fulfilled. Farewell.

Your most devoted
Thomas Hobbes

Paris, 30 March 1641

Italics in the text represent words written in larger script in the MS, and numerals underlined.

[1] See Letter 33, pp. 94–5, 97.

[2] hyposthesim *MS: the copyist wrote* hypostasim, *Hobbes deleted* a *and inserted* he, *leaving the first* s *undeleted*.

[3] See Letter 33, pp. 95, 97.

[4] Jean de Beaugrand (*c.*1595–1640) studied under Viète and became mathematician to Gaston d'Orléans in 1630. A friend of Fermat and a member of Mersenne's circle, he published a treatise on weight and gravity, *Geostatice*, in 1635. Between Feb. 1635 and Feb. 1636 he was in Italy, where he met Cavalieri and Galileo. In the later 1630s he had a public quarrel with Descartes and issued anonymous pamphlets accusing him of plagiarism.

[5] i.e. the warning that Descartes is accusing him of plagiarism.

[6] est *MS*.

[7] Hobbes had returned to England by Nov. 1630 (see Letter 8).

[8] See Letters 29, 30, 33.

[9] Contraction expanded. All previous printed versions of this letter have given this mistakenly as 'Artem'. A logic textbook, the 'Introduction to the Aristotelian categories', by the Neoplatonist philosopher Porphyrios (AD 232 or 233–*c.*305).

[10] Concealed by binding.

[11] Concealed by binding.

[12] Concealed by binding.

[13] Abbedinem *MS*.

[14] quanquam *MS: the copyist wrote* quam duam; *Hobbes has deleted* duam *and added* quam, *with the caret striking through the last limb of the* m *in the* quam *written by the copyist*.

[15] abbedo *MS*.

[16] See Letter 33, pp. 96, 99.

[17] See ibid., pp. 96, 99.

[18] *The copyist wrote* strauit *leaving a gap for the beginning of the word; Hobbes added* common.

[19] efficiat *MS*.

[20] *Three letters before* ne *have been deleted, possibly* nec.

[21] Concealed by binding.

[22] Concealed by binding.

[23] Concealed by binding.

²⁴ For 'minuto secundo' Hobbes apparently means 'minuto'. On these terms, see Letter 31 n. 3.

²⁵ See Letter 29, pp. 54–5, 57–8. The sign rendered √ here is a capital 'R' with a bar through its oblique leg, an abbreviation for 'radix' ('root').

²⁶ Page edge torn.

²⁷ Page edge torn.

²⁸ ad *MS*.

²⁹ Page edge torn.

³⁰ See Letter 30, pp. 64–5, 72–3.

³¹ See Letter 33, pp. 95–6, 98.

³² *The final letter of* discursu *has been altered by Hobbes from another letter (heavily deleted).*

³³ See A&T vi, pp. 98–9.

³⁴ *Written as* insequentibus *with a dividing line added by Hobbes.*

LETTER 35   2/12 APRIL 1641

Hobbes to John Scudamore, first Viscount Scudamore, from Paris

BL MS Add. 11044, fos. 180–1 (original).
Printed in Zagorin, 'Thomas Hobbes's Departure from England', pp. 159–60.

Right Honorable and my very good Lord.

I cannot deny but your Lo.ᵖ has iust cause to suspect my nature, of inciuility, or wᶜʰ is worse, ingratitude. But yet, my Lord, I am reasonably wel prouided of an excuse. I came to London last Michaelmas,¹ wᶜʰ was .6. weekes before my Lord came thither from yorke,² and made full account to haue wayted all that time vpon your Lo.ᵖ hauing then no other businesse in towne but to expect my Lords Comminge. But it was my fortune to go into a shop in Fleetestreete the master whereof, I not knowing it lay then sicke and dyed the next day, of the Plague. So there are 6 weekes³ honestly discounted. In the end of that time I went to your Loᵖˢ house in Sᵗ Martins,⁴ but found no body at all there, and thereupon made account to come againe a day or two after, but in the meane time I was seased so violently wᵗʰ a resolution of comming hither, as I departed wᵗʰin .3. dayes after, makeing nobody acquainted but my Lord, and one of his seruants who was to send the little mony I had after me by exchange and to see my trunke shipped. That wᶜʰ I can least excuse is my staying here so long wᵗʰout writinge. And of this fault I lay part vpon Monsʳ du Bosc. I told him I was so much behind hand with your Loᵖ in yᵉ duties I owe you, that I would gladly write to your Lop when he did; that my excuse might passe w^(th) the lesse examination. He promised to let me know when he writte, and I vrged him to write, w^(ch) he did and forgotte to tell me. By this meanes sentence came to be passed vpon me in yor Lo^ps answer to his. I pray you my Lord do not beleeue I had so little discerninge of your noble nature, or my particular obligation, as that I should neuer haue made acknowledg^t thereof, without this admonition out of yor letter to Monsr du Bosc. Truely I did intend it from weeke to weeke, and but wayted for some handsome occasion to present my excuse the better. The reason I came away was that I saw words that tended to aduance the prerogatiue of kings began to be examined in Parlament.⁵ And I knew some that had a good will to haue had me troubled, and might for any thing I saw in their honestyes make both the wordes and the witnesses. Besides I thought if I went not then, there was neuerthelesse a disorder comming on that would make it worse being there then here.⁶ Here I liue contentedly w^(th) my old frend Monsr du Bosc, who so much engrosses your Lo^ps seruice, as there would be no place for my endeauor though I were able, yet if you will be pleased to accept of the will for the deed I may still retayne the title of

> your Lordships most humble and most obliged seruant
> Tho: Hobbes

Paris April. 12. 1641 st°. n°.

[*endorsed:*] 1641 April 12/ 2 L^(re) from mr Hobbes

[*also endorsed:*] letter from Mr Hobbes 1641 to Ld Scudamore

¹ 29 Sept./9 Oct.
² The third Earl of Devonshire ('my Lord') had attended the King at York in Sept.–Oct. On 18 [/28] Oct. he was at Hardwick, when he wrote to Sir Edward Nicholas that he had received the King's command to attend Parliament on 20 [/30] Oct.: 'Not intending to haue come so soone to the towne, I know not how I can possibly make so much haste [>now] as to be there by that time' (OCC Nicholas papers, letters, unclassified).
³ i.e. 40 days: quarantine.
⁴ A street (now St Martin's Le Grand) to the north of St Paul's, running from what is now Cheapside into Aldersgate; on the site of the former college of St Martin's there were many 'highly priced' houses (Stow, *Survey*, p. 330).
⁵ This probably refers to the debate on 7/17 Nov. when, according to Sir Simonds D'Ewes's journal, John Pym included in a list of grievances 'Frequent preaching for Monarchy, Doctor Beale and others'; Sir Thomas Peyton recorded: 'Preaching for

absolute monarchy that the King may do what he list' (D'Ewes, *Journal*, pp. 8–9 and n.). Geoffrey Palmer's journal entry for this speech included 'Bookes & preaching y^t tende y^t waie & sett descention betwene King & state' (CUL MS Kk. 6. 38, fo. 16^r). The Doctor Beale mentioned by Pym was William Beale, Master of St John's College, Cambridge, against whom articles were exhibited in Parliament in Aug. 1641; article 3 stated that he had 'preached in St. *Maries* against the *Subjects* freedome and liberty' (*Articles against Beale*, p. 2). Hobbes was evidently worried that a similar view would be taken of his *Elements of Law*.

⁶ Three sentences, from 'The reason I came away' to 'worse being there then here', are underlined in the MS, but in a different ink from Hobbes's.

LETTER 36 [11/] 21 APRIL or [18/] 28 APRIL 1641

René Descartes to Marin Mersenne for Hobbes, from Endegeest

MS unknown.

This French translation (of the original Latin) printed in Descartes, *Lettres*, ed. Clerselier, iii, pp. 165–7; A&T iii, pp. 353–7; Descartes, *Correspondance*, iv, pp. 332–4; *MC* x, pp. 588–91. Latin translation of this French translation printed in Descartes, *Epistolae*, iii, pp. 84–6.

Qvant à ce que vous me mandez de l'Anglois, qui dit que son Esprit & ma matiere subtile sont la mesme chose, & qu'il a expliqué par son moyen la lumiere & les sons dés l'année 1630.¹ ce qu'il croit estre paruenu jusques à moy, c'est vne chose puerile & digne de risée. Si sa Philosophie est telle qu'il ait peur qu'on laluy dérobe, qu'il la publie; pour moy, ie luy promets que ie ne me hasteray pas d'vn moment à publier la mienne à son occasion. Ses derniers raisonnemens que vous m'ecriuez sont aussi mauuais que tous les autres que j'ay veus de luy. Car premierement, encore que l'Homme & Socrate ne soient pas deux diuers supposts,² toutesfois on signifie autre chose par le nom de Socrate que par le nom d'Homme, à sçauoir les differences³ indiui-duelles ou particulieres; de mesme le mouuement determiné n'est point different du mouuement, mais neantmoins la determination est autre chose que le mouuement.

Secondement, il n'est pas vray que la cause efficiente du mouuement soit aussi la cause efficiente de la determination;⁴ par exemple, ie iette vne balle contre vne muraille, la muraille determine la balle à reuenir vers moy, mais elle n'est pas la cause de son mouuement.

Troisiémement, il vse d'vne subtilité tres-legere, quand il demande si la determination est dans le mouuement, comme dans vn suiet;⁵

comme s'il estoit icy question de sçauoir si mouuement est vne substance ou vn accident; comme on dit que la quantité est le sujet des autres accidens; Et quand j'ay dit que le mouuement estoit à la determination du mouuement, comme le corps plan est à son plan ou à sa surface,[6] je n'ay point entendu par là faire comparaison entre le mouuement & le corps, comme entre deux substances, mais seulement comme entre deux choses concretes, pour monstrer qu'elles estoient differentes de celles dont on pouuoit faire l'abstraction.

Enfin c'est tres-mal à propos qu'il conclud, qu'vne determination estant changée, les autres le doiuent estre aussi; parce, dit-il, que toutes ces determinations ne sont qu'vn accident, sous diuers noms;[7] Si cela est, il s'ensuit donc que selon luy l'Homme[8] & Socrate ne sont qu'vne mesme chose sous deux noms differens, & partant pas vne difference indiuiduelle de Socrate ne sçauroit perir, par exemple, la connoissance qu'il a de la Philosophie, qu'en mesme temps il ne cesse d'estre Homme. Ce qu'il dit en suitte, à sçauoir, qu'vn mouuement n'a qu'vne determination,[9] est le mesme que si ie disois qu'vne chose estenduë n'a qu'vne seule figure, ce qui n'empesche pas que cette figure ne se puisse diuiser en plusieurs parties, comme la determination le peut aussi estre.

Ce qu'il reprend en la Dioptrique, page 18[10] fait voir seulement qu'il ne cherche que les occasions de reprendre, puisqu'il me veut imputer iusques aux fautes de l'Imprimeur; Car i'ay parlé en ce lieu-là de la proportion double, comme de la plus simple, pour expliquer la chose plus facilement, à cause que la vraye ne peut estre determinée, pource qu'elle change à raison de la diuersité des sujets. Mais si dans la figure, la ligne HF n'a pas esté faite justement double de la ligne AH, c'est la faute de l'Imprimeur, & non pas la mienne. Et en ce qu'il dit estre contre l'experience, il se trompe entierement; à cause qu'en cela l'experience varie, selon la varieté de la chose qui est iettée dans l'eau, & de la vitesse dont elle est meuë. Et ie ne me suis pas mis en peine de corriger en ce lieu-là la faute de l'Imprimeur, pource que j'ay crû aisément qu'il ne se trouueroit point de Lecteur si stupide, qu'il eust de la peine à comprendre qu'vne ligne fust double d'vne autre, à cause que la figure en represente vne qui n'a pas cette proportion, ny qui fust aussi si peu iuste, que de dire que pour cela je meritois d'estre repris. Enfin lors qu'il dit que i'approuue cette partie de ses écrits que ie ne reprens point, & dont ie ne dis mot, il se trompe encore; Car il est vray que c'est que ie n'en ay pas fait assez de cas, pour croire que ie deusse m'employer à la refuter.

As for what you send me by the Englishman, who says that his spirit and my subtle matter are the same thing, and that he gave an explanation in his own way of light and sound as early as 1630[1]—an explanation which, he thinks, then reached me—it is childish and ridiculous. If his philosophical system is such that he is afraid of other people stealing it from him, let him publish it; for my own part, I promise him that I shall not try to publish mine a moment sooner on his account.

His most recent arguments, which you tell me about in your letter, are as bad as all the other ones I have seen by him. For, firstly, even though 'man' and 'Socrates' are not different substances,[2] nevertheless we signify different things by using the names 'Socrates' and 'man', namely individual or particular *differentiae*.[3] In the same way, determined motion is not at all different from motion, but nevertheless determination is something different from motion.

Secondly, it is not true that the efficient cause of motion is also the efficient cause of determination.[4] For example, when I throw a ball against a wall, the wall determines the ball to return towards me, but it is not the cause of its motion.

Thirdly, he makes a very trivial quibble when he asks whether the determination is in the motion as if in a subject[5]—as if it were a matter here of knowing whether motion is a substance or an accident. For there is nothing awkward or absurd about saying that one accident is the subject of another accident, as when one says that quantity is the subject of other accidents. And when I said that motion was to the determination of motion as a flat body is to its plane or surface,[6] I did not mean to make any comparison thereby between motion and a body (as between two substances), but merely between two concrete things, to show that they were different from the things of which one can frame abstract concepts.

Finally, he draws a very improper conclusion when he says that if one determination is changed, the others must be changed too—because, he says, all these determinations are merely one accident under different names.[7] If that is true, it follows that in his view 'man'[8] and 'Socrates' are merely one thing under two different names, so that not a single individual *differentia* of Socrates could perish (for example, his knowledge of philosophy) without at the same time his ceasing to be a man.

What he says next, namely, that a motion has only one determination,[9] is as if I were to say that an extended thing has only one shape. That does not mean that that shape cannot be divided into several parts; and so can determination.

His objection to 'Dioptrique', p. 18,[10] merely shows that he is just looking for opportunities to reprove me, since he wants to blame me even for the errors of the printer. For I discussed double proportion in that passage because, being the simplest proportion, it allowed me to explain the matter more easily (since the correct proportion cannot be determined, because it varies according to the different kinds of objects involved). But if the line HF was not made exactly double the line AH in the diagram, that is the printer's fault, not mine. And when he says it is contrary to experience, he is completely mistaken; for experience varies in this matter, according to the variety of the objects which are thrown into the water, and the speed at which they move. And I did not bother to correct the printer's error in that passage because I was content to believe that there would never be any reader so stupid as to have difficulty in understanding that one line was double the other, just because the diagram showed a line which did not have that proportion; nor did I think there would ever be a reader so unfair as to say that I had earned a reproof on that account.

Finally, when he says that I approve of that part of his writings to which I do not object, and on which I say nothing, he is wrong again. The true explanation, rather, is that I did not take that part of his writings seriously enough to think that I was obliged to spend my time refuting it.

Clerselier prints this letter immediately after his French translation of the Latin section of Descartes's letter to Mersenne, [22 Feb./] 4 Mar. 1641 (Letter 33), under the heading 'And in another letter one finds the following, given here in translation' ('Et dans vne autre Lettre on trouue ce qui suit, dont voicy la version' (Descartes, *Lettres*, iii, p. 165)). The fact that this is a translation indicates that this was another of Descartes's Latin sections or enclosures in his letters to Mersenne, intended for Hobbes. (The reasons for thinking that the Latin version printed in Descartes, *Epistolae*, iii, pp. 84–6, is a retranslation from the French are convincingly set out in A&T iii, pp. 353–4.)

This letter replies to Hobbes's letter to Mersenne of [20/] 30 Mar. (Letter 34), and appears to have been enclosed in another letter from Descartes to Mersenne which, although itself undated, contains the information that Descartes has spent three or four weeks since writing his previous letter (which was dated [21/] 31 Mar.) (see *MC* x, p. 582). It can therefore be dated to either [11/] 21 or [18/] 28 Apr.

[1] See Letter 34, pp. 102–3, 108.
[2] See ibid., pp. 103, 108.

[3] The French term 'differences' here is taken to stand for the term '*differentiae*' in scholastic logic, i.e. the distinguishing features of a thing which qualify it for a given description.

[4] See Letter 34, pp. 103, 108.

[5] See ibid., pp. 103, 109.

[6] See Letter 33, pp. 96, 99.

[7] See Letter 34, pp. 104, 109.

[8] 'L'Homme' ('man') here stands presumably for 'Homo', which in this context would have been better translated as 'un Homme', 'a man'.

[9] See Letter 34, pp. 104, 109.

[10] See ibid., pp. 107, 112.

LETTER 37   23 JULY/2 AUGUST 1641

Hobbes to William Cavendish, third Earl of Devonshire, from Paris

MS (original) unlocated.
Printed in facsimile in *EW* i, plate facing p. 5; Tönnies, 'Analekten', pp. 302–3.

Right Honorable and my very good Lord.

I haue seene the Nottinghamshire *petition against BBs*.[1] In it there are reckoned vp abondance of abuses committed by Ecclesiasticall persons and their Officers, wch can neyther be denyed nor excused. But that they proceed from y^e *Episcopacy* it selfe, is not so euidently proued.[2] Howsoeuer since the Couetousnesse and supercilious behauior of the persons, *haue* made the people weary of that forme, I see nothing to be misliked in the *new way* propounded. If it displease any that there are to be so many Lay Commissioners[3] for church matters and so few ministers, I thinke it will be those that haue most desired the change and made account to haue the Episcopall authority diuided amongst them. I am of the opinion, that Ministers ought to minister rather then gouerne; at least that all Church gouerment depend on the state, and authority of the Kingdome, w^thout wch there can be no vnity in ye church. your Lo^p may perhaps thinke this opinion, but a *fancy of Philosophy*. but I am sure that Experience teaches, thus much, that the dispute for [precedence][4] betwene the *spirituall* and *civill power*, has of late more then any other thing in the world, bene the cause of *ciuill warres*, in all *places of Christendome*. For want of other discourse I haue taken this to bring me on in my letter so farre as I may make vp the rest wth the presenting of my duty to you, and the acknowledgt of yor great fauor to me, that am

> your Lordships most humble and most obedient servant S^r
> Th: Hobbes
> to the Earl of Deuonshire

Paris July 23/Aug. 2. 1641

[*addressed:*] To the Right Honorable my very good Lord [the *?*] Earle of Deuonshire London

[*annotated:*] to the Earl of Devonshire

Tönnies writes that this letter is in BL MS Harl. 6796 ('Analekten', p. 303). It is possible that he saw it there, and that it has since been removed; but I suspect that he was writing from memory, and confusing it with Letter 31.

The material presented in italics in the text is underlined in the MS; it is not possible to tell whether these underlinings are original.

[1] *A Petition presented to the Parliament from the Countie of Nottingham. Complaining of Grievances under the Ecclesiasticall Government by Archbishops, Bishops, &c* (1641): a pamphlet consisting mainly of Puritan objections to Laudian policies in the Church. The preface claimed that the petition had been signed by 'above 1500. hands of Esquires, Gentlemen, and Yeomen' (sig. A2^v).

[2] The last section of the petition is entitled: 'A humble Remonstrance Shewing how our Grievances under th'Ecclesiasticall government [. . .] Doe arise from the Inconveniences of the Forme or Constitution of the said Government it selfe' (p. 16).

[3] On 12/22 July 1641 new clauses were added to the Root-and-Branch Bill in committee, proposing that all ecclesiastical jurisdiction in England should be exercised by nine lay commissioners (see Gardiner, *History of England 1603–1642*, ix, pp. 407–8).

[4] precedence *omitted in MS*. Some such word as 'precedence' or 'primacy' seems to be required.

LETTER 38   [1/] 11 JULY 1645

Samuel Sorbière to Hobbes, from Lyon

BN MS f.l. 10352, part 1, fos. 83^v–84^r (transcript).

Viro Clarissimo, Doctissimóque D. Thomae Hobbio, Samuel Sorberius.

Vir Clarissime, non siuit aduersa valetudo, vt Lutetiae degens[1] eâ fruerer vberiùs felicitate quam mihi clarissimus Martellus noster procurauit, cùm aditum ad te fecit; nec per prae[>pro]peram profectionem licuit, vt gratias agens non spreti consortij nostri testatum relinquerem cultum, quo te, tuíque similes Heroas prosequor. Eo me sane nomine beatum puto, quod dum humanam foedè jacentem vitam cernerem, dum reputarem ineptiam plerorumque Mortalium, subirétque non rarò existimare pauxillulum a brutis hominem animantibus differre, obuiam tu factus, cujus viuida vis animi processit longè flammantia moenia Mundi, atque omne immensum peragrauit mente, animoque,[2] qui altius vt de genere nostro sentirem effecisti. Hujuscemodi factos viros plures Vtinam occurrerent, & vel vnus esset in singulis Prouincis! Id sperare ego non ausim; itaque dum vereor ne redux in Hollandiam rursum nimis humana omnia contemnere incipiam & bonae mentis studium neglegam, rogaui Martellum vt Iconem tuam, magni Gassendi, optimíque Mersenni mihi impetraret quam summopere jam efflagito, ratus aequi boníque te consulturum expetitionis meae libertatem. Non solùm enim scripta me mouent & ad virtutem impellunt, afficit quoque me vultus virorum maximorum, a quibus in me veluti effluuium, diffusámque vim insitam sentio. Vale, Vir Clarissime, & me tui summum cultorem vicissim redama.

Lugduni[3] V. Eid. Quintil. 1645.

Translation of Letter 38

Samuel Sorbière to the very distinguished and learned Mr Thomas Hobbes.

Distinguished Sir, while I was staying in Paris,[1] ill health prevented me from enjoying more fully the pleasure which our distinguished friend de Martel had procured for me when he introduced me to you. And my departure was so sudden that I was prevented from leaving behind, in gratitude for our undivided friendship, evidence of the worship with which I honour you and heroes like you. I think I too am blessed with the title of 'hero', since while I was considering the grovelling baseness of human life, while I was contemplating the stupidity of most mortals, often thinking that man differed by next to nothing from brute animals, you appeared: 'the quick vigour of your mind ventured far beyond the flaming ramparts of the world, and voyaged in mind and spirit through the immeasurable universe'.[2] Thus you made me think more highly of human kind. I wish that there were more men made in your mould, and that there might be at least one in each country! But I dare not hope for that; and since I fear that when I return to Holland I may start to despise all things human again excessively and neglect the cultivation of a good mind, I have asked de Martel to send me portraits of you, the great Gassendi, and the excellent Mersenne. I ask for this most earnestly, in the belief that you will approve and look favourably on the boldness of my request. For I am moved and impelled to be virtuous not only by writings but also by the faces of great men; I feel, as it were, an emanation, a natural force which radiates from them to me.

Farewell, distinguished Sir, and return the love of your most devoted admirer.

Lyon,[3] 11 July 1645

---

[1] Sorbière stayed briefly in Paris in the early summer of 1645 (see the Biographical Register).

[2] The passage placed in quotation marks in the translation is an almost unaltered quotation of Lucretius, *De rerum natura*, 1, lines 72–4; line 62 has also been adapted earlier in the same sentence. Reading (literally) between these lines, we find that Sorbière is implying that Hobbes has overthrown religious superstition. The original text of lines 62–3, 66–7, and 72–4 is:

> Humana ante oculos foede cum vita iaceret
> in terris oppressa gravi sub religione
>
> .   .   .   .   .   .
>
> primum Graius homo mortalis tollere contra
> est oculos ausus primusque obsistere contra
>
> .   .   .   .   .
>
> ergo vivida vis animi pervicit, et extra
> processit longe flammantia moenia mundi
> atque omne immensum peragravit mente animoque

('While human life could be seen grovelling, crushed to the earth by the weight of superstition [. . .] a Greek was the first mortal who dared to raise his eyes in defiance [. . .] so the quick vigour of his mind prevailed, and he ventured far beyond the flaming ramparts of the world, and voyaged in mind and spirit through the immeasurable universe.')

[3] 'Lugduni' here must be Lyon, not Leiden; although mainly resident in Holland from 1642 to 1650, Sorbière was in Lyon in late June 1645 (see *MC* xiii, p. 454).

LETTER 39   [29 JULY/] 8 AUGUST 1645

Hobbes to Edmund Waller, from Rouen

MS owned by Mr Richard Waller (original).
Printed in Wikelund, 'Thus I passe my Time', pp. 263–8.

Noble sir
  Though at the foot of my letter (which commonly is first look't at) you find from Roüen, and from me, I pray you beleeue that in my absence I haue left your sonne[1] and Nephew[2] such directions as they will not loose their time. And I hope wthin this fortnight to be wth them againe. I came hether to see my lord of Deuonshire, but am no lesse in other Company then his; where I serue when I can be matched as a gladiator; My odde opinions are bayted. but I am contented wth it, as beleeuing I haue still the better, when a new man is sett vpon me; that knowes not my paradoxes, but is full of his owne doctrine, there is something in the disputation not vnpleasant. He thinkes he has driuen me vpon an absurdity when t'is vpon some other of my tenets and so from one to another, till he wonder and exclayme and at last finds I am of the Antipodes to ye schooles.[3] Thus I passe my time in this place. I beleeue you passe much of yours in meditating how you may to your Contentment [>and w^{h}out blame] passe the seas.[4] If the newes we heare lately be true,[5] other men will haue the same meditation. My lady kingsmill[6] has expected a letter from you. Shee will not be brought to write first, and bad [be *deleted* >mee] tell you she was to stout to descend to that. I was told you had an inclination to put a booke Called de Ciue into English.[7] I can not hope it should haue that honor, and yet now I thinke of it, the honor will come all to the English booke, [if *deleted*] when it is of your doing, but so will the enuy [too *deleted*] also. I will not presse you to it but I must thanke you for hauing once entertayned the thought, wch alone I esteeme as a great obligation to [ye *deleted*]

  your most humble and most obedient seruant
  Tho: Hobbes

Rouen Aug. 8: 1645

[*addressed:*] A Monsieur
  Monsieur Edward Waller Gentilhomme Anglois à Calais

¹ Robert Waller, who died young.

² Unidentified; probably a son of Waller's brother-in-law Nathaniel Tomkins, who had been executed for his part in their conspiracy of the previous year.

³ = scholastic philosophy.

⁴ As a result of his part in a plot to seize London for the King, Waller had been imprisoned in May 1644 and then exiled by an ordinance of 4/14 Nov. 1644. The ordinance was not revoked until Nov./Dec. 1651, and Waller did not return to England until Jan. 1652.

⁵ Probably the defeats inflicted on royalist forces at Naseby on 14 [/24] June and Langport in July (see Wikelund, 'Thus I passe my Time', p. 266n.).

⁶ Either the widow of Sir William Kingsmill (d. 1619 or 1620), or Bridget, the widow of Sir Henry Kingsmill (d. 1624 or 1625) (see Wikelund, 'Thus I passe my Time', pp. 266–7n.).

⁷ Cf. *ABL* ii, p. 277: 'I have heard him [sc. Waller] say that he so much admired Mr. Thomas Hobbes' booke *De Cive*, when it came forth, that he was very desirous to have it donne into English, and Mr. Hobbes was most willing it should be done by Mr. Waller's hand, for that he was so great a master of our English language. Mr. Waller freely promised him to doe it, but first he would desire Mr. Hobbes to make an essaye; he (T.H.) did the first booke, and did it so extremely well, that Mr Waller would not meddle with it, for that nobody els could doe it so well. Had he thought he could have better performed it, he would have himselfe been the translator.'

LETTER 40   [6/] 16 MAY 1646

Hobbes to Samuel Sorbière, from Paris

BN MS f.l. 10352, part 2, fos. 79ᵛ–80ʳ (transcript).

Printed in *Illustrium virorum epistolae*, pp. 573²–5² (sigs. Bb2–3ʳ); Tönnies, 'Siebzehn Briefe', pp. 67–8; Robertson, 'Some Letters', p. 441; *MC* xiv, pp. 280–1 (extract); translated in *HW* ii, pp. 300–1.

Thomas Hobbesius Samueli Sorberio suo.

Ex literis tuis ad D. Martellum nostrum, quibus te venisse Hagam cognoui incolumem, hoc ipso die (mi Sorberi dilectissime) cepi voluptatem, quam tua bonitas et timor itinerum, incommoda, atque pericula sola recordantis, non patiebantur esse mediocrem. Itaque quòd molestis illis cogitationibus primo tempore me liberaueris, id quoque amicissimè à te factum est. Quòd in ijsdem literis praefationem meam¹ laudas, secunda voluptas erat, nam et delector judicio tuo, et quamquam nimium laudas, tamen affectus quo id facis, ad id quod ago, vtilis est, nam vt Typographo spes fiat fore vt liber ille vaeniat, laudatoribus, & magnis, et quibus credi possit opus est. Itaque et D. Gassendus, et R. P. Mersennus librum illum hyperbolicè laudauerunt, mihi certe potiùs quam sibi satisfacientes; quorum vtriusque literas jam pridem te puto accepisse.[2] Quae editionem impedire posse videntur; sunt primò si ejusmodi librum scierint sub praelo esse ij qui dominantur in Academijs, ad quorum pertinet existimationem nequis in ea doctrina quam profitentur viderit quod illis prius non vidissent. Itaque tacitè peragendum est, nec quaerenda testimonia nisi quae obtineri posse certo scias. Neque ergo si prohiberi potest, Typographo permittendum est, homines suo ipsius judicio doctos de libri vtilitate consulere. Deinde cauendum est ab ijs qui cum pleraque probent, reliqua improbant, nam Magistros agunt, ac laude quam priuatim ipsi mihi tribuunt contentum me debere esse putant, publicam invidebunt. Praeterèa, si id agi vt edatur liber meus (vel hic, vel quilibet alius) sentiat vel suspicetur D. Des-Cartes, certò scio impediturum esse si potest, quod unum velim mihi credas qui scio. Caeteram cautelam omnem tibi permitto. Nam et prudentiam, et voluntatem in me tuam penitus perspectam habeo. Cùm spem edendi videris aliquam, fac me quaeso certiorem quamprimum potes, vt eam spem, si fieri possit, mecum Montalbanum[3] feram, illuc iturus sum cum D. Martello, qui et causa mihi eundi maxima est, quanquam accedat altera haec, vt perficiendae parti primae meorum elementorum,[4] majore otio vacare possim. Ibimus circa finem mensis proximi, aut aliquanto citius. Vale

Tuus Deuinctissimus
Tho. Hobbes.

Maij 16. 1646. Parisijs.

Translation of Letter 40

Hobbes to his friend Sorbière.

My dearest Sorbière, I have gained great pleasure from learning today, from your letter to M. de Martel, that you have arrived safely at The Hague. Your goodness, together with the fear of travelling felt by one who considers merely its discomforts and dangers, caused my pleasure to be especially great. And so your freeing me at the first opportunity from those worrying thoughts was also a very friendly thing to do. Your praise of my preface[1] in the same letter was an additional pleasure: both because I am pleased by your judgement and because, although you praise it too much, your goodwill in so doing is useful for my undertaking. For in order to give the printer hope that the book will sell, I need to have it praised by people who are important and whose word can be believed. Accordingly, both M. Gassendi and the reverend Father Mersenne praised it excessively—satisfying me, at least, rather than themselves. I think you have already received a letter from each of them.[2]

The following things may, I think, hinder the publication of the book. First, if the people who hold sway in the universities learn that a book of this sort is in the press. For their public reputation demands that in the subject which they teach no one should have discovered anything which they have not already discovered. So you must proceed quietly, and not ask for testimonials except when you are sure that you can get them. Nor, accordingly, if it can be prevented, should the printer be allowed to get judgements on the book's importance from people who, in his own opinion, he considers to be learned men. Then you must beware of those who approve of most of it but disapprove of the rest. Such people will treat me as if I were their pupil; they will expect me to be content with the praise they give me in private, and will begrudge me public praise. Furthermore, if M. Descartes hears or suspects that a book of mine (this or any other) is being assessed for publication, I know for certain that he will stop it if he can. Please believe me on this one thing, for I do know. I leave all the other precautions to you, as I am fully aware of both your prudence and your goodwill towards me.

When you see some hope that it will be published, please let me know as soon as possible, so that I may take that hope with me to Montauban.[3] I am about to go there with M. de Martel; he is the main reason for my going there, but I do have another reason, which is that I aim to be able to devote my time more freely there to finishing off the first part of my Elements.[4] We shall leave around the end of next month, or a little sooner.

Your most obliged
Thomas Hobbes

Paris, 16 May 1646

---

[1] The preface by Hobbes to the 2nd edn. of *De cive*.

[2] The commendatory letters to Sorbière from Gassendi and Mersenne (*HW* ii, pp. 85–6) were first printed in the 3rd edn. of *De cive* (sigs. **10–11).

[3] The Protestant hill-town, north of Toulouse, from which de Martel's family stemmed (see the Biographical Register, 'de Martel').

[4] The first section of Hobbes's tripartite 'elements of philosophy', eventually published as *De corpore*.

LETTER 41 [11/] 21 MAY 1646

Samuel Sorbière to Hobbes, from The Hague

BN MS f.l. 10352, part 1, fo. 98 (transcript).
Printed in Tönnies, 'Siebzehn Briefe', p. 68 (extract); translated in *HW* ii, p. 301 (extract).

Viro Clarissimo, Nobilissimóque D. D. Thomae Hobbio, Samuel Sorberius.

Quàm gratum fecerim Viris summis, solidóque philosophantibus Boswellio,[1] [Johnsonio][2], Bornio,[3] [*word deleted*] Regio,[4] Heereboordio,[5] caeteris vbi de libri tui necnon partium operis priorum[6] editione spem dedi, vix credas, quanquam verissimè narranti. Omnes enim te vnum, Gassendúmque spectant, in te oculos habent, ex quo mons ille parturijt ridiculum murum, nósque tanto hiatu vocatos lusit.[7] Para igitur missurus quamprimùm quae egregia ostendisti circa Opticam plurima,[8] & pande prorsus quidquid in Vniuersa natura tanta solertia detexisti. Regij Physicam[9] Elzevirius Amstelodamensis[10] qui tua quoque idem excudet, & Cartesiana excudit,[11] jam sub prelo suo versat. Spero multa saniora in illo Opere haberi; Sed vereor ne praeclarus ille vir tam bene in rem naturalem affectus non satis ingenio suo largiatur. Nam ille nimis δουλεύει τῇ ὑποθέσει scilicet Cartesianum acumen, adyta illa Naturae penetrasse, quae nemo fortasse vnquam homo perspecta penitus, compertáque habebit. Gratias quidem ingentes ago, & vehementer laudo molientium conatus aliquid famâ dignum, sed doleo viros sapientes vbi tam audacter minus certa affirmant viam sibi praecludere ad vlteriorem inquisitionem, atque nobis ita spem adimi aliquando frui ταῖς δευτέραις φροντίδεσι σοφωτέρων, verùm haec obiter. Ad Clarissimum Martellum fusiùs scribo & narro quid egerim cum Typographo. Tu vale & me ama qui te prae caeteris mortalibus vnicè colo, venerórque. Raptim dabam Hagae Comitis XXI Maj 1646.

Translation of Letter 41

Samuel Sorbière to the most distinguished, noble, and learned Mr Thomas Hobbes.

You may hardly believe (even though you hear it from the most truthful of sources) what pleasure I gave to those excellent men and sound philosophers Boswell,[1] Johnson,[2] Bornius,[3] Regius,[4] Heereboord[5] and others, when I told them they might hope for the publication of your book—and also of the earlier parts of your work.[6] For they are all looking to you and Gassendi; and they have their eyes on you now that that mountain has brought forth the ridiculous mouse and made fools of us, having summoned us after such a long interval.[7] So please get ready to send off as soon as possible those various outstanding demonstrations which you have made in optics,[8] and set out in full whatever you have so ingeniously discovered in general physics.

The Amsterdam Elsevier,[10] who printed Descartes's works[11] and is also printing yours, is just going to press with Regius' Physics.[9] I hope there are many sound things in that book of Regius'; but I fear that that distinguished man, whose thoughts in natural science are so well grounded, may not give us enough of his own way of thinking in his treatment of the subject. For he is too much 'enslaved to the hypothesis', namely that the sharp mind of Descartes has penetrated that innermost sanctuary of nature, which perhaps no man will ever fully inspect or know with certainty. I have enormous gratitude and enthusiastic praise for the efforts of those who struggle to produce something worthy of fame; but I am sad to see wise men proposing rather dubious things so boldly, thereby preventing themselves from investigating the matter further, and depriving us of the hope that we might one day enjoy 'the second thoughts of wise men'. But all this is by the way, of course. I am writing at greater length to the most distinguished M. Martel, and telling him what I have done in my dealings with the printer. Farewell, and love me—I who worship and respect you alone above all other mortals.

From The Hague, written in haste, 21 May 1646.

---

[1] Sir William Boswell (d. 1649), British Ambassador at The Hague since 1633, and a man of wide scholarly interests. He was one of the literary executors of Bacon's estate, and possessed the Bacon MSS eventually published by Isaac Gruter as *Scripta in naturali et universali philosophia* (1651). Sorbière had corresponded with Boswell on scientific matters from Paris in 1639 (BN MS f.l. 10352, part 1, fos. 15ᵛ–17ʳ). Sir Charles Cavendish, who met Boswell in Mar./Apr. 1645, recorded that he admired Descartes, but not uncritically (BL MS Add. 4278, fo. 203ʳ).

[2] *Jonshonio MS.* Samson Johnson (b. 1603), Fellow of Magdalen College, Oxford (1625–37), created DD 1636, and rector of Fobbing, Essex, until sequestered in 1645 (Foster). A liberal theologian, he was an admirer of Grotius, corresponding with him from London in 1635 and addressing him as 'My incomparable patron' ('Patrone mi Incomparabilis' (Brant, *Clarorum virorum epistolae*, pp. 135–7)). From *c.*1637 he served as

chaplain to Elizabeth, Queen of Bohemia, in Holland, but was dismissed at Parliament's insistence (as a Laudian) in 1642 (Oman, *Elizabeth of Bohemia*, p. 349). He became a professor at the newly founded University of Breda in 1646, and was the 'English preacher' there from 1646 to 1655 (de Vrijer, *Henricus Regius*, p. 160n.). According to Sorbière he was persuaded by a reading of Gassendi's *Disquisitio metaphysica* to abandon Cartesianism (Gassendi, *Opera omnia*, vi, p. 470A); but Baillet records that he later became a Cartesian again (*Vie de Descartes*, ii, p. 210). In Aug. 1652 Hyde wrote to Nicholas that when he had last seen his 'old friend Dr Johnson' he had expressed 'a great reverence for Mr Hobbs, and it seems is of his faith in all things' (Ogle *et al.* (eds.), *Calendar of Clarendon State Papers*, ii, p. 142).

³ Henricus Bornius (Henrick Born) (1617–75), who had studied philosophy and theology at Leiden and Utrecht. Later in 1646 he became Professor of Logic and Ethics at Breda, and in 1651 he returned to teach at Leiden. Regarded as a defector from Cartesianism (Thijssen-Schoute, *Nederlands Cartesianisme*, p. 96), he was in contact with Regius and Gassendi in the mid-1640s.

⁴ Henricus Regius (Henrick de Roy) (1598–1679), who studied at Franeker and Leiden, before practising as a physician at Naarden and Utrecht. He taught medicine at Utrecht, becoming an enthusiastic Cartesian in the early 1640s; but in 1647 he broke publicly with Descartes, asserting that the mind might be merely a mode of a corporeal substance.

⁵ Adrian Heereboord (*c.*1614–61), who studied philosophy at Leiden, became a lecturer in rhetoric there in 1640 and Professor of Philosophy in 1644. Originally one of the first to introduce Descartes's theories at Leiden, he later became a very lukewarm Cartesian, with a strong element of scholasticism.

⁶ The two earlier sections of Hobbes's tripartite system, eventually published as *De corpore* and *De homine*.

⁷ This scornful reference to Gassendi (using the proverbial Latin phrase for those who promise much and deliver little) is puzzling. It can scarcely refer to Gassendi's most recent work, the *Disquisitio metaphysica* (1644): not only was that a large volume, but its publication was arranged by Sorbière himself. Since Sorbière seems mainly concerned here with expectations for a major new work on physics, he may be referring to Gassendi's only published work in that field, the slender volume *De motu impresso* (1642).

⁸ See Letter 42 n. 12.

⁹ *Fundamenta physices* (1646). Huygens told Mersenne on [11/] 21 Aug. 1646 that the book had been printed (*MC* xiv, p. 413), and copies went on sale at the beginning of Oct. (de Vrijer, *Henricus Regius*, p. 166).

¹⁰ Louis Elsevier (d. 1670), a member of the numerous family of printers and book-sellers from Leiden; he had established a printing house in Amsterdam in 1638.

¹¹ Louis Elsevier had published the 1st edn. of Descartes's *Principia* in 1644.

LETTER 42   [22 May/] 1 JUNE 1646

Hobbes to Samuel Sorbière, from Paris

BN MS f.l. 10352, part 2, fos. 80ᵛ–81ʳ (transcript).
Printed in Tönnies, 'Siebzehn Briefe', pp. 68–70; Robertson, 'Some Letters', pp. 441–2; *MC* xiv, pp. 303–4 (extract); *HW* ii, pp. 302–3.

Viro Clarissimo Eruditissimo D. Samueli Sorbierio S.P.D. Thomas Hobbes

Literis tuis quas a D. Martello proximé accepi magnopere laetatus sum. Fructum enim omnis operae et laboris praeteritae amplissimum fero, quod placeant ea quae scripsi viris illis tantis quos nominasti, et tibi; quoque spem fecisti fore vt edantur. Quod scribis [videri][1] Elzeuirio,[2] si prodeat liber tanquam pars [majoris][3] operis nondum editi, homines illum minus libenter emptores esse, ego idem censeo, quare mutetur titulus, fiatque simpliciter DE CIVE.[4] Caeterùm mutationem tituli sequitur necessitas ea loca tollendi, in quibus mentio aliqua fit sectionis praecedentis, quae quidem loca nec multa sunt, nec talia quae non possunt tolli facillimè, excepto initio Capitis primi, quod poterit esse hujusmodi. *Naturae humanae facultates ad quatuor genera reduci possunt, Vim Corpoream, Experientiam, Rationem, Affectum. Ab his sequentis doctrinae initium capientes inquiremus primo loco quid animi habeant homines illis facultatibus praediti, alteri aduersus alteros. Et an.*[5] Item initio Capitis quinti pro his verbis *Ostensum est sectione praecedente* substitui haec possunt, *Manifestum per se est.*[6] Caeteris locis cum mentio sectionis praecedentis sub parenthesi tantummodo fiat poterit ea sine hiatu, sine incommodo deleri, vt pag. 4. linea. 21.[7] et pag. 17. linea. 15.[8] et fortasse vno vel altero loco alias. Tollantur ergo eae parentheses, et fiat titulus vt dixi breuis simplexque DE CIVE. sed cauendum est ne superiorum capitum articulorumue citationes deleantur. Itaque nisi vbi vox Sectio occurrit, nil mouendum est.

Quod in Elementorum meorum sectione prima[9] tamdiu versor, partim quidem causa est pigritia, sed maximè quod in sensibus meis explicandis non facile placeo [mihimet][10] ipsi. Nam quod in doctrina morali fecisse me spero, id quoque in Philosophia prima, et in Physica facere studeo ne locus sit relictus contrascriptoris. Attamen de ea absoluenda intra annum vertentem modo viuam et valeam minime dubito. Itaque vt ei rei magis vacem stat secedere Rus, praesertim Montalbanum,[11] nostri Cl. Martelli gratiâ, Expectatio amicorum excitat industriam meam aliquantulum, sed tu me blanditijs tuis ad scribendum potenter adigisti atque impulisti. Accedit quoque quod ipse Opticae meae (quam anglicè scriptam dedi Marchioni de NeuCastel)[12] firmitate et robore delectatus, cupiam primo tempore emittere eam latinè. D. Johnsonnius[13] promisit mihi breui se missurum, D. Regij Systema Physicum.[14] vt id fiat quam primum quaeso adjuua. Vidi enim jam quaedam dogmata ejus Physica, in libro quodam medico,[15] quae mihi valde placuerant. Vir optime Vale.

Parisijs Junij. 1º 1646.

[*postscript:*] D. Gassendo salutem tuo nomine dicam cras. aegrotat a febre quae tamen nunc leuiuscula est. Mersennus nondum redijt.[16]

Translation of Letter 42

Thomas Hobbes sends greetings to the most distinguished and most learned M. Samuel Sorbière.

Your letter, which I have just received from M. de Martel, has given me great pleasure. For I am earning a splendid reward for all my past labour and effort if my writings please people as eminent as those you have named—and you. You have also aroused the hope that my book will be published. I agree with what you say Elsevier[2] thinks,[(1)] that if a book is issued as only part of a larger[(3)] work, as yet unpublished, people are less willing to buy it. So the title should be changed, and it should be simply *De cive*.[4] As a consequence of this change of title, you should also remove those passages in which a previous section of the Elements is mentioned. There are not many of these passages, and they are of such a sort that it will be very easy to remove them. The only exception is the beginning of the first chapter, which could be done like this: 'The faculties of human nature can be reduced to four kinds: bodily strength, experience, reason, and emotion. In the doctrine which follows we shall take our starting-point from these, and shall investigate in the first place what attitude men bear towards one another, given that they are endowed with these faculties. And whether . . .'.[5] Again, at the beginning of chapter 5 the words 'It has been shown in the preceding section' can be replaced by 'It is self-evident'.[6] In the other places where a previous section is mentioned it happens only within parentheses; thus it will be possible to remove them without inconvenience and without leaving a gap in the sentence (e.g. p. 4, line

21;[7] p. 17, line 15;[8] and perhaps one or two other places elsewhere). So those phrases in parenthesis should be removed, and the title should be, as I said, *De cive*, which is short and simple. But care should be taken not to remove references to earlier chapters or paragraphs. So: nothing should be removed except where the word 'section' occurs.

The reason why I am taking so long over the first section of my Elements[9] is partly laziness, but mostly the fact that I find it difficult to explain my meanings to my own[(10)] satisfaction. For I am seeking to achieve in metaphysics and physics what I hope I have achieved in moral theory, so that there may be no room left for any critic to write against me. However, I do not doubt that I shall finish it before the end of the year, provided I live and am in good health. So, to give me more time for it, it is resolved that I should leave for Montauban,[11] thanks to our distinguished friend M. de Martel. The expectation of my friends makes me a little bit more industrious, but you with your coaxing have powerfully forced and impelled me to write. In addition, I myself am so satisfied with the firmness and strength of my 'Optics' (which I wrote in English and dedicated to the Marquis of Newcastle),[12] that I want to publish it in Latin at the first opportunity.

Mr Johnson[13] promised me that he would send me shortly Regius' 'Physical System'.[14] Please help him to do this as soon as possible. I have already seen some of Regius' teachings about physics in a medical book,[15] and I liked them very much. Best of men, farewell.

Paris, 1 June 1646

[*postscript:*] I shall give your greetings to Gassendi tomorrow. He is ill with a fever, but it is slightly better now. Mersenne has not yet returned.[16]

The quotations presented in italics here are over-lined in the MS.

[1] videre *MS*.

[2] See Letter 41 n. 10.

[3] magoris *MS*.

[4] The 1st edn. (Paris, 1642) had been published under the title *Elementorum philosophiae sectio tertia de cive*.

[5] For the passage replaced here, see *HW* ii, I. 1, pp. 89–90 n. 11.

[6] Ibid. ii, V. 1, p. 130 n. 7.

[7] Ibid. ii, I. 2, p. 91 n. 4.

[8] Ibid. ii, II. 10, p. 102 n. 6.

[9] See Letter 40 n. 4.

¹⁰ mehi met *MS*.

¹¹ See Letter 40 n. 3.

¹² Hobbes's English Optical MS, entitled 'A Minute or first Draugt of the Optiques', BL MS Harl. 3360. A revised Latin version of part 2 of this work was eventually published as part 1 of *De homine* (1658).

¹³ See Letter 41 n. 2.

¹⁴ See Letter 41 n. 9. Johnson's letter does not apparently survive.

¹⁵ This may refer to either of two earlier works by Regius: *Spongia* (1640) or *Physiologia* (1641).

¹⁶ Mersenne was travelling through the south and south-west of France; he left Paris on [10/] 20 Apr. and returned by [16/] 26 Aug. (see *MC* xiv, pp. 212–16).

LETTER 43   [22 AUGUST/] 1 SEPTEMBER 1646

Samuel Sorbière to Hobbes, from The Hague

BN MS f.l. 10352, part 1, fos. 91ᵛ–92ʳ (transcript).
Printed in Tönnies, 'Siebzehn Briefe', p. 192; translated in *HW* ii, p. 304.

Clarissimo Viro D.D.¹ Samuel Sorberius.

En tibi Epigramma quod in Effigiem tuam adornauit Henricus Bruno² Ephorus Hugeiniorum literatissimus & nominis tui cultor inprimis, quae postrema virtus communis illi cum omnibus bonae mentis, & solidae eruditionis amantibus; quis enim Musas hodie colit qui quantum praestiteris et quotidie ad promouendas Artes ignoret? Vtinam diutissimè, in firmissima Valetudine Lutetiam, ornamentum Galliae, ornes quò te adeat semper Oraculum vndiquaque curiosorum hominum coetus³ ille doctissimus. Ego Leydae pedem figo, vnde quid moliantur nostrates certiorem te si velis faciam subinde. Tu vicissim cùm ad Reuerendissimum Riuetum⁴ scribes, beare me poteris Epistolis, vnde intelligam me a te amari, neque prorsus affectum nostrum in rem literariam sperni [Ita *deleted*] Vale

Hagae Comitis Kal. Septemb. 1646.

Translation of Letter 43

To that very distinguished man, the most learned Mr¹ Hobbes, from Samuel Sorbière.

Here is the epigram which Henricus Bruno has written to adorn your portrait.² He is the guardian of the Huygens family, a man steeped in fine literature, and one of your leading admirers. That last virtue is one he shares with all those who love good sense and sound learning; for what worshipper of the Muses nowadays is not aware of how much you have contributed, and still contribute each day, to the improvement of the arts? May you continue, for a very long time and in the very best health, to be an ornament to Paris, that ornament of France, so that that extremely learned gathering[3] of enquiring minds, drawn from all regions, may always consult you as its oracle. I am staying in Leiden, and, if you like, I shall let you know immediately of any projects our friends here may undertake. In return, when you write to the most reverend M. Rivet,[4] you can bless me with a letter, to let me know that you love me, and that our literary friendship has not weakened. Farewell.

The Hague, 1 September 1646

[1] Warrender takes 'D.D.' to mean 'dono dedit', the phrase used when making a present of something—in this case, the poem by Bruno (*HW* ii, p. 304n.). But the same abbreviation occurs in the salutations of other letters in this MS which did not accompany presents. As 'D.' on its own in these salutations clearly stands for 'Domino' ('Mr'), I take 'D.D.' to stand for 'Doctissimo Domino' ('most learned Mr').

[2] Henricus Bruno (d. 1664), a prolific minor neo-Latin poet, was employed by Constantijn Huygens as a tutor to his sons from 1639; he later became rector of the Latin school at Hoorn (see *HOC* i, p. 3). The epigram referred to here must be the first of the three poems by Bruno printed in the prefatory material to the second edition of *De cive* (*HW* ii, p. 71). Since it refers to the 'colours' of the portrait, it was evidently not written originally for the engraving in that edition; it must have been composed to be displayed under (or written on) the picture of Hobbes which Sorbière had procured from de Martel (see Letter 38). At this stage Sorbière was still not contemplating including an engraved portrait of Hobbes in the edition (see Letter 47).

[3] This may refer to the gatherings in Mersenne's rooms, or it may be a more general collective noun for all the learned men who visited Paris.

[4] André Rivet (1573–1651), Protestant divine, Professor of Theology at Leiden (1620–32), thereafter director of the University of Breda. Although *c*.4,350 letters from Rivet's correspondence are extant, no letter to him from Hobbes is known to exist (see Dibon, *Inventaire de la correspondance de Rivet*).

LETTER 44   [late SEPTEMBER] 1646

Samuel Sorbière to Hobbes [from The Hague]

BN MS f.l. 10352, part 1, fos. 90ᵛ–91ʳ (transcript).
    Printed in Tönnies, 'Siebzehn Briefe', pp. 70–1; *MC* xiv, p. 427 (extract); translated in *HW* ii, p. 303.

Viro Nobilissimo, Sapientissimóque D. Thomae Hobbio, Samuel Sorberius.

    Aegrè fero Elzevirium[1] tandiu libri tui Editionem distulisse; attamen illo vel inuito factum, quippe Regij Physicam[2] cùm prae manibus haberet ab Auctore additamenta subinde[3] missa, quae dilationem Operis tediosam sanè intulerant. Iam verò in Indice[4] praelum sudat, & spes est ante dies quindecim exactos missurum me primum specimen; Sed en illud tibi quod dum haec scribo nanciscor Elzeuirio ipso deferente. Para itaque quam affectam habebas Anglicè partem,[5] vt per amicam occasionem mittas, atque vnà vrge quaeso, vt curae nostrae mandet D. Gassendus Physicam suam,[6] cui inhiant Typographi nostri Lugdunensibus longè anteponendi, siue elegantem, siue properatam Editionem velit. Sed an tibi, Vir Maxime, iam satis supererit temporis Principi[7] admoto vt lineam quotidie quae supersit, ducere possis?[8] ô quàm te digna injecta est provincia? quàm felix futura est Patria tua cum praeceptis tuis imbutum Regem sapientissimum obtinebit? Gaudeo & tibi ex animo gratulor; quidquid jacturae forsan ex dilata Elementorum tuorum parte promissa simus passuri. Verùm vnicè doleo vicem Nobiliss. Martelli Montalbanum[9] repetentis, qui in illa diuulsione mirum quàm acerba experietur. Equidem optandum esset vt generosissimus ille vir Lutetiae pedem figeret, quod tu in illo fastigio in Aula positus circumspice quâ ratione tandem consequi posset, atque vnâ operâ Prataeo nostro[10] Medico Lugdunensi, fortissimi pectoris in aduersissima fortuna viro, si qua possis prospice; est enim inter paucos qui bonam mentem colunt, nec non D. Gassendo notus, & opinor charissimus. Ego luctor adhuc, vt si fortè emergam, & cum uxorcula[11] Leydam propero, vbi domus mea excipiendis studiosis erit aperta; si quos igitur nôris nobiles Britannos Academiam petituros, rogo ad me mittas. Vale Vir Sapientissime,

1646.

Translation of Letter 44

Samuel Sorbière to the most noble and wise Mr Thomas Hobbes.

I am sorry that Elsevier[1] has delayed the publication of your book for so long; but it has happened against his will, because while he was working on Regius' Physics,[2] he received some late[3] additions to the text from the author, which caused an extremely tiresome delay to that work. In fact his press is now hard at work on the table of contents,[4] and it is hoped that he will send me the first copy of the book within a fortnight. But here is that table of contents, which has just come into my hands, delivered by Elsevier himself, while I was writing this. So please make ready the part which you had drawn up in English,[5] so that you can send it to me when a favourable opportunity arises; and together with that, please urge M. Gassendi to send me his Physics.[6] Our printers here are longing for it; and they are far preferable to the ones at Lyon, if he wants either elegant or speedy printing.

But, most excellent Sir, now that you have been promoted to the service of the Prince,[7] will you have enough time left to keep your hand in with the work which needs to be done every day?[8] How worthy of you is that duty which has been laid upon you! How fortunate your country will be when it receives a King full of wisdom and imbued with your teachings! I am glad, and congratulate you with all my heart, whatever loss we may perhaps suffer through the delay to the promised part of your Elements. My real regret is only for the most noble M. de Martel on his return to Montauban,[9] who will be bitterly disappointed to an extraordinary degree at having you thus torn away from him. Indeed, one might hope that that most noble man might take up residence in Paris: can you, in your exalted position at Court, please think about how that could eventually be arranged? And while you are working on that, please also see if you can do anything for my friend du Prat,[10] the doctor from Lyon, a man of great strength of spirit in adversity. He is one of that small number of people who cultivate good sense; he is also known to M. Gassendi, who I think is extremely fond of him.

I am still struggling to get on, and am about to move to Leiden with my dear wife,[11] where my house will be open to welcome people interested in learned studies; so if you know any British noblemen who are going to visit the university there, please send them to me. Farewell, wisest Sir.

1646

This letter is dated Aug. 1646 by Tönnies, and the sequence proposed by Tönnies is followed by Warrender in *HW* ii. However, the enclosure of Elsevier's first printed sheet of *De cive* with this letter, and Sorbière's references to Hobbes's employment by Prince Charles, to his own plan to settle in Leiden, and to du Prat, clearly show that this is the letter which Hobbes received on or shortly before [24 Sept./] 4 Oct., when he wrote Letter 45.

¹ See Letter 41 n. 10.
² See Letter 41 n. 9.
³ 'subinde', translated here as 'late', could mean 'frequent', 'repeated'.
⁴ The 'Index Capitum' before ch. 1 of *De cive*.
⁵ See Letter 42 n. 12.
⁶ This refers to bks. 12–25 of Gassendi's MS philosophical project (most of which books survive in the Bibliothèque municipale, Tours, MSS 707, 709–10) (see Pintard, *La Mothe le Vayer*, pp. 42–3). Some of this material appeared in the *Animadversiones* (1649); nearly all of it was eventually printed as part 2, 'Physica', of the *Syntagma* (Gassendi, *Opera omnia*, i, pp. 125–752; ii, pp. 1–658).
⁷ Prince Charles, who had arrived in Paris in July 1646.
⁸ Literally, 'to draw the daily line': an allusion to the proverb 'no day without its line' ('nulla dies sine linea'), which Pliny explains as follows: 'it was the constant practice of Apelles [the Greek artist] never to spend any day, however busy, without practising his art by drawing a line' ('Apelli fuit alioque perpetua consuetudo, numquam tam occupatam diem agendi, ut non, lineam ducendo, exerceret artem' (*Historia naturalis*, 35. 10. 36, sect. 84)).
⁹ See Letter 40 n. 3.
¹⁰ Abraham du Prat; 'nostro' is Sorbière's use of first person plural for first person singular.
¹¹ Sorbière had married Judith Renaud on [14/] 24 June 1646.

LETTER 45   [24 SEPTEMBER/] 4 OCTOBER 1646

Hobbes to Samuel Sorbière, from Saint-Germain

BN MS f.l. 10352, part 2, fos. 84ᵛ–85ʳ (transcript).
Printed in Tönnies, 'Siebzehn Briefe', pp. 193–4; Robertson, 'Some Letters', pp. 442–3; *MC* xiv, p. 504 (extract); translated in *HW* ii, pp. 305–6.

Thomas Hobbius, Samueli Sorberio suo s.

  Clarissime Charissimeque Sorberi, cum a te ad Martellum nostrum diu nullae literae venissent, cogitabam mecum modo Typographum resipuisse, Modò folium aliquod libri¹ vel annotationum interijsse. Nam de valetudine tua et tuorum nolui; de conatu tuo non potui dubitare. Sed quidquid erat impedimenti cùm nescire molestè ferrem, Rogaui D. Martellum vt de ea re ad te scriberet. Id quod nunc factum nollem. Accepta enim Epistolâ tuâ,² tantas tibi gratias debere me sentio, vt querelarum praeniteat et pudeat, si tamen ille quicquam questus est, nam rogaui vt quaereret, non vt quaereretur.

Literas tuas ad D. Gassendum, et P. Mersennum (vnâ cum Epigrammate D.[i] Bruno[3]) illis curaui tradendas.

Quod attinet ad folium impressum quod misisti, valde mihi placet et character literarum, et volumen, neque erratum typorum, quod alicujus sit momenti, vllum reperio, praeter vnum (sed magnum) pag. 14. l. 2. vbi pro *Duritas*, ponitur *Claritas*.[4] Dixi conclusionis *duritatem* prae-missarum memoriam expellere: id quod verum est. Contra fuisset si dixissem *Claritatem*. duae illae voces scripturam habent ferè similem; propter quam causam, et quia forte putabat typorum compositor vocem hanc *Duritas* non esse Latinam, (nam saepius dicitur Durities) factum est, vt pro Claritate accepta sit. Vox Duritas latina est et Ciceroniana cum sermo sit de dictis duris, quamquam de corporibus duris, *Durities* potius vsurpetur. Quod scribis te sedem Lugduni (Leydae) fixurum, vehementer gaudeo, cum tui causa qui conuersabere cum doctissimis viris, tum mei, qui amicis meis illic euntibus quo gratum facere possum tua ope habiturus sum. Scripsi nuperrimè (ante tamen quam acciperem literas tuas) Londinum, ad Comitem Deuoniae patronum meum, cui filius est Sexe[nnis][5] et vnicus, ad quem instituendum opus est viro, ex tua, Gassendi Martelli commendationes cognoui esse D. Du Prat.[6] Si ille conditionem merito ejus conuenientem proposuerit, enitar quantum possum, vtriusque causa, vt se Lugduno Londinum trans-ferat.

Quod mihi de praesente loco[7] gratulatus sis, agnosco beneuolentiam tuam. Sed caue ne eam rem majoris putes esse quam est. Doceo enim Mathematicam, non Politicam. Nam praeceptis Politicis quae habentur in libro qui imprimitur, imbui illum, ipsius aetas nondum sinit, et judicia eorum quorum consilijs aequum est regi illum, semper prohibebunt. Si quid ego diuturno officio gratiae apud eum collegero, scias me ea vsurum omni, non tam ad meas quam ad amicorum meorum commoditates, et ad tuorum quoque, si aliquos commen-daueris. Sed multum sperare neque humilitas mea neque aetas patitur. Vale Charissime Sorberi et ama

Tuum
Th. Hobbes.

Dab. S. Ger. Octob. 4. 1646.

Translation of Letter 45

Thomas Hobbes to his friend Samuel Sorbière, greetings.

Most distinguished and dearest Sorbière,

Since our friend de Martel has not received any letters from you for a long time, I have been wondering whether the printer has changed his mind, or whether some sheet of the book[1] or the notes has been lost. For I did not want to entertain doubts about your own health or your family's; and I could not doubt your application to the task. But since I was troubled by not knowing what the problem was, I asked M. de Martel to write to you about it. And now I wish I had not done so. Having received your letter[2] I feel so obliged to you that it puts my complaints in a poor light and makes me ashamed for them—assuming that he did complain; for I asked him to enquire, not to complain.

I have made sure that your letters to M. Gassendi and Father Mersenne (together with a short poem by M. Bruno[3]) are delivered to them.

As for the printed sheet which you sent me, I very much like the style of the type-face and the size of the print. I have not found any misprints of any importance except for one (which is however a major one): on p. 14, line 2 'Claritas' is printed instead of 'Duritas'.[4] I said the *difficulty* of a conclusion makes us forget the premisses, which is true. It would be the opposite of the truth if I said the *clarity*. The two words are written rather similarly; and because of that, and perhaps because the compositor thought this word 'duritas' was not a Latin word ('durities' being the more common form), it came about that it was read as 'claritas'. 'Duritas' is not only Latin but Ciceronian, where hard or difficult statements are concerned, although 'durities' is preferred in the case of hard objects.

I am thoroughly delighted by your news that you are going to stay in Leiden—both for your sake, because you will be able to converse with extremely learned men, and for my own, because by your help I shall be able to do a favour to all those of my friends who go there. I have just sent a letter (before I received your letter, however) to London, to my patron the Earl of Devonshire; he requires a tutor for his only son, who is 6 years old.[5] I know about M. du Prat[6] from the recommendations of Gassendi, de Martel, and yourself. If the Earl proposes terms suitable to his merits, I shall try hard, for both their sakes, to help him move from Lyon to London.

I acknowledge your goodwill in congratulating me on my present employment;[7] but beware of thinking it more important than it is. For I am only teaching mathematics, not politics. I would not be able to teach him the political doctrines contained in the book which is being printed, both because he is too young, and because my doing so will always be forbidden by those whose counsels, justly, govern him. If I earn any favour with him for my daily services, I shall use it all, I assure you, not so much for my own benefit as for that of my friends—and of your friends too, if you recommend any to me. But neither my humility nor his age will allow me to hope for very much. Farewell, dearest Sorbière, and think fondly of

Your
Thomas Hobbes

Saint-Germain, 4 October 1646

Words presented in italics here are over-lined in the MS.

[1] *De cive* (see Letters 40–2, 44).

[2] Letter 44 (see the general note there).

[3] See Letter 43 n. 2. This short poem was either the one referred to there, or else (more probably) another poem celebrating the portraits of Mersenne and Gassendi which Sorbière had also procured from de Martel (see Letter 38).

[4] *De cive*, I. 10, annotation (*HW* ii, p. 95 n. 5). The 2nd edn. was issued with this error uncorrected in the text, but listed in the errata (*HW* ii, p. 88).

[5] The copyist left a long gap, and wrote 'Sexe' in the middle of it. Tönnies conjectures 'Sexe annorum'. Evidently the original was very hard to read: when Sorbière himself quoted this sentence in a letter to Abraham du Prat he wrote merely 'filius est vnicus' (BN MS f.l. 10352, part 1, fos. 95ᵛ–96ʳ). The third Earl of Devonshire's eldest son, William Cavendish, future fourth Earl and first Duke, was born on 25 Jan. [/4 Feb.] 1640.

[6] Abraham du Prat: cf. Sorbière's request to Hobbes in Letter 44.

[7] As mathematics tutor to Prince Charles.

LETTER 46   [12/] 22 OCTOBER 1646

Hobbes to Samuel Sorbière, from Saint-Germain

BN MS f.l. 10352, part 2, fos. 85ᵛ–86ʳ (transcript).
Printed in Tönnies, 'Siebzehn Briefe', pp. 195–6; Robertson, 'Some Letters', pp. 443–4; *MC* xiv, p. 558 (extract); translated in *HW* ii, pp. 305–6.

Amice Charissime, accepi jam duas a te Epistolas in quarum priore,[1] quam acceperam ante dies circiter viginti, folium primum incluseras, atque etiam duas Epistolas alteram ad R. P. Mersennum, alteram ad.

D. Gassendum, quas ambas illis dari curaui diligenter; et statim rescripsi; In posteriore[2] accipio nunc tria simul folia prima, cum Literis ad D D. Martellum et Prataeum quas ad eos jam transmittam. In superiore mea Epistola notaui Erratum Typorum vnum pag. 14. l. 2. nempe *Claritas* pro *Duritas*.[3] In secundo folio noto jam duo alia magni momenti; quaeque sententiam corrumpunt, pag. 48. lineis. 19. et 23. nimirum vox *quaerere* lin. 19. & vox *Ergo* linea 23. quae ambae delendae sunt,[4] nam illis stantibus sensus nullus est, deletis optimus est. Nescio quomodo voces illae irrepserint. aut, quia periodus longa non satis a typorum compositore comprehendebatur, illi visum est sic emendare, aut ego relegendo illum locum ita putaui locum emendandum esse, cùm non esset opus, nam in exemplari impresso Parisijs[5] illae voces non sunt. Video periculum magnum esse ne in alijs quoque locis similiter erretur, cùm neque mea scriptura satis distincta sit, neque ego neque tu praesentes simus; sin accidat vt reliquum libri sine magnis mendis impressum fuerit, non grauabor meis impensis paginam illam 48 cum adhaerentibus, denuò imprimere. Alioqui colligenda sunt errata, et ante initium libri, in conspectum danda sunt vt ab ipsis lectoribus corrigi possint. Expecto jam vt Physica Regij[6] parisijs venalis fiat; Et si enim de spe mea, verba illa (copie de celuy de Mr des Cartes)[7] aliquantum detriuerint, cupio tamen videre quid sit cujus [causa][8] librum illum tanta fama antecessit. Agam quantum potero cum D. Gassendo vt quicquid imprimendum habet vobis transmittat, sed agam cum fuero Parisijs, id est, vt opinor circa medium Nouembrem, quamquam si in ea re tuis literis non moueatur, minus mouebitur sermone meo. Nil aliud occurrit quod scribam, nisi vt gratias agam tantis officijs, tantaque beneuolentia dignas; quod est omnino impossibile; crede tamen animum mihi esse gratissimum amantissimum tui, etsi non sum ita blandus, vt ad millesimam partem blanditiarum quae sunt in Epistolae tuae fine attingere possim. Jamais homme ne receut si grand compliment que vous m'aues fait; mais je ne le [recoy?][9] point, neantmoins je vous en remercie. Vale.

Tuus
Thom. Hobbes.

St Germ. Oct. 22. 1646.

Translation of Letter 46

Dearest friend,

I have already received two letters from you. In the first,[1] which arrived roughly twenty days ago, you enclosed the first printed sheet, together with two letters, one for the Revd Father Mersenne, the other for M. Gassendi. I took great care to deliver both letters to them, and I replied to you immediately. Now in your second letter[2] I have received the first three sheets, together with letters to MM. de Martel and du Prat, which I shall immediately send on to them. In my previous letter I recorded one misprint, on p. 14, line 2, which was 'Claritas' ['clarity'] instead of 'Duritas' ['hardness'].[3] I have now observed two other misprints (both very important ones, corrupting the meaning of the text), on the second sheet: p. 48, lines 19 and 23. The words 'quaerere' ['to enquire'] (line 19) and 'Ergo' ['therefore'] (line 23) should both be deleted;[4] so long as they remain, the passage makes no sense, but if they are deleted it makes excellent sense. I do not know how those words crept in: either the compositor saw fit to correct the passage because he had not adequately understood that long sentence; or else I thought it should be corrected when I was rereading the passage, when in fact it did not need to be corrected (for the Paris edition[5] does not contain those words). I see there is a great danger that he will make similar mistakes in other passages, both because my writing is not clear enough, and because neither of us is there with him. If it so happens that the rest of the book is printed without any major corrections needing to be made, I shall not mind paying to have that page 48, together with the rest of its sheet, reprinted. Otherwise a list of errata should be made and inserted before the beginning of the book, so that they can be corrected by the readers themselves.

I am now waiting for Regius' Physics[6] to go on sale in Paris. Although my hopes have been somewhat diminished by those words 'a copy of that of M. Descartes',[7] I am still keen to see why[8] that book has enjoyed such a high reputation in advance.

I shall do my best to persuade M. Gassendi to send you anything of his which is ready for the press; but I shall do this when I am in Paris, that is, I think, in about mid-November. However, if your letter fails to persuade him, my talking is even less likely to succeed.

There has not been anything else for me to write about, except to give you my thanks for helping me so much, thanks which must be worthy of such great kindness—which is quite impossible. Nevertheless, be assured that I am immensely grateful to you and fond of you, even if I am not polished enough to manage one-thousandth of the compliments which I find at the end of your letter. No one has ever been paid such a great compliment as that which you have paid me; I cannot accept[9] it, but nevertheless I thank you for it. Farewell

Your
Thomas Hobbes

Saint-Germain, 22 October 1646

Words presented in italics here are over-lined in the MS.

[1] Letter 44.
[2] This letter apparently does not survive.
[3] See Letter 45 n. 4.
[4] *De cive*, III. 11 (*HW* ii, p. 113 nn. 1, 3). The 2nd edn. was issued with these errors uncorrected in the text but listed in the errata (*HW* ii, p. 88).
[5] The 1st edn. (Paris, 1642).
[6] See Letter 41 n. 9.
[7] The words quoted here do not appear on the title-page, but may perhaps derive from a bookseller's advertisement.
[8] tanta *MS*. This emendation is adopted from Tönnies.
[9] *Uncertain reading: perhaps* reccoy.

LETTER 47   [21/] 31 OCTOBER 1646

Samuel Sorbière to Hobbes, from Leiden

BN MS f.l. 10352, part 1, fos. 93ᵛ–94ʳ (transcript).
Printed in Tönnies, 'Siebzehn Briefe', pp. 194–5 (extract); translated in *HW* ii, p. 306 (extract).

Clarissimo Viro D.D. Hobbio Samuel Sorberius.
     Heri tuas accepi 4ᵒ. Octobris datas[1] juxta quas curabo vt in Indice Erratorum Typographi nisi aliter fieri possit, emendetur illa pagina 14. duritas.[2] Gaudeo autem tibi Editionis formam & characterem literarum probari. Habes hîc iterum specimina, quae plura non mittam nisi ita significes gratum, donec librum integrum, sed aliâ viâ commodiori transmittam. Bruno carmina in librum tuum dedit, atque in Iconem tuam,[3] quam aere incidi curassem si formam in 4ᵒ. Typographus retinuisset.[4] Addetur ea caeteris Operibus tuis quae auidè expeto & expecto. Vtinam D. Gassendus suarum partem tradat, quibus nullum

jam a Morinis[5] periculum. Ad Prataeum[6] scribo, quem breui puto Lutetiam venturum; fortasse Gassiono Medicus Castrensis futurus;[7] suadeo tamen vt consilio tuo vtatur circa eligenda vitae sorte. Nisi fata aliò me traxissent, stationem, domo illustrissimi Comitis[8] commodiorem non optarem. De incomparabili Martello nostro dudum nihil audio, & vbinam sit, quid rerum agat scire aueo. Tu Vale et me amare perseuera;

Lugduni Batauorum pridie Kal. Nouemb. 1646.

Translation of Letter 47

From Samuel Sorbière to the very distinguished and most learned Mr Hobbes.

Yesterday I received your letter of 4 October,[1] and in accordance with its instructions I shall take care that that word 'duritas' ['hardness'] on p. 14 is corrected in the list of errata,[2] unless it can otherwise be changed. But I am glad that you like the size and style of the type-face. Here is another set of proofs; I shall not send any more (unless you say you would like me to) until I can send you the entire book by some other, more convenient method. Bruno has contributed poems on the subject of your book and your portrait.[3] I would have had the portrait engraved in copper if the printer had retained the quarto format:[4] let it be added to your other works, which I avidly long for and await. I wish M. Gassendi would deliver some part of his works, which cannot be threatened now in any way by people like Morin.[5] I shall write to du Prat,[6] who I think will be in Paris soon. He may perhaps become military physician to the Marshal de Gassion;[7] but I am advising him to take your advice on what career he should choose. Had fate not decreed otherwise, I myself could not hope to find any more pleasant position than one in the household of that most illustrious Earl.[8] I have heard nothing about our friend the incomparable M. de Martel for a long time, and am avid to know where he is and what he is doing. Farewell, Sir, and continue to love me.

Leiden, 31 October 1646.

[1] Letter 45.

[2] See ibid., n. 4.

[3] Probably the second and third of the three poems printed in the prefatory material to the 2nd edn. of *De cive* (*HW* ii, pp. 71–2); cf. Letter 43 n. 2.

[4] See Letter 43 n. 2. The first edition of *De cive* was quarto, the second duodecimo.

⁵ Jean-Baptiste Morin (1583–1656), mathematician and astrologer, Professor of Mathematics at the Collège de France from 1630, and author of a polemical criticism of Gassendi, *Alae telluris fractae* (1643). A reply to this, written in 1643 by Gassendi but not intended for publication, circulated among Gassendi's friends and was eventually published as *Apologia* in 1649 (see Sortais, *La Philosophie moderne*, ii, pp. 169–70). For Morin's subsequent dispute with Gassendi (and/or his pupil Bernier) see the Biographical Register, 'Gassendi'.

⁶ Abraham du Prat.

⁷ Jean de Gassion (1609–47), prominent Huguenot and lieutenant-general of the French army in Flanders under the duc d'Orléans. Abraham du Prat's brother Pierre was already employed as chaplain to de Gassion (Pintard, *Libertinage*, p. 333); Pierre later published a laudatory work, *Le Portrait du mareschal de Gassion* (1664), and prepared a biography of de Gassion in 1666 (BL MS Harl. 1589).

⁸ William Cavendish, third Earl of Devonshire (see Letter 45 n. 5).

LETTER 48   [1/] 11 NOVEMBER 1646

Hobbes to Samuel Sorbière, from Paris

BN MS f.l. 10352, part 2, fo. 87ᵛ (transcript).

Printed in Tönnies, 'Siebzehn Briefe', p. 196; Robertson, 'Some Letters', p. 444; *MC* xiv, p. 603 (extract); translated in *HW* ii, pp. 307–8.

Thomas Hobbius Samueli Sorberio S.

Domine Charissime, amicissime, Accepi heri literas tuas datas prid. Kal. Nov.¹ atque vna duo folia, in quibus [corrigendum]² est nullum praeterquam quae ipse in margine [correxisti]³ leuia, consentio tibi, ne alia mittas, donec totus liber impressus sit. De icone incisâ gratias tibi ago, et ne libro praeponatur facile patior.⁴ Epistolam tuam ad Prataeum⁵ ferendam cras dabo. Martellus noster Montalboni⁶ est, scripsit inde ad me semel, exierat Parisijs circa finem septembris, do ad eum literas hodie in quibus id quod de illo ad me scripseras refero. D.º Gassendo salutem tuo nomine dixi hodie. in morbum a quo paulo ante conualuerat, rursus ceciderat, nunc autem rursus conualescit. Conueniendi Mersennum et salutem tuam ei impertiendi, mihi S.ᵗ Germanum repetenti tempus non est. Faciam proximo tempore. ab initio Decembris vsque ad Festum Paschalis futuri sumus Parisijs, illic si Prataeum tuum conuenire potero, amicitiam cum eo facere conabor; cura vt valeas.

Tui amantissimus
Thom. Hobbes.

Parisijs die 11.º Nouemb. 1646.

Translation of Letter 48

Thomas Hobbes to Samuel Sorbière, greetings.

Dearest and most loving friend, I have received your letter dated 31 October,[1] together with two printed sheets, in which there is nothing that needs to be corrected[(2)] except those minor things which you have corrected[(3)] in the margin. I agree that you should not send any other sheets until the whole book has been printed. I am grateful to you for what you say about the engraved portrait, and I really shall not mind if it is not put at the beginning of the book.[4] I shall send off your letter for du Prat[5] tomorrow. Our friend de Martel is at Montauban;[6] he has written to me once from there, saying that he had left Paris at about the end of September. I am sending him a letter today, in which I refer to what you wrote to me about. I gave M. Gassendi your greetings today. Having just recovered from his fever he then had a relapse, but he is now recovering again. Since I have to go back to Saint-Germain now, I do not have time to visit Mersenne and give him your greetings. I shall do it next time. We shall be in Paris from the beginning of December until Easter; if I can meet your friend du Prat there, I shall try to make friends with him. Be sure to keep well.

Your most loving
Thomas Hobbes

Paris, 11 November 1646

Warrender mis-dates this letter '2 Nov.'

[1] Non. *MS* (Letter 47).
[2] The copyist has left a gap for this word.
[3] corexisti *MS*.
[4] The translation is deliberately expansive here; Hobbes means that he is grateful to Sorbière for expressing a willingness to have an engraving made (see Letter 47). He cannot be thanking Sorbière for sending a copy of the engraving which was printed in the 2nd edn. of *De cive*; Letter 52 makes it clear that he saw this engraving for the first time in Mar. 1647.
[5] Abraham du Prat.
[6] See Letter 40 n. 3.

Adrian May to Hobbes

BL MS Harl. 6016, fos. 126ᵛ–128ʳ (transcript).

Mʳ Adrian Mayes letter to Mʳ Hobbes

Sʳ,

   Vpon some occasion much like this, you were pleased to desire of me
by way of Obseruation, what [>is] *Sense*, not taking yᵉ seuerall fiue
Organs, but seeking further, making them, but the Instruments of it; to
all wᶜʰ I submitt, euen to this also of giuing my opinion here, wherein
yo.ʳ owne knowledge is most excellent. They, like yo.ʳ selfe, that are
deepely learn'd, oft aduantagiously iette out¹ vpon the foundation by
enforcing consequence, as the whole trueth by any part be inferred by a
longe circuyte of deduction: yea my meere coniecture hath often had
successe, & reward in my desires to attende yᵉ Prince,² when his
Highnesse voluntary choyce in their equall pleasantnesse, hath
preferred one walke in S.ᵗ Germans before another. If all coniecture
proue friuolous, then Nature hath giuen us a vayne guift, & morality
uselesse precepts about it, which will proue a bold censure, when by
this surmising faculty Naturall man ascertayneth the true God, whom
afterwards he cannot conceiue without diuine reuelation. But in better
complyance wᵗʰ yo.ʳ directions, Obseruation shall bee my building, an
edifice immediately raysed on matter of fact: & in deede I like this
proceeding the better, because it is inferred, yᵗ all worldly thinges are
thereto lyable, where tis sayde, that yᵉ Kingdome of Heauen is not to be
had by Obseruation: 'tis true, some reasons of nature are not yet
founde, but 'tis [>because] man may be out of distance, or his
obseruation wanteth strictnesse, as a childes comparatiuely wᵗʰ his, or
his with his owne in yᵉ progresse of his life.

   These seuerall parts, we use, are but instruments, were they Senses,
they would be perfect of themselues, & yᵉ dismembred hande would
feele; but it being not soe, they are but Organs, though wᵗʰout them yᵉ
seuerall Senses are [>not] to be had. 'Tis requisite in the body, there
be a temperate complexion betwixte heate, & colde, least the Channells
be suffocated, or obstructed by excesse of either, & a supplenesse
betwixt hard, & soft must goe alonge with it; for if either of these be
oppressiue in the Organs, yᵉ Sense is destroyed, though the hande,

eyes, Eares, & ye rest of them remayne, as wee commonly see, & attribute the losse of them to cold, & ye like; in default whereof stones are depriued of Sense; for though they admitt heate, cold, & a mollification,³ yet 'tis casuall, not constantly, conteyning these qualityes in a temperature, as Nature usually contriueth itt for this Sensitiue purpose, who is ye best Judge. Besides ye Obiect may be stronge, soe that after a while, wee can neither see, feele, nor heare, & euen when ye Obiect is competent, it must not be [contended *altered to* contested] with, for that may be fixt, & sense is of a reposing Nature, & soe giues ouer of itt selfe. Also a through⁴ tranquillity, & a stande in man is materiall, as longe, as it can be helde; for once earnestly thinking of one passage in this discourse, I founde an aptnesse in my selfe to hold euen my breath. Beyond this there must be life, from whence commeth inward motion a maine p[ar]^t5 of *Sense*; notwithstanding Trees haue it not by reason of their outward cold, & grosse composition, wch disableth them, yett if I might say it w^thout standing to it, I would offer to you, y^t Trees haue vnactuall *Sense* in them, but constreyned by their constitution, wch may as well be argued, as y^t life is not Act, when the puissance thereof lyeth in the Seede. When the bones are iniured by some kinde of violence, & the fell'd body layde in the Shade, sensible Creatures are produced by ye operation, & influence of ye Sun, yet it worketh not soe on Stones, though prepared before by the like violence, & iniury. And *Sense* may be founde lurking soe euen in Creatures, that haue itt. who hath not seene diuerse men by nature, or accident depriued of one, or more *Senses*? yett in being; & I am inclinable, to beleaue itt possible, y^t a man may want them all, & yett liue; can I say, *Sense* is not then in him, because obstructed wth heate, or cold excessiue, more then I can say it, when but one, or more of the fiue are wanting? But I'le waue this speculatiue opinion of mine, nor will I trouble you wth y^e *Sensitiue* vitall motion in a Horse-hayre in water,⁶ or wth that shrinking Plant in touch,⁷ boeth soe generally receaued, but mainely sticke to my enioyned Obseruation. These proportions concurring auayle nothing after all this; for I fynde yett noe discernement of *Sense* without attention; & therefore I beleaue, feeling lyeth in the Mynde, wch I take to be a sprightly Substance pure, & cleare, seated in ye Nobler parts of the body more agreeable to it's temperature, euer in readynesse ably to passe, & returne in an instant to, & from ye outermost of ye Organs wth such speedynesse, that I haue it in admiration. When the body dyeth, ye mynde, & Sense departeth togeather, & when it sleepeth soundly, which cannot be taken for slumbering, ye Mynde in ye waking

Body kindely moueth first, as naturally it is, when ye Body hath noe disturbance, nor any Obiect to moue *Sense*; & when ye Body is in any way prouok'd, all's but haring,[8] till the due tyme of the Mynde. I am sure, ye Mynde can be soe cloyster'd vp by Art, that a lymbe may be cutt off without *Sense*, till ye Mynde be enlarg'd agayne; & ye awaking Body may be runne through without feeling it for the present, if ye mynde be employ'd, as many men haue bin wounded without feeling ye stroake. If ye Mynde to an Extasy be strongly fixt on a choyce, & inuiting Obiect, I am persuaded a man may endure the Racke.

But to proceede more playnely, & familiarly, & on Touch, which agreeth at large with all the other *Senses*: my Cloathes are on me all ouer, yet I feele them not, till I mynde them, & when I doe, 'tis part after part; & all the while I writt this same, I felt ye penne no more, then it felt mee, till I thought on it. And in Madnesse, which is ye Mynde distracted, there is noe *Sense*, almost noe more, then in a Sober diuerted, who cannot say, he hath sensibly heard ye braying of euery *Asse*, as loude, & offensiue, as it is: or the Musique in its continuance, how pleasant, or Harmonious soe ere it bee. The fingers are most generally employed in feeling, sett the two foremost to feele exactly each other in an instant, & see the confusion, but to make a discernement, ye Mynde will side, & giue ye motion: putt them togeather as gently, as may be, yett *Sense* will be first on one side, & impartially [move *deleted* > force] ye motion on boeth sides, still y^e *Sense* will be of one; 'tis true, ye passage will be most quicke, yett ye chaunge may be perceaued. Had I not promised you ordinary matter, which insisteth grossely, & for prosecution of nicety to be noe Opiniatour, I would auerre the Sensible inward motion, when ye mynde passeth from one finger to another; hereof lett euery man aduise wth his owne heart, when 'tis strucke wth any stronge Passion. But to come into my low path agayne; when ye Witts are a wooll-gathering, I pray, where are y^e *Senses*? Soe that in my Oberuation, by ye Mynde is ye discernement of *Sense* in a body well disposed; & *Sense* is not there to be founde, when ye body is dead, or ye Mynde distracted with madnesse, or naturally reposed, or being att large will not attende, or is diuerted, or when ye body is sounde asleepe. And actuall Sense is in all ye Bodyes, y^t haue a Mynde, & is in none without it, where else I cannot better place itt in any other part of man hitherto mentioned by man: *Soe that the mynde heeding the Obiect discerneth it's qualityes by, & through the healthfull organs*, wch I your humble Seruant define to be *Sense*.

Adrian May

This letter is dated by reference to May's remark about attending Prince Charles at Saint-Germain; the Prince was there from July 1646 to June 1648.

Hobbes touches on some of the questions raised in this letter in *De corpore*, XXV, 'Of Sense and Animal Motion', especially in sects. 5–6, where he discusses the claim that all bodies are endued with sense, arguing that sense requires change and motion in its objects (so that someone who saw only one stationary object 'would seem to me, whatsoever others may say, to see, no more then I seem to myself to feel the Bones of my own Limbs by my Organs of Feeling'), and also arguing that the strongest sensation-causing motion will always predominate over others ('And hence it is, that an earnest studying of one Object, takes away the Sense of all other Objects for the present'). We know that Hobbes had reached ch. XIII of *De corpore* by April or May 1645 (see Pacchi, *Convenzione e ipotesi*, pp. 22–7); on [22 May/] 1 June 1646 Hobbes told Sorbière that he was proceeding slowly with it (see Letter 42); and on [23 July/] 2 Aug. 1648 Sir Charles Cavendish wrote to John Pell that Hobbes had taken up work on *De corpore* again (BL MS Add. 4278, fo. 273ʳ). It seems likely, therefore, that Hobbes had asked May for his opinion when he was preparing to write ch. XXV.

However, in the prose 'Vita' Hobbes describes a preoccupation with the problem of sensation which went back to his earliest awakening of interest in the natural sciences: 'By his nature, and from his earliest years, he was drawn to reading historians and poets [. . .]. But later, at a meeting of learned men, when mention was made of the cause of sensation, somebody asked "What is sense?", and he did not hear any reply; he wondered how it could come about that people who, on account of their alleged wisdom, so scornfully despised other men, should yet have no knowledge of the nature of their own senses. From that time on he thought frequently about the cause of sensation; and by good fortune it occurred to him that if all physical things and their parts were at rest together, or were always moved in a similar motion, the distinctions between all things would be removed, and so, consequently, would all sensation. So that therefore *the cause of all things was to be sought in the differences between their motions*' ('Naturâ suâ, & primis annis, ferebatur ad lectionem Historiarum & Poetarum [. . .]. Postea autem cum in congressu quodam virorum doctorum, mentione facta de causa sensionis, quaerentem unum quasi per contemptum *Quid esset sensus*, nec quemquam audisset respondentem, mirabatur, qui fieri potuerit, ut qui Sapientiae Titulo homines caeteros tanto fastu despicerent, suos ipsorum Sensus, quid essent, ignorarent. Ex eo tempore de causa Sentiendi saepe cogitanti, forte fortunâ mentem subiit, quòd si res corporeae & earum partes omnes conquiescerent, aut motu simili semper moverentur, sublatum iri rerum omnium discrimen, & (per consequens) omnem Sensionem; & propterea *Causam omnium rerum quaerendam esse in diversitate Motuum*' (*Thomae Hobbes angli vita*, pp. 18–19: *OL* i, pp. xx–xxi)).

Words presented in italics here are written in a larger script in the MS.

¹ = jet out, to build out or build upwards (*OED* jet *v.*² I.2, citing an example from 1632: 'John Gryffin hath Jetted out his chamber Windowes over the Lords Wast').

² Prince Charles.

³ = softening.

⁴ = thorough.

⁵ Contraction expanded.

⁶ This popular belief was rebutted by Martin Lister in the *Philosophical Transactions*, 7/83 (20 May 1672), pp. 4064–6, in a communication which began: 'It hath been credibly

reported, that *Horse hairs* thrown into water will be animated; and yet I shall shew you by an unquestionable observation, that such things as are vulgarly thought animated Hairs are very Insects.' Lister identified the 'insects' as a type of worm or larva called *Seta aquatica*.

⁷ The shrub *Mimosa pudica*, of which the leaves fold together when touched.

⁸ = scaring or startling (*OED* hare *v.*2, citing an example from 1659: 'Who ... so staggered and hared him, that he could not make one word of answer').

LETTER 50   [18/] 28 FEBRUARY 1647

Hobbes to Samuel Sorbière, from Paris

BN MS f.l. 10352, part 2, fos. 88ᵛ–89ʳ (transcript).
Printed in Tönnies, 'Siebzehn Briefe', p. 197; Robertson, 'Some Letters', p. 444; *MC* xv, p. 115 (extract); translated in *HW* ii, pp. 308–9.

Samueli Sorberio suo Th. Hobbius s.

Mi Sorberi dilectissime, quo diutiùs jam quàm meum desiderium atque amicitia tua [requirebant]¹ scribendi ad te officium praeter-miserim, causa est tua Epistola vltima,² quâ admonebar ne librum meum amplius foliatim expectarem sed totum simul viâ aliquâ quae videretur tibi commodissima. Illud igitur de hebdomade in heb-domadem expectans nolui crebris literis videri flagitare quod sciebam te quamprimum fieri posset sponte facturum. Nunc cum tres menses elapsi sunt & quo impressio libelli tantuli finiri poterat, cùmque amicus tuus D[ominu]s³ Musart,⁴ operam suam in mittendis ad te his literis vltro mihi obtulit, praetereunda commoditas ea non videbatur. Itaque te oro, vt si quid impressioni oblatum impedimentum sit, certiorem me facias. tuorum denique erga me officiorum cumulo hoc addas vt rescribas, tum vt quando liber ille expectandus sit, tum quod me amare non desisti certo sciam. Mersennus at Gassendus te salutant beneque valent. Te bene valere et cupio & spero.

Tui amantissimus
Tho. Hobbes

Parisijs. Feb. 28 1647

[*postscript:*] Ad Martellum nostrum scripsi saepius. nihil rescribit neque vbi sit, neque an sit scio.

Translation of Letter 50

Thomas Hobbes to his friend Samuel Sorbière, greetings.

Dearest Sorbière, the reason why I have ignored my duty of writing to you for so long (longer than both my desire and your friendship required[(1)]) lies in your last letter.[2] In it, you warned me not to expect to receive any more of my book sheet by sheet, but rather to wait until I could receive it complete, by whatever means seemed most convenient to you. Accordingly, while I have spent week after week waiting for it, I have not wanted to appear to be goading you with frequent letters into doing something which I knew you would do of your own accord as soon as you could. But now, since three months have passed, by which time the printing of such a small book could easily have been completed, and since your friend M.[(3)] Musart[4] offered to lend me his help in sending you this letter, I thought I should not let the opportunity pass. So I beg you to let me know if any obstacle has arisen to the book being printed. Finally, to add to all the kind services you have done me, please send me a reply, so that I may be sure not only of when to expect the book, but also that you have not ceased to love me. Mersenne and Gassendi are well, and send you their greetings. I wish and hope that you are in good health.

Your most loving
Thomas Hobbes

Paris, 28 February 1647

[*postscript:*] I have written quite frequently to our friend de Martel. He does not reply. I do not know where he is, or whether he is alive.

---

[1] requirebat *MS*.

[2] Letter 47.

[3] Contraction expanded.

[4] Unidentified. Probably not Charles Musart (1582–1653), the Jesuit theologian and philosopher. M. Musart, described here as Sorbière's friend, is referred to elsewhere in Sorbière's correspondence as 'Mussardus', 'Mujssardus', and 'Monsr Muysart' (BN MS f.l. 10352, part 1, fos. 100^r, 95^v; MS f.fr. 3930, fo. 256^r): this suggests the Flemish name 'Muyssard'. Each time he is mentioned, it is as the bearer of letters, from Lyon to Leiden, from Geneva to The Hague, or from Leiden to The Hague; this suggests that he may have been a merchant.

[22 FEBRUARY/] 4 MARCH 1647

Samuel Sorbière to Hobbes, from Leiden

BN MS f.l. 10352, part 1, fo. 104ᵛ (transcript).
Printed in Tönnies, 'Siebzehn Briefe', p. 198; translated in *HW* ii, p. 309.

Viro Nobilissimo, Sapientissimóque D. Thomae Hobbio, Samuel Sorberius.

Mirum est, Vir Clarissime, te nullas a nobis dudum Epistolas, neque illud ipsum Exemplar libri tui accepisse,[1] quod compactum tradidi 29.° Januarij nostrati cuidam Lutetiâ transituro. Habeo penes me alia 20. Exemplaria incompacta, quae solutâ glacie Elzevirius Leidensis[2] sarcinis suis addet & ad te mittet per Petitum viduae Camusatae[3] generum. Ecce interea folium primum, titulum & effigies tuam, minùs bene tamen expressam continens. Brunonis nostri versus[4] desunt quos in alijs habebis. Caeterùm libri tui tam multa jam distracta sunt Exemplaria, vt Typographus reliqua opera tua summopere expetat; quae igitur adfecti habes, rogo te, mittas quamprimùm, Vale Vir Maxime, & nos ama semper,

Lugduni batauorum IV. Nonis Mart. 1647.

[*postscript:*] Si quid literarum ad nos perscribas dirige, quaeso, A la Haye chez M. Renaud[5] *in de* [*poorte*][6] *by graff Willem*.

Translation of Letter 51

Samuel Sorbière to the most noble and wise Mr Thomas Hobbes.

I am surprised, most distinguished Sir, that you have not received any letters from me yet, nor that copy of your book,[1] which, when it was bound, I gave on 29 January to a friend of ours who was about to travel to Paris. I have with me another twenty unbound copies, which the Leiden Elsevier[2] will add to his consignment and send to you, when the ice has melted, via M. Le Petit, the son-in-law of the widow Camusat.[3]

Here meanwhile is the first sheet, which contains the title-page and your portrait—albeit not so well printed. Our friend Bruno's verses[4] are missing here, but you will have them in the other copies. Otherwise, so many copies of your book have already been printed, that the printer is desperately longing for the rest of your works. So I beg you to send as soon as possible those which you have completed. Farewell, most excellent man, and love me always.

Leiden, 4 March 1647

[*postscript:*] If you write any letters to me, please send them to The Hague, care of M. Renaud,[5] at Count William's gate[(6)].

---

[1] *De cive*: Sorbière is replying to Hobbes's complaint in Letter 50.

[2] Probably Bonaventura Elsevier (d. 1652), who was in charge of the Leiden branch of the family business; or else his nephew and partner Abraham (d. 1652), who ran the printing there.

[3] Pierre Le Petit (*c*.1617–86), active as a printer and bookseller in the rue Saint-Jacques, Paris, 1642–86, and royal printer, 1647–86. In 1643 he married Denise Camusat, daughter of Jean Camusat, printer to the Académie française. Her mother, also Denise, continued the business after Jean Camusat's death, working in co-operation with Le Petit, who took over from her as printer to the Académie towards the end of 1647 (Lepreux, *Gallia typographica*, pp. 326–7). Le Petit had special connections with the Elseviers: Daniel Elsevier (Abraham's son) had spent two and a half years working with Le Petit in Paris in the early 1640s (Davies, *World of the Elseviers*, p. 83).

[4] See *HW* ii, pp. 71–2.

[5] Sorbière's father-in-law, Daniel Renaud, a Huguenot merchant resident in The Hague.

[6] *poote* MS.

LETTER 52   [12/] 22 MARCH 1647

Hobbes to Samuel Sorbière, from Paris

BN MS f.l. 10352, part 2, fo. 91 (transcript).
Printed in Tönnies, 'Siebzehn Briefe', pp. 199–200; Robertson, 'Some Letters', pp. 445–6; *MC* xv, pp. 142–3 (extract); translated in *HW* ii, pp. 310–12.

Eruditissimo Viro D. Samueli Sorberio Amico Sincero Suo, Thomas Hobbes.

Literas tuas, Vir Clarissime, datas Lugduni Batauorum 4º Nonas Martij[1] accepi traditas mihi à Mersenno vnâ cum primo folio in quo est imago mea.[2] Quam quidem certò scio a te optima in me voluntate Libro praefixam. Veruntamen ita se res habet, temporaque eiusmodi sunt, vt magno emptum vellem vt vel praefixa non esset, vel saltem Subscriptio illa *Serenissimo Principi Walliae à studiis praepositus*, sublata exculpta vel abcissa esset. Primò enim id quod est maximum qui hodie rerum Angliae potiuntur, causas omnes quibus Stirpum Regiam in inuidiam apud plurimos conijciant vndiquaque sedulò conquirunt, atque arripiunt. Cùm ergo viderint doctrinae Ciuili adeo ab opinionibus fere omnium hominum abhorrenti praeferri nomen ejus, jactabunt se inimici magnificè & etiam odiosè in eo quod quale Imperij jus expectat, arrogaturusque sibi sit jam nunc videtur praemonstrare. Quare quidquid inde mali eueniet, vel euenire posse praetendi poterit ab illis qui in Aula Principis omne peccatum meum interpretationibus & Scholijs suis inflammare parati sunt, id omne cum meo summo dedecore ineptiae, & vanae gloriae meae imputabitur. Secundò hoc titulo reditus meus in patriam si me quando redeundi voluntas ceperit praeclusus est; nec cur redire [>non] velim si liceat quomodocunque pacatâ Angliâ non video; non sum enim Praeceptor Principis Walliae, nec omnino Domesticus (quae causa tertia est quare nollem titulum illum subscribi) sed qualis quilibet eorum qui docent in mensem, itaque mentitum me esse liceat [dicere]³ prae ambitione, qui mihi malè volunt, sunt ij non pauci. Doleo ergo tot Exemplaria jam emissa, diuenditáque esse. Sed quia id corrigi non potest, demus, quaeso, operam vt ab ijs Exemplaribus quae apud Elzeuirios⁴ reliqua sunt Effigies vel Inscriptio, mallem vtraque quamprimùm tollatur, idque priusquam vlla in Angliam transmittantur. Hoc ab Elzeuirijs [>vel] prece vel pretio impetrandum est, pretio si videbitur Liber minoris venalem fore sublatâ imagine vel inscriptione, quod non credo, sed tamen pretio si necesse est. Agam interea hic cum Petito⁵ Bibliopola vt eam tollat ex suis si quae habuerit ([non]⁶ enim allati sunt 21. illi Libri quos scribis esse in sarcinis Elzeuirianis, neque venit ille cui tradideras librum compactum) & scribam ad Bibliopolam quemdam Londiniensem Amicum meum⁷ vt idem fieri curet si qua istic exemplaria venalia esse contigerit. D. Brunonis⁸ beneuolentiam gratissimè amplector, neque in votis quicquam magis habeo quàm vt officio meo officia ejus mereri possem; tamen hoc tempore nullos versus Libro praeponi volo quos non antè viderim, tum ne quod animo & ingenio factum est bono, temporibus fiat mihi non bonum, tum etiam ne auiditas gloriae illius in testimonium ducatur, tanquam etiam indebitum illum titulum cupiuerim Praeceptoris Principis. Non est in toto hoc negotio quod meâ culpâ admissum sit cui status rerum nostrarum minimè cognitus erat. Est quod à te corrigi possit, & propterea quod te oro, obsecróque, nimirum id quod dixi antè, vt quamprimùm hanc acceperis Epistolam Elzeuirum Lugdunensem conuenire velis, atque impetrare primum ab eo vt ex illis quae ipse habet Exemplaribus Effigiem tollat, deinde per eum vt frater ejus qui est Amstelodami idem faciat, vel si quo alio modo desiderium meum hac in re adimplere possis, vt id facere velis.⁹ Molesta est haec Epistola propter materiam, non faciam ergo vt molesta quoque sit prolixitate. Nihil addo nisi vt valeas, meque adhuc, ac nunc quùm maxime opus est, ames.

Tui amantissimus
Thomas Hobbes.

Parisijs 22. Martij 1647.

[*postscript:*] Mersennus & omnes amici nostri permagni dicunt interesse & mei & Principis Walliae vt inscriptio vel potiùs tota Effigies tollatur. Si vt fiat opus pecuniâ sit non nimis magnâ, soluam libenter. Iterumque Vale.

Translation of Letter 52

Thomas Hobbes to his true friend, the very learned Samuel Sorbière.

Most distinguished Sir, I have received from Mersenne your letter of 4 March from Leiden,¹ enclosing the first sheet, which contains my portrait.² I am sure you put this in at the beginning of my book with the best of intentions towards me. Nevertheless, the matter is such that, given the times we are in, I would willingly have paid a great deal for it not to have been put in, or at least for that inscription beneath it, 'Academic Tutor to His Serene Highness the Prince of Wales', to have been removed, erased, or cut out. For, in the first place, and most importantly, those who are at present in power in England are assiduously searching for and seizing upon any pretexts on which to stir up popular ill feeling against the royal family. So when they see his name set before a political theory which offends the opinions of almost everyone, his enemies will attack him in a haughty and hateful way, claiming that he is now revealing what sort of sovereignty he expects, and intends to demand. Then whatever ill consequences follow from that (or will be said to be capable of following from it, by those people at the Prince's Court who are ready to aggravate my every fault with their own interpretations and glosses), they will all be blamed on my carelessness and vanity, to my great dishonour.

Secondly, this title will prevent me from returning to my own country, if the desire to return ever comes over me—and I do not see why I should not wish to return, if it is permitted, when England has somehow or other been pacified. After all, I am not the Prince of Wales's tutor, nor any sort of servant of his—which is a third reason why I do not want that title to be inscribed there—but just like one of those teachers who are hired on a monthly basis. So my enemies will be able to say[3] that I lied out of ambition; and they are not few.

I am very sorry, therefore, that so many copies have already been issued and distributed for sale. But since that cannot be changed, please let us try hard to ensure that in the copies which are left with the Elseviers[4] either the portrait or the inscription (or preferably both) is taken out as soon as possible, before any of them are shipped to England. We must get the Elseviers to do this, either by pleading with them or by paying them. We shall have to pay them if they think the book will be less vendible without the portrait or the inscription; I do not think it will, but still we must pay them if necessary. Meanwhile I shall arrange here with the bookseller Le Petit[5] that he should remove it from his copies, if he gets any (for those twenty-one copies which you say are in the parcel from the Elseviers have not[6] arrived, nor has the man to whom you gave the bound copy). And I shall write to a certain London bookseller, who is a friend of mine,[7] asking him to ensure that the same thing is done there, if there happen to be any copies on sale there.

I accept with extreme gratitude the kindness of M. Bruno,[8] and my greatest prayer is that I might be able to become worthy of his kind service by doing him some service in return. However, at present I do not want any verses to be prefixed to my book which I have not seen in advance. Otherwise I fear that something done cleverly and with a good intention might, in present circumstances, turn into something damaging to me; and I fear that his eagerness for fame might be used as evidence to suggest that I wanted that undeserved title of tutor to the Prince.

Nothing in this whole business can be blamed on me; I hardly knew what was going on. There is something you can do to correct it, and so I beg and beseech you to do as I have said: as soon as you receive this letter go and see the Leiden Elsevier, and first of all make him remove the portrait from those copies which he has; then, through him, make his brother at Amsterdam do the same; or if you can carry out my wish in this matter in any other way, please do so.[9] This is a tiresome letter because of its contents; so I shall not make it tiresome because of its length as well. I shall only add that I hope you are well, and that I hope you still love me, now that I am in greatest need of your love.

Your most loving
Thomas Hobbes

Paris, 22 March 1647

[*postscript:*] Mersenne and all our friends say that it is of the utmost importance both to me and to the Prince of Wales that the inscription, or rather the whole portrait, should be removed. If not too great a sum of money is needed for this, I shall willingly pay. Farewell again.

---

[1] Letter 51
[2] For the engraving, which bears the inscription quoted by Hobbes below, see *HW* ii, pl. 4.
[3] dicere *omitted in MS. Tönnies emends* liceat *to* dicet.
[4] The Elseviers of Amsterdam and Leiden (see Letters 41 n. 10, and 51 n. 2, respectively).
[5] See Letter 51 n. 3.
[6] nam *MS.*
[7] Probably Andrew Crooke (see the Biographical Register, 'William Crooke').
[8] See Letter 43 n. 2.
[9] The portrait was in fact removed from many copies (see *HW* ii, p. 43 n.).

LETTER 53   [2/] 12 AUGUST 1647

Samuel Sorbière to Hobbes, from Leiden

BN MS f.l. 10352, part 1, fo. 111 (transcript).
Printed in Tönnies, 'Siebzehn Briefe', p. 203; translated in *HW* ii, p. 313.

Clarissimo Viro D. Thomae Hobbio, Samuel Sorberius.
   Haec ad te post quadrimestre silentium scribo, Vir Summe, ne me tui, vel potius officij mei oblitum putes. Nihil per id tempus literarum dedi, qui vereor ne multa vel intempestiua scriptione molestus fiam; at velim tamen aequi boníque consulas si ter, quaterve singulis annis testatum faciam quantum te semper colam, & vnà affectûs in me tui non imminuti symbolum aliquod efflagitem, rogitémque insuper quomodo valeas, quovsque opus illud tuum[1] perduxeris, quandonam vel totum vel partem missurus sis, quando nos beabit D. Gassendus Operum suorum Editione, quomodo charissimum Caput valeat vt nostri

meminerit: Quid de optimo Martello audiueris, & quae talia te vno certiorem faciente rescire[2] possum. His igitur vt nunc breui Responso satisfacias te summopere obsecro, Vir Summe, & vt me amare pergas. Vale.

Lugduni Batauorum 12.º Augusti 1647.

Translation of Letter 53

Samuel Sorbière to that most distinguished man, Mr Thomas Hobbes.

Most excellent Sir, I am writing this letter to you after a silence of four months, lest you think that I have forgotten you—or rather, forgotten my own duty. I have sent you no letters during that period because I have been afraid of bothering you with writing either too much, or at an inopportune moment; but I hope you will think it fair and agreeable if I write three or four times each year to confirm how much I shall always honour you. At the same time I should like to ask you for some sign that your kindly regard for me has not diminished; and also to enquire further about your health; about how much progress you have made on that work of yours;[1] about when you will send either part of it or the whole thing; about when M. Gassendi will bless us with an edition of his works; and about how that dearest fellow is, and whether he remembers us. I shall also be able to learn[(2)] what you may have heard of the excellent M. de Martel, and other news of that kind which someone may have told you. So now I utterly beseech you, most excellent Sir, to send a brief reply to these questions, and continue to love me. Farewell.

Leiden, 12 August 1647.

[1] See Letter 41 n. 6.

[2] Tönnies emends this to 'nescire'; 'rescire' should more properly be 'resciscere', but since Sorbière uses the verb 'rescire' elsewhere, this is clearly not a scribal error.

Samuel Sorbière to Hobbes, from Leiden

BN MS f.l. 10352, part 1, fo. 111ᵛ (transcript).
Printed in Tönnies, 'Siebzehn Briefe', p. 204 (extract); translated in *HW* ii, pp. 313–14 (extract).

Heri adfuit nobis Elzevirius[1] Typographus tuus, qui rogauit vt significarem tibi nulla superesse ampliùs libri tui[2] Exemplaria cùm tamen vndique centena ab ipso expetantur; itaque cogitare se de noua Editione adornanda, cui si quid inserendum, demendumue optares, posses mihi significare per Tabellarium, vel per amicam mittere occasionem; qua etiam vellem ego vtereris ad Partem aliam Operum tuorum, quam adfectam habebis tradendam, imò & ad ea quoque nobis procuranda quae D. Gassendus fidei & diligentiae nostrae[3] committere vellet. Vrge, quaeso, Virum illum amicissimum ne tamdiu expectatione Scriptorum ejus torqueamur. Non deerunt nobis noti & fidi Amici, qui ad nos profiscantur; vbi verò penes me erunt scripta illa, spondeo fore vt quàm breuissimo temporis spatio elegantissimè excudantur. An lucem adhuc viderit Liber de Vita Epicuri[4] planè ignoro, cujus quidem si copiam mihi faceres, pretium statim refunderem. Si quid de Martello acceperis, scire aueo, & responsum a te istis quamprimùm expecto, vt & superioribus meis ante octiduum datis.[5] Vale, Vir admirande, & nos ama, qui aeternùm te Numinis alicuius instar venerabimur.

Lugduni Batauorum 19.° Augusti 1647.

Translation of Letter 54

Your printer, Elsevier,[1] was at my house yesterday and asked me to tell you that there are no more copies left of your book,[2] although he is getting requests from everywhere for hundreds of them. He said he is therefore thinking of preparing a new edition, and that if you want to add anything to it, or take anything out, you can let me know, either by the public post, or through some favourable opportunity. I wish you would also use that opportunity to send me the other part of your works which you have in a finished state, and also to procure for us those things which M. Gassendi is willing to commit to our loyalty and our[3] diligence. Please urge that man, who is my very dear friend, not to torture us by making us wait so long for his writings. There will be plenty of faithful friends of his, known to me, who will travel here; and as soon as those writings are in my possession, I solemnly promise that in the shortest possible time they will be printed in a very fine edition. I simply do not know whether his book on the life of Epicurus[4] has been published yet; if you can buy a good quantity of them for me, I shall immediately refund what you pay for them. I am avid to know whether you have received any news of de Martel; and I also await your answer, as soon as possible, to this letter—as also to the earlier letter which I sent you a week ago.[5] Farewell, admirable Sir, and love me, who shall eternally worship you like some divine being.

Leiden, 19 August 1647.

---

[1] See Letter 41 n. 10.

[2] The 2nd edn. of *De cive*.

[3] As often in his letters, Sorbière seems to use the first person plural for first person singular. But since he has just also used the first person singular, I translate 'noster' here as 'our'.

[4] *De vita et moribus Epicuri* (Lyon, 1647).

[5] Letter 53.

LETTER 55   [24 SEPTEMBER/] 4 OCTOBER 1647

Samuel Sorbière to Hobbes, from Leiden

BN MS f.l. 10352, part 1, fos. 114ᵛ–115ʳ (transcript).
Translated in *HW* ii, p. 314 (extract).

Clarissimo Viro D. Thomae Hobbio, Samuel Sorberius.

Binas ad te scripsi eodem argumento.[1] Elzevirius libri tui [nouam][2] Editionem cogitat,[3] & quid a te addi vel demi queat scire laborat. Ego insuper ingenti teneor desiderio resciendi an caeterorum Operum tuorum parte aliqua nos beabis breui; an idem D. Gassendus praestiturus sit de suis; quid de Martello nostro acceperis, & alia quae pro tua comitate, otium nactus, edocere poteris. Vale, Vir admirande, Seculi nostri decus primarium, verae Philosophiae spes altera, & me ama.

Lugduni Batauorum IV Octobris 1647.

Translation of Letter 55

Samuel Sorbière to the most distinguished Mr Thomas Hobbes.

I have written two letters to you on the same subject.[1] Elsevier is thinking of a new[(2)] edition of your book,[3] and is anxious to know what additions or omissions you may make. Besides, I am extremely eager to find out whether you are soon going to bless us with some part of your other works; whether M. Gassendi is going to publish some part of his; what news you have heard from our friend de Martel; and other things which, out of kindness, you may be able to tell me about when you have time.

Farewell, admirable Sir, the leading ornament of our age, the new hope of true philosophy, and love me.

Leiden, 4 October 1647

[1] Letter 54, and another letter which apparently does not survive.
[2] nonnam *MS*.
[3] See Letter 54, and on the preparation of the 3rd edn. in 1647 see *HW* ii, pp. 45–7.

LETTER 56   [17/] 27 NOVEMBER 1647

Hobbes to Samuel Sorbière, from Saint-Germain

BN MS f.l. 10352, part 2, fo. 93ᵛ (transcript).
Printed in Tönnies, 'Siebzehn Briefe', pp. 206–7; Robertson, 'Some Letters', pp. 446–7; *MC* xv, pp. 552–3; translated in *HW* ii, pp. 314–15.

Eruditissimo, Praestantissimóque Viro D. Samueli Sorberio, Thomas Hobbes S. P. D.

Literas tuas datas quarto die Octobris[1] accepi hebdomade proximè superiore. In qua quoniam libri mei editionem alteram Elzeuirium[2] cogitare scribis, ecce mitto tibi inclusum in hac Epistola folium, in quo quid mutatum esse velim, annotaui. Nihil autem in eo folio continetur praeter Errata quaedam prioris impressionis, non enim habeo quicquam quod addam, aut demam. Aliam partem Philosophiae Elementorum[3] nondum paratam vllam habeo; nam circa medium mensem Augusti in febrem incidi grauissimam & continuam, ita vt non modò corpore aeger, sed etiam mente laesus, ne Amicos quidem qui me visebant lecto astantes recognoscere potui. Febris ea in lecto me detinuit pro hebdomadas sex, postea abiens erupit in Apostemata quae hebdomadas quatuor alteras lecto me affixerunt, postremo sanatis

Apostematibus superuenit Ischiadica, eáque maximis cum doloribus. Nunc autem aliquanto me tractat mitiùs, sinitque vt animum ad Amicorum res conuertam aliquando. Per tempora morbi priora accepi à te Epistolam vnam, in qua inuoluta erat altera ad D. du Prat,[4] quam (vbi coepi paulum à febre & delirio respirare) dedi cuidam ex Amicis meis Parisios ferendam, dandámque Tabellario publico. Nisi morbus interuenisset, perfecissem, credo, partem Philosophiae primam quae est de Corpore; vt autem nunc se res habet, eam partem circa festum Pentecostes expectare poteris; nihil est quo ampliús te detineam, cum valetudine & perge me amare.

Dabam Germani 27. Nouembris 1647.

Translation of Letter 56

Thomas Hobbes sends greetings to the most learned and distinguished M. Samuel Sorbière.

I received last week your letter dated 4 October.[1] Since you say in it that Elsevier[2] is thinking of a second edition of my book, I enclose here in this letter a sheet of paper on which I have noted what I want to be changed. There is nothing on this sheet except errors of the previous printing; for I have nothing to add or subtract. I do not have any other part of the Elements of Philosophy[3] ready; in about mid-August I fell ill with a very severe and continuous fever, which not only weakened my body but also injured my mind. So much so that I could not recognize some friends who came to visit me when they stood at my bedside. That fever kept me in bed for six weeks; then as it subsided it broke into abscesses which kept me in bed for another four weeks; then when the abscesses had been cured they were replaced by a swelling of the hip-joints which was immensely painful. Now that that is calming down a little it allows me to turn my mind now and then towards my friends' affairs. During the earlier period of my disease I received one letter from you enclosing another to M. du Prat,[4] which (when I began to recover a little from the fever and delirium) I gave to one of my friends to take to Paris and give to the public carrier. If the disease had not intervened I should, I think, have completed the first part of my 'Philosophy', which is about body; but as things now are, you can expect to receive that part at about Whitsun. I have no reason to detain you further; be in good health and continue to love me.

Saint-Germain, 27 November 1647

¹ Letter 55.
² See Letter 41 n. 10.
³ See Letter 41 n. 6.
⁴ Abraham du Prat.

LETTER 57   [7/] 17 FEBRUARY 1648

Hobbes to Marin Mersenne, from Saint-Germain

BN MS f.fr. n.a. 6206, fos. 143–4 (original).
Printed in Tönnies, 'Analekten', pp. 172–3; Pascal, *Œuvres*, ed. Brunschvicg and Boutroux, ii, pp. 212–14; *MC* xvi, pp. 107–10.

Reuerende Pater. Cùm venissem te visurus, negauitque Janitor te ad accipiendos amicos [*word deleted*] satis firmae valetudinis esse, discessi tristis metuens ne grauius aegrotares quam sperassem. eam tristitiam literae tuae propria manu scriptae abstulerunt. Librum quem mihi dedisti de Vacuo¹ perlegi quantum potui attentissimè. nouae authoris de elementorum mixtione cogitationes, experimentis Toricelli, et Paschalis non satisfaciunt,² neque si satisfacerent, ob eam rem possibilitatem Vacui tollunt, quia positio Vacui ijsdem experimentis satisfacit facilius elegantiusque. Sed profectò illius ordinis homines, vt qui soli docti, et rectè philosophari soli videri cupiunt, hoc omnino habent, vt quicquid ab aliorum ingenijs noui existat, id [*two words deleted*] summo conatu oppugnent. Itaque de Vacuo censeo summatim idem quod antè censui, esse nimirum loca quaedam, nunc haec nunc illa in quibus corpus nullum inest, et [*word deleted* > haec] contingere ex natura siue actione naturali solis, ignis, aliorumque, si qua sunt, corporum calefacientium. horum enim actio talis est, vt corpora vicina agitent partesque ipsorum dissipent vnam in alteram illidentia.[ex *deleted*] qua actione vacua quaedam spatiola necessariò oriuntur. Habet etiam libellus hic, dictiones quasdam, quas nulla sequitur rerum imaginatio, quales sunt *legereté mouuante*, *pesanteur effectiue*,³ *Esprits de feu*,⁴ cùm nihil dici possit *Mouens* neque *Effectiuum* praeter Corpora, leuitas autem et grauitas accidentia sint, nimirum, potentiae passiuae. et quod attinet ad *spiritus ignis*, siue *spiritus ignitos*, imaginari nullo modo possum, ignem ipsum, separatum a carbone, ligno, aliaue materia combustibili aliud esse praeter spiritum hoc est corpus subtilissimum, ab ipso combustibili velociter [*word deleted*] euolans siue expulsum,⁵ qua velocitate aer vicinus impulsus, motu [>vsque] ad oculum pertinente, facit vt concipiamus inde Lumen propter quod appellamus ignem id quod antè carbonem dicebamus. Videtur autem sibi etiam aliquando contradicere.

nam in capite de Thermometro, cùm rationem ex aethere suo reddidisset quare aqua videtur descendere, (nempe, aethere qui in ea erat ascendente) redditurus rationem quare cessante calore eadem aqua denuo ascendit, dicit tum, *aetherem repetere illam eandem mixtionem quam antè habuit, vt rem mundo propriam siue naturalem*. pag. 19. l. 25.[6] Hoc autem fieri non potest nisi aethere descendente. Dicit autem postea. pag. 30. li. 17 *Eam esse Aetheris Inclinationem vt supra aerem atque alia omnia Elementa ascendat*.[7] id quod antedictis est Contradictorium. plura de hac re hoc tempore non scribam, quia causam quare Argentum viuum semper subsistit in tubo ad certam vnamque ab argente viuo quod in vate est distantiam nondum perspicio, ergo cogitandum est de ea, donec te reuisam, quod erit fauente Deo circa medium tempus quadragesimale. Interea ἔρρωσω

Paternitatis tuae Reud^{ae} obseruantissimus
Tho: Hobbes

St Ger. feb. 17. 1648

[*postscript:*] Quoniam dicitur, in tubo vnde argentum viuum descendens locum relinquit vacuum, fieri per illum locum visionem, ex quo sequatur actionem lucidi corporis propagari per vacuum, id quod mihi impossibile videtur, experiaris velim si potes qua figurâ rerum per illud vacuum perspectarum imagines apparent, ne forte transmissio illa radiorum fiat non per ipsum vacuum, sed per corpus tubi qui vacuum includit, actione circulari. cupio etiam scire quale miraculum illud sit de quo scribis naturale Indorum.[8]

[*addressed:*] Au Reuerend pere, le pere Mersenne, aux Minimes pres La place Royale a Paris

Translation of Letter 57

Reverend Father,
    When I came to see you, and the door-keeper said you were not well enough to receive your friends, I went away sorrowing, fearing that your illness was more serious than I had hoped. But your letter, written in your own hand, removed that fear from me. I have read through, with the utmost attention I could manage, the book about the vacuum[1]

which you gave me. The author's new theories about the chemical combination of elements do not adequately account for the experiments of Pascal and Torricelli;[2] and even if they did adequately account for them, they would not therefore remove the possibility of a vacuum, since the supposition of a vacuum accounts for those experiments more simply and more elegantly. But of course people of that sort, who want to appear to be the only learned men and the only true philosophers, always behave in this way: whenever any new discovery is made by others, they try their hardest to argue against it.

So, to sum up my opinion about the vacuum, I still think what I told you before: that there are certain minimal spaces here and there, in which there is no body, and that these spaces occur because of the nature, or natural actions, of the sun, fire, and other heat-producing bodies (if there are any others). For the action of these bodies is such that they agitate the bodies which are next to them, and dissipate their component parts by making them strike against one another. Certain small empty spaces are necessarily formed by this action.

This little book also contains some expressions which do not produce any mental images of things: for example, 'moving lightness', 'effective weight',[3] and 'spirits of fire'.[4] Nothing can be called 'moving' or 'effective' but bodies; whereas 'lightness' and 'heaviness' are accidents, that is, passive powers. And as for 'spirits of fire' or 'fiery spirits', I cannot imagine that fire itself separated from coal, wood, or some other fuel is anything other than a spirit (that is, a very subtle body), flying off or driven off at great speed from the fuel itself.[5] The neighbouring air is driven by the speed of this spirit, and when the resulting motion reaches our eyes it makes us conceive of a light, because of which we describe as 'fire' what we previously described as 'coal'.

The author of this book also seems to contradict himself in places. In his chapter on the thermometer, for example, he used his theory of the ether to explain why the water is seen to descend (his theory being that the ether which was contained in the water rises). Then, when he had to explain why the water rises again when the heat-source is removed, he says, 'the ether seeks to form the same chemical combination which it had before, since that is its fitting or natural place in the world' (p. 19, line 25).[6] But this cannot happen unless the ether descends. Later, however, he says (p. 30, line 17) 'the inclination of the ether is to ascend above the air and all the other elements',[7] which is the opposite of what he said before.

I shall not write any more about this subject at the moment, because I do not yet understand why the mercury always stays in the tube at the same distance from the mercury in the vessel. So I must think about this, until I see you again—which, God willing, will be at about the middle of Lent. Meanwhile, reverend Father, farewell.

Your most devoted
Thomas Hobbes

Saint-Germain, 17 February 1648

[*postscript:*] It is said that one can see through the empty space which is left in the tube when the mercury descends, from which it follows that the action of a light-producing body is being propagated through a vacuum (which I think is impossible). So I should like you to find out if you can what shape the images of the objects which are seen through that vacuum have, in case the rays of light are being transmitted not through the vacuum itself but, in a circular action, via the body of the tube which contains the vacuum. I should also like to know what that wonderful natural phenomenon from the Indies is which you write about.[8]

[*addressed:*] To the reverend Father Mersenne, at the house of the Minims, near the Place Royale, Paris

---

[1] Étienne Noël, *Le Plein du vuide* (1648). Noël (1581–1660) was a Jesuit priest and a friend of Descartes. After reading Pascal's first report on the Torricellian experiment (*Expériences nouvelles touchant le vide*, 1647), Noël had written to Pascal, arguing that the apparent vacuum was in fact filled with purified air, which had entered through the pores in the glass (Pascal, *Œuvres*, ed. Brunschvicg and Boutroux, ii, pp. 82–9). He expanded this argument in *Le Plein du vuide*. Since examples of the 1st edn. of that work are very rare, I give references in the following notes to the reprinting of the entire work in Pascal, *Œuvres*, ed. Bossut, iv, pp. 108–46.

[2] On the experiments by Torricelli and Pascal see de Waard, *L'Expérience barométrique*. Noël's thesis was that air is normally a mixture of two elements, air and ether. The latter, which consists of 'elementary fire', can be separated from air; in its separated form it can penetrate glass, thus filling the apparently empty space at the top of the tube in the Torricellian experiment.

[3] *Le Plein du vuide*, sect. 8. To illustrate his argument that when any body moves, its place is taken by another body, Noël writes: 'This is a familiar experience with a sand-caster, when the air, with its moving lightness, pushes the sand from the bottle, and the sand, with its effective weight, pushes the air into the upper part of the bottle' ('Cette expérience est familiere en un poudrier, quand l'air, par sa légéreté mouvante, pousse le sable en la bouteille où il étoit; & le sable, par sa pesanteur effective, pousse l'air en la

bouteille supérieure' (Pascal, *Œuvres*, ed. Bossut, iv, p. 122)). Noël goes on to attribute 'légéreté mouvante' to the ether, and 'pesanteur effective' to the mercury (ibid., iv, p. 125).

[4] Ibid., sect. 6, p. 119. Noël also uses the phrases 'esprits solaires', 'esprits ignés', and 'esprits lucides' (sect. 3, pp. 114–16).

[5] Noël argues that the air contains an 'elemental fire' ('feu élémentaire') which is 'invisible, and therefore very different from flames or burning coal' ('invisible, & par suite fort différent de la flamme & du charbon allumé' (ibid., sect. 3, p. 114)).

[6] 'l'air & l'eau reprennent leur mélange naturel & propre au monde' (ibid., sect. 6, p. 119).

[7] 'L'inclination de l'*ether* est de monter par-dessus l'air & tous les autres éléments' (ibid., sect. 9, p. 125).

[8] On [22 Feb./] 3 Mar. 1648 Jean Columbi referred, in a letter to Mersenne, to 'the news you imparted to me about the great agility of Indians' ('la nouuelle dont vous m'auez faict part concernant ceste grande souplesse des Indiens'), and on [24 Feb./] 5 Mar. Bourdelot wrote to another correspondent: 'Father Mersenne says that, according to a letter he has received, there are jugglers in the Indies who levitate above the ground, up to the height of the first storey of houses' ('Le pere Mersen dit qu'on luy escrit qu'aux Indes il y a des charlatans qui s'esleuent de terre jusqu'au premier estage des maisons' (*MC* xvi, pp. 149, 152)). This evidently refers to a version of the Indian rope trick (for an early description of which see Ibn Battuta, *Travels*, p. 296). The source of Mersenne's information was Constantijn Huygens, who wrote to him on [27 Mar./] 6 Apr. 1648: 'I shan't be able to give you any more details about those wonderful jugglers in the Indies; my informants live a long way away' ('Je ne scauray vous dire plus de circonstance de ces merueilleux basteleurs des Indes: mes rapporteurs viuent loing d'icy' (*MC* xvi, p. 219)).

LETTER 58   2/12 MAY 1648

Hobbes to William Cavendish, third Earl of Devonshire, from Saint-Germain

MS (original) unlocated.
Reproduced in facsimile in Thibaudeau (ed.), *Catalogue of the Collection of Alfred Morrison*, ii, pl. 89.
Printed in HMC, *Ninth Report*, p. 439b (extract).

Right Honorable and my singular good Lord

I haue receaued your lops letter sent by Sr John Cooke,[1] who comming to Paris left it wth monsieur du Bosc, because he meant to stay at Paris but a day or two, and then wthout comming hether to go to Orleans. I writte to mons^r du Bosc to signify to him that I should be very glad, that if he had any occasion to vse my service he would be pleased to write to me from Orleans or wheresoeuer he shall be, and that I would most readily obey all his Commands, eyther here or at Paris whether I would go on purpose to do whatsoeuer he shall employ me in. Monsr du Bosc hath also assured me, that he will do him all the seruice he can. Though I doubt S:^r John Cooke doth remember we were of Contrary opinions touching the proceedings wch were then when I saw him last,[2] yet I am resolued never to say any things that may put him in mind of any errour of his iudgem^t, for that I beleeue hee is now of my opinion, and also because he is your Lo^Ps frend.

I haue written to Monsr du Bosc of yor Lo^Ps kindnesse, and that I haue ten pieces ready for him,[3] whensoeuer he shall send to me for it, or that I shall my selfe come to Paris. It is a great allowance, 50^l a year for a young vniuersity scholler vnlesse he hath better learning then is vsually taught in the vniuersity. That wch is requisite for my young Lord, is the latine tonge and the Mathematiques, I meane whilest he is yonge, for other knowledge, as the knowledge of the passions and manners of men, of the nature of Gouerment, and the reading of history or Poets otherwise then to exercise his latine tongue he is and will be a great while too young. If the young man propounded by Mr Payne can teach him Latine well, and the beginnings of Mathematiques, and be such a one as will imprint [>in] him piety without superstitious admiration of Preachers, he may then deserue his allowance. In these partes I find none yet that can do this. And seeing your Lo^p may perhaps come ouer, I thinke it best to reserue that businesse till you come. If I vnderstand your letter, you aske me what inclinations I haue to the place you are now in. I haue no inclinations to the place where there is so little security, but I haue such inclinations to your Lo^p as I will come to any place (if I may haue a passe) where your Lo^p shall be. I am now tyed to Mr Ridgely[4] but t'is thought the occasions there, will cause his remoue hence thither, or to some other place. W^ch if it fall out, I shall desire nothing so much as to be where you are, and to serue you in that employment you seeke another for. When I consider how dangerous a time there is like to be for peaceable men, I am apter to wish you on this side, then my selfe on that side the sea. Assoone as I heare of Mr Ridgeleyes resolutions I will not fayle to aduertise you. So I take leaue and remayne

Your Lo^p most humble and most obedient seruant

St Germ. May 2/12 1648.

[1] Sir John Coke of Melbourne, Derby., was the eldest son of Sir John Coke, Charles I's Secretary of State (1563–1644). Although the father had angered Parliament with his defences of regal authority, the son took the parliamentarian side in the Civil War.

[2] 'I doubt', in normal 17th-cent. usage (including Hobbes's) meant 'I suspect'—i.e. believe to be probably true. Hobbes may be referring here to the elections to the Short Parliament in 1640. In the borough of Derby, an attempt by the Earl of Devonshire to impose Hobbes as a candidate was rejected by the burgesses. On 26 Jan. [/5 Feb.] 1640 Sir John Coke senior wrote to his son that 'Mr Fulwood telleth me that Derbymen are resolved to give no way to the election of Mr. Hobs; and he thinketh your brother may be introduced. But I shall not persuade him to put himself in contestation with my lord. Only if you find that Hobs cannot prevail, do what you can for your brother' (HMC, *Cowper*, p. 251). The brother, Thomas, was eventually nominated as a candidate by the Countess of Devonshire, but was not elected (he was MP for Leicester in the Long Parliament, and a royalist); nevertheless, Hobbes may have been aware that the Coke family had had an interest in blocking his own election. However, when Sir John Coke junior was elected MP for the county of Derby. in Nov., the candidate he defeated, John Manners of Haddon, had been an opponent of the Earl of Devonshire's candidate, Sir John Harpur of Swarkeston, in the election of the Short Parliament. See Beats, 'Politics and Government in Derbyshire', pp. 72–3; Fletcher, 'Petitioning in Derbyshire', p. 33; Gruenfelder, 'Election to the Short Parliament', p. 201.

[3] From what follows, it appears that the Earl of Devonshire had asked du Bosc to find a young French graduate to become tutor to his son in England, and had sent the money for the first instalment of the tutor's wages to Hobbes, to be transmitted to du Bosc.

[4] Unidentified. Possibly William Rugeley (or Rudgeley) of Dunton (War.), who died in 1655; he was the son of Sir Rowland Rugeley (see the genealogy in BL MS Add. 37141, fo. 274ʳ). William Rugeley was a royalist who compounded for delinquency in arms in Mar. 1647, was summoned to pay his fine in May 1649, had it reduced in July of that year, and paid it in 1650 (Green (ed.), *Calendar of Committee for Advance of Money*, ii, p. 1072; iii, p. 1694). However, that sequence of dates suggests that he was occupied with his affairs in England during that period, and not in France, as this letter implies. There is one Ridgley or Ridgeley with whom Hobbes can be at least indirectly connected. Thomas Ridgeley (MD Cambridge 1608, Fellow of the Royal College of Physicians 1622) was a distinguished physician and a personal friend of Sir Gervase Clifton, with whom he corresponded in the 1630s, sending not only medical advice but also recommendations of books (NUL MSS Clifton C 382–5; BL MS Lansdowne 238, fo. 149). But Thomas Ridgeley was 80 when he died in 1656 (Munk *et al.* (eds.), *Roll*, i, p. 169), and it may be doubted whether he was travelling on the Continent in his seventies. A more likely candidate is his son, Luke (d. 1697), also a physician, who proceeded MD at Cambridge in 1646 and was admitted as a candidate of the Royal College of Physicians in Nov. 1649 (ibid., i, p. 249). A pass was issued for Dr Luke Ridgley and Edward Cooke to travel to Utrecht in 1650 (*CSPD* 1650, p. 536), and another pass in 1653 for Edward Conway, his wife Anne, Francis Finch, and Dr Ridgley to travel 'beyond seas' (*CSPD* 1652–3, p. 445); but it is not known whether he was in France in 1648. Against this identification, however, must be put the fact that Hobbes refers to 'Mʳ', not Dr, Ridgely. Luke Ridgley had two brothers, Thomas and George (Masson, *Life of Milton*, ii, p. 101 n.); so perhaps Hobbes's patron or temporary employer was one of these.

Hobbes to Marin Mersenne, from Saint-Germain

MS in the Houghton Library, Harvard, autograph file (original).
Printed in H. Brown, 'The Mersenne Correspondence'; *MC* xvi, pp. 333–4; facsimile
of MS printed in Maggs' catalogue 471 (1925), item 2835, pl. 17.

Mon Reuerend Pere,

L'enclose est une lettre que i'ay escrit a Monsieur Martel, en
response d'une sienne, que i'ay receu de Bourdeaux il y a un mois.[1] Il
ne m'a pas donné aucune addresse a Bourdeaux c'est pourquoy i'ay
addressé la mienne a Mountauban,[2] pensant que ses amis l'envoyeront
a luy. Je vous prie de l'envoyer par telle voye que vous iugerez la
meilleure.

J'ay reuieu mes papiers de l'Optique,[3] ou ie ne trouue aucune regle
generale pour le lieu de l'image, mais qu'il change selon la figure du
miroir. tellement que ie ne scaurois vous monstrer mon sentiment la
dessus, sans transcrire tout ce que i'ay escrit.

Toutes les experiences faites par vous et d'autres, auec l'argent vif,
ne concluent pas qu'il y a du vuide, parceque la matiere subtile qui est
dans l'air estant pressée passera a trauers l'argent vif et trauers tout
autre cors fluide ou fondu, que ce soit. Comme la fumee passe à trauers
l'eau.

N'ayant autre chose pour vous escrire, ie vous souhaitte parfaicte
santé et bon succes en vos trauaux, et demeure

vostre treshumble et tresaffectioné seruiteur
Tho: Hobbes

St. Germ. may. 25. 1648

Translation of Letter 59

Reverend Father,

The enclosed is a letter which I have written to M. de Martel, in
reply to one of his, which I received from Bordeaux a month ago.[1] He
did not give me any address at Bordeaux: that is why I have addressed
mine to Montauban,[2] thinking that his friends will send it on to him.
Please send it by whatever means you think best.

I have looked again at my papers on optics.[3] I do not find any general rule there for the place of the image; rather, it changes according to the shape of the mirror. So I would not be able to show you what my opinion is on that subject, without copying out everything I have written.

All the experiments which you and others have made with mercury do not prove that a vacuum exists, because when the subtle matter which is in the air is pressed, it will pass through the mercury, and through any other fluid or molten body whatsoever—just as smoke passes through water.

Not having anything else to write to you, I wish you perfect health and complete success in your labours, and remain

Your most humble and affectionate servant
Thomas Hobbes

Saint-Germain, 25 May 1648

From the early pagination number '131' at the head of the page, it appears that this MS was formerly pp. 131–2 of the bound volume of Mersenne correspondence, BN MS f.fr. n.a. 6206. This letter is listed in the index to that volume with the entry '131–4', indicating that there was also an outer sheet bearing the address (now lost).

[1] Neither letter apparently survives. De Martel (who was pursuing a lawsuit in Bordeaux) had still received no reply from Hobbes by [18/] 28 July, despite having written to him several times (see his letter to Mersenne of that date in *MC* xvi, p. 436).

[2] See Letter 40 n. 3.

[3] This probably refers mainly to the English Optical MS (BL MS Harl. 3360).

LETTER 60 [9/] 19 JUNE 1648

Hobbes to Marin Mersenne, from Saint-Germain

BN MS f.fr. n.a. 6206, fo. 73 (original).
Printed in Tönnies, 'Analekten', pp. 174–5; *MC* xvi, pp. 364–6.

Mon Reuerend Pere

Je ne trouue rien dans mon discours touchant La Refraction,[1] contre mon sens, si ce n'est des fautes de l'impression, Lesquelles ie ne scauray Corriger toutes, sans le lire tout entierement et auec tresgrand soin, et plus de temps que ie ne scauray employer a present. J'ay corrigé la derniere figure qui est au page .589. faussem^t [tirée *deleted*] marquée[2] J'ay corrigé aussi quelques lettres au page 472.[3] pour celuy de Monsieur Verner,[4] ie croy qu'il est bien, mais ie ne l'ay pas examiné diligement.

Ce que Monsr Werner a fait touchant la monnoye,[5] est en Anglois, et fort long et mal aisé a lire, ny scay ie entre quelles mains il l'a laissé; pour moy, l'ayant leu je le rendi a mons^r Candish,[6] qui me l'auoit presté.

Pour les points lesquels vous m'auez proposé a mediter, ie les ay oublié. si vous me les proposerez encore vne foys ie feray tout ce que ie pourray pour vous satisfaire.

Quand le Prince sera de retour a St Germains,[7] s'il fait quelque demeure icy (car ie ne scay sil retournerà bien tost en Angleterre) ie tascheray de [l' *deleted*] essayer [> sa lunette] (sil est possible) auec vous en vostre maison. mais ie doute qu'il sera bien difficile, si ie n'y mene auec moy celuy qui en a la garde.

Je uous enuoye aussi vn papier dans lequel i'ay tasché d'expliquer la maniere de Reflexion, et Comment ces trous dont vous parlez n'empeschent pas que [> les] angles de l'incidence et la Reflexion ne soyent egales.[8]

Voyla tout ce que i'ay pour le present a respondre a la vostre du 15me de Juin.[9] Excepté que ie suis fort marri de vostre mal de dents, dont ie suis [*word deleted* > le] plus sensible pour auoir esté fort souuent trauaillé du mesme mal. Dieu vous en guerie bien tost, et vous garde aussi de toute autre Maladie

Vostre seruiteur tres humble
Tho: Hobbes

St Germ. Juin. 19.me vendredi. 1648

Translation of Letter 60

Reverend Father,

In my treatise on refraction[1] I find nothing that misrepresents my argument, apart from printing errors; and I would not be able to correct all of them without reading the whole thing very carefully, and giving it more time than I am able to spend on it at present. I have corrected the last diagram, which is wrongly marked on p. 589.[2] I have also corrected some letters on p. 472.[3] As for Mr Warner's treatise,[4] I think it is all right, but I have not checked it carefully.

What Mr Warner wrote about coinage[5] is in English, and very long and difficult to read; nor do I know who he left it with. For my part, after I had read it I gave it back to Mr Cavendish,[6] who had lent it to me.

As for the questions which you asked me to think about, I have forgotten them. If you put them to me again, I shall do everything I can to satisfy you.

When the Prince returns to Saint-Germain,[7] if he stays here for any length of time (for I do not know whether he will go back soon to England) I shall see if I can try out his glass, if possible, with you in your house. But I suspect it will be very difficult to arrange, unless I bring with me the person who is its keeper.

I am also sending you a paper in which I have tried to explain how refraction works, and how it is that those holes which you speak of do not prevent the angles of incidence and of reflection from being the same.[8]

That is all I have, for the moment, by way of reply to your letter of 15 June.[9] Except that I am very sorry about your toothache; I sympathize with you all the more strongly because I have very often been troubled by the same illness. May God cure you of it soon, and keep you from all other illnesses too.

Your very humble servant,
Thomas Hobbes

Saint-Germain, Friday 19 June 1648

[1] The 'Optica', bk. 7 of the section on optics in Mersenne, *Universae geometriae synopsis* (1644), pp. 567–89 (*OL* v, pp. 217–48) (cf. Letter 32 n. 2). It appears that Mersenne was planning to republish it, and had asked Hobbes to correct any faults in the text.

[2] Hobbes, 'Optica', prop. 14, second diagram. The editors of *MC* think that 'faussement marquée' ('wrongly marked') here refers to the page number 589, which should in fact be 591; but the deleted 'tirée' ('drawn'), and the fact that Hobbes thought 'page' was masculine, make it evident that he is referring to an error in the diagram.

[3] *Universae geometriae synopsis*, pp. 472–5, presents a discussion of telescopes by Hobbes, as part of Mersenne's preface to the optical section of the book (not in *OL*).

[4] Warner's treatise on refraction, bk. 6 of the optical section of the book (*Universae geometriae synopsis*, pp. 549–66).

[5] Warner (see Letter 16 n. 3) wrote several works on coinage (at the behest of his patron Sir Thomas Aylesbury, who was Master of the Mint). These included a treatise on the analysis and comparison of bullion (BL MS Harl. 6754, fos. 2–27) and a treatise on money, commodities, and exchange (ibid., fos. 28–39). The work referred to here is probably his treatise 'of the commixture of metalls for the Mint', of which extracts copied by Sir Charles Cavendish are in BL MS Harl. 6755, fos. 15–18ʳ. In 1656 Hobbes recalled that the only papers by Warner he had seen were his treatise on refraction and 'another Treatise of the Proportions of Alloy in Gold and Silver Coine' (*Six Lessons*, p. 59: *EW* vii, p. 342).

⁶ 'Candish' was the 17th-cent. pronunciation (and, frequently, spelling) of 'Cavendish'.

⁷ Prince Charles had left in the first week of June, and did not return until Oct. 1651.

⁸ This paper does not apparently survive.

⁹ This letter does not apparently survive.

LETTER 61   [4/] 14 JUNE 1649

Hobbes to Samuel Sorbière, from Paris

BN MS f.l. 10352, part 2, fo. 100ʳ (transcript).

Printed in *Illustrium virorum epistolae*, pp. 571²–572² (sig. Bb1); Tönnies, 'Siebzehn Briefe', pp. 207–8; Robertson, 'Some Letters', p. 447.

Thomas Hobbius Samueli Sorberio S. P.

Duplici gaudio me affecit (ornatissime Sorberi) Amicus tuus Dominus Guatelier,¹ qui et te saluum esse nuntiauit, et mihi à te salutem dixit. Ego tibi rescribo imprimis vota mea, vt bene valere, laetus viuere, et mihi bene velle perseueres. Deinde, si tanti est, curas meas, id est studia Philosophica quae tu alijque amici mei & voce flagitant, et silentio interdum videntur flagitare.

Quantum cura valetudinis, et erga amicos quos hic habeo praesentes, officiorum meorum ratio sinit, tantum operae scriptionis impertio, scriptioni inquam, non enim jam quaerendae sed explicandae demonstrandaeque veritatis labor editionem moratur. Puderet me tantae tarditatis, nisi certus essem, rationem ejus in ipso opere, satis constitutam esse. Veruntamen non ita longe abesse videor à fine primae partis² (quae et maxima est, & speculationis quam caeterae partes profundioris[)]³, vt non possim (Deo fauente) eo peruenire ante exactam hanc aestatem. Interea tabulis [*word deleted*] aeneis figuras quibus vtor in Demonstrationibus meis quotidiè incidi curo, vt simul ac scribere desierim, omnia praelo parata sint. Accipio quandoque literas ab amico nostro Domino Martello, & accepi nuper, degit plerumque credo, Buldigalae. Bene valet, & me amat. Tu quoque vale (Optime Sorberi) & me ama.

Tui Amantissimum
Th. Hobbes

Parisijs Iunij 14 1649

Translation of Letter 61

Thomas Hobbes sends greetings to Samuel Sorbière.

Most distinguished Sorbière, your friend M. Guatelier[1] gave me a double pleasure when he brought me both your greetings and the news that you were well. I reply first of all with my prayers that you may continue to be well, and to be happy, and to wish me well. My own concerns, if they are of any importance, come second—that is, my philosophical studies, which you and other friends of mine entreat of me both by your words and (at times, it seems) by your silence.

I give as much time to the task of writing as is permitted by my health, and by the amount of duties I owe to those of my friends who are present here. I say the task of writing: for it is not the effort of finding out the truth but that of explaining and demonstrating it which is holding up publication. I should be ashamed of such tardiness, were I not certain that it is sufficiently justified by the book itself. Nevertheless, I think I am close enough to the end of the first part[2] (which is both the largest part and the part which contains the deepest speculations)[3] that I shall be able, God willing, to finish it before the end of this summer. Meanwhile I am getting the figures which I use in my demonstrations engraved on brass plates every day, so that everything will be ready for the press as soon as I stop writing.

I occasionally receive letters from our friend M. de Martel, and I received one recently. I believe he is mainly staying in Bordeaux. He is well, and loves me. And I hope that you, most excellent Sorbière, are well and love me too.

Your most loving
Thomas Hobbes

Paris, 14 June 1649

---

[1] Unidentified; I have not found him mentioned elsewhere in Sorbière's correspondence.

[2] *De corpore*.

[3] ~) *omitted in MS.*

LETTER 62 [12/] 22 SEPTEMBER 1649

Hobbes to Pierre Gassendi, from Paris

BN MS f.l. n.a. 1637, fos. 189–90 (original).
Printed in Gassendi, *Opera omnia*, vi, p. 522A; *OL* v, p. 307.

Domine, Libellum hunc *de seirio*,[1] Antwerpiâ ad me misit Dnus Cauendyshe,[2] mittendum tibi si tanti putarem. Ego vero an tanti sit necne tui potius quam mei iudicij esse volo. Promittunt etiam nescio quid nomina illa Vlug Beigus, et Tamerlanes Magnus, et incogniti illi Characteres. Itaque omnino mittendus erat. Quid de eo censeas scire velim, si tibi vacat. Vacare autem videtur. Nam Philosophiae tuae finita est Impressio,[3] et exemplaria eius huc aduecta nunc sunt in Telonio. Quorum exemplarium vnum, quam primum potero, missurus sum Hagae Comitis, Dno Sorberio Expetenti. a quo etiam iussus sum te salutare. Ego pro aetate satis bene valeo, et mihi nimirum indulgo, seruans me, si forte contingat, reditui in Angliam. Opto interea praesentiam tuam, qua si cariturus sum, cupio non modo vt valeas, sed vt id ipsum te valere sciam, qui quantum ego in hominem inspicere possum, scientiâ omnes mortales, et scientiam virtute superas:—

Seruus tuus
Tho: Hobbes:—

Parisijs sept. 22 1649:—

[*addressed:*] A monsieur
Monsieur Gassendi a Disne[4]

[*endorsed:*] Hobbes 22. Septemb 1649

Translation of Letter 61

Sir,

Mr Cavendish[2] sent me this little book about Sirius[1] from Antwerp, asking me to send it to you if I thought it sufficiently important. I should really prefer you to decide, rather than me, whether it is or not. For I do not know what those names 'Ulug Beg', 'Tamerlane the Great', and those unknown characters hold in store. So it was altogether necessary to send it to you. I should like to know your opinion of it, if you have some free time. I think, however, that you will have some free time: they have finished printing your philosophy,[3] and copies of it have been delivered to the customs-house here. Of those copies, I am to send one as soon as I can to The Hague, to M. Sorbière, who is eagerly awaiting it—and who has asked me to send you his greetings. I am in fairly good health for my age, and I am certainly looking after myself, preserving myself for my return to England, should it happen by any chance. Meanwhile I wish you were here; for when we are apart, my desire is not only that you should be in good health, but that I should know that you are. For, according to my judgement of men, your knowledge is greater than all mortals', and your virtue is even greater than your knowledge.

Your servant,
Thomas Hobbes

Paris, 22 September 1649

[*addressed:*] To M. Gassendi, at Digne[4]

The letter is incorrectly dated 21 Sept. by Molesworth.

[1] This must refer to John Bainbridge, *Canicularia*, ed. John Greaves (Oxford, 1648). The work consisted principally of an unfinished treatise by Bainbridge (1582–1643), the Savilian Professor of Astronomy at Oxford, on the theories of classical astronomers about Sirius, the 'dog star', and the 'dog days', the period of the year when Sirius is in the ascendant. To this John Greaves (1602–52), Bainbridge's successor in the Savilian chair, added a demonstration of the helical motion of Sirius across the heavens, and notes on other stars drawn from a Persian MS of astronomical observations by Ulug Beg, the grandson of Timur Leng (Tamerlane, Tamburlaine). Greaves was a scholar of Arabic and Persian, and Bainbridge had also studied Arabic; the Savilian statutes required the Professor of Astronomy to prepare editions of the early Arab astronomers. Extracts from Ulug Beg's MS (Bodl. MS Savile 46) are printed in Persian, the 'unknown characters' to which Hobbes refers.

[2] Sir Charles Cavendish, who had settled with his brother in Antwerp in the autumn of 1648 (see the Biographical Register).

[3] *Animadversiones* (Lyon, 1649).

[4] Digne, in the Basses-Alpes, north-west of Nice; Gassendi was a canon of the cathedral there.

Addendum: for Letter 62A (Hobbes to Sir Charles Cavendish, late September 1649), see p. 776.

LETTER 63   27 MAY [/6 JUNE] 1651

Ralph Bathurst to Hobbes [from Oxford?]

MS unlocated.
Printed in Warton, *Life of Bathurst*, p. 49 n. (extract).

I hope[1] your learned booke of Optickes,[2] and that other *de corpore*, if it be yet finished, may no longer lie concealed: especially since now the best wits, as well here as in other countries, are so greedy to listen after workes of that nature, and to vindicate themselves from the chimericall[3] doctrines of the schools; under which, to the bane of true knowledge, they have for these many hundred years so miserably laboured. And thus much I am the rather bold to suggest to you, because if by your other workes already published, you have gained so high an esteem:—[4] how much more shall those be received with honour, in whose argument no man's *Diana*[5] will be brought into[6] question.

Warton introduces the letter as follows: 'I have a letter before me of Bathurst to Hobbes, at Paris, dated May 27, 1651, by which it appears that Hobbes sent him two copies of his *Leviathan*, in acknowledgement for the Iambics. Among other things, he tells Hobbes—'. Bathurst had written the poem in praise of Hobbes ('the Iambics') printed in *Humane Nature* (sig. I2), the 1650 Oxford edition of the first part of the *Elements of Law* (*ABL* i, p. 371).

A copy of Warton's book in the Old Library, Trinity College, Oxford, pressmark E 8 27, has annotations by someone, probably James Ingram (President of the College, 1824–50), who was able to compare the printed text with Bathurst's MS draft. These annotations are given in the notes below (siglum: 'Ing').

Against the last sentence of the letter Ingram wrote: 'vid. MS *penes me*' ('see the MS, in my possession'). Ingram's papers are now at the Bodleian Library, but this Bathurst letter has not been found among them. I am grateful to Steven Tomlinson (who is currently cataloguing the Ingram papers) for this information.

The text here is from CUL VI. 12. 28, collated with a photocopy of OTC E 8 27.

[1] vide MS. imperfect in this part & designed by Tom perhaps *Ing*. ('Tom' here means Thomas Warton.)

[2] The English Optical MS (BL MS Harl. 3360). Bathurst had probably heard of this work from William Petty, who had copied out the MS in Paris in early 1646.

[3] altered as a correction in the original MS from '*superficiall*' Ing.

[4] esteeme, even when almost a whole order of men thought it concern'd them to cry downe your opinions, *how much* &c *Ing*.

[5] The goddess of the Ephesians, symbolizing here any religious mystery which it was in the vested interests of certain people to preserve. (When St Paul visited Ephesus, the

silversmiths who made images of Diana rose against him, saying 'this our craft is in danger to be set at nought' (Acts 19: 24–8).)

⁶ '*call'd in*'—originally, which proves the attention paid to elegance of composition *Ing*.

LETTER 64   [25 OCTOBER/] 4 NOVEMBER 1653

François du Verdus to Hobbes, from Paris

Chatsworth, Hobbes MSS, letter 1 (original).

Monsieur

Si vous m'aués oublié je me plains de vous; si vous aués eü des affaires qui vous ayent empesché de me doner des marques de vostre souuenir; je me plains de Vos affaires. Aprés tout c'est que vous m'aués tenu au filet fort long temps, Et que dépuis la Sᵗ Michel il s'est passé cincq semaines que j'ay toujours attendû de vos Nouuelles dans le desir ou je suis d'en sçauoir; je ne scaurois dire si l'inquietude que j'ay pour vostre Philosophie est fort grande: mais celle que j'ay pour vostre persone ne sçauroit l'estre dauantage. S'il vous plait de me temoigner que cette espece de soins ne vous deplait pas, je vous prie que vous adressies vostre Lettre chez Mʳ Grelin¹ Boulenger au fauxbourg sᵗ Germain au coin du jeu de Mets. quand Mʳ Gassendi aura fait imprimer ses 4 uolumes in fol. de sa ph[ilosoph]ie² nous vous l'enuoy-erons si vous le voulés; et quand Mʳ Martel sera ou a paris ou a Bourd:ˣ nous vous dirons de ses Nouuelles. Il doit aller en l'une ou en l'autre mais en quelque lieu qu'il soit a present il me chargea nagueres de vous asseurer de ses seruices en vous jurant que je suis a la vie et a la mort

Monsieur
vostre tres humble et tres obeissant seruiteur
Duuerdus

A Paris le 4ᵉ Nou.ᵇ 1653.

[*endorsed by James Wheldon:*] Mons.ʳ du Verdus No 4ᵗʰ. 1653

Translation of Letter 64

Sir,

If you have forgotten me, I have a grievance against you; if your affairs have prevented you from giving me any sign that you remember me, I have a grievance against your affairs. After all, you have kept me on the hook for a very long time; since Michaelmas five weeks have gone by while I have been waiting for your news, wishing as I do to know what they are. I cannot say that I am particularly worried about your philosophy; but I could not be more worried about your person. If you are willing to give me some indication that you do not dislike this sort of attention, please address your letter to M. Grelin,[1] baker, in the faubourg Saint-Germain at the corner of the Jeu de Mets. When M. Gassendi has had the four folio volumes of his philosophy[2] printed we shall send you a copy if you want one; and when M. de Martel is in Paris or Bordeaux we shall tell you his news. He is due to go to one or the other of these towns, but wherever he may be at the moment he instructed me not long ago to assure you of his desire to serve you. I am, Sir, in life and death,

Your most humble and obedient servant
du Verdus

Paris, 4 November 1653

---

[1] Unidentified.

[2] Contraction expanded. Gassendi was trying to complete his *Syntagma*, a systematic exposition of his philosophy, some of the material for which had been published in his *Animadversiones* (1649). The *Syntagma* was eventually published posthumously in the *Opera omnia* (1658).

LETTER 65   [28 APRIL/] 8 MAY 1654

Samuel Sorbière to Hobbes, from Paris

Chatsworth, Hobbes MSS, letter 2 (original).

Monsieur,
 Il y a quelque temps que je uous ay escrit dans un pacquet que M. Martel uous adressa, pour uous tesmoigner que je suis tousjours intimement uostre seruiteur. J'espere que ceste uerité uous aura esté persuadee: desorte que maintenant je ne prens la plume que pour uous supplie de m'enuoyer promptement par l'adresse à M. Martel ou telle autre bien asseuree vostre discours sur la poësie en forme de preface aux oeuures de l'un de uos amis.[1] Je uous [prie][2] de me le faire copier en sa langue, si tant est que uous n'ayès pas ceste fueille separee; car j'en ay parlé à un homme de condition grand amateur de uos pensees, & il

m'importe de le luy faire [auoir]³ au plustot. J'attends de uous ceste faueur, & suis,

Monsieur,
Vostre tres humble & tres obeissant seruiteur
Sorbiere

De Paris le 8. de May 1654

[*postscript:*] Je loge Ruë de la Jussienne à la ville de Mante⁴

[*addressed:*] A Monsieur
Monsieur Hobbes; chez Monsʳ Andrew Crooke⁵ at the green dragon in Sᵗ Pauls church-yard London

[*endorsed by James Wheldon:*] Mons.ʳ de Sorbierre May 8. 1654

Translation of Letter 65

Sir,
   Some time ago I wrote a letter to you, enclosed in a parcel which M. de Martel sent you, to tell you that I am still your devoted servant. I hope you have been persuaded of this truth; so now I am writing only to beg you to send me soon (via M. de Martel, or some other reliable address) your discourse on poetry, which you wrote in the form of a preface to the works of one of your friends.¹ I beg⁽²⁾ you to have it copied for me in its original language (if it is not separately available in print); for I talked about it to a gentleman of quality who is a great admirer of your thinking, and I am concerned that I should be able to let him have⁽³⁾ it as soon as possible. Expecting this favour of you, I am, Sir,

Your most humble and obedient servant
Sorbière

Paris, 8 May 1654

[*postscript:*] I am staying in the rue de la Jussienne in the town of Mantes.⁴

[*addressed: see text*]

---

¹ Hobbes's 'Answer' to the Preface to Sir William Davenant's *Gondibert* (1st edn., Paris, 1650; 2nd and 3rd edns., London, 1651; *EW* iv, pp. 441–58; and see also Letter 184 n. 2). Hobbes seems to have complied with this request: Sorbière summarized the

argument of the 'Answer' in a letter to Michel de Marolles of [5/] 15 Sept. 1656 (*Lettres et discours*, pp. 396–9).

² prie *or some such word omitted in MS.*

³ aoir *MS.*

⁴ A small town on the Seine near Rouen, thirty-six miles from Paris.

⁵ See the Biographical Register, 'William Crooke'.

LETTER 66   10/20 JULY 1654

Hobbes to Pierre Gassendi, from London

Historical Society of Pennsylvania, Philadelphia, Simon Gratz Collection, British authors, case 10, box 30 (original).

Monsieur

Ayant appris par vne lettre de Monsieur du Verdus que vous estiez a paris et en bonne santé, vous me permetterez de m'en resiouir auec vous, Car en veritè considerant vostre maladie La quelle me sembloit estre aux poulmons, et fort dangereuse, i'en auoy gran peur; mais aceste heure ie n'ay autre crainte que celle que me donne la mortalite de tous les hommes, et me contente de ce que Dieu n'a pas voulu oster du monde [>si tost] vne chose si pretieuse, et conte par auance vne vintaine d'années de vostre vie au moins. Monsieur du Verdus m'a escrit [encore *deleted* >aussi] que ie n'ay rien perdu de l'estime que vous auiez de moy en des termes plus magnifiques que ie ne merite pas. Si vostre charité vous trompe, l'erreur me plaïst, et ie fairay tout ce que ie peux pour vous ne detromper pas. Mon plus grand merite pour tant, [n'est *deleted* >ne] me semble autre que d'entendre vostre doctrine, et d'imiter tant que puis vostre honestetè de meurs, et distinguer la vostre d'auec la fausse, pompeuse et histrionique doctrine et vie de ceux qui veulent malgré le monde en estre les seuls maistres. Dieu vous conserue long temps en vne santé parfaite. cest prie pour tout le monde cela; non seulement pour moy mesme que suis

Monsieur.
Vostre treshumble et tresobeissant seruiteur
Tho: Hobbes

de Londres ce 10. de Juillet 1654 stilo nostro.

[*addressed:*] Pour Monsieur Gassendi

Translation of Letter 66

Sir,

A letter from M. du Verdus[1] informed me that you were in good health and staying in Paris; allow me to share the happiness of your good health with you, because, to tell the truth, I was very anxious about your illness, which I thought was a disease of the lungs,[2] and a very dangerous one. But now I feel no anxiety—except that which I feel when I consider the mortality of all men. I am glad that God did not decide to rob the world of such a treasure, and I reckon on at least another twenty years of your life. M. du Verdus also told me in his letter (in terms more laudatory than I deserve) that you continue to hold me in the same high esteem. If your good nature is deceiving you, I am pleased by your mistake, and I shall do whatever I can to make sure you are not undeceived. I think, however, that the most I deserve is to hear your teaching, to imitate, so far as I can, your virtuous way of life, and to distinguish them from the false, pompous, and histrionic life and teaching of those who, in spite of everyone else, desire to be the only authorities in those subjects.

May God keep you in perfect health for many years. That is my prayer, for the sake of everyone, and not just for the sake of

Sir,
your most humble and obedient servant,
Thomas Hobbes.

London, 10 July 1654, our style.

[*addressed:*] For M. Gassendi

---

[1] Possibly the letter of 16 [/26] May 1654 (now unlocated), in which du Verdus 'dwells on his relations with Gassendi' (see the section on missing letters in the Textual Introduction (p. lv)).

[2] Gassendi died of pneumonia in the following year. Guy Patin, who treated him in his final illness, wrote that the lungs were 'the weakest part of his body, by his very nature' ('la partie la plus foible de son corps, naturellement à lui' (*Lettres*, ii, p. 154, [13/] 23 Feb. 1655)).

LETTER 67   [25 JULY/] 4 AUGUST 1654

François du Verdus to Hobbes, from Paris

Chatsworth, Hobbes MSS, letter 3 (original).

Monsieur

Il y a long temps que je ne vous ay doné de mes nouuelles; mais en uerité il y a tres long temps que je n'en ay recëu des vostres. j'en suis en peine; Et je le suis dautant plus que je ne trouue icy persone que je conoisse qui dépuis moy, ait eu de vos Lettres. Ils sçauent neanmoins de l'état de vostre fortune plus que je n'en scay; s'il est uray ce qu'ils [m' *deleted* >m'en] ont dit que vous vous soyiés marié.[1] si cela est je vous en felicite de tout mon coeur. je sçay que vous estes fort prudent; Et posé que vous ayiés pris une feme, je suis certain que vous n'aurés pas fait come ceux qui prennent une hacquenée pour aller l'amble uers le paradis. C'est le terme dont nous nous seruons; et vous l'entandés sans doute. Vous aurés pris une persone vertüeuse; pour vous ayder et vous seruir; et par les conditions de vostre Contract vous aurés pouruû je m'asseure qu'elle eust interest a uostre conseruation. C'est ce que j'ay allegué a Ceux de mes amis que j'ay uus dans cette Erreur que le Philosophe ne deuoit jamais prendre femme; n'en y ayant point (disent ils) qui puisse estre la juste moitié d'un grand personage. Et sur ce sujet je leur ay dit ce que faisoit un tres habile home de mes amis; il donoit a ses valets quelque ecû de gages plus que les autres maistres et de bones Estrenes tous les ans tellement qu'ils auoient interest a le uoir atteindre a l'autre année. il faisoit une honeste pension a son medecin qui par ce moyen auoit interest à le conseruer en santé Car par leurs conuentions, qu'il fust sain, ou qu'il fust malade le medecin n'y auoit ni plus ni moins. Voyla uostre Apologie come je la fais. Quoy qu'il en soit si vous aués changé la condition de garçon en celle d'home marié, come ce ne peut estre que pour une persone de grand merite, je vous prie qu'au moins j'en sois eclaircy et que par une Lettre que je prendray la liberté de vous adresser, je déclare a qui vous touche de si prés, combien je vous suis acquis.

Apres vous auoir rendû ce respect, il faut que je me confesse ingenûment a vous Monsieur, d'un soupçon que j'ay eu de vous. je vous écriuis les deux dernieres fois que j'auois remis entre les mains de Mr de Martel les trois volumes de la Philosophie d'Epicure de Mr

Gassendi² pour vous les faire tenir. il m'auoit promis qu'il le feroit par le moyen de Mʳ de Scorbiac³ Conseiller en la Chambre de l'Edit de Castres⁴ son Cousin Germain, autrefois compagnon d'étude, et maintenant grand amy de nostre Ambassadeur Mʳ de Bourdeaux:⁵ Cependant Mʳ de Martel a encore Ces liures dans sa mâle bien empacquetés et le pacquet bien cacheté, je luy en ay donc fait reproche fort souuent; et il m'est échapé de luy dire une fois entre autres que si vous croyiés de moy, que j'eusse manqué a vous rendre ce petit office, vous pourrès ne plus faire compte de moy. A cela il m'a repondu que sans doute vous auriés jugé autrement de mes manieres d'agir, et m'a promis de vous bien rendre compte de tout. Auec celà je le uois luy mesme bien embarrassé a cette heure que le pere ou le frere de Mʳ de Bourdˣ est a la Cour, et qu'il ne scait par qui vous envoyer ces Liures. Si vostre Libraire auoit icy un Correspondant affidé, ce seroit la meilleure chose du monde, non seulement le Gassendi mais toute autre chose que vous voudriés nous vous l'envoyrions. il s'est imprimé a Tholose une Philosophie entiere du P Maignan Minime, en 4 uolumes in 8°.⁶ Mʳ de Carcaui⁷ m'a promis de me la faire uoyr; si c'etoit quelque chose de solide, des qu'il y en auroit [>a uendre] en cette ville nous vous [en *deleted*] l'enuoyerions. Nous pourrions mesme de temps en temps vous dire quelque chose des Porismes [>des anciens] restitües par Mʳ de fermat;⁸ des nombres magiques de Mʳ de Pascal;⁹ et des autres choses dont on s'entretient les samedy-apres-disné chez Mʳ le Pailleul¹⁰ en la rüe Sᵗ André ou nos Geometres de cette ville ont bien uoulû que je me trouuasse. En un mot je ne suis en peine que des moyens; quant au desir de vous rendre toute sorte de seruices je vous prie d'en juger par l'estime que je fais de vous Monsieur, que je tiens sans exception quelquonque le seul Philosophe qui soit au monde, pour auoir allié ensemble une Geometrie tres solide a [une *deleted* >la] conoissance claire et distincte que vous aués de la Nature.

Certes c'est en uertû de cette estime et seulement pour entendre uostre Leuiatan qu'enfin apres auoir icy trouué un Docteur qui scait uostre langue je me suis mis entre ses mains, et qu'aprés en auoir receu les reigles de la Prononciation, la Conjuguaison des auxiliaires, les Pronoms et Particules en un mot les reigles de la Gramaire je me suis mis a écrire sous luy [>mot a mot] uostre liure dont je fais une version interlineaire dont j'écris tous les jours ponctuellement sur la ligne ce qui m'a esté dicté, dans mon Liure le seul que j'aye trouué a acheter en tout Paris. Je vous en diray mesmes cela de particulier. Mon Docteur tout scauant qu'il est en celà, mais d'ailleurs ne scachant pas vos

Principes ne m'a sceu expliquer le terme *limbs* qui se trouue tout au comencement de vostre Introduction ou vous insinüés que la vie est seulement un mouuement de ce *limbs*. for seeing life is but a motion of limbs:[11] Et ce qui est rare c'est que ni le mot ne se trouue dans le Dictionaire de Robert Sheruood; ni il ne se trouue dans le Dictionaire de Cotgraue[12] ni il n'est conû par cincq ou six Anglois qui sont icy gens de lettres d'ailleurs, a qui on en a demandé le sens[13] et qui n'ont sceu en rendre raison. Vous trouuerrés bon Monsieur que moy qui suis resolû de ne pas perdre un seul mot de ce bel ouurage et qui dans moins de trois mois fust ce a force de trauail espere de l'auoir tout étudié, si dis-je je vous demande l'explication de ce mot. Au reste je commence a comprendre qu'est ce qui oblige tous ceux qui parlent de cet ouurage a l'estimer également et pour la solidité de la doctrine et pour la beauté des expressions. je vois, au moins j'apercois quelle part le tour de vos phrases doit estre latin come la ou parlant des penseés qu'on a en ueillant vous dites *de nos ueillantes penseés*;[14] et les endroits ou le tour du langage ueut estre grec come en ces expressions *du des homes coeur*[15] &^{c} τῆς τῶν ἀνθρώπων καρδίας. Mais je m'emporte et je pourrois bien vous ôter un peu trop de ce temps si cher et si precieus que vous auriés destiné a toute autre chose. a celà prés je ne me lasserois point de vous dire que c'est vous Monsieur que j'estime, que j'étudie, que j'apele mon Maistre et dont en effect je seray toujours tres sincerement

Monsieur
Vostre tres humble et tres obeissant seruiteur
Duuerdus

A Paris le 4e Aoust 1654

[*postscript:*] Si vous me faites l'honeur de m'écrire s'il vous plait que ce soit auec cette suscription. A Mr Duuerdus, chez Mr Mallet[16] Mathematicien sur le fossé de la Porte St Germain, proche la Main d'or à Paris.

[*endorsed by James Wheldon:*] Monsr du Verdus Aug. 4. 1654

Translation of Letter 67

Sir,

I have not told you my news for a long time; but in fact I have not received any news from you for a long time either. This grieves me, all the more so because I cannot find anyone among my acquaintance here who has had any letters from you since I last received one. Nevertheless, they know more about how your affairs are going than I do, if what they told me is true—that you have got married.[1] If that is so then I congratulate you with all my heart. I know you are a very prudent man; given that you have taken a wife, I am sure that you will not have followed the example of those who take an ambling mare for a slow journey to heaven. That is the phrase we use; no doubt you see what it means. You will have taken someone virtuous, to help you and serve you; and I am sure that under the terms of your contract she will have an interest in your preservation.

This is what I told those of my friends who, I found, held the erroneous view that a philosopher should never take a wife—on the grounds, they say, that no woman can ever adequately fulfil the role of being one half of such a great person. A propos, I told them what a clever friend of mine did: he gave his servants wages which were a crown or so more than those of other masters, and gave them good New Year's gifts every year, so that they had an interest in seeing him last till the following year; and he gave an annual payment to his doctor, who thereby had an interest in keeping him in good health. Under the agreement they had made, his doctor was paid neither more nor less whether he was healthy or sick. That is the defence I made on your behalf. At all events if you have changed your status from bachelor to married man, as it can only be for a very worthy lady, I beg you at least to let me know about it. And please allow me, in a letter which I shall take the liberty of sending you, to tell the person who is now so closely related to you how utterly devoted to you I am.

After paying you these respects, Sir, I am obliged to make an honest confession of a doubt which I have had about you. In my last two letters I told you that I had sent the three volumes of M. Gassendi's work on the philosophy of Epicurus[2] back to M. de Martel, to have them delivered to you. He had promised me that he would have this done through M. de Scorbiac,[3] *conseiller* of the Chambre de l'édit at Castres[4] (his cousin and erstwhile fellow student), who is now a great friend of our Ambassador M. de Bordeaux.[5] However, M. de Martel still has those books in his trunk, well wrapped up as a parcel and the parcel well sealed. I have frequently reproached him over this, and once I could not restrain myself from saying, among other things, that if you thought I had failed to perform this small service for you you would not be able to put your trust in me any more. To which he replied that he was sure you would have thought differently of my way of behaving, and he promised to explain everything to you properly. Accordingly I know that he feels very awkward now that M. de Bordeaux's father or brother is at Court, and he does not know whom he can use to deliver these books to you.

If your bookseller had a reliable correspondent here, that would be quite the best solution, and we could send you not only the Gassendi but also anything else you wished for. The complete Philosophy of Father Maignan (a Minim friar) has been printed at Toulouse, in four volumes, octavo.[6] M. de Carcavi[7] promised he would show it to me. If it is a solid piece of work we could send you a copy as soon as it goes on sale in this city. We could also tell you something about the Porisms of the Ancients which M. de Fermat has reconstructed;[8] about M. de Pascal's magic numbers;[9] and about the other things which we discuss on Saturday evenings at M. Le Pailleur's[10] house in the rue S. André, where the geometers of this city have kindly invited me. To sum up, I am anxious only about the means to employ; as for my desire to do you every kind of service, I beg you, Sir, to judge how great it is by the high regard which I have for you. I hold you to be, without any exception whatsoever, the only philosopher in the world, for your achievement of joining together a firmly argued geometry and the clear and distinct knowledge of nature which you possess.

Indeed, it is because of this high regard for you and solely in order to understand your *Leviathan* that I have at last put myself under the tuition of a doctor I found here who knows your language. Having learned from him the rules of pronunciation, the conjugation of auxiliary verbs, the pronouns, and particles—in short, the rules of English grammar—I have begun under his direction to write out your book word by word. I am making an interlinear translation, writing punctually each day what he dictates to me, which I insert above the line in my copy of the book; it was the only copy I could find on sale in the whole of Paris (a fact which I should like to point out to you).

My doctor, learned though he is in the subject, but not being familiar with your principles, could not explain the term 'limbs' to me; it appears right at the start of your Introduction, where you suggest that life is only a motion of this 'limbs': 'for seeing life is but a motion of limbs ...'.[11] The odd thing is that the word is not given in Robert Sherwood's Dictionary, nor in Cotgrave's,[12] nor is it known by five or six Englishmen here (who, what is more, are men of letters); they were asked what it meant[13] but could not explain it. You will be pleased, Sir, if I, who am determined not to miss a single word of this fine book, and who hope to complete my study of it within three months (by sheer hard work if necessary)—if, I say, I ask you to explain this word to me. Otherwise, I am beginning to understand what it is about this book which obliges all who talk about it to praise it both for the strength of its doctrines and for the beauty of its expressions. I can see (or, at least, glimpse) how far the turn of phrase you use is essentially Latin: as when, talking of the thoughts which we have while we are awake, you say 'our waking thoughts'.[14] And in places the turn of speech imitates Greek, as in expressions such as 'of man's heart'[15] (τῆς τῶν ἀνθρώπων καρδίας). But I am getting carried away, and perhaps I am depriving you of a little too much of your valuable and precious time, which you will have intended to spend on other things. Were it not for that, I should never stop telling you that you, Sir, are the person I admire, study, and call my master; and I shall indeed always remain, with all my heart, Sir,

Your most humble and most obedient servant
du Verdus

Paris, 4 August 1654

[*postscript:*] If you do me the honour of writing to me, please address your letter as follows: M. du Verdus, at the house of M. Mallet,[16] mathematician, at the moat of the Porte Saint-Germain, near the Main d'Or, Paris.

[1] Hobbes never married.

[2] *Animadversiones* (1649).

[3] Thomas de Scorbiac or d'Escorbiac, member of a prominent Protestant family of Montauban and Castres. His father, Samuel, married Anne de Thomas (whose sister, Marguerite, married de Martel's father) (see Tournier, *Les Réfugiés du pays castrais*, pp. 224n., 313n., and the entry on de Martel in the Biographical Register). Thomas de Scorbiac succeeded his father as a *conseiller* of the Chambre de l'édit at Castres (see below, n. 4) in 1638; in 1650 he became a member of the 'academy' of Castres (a literary and philosophical society of which his uncle, the poet Jean de Scorbiac, was a founding member); and in 1651 he edited the treatise on physiology by his teacher, William Duncan (*Physiologia Gullielmi Duncani* (Toulouse, 1651)) (see Niderst, *Madeleine de Scudéry*, pp. 123–5). In 1665 he opposed, unsuccessfully, the take-over of the Protestant College of Castres by the Jesuits (Combes, *Particularités historiques*, p. 69).

[4] A court composed of Protestants and Catholics in equal numbers, set up in accordance with the Edict of Nantes to ensure unbiased treatment for Protestants. The court at Castres covered the jurisdiction of the Parlement of Toulouse.

[5] Antoine de Bordeaux (*c.*1621–60), sent by Mazarin as an emissary to England in Dec. 1652; he received the title of Ambassador in Mar. 1654 and negotiated the Anglo-French treaty of Nov. 1655.

[6] *Cursus philosophicus* (4 vols., Toulouse, 1653). Emmanuel Maignan (*c.*1601–76), a native of Toulouse, took his vows as a Minim friar in 1619. He taught philosophy and theology at the order's convent in Rome (1636–50), where he developed an interest in experimental science, and returned to Toulouse in 1650. The *Cursus philosophicus* expounds a modified scholasticism.

[7] Pierre de Carcavi (*c.*1600–84), mathematician, member of the Parlement of Toulouse (1632), resident since 1636 in Paris, where he entered the service of the duc de Liancourt (1648). An old friend of Fermat from his early years in Toulouse, he also corresponded with Huygens and acted as intermediary between Roberval and Descartes in 1649, reporting Roberval's objections to Descartes's *Géométrie*.

[8] Pierre Fermat (1601–65), member of the Parlement of Toulouse and one of the founders of modern algebraic geometry, attempted to reconstruct the *Porisms* of Euclid, a lost work mentioned by Pappus (see Fermat, *Œuvres*, i, pp. 76–84).

[9] In 1654, in his 'Address to the Parisian Academy' (the group which met at Le Pailleur's house (see below, n. 10)), Pascal announced that he was preparing to publish a treatise, which was 'completely ready' ('entièrement préparé'), on magic squares (Pascal, *Œuvres*, ed. Brunschvicg and Boutroux, iii, pp. 305–8). A version of this treatise was eventually published in Arnauld, *Œuvres*, xlii, pp. 345–66. See Pascal, *Œuvres complètes*, ed. Lafuma, pp. 95–100.

[10] Jacques Le Pailleur (d. 1654), mathematician and *libertin*; his date of birth is unknown. A friend of the poet Saint-Amant in the 1620s, he was at first best known as a lover of music and dance and a composer of burlesque poetry (see Pintard, *Libertinage*, pp. 349–50). He was largely self-taught in mathematics. In 1646 he contributed (as did Hobbes) a demonstration to Pell's *Controversiae pars prima* (p. 54). As early as 1635 Pascal's father had shown him some of his son's work in geometry, and in 1648 Pascal sent Le Pailleur a long letter on Noël's *Le Plein du vuide* (Pascal, *Œuvres*, ed. Brunschvicg and Boutroux, ii, pp. 179–211). After Mersenne's death, Le Pailleur continued the regular meetings of scientists at his own house (see the Biographical Register, 'Mylon'); he died on 25 Oct./4 Nov. 1654.

[11] *Leviathan*, p. 1.

[12] The *French-English Dictionary* by Randle Cotgrave and the *Dictionaire anglois & françois* by Robert Sherwood were published together (London, 1650). 'Limb' does not appear in Sherwood's dictionary, because he spells the word as 'Limme' instead.

[13] The impersonal construction 'they were asked what it meant' suggests an explanation of this bizarre statement: no doubt the enquiry was made through a third party, who garbled the word in the process.

[14] *Leviathan*, p. 6.

[15] Ibid., p. 2.

[16] Philippe Mallet (*c.*1606–79), a teacher of mathematics in Paris, author of a *Cursus mathematicus*, and of a treatise on fortification in French verse (Poggendorff, *Handwörterbuch*). He was perhaps also the 'M. Mallet' described by Oldenburg in 1659 as 'a reasonable good Chymist' (*OC* i, p. 215).

François du Verdus to Hobbes, from Paris

Chatsworth, Hobbes MSS, letter 4 (original).

Monsieur

Plus je uis dans le monde, plus je conois qu'il est uray ce que dit Mr Bacon dans sa Parabole du Sphinx, que l'home est un Enigme dificile a expliquer.[1] je vous écriuis le 8e de ce moys;[2] et aprés vous auoir felicité de vostre mariage (s'il est uray) je me pleignis a vous du peu d'amitié qu'il semble que Mr de Martel aye pour vous Monsieur, et pour moy. j'auois bien oüy dire qu'en certaines rancontres, des choses qu'on ueut s'excuser de faire on dit au comancement *qu'il n'est pas* encore temps; et aprés; *que le temps en est passé*: Mais qu'ou il s'agit de faire plaisir a nos amis, on fist ce que m'a fait Mr de Martel qui a retenû plus de quatre mois vostre Epicure par Mr Gassendi;[3] en uerité je ne m'y serois pas attendû. Je vous dis cecy parce-que l'affaire me touche au coeur: il se peut faire que vous etiés pressé de lire ces Liures pour y examiner et refuter quelqu'une de ces opinions qu'il y a qui y sont si mal établies, ou pour autre dessein quel qu'il soyt. Tant y a Mr de Martel m'assura hier de fraische date qu'ayant un home assuré pour enuoyer en Angleterre ce qu'il uoudra, et en f[aire *page torn*] venir tout ce dont il aura besoin, sans faute il vous enuoyeroit vos Liures dans cette semaine. Il receut mesmes quelque comission de moy; Et come je me suis enfoncé dans l'Etude de vostre langue, il me promit de me faire uenir [▷ pour mon usage] diuers liures, dont je luy donay le memoyre. Ils uiendront quand il plairra a Dieu. Cependant uoicy au uray deux mots d'une resolution que j'ay prise. La Guerre ayant esté en Guyenne,[4] il faudroit que j'y retournasse si je uoulois remettre mon Bien-en-fonds, et en tirer du reuenû. Ne pouuant me resoudre si tot a une telle retraite, soit que je sois acoutumé aux Grandes villes; ou que je craigne qu'il n'arriue de delà quelque autre souleuement auant lequel ce seroit fort a contretemps que j'aurois reparé mon Bien; je me tiens icy a étudier. Si Mylord Protecteur, le Roy de Süede, les Protestans d'Allemagne et ceux que nous auons en france prenent leur temps, et que j'en pressente quelque chose,[5] mon dessein est de me retirer a Londres ou je ne jureray que par vostre Philosophie et par la Sagesse des Anciens de Mr Bacon. Voyla mes ueües. Mais Monsieur

tandis que je suis icy j'ay a vous prier de deux choses: l'une; que si vous
ne m'enuoyés plus de vos Cayers (a moy qui n'en ay point reçeu depuis
le Cahyer L⁶ et qui neanmoins vous ay esté fidelle, et le seray, et n'en ay
rien fait uoir, non pas mesmes a Mʳ [de *page torn*] Martel) au-moins
vous me disiés des nouuelles tant de vostre santé que de vos études.
l'autre: que si le Liure de la Sagesse des Anciens de Mʳ Bacon se trouue
en langue Angloise,⁷ vous m'obligiés de me l'enuoyer par le premier
Courrier, soit en blanc, ou rellié: toutefois j'aymerois mieux qu'il fust
en blanc, et de beau papier je le ferois rellier icy a ma mode et ce seroit
mon second-vade-mecum; vostre liure de Ciue de l'impression de
hollande⁸ étant mon Breuiaire ordinaire. je ne vous ferois pas cette
priere, si je ne sçauois combien vous estimés les ecrits de Mʳ Bacon, et
si en mon particulier je n'auois trauaillé sur ce liure de la Sagesse des
Anciens. Dés l'anneé passeé je vous écriuis ce me semble que j'auois
traduit ce Liure en francois; dépuis, j'ay fait encore plus; j'en ay
expliqué diuers endroits ou par tout j'ay discourû dans les ueües que
vous m'aués donées. sur tout je me suis étendû a propos du Typhon sur
l'vnité de la puissance de l'Etat,⁹ vous alleguant par tout et expliquant
vos sentimens que le peuple les puisse entendre. mesmes l'amitié que
j'ay pour vous (et permettés moy ce terme je le dis auec tandresse) m'a
fait auancer (c'esté l'explication sur le Promethée du peu de progrés
que lon fait dans les Sciences)¹⁰ que nostre Siécle aymoit bien peu les
Doctrines saines et utiles; qu'on n'y eust pas uû tous les Souuerains de
l'Europe a l'enuy l'un de l'autre [>vous faire] de grands regales, a vous
qui auiés si bien étably leur authorité; et qui sur un sujet de cette
importance auiés écrit plus fortement que qui que ce soit, et si
fortement que tous les articles de uostre liure [>fondes sur deux
principes dont on ne scauroit douter] sont dans un enchaisnement
[*page torn* pa]reil a celuy ou doiuent estre les propositions Géo-
metriques. Ce que je vous dis est uray. Tant y a qu'ayant trauaillé sur le
Liure de la Sagesse des Anciens, et regardant l'angleterre come un
Lieu qui peut estre [>me] sera un asyle; pour y estre mieux reçeu j'ay
enuie de faire imprimer en Anglois ce liure de la Sagesse des Anciens;
auec une uersion interlineaire mot a mot; mon autre uersion un peu
moins forcée et mes explications. Pour cela donc je vous prie encore
une fois, que [>le] plutot que vos autres occupations vous le
permettront vous m'obligiés de me l'enuoyer; et que vous preniés la
peine de me l'adresser chez Mʳ Mallet¹¹ Ingenieur du Roy sur les fossés
de la porte Sᵗ Germain proche de la main d'or au fauxbourg Sᵗ
Germain. J'y loge; et y attens de vos Nouuelles. Dieu veüille qu'elles

soyent bonnes. Et je le prie qu'il vous tiene en santé; et [>que] vous donant une longue et heureuse vie il conserue pour le bien de nostre Siécle le seul philosophe qui soit au Monde. a ces mots le seul Philosophe qui soit au monde je me souuiens que je vous parlay dernierement du Cours de Philosophie du P. Maignan.[12] Mr de Carcauj[13] me l'a fait uoyr; En uerité cet autheur est un bon home. sa Metaphysiq est toute pleine de Quiddités, et d'Entités; et dans sa Physique [traitant *deleted* >au lieu ou il traitte] de la distinction de la Quantité et de la Matiere; il fait un grand discours sur le [>grand] mystere [des Gouttes? *deleted*].[14] Apres tout ou qu'on suprime son Liure, a quoy je conclûs et je l'ay deja suprimé pour mon regard; ou qu'on y corrige tout ce fatras [>de chôses] qu'il y a a corriger dans les liures ou il a étudie *amongst which the frequency of insignificant speech is one.*[15] Je suis

Monsieur
Vostre tres humble et tres obeissant seruiteur
Duuerdus

A Paris le 20e Aoust 1654

[*endorsed by James Wheldon:*] Monsr du Verdus 20 Aug. 1654

Translation of Letter 68

Sir,

The longer I live in the world, the more fully I understand the truth of what Mr Bacon says in his parable of the Sphinx, that man is a riddle hard to explain.[1] I wrote to you on the eighth of this month:[2] having congratulated you on your marriage (if the news of it is true), I complained about the low degree of friendship which M. de Martel seems to feel towards you, Sir, and towards myself. I had indeed heard it said that on certain occasions, when people want to excuse themselves for not doing something, they say to start with that 'it isn't the right time for it yet', and then later they say 'the right time has passed'. But where it is a matter of doing something to make our friends happy, I really would not have expected that anyone would treat me as M. de Martel has done, keeping your copy of M. Gassendi's *Epicurus*[3] for more than four months. I say this to you because the matter affects me very deeply: you may perhaps have been in a hurry to read these books in order to judge and refute some of the theories they contain which are so ill-founded—or for any other reason. Whatever the case,

M. de Martel gave me fresh assurances yesterday that he would send you your books this week without fail, now that he has a reliable person through whom to send whatever he wishes to England and to get whatever he needs sent from there. He also undertook to do some things for me: since I am engrossed in the study of your language, he promised to have various books (which I listed for him) sent over for my use. They will arrive when God wills.

However, let me say a word or two in all seriousness about a resolution I have made. Since there has been a war in Guyenne[4] I ought to return there if I am to restore my estates and get any income from them. But I cannot come to a speedy decision to confine myself there, either because I am used to living in large cities, or because I am afraid that some further uprising may occur there which would make my restoration of my property seem very untimely. So I remain here, in order to pursue my studies. If the Lord Protector, the King of Sweden, the Protestants of Germany, and the Protestants we have in France take their opportunity, and if my presentiment about that is correct,[5] it is my intention to retire to London, where I shall swear by nothing but your philosophy and Mr Bacon's *De sapientia veterum*. Those are my plans. But, Sir, there are two things that I should like to ask you to do while I am still here. One is that even if you no longer send me your sheets from the printers (I have received nothing since signature 'L',[6] although I have been faithful to you and shall continue to be so, having shown them to nobody, not even M. de Martel), at least you might send me some news, of your health as much as of your studies. And secondly, if Mr Bacon's book *De sapientia veterum* is available in an English translation,[7] I should be grateful if you could send it to me by the first post, either unbound or bound. (I should prefer it unbound, however, and printed on good paper; I should have it bound to my own taste and it would become my second vade-mecum, the Dutch edition of your *De cive*[8] being my usual breviary.) I would not ask this of you if I did not know how highly you regard Mr Bacon's writings, and if I had not, for my own part, done some work on this book, *De sapientia veterum*. I think I told you in a letter last year that I had translated this book into French. Since then I have done even more: I have written explanations of various passages in it, and throughout my explanations I have elaborated on the interpretations which you gave me. Above all, on the subject of Typhon I have written at length about the unity of the power of the state,[9] constantly citing you and explaining your views so that ordinary people can understand them. Moreover, the friendship which

I feel towards you (allow me to use this word—I say it with affection) has made me put forward the following claim in my commentary on the subject of Prometheus, concerning the small amount of progress achieved in the sciences.[10] I argue that our century has had very little regard for sound and useful theories, given that we have not seen all the sovereigns of Europe competing with one another to heap rewards on you for having established their authority so well—you who have written more cogently than anyone else on a subject of such importance, so cogently that all the parts of your book's argument, based on two principles which could not be doubted, are linked together in the same way that geometrical propositions should be. What I am telling you is the truth. Anyway, since I have worked on the book *De sapientia veterum*, and since I look upon England as a place which will perhaps afford me a safe haven, in order to be better received there I should like to have this book printed in English, together with an interlinear word-by-word translation, my other, rather less stilted, translation, and my commentary. So with that in mind I beg you again to do me the favour of sending it to me as soon as your other affairs will permit. Please address it to me at the house of M. Mallet,[11] Royal Engineer, at the moat of the porte Saint-Germain, near the Main d'Or in the faubourg Saint-Germain. That is where I am staying, and where I shall expect to receive your news. May it please God to let your news be good. And I pray to God to keep you in good health and give you a long and happy life, preserving for the good of our century the only true philosopher in the world.

Writing these words 'the only true philosopher in the world', I remember that I told you in my last letter about Father Maignan's *Cursus philosophicus*.[12] M. de Carcavi[13] has shown it to me, and the truth is that the author is a great booby. His metaphysics is absolutely full of quiddities and entities, and in his physics where he discusses the distinction between quantity and matter he discourses at length on the great mystery of droplets.[14] In the end one has to either put his book away (which is my own view, having already put it out of my mind), or correct the entire mishmash of things which need to be corrected in the books from which he has acquired his knowledge—'amongst which the frequency of insignificant Speech is one'.[15] I am, Sir,

Your most humble and obedient servant
du Verdus

Paris, 20 August 1654

¹ *De sapientia veterum*, ch. 28, does not quite say this; it treats the story of the Sphinx as a parable concerning the nature of science, and says that the science of man contains many riddles (Bacon, *Works*, vi, pp. 677–80).

² Letter 67 (dated [25 July/] 4 Aug.).

³ See Letter 67 n. 2.

⁴ The Fronde had been particularly turbulent in Guyenne, but the region was largely pacified by July 1653.

⁵ Meaning, presumably, if Cromwell, Charles X of Sweden, and the other Protestants combined in a war to overthrow Louis XIV.

⁶ This probably refers to proofs of *De homine*. This book was not published until 1658; but as there is no separate entry for it in the Stationers' Register, it was apparently covered by the entry of 18 [/28] Mar. 1653 for 'Elementorum Philosophiae', in Latine and English' (i, p. 416), which would have enabled the printing to be well advanced prior to the date of this letter. The signatures of the 1658 edition extend to 'M' (4to: A² B-M⁴).

⁷ *The Wisedome of the Ancients*, tr. Sir Arthur Gorges (London, 1619).

⁸ The 2nd or 3rd edn. (both Amsterdam, 1647).

⁹ Ch. 2 of *De sapientia veterum* treats the story of Typhon, who rebelled against Jupiter, as a parable concerning the nature of rebellion (Bacon, *Works*, vi, pp. 630–1).

¹⁰ Ibid., ch. 26, treats the story of Prometheus as a parable concerning the human condition, and argues that the progress of arts and sciences is held back by those who think that knowledge of them has already been perfected (pp. 668–76).

¹¹ See Letter 67 n. 16.

¹² See ibid., n. 6.

¹³ See ibid., n. 7.

¹⁴ Maignan uses drops of water as an analogy to show how the same essence can be contained in different *entia* (*Cursus philosophicus*, i, pp. 303–4).

¹⁵ *Leviathan*, p. 4, where Hobbes says this is something that needs to be amended in the universities.

LETTER 69   [26 AUGUST/] 5 SEPTEMBER 1654

Thomas de Martel to Hobbes, from Paris

Chatsworth, Hobbes MSS, letter 5 (original).
Printed in von Brockdorff, 'Fünf Briefe', pp. 11–13.

Monsieur

Vous me cognoissez assez pour Juger que si j'estois coupable comme Je vous ai peut estre paru Je n'aurois pas mesme la hardiesse de vous demander pardon d'un manquement qui n'en deuroit Jamais trouuer en vous s'il estoit veritable apres les bontez que vous auez eues pour moi bien loin de pretendre de me justifier si vous me le permettez, Vous n'auez pas oublié auec quel regret Je vous laissai à mon depart malgré moi en un estat auquel bien que vous fussiez en effect hors de

danger de Vostre Indisposition mon affection ne me permettoit pas
d'estre sans beaucoup d'apprehension, et certainem[t] J'en fus en des
Inquietudes Incroiables Jusqu'a ce que Je sceus vostre entiere guerison,
mais Je ne fus pas chez moi[1] que la guerre y fut portée qui rompant tout
commerce auec Paris à peine me laissa Informer de vostre retour en
Angl.[re] ou vostre seule satisfaction et l'Interest de vostre repos pend[t] les
troubles de ce Roiaume et surtout de Paris me donna de la Joie de vous
scauoir bien que Je perdisse presque toute esperance de vous reuoir,
qui ne m'a pas esté un mediocre desplaisir, Dans ce temps neantmoins
Je hazardai quelques letres dont Je n'ai pas sceu l'euenement, Depuis la
paix immediatem[t] apres la peste nous affligea de sorte qu'il n'a pas este
estrange que ce qui nous priuoit du commerce des plus voisins m'ostat
le vostre, Eschapé de ce fleau et venu aussi tost [> apres] ici ou Je vous
ai trouué si fort à dire que Je n'y ai point gousté la mesme satisfaction
qu'autrefois bien que hors de vostre conuersation J'en eusse plus de
subiet, mon premier soin fut de scauoir vostre estat de tous ceux qui s'y
Interessoient presque comme moi; et Je vous ai mesme obligation de
m'en auoir appris vous mesme quelque chose par vostre letre du mois
de 10.[bre2] que Je ne receus qu'en mars au quel temps M[r] Du Verdus
m'aiant baïllé la Phi'e d'Ep.[re] pour vous faire tenir par la voie de nostre
Ambassadeur[3] Je vous fis reponse que Je mis dans le paquet de ces
liures, qui m'a demeure Jusques à present partie par la faute d'autrui,
partie un peu par la mienne, croiant toutes les sepmaines vous
l'enuoyer sans trouuer commoditè ou la laissant eschaper, ne vous
osant cepend[t] escrire que ces liures ne fussent enuoyez, voila, M[r], la
Cause ou l'occasion d'un silence de trois annees, ne contant pas les
letres que Je vous ai escrites si uous ne les auez pas receues, ou si J'ai
failli en quelque chose Je ne puis estre accusé que de quelque
Negligence dont la cause Je vous asseure est si raisonnable qu'elle
porte sa grace, car si J'en ai esté capable en vostre endroit, bien que Je
recognoisse qu'il n'y a sorte de deuoir, de respect et d'office que Je ne
vous doiue rendre, la seule veneration neantmoins que vous scauez que
J'ai pour vous m'a dispensé d'estre si regulier pour des simples
Ciuilitez, qui satisfont si peu ceux qui ont des hauts sentiments pour
ceux à qui ils les doiuent, tels que J'en ai pour vous. S'il se fut agi de
vous seruir, si seulem[t] mes letres vous eussent peu estre agreables
d'elles mesmes sans me considerer par l'Inclination que vous auez
pour moi, Je veux dire que si J'eusse peu vous escrire en philosophe
approchant de celui que vous estes J'aurois este sans doubte le plus
assidu à vous escrire, Mais si vous m'apprenez que vous auez eu

agreable que Je vous rendisse raison de tout ce qui m'auroit peu rendre suspect dans vostre esprit du peu de recognoissance, desormais quand mes letres vous deuroient estre Importunes Je ne m'aquiterai pas moins de ce deuoir que des plus essentiels qui sont vne Estime si particuliere de vostre grand genie et de vostre vertu aussi extraord^{re} que Je n'en ai point de pareille pour homme que Je cognoisse par moi mesme, par reputation ou par ses ouurages, et vne si profonde recognoissance pour tout ce que Je doibs à vostre bonté de m'auoir souffert dans sa conuersation et donné par la moien d'apprendre des choses que Je n'eusse Jamais acquises par aucun estude, ou meditation, ou experience que Je ne serai pas satisfaict si Je ne passe la mer tost ou tard pour vous l'aller tesmoigner, et vous embrasser encore une fois, pour ne mesler pas de subiets si differents et ne faire pas celle ci trop longue Je ne vous dis rien touchant vostre trauail quelque curiosité que J'en aie, Je le reserue à une autrefois, Je vous supplie cepend^t m'app[rendre *page torn*] l'Estat de vostre santé, Je loge a l'hostel d'Aniou rue Dauphine.

Au reste Je doubte si peu que vous ne soiez satisfaict de moi apres cette lecture que J'ose bien vous prier de commander à quelquun des vostres de chercher un honneste logem^t d'un couple de chambres pour la femme de M^r le Maire,[4] qui doibt passer en Angleterre dans peu de Jours, estant de ce pais la, c'est vne fort honneste Damoiselle dont le mari est chez Mr Heruard[5] fort cognu de M^r Du Prat Je souhaiterois, que ce logem^t fut prest quand elle arriuera en enuoyant demander des nouuelles chez vous, bien que ce ne soit pas une commission digne de vous, Je n'ai pu neantmoins la lui refuser, sur tout la chargeant du liure de Mr Gassend qu'elle vous rendra, Je vous prie me croire toute ma vie plus que personne du monde

Monsieur
Vostre treshumble et tresobeiss^t seruiteur
De Martel

A Paris ce 5 7.bre 1654

[*addressed:*] For Mr Hobbes at the greene dragon in Paules Church-yerd[6] London

[*endorsed by Hobbes:*] Monsr Martell Sept. 5. 1654 Mad:^{lle} le Maire Hostel d'Aniou rue Dauphine

Translation of Letter 69

Sir,

You know me well enough to conclude that if I were as blameworthy as I may perhaps have seemed to be, I would not even have the audacity to ask your forgiveness for a sin of omission which, if it were real, would never deserve to be forgiven by you, after all the kindnesses you have shown me. Still less would I claim (if you will allow it) to justify my actions. You have not forgotten how sorry I was, when I was forced to go away, to leave you in such a poor state that my love for you obliged me to feel extremely anxious on your behalf, even though your health was in fact no longer in danger. Indeed, I suffered from unimaginable anxieties until I learned that you were completely well again. However, no sooner had I returned home[1] than the war reached that region: it cut off all communication with Paris, and only just allowed me to learn of your return to England. It gave me great happiness to know that you were content and enjoying the benefit of a tranquil life while this kingdom (and especially Paris) was undergoing these disturbances, even though I lost almost all hope of seeing you again, which caused me considerable distress. Nevertheless, during this period I ventured to send you some letters; I do not know what became of them. Immediately after peace was settled we were afflicted by the plague, and it is not surprising that it should have prevented me from communicating with you, when it was cutting off our communication with our closest neighbours. Having escaped that scourge I returned immediately afterwards to Paris, where I missed you so much that I could not take the same pleasure in being there as I had before, even though, deprived of your company, I had more opportunity to do so. My first concern was to find out how you were from all those who were almost as interested in this as I was; and for that matter I am obliged to you for having given me some news of this yourself, in the letter which you wrote in December,[2] but which I did not receive till March. By then M. du Verdus had sent me the 'Philosophy of Epicurus' to get it delivered to you by means of our Ambassador;[3] I wrote you a reply which I put in the parcel containing these books, but up till now the parcel has stayed in my possession. This is partly through the fault of other people and partly through my own fault; each week I have thought I would be able to send it to you, but have either failed to find or failed to take up an opportunity of doing so.

That, Sir, is why (or how) I have been silent for three years (ignoring, that is, the letters I wrote to you, if you did not receive them). If I have failed to some extent, I can only be accused of a certain amount of neglectfulness whose cause, I assure you, is so reasonable that it brings its own pardon with it: if I have been capable of neglecting you, despite my awareness that I owe you every kind of duty, respect, and service, nevertheless the sheer veneration which you know I feel for you has relieved me of the duty of strict adherence to the mere observances of good manners—observances which give us so little satisfaction when we have feelings of soaring admiration towards those to whom they are due, as I do towards you. If it had been a matter of doing you some service; if my letters had only been capable of giving you pleasure in their own right, and not by virtue of your indulgence towards me; if, in other words, I had been capable of writing as a philosopher at anything like your own level, I should undoubtedly have been the most assiduous of correspondents. But if you tell me that you have accepted my explanation of everything that may have made you think me unmindful of you, from now on when I have a duty to pester you with my letters I shall meet that obligation as fully as I do the most essential obligations that I am under—of which the first is the special esteem which I feel for your great intellect and extraordinary virtue, an esteem which is greater than any I feel for anyone that I know, or know of, or whose works I have read. And the second is the gratitude I feel for all the benefits I have gained from your kindness in letting me enjoy your conversation, from which I was able to gain knowledge which I should otherwise never have acquired by any reading, contemplation, or experience. So deep is my gratitude that I shall not be content unless, sooner or later, I cross the sea in order to express it to your face, and embrace you once more. In order not to intermingle such different topics, and in order to keep this letter from growing too long, I ask you nothing about your work, however much curiosity I have to hear of it. I shall reserve that topic till another occasion; but I beg you meanwhile to tell me if you are well. I am staying at the hotel d'Anjou in the rue Dauphiné.

Moreover, I am so sure that you will be satisfied about my conduct after reading this letter that I am bold enough to ask you to tell one of your household to find some decent lodgings (two rooms) for M. le Maire's wife,[4] who is due to go into England in a few days' time. She is English herself, and a very respectable lady; her husband is staying with M. Hervart,[5] whom M. du Prat knows well. I should like the lodgings to be ready when she arrives. I know this request is not worthy of being addressed to you, but I could not refuse to make it, especially since I have entrusted M. Gassendi's book to her, which she will give you. I beg you to believe, Sir, that I am, for all my life, and more than anyone in the world,

Your most humble and obedient servant,
de Martel

Paris, 5 September 1654

[*addressed: see text*]

[1] Montauban (see the Biographical Register).

[2] This letter does not apparently survive.

[3] See Letter 67, at nn. 2, 5.

[4] Unidentified. Possibly Jean Maire, the printer and bookseller of Leiden who published Descartes's *Discours* in 1637, and was active until *c*.1656. He is conflated in the index of *MC* with Jean Le Maire (b. 1581), the engineer, scientist, and musical theorist whose work on notation and the development of an 'almeric lute' attracted Mersenne's interest (see *MC* v, pp. 216n., 219, 235n., 479; ix, p. 16). Since a copy of one of this Le Maire's MSS survives in a group of Sir Charles Cavendish's papers (BL MS Harl. 6796, fos. 175-7ʳ: reproduced in *MC* ix, pp. 565-9), it is possible that he had some contact with Hobbes; but a modern study of Le Maire's work implies (though without presenting the evidence) that he died not long after 1647 (Cohen, 'Jean Le Maire', p. 176). Alternatively, the le Maires mentioned here may have been members of the family of Pierre de la Maire or de la Mare, a French musician in the service of Queen Henrietta Maria who died in 1649 (Ashbee (ed.), *Records of Court Music*, iii, pp. 245-51; v, p. 23: I am grateful to Dr Richard Luckett for this reference). Other candidates for identification are less promising. A John and Mary Le Maire of Amsterdam are mentioned in an application by their daughter, Susanna Cooper, for denization in 1661 (*CSPD* 1661-2, p. 175); a Cornelius la Maire, a merchant from Amsterdam, was staying in London in May 1656 (BL MS Add. 34015, fo. 5ʳ). The C. le Maire whose *Paris ancien et nouveau* was published in 1685 might also be considered: the accounts he gives of the Bourdelot 'academy' and other gatherings of the 1650s are detailed enough to suggest personal knowledge (iii, pp. 442-5). But the minute attention paid by that author to Catholic churches and religious orders makes it unlikely that he can have been the le Maire referred to here, whose connection with a Protestant patron (and an English wife) strongly suggests that he was a Huguenot.

[5] Barthélemy Hervart or Herward (d. 1676), born in Augsburg but established as a banker in Paris. Admired by Mazarin for his actions during the Fronde, when he persuaded Turenne's troops in Germany not to invade France, he was made *intendant des finances* in 1656 and *contrôleur général des finances* in 1657. He was a zealous Protestant, and a patron of his co-religionists. Abraham du Prat had entered his service in 1647 (BN MS f.l. 10352, part 1, fos. 107ᵛ-109).

[6] Andrew Crooke's shop: see the Biographical Register, 'William Crooke'.

LETTER 70   [4/] 14 SEPTEMBER 1654

Abraham du Prat to Hobbes, from Paris

Chatsworth, Hobbes MSS, letter 6 (original).

Monsieur

Apres vous auoir tesmoigné ma veneration par un long silence, vous me permetrés s'il vous plaist, de ioindre à ce culte muet, celui de ma plume pour quelques momens seulement, et qu'elle soit auiourduy l'interprete de mes pensées. Quand i'auois l'honneur de vous voir en cette ville, ie rendois de temps en temps hommage à vostre scauoir et à vostre vertu, et ie vous declarois auec plaisir l'empire absolu que vostre teste auoit acquis sur la mienne, et sur mon coeur aussi. Mais à present que ie ne puis le faire de bouche, à cause de la distance des lieux, ie suis contraint d'employer l'escriture qui est le seul moyen qui me reste pour vous asseurer de leur entiere sousmission. Vous n'aués qu'a publier bien tost vos sentimens touchant les choses naturelles, et ie vous promets de les receuoir auec le mesme respect que si c'estoyent des Edicts et des Ordonnances du Prince. Je ne pense pas de rien faire contre le bon sens si ayant la cognoissance que i'ay de la verité de vos principes, et du soin exa[ct *page torn*] auec lequel vous aués acoustumé de considerer et de supputer toutes choses, ie ne conte point apres vous, et si ie n'examine pas beaucoup les consequences que vous en tirés si iudicieusement. Mais, Monsieur, si par l'euidence de vos demonstrations, vous vous estes rendu maistre de ma teste, qui auoit esté imprenable à tous les anciens Philosophes et Modernes, et qui ne s'estoit iamais voulu rendre à leurs systemes, quelque ordre et quelque force qui semblat les acompagner, l'excellence de vostre vertu vous a gagné tout à fait mon coeur. Il est vray que Monsieur D'Heruart[1] et quelques autres de mes amis y ont aussi part, et que vous ne le possedés que par indiuis auec eux, mais si ie [> le] leur ay donne, c'est pour vous en acquerir d'autres plus vtiles et de plus grand reuenu que le mien, et à condition que chacun d'eux vous donnera le sien tout entier, et qu'il vous aimera s'il est possible, aussi passionnement que

Monsieur
Vre tres humble et tres obeissant seruiteur
A. Du Prat

A Paris ce 14 septembre 1654

[*postscript:*] Celui qui vous rendra la presente est un gentilhomme de mes amis, parent de Monsieur D'Heruart, et tres honeste homme. Je vous prie de me donner de vos nouuelles et de vostre Philosophie. Mrs Martel, Sorbiere et moy, nous entretismes hier de diuerses choses, et entre autres de la nature et des causes du plaisir et de la douleur. Je leur auouuay franchement que ie n'y entendois rien, et qu'il faloit pour expliquer ce mystere non un *Dauus*, comme moy, mais un *Oedipus*, comme vous.² Si vous vouliés prendre la peine de nous l'esclaircir, vous nous obligeriés infiniment. J'ay enfin rendu à M^r des Verdus les papiers que vous m'auies laissé a vostre depart. [Il *deleted*] Je les ay trouués lors que ie les croyois entierement perdus, et que ie desesperois de les pouuoir recouurer.

[*addressed:*] A Monsieur
Monsieur Hobbes at the Green Dragon in St Pauls Church-yard London

[*endorsed by James Wheldon:*] Monsr du Prat. Sept. 14. 1654

Translation of Letter 70

Sir,
    As I have shown my veneration for you by a long silence, allow me, please, to add just for a few moments the worship of my pen to that silent devotion, and let it be the interpreter of my thoughts. When I had the honour of seeing you in Paris I paid homage from time to time to your learning and your virtue, and was happy to proclaim your mind the absolute ruler of my own—and of my heart also. But now that distance prevents me from doing this by word of mouth, I am forced to use writing instead, the only means I still have of assuring you of my heart and mind's total submission. You have only to publish soon your opinions concerning nature for me to accept them, I promise you, as respectfully as if they were the edicts and proclamations of my prince. I think it is not unwise of me if, knowing as I do how true your principles are and how carefully and precisely you have always contemplated and calculated everything, I do not reckon up after you and do not inspect very thoroughly the consequences which you draw from your principles so judiciously. But, Sir, if the obvious truth of your proofs has made you ruler of my mind, which had been impregnable against all the ancient and modern philosophers, and had never wished to yield to their systems, whatever order and strength seemed to accompany them, the excellence of your virtue has completely won you my heart. It

is true that M. Hervart[1] and a few others of my friends have some share of it also, and that you possess it only by joint ownership with them. But if I have given my heart to them, it is in order to gain other hearts for you which will be more useful and yield you greater revenues than my own, and it is on the condition that they should each give you entire ownership of his own heart and love you, if it is possible, as intensely as does

Sir,
Your most humble and most obedient servant
A. du Prat

Paris, 14 September 1654

[*postscript:*] The person who will bring you this letter is a gentleman who is a friend of mine and a relative of M. Hervart, and a very worthy man. Please give me news of yourself and your philosophy. De Martel, Sorbière, and I discussed various things yesterday, and among others the nature and causes of pleasure and pain. I frankly declared to them that I did not understand the subject at all, and that in order to solve this mystery we had need not of a Davus like myself but of an Oedipus like you.[2] If you were willing to take the trouble to explain it to us we should be immensely grateful. I have at last given M. du Verdus the papers which you left with me on your departure. I found them when I thought they had been completely lost and despaired of being able to recover them.

[*addressed: see text*]

[1] See Letter 69 n. 5.
[2] A proverbial phrase from Terence, *Andria*, line 194: 'Davus sum, non Oedipus', meaning 'I am Davus, a simple fellow, not a solver of riddles like Oedipus'.

LETTER 71   [13/] 23 SEPTEMBER 1654

François du Verdus to Hobbes, from Paris

Chatsworth, Hobbes MSS, letter 7 (original).

Monsieur
    Je vous écris auec une plume que je uiens d'emprunter et auec d'autre ancre que la miene. C'est a dire que je uiens de conduire ma

mâle, et que je uais monter en Carrosse pour aller a Bourdeaux. je menage donc ce temps pour vous doner a conoitre combien vous me tenes au coeur; Et vous prier d'estre assuré de mes tres humbles respects et seruices. Je vous prie aussi Monsieur, que vous me fassiés l'honneur de m'écrire et qu'a l'acoutumée vous ayiés la bonté de m'enuoyer uos écrits a mesure qu'ils s'imprimeront. vos lettres s'il vous plait de les adresser au mesme lieu chez Mr Mallet[1] Mathematicien en la rüe neuue des fossés proche la porte St Germain, me seront rendües ponctüellement: j'y laisse un correspondant habile et fidelle. Au reste je dois m'acquiter icy du remerciment pour le petit liure The Wisdome of the Ancients[2] d'autant plus que vous aués eü de la peine a le chercher; ce que je scay premierement par vostre lettre, et en second lieu par diuerses autres qu'ont receües de mes amis ayants la mesme curiosité ausquels on a [dit *deleted* >écrit] que ce Liure ne se trouuoit plus. Je vous rends aussi graces trés humbles de la bone uolonté auec laquelle vous m'auertissés qu'il auoit esté traduit. Car pour celà je le scauois, et que la 1ere Traduction qu'en fit J Baudoüin[3] est [>pour le sens] peu fidelle, et pour l'expression pis que Gascone. Mais Adieu; il faut partir; je suis de coeur et seray toute ma vie

Monsieur
Vostre tres humble et tres obeissant seruiteur
Duuerdus

A Paris le 23e 7.bre 1654

[*endorsed by Hobbes:*] Monsr du Verdus 23 Sept. 1654 Chez Monsr Mallet Mathematicien en la rue neuue des fosses proche la Porte St Germain

Translation of Letter 71

Sir,

I am writing to you with a pen which I have just borrowed, and with somebody else's ink. That is, I have just sent off my trunk, and I am about to get into a coach to go to Bordeaux. So I have saved these moments in order to let you know how devoted to you I am, and to assure you of my most humble respects and my desire to serve you. Also I beg you, Sir, to do me the honour of writing to me, and to have the goodness, as usual, of sending me your works successively as they are printed. Please address your letters to the same place, the house of M. Mallet[1] in the rue Neuve des fossés near the porte Saint-Germain; I am leaving an intelligent and loyal correspondent there, who will forward them punctually to me.

The other thing I must do in this letter is to fulfil my obligation to thank you for the little book *The Wisdom of the Ancients*,[2] especially because it was difficult for you to find a copy. I know that first from your letter, and secondly from various other letters received by friends of mine who wanted the same thing, and who were told that the book was no longer available. I give you humble thanks also for your kindness in warning me that it had already been translated. I knew that already; the first translation, by J. Baudouin,[3] is not very faithful to the original where the meaning is concerned, and where the style of the French is concerned it is worse than Gascon. But farewell; I must go. I am, Sir, with all my heart and shall be for all my life

Your most humble and most obedient servant
du Verdus

Paris, 23 September 1654

[1] See Letter 67 n. 16.
[2] See Letter 68 n. 9.
[3] Bacon, *La Sagesse des anciens*, tr. Jean Baudouin (Paris, 1619).

LETTER 72   [14/] 24 APRIL 1655

Thomas de Martel to Hobbes, from Paris

Chatsworth, Hobbes MSS, letter 8 (original).
Printed in von Brockdorff, 'Fünf Briefe', pp. 13–14.

Monsieur
Je ne scai par quel malheur tout ce que Je vous enuoye ou que vous m'adressez s'esgare ou ne vous est rendu que bien tard comme le chapeau que Je me chargai de vous faire tenir, pour les Caiers[1] que vous m'adressiez pour M.ᵣ Du Verdus quelque enqueste que J'en aie faicte par tout ou je pouuois soupçonner qu'ils auroient demeuré Je n'en ai jamais eu nouuelles, et Je Juge par ce que vous escriuez à M.ᵣ Du Prat[2] comme J'auois desia faict auparauant par les letres de M.ˡᵉ le Maire[3] que vous n'auez receu aucune de mes letres dont quelques vnes accompagnoient celles de M.ᵣ Du Verdus, J'en soupçonne la cause dont Je me garentirai à l'auenir, quoi qu'il en soit Je n'ai point manqué de temps en temps de vous faire cognoistre que vous m'estes tousiours

aussi present que ce que Je tiens de vous le merite soit par son propre prix, soit par l'obligation de mon ressentiment, vous asseurant que J'ai de la peine à me retenir de ne vous Importuner pas de mes letres, estant bien mal aisé que presque à chasque pas de ma vie aiant occasion de me souuenir de ce que vous m'auez appris pour reigler la dessus autant que Je puis ma conduite, Je ne sois porté malgré moi à vous exprimer plus frequemment les mouuemˢ qui fairoient que Je vous [*page torn* embrass]erois de tout mon coeur si J'estois prez de vous, Je laisse toutes les occasions de philosopher soit auec moi mesme soit auec les autres, ou J'ai tousiours recours à vos oracles, et comme ils me manquent souuent par ma faute ou autrem˕ si J'osois combien de fois seriez vous consulté, mais quand Je pense que pour ceux que Je tirerois sur quelques matieres Je differerois ceux qu'on attend de vous sur toutes [>les] choses qu'une profonde speculation et tresexacte nous peut descouurir je fais conscience de vous desrober du temps que vous employez si utilem˕ à parfaire vos ouurages pour lesquels Je vous souhaite de tout mon coeur un profond repos et vne longue et vigoureuse santé ce que mon affection ne vous souhaiteroit pas moins grand quand vous n'auiez resolu de viure que pour vous mesme, Ce sont les voeux que faict sans cesse pour vous celui qui vous estime par dessus tout le reste des hommes, qui se tient heureux de vous auoir cognu, et qui est et sera toute sa vie comme vostre plus obligé

Monsieur
Vostre plus humble et plus obeissant seruiteur
De Martel

A Paris ce 24 Apr. 1655

[*addressed:*] For M.ʳ Hobbes at the Greene Dragon in Paules Churchyard London

[*endorsed by James Wheldon:*] Mons.ʳ de Martell. Apr. 24. 1655

Translation of Letter 72

Sir,

I do not know what misfortune brings it about that everything I send you (or you send me) goes astray; or else what I send you is delivered very late, such as the hat which I undertook to convey to you. As for the printed sheets[1] which you sent me to give to M. du Verdus, I have had no news of them, even though I have enquired wherever I could imagine they might have got held up. From what you write to M. du Prat[2] I conclude, as I had previously done from Mlle le Maire's[3] letters, that you have not received any of my letters, some of which were sent together with those of M. du Verdus. I have a suspicion about the reason for this, and I shall try to guard against it in future. Anyway, I have certainly not failed to write to you from time to time to let you know that you are still much in my thoughts, as you should be, considering how much I retain of what you have imparted to me— whether because of its own value or because of the debt of gratitude which I owe you. It grieves me, I assure you, that I have to restrain myself from pestering you with my letters; and since, at almost every step throughout my life, I am reminded of how you have taught me to regulate my actions (so far as I can), it troubles me that I do not give in to the desire to express more often those feelings which would make me embrace you with all my heart if I were with you. I shall not mention all the opportunities I have to philosophize, either by myself or with others, when I always have recourse to your oracular judgements; and since I often lack them, either through my own fault or otherwise, how often would I consult you yourself, if only I dared! But then, when I think that in drawing out your thoughts on some subjects I should be delaying those pronouncements which we expect from you about all those things which can be revealed to us by profound and very discriminating contemplation, my conscience tells me not to deprive you of the time which you spend so profitably in perfecting your works. For that purpose I wish you a very tranquil life and long-lasting, robust good health; my love for you would wish you this even if you had resolved to live only for your own sake. Such are the prayers made constantly on your behalf by someone who esteems you far above the rest of mankind, who calls himself happy to have known you, and who is and shall be for the rest of his life,

Sir,
Your most humble and most obedient servant,
de Martel

Paris, 24 April 1655

[*addressed: see text*]

[1] See Letter 68 n. 6.
[2] Abraham du Prat; this letter from Hobbes does not apparently survive.
[3] See Letter 69 n. 4.

Henry Oldenburg to Hobbes

R.Soc. MS MM 1 Oldenburg, 'Liber epistolaris', fo. 6 (autograph copy).
Printed in *OC* i, pp. 74–5.

To my most honored friend M.ʳ T. Hobs.

As I found no trouble at all in ye reading of yʳ hand, wᶜʰ in ye close of yʳ letter you seemed to apprehend, I might, so I hope, you will find none in the receaving of these my thanks, wᶜʰ I was bound to send you for yʳ favor. Giue me leave, to adde to yᵐ, [here *deleted*] yt my friends¹ question did not at all call in question the use of ye Mathematiques, but supposing yt as granted and vnquestionable, desireth only a direction to such authors, as haue written of their uses particularly; For, ye benefit of a science [being *deleted*] knowne not only in grosse, but also by retaile and in parcels, moue ye mind to a more eager and vigorous pursuit of acquiring ye same. Neither have all men yt felicity of nature, as to invent much to things already invented, but many are glad to take from ye pregnancy of others, and breed it vp in stead of their owne issue. Low men must climbe vp to ye shoulders off ye tall, if they will see a farre off. Neither is the question made for any use of trade, but of enriching and entertaining ye mind, both wᵗʰ ye theory and the particular knowledge of ye use of yt theory. These two joined together cannot but procure indeed ye end of all things, you mention, pleasure; seing this demonstratif knowledge stayeth and satisfieth the mind as much as food doth an hungry stomach: and the same diffusing itself through and to ye good of all ye parts of ye body politique, as good meat well concocted doth to all ye limmes of ye body naturall, [& *deleted*] must needs beget ye greatest contentmt yt any sublunary thing can doe. The only desire of my questionist was, and is still, to know ye best authors, yᵗ haue specified those uses, wch he hath only a general knowledge off. That looking-glasse, you sent me among ye rest, is a very excellent one, and I should think is the compleatest of any, yt euer I saw, if besides those things, you mention, and the secrets of nature, it might shew one secret more, wch is about ye state of man after this life. This I judge a secret of yᵗ weight yᵗ, if we were [once]² resolued and established in it, we should enjoy ourselves wᵗʰ much more setlednes and security, yⁿ now we doe. But I dare not digresse into this point for fear of troubling you. I shall therefore end wth repeating my former intreaty, yt, if a second letter inconuenience you not, you would fauor us wth ye culling out of such authors, and send their names: wch is a thing, you will oblige my friend and self very much in, who both doe value y^r knowledge, and honor yr worth, as I in particular rest,

Y^r humble and obliged serv^t
H.O.

A. 1655. jun. 6.

¹ The editors of *OC* suggest that this may have been Robert Boyle, who has a section on the usefulness of mathematics in his book *The Usefulnesse of Experimental Naturall Philosophy* (1663), on which he was already working at this time. See also the Biographical Register, 'Oldenburg'.
² one *MS*.

LETTER 74   [24 SEPTEMBER/] 4 OCTOBER 1655

Abraham du Prat to Hobbes, from Paris

Chatsworth, Hobbes MSS, letter 9 (original).

Monsieur

J'ay esté bien aise d'apprendre que M^r des Verdus ait entrepris il y a long temps la traduction de vostre Philosophie.¹ Il s'en acquitera sans doute plus dignement que ie n'aurois fait. Je lui cede tres volontiers ce dessein ou ie ne trauaillois qu'auec crainte et tremblement. Vostre ouurage ne pouuoit manquer de traducteurs. Je vis il y a deux iours un honeste homme qui me dit qu'il auoit eu la mesme pensée que moy, et qu'il n'en auoit esté detourné que parcequ'il sceut que i'auois commencé cette version. les libraires de cette ville ont voulu donner de l'argent à Mr Roure² qui enseigne icy la Philosophie de M^r des Cartes [>pour traduire vostre liure]. Mr Sorbiere (qui sera icy dans dix ou douze iours) m'a escrit qu'il a enuie de mettre en francois vostre Philosophie. Quand vous la ferés rimprimer, obligés vostre libraire de fournir de meilleur papier et des characteres plus nets et plus gros. Mr Gassendi vous baise tres humblement les mains. Il y a auiourduy quarante et trois iours qu'il est malade d'une fieure continuë acompagnée du commencement d'une grande inflammation du poulmon, et [>presque] tousiours d'orthopnée.³ Il a esté saigné douze fois. Il est à present presque sans fieure, et hors de danger pour quelque temps. Tous ses amis lui conseillent de retourner au printemps en Prouence, dont l'air chaud et sec lui [est *deleted*] sera plus salutaire que celui de Paris. Je vous prie de m'enuoyer par voye d'ami deux exemplaires de la Philosophie de *Epicuro-Gassendo-Carletoniana*[4] Mr Gassendi m'a prié de vous en escrire. Mr de la Boulaye[5] Gentilhomme qui vous rendra la presente, s'en chargera peutestre, et les pourroit mettre auec ses hardes, ou au moins un si les deux occupent trop de place. Ce M[r] de la boulaye est un Gentilhomme qui est estimé a Paris [>de tous] les honestes gens. Il a voyagé iusques sur les [confins *deleted* >frontieres] de la Chine, et a fort iudicieusement obserué tout ce qu'il y a de considerable dans tous les pays où il a passé. Je m'asseure que vous ne receurés pas moins de satisfaction de sa conuersation que Mrs Martel, Sorbiere et moy, qui l'auons tousiours trouuée charmante. Il est du nombre de ceux qui se disent citoyens du monde. Je vous prie de me faire scauoir si Harueus est en vie, et s'il a fait quelque ouurage nouueau,[6] et qui est highmorus[7] qui a escrit de l'Anatomie. Si vos Medecins ont mis quelque liure en lumiere que vous estimiés, vous m'obligerés de m'en faire part. On a apporte icy un liure de *Praeadamitis*[8] qui a esté incontinent deffendu, et qui n'a pas laissé pour cela d'y trouuer plusieurs approbateurs. Vn Mathematicien de cette ville[9] m'a dit qu'il auoit fait quelques obseruations sur quelques endroits de vostre [liure *deleted*] Geometrie. Si c'eut este [>sur] une matiere [que i'eusse peu entendre *deleted* >de ma portée], ie les aurois leuës pour vous dire ce qui en est. [>Je vous les enuoyeray quand vous voudrés.] Je vous prie de m'expliquer ce que vous dites en la page 25. Ligne 4. Sed in Contingentibus etsi vera sit, *Omnis coruus niger est*, falsa tamen erit, *Si quid coruus sit, id nigrum est*.[10] Je vous prie de m'enuoyer un exemplaire de la seconde impression,[11] et [>de] c[roire *page torn*] que ie suis et seray toute ma vie

Monsieur
Vostre tres humble [et tres *page torn*] obeissant seruiteur
[A. Du Prat *page torn*]

a Paris ce 4 Octobre 1655

[*addressed:*] A Monsieur
Monsieur Hobbes at the greene dragons in Pauls churchyard A Londres

[*endorsed by James Wheldon:*] Oct. 4th. 1655

Translation of Letter 74

Sir,

I was very happy to learn that M. du Verdus had long ago undertaken to translate your philosophical system.[1] I am sure he will acquit himself more worthily than I should have done. I hand over this project to him very willingly, having been working on it only with fear and trembling. Your work could not possibly lack for translators. Two days ago I met a worthy fellow who told me he had had the same idea as myself, and that he had been put off proceeding with it only because he knew I had begun my translation. The booksellers in this city wanted to pay M. du Roure,[2] who teaches Descartes's philosophy here, to translate your book. M. Sorbière (who will be here in ten or twelve days' time) wrote to me that he wanted to translate your philosophical system into French. When you have it reprinted, tell your bookseller to provide better paper and clearer, larger type.

M. Gassendi send you his humble greetings. He has been ill now for forty-three days with a continuous fever, accompanied by the initial stages of a great inflammation of the lungs, with orthopnoea most of the time.[3] He has been bled twelve times. At present he is almost without fever, and out of danger for some time. All his friends are advising him to go back to Provence in the spring, where the warm, dry air will be better for him than the air in Paris. Please send me, via a friend, two copies of the 'Epicuro-Gassendo-Carletonian Philosophy'.[4] M. Gassendi asked me to write to you about it. M. de la Boulaye,[5] who is a gentleman, and the bearer of this letter, will perhaps take the books; he could pack them with his clothes—or at least one copy, if two take up too much space. This M. de la Boulaye is a gentleman who is highly regarded in Paris by all the better sort. He has travelled as far as the borders of China, and has observed with a penetrating judgement all the things that are worthy of note in all the countries where he has been. I am sure that you will get as much satisfaction from his conversation as de Martel, Sorbière, and myself, who have always found it fascinating. He is one of those people who describe themselves as citizens of the world.

Please tell me whether Harvey is still alive, and whether he has written any new books;[6] please tell me also who Highmore[7] is, who has written about anatomy. If your medical experts have published anything that you think well of, I should be grateful if you could let me know. A book called *Prae-Adamitae*[8] has arrived here; it was immediately banned, but for all that it has not failed to find several admirers. A mathematician from this city[9] told me that he had written some critical comments on certain passages in your Geometry. If it were on a subject that lay within my capabilities, I should have read them in order to tell you what they contain. I shall send them to you whenever you wish. Please explain what you say on p. 25, line 4: 'but in Contingent Propositions, though this be true, *Every Crow is Black*; yet this, *if any thing be a Crow the same is Black*, is false'.[10] Please send me a copy of the second impression,[11] and believe me when I say that I am, Sir, and shall be for the rest of my life,

Your most humble and most obedient servant
A. du Prat

Paris, 4 October 1655

[*addressed: see text*]

The writer of this letter is identified as Abraham du Prat by his handwriting.

[1] Meaning the entire tripartite 'elements': *De corpore*, *De homine*, and *De cive*.

[2] Jacques du Roure was one of the first publicists of Descartes's philosophy: his *La Philosophie divisée en toutes ses parties* (1654) praised Descartes above all others and included a compilation of Descartes's writings on method (see Bouillier, *Histoire de la philosophie cartésienne*, i, pp. 506–7).

[3] Orthopnoea, traditionally regarded as the third stage of asthma, is a condition in which the patient has difficulty breathing except when standing, or with the shoulders held back. Having suffered a severe illness in Feb. 1655, Gassendi fell ill again in Sept. and was treated again by Guy Patin, a firm believer in the efficacy of bleeding. Patin wrote that Gassendi died 'because of the extreme weakness of his natural heat' ('propter summam caloris nativi imbecillitatem' (*Lettres*, ii, pp. 215–16)). He died on 15/25 Oct.

[4] Walter Charlton, *Physiologia Epicuro-Gassendo-Charltoniana* (London, 1654), which the author described as 'a fabric of science natural, upon the hypothesis of atomes, founded by Epicurus, repaired by Petrus Gassendus, augmented by Walter Charlton'.

[5] François le Gouz, sieur de la Boullaye (1610–66). In 1643 he sailed to England to fight for Charles I; but after the death of his two French companions he embarked instead on travels through England, Ireland, Holland, Denmark, and Poland. In 1645 he travelled to Turkey, Persia, and India, returning to France via Syria, Egypt, and Italy. His account of these journeys, *Les Voyages et observations*, was published in 1653. In 1664 he was sent on a French trading mission to Persia; he went on to India again, and took a boat from Patna to Dacca, intending to go on to China, but was killed by robbers on board ship (see Castouret des Fosses, *La Boullaye le Gouz*, pp. 47–55). The fact that he returned to England in 1655 was hitherto unknown. In Dec. 1655 Sorbière wrote to Jean Bertet that he had recently seen his friend 'La Boulaye' again, 'who, on his return from England, has as much admiration for Hobbes as he has contempt for Cromwell' ('qui

215

redux ex Anglia tam miratur Hobbium quàm despicit Cromwellum' (BN MS f.l. 10352, part 1, fo. 226ʳ)).

⁶ Harvey died on 3/13 June 1657, having published nothing since *De generatione animalium* (1651).

⁷ Nathaniel Highmore (1613–85) studied medicine at Trinity College, Oxford, proceeding BA in 1641; in 1642–3 he was befriended by Harvey, who urged him to publish his medical researches, and in 1643 he was created DM. Most of his career was spent as a practising physician at Sherborne, Dorset. In 1651 he published two works: *Corporis humani disquisitio anatomica* (a textbook on anatomy which expounded Harvey's theory of the circulation of the blood) and *The History of Generation*, a study in embryology, dedicated to Boyle. See Frank, *Harvey and Oxford Physiologists*, pp. 97–101.

⁸ Isaac La Peyrère's *Prae-Adamitae*, which argued that men had existed before Adam (and that the Book of Genesis was therefore fabulous) was published in five edns. in 1655: three in Holland, one in Basel, and one at an unidentified place. It was publicly condemned in Holland on [16/] 26 Nov. and anathematized by the Bishop of Namur on [15/] 25 Dec.; the author was arrested in Feb. 1656 (Popkin, *Isaac La Peyrère*, p. 14).

⁹ Unidentified; possibly André Tacquet, whose comments on *De corpore*, XIII–XXIV were published in Moranus, *Animadversiones*, pp. 13–29.

¹⁰ *De corpore*, III. 11: having distinguished between necessary and contingent propositions (examples would be, respectively, 'Every crow is a bird' and 'Every crow is black': the latter may be true, but if we found a white crow we should still call it a crow), Hobbes uses this distinction to show that hypothetical propositions ('If there is an x it is y') do not necessarily follow from universal ones ('Every x is y').

¹¹ There was no new edition of *De corpore* until its inclusion in Hobbes's *Opera philosophica* (1668).

François du Verdus to Hobbes, from Bordeaux

Chatsworth, Hobbes MSS, letter 10 (original).

Monsieur

J'ay reçeu par les soins de Nôtre Amy le Sage Monsieur de Martel, la lettre que vous m'aués fait l'honneur de m'écrire de Londres du 15ᵉᵐᵉ 8.ᵇʳᵉ;¹ J'atendray vos ordres pour publier la uersion que j'ay faite de uôtre liure de Corpore. J'ay tant eu de satisfaction a le mettre en nostre langue, que j'ay résolu quelques affaires qu'il me suruiene, ou quelque employ que ie puisse auoir dans le monde, de traduire les deux autres sections de vôtre Philosophie.² J'espere mesmes d'en faire autant de vôtre Liure Anglois,³ où désormais il n'y a que quelques mots qui m'arrétent faute d'un bon Dictionaire. Ce que ie souhaiterois Monsieur, seroit de pouuoir aler a vous, pour vous faire agreër la version que j'ay faite. Il y a long temps que i'ay ce dessein; et ie l'executeray s'il plait à Dieu que je réspire de mes affaires. Cepandant je puis vous assurer que cette version est francoise et qu'elle est fidelle: je veux dire qu'elle n'est point paraphraseé qui est ce que vous condamniés ce me semble en quelque autre;[4] que la diction y est pure, point figureé, gardant par tout le caractére de vos expressions; et ce qui étoit nécessaire pour la rendre telle que je n'y ay rien traduit sans l'auoir bien étudié, et si je ne me trompe, sans l'auoir bien entendu. Mais Monsieur aprés toute l'aplication d'esprit que j'ay aportée a cette étude que j'aye la conception si dure de ne comprendre pas surquoy [soit][5] fondé l'Elenchus[6] qu'on vous dit qui s'en imprime à Oxford! Mais [>aussi] ce Grand Docteur[7] qui ua s'immortaliser par ce chef d'oeuure, ne seroit ce pas [aussi *deleted*] un homme comme Le vindex,[8] écriuant sur le raport d'autruy auec cette difference que l'un écrit un Libelle, et l'autre une Chicane. Car de maliçe il faut qu'il en ait sa bone part aussi bien que l'autre n'étant pas possible qu'en tels procedés l'ignorance soit sans maliçe. Certes on a peine a croire que ces Philosophes de [quel *deleted*] certaines Écoles ie ueux dire ces Sophistes ou plutot les 'perroquets' qu'on y a sifflés sans qu'ils ayent jamais fait reflection a l'interet des Pédans qui les ont amusés pour les tenir long temps sous leur férule on ne sçauroit croire dis-je combien ils haïssent un Philosophe Geometre. Cent fois j'en ay ueu qui me chicanoient des choses toutes uisibles d'elles mesmes, m'aportant contre, quelque distinction a quoy sur ma parole ils n'auoient point d'ideé claire et distincte qui répondit. Il m'est arriué quelque-fois d'auançer bonement, Que puis que les Corps agissent selon [leurs grandeurs et leurs figures *altered to* leur grandeur et leur figure] et par leurs mouuemens qui sont les Objects de la Geométrie et des Mécaniques, il est impossible d'estre Philosophe a moins que d'estre Géométre Et aussi tot j'ay ueu ces Gens-là s'éfaroucher croyans qu'une Philosophie Geometrique c'est a dire que la uraye Philosophie [tendit *deleted* >tende] a ranuerser les uerités les plus importantes. Mesmes quand je luy ay allegué que du vray on ne peut rien inferer que de vray [Et que mesmes je leur ay fait *deleted* >jusqu'a leur faire] uoir dans l'Écriture Sainte la Nécessité qu'il y a d'estre Geométre pour estre Philosophe où il est dit Que Dieu á fait toutes choses *En poids En nombre En mesure*[9] Car (dis-je a ces Messieurs là) *la Mesure* ueut dire l'étenduë et la grandeur du Corps, *le nombre* ueut dire en Effect le nombre de ses Angles, qui fait la figure; Et *le Poids* c'est l'effort a tendre uers quelque part: bien loin de se rendre a de si bones raisons, j'ay sçeu qu'ils m'auoient uoulû faire passer dans le monde pour un homme ayant des sentimens particuliers sur de mauuais principes. Tout cecy est á propos du vindex et de l'Élenchus il faut que l'autheur de celuy-cy soit vn Chicaneur obstiné, come l'autre étoit un Calomniateur peruers et malin. De uray je ne trouue rien que de démontré dans vôtre Chapitre 16.eme sinon qu'il me semble que dans [le *deleted* >son] Corollaire de l'article 1er vous ayés oublié a nomer une ligne. Car uoicy ce Corollaire.

Si l'impétuosité est par tout la mesme; Et qu'on prene telle ligne droite qu'on uoudra pour la mesure du temps: les impétuosités apliqueés ordonément a cette ligne droite désigneront un parallellogramme, qui représentera la vitesse de tout le mouuement. Que si l'impétuösité comançant au repos croit uniformement, c'est a dire toujours en mesme raison auec les temps employés: Toute la vitesse du mouuement sera representée par un Triangle, dont l'un des côtés est tout le Temps; et l'autre la plus grande impétuosité acquise dans ce temps là: ou par un parallellogramme, ayant pour l'un des côtés tout le temps du transport du mobile, et pour son autre côté la moitié de la plus grande impétuösité; ou enfin par un parallellogramme, dont l'un dés côtés est milieu proportionel entre l'impétuosité la plus grande, ie ueux dire qui a esté acquise la derniére, et la moitié de cette mesme impétuosité.^{10}

Où je vous auouë, Monsieur, que je ne uois pas Quel doit estre ce parallellogramme, dont l'un des côtés soit moyen proportionel etc: si vous ne m'en dites l'autre côté. Et faute de sçauoir quel est cet autre côté, je n'entans pas aussi ce que vous dites a la fin du Corollaire: Car ces deux parallellogrammes sont égaux et entre eux, et au Triangle qui se fait de tout le temps et de l'impétuösité accreüe comme il a esté démontré dans les Élemens de la Geométrie.

J'ay bien trouué encore ailleurs quelque autre chose qu'il m'à semblé que vous pouuiés ou expliquer ou énoncer autrement. Ainsi dans vôtre figure du Prédicament de la Quantité vous dites Que le Mouuement est quantité continuë par accident dautant qu'il l'est à [raison *deleted* >cause] de la ligne et du Temps et reprenant vôtre discours dans la page 17eme vous dites que le Temps n'est capable d'égalité et d'inégalité c'est a dire aussi qu'il n'est quantité qu'a [raison *deleted* >cause] de la ligne et du mouuement.^{11} Et voylà donc le Temps quantité a [raison *deleted* >cause] du mouuement et le mouuement quantité a cause du Temps En quoy il semble qu'il y ait un Cercle. Je sçay qu'on ne peut conçeuoir de mouuement qu'on n'y conçoiue le passé et l'auenir; comme vous démontrés dans l'article 11^{éme} du chapitre du Corps et de l'accident;^{12} et qu'autrement le Corps seroit en repos. Et je sçay ce que vous dites au Chapitre de la Quantité[13] touchant l'exposition du temps: Mais toujours semble-t-il qu'il y ait un Cercle a l'endroit que je vous marque.

Je trouue aussi dans la ligne 8^{éme} de la page 68^{éme} le mot *Ejus*, et dans la ligne 13eme de la mesme page le mot *Illius* qu'il me semble qui vous ayent échapé. Car Monsieur quand un Corps se meut, de quelque façon qu'on le considére ou comme point ou comme ligne ou comme surfaçe ce n'est pas sa propre largeur ni sa propre épaisseur ou pro-fondeur qu'il décrit: mais bien celle d'un autre solide qui répond a tout l'espaçe parcourû par son mouuement. Et c'est pourquoy j'ay ôté cet *Ejus* dans ma Traduction que uoicy.

12. Si l'on ne considére point la grandeur du Corps qui se meut, qui neanmoins à toujours quelque grandeur pour petit qu'il soit: nous apelons le chemin par où il passe, *la ligne* ou la dimension une et simple et l'espace qu'il parcourt *la longeur*; et le corps mesme qui se meut *le point.* qui est le sens auquel on prend ordinairement la Terre pour un point et qu'on nome son chemin d'un an autour du Soleil La Ligne Ecclyptique. Que si aprés cela nous considerons le corps qui se meut comme long; Et que nous suposions qu'il se meuue, de maniére que toutes ses parties décriuent autant de lignes, c'est a dire chacune la siene: nous dirons que la uoye de chacune de ses parties est *la largeur*; Et que l'espaçe qu'il acheue est *la Surfaçe*, ayant deux dimensions la longeur, et la largeur, dont chacune s'est ajusteé toute entiére a toutes les parties de l'autre.

Derechef si nous considerons le Corps comme ayant la surfaçe; et que nous suposions qu'il se meuue en sorte que chacune de ses parties décriue une ligne: nous dirons que la uoye de chaque partie est *la grosseur* ou *profondeur* et que l'espaçe qui est acheué est *le solide*, ayant trois dimensions, dont les deux comment qu'on les prene se sont ajusteés toutes entiéres a chacune des parties de la troisiéme.[14]

Je pourrois encore douter de vôtre motif quand vous aués mis au chapitre 20.eme l'article Quadratura Circuli falsa ex falsâ hypothesi s'il n'etoit du Philosophe de donner aussi bien des exemples du faux raisonement que du uray. d'ailleurs c'est a faire a l'homme de coeur d'auouër franchement qu'il a tenu a peu qu'il ne fût déçeu. homo sum; humani a me nil alienum puto.[15]

Du reste Monsieur il n'y a qu'une chose dans vos Écrits qui me fasse peine: Que la Grandeur, ou Quantité, ou Étandue soit un Accident du Corps.[16] Car de uouloyr que tous les autres accidens soyent engendrés et périssent, sans que leur sujet soit détruit, et dire

que cela n'arriue pas a la quantité, puis qu'un mesme corps à toujours
une mesme grandeur ou étenduë: c'est assés prouuer ce me semble
que la quantité du Corps n'est rien que le Corps luy mesme; de
mesme que la substançe du corps n'est rien autre chose que le Corps.
pour moy j'ay toujours creû ces mots synonimes Le Corps, La
Quantité, La Substançe J'ay creu que nous apelions les choses Corps,
en ce qu'elles sont parties reëlles du Monde; que nous les apelions
quantités, en tant qu'on peut les comparer les unes aux autres, et les
trouuer plus grandes ou plus petites; Et que nous leur donions le nom
de substance, en ce qu'elles sont sujetes a diuers accidens; c'est a dire
a se montrer a nous tantot d'une façon tantot d'une autre; Et vous
estes de l'auis de la premiére et de la troisiéme de ces acceptions dans
votre Chapitre Of the signification of spirit etc.[17] Come donc nous ne
disons pas que l'estre substançe c'est a dire l'estre sujet a diuers
accidens soit un accident au Corps: Car si c'étoit un accident le Corps
seroit donc aussi sujet a cet accident; et par la mesme raison il luy
seroit encore accident d'estre sujet a cet accident ce que doneroit en
galimatias et iroit a l'infiny. Aussi l'estre quantité, c'est a dire l'estre
sujet a estre comparée aux autres corps n'est point un accident au
Corps; Et j'oseray vous dire Monsieur que si Nous reçeuions cette
distinction Que les autres Accidens sont accidens séparables et la
quantité inséparable on pourroit nous dire aussi bien que la Substançe est un Accident du Corps: mais Inséparable.

Mais je passe sur tout cela et sur ce qu'il me semble qui s'en en suiue
nécessairement de l'Espaçe plein, qui n'a point de bornes, dont
quelqu'un neanmoins pourra s'imaginer que ma croyançe ne uient que
d'un faux préjugé: je passe dis-je sur cela pour vous dire s'il vous plait
Monsieur auec la mesme ingénuité mes autres sentimens de vôtre
Philosophie. Je trouue donc Monsieur que vous estes le seul qui ayés
baty un Corps de Philosophie de maniére qu'en uray Geometre vous
comançés par des définitions toutes claires d'elles mesme; que sur ces
définitions vous bâtissés un premier Article; que du premier vous
inferés le second; du premier et du second le troisiéme Et ainsi de
suite: de maniére qu'il n'y a rien dans vôtre Ouurage que vous n'ayé
demontré. vous estes le seul qui nous ayés doné une uraye Méta-
physique vous estes le seul qui tout en alant a uôtre but sans vous
diuertir en chicanes ayés tranché en peu de mots toutes les Con-
trouerses de l'École. Vous estes le seul qui par les définitions que vous
[ayés *deleted* >aués] donées et par la suite de vos démonstrations ayés
montré qu'en effect vous aués ueu les choses dans les choses mesme. Et

je vous prie pour ne rien dire de la définition du Point dans Euclide, où il fait entrer le nul; cujus pars nulla;[18] Et où il semble par conséquent définir le rien; come en effect ôté de la longueur, la largeur, la profondeur il ne nous reste point d'idée: quelle définition est ce que celle de la ligne droite; au prix de la uostre, Cujus extrema saluâ ratione ejus ad aliam diduci non possunt?[19] Il en faut dire autant des paralleles, des Asymptotes, de l'angle, de la figure, en un mot de tout ce que vous aués définy. Auant vos définitions de deux choses, l'une: ou lon n'entendoit point la chose; ou lon n'y parloit qu'un jargon. Car on pouuoit bien sçauoir par exemple ce que c'est que la ligne droite: mais d'ideé claire et distincte qui répondit a ces termes Quae ex aequo sua interjacet signa,[20] pour moy, je n'en auois point. Mais ce que vous me dites c'est Nature elle mesme qui me le dit. Sur tout, ce qu'on ne peut vous ôter Monsieur, c'est qu'auant vous il n'y auoit point de Geométrie. C'est vous qui en estes l'auteur. Car quoy que vous auouiés vous mesme que cette partie de la Philosophie eût esté bien cultiueé de tout temps par les meilleurs esprits; neanmoins comme à la reserue de peu d'Élemens Toute la Geométrie est fondée sur les raisons des grandeurs: j'ay raison de dire Qu'il n'y auoit point de Geométrie auant la sciençe des raisons. Or cette sciençe Monsieur c'est de vous que nous la tenons qui n'auions pas seulement de définition de la mesme raison. Car la 5ème définition du 5ème Liure d'Euclide non seulement etoit obscure [qui vouloit qu'on *deleted* >selon laquelle on deuoit] juger de la mesme raison de quatre quantités par l'excés ou le défaut de leur Equimultiples: non seulement Elle jetoit dans l'impossible quand pour s'éclairçir de la mesme raison de quatre quantités il faloit estre assuré qu'il y auroit excés ou défaut tout a la fois des multiples de la premiére a ceus de la séconde et des multiples de la 3.ème a ceux de la 4ème, selon toute multiplication: mais encore elle faisoit un Cercle auec la 15.ème proposition de ce mesme 5.ème Liure: Ce qui en effect auoit tellement embarassé nos Geometres que chacun comançoit a se faire un 5ème Liure a sa mode; et ils s'y trompoient tous tant qu'ils sont quand vous nous aués doné vôtre définition de la mesme raison, sur quoy désormais doit estre fondeé la Geométrie. Je ne vous diray point Monsieur, quelles uérités surprenantes vous en aués déduites. Et pour la sciençe des mouuemens que vous aués porteé au dernier point de perfection Et pour la comparaison des lignes courbes aux lignes droites qui est une chose qu'auant vous aucun Geométre n'auoit entrepris. Ce que je vous diray (mais c'est touchant votre 3ème Section des Elémens de la Philosophie)[21] C'est qu'aprés que vous aués esté le premier Et le

seul qui nous ayés démontré les urays principes des Offices de la vie
Ciuile: il est bien aisé a conoitre que ce siécle icy tout ciuilisé qu'il est
pour les arts et les sçiençes, est un siécle barbarë pour les meurs, où le
bruit des armes empéche qu'on n'entende la voix de la raison Et ou
(pour parler auec vôtre Sage Mr Bacon) on est si étourdy du Cor des
Baccantes qu'on n'écoute point la Lyre d'Orphée;[22] Quand tous les
Roys et tous les États de toute la Terre, n'ont pas fait a l'enuy les uns
des autres à qui vous doneroit de plus grandes recompenses. Car
Monsieur vous estes le seul qui ayés bien démontré sur la Nature de la
Societé Ciuile, Que l'autorité de l'Etat est absoluë et indiuisible Qui est
une chose dont il est absolûment nécessaire que les sujets soyent bien
persüädés; Et qu'ils ne peuuent bien sçauoir qu'ils ne haïssent la
guerre Ciuile; et ne soyent bien replus a viure en paix entre eus sous la
Puissançe de l'Etat: Ce qui maintient cette Puissançe.

Voylà Monsieur, Ce que j'auois à vous dire touchant la grande
Oeuure de vôtre Philosophie. C'est en ces termes que j'en parle a tout
le monde; car j'ay les maniéres libres, et ne sçaurois dissimuler mes
sentimens si justes: Et c'est en ces termes que je vous en parleray s'il
vous plait dans l'épitre dédicatoire que je vous feray de ma Traduction
de vôtre Liure du Corps. Certes Monsieur je ne trouue que vous seul
au Monde qui soyés digne de vous mesme; Et pour cela je vous prie de
trouuer bon que je vous dédie ce Trauail. J'y suis encore obligé par
cette confiançe pleine de tendresse et d'éstime que vous me
témoignates que vous auiés en moy, Quand malade a Paris qu'on vous
croyoit a l'extremité vous me uoulûtes confier le Manuscrit de vos
Oeuures; me priant mesme d'y mettre la derniére main selon vos
sentimens que vous m'auiés expliqués; et de les publier si Dieu
disposoit de vous. Mais le Ciel qui vous uoyoit si nécessaire pour le
bien public, ueilla d'un soin particulier a la conseruation de vôtre vie si
illustre; et mes veux furent exauçés, Que ce ne fût pas là la fin de vôtre
amitié pour moy. Je repons Monsieur a cette Amitié qui m'est si chére
auec des sentimens singuliers d'estime et de uénération; et par ma
volonté ferme et constante d'estre toute ma vie

Monsieur
Votre tres humble, et trés obeissant seruiteur
duuerdus

A Bourdeaux le 23e xbre 1655

[*postscript:*] Je vous souhaite de tout mon coeur les bones festes et la bonne année. ie voudrois bien uoyr le vindex, et l'Elenchus quand il sera imprimé: mais ne me les enuoyés pas que je ne vous écriue par qui, et par quelle uoye. C'est de vôtre Liure de homine que j'atendray s'il vous plait des nouuelles, et vos Cahyers[23] si vous uoulés.

[*endorsed by James Wheldon:*] Monsr du Verdus Dec. 23. 1655

Translation of Letter 75

Sir,

   Through the good offices of our wise friend M. de Martel I have received the letter which you did me the honour of writing to me from London on 15 October.[1] I shall await your instructions about publishing the translation which I have done of your book *De corpore*. It gave me so much pleasure to translate it that I have decided to translate the two other sections of your philosophical system,[2] whatever business I may have to deal with and however I may be occupied in the world. I am even hoping to do the same with your English book,[3] in which I have reached the stage where there are only a few words that bring me to a halt, in the absence of a good dictionary. What I should like to do, Sir, is to go and see you, to get your approval for the translation which I have done. I have had this plan for a long time, and I shall carry it out if it pleases God to give me some respite from my affairs. Be that as it may, I can assure you that this translation is in proper French and is faithful to the original (I mean it does not paraphrase it, which I seem to remember is what you found fault with in some other translation);[4] its diction is pure and non-figurative, retaining the character of your own expressions throughout. In order to achieve this I translated nothing without having studied it well, and, unless I am mistaken, without having also understood it well.

   But, Sir, after all the mental application which I have brought to bear on this study, how dim-witted I must be not to understand what the basis is[(5)] of that *Elenchus*[6] which people have told you is being printed at Oxford! No doubt, however, this great doctor[7] who is going to immortalize himself with this masterpiece is someone just like 'Vindex',[8] writing at second-hand—but with this difference, that one of them lampoons you and the other splits hairs with you. He must have his fair share of malice, just like the other one; for in such dealings ignorance cannot possibly be unaccompanied by malice. These philosophers who belong to certain schools, I mean these sophists, or rather, these parrots who have been whistled into their cages, without ever thinking about the intentions of the pedants, their masters, who have beguiled them into captivity in order to keep them for a long time under their rods—these people hate a philosopher who is a geometer more than one can imagine. I have seen them a hundred times quibbling with me about things which are completely self-evident, raising as an objection against me some distinction or other without, I swear, having any clear and distinct idea corresponding to it in their minds. Sometimes I have just told them plainly that since bodies act in accordance with their size and shape and by means of their motions, which are the subject-matter of geometry and mechanics, it is not possible to be a philosopher without also being a geometer. At that, I have seen these people take fright immediately, thinking that a geometrical philosophy (the true philosophy, in other words) tends to overturn the most important truths. I told them that from truths one can only infer other truths, and I even showed them from Holy Scripture itself that one has to be a geometer in order to be a philosopher, using the text 'And God made all things by number, weight, and measure.'[9] For (I told them) 'measure' means the size and extension of bodies, 'number' means in effect the number of the bodies' angles, which makes their shape, and 'weight' is the force by which they tend in some direction. Yet despite all this, far from yielding to such good arguments, they wanted, I knew, to give me the reputation of someone holding peculiar opinions based on bad principles. All this is apropos of 'Vindex' and the *Elenchus*; the author of the latter must be an obstinate quibbler, just as the former was a perverse and malicious slanderer.

To tell the truth, I think everything in your Ch. XVI is demonstrated to be true, except that in the corollary of the first section I think you have forgotten to specify a line. Here is that corollary:

'If the *Impetus* be the same in every point, any straight line representing it may be taken for the measure of Time; and the Quicknesses or *Impetus* applyed ordinately to [that straight line] will designe a parallelogram which shall represent the Velocity of the whole motion. But if the *Impetus* or Quickness of Motion begin from Rest, and increase Uniformly, that is, in the same proportion continually with the times which are passed, the whole Velocity of the Motion shall be represented by a Triangle, one side whereof is the whole time, and the other the greatest *Impetus* acquired in that time; or else by a parallelogram, one of whose sides is the whole time of Motion, and the other, half the greatest *Impetus*; or lastly by a parallelogram having for one side a mean proportional between [the greatest impetus, I mean, that which was acquired last, and half that impetus].'[10]

Here, Sir, I must say that I do not see what this parallelogram should be (one of whose sides is the mean proportional etc.), if you do not tell me what the other side is. And without knowing that, I do not understand either what you say at the end of the Corollary: 'For both these parallelograms are equal to one another, & severally equal to the triangle which is made of the whole line of time, and the greatest acquired *Impetus*; as is demonstrated in the Elements of Geometry.'

Elsewhere, I have found a few other things which I thought you might explain or expound differently. For example, in your 'Form of the Predicament of Quantity' you say that motion is 'continual quantity by accident', it being so by means of *line* and *time*; resuming your argument on p. 17, you say that time is not capable of equality or inequality, which also means that time is quantity only by means of *line* and *motion*.[11] So there you are saying that time is quantity by means of motion, and motion is quantity by means of time; which I think involves a circular argument. I know that one cannot conceive of motion except by conceiving of the past and the future, as you demonstrate in section 11 of your chapter 'Of Body and Accident',[12] and that otherwise matter would be at rest. And I know what you say about the 'exposition' of time in your chapter 'Of Quantity'.[13] But I still think there is a circular argument in the passage which I have pointed out to you.

I notice also that 'ejus' appears in line 8 of p. 68, and 'illius' in line 13 of the same page; I think this has escaped your attention. For surely, Sir, when a body moves, whether one considers it as a point, a line, or a surface, it is not its *own* breadth, thickness, or depth that it describes, but that of another solid, corresponding to the whole space traversed by its motion. That is why I have removed the word 'ejus' in my translation, which goes as follows:

'12. Leaving completely out of consideration the size of a body which is moved (even though it always has some size, however small), we call the path on which it travels a "line", or one single dimension, we call the space it travels "length", and we call the moving body itself a "point". That is the sense in which one normally treats the earth as a point and calls its annual path round the sun "the ecliptic line". Then, if we consider the moving body as possessing length, and if we suppose that it is moved in such a way that all its parts describe so many lines (that is, each part describing its own line), we say that the path travelled by each one of its parts is "breadth", and that the space it makes is "surface", which has two dimensions—length and breadth—each of which is added whole to all the parts of the other. Again, if we consider the body as having a surface, and if we suppose that it is moved in such a way that each of its parts describes a line, then we say that the path of each part is "thickness" or "depth", and that the space it makes is "solid", possessing three dimensions, of which any two are added whole to each of the parts of the third.'[14]

I might also suspect your motive for putting the section 'A false squaring of the circle from a false hypothesis' in ch. XX, were it not the philosopher's job to give examples of false reasoning just as much as of true reasoning. Besides, it is the action of a generous spirit to admit freely that he has held beliefs which he later learned were false. 'I am a man; and I regard no human failing as foreign to me.'[15]

Otherwise, Sir, there is only one thing in your writings which I have trouble with, namely your claim that magnitude or quantity or extension is an accident of body.[16] For if you say that all other accidents come into being and pass away without their subjects being destroyed, and that this does not happen with quantity, since the same body always has the same magnitude or extension, I think this is sufficient to prove that the quantity of a body is nothing other than the body itself, just as the substance of a body is nothing other than the body itself. For my own part, I have always believed that the words 'body', 'quantity' and 'substance' were synonyms. In my opinion we call things 'bodies' in so far as they are real parts of the world; we call them 'quantities' in so far as we can compare them with one another and find them to be larger or smaller; and we call them 'substances' in so far as they are the subjects of various accidents, in other words in so far as they appear to us sometimes in one manner and sometimes in another. You agree with me about the first and third of these meanings in your chapter 'Of the Signification of Spirit . . .'.[17] Since, therefore, we do not say that 'to be a substance', that is, 'to be the subject of various accidents', is an accident of body (because if it were an accident, body would also be the subject of that accident, and by the same token being the subject of that accident would also be an accident of it; this would become nonsensical and would go on *ad infinitum*), it follows also that 'to be a quantity', that is, ' to be subject to comparison with other bodies', is not an accident of body either. And, Sir, I would go so far as to say that if we accepted the distinction that the other accidents are separable and quantity is inseparable, we should also have to say that substance is an accident of body, though an inseparable one.

However, I shall pass over all that, together with the implication which necessarily follows from it that space is an infinite plenum; people might imagine that my belief in this is the product of a false prejudice. I shall, I say, pass over all that in order to tell you, Sir, in the same ingenuous spirit (if you do not mind), what my other thoughts are about your philosophy. I find, Sir, that you are the only person to have constructed a body of philosophy in such a way that, like a true geometer, you begin with definitions which are completely clear in themselves; you build the first proposition on these definitions; you infer the second proposition from the first, the third from the second, and so on; so that there is not a single thing in your book that has not been demonstrated by you. You are the only person to have given us a true system of metaphysics, and the only one to have settled, in a few words, all the scholastic controversies—all the while following your own course, without being diverted into quibbling disputes. You are the only person to have shown, by the definitions you have given and by the subsequent demonstrations which you draw from them, that you have indeed considered things in themselves. And, I insist, this is to say nothing of Euclid's definition of a point, where he uses the term 'nothing' ('that whose part is nothing'),[18] and where, consequently, he seems to define nothing—since, when length, breadth, and depth are removed, we are indeed left with no idea at all. And what is his definition of a straight line worth, compared with yours: 'whose extreme points cannot be drawn further asunder [. . .] without altering the proportion of that line to any other line given'?[19] The same must be said about parallel lines, asymptotes, the angle, shape, in short about everything you have defined. Before your definitions appeared, one of two things happened: either people did not understand the matter at all, or they just talked gibberish about it. For it was quite possible, for example, to know what a straight line was; but as for having a clear and distinct idea corresponding to the words 'which lies evenly with the points on itself',[20] I for one had no corresponding idea at all. But when you write, it is Nature herself who is speaking. Above all, Sir, you have the honour, which no one can take away from you, of having been the first true founder of geometry. You are its creator. For, although you yourself say that this part of philosophy has been well cultivated by the best minds in all ages, nevertheless since geometry, apart from a few elements, is founded on proportions of quantities, I am right to say that there was no geometry before the science of proportions. And you, Sir, are the one who has given us this science, since previously we did not even have a definition of proportion itself. Not only was the definition given by Euclid (book 5, def. 5) obscure, when it required one to judge whether four quantities were in the same proportion by the excess or deficiency of their equimultiples; not only did that definition pose an impossibility, when it required that in order to know whether four quantities were in the same proportion one should ascertain at one and the same time that the multiples of the first would exceed or fall short of the multiples of the second, and those of the third exceed or fall short of those of the fourth, in any multiplication of them; but also it formed a circular argument with proposition 15 in book 5. Our geometers, indeed, had found this so awkward that each of them was beginning to write a book 5 in his own style; and, being what they are, they were all getting it wrong, until you gave us your definition of the same ratio, on which geometry must henceforth be founded.

I shall not tell you, Sir, what astounding truths you have derived from it. Nor shall I talk about the science of motions which you have developed to the peak of perfection; nor the comparison between curved and straight lines, which is something that no geometer before you had undertaken. What I shall say (but this is concerning your third section of the *Elements of Philosophy*)[21] is that after you were the first and the only person to demonstrate the true principles of the duties of civil life, it is obvious that our century, civilized though it may be in the arts and sciences, is barbarously uncivilized in its manners, when it lets the clash of arms drown the voice of reason—and when, to quote your wise author Bacon, we are so deafened by the chorus of Bacchae that we cannot hear Orpheus' lyre.[22] So it is that all the kings and states of the world have failed to compete with one another to heap the highest rewards on you. For, Sir, you are the only person to have demonstrated, from the nature of civil society, that the authority of the state is absolute and indivisible. That is something which it is absolutely necessary for subjects to be well convinced of, and which they cannot truly understand without hating civil war and without being content to live in peace among themselves under the power of the state. And that is what maintains that power.

That, Sir, is what I wanted to say about the great corpus of your philosophy. I describe it to everyone in these terms, since I am open in my behaviour and could not conceal feelings which so befit their object; and, if you do not mind, I shall write about it in these terms in my dedicatory epistle (which I shall address to you) before my translation of *De corpore*. Truly, Sir, I can think of no one in the world who is worthy of your work except yourself; for that reason I beg you to agree to my dedicating the work to you. I am still further obliged to acknowledge you in this way by the trust, full of esteem and affection, which you showed in me when, lying so ill in Paris that we thought your time had come, you wanted to entrust the manuscript of your works to me, asking me even to put the final touches to it in accordance with the theories you had explained to me, and to publish it if God took you from us. But Heaven took special care to preserve your illustrious life, knowing how indispensable you were to the good of society; and my prayer that that should not be the end of your friendship towards me was answered. To this friendship, Sir, which is so dear to me, I respond with feelings of special esteem and veneration, and with a firm and constant resolution to be, for the rest of my life,

> Sir,
> your most humble and most obedient servant,
> du Verdus

Bordeaux, 23 December 1655

[*postscript:*] I send you my sincerest greetings for Christmas and the New Year. I should very much like to see 'Vindex', and the *Elenchus* when it is printed. But do not send them to me until I write to let you know how and through whom. Please send me news (and, if you wish, your printed sheets) of your book *De homine*.[23]

---

[1] This letter does not apparently survive.

[2] Du Verdus's translation of *De cive* was published in 1660 as *Les Elemens de la politique*; the printer's notice to the reader there announced (sig. i3ʳ) that du Verdus had completed translations of *De corpore* and *De homine*, but these last two were never published.

[3] *Leviathan*.

[4] This could refer to Sorbière's translation of *De cive*, *Les Fondemens de la politique*; but du Verdus was familiar with that book, and did not refer to it elsewhere in such distant and vague terms (see Letter 84 n. 7). More probably he is recalling a comment by Hobbes on the unauthorized English translation of *De cive*, *Philosophicall Rudiments* (*HW* iii), which, for reasons too elaborate to be entered into here (but which will be presented in my biography of Hobbes) can confidently be assigned to the young poet Charles Cotton.

[5] soit *or some such word omitted in MS*.

[6] Wallis, *Elenchus geometriae hobbianae* (Oxford, 1655): the dedicatory epistle is dated 10 [/20] Oct.

[7] John Wallis (1616–1703), the son of an Anglican priest, matriculated at Emmanuel College, Cambridge, in 1632, proceeded BA (1637), MA (1640), and was ordained (also in 1640). In the early years of the Civil War he deciphered captured royalist documents for the parliamentarian side, and in 1644 he was appointed secretary to the Westminster Assembly. In the same year he was given a fellowship at Queens' College, Cambridge, which he had to vacate on his marriage one year later. In the later 1640s he was in London, where he got to know Robert Boyle and other scientists and mathematicians. He was installed as Savilian Professor of Geometry at Oxford, in place of the ejected royalist Peter Turner, in 1649; in 1654 he was admitted Doctor of Divinity, and in 1657 he was made Keeper of the Archives of the university. A talented mathematician who corresponded with many continental mathematicians (including Fermat and Huygens), he specialized in algebraic geometry and published his most important work, *Arithmetica infinitorum*, in 1656.

[8] 'Vindex' was the soubriquet used by Hobbes and Wallis to refer to Seth Ward, whose book *Vindiciae academiarum* (1654)—the book referred to here—contained an appendix criticizing Hobbes. Ward (1617–89), the son of an attorney, matriculated at Sidney Sussex College, Cambridge, in 1632, proceeded BA (1637) and MA (1640), and became a Fellow there (also in 1640). In 1643 he was appointed Mathematical Lecturer to the university; he was a particular admirer of William Oughtred, whose *Clavis mathematicae* he introduced as a textbook in Cambridge. A firm Anglican, he was ejected in 1644 for refusing to take the Covenant; but in 1649 he was installed as Savilian Professor of Astronomy in place of the ejected John Greaves (at Greaves's own suggestion), and took the Engagement oath. In 1654 he was created Doctor of Divinity. His two main scientific works were on the geometry of planetary motion: *In Bullialdi astronomiae fundamenta inquisitio* (1653) and *Astronomia geometrica* (1656). He first criticized Hobbes in his *Philosophicall Essay towards an Eviction of the Being and Attributes of God* (1652), before publishing a full-scale attack on *Leviathan*, entitled *In Thomae Hobbii philosophiam exercitatio epistolica* (1656). He became Bishop of Exeter in 1662, and Bishop of Salisbury in 1667.

[9] Wisd. 11: 20.

[10] *De corpore*, XVI. 1. Hobbes emended this section accordingly in the English translation of 1656, *Of Body*; the passages presented in square brackets in the translation here represent those offending passages in the original Latin which were altered in *Of Body*. The first passage became 'any straight line making an Angle with it, and representing the way of the Bodies motion'; the second became 'the whole time & the half of that time, & for the other side the half of the greatest *Impetus*'. Hobbes also issued instructions for the correction of these passages in a note at the end of *Examinatio et emendatio* in 1660 (p. 186; not in *OL*), and the correction was incorporated in the 2nd edn. of *De corpore* in the *Opera philosophica* of 1668.

[11] *De corpore*, II. 15.

[12] Ibid., VIII.

[13] Ibid., XII.

[14] Ibid., VIII. 12. The translation here is from du Verdus's French, since *Of Body* obscures both the problem du Verdus identifies and the emendation he proposes. The offending passages in the Latin are 'via uniuscuiusque partis, ejus corporis *Latitudo*

[. . .] vocatur' and 'uniuscuiusque partis via corporis illius *Crassities* [. . .] vocatur'. According to the punctuation of the first passage and the word-order of the second, the meanings should be 'the path of each part is called the *breadth* of that body' and 'the path of each part is called the *thickness* of that body'. *Of Body* seems to accept du Verdus's objection, since it ignores punctuation and word-order to translate as follows: 'the Way of every part of that Body is called BREADTH' and 'the Way of every part of that Body is called THICKNESS'; but the passages were not emended in the 2nd edn. of *De corpore* in the *Opera philosophica* of 1668.

[15] Terence, *Heauton timoroumenos*, line 77.

[16] *De corpore*, VIII. 4.

[17] *Leviathan*, ch. 34.

[18] Euclid, *Elements*, bk. 1, def. 1.

[19] *De corpore*, XIV. 1. The words omitted by du Verdus (and indicated by the elision in the translation here) are 'salva quantitate, id est' ('without altering the quantity, that is').

[20] Euclid, *Elements*, bk. 1, def. 4. Du Verdus's Latin appears to be an adaptation from Clavius' translation: 'Recta linea est, quae ex aequo sua interiacet puncta' (p. 30). The translation here of this notoriously difficult phrase uses the English version by Sir Thomas Heath.

[21] *De cive*.

[22] In ch. 11 of *De sapientia veterum* Bacon compares Orpheus' taming of the beasts through his music, which was undone by the intrusion of the Bacchantes, to the pacifying of kingdoms through the teaching of moral philosophy, which is undone by wars and sedition (*Works*, vi, pp. 646–8).

[23] See Letter 68 n. 6.

LETTER 76   [20 FEBRUARY/] 1 MARCH 1656

François du Verdus to Hobbes, from Bordeaux

Chatsworth, Hobbes MSS, letter 11 (original).

First enclosure: Chatsworth, Hobbes MSS, letter 82 (original).
Second enclosure: Chatsworth, Hobbes MSS, letter 32 (original).

Monsieur,

Je vous écriuis il peut y auoir six semaines ou du mois une longue lettre[1] que j'adressay a Mr Martel le priant de vous la faire tenir. Il l'aura fait sans doute Et vous aurés ueû que sur vos ordres je suspans l'edition de la Traduction que j'ay faite de vostre Liure de Corpore. vous aurés ueû aussi le dessein que j'ay de vous dédier cette version Ce que je vous prie d'agreër. J'ose vous dire qu'elle est exacte Et (si ce n'est pas trop me uanter) que ceux a qui j'en ay leu quelque chose trouuent que j'y ay eu du genie et de la bone fortune. Je ne vous done pour exemple que votre premiere periode de votre Epitre liminaire a M^r le

Comte de Deuonsire (si Comes Deuoniae ne se traduit pas ainsi je vous prie apprenés moy le mot françois[)][2] mais voicy cette période. Monseigneur Je vous presente cette premiére section des Elemens de la Philosophie, que j'ay fait long temps atendre aprés l'edition de la Troisieme et qu'enfin j'ay acheuée; et je vous l'offre qu'a l'auenir elle soit un Monument de vos bontés enuers moy et du respect que j'ay pour vous.[3] vous uoyés Monsieur que tout y est et qu'auec cela le tour y est francois sans parenthese ni transposition qui est une des délicatesses de nostre langue. Mais je suis encore plus exacte dans le corps de l'oeuure car j'y rends tout mot a mot et si j'y eusse trouué le benignitatis de l'epitre j'eusse traduit benignité.

Ce que je vous disois aussi dans ma lettre que j'adressay a Mr Martel: C'est que je uerrois d'auoir le sentiment de nos Geometres sur vostre Liure. Quand je seray a Paris j'en scauray dauantage Car Mr Roberual[4] par exemple et Mr Pascal m'en parleront uolontiers, qui mal-aysément se resoluent a écrire de peur de se couper. Cepandant Mr Mylon m'en a écrit a deux diuerses fois sur la semonçe que je luy en fis. La premiere fois il m'enuoya son premier Memoire. la s[econ]de[5] fois le second[6] Mais voicy come je répondis au premier.

Au 1er et 2^d nombres. Que dans uostre définition. Deux lignes quelles qu'elles soyent (soit droites ou courbes) et mesme deux surfaçes sont paralleles sur lesquelles deux lignes droites tombans quelque part que ce puisse estre et faisans angles égaux auec l'une ou l'autre d'elles seront égales entre elles.[7] que dans cette définition dis-je c'est qu'il faut entendre que les lignes tombans sur les paralleles y soient interceptées Ce qui est fort aisé a entendre; et qu'en un besoin on peut enonçer ainsi. Deux lignes quelle que ce soit, droites ou courbes et mesme deux surfaçes sont paralleles entre lesquelles deux lignes droites interceptées quelque part que ce soit qui y font angles égaux sur l'une ou l'autre sont égales entre elles.

Au 4e[8] Que ce qu'il ne uous accorde que come une hypothese vous le démontrés en ce qu'il ne peut y auoir de dureté infinie.[9] Et que ce qu'il ueut que DesCartes ait dit mieux In Circulum l'a jetté dans l'absurde que nous trouuons dans l'art. 34 de sa seconde partie qu'en ce mouuement en cercle il se fait une diuision infinie de la matière Car affin que cela fut il faudroit que les [cotes *deleted* >extremités] de ses cercles ne receussent point du tout d'impression de la matiere qui se meut [au ded *deleted*] entre deux c'est a dire que la resistance de ces cercles là fut infinie.[10]

Au 5eme Que ce qu'un côté du parallelograme a esté obmis, c'est une faute d'impression et que le mot Semissem y etant deux fois l'Imprimeur a pris le premier [> semissem] pour le second et a sauté au mot nam haec &c.[11]

Au 6eme et 7eme Qu'il se trompe en disant que vous prenés qu' AJ soit accelerata pars acceleratae AH. qu'au contraire vous prenés AJ parcouruë uniformement; que ce que l'a brouïllé c'est qu'il ne distingue pas AB d'elle mesme Et que quand vous dites Dico esse ut AH ad AB ita AB ad AJ vous entendés que AH qui est toute la longueur parcouruë par le mouuement hasté dans le temps AC, est à AB qui est toute la longueur parcouruë uniformement dans le mesme temps comme AB prise comme une longueur parcouruë par le mouuement hasté et laquelle est partie de AH, est a AJ prise come longueur parcouruë uniformement &c.[12]

Au 8eme Que si vous estes contraire a Mss Roberual et DesCartes ils sont contraires a la verité[13] Ce que vous dites de la refraction etant fort bien demontré.

Au 9eme Que je n'ay point l'esprit de comprendre en quoy vous vous trompés au chap. 18eme. Que si vous uous y estes trompé (ce que j'ay peine a croire) il ne doit pas se fascher qu'on l'ait découuert puis qu'au contraire vous mesmes Monsieur en serés bien aise qui estes un home ingenu Et aymant la verité. Et qu'enfin ie le prie de m'enuoyer cette prétenduë démonstration de Mr Zulichem.

Il me l'a donc enuoyée dans son second Memoire. Je la reçeus par le dernier courrier Et je vous l'enuoye[14] sans perdre temps que vous preniés la peine d'y faire réflection.

Au reste Monsieur j'ay a vous dire de Mr Mylon Qu'il parle de vous auec toute sorte d'estime et de bone uolonté voicy quelque chose de sa première lettre. On dit icy que vous aués traduit la Physique de M^r hobbes pour la faire imprimer; vous obligerés toute la france. Je scay bien que l'ecole ne done pas trop son aprobation a cet Ouurage et croy que Joh: Wallesius STD et Geometra in Acad. Oxon. professor Saluïenus l'aura combatu par Aristote:[15] mais ni vous ni l'autheur ne vous en souciés pas beaucoup. vous ne prétendés de plaire qu'a ceux qui sont hors des préjugés et conduisent bien leur raison. J'ay leu ce liure de Mr Hobbes auec tres grand plaisir Et y ay tout admiré horsmis les endroits que je vous cotte sur l'entre-papier. receués le come d'une persone tres affectionée a l'autheur et si je me suis méconté faites moy la faueur de me montrer ma faute.

Et dans sa seconde lettre Quand il me dit Que pour décrier le meilleur liure du Monde il ne faut que dire qu'il y a des paralogismes je vois effectiuement que c'est un trait de sa bone uolonté qu'il souhaiteroit que les Chapitres De Dimensione Circuli et des droites égales aux paraboliformes[16] ne fussent pas dans le vostre; luy qui n'a pas la mesme opinion de ces Chapitres là Que du reste du Liure qu'il admire.

Ce qu'on m'écrira de plus ou que je scauray autrement sur votre sujet je vous l'écriray de mesme en confidançe. Car je suis asseuré Monsieur Que vous receurés toutes choses de ma part auec [les *deleted*] autant de bonté que j'ay d'estime et de uénération pour vous. Cepandant soit que vous ueuïlliés me dire en quoy se trompe Mr Zulichem (que je croiray toujours qui se trompe jusqu'a ce que vous m'ayés dit que non); soit que vous me ueuilliés enuoyer vos Cahiers de homine[17] que je souhaiterois de reçeuoir a mesure qu'ils s'imprimeront pour y trauailler en mesme temps et auoir vos Trois sections traduites tout a la fois: ou qu'enfin vous ueuilliés de temps en temps m'aprendre de vos Nouuelles que je prie Dieu qui soyent toujours bones Je vous prie Monsieur écriués moy de droiture. Car j'ay esté auerty que le Comis de Paris enuoye les lettres de Bordeaux a Londres et celles de Londres a Bordeaux. Obligés moy donc de mettre ainsi le dessus a vos lettres. / A Monsieur Monsieur de Cheneuas[18] Maistre de Bureau de la Poste pour M^r de St Hilaire A Bourdeaux. /.

S^t hilaire est un nom suposé que j'ay doné a Mr Cheneuas parce qu'on me faisoit perdre de mes lettres. sous cette suscription les vostres me seront renduës ponctuellement Et je les reçeuray auec mes sentimens inuiolables d'estime et d'amitié qui suis a la vie et a la mort

Monsieur
Vôtre tres humble et tres obeissant seruiteur
du uerdus.

A Bordeaux le 1er Mars 1656.

[*endorsed by James Wheldon:*] Mar. 1.st 1656 Mon^sr du Verdus

[*enclosed: Mylon's objections to* De corpore *in Mylon's hand, with an annotation in du Verdus's hand,* '1er Memoyre de Mr Mylon':]

Ad physicam Domini hobs.

1. Chap. 14. Art. 12. La definition des paralleles doit estre supplée
2. pag. 114. Linea 13. Il ne conclut pas juste par ce qu'il se fonde sur Sa definition des paralleles[19]

3. pag. 114. Art. 13 me semble obscur[20]

4. Chap. 15. Art. 7. on peut Luy accorder comme vne hypothese que Motus siue Conatus tam In vacuo, quam In pleno propagatur In Infinitum: Il me semble que Monsr DesCartes dit mieux quod propagatur Iste motus In Circulum.[21]

5. pag. 128. Linea 6. Il compose vn parallelogramme auec vn seul costé. Il doit estre ainsi. Vel denique per parallelogrammum cujus vnum latus medium proportionale Inter Impetum maximum (siue vltimò acquisitum) et et [*sic*] Impetus ejusdem maximi semissem, alterum verò latus sit medium proportionale Inter totum tempus et ejusdem totius temporis Semissem, nam Duo haec parallelogramma et Inter se, et [*blotted* tri]angulo quod fit ex tempore toto et Impetu crescente sunt aequalia.[22]

6. Ad cap. 16. Artic. 17. Enunciatur generaliter, demonstratur vero singulariter, vel non Intelligo. Nam In fig. 8ª AB est Longitudo vniformis respondens tempori AC. AH est Longitudo accelerata respondens eidem tempori AC. Iam sumitur AI Longitudo accelerata, pars accelerata AH; debet etiam sumere Longitudinem vniformem vt AO quae sit pars Vniformis AB, atque demonstrare differentiam totius AH supra totam AB esse ad differentiam partis AI supra partem vt AO; vt ratio Longitudinum vt AH, AB (vel quod Idem est vt ratio partium Longitudinum AJ. AO) ad rationem temporum AC, AM.

7. Articulo 17. Cap. 16. Non Intelligo demonstrationem.

8. pag. 114. Linea 4. Il est tout contraire a M. DesCartes et a M. Roberual pour la refraction.[23]

9. Cap. 18. Le probleme general qui donne des lignes droites egales aux Paraboles, seroit tres beau s'il estoit vray, mais ce qui me fasche, Monsieur Hugens de Zulichem en a demonstré La fausseté il en doit escrire d'hollande a Monsr. hobs. Je vous l'Enuoyeray quand Il vous plaira si vous auez La Curiosité de voir cette demonstration.

[*The following text, written in Mylon's hand on a single folio sheet and endorsed by James Wheldon, 'Monsr. Mylon 1656', is probably to be identified with the geometrical demonstration enclosed with the second commentary by Mylon and forwarded by du Verdus to Hobbes:*]

Soit vn triangle rectangle ADC dont AD soit 5. CD soit 12. et AC soit 13. autour duquel Soit vne parabole Conique ABC, son Axe AD, sa base en ordonnèe DC, soit diuiseè egalement AD en E, et soit tireè L'ordonneè EB Laquelle soit prolongée de sorte que EF soit egale à

DC, soit prise eg moyenne proportionelle entre EF, et EB. tirant Ag, gc
Je Dis que Ag plus gc n'est point egale à La parabole ABC.

Soit descrit le Cercle AJC dont le Centre soit dans l'axe AD
prolongé. L'arc AJC sera hors la parabole ce qui est aisé a demonstrer
comme a fait M.^{r} hugenius dans la prop. 17. du Liure de Circuli
magnitudine. Soient tirées les droites AK, CK qui touchent le cercle
AJC en A et C. Soit tireé Kh diuisant egalement AC en h. Le point h
sera l'Intersection de EF, AC, a cause des paralleles ef, DC, et de la
Ligne AD my partie en E.

A Cause de la similitude des triangles DCA, hAK, comme DC à CA,
ainsi hA à AK ou ainsi 2hA, à 2AK, c'est a dire ainsi CA; à AK plus KC.
donc AK + KC sera $\frac{169}{12}$. donc $\frac{2}{3}$AC + $\frac{1}{3}$AK + $\frac{1}{3}$CK sera $\frac{481}{36}$ qui sera plus
grand que l'arc de Cercle AJC par La $9.^{eme}$ prop. de hugenius de Circuli
magnitudine.

Mais EB est $\sqrt{72}$. car AD est à AE comme CD.q^{ré} à EB.q^{ré}

Donc Eg.q^{ré} est $\sqrt{10368}$ lequel est vn peu plus grand que $\frac{1018233}{10000}$.
Mais AE.q^{ré} est $\frac{25}{4}$.

Donc AE.q^{ré} + eg.q^{ré} c'est a dire Ag q^{ré} sera plus grand que $\frac{4322932}{40000}$
Et la droite Ag sera plus grande que $\frac{2079}{200}$.

Or la Racine quarreé prochainement moindre du nombre $\frac{1018233}{10000}$ est
$\frac{1009}{100}$.

Soit pris $\frac{1010}{100}$ ou $\frac{101}{10}$ pour valeur trop forte de la droite eg, car le quarré
quarré de $\frac{101}{10}$ est plus grand que 10406. qui est plus grand que 10368 qui
est la valeur de eg.q^{ré} q^{ré}.

Donc fg sera plus grande que $\frac{19}{10}$. Mais [fc quarré]^{24} est $\frac{25}{4}$.

Donc Fg.q^{ré} + FC.q^{ré} c'est a dire cg q^{ré} sera plus grand que $\frac{3944}{400}$

Donc cg sera plus grande que $\frac{62}{20}$

Donc Ag + gc sera plus grande que $\frac{2699}{200}$ qui est plus grand que $\frac{481}{36}$
Car. $\frac{481}{36}$ vaut $\frac{96200}{7200}$ Et $\frac{2699}{200}$ vaut $\frac{97164}{7200}$

Donc $\frac{2699}{200}$ est plus grand que la valeur de $\frac{2}{3}$AC + $\frac{1}{3}$AK + $\frac{1}{3}$CK

Et partant si la parabole [>ABC] est egale à Ag + gc, elle sera aussi
[>beaucoup *deleted*] plus grande que $\frac{2}{3}$AC + $\frac{1}{3}$AK + $\frac{1}{3}$CK.

Et par consequent [ag + gc sera beaucoup pl *deleted*] la mesme
parabole ABC est beaucoup plus grande que l'arc AJC. ce qui est
absurd. Donc la Construction precedente n'est pas vraye ce qu'il falloit
demonstrer.

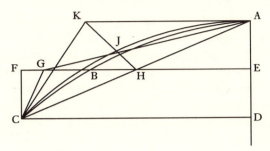

Translation of Letter 76

Sir,

I wrote a long letter to you, perhaps six weeks or a month ago,[1] which I sent to M. de Martel, asking him to convey it to you. No doubt he has done so, and you have seen that, obeying your request, I am suspending publication of my translation of your book *De corpore*. You will also have seen that I plan to dedicate this translation to you—something which I beg you to accept. I am so bold as to tell you that it is exact, and (if this is not boasting too much) that, according to those who have heard me read some extracts, it is a talented and felicitous translation. I shall give you just one example, the first sentence of your dedicatory epistle to the Earl ['M. le Comte'] of Devonshire (if that is not the correct translation of 'Comes Devoniae', please tell me what the French term is)[2]. Here is the sentence: 'My Lord, I present to you this first section of the Elements of Philosophy, which I have long deferred after the publication of the third, and which I have at last finished; and I present it to you so that it may be in future a monument of your bounty to me and my respect for you.'[3] You see, Sir, everything is there, and at the same time the turn of phrase is French, with no parenthetical or transposed clauses—which is one of the finer points of our language. But my translation is even more exact in the body of the work, since there I give a word-for-word rendering of everything; if I had found the dedicatory epistle's word 'benignitatis' ['of bounty'] there, I would have translated it as 'benignity' ['benignité'].

What I also told you in the letter which I sent to M. de Martel was that I would try to get the judgements of our geometers on your book. I shall find out more when I am in Paris; for M. Roberval,[4] for example, and M. Pascal, who are afraid to write for fear of contradiction, will be happy to talk to me about it. However, M. Mylon wrote to me about it on two separate occasions, after I had admonished him about it. He sent me his first commentary the first time, and his second,[(5)] the second.[6] But here is how I replied to the first one:

To his first and second points: these concern your definition, 'any two lines whatsoever, strait or crooked, as also any two superficies, are PARALLEL; when two equal strait lines, wheresoever they fall upon them, make always equal angles with each of them'.[7] In this definition, I say, one must understand that the lines falling on the parallel lines are intersected there. This is very easy to understand; and if need be one can put it as follows. 'Any two lines whatsoever, straight or curved, and likewise any two surfaces, are parallel, when any two straight lines between them, intersected anywhere, make equal angles and are of equal length.'

To his fourth[8] point: that which he grants you only as a hypothesis, is in fact demonstrated by you, in that there cannot be such a thing as infinite hardness.[9] And that which he claims Descartes expressed better in his section on the circle has made him fall into the absurdity which we find in part 2, section 34: namely that in this circular motion matter is infinitely divided. For in order for that to happen, the extremities of his circles would have to receive no impression whatsoever from the matter which moves between them— in other words, the resistance of those circles would need to be infinitely great.[10]

To his fifth point: the fact that one side of the parallelogram was omitted is a printing error. And because the word 'semissem' ['half'] occurred there twice, the printer mistook the first 'semissem' for the second, and jumped to the words 'nam haec . . .' etc.[11]

To his sixth and seventh points: he is mistaken in saying that you take AJ as the accelerated part of the accelerated motion AH. On the contrary, you take AJ as traversed in uniform motion. What has confused him is his failure to distinguish between AB and itself. And when you write 'I say, that as AH is to AB, so will AB be to AJ,' you mean that AH (the entire length traversed by accelerated motion in the time AC) is to AB (the entire length traversed by uniform motion in the same time) as AB (taken as a length which is traversed by accelerated motion, and which is part of AH) is to AJ (taken as a length traversed by uniform motion), and so on.[12]

To his eighth point: if your theories contradict those of MM. Roberval and Descartes, then their theories contradict the truth.[13] What you say about refraction is very well demonstrated.

To his ninth point: I do not have the wit to understand what your error may be in ch. XVIII. If you have made an error there (which I find hard to believe), then he should not worry about the fact that someone has exposed it: on the contrary, you yourself, Sir, will be very happy to see it exposed, since you are an intellectually honest man and a lover of truth. And finally I ask him to send me that so-called demonstration by M. Huygens.

So he did send it to me, enclosed in his second commentary. I received it by the last carrier, and without further delay I send it to you,[14] so that you may take the trouble to think about it.

Otherwise, Sir, I must tell you that M. Mylon speaks about you with very high esteem and goodwill. Here is an extract from his first letter: 'It is said here that you have translated Mr Hobbes's "Physics" for publication; you will do a service thereby to the whole of France. I know that the universities do not approve too highly of this work, and I believe that the geometer Dr John Wallis, Savilian Professor in the University of Oxford, has used Aristotle to attack it;[15] but neither you nor the author can be very worried by that. You are only claiming to please those who are free of prejudice and reason correctly. I have read this book by Mr Hobbes with very great pleasure, admiring everything in it (with the exception of the points which I list for you on the enclosed paper). Receive this as from someone who is very well disposed towards the author; and if I have made any mistakes, please do me the favour of demonstrating my errors.'

And in his second letter, when he says that in order to denigrate the best book in the world, one need only say that it contains some paralogisms, I see that it is indeed a sign of his goodwill that he would prefer it if your book did not contain the chapters 'Of the Dimension of a Circle' and 'Of the Equation of Strait Lines with the Crooked Lines of Parabolas and other Figures made in Imitation of Parabolas':[16] he does not have the same opinion of those chapters as he does of the rest of the book, which he admires.

If there are any other judgements concerning you which I receive in letters, or learn about by other means, I shall also write to you about them in confidence. For I am sure, Sir, that you will accept everything I send you with as much goodwill towards me as I feel esteem and veneration towards you. Anyway, should you wish to tell me what error M. Zuylichem has committed (and I shall always assume that he is in error unless you tell me otherwise); should you wish to send me your sheets of *De homine*,[17] which I should like to receive as they are printed, in order to work on them at the same time and have your three sections translated simultaneously; or, finally, should you wish from time to

time to tell me your news—which I pray to God may always be good —
please write to me, Sir, directly. For I have been told that the Paris post
office sends letters from Bordeaux to London, and letters from London
to Bordeaux. So please address your letters as follows: 'To M. de
Chenevas,[18] Director of the Post Office, for M. de St Hilaire, at
Bordeaux'.

St Hilaire is a fictitious name which I have given to M. Chenevas
because people were intercepting my mail. Addressed like this, your
letters will be delivered on time; and I shall receive them with the
feelings of unalterable esteem and friendship of one who is, in life and
death,

Sir,
Your most humble and obedient servant,
du Verdus

Bordeaux, 1 March 1656

[*enclosed: Mylon's objections to* De corpore *in Mylon's hand, with an
annotation in du Verdus's hand,* 'M. Mylon's first commentary':]

On Mr Hobbes's Physics

1. XIV. 12: the definition of parallels must be supplemented.

2. Page 114, line 13: he reaches a false conclusion, because his
argument is based on his definition of parallels.[19]

3. Page 114, article 13: this seems obscure to me.[20]

4. XV. 7: one can grant him, as a hypothesis, that 'motion or
endeavour, whether in space which is empty, or in space which is filled,
is propagated to an infinite distance'; but I think M. Descartes argues
better when he says that 'that motion is propagated in a circle'.[21]

5. Page 128, line 6: here he constructs a parallelogram with only one
side. It should go like this: 'or lastly, by a parallelogram, one of whose
sides is a mean proportional between the greatest impetus (or the last
impetus to have been acquired) and half that greatest impetus, and
whose other side is the mean proportional between the whole time and
half that whole time. For both these parallelograms are equal to one
another, and severally equal to the triangle which is made of the whole
line of time and the increasing impetus'.[22]

6. XVI. 17: the proposition is made in general terms, but the
demonstration is true only in a particular case; or else I do not

understand it. For in fig. 8, AB is a uniform length corresponding to the time AC. AH is the accelerated length corresponding to the same time AC. The accelerated length AI is taken to be part of the accelerated length AH; so one should also take the uniform length AO as part of the uniform length AB, and demonstrate that the ratio between the difference between the whole of AH and the whole of AB, and the difference between the part AI and the part AO, is the same as that between the ratio between the lengths AH and AB (or the ratio of the parts of those lengths, AI and AO) and the ratio between the times AC and AM.

7. XVI. 17: I do not understand this demonstration.

8. Page 114, line 4: his account of refraction is the opposite of that of M. Descartes and M. Roberval.[23]

9. XVIII: the general problem which he uses to equate straight lines with parabolas would be fine if it were true; but the trouble is, M. Huygens of Zuylichem has demonstrated that it is false. He is due to write about that from Holland, to Mr Hobbes. If you are curious to see this demonstration of his, I shall send it to you whenever you like.

[*Second enclosure from Mylon*]

Let there be a right-angled triangle ADC, of which AD is 5, CD is 12, and AC is 13. Round it, let there be a conical parabola ABC, with AD as its axis and DC as its base or ordinate. Let AD be bisected at E, and let the ordinate EB be drawn and continued so that EF is equal to DC. Let EG be the mean proportional between EF and EB. Drawing AG and GC, I say that AG plus GC is not at all equal to the parabola ABC.

Let the circle AJC be drawn, the centre of which lies on the continuation of the axis AD. The arc AJC will lie outside the parabola: that is easily demonstrated, as Mr Huygens has done in proposition 17 of his book *De circuli magnitudine*. Let the straight lines AK and CK be drawn, touching the circle AJC at A and C. Let KH be drawn, bisecting AC at H. The point H will be the intersection of EF and AC, because EF and DC are parallel lines, and because E is the mid-point of the line AD.

Because of the similarity of the triangles DCA and HAK, as DC is to CA, so HA is to AK, or 2HA is to 2AK; in other words so is CA to AK plus KC. Therefore AK + KC will be $\frac{169}{12}$.

Therefore $\frac{2}{3}$AC + $\frac{1}{3}$AK + $\frac{1}{3}$CK will be $\frac{481}{36}$, which is greater than the arc of the circle AJC, according to the ninth proposition of Huygens's *De circuli magnitudine*.

But EB is $\sqrt{72}$; for AD is to AE as CD^2 is to EB^2.

Therefore EG^2 is $\sqrt{10{,}368}$, which is slightly greater than $\frac{1{,}018{,}233}{10{,}000}$.

But AE^2 is $\frac{25}{4}$.

Therefore $AE^2 + EG^2$, that is, AG^2, will be greater than $\frac{4{,}322{,}932}{40{,}000}$.

And the straight line AG will be greater than $\frac{2{,}079}{200}$.

Now, the closest square root lower than the number $\frac{1{,}018{,}233}{10{,}000}$ is $\frac{1{,}009}{100}$.

Let $\frac{1{,}010}{100}$ or $\frac{101}{10}$ be taken as slightly more than the value of the straight line EG, since the fourth power of $\frac{101}{10}$ is greater than 10,406, which is greater than 10,368, which is the value of EG^4.

Therefore FG will be more than $\frac{19}{10}$. But $[FC^2]^{24}$ is $\frac{25}{4}$.

Therefore $FG^2 + FC^2$, that is, CG^2, will be greater than $\frac{3{,}944}{400}$.

Therefore CG will be greater than $\frac{62}{20}$.

Therefore AG + GC will be greater than $\frac{2{,}699}{200}$, which is greater than $\frac{481}{36}$.

For $\frac{481}{36}$ equals $\frac{96{,}200}{7{,}200}$. And $\frac{2{,}699}{200}$ equals $\frac{97{,}164}{7{,}200}$.

Therefore $\frac{2{,}699}{200}$ is greater than the value of $\frac{2}{3}AC + \frac{1}{3}AK + \frac{1}{3}CK$.

And by the same token, if the parabola ABC is equal to AG + GC, it will also be greater than $\frac{2}{3}AC + \frac{1}{3}AK + \frac{1}{3}CK$.

And consequently the same parabola ABC is much greater than the arc AJC: which is absurd. Therefore the foregoing construction is false: QED.

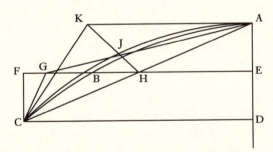

Commentary on the second enclosure. Hobbes's assertion appears to be that the length of the arc ABC of the parabola equals AG + GC, where G is defined by $EG^2 = EB.EF$, and E is the bisector of the axis AD. This is refuted here by Mylon. Two propositions of Huygens are used: (1) that the circle through A and C with centre on the axis AD lies outside the parabola, up to the point where the circle and parabola meet at C, and (2) that the length of the arc AC of this circle is less than $\frac{AK}{3} + \frac{CK}{3} + \frac{2AC}{3}$. Combining these propositions one has:

length of arc of parabola ABC < length of circular arc ABC < $\frac{AK}{3} + \frac{CK}{3} + \frac{2AC}{3}$.

Using Pythagoras' theorem, Mylon then shows that AG + GC > $\frac{AK}{3} + \frac{CK}{3} + \frac{2AC}{3}$ for the particular lengths AD = 5, CD = 12, and hence that Hobbes's assertion is false.

Simple proofs of Huygens's propositions are as follows: Choose AD as the x-axis and AK as the y-axis, and let the equation of the parabola be $y^2 = 4ax$. Suppose D is the point $x = b$. The coordinates of C are therefore $\{b, \sqrt{(4ab)}\}$. Suppose the centre of the circle, which lies on the x-axis, is $(c,0)$. Then its equation must be of the form $(x-c)^2 + y^2 = c^2$, and, since it passes through C, we have $c = 2a + \frac{b}{2}$. The circle is therefore given by $y^2 = (4a+b)x-x^2$, and it will lie outside (to the left of) the parabola if $(4a+b)x-x^2 \geqslant 4ax$, i.e. if $0 \leqslant x \leqslant b$. This proves (1).

To prove (2), suppose the angle subtended at the centre of the circle by its arc AC is 2θ. Simple trigonometry shows that the tangents AK and CK have length $r\tan\theta$, and the chord AC has length $2\sin\theta$. Since the length of the arc is $2r\theta$, the proposition amounts to $\tan\theta + 2\sin\theta \geqslant 3\theta$. Equality holds at $\theta = 0$, and it is easy to check that the derivative of $\tan\theta + 2\sin\theta - 3\theta$ is positive in the range $0 < \theta < \frac{\pi}{2}$. G.M.

[1] This letter does not apparently survive. The odd construction 'du mois' here may perhaps be a slip for 'deux mois' ('two months').

[2] $\sim$) omitted in MS.

[3] The sentence in the 1656 English translation, which keeps more closely to the 'parenthetical and transposed clauses' of the original, is as follows: 'This first Section of the *Elements* of *Philosophy* , the Monument of my Service, & your Lordships bounty, though (after the third Section published) long deferred, yet at last finished, I now present (my most excellent Lord) and dedicate to your Lordship.'

[4] Gilles Personne de Roberval (1602–75) was a mathematician of humble origins, who seems to have received little formal education before he reached Paris in 1628 and joined Mersenne's circle. He became Professor of Philosophy at the Collège de maître Gervais, Paris, in 1632, and in 1634 won the competition for the Ramus chair at the Collège royale. He remained at the Collège royale for the rest of his life, succeeding Gassendi in the chair of mathematics there in 1655, and in 1666 he was a founder member of the Académie royale des sciences. He published only two scientific books, the *Traité de méchanique* (1636) and *Aristarchi Samii de mundi systemate* (1644); his mathematical researches were concentrated on the geometry of infinitesimals, but he was secretive with his discoveries (some of which circulated in MS: see the entry for du Verdus in the Biographical Register) and was often involved in quarrels with other mathematicians over questions of precedence and plagiarism.

[5] Contraction expanded.

[6] The first commentary is printed as the first enclosure to this letter; the second contained the geometrical demonstration which is printed as the second enclosure.

[7] *De corpore*, XIV. 12.

[8] Du Verdus seems to have inadvertently omitted his reply to the third point.

[9] Descartes, *Principia* , part 2, sect. 34 (A&T viii, pp. 59–60). Cf. the claim made in *De corpore*, XXII. 2 that the terms 'soft' and 'hard' 'are used onely comparatively; and are not different kinds, but different degrees of Quality' ('dicuntur tantum comparative, nec sunt diversa genera, sed diversi gradus qualitatis').

[10] In *Principia*, part 2, sect. 33, Descartes argued that in a plenistic universe, every individual motion is part of a chain of motions which is ultimately circular: when one part moves from space A to space B, it displaces another part, and so on— with, at the end of the chain, another part moving into space A. Descartes allowed for the idea that the spaces might be of different sizes by arguing that this was compensated by the different speeds at which matter would move into them. (An analogy to this would be

water moving at different speeds through pipes of different diameters.) In sect. 34 Descartes argued that matter must therefore be capable of travelling through an infinite variety of sizes of spaces, and that this implied that matter was infinitely divisible. Du Verdus's objection is obscure; he seems to be conflating the 'circles', i.e. circular motions, of Descartes's account, with the physical limits on the motion of the quantities of matter (in the water analogy, the sides of the pipe).

[11] See Letter 75 n. 10.

[12] See *De corpore*, XVI. 17, and Mylon's sixth and seventh objections in the first enclosure to this letter.

[13] For Descartes's theory of refraction, see the second discourse of his 'Dioptrique'. Roberval's views on refraction were not the same as those of Descartes (with whom, in any case, he tended to disagree whenever possible). In the posthumously published version of du Verdus's compilation of Roberval's teachings, Roberval criticized Descartes's theory of refraction and argued that the motion of light is slower in a denser medium (Roberval, *Ouvrages de mathématique*, pp. 13–14: for the history of this work, see the Biographical Register, 'du Verdus'). In his notes for a treatise on refraction, however, Roberval avoided giving any physical explanation for the phenomenon (BN MS f.fr. n.a. 5175, fos. 14–21). And in the treatise which he planned to publish as a companion to Mersenne's two treatises on optics, *L'Optique et la catoptrique*, he explicitly refused to offer a physical theory of the transmission of light (BN MS f.fr. 12279, 'Liure troisieme de la dioptrique', fos. 3, 8^r).

[14] See the second enclosure to this letter.

[15] The reasons for this claim are obscure.

[16] Chs. XX and XVIII respectively.

[17] See Letter 68 n. 6.

[18] François Chenevas is mentioned in a decree of Mar. 1665 as one of several joint holders of the four offices of *maître des courriers* at Bordeaux (see Vaillé, *Histoire générale des postes françaises*, iii, p. 275).

[19] The reference is to XIV. 12, coroll. 5, first sentence. Hobbes cited these comments in *Six Lessons*: 'The same [sc. criticism] was observed also upon this place by one of the prime Geometricians of *Paris*, and noted in a Letter to his friend in these words *Chap. 14 Art. 12 the Definition of Parallels wanteth somewhat to be supplyed*. And of the Consectary, he says *it concludeth not, because it is grounded on the Definition of Parallels*' (p. 25: *EW* vii, p. 255).

[20] XIV. 13.

[21] See n. 10 above. The words attributed to Hobbes here are a summary of the argument of XV. 7, rather than a direct quotation.

[22] This is adapting XVI. 1, coroll.; the translation here adapts *Of Body*, p. 161.

[23] Mylon appears to have copied out the wrong reference for this objection. Hobbes's account of refraction is in XXIV, pp. 215–22.

[24] fc *MS*.

LETTER 77   [22 MARCH/] 1 APRIL 1656

Abraham du Prat to Hobbes, from Paris

Chatsworth, Hobbes MSS, letter 13 (original).

Monsieur,

J'ay differé iusques à cette heure de respondre à vostre lettre[1] par laquelle vous me donnés aduis que vous m'aues [>fait] la faueur de m'enuoyer la Philosophie Epicuro-Gassendo-Carletoniene,[2] parce que i'esperois de iour en iour de la receuoir. Mais à present que ie crains qu'elle ne soit perduë, ie me sens obligé de vous remercier de vostre bonne intention, encore qu'elle n'aye pas esté fidellement executée par ceux entre les mains de qui vous [avez]³ mis ce liure. Mr Car,[4] Prestre anglois que i'ay veu, m'a dit qu'il en auoit oui parler, et qu'on ne lui en auoit rien escrit. On m'a dit qu'on a imprimé en Hollande un nouueau Systeme de Philosophie, composé par le Secretaire de Rotterdam,[5] et dedié au Roy de france. Il n'en est venu en cette ville qu'un seul exemplaire pour le Roy. Si vous faites rimprimer vostre Philosophie,[6] il faut prendre garde que le papier soit meilleur, [>et] les characteres plus grands. Mr de Roberual[7] fit auanthier une oraison inaugurale en presence du Cardinal antonio,[8] et de plusieurs gens scauans, dans laquelle il monstra que la Mathematique estoit vtile en tous les arts et toutes les sciences, et que rien ne se faisoit que par ses loix, à scauoir pondere, numero et mensura.[9] Il est à present professeur du Roy en Mathematique,[10] et commencera ses lecons apres Pasques. Sa harangue ne respondit pas à ce qu'on s'attendoit de lui. Plusieurs disoyent qu'il est aussi mauuais Orateur, qu'excellent Geometre, et qu'il a fait voir en lui mesme que la Mathematique et l'art Oratoire sont incompatibles, et se rencontrent rarement dans un mesme suiet. Cela n'est pas vniuersellement vray, puis que [>dans] vostre liure de Ciue, et [>dans] vostre Philosophie, on y voit la solidité du raisonnement coniointe auec les ornemens de l'Eloquence. Ne verrons nous iamais vostre leuiathan en latin ou en francois? L'Angleterre iouira elle toute seule de cet excellent ouurage, et n'y aura il personne qui aye la bonté d'en faire part à ses voisins? Je vous prie me faire scauoir si Mʳ Haruaeus fit imprimer quelque chose.[11] Nous auons veu icy Anatomia hepatis [>Griffonii imprimè a Londres].[12] Mʳ Pecquet escrit a present de la circulation du serum, de la fermentation et de la Cataracte.[13] On imprime un traité de la lumiere par M^r de la chambre.[14] Je suis Monsieur

Vostre tres humble et tres obeissant seruiteur
Du Prat

a Paris ce 1 Auril 1656.

[*endorsed by James Wheldon:*] Monsr du Prat Ap. 1:^st 1656

Translation of Letter 77

Sir,

I have delayed until now replying to your letter,[1] in which you inform me that you have done me the favour of sending me the *Physiologia Epicuro-Gassendo-Carltoniana*,[2] because I was hoping from day to day to receive it. But now that I am afraid it has been lost, I feel obliged to thank you for your good intention, even though it was not faithfully carried out by those to whom you had entrusted[(3)] the book. The English priest Mr Car,[4] whom I have seen, told me that he had heard nothing of it, and that no one had written anything to him about it. I have been told that a new 'System of Philosophy' has been printed in Holland, written by the Secretary of Rotterdam,[5] and dedicated to the King of France. Only one copy, for the King, has reached this town. If you have your Philosophy[6] reprinted, you should make sure that they use better paper and larger print. M. Roberval[7] made an inaugural speech the day before yesterday in the presence of Cardinal Antonio[8] and several learned people; in it, he demonstrated that mathematics is useful for all the arts and sciences, and that nothing happens except by 'number, weight, and measure'.[9] At present he is Royal Professor of Mathematics,[10] and will begin his lectures after Easter. His speech did not match up to what had been expected of him. Several people said that he was as bad at oratory as he is good at geometry, and that he showed by his own example that mathematics and the art of oratory are incompatible, and are seldom found together in a single person. But that is not universally true, since one can see in your *De cive* and your Philosophy solid reasoning combined with the ornaments of eloquence. Shall we never see your *Leviathan* in Latin or French? Will England have the enjoyment of this excellent work all on her own, and will no one have the kindness to share it with her neighbours? Please let me know whether Mr Harvey had something printed.[11] Here we have seen Glisson's *Anatomia hepatis*, printed in London.[12] M. Pecquet is writing at present about the circulation of serum, fermentation, and cataracts.[13] The treatise on light by M. de la Chambre is being printed.[14] I am,

Sir,
your most humble and obedient servant,
du Prat

The author of this letter is identified as Abraham du Prat by the handwriting.

[1] This letter has not apparently survived.

[2] See Letter 74 n. 4.

[3] avez *or some such word omitted in MS.*

[4] Miles Pinkney, alias Thomas Carre (1599–1674), entered Douai College in 1618, was ordained priest in 1625, and from 1634 was chaplain to the English Augustinian convent in Paris. He was much favoured at the French Court, especially by Richelieu. He enjoyed a close friendship with the poet Richard Crashaw, and was editor of his *Carmen Deo nostro* (Paris, 1652); he also translated into English several devotional works by François de Sales and Jean-Pierre Camus. See Gillow, *Literary and Biographical History*; Anstruther, *Seminary Priests*, ii; Warren, *Crashaw*, pp. 52–5; and le Maire, *Paris ancien et nouveau*, i, pp. 292–5.

[5] Van Berlicom, *Elementorum de rerum naturalium gravitate libri XII* (Rotterdam, 1656). Andreas van Berlicom (*c*.1587–1656) studied philosophy and law at Leiden, became *Secretaris* of Rotterdam in 1628, and was appointed curator of the Latin school there in 1641; he had some contacts with both Descartes and Huygens (see A&T ii, pp. 642; *HOC* xi, pp. 261–2). He remained *Secretaris* until his death in July 1656 (Unger, *De regeering van Rotterdam*, p. 130). One of the two entries on him in the *Nieuw nederlandsch biografisch woordenboek* (vi) says that his *Elementorum* was published in 1654, but this must be an error: the dedicatory epistle to Louis XIV is dated Oct. 1655. The book is a treatise on metaphysics, astronomy, and biology, arranged somewhat spuriously in Euclidean sequences of 'definitions' and 'theorems', and expounding a broadly mechanistic physics which distinguishes between several different kinds of fundamental motion.

[6] *De corpore*.

[7] See Letter 76 n. 4.

[8] Antonio Barberini (1608–71), nephew of Pope Urban VIII, Cardinal (1628), poet and literary patron.

[9] Wisd. 11: 20.

[10] Roberval had succeeded Gassendi as Professor of Mathematics at the Collège royal.

[11] See Letter 74 n. 6.

[12] *Anatomia hepatis* (1654). Francis Glisson (1597–1677) was Professor of Physic at Cambridge, though from the 1640s he resided mainly in or near London. He became a Fellow of the Royal Society in 1661 and President of the Royal College of Physicians in 1667. His *Anatomia hepatis* was the first modern treatise devoted to the anatomy of the liver in its normal and morbid conditions.

[13] Jean Pecquet (1622–74), who had qualified as MD at Montpellier in 1652, lived in

Paris as personal physician to Fouquet; he was famous for his work on chyle and the lymphatic system. His first work on that subject, *Experimenta nova anatomica* (1651), was later issued in an expanded version (1661). 'Fermentation' here probably refers to the decoction of the blood or some other process attributed to the liver. 'Serum' is the serum of the blood, the fluid which separates from the clot during coagulation. Pecquet did not publish any new work specifically on these topics; but he did later publish a short work on ophthalmology, *Réponse sur une nouvelle découverte touchant la vueue* (1668).

[14] The 2nd edn. of Cureau de la Chambre's *Traité de la lumière* was published in 1657. Marin Cureau de la Chambre (1594–1669) became personal physician to the Chancellor, Séguier, in 1634. He published several non-experimental works on topics in physics (his theory of light, for instance, was essentially Neoplatonist) and a very popular two-part work on psychology (*L'Art de connoistre les hommes*, 1659, and *Le Système de l'âme*, 1664). He was famed more as a stylist than as a scientist, and was a founder member of the Académie française as well as of the Académie royale des sciences. See Kerviler, *Le Maine à l'Académie française*, pp. 3–94.

LETTER 78   [26 MARCH/] 5 APRIL 1656

François du Verdus to Hobbes, from Bordeaux

Chatsworth, Hobbes MSS, letter 14 (original).

Monsieur

Que vous estes genereus! et que vous sçaués obliger de bone grace! Je ne puis me lasser de lire et relire cette belle lettre que j'ay reçeuë de vous Monsieur du 10ᵉ Mars 1655/56.[1] Me conuier, come vous me conuiés a aler a vous, vous doner des soins par auançe de la façon que j'y uiuray, m'y destiner l'habitude des persones qui y ont de tout ce qu'il y a de meilleur, et sur tout me doner cette permission que je desirois passionement, de vous dedier la seule chose que j'ayma d'auoir faite au monde, la Traduction de vos Écrits:[2] aprés cela vous aués mon coeur. Mais il faut qu'une fois en ma vie je vous compte mes douleurs; que vous scachiés ce qui me retient pour quelque temps d'aler a vous. Car enfin ce n'est que pour quelque temps. Tost ou tard je franchiray tous ces obstacles et je me done a vous aussi tot au moins pour deux ans; heureux si j'y passois toute ma vie. Voicy donc mon histoire en abregé. Je nacquis en l'an 1621 le 25ᵉ d'auril. deffunt Mr. Duuerdus mon Pere mourut deux mois apres me laissant son heritier vniuersel à condition des legats qu'il [faisoit *deleted*] fit a deux seurs que j'auois et me dona pour Tuteur un de ses Cousins germains nomé Lancelot de Calmeilh.[3] Ma Mére Marie de Blanc mourut 4 ou 5 ans aprés s'étant mariée au baron du Tirac fils du presidant Cadillac[4] sans en auoir eu d'enfans. l'une de mes soeurs mourut quelque 18 ans aprés s'étant mariée au Baron de Carbonieux[5] (qui dépuis a espousé la fille du marquis de flamarens[6]) et n'en eut point d'enfans. l'autre soeur se mit en Relligion dans le Conuent des filles de s^{te} vrsule[7] a l'age de 15 ans Ainsi tout le bien de mon Pere et de ma Mere me reuint, et mon Tuteur en a toujours iouy. Ces biens là consistoient en un office de Conseiller de feu mon Pere au Parlement de Bordeaux,[8] en quelques 40 mille francs en argent ou en obligations [>actiues], en une maison [>du reuenu] de 150 toneaux de vin de 16 cents boisseaus de blé froment &^{c} c'est a dire de quelque six mille liures de ferme en ses meubles qui etoient superbes pour sa condition. Le Tuteur se trouuant cette bone proye et donant ordre que je ne pûsse jamais l'en dépouïller, uandit 1^{erement} tous les meubles de mon Pere en faisant faire un Inuantaire a sa mode. 2° fit perdre une partie des somes [>du prix] de l'office de Con[seill]^{er9} y faisant faire un procés par collusion il est uray que tout autre que moy en auroit tiré plus de 20 mil ecus mais l'embarras y est grand, et beaucoup d'auances a faire. 3° s'acomoda auecque les debiteurs fit sa condition auec tous et les laissa sans les poursuiure [>ou les poursuiuit collusoirement] en ayant exigé ce qu'il peut. 4° fit aler le bien en fonds a la ferme par collusion a vil prix a un valet de deffunct mon ayeul, lequel [>valet] luy pretoit le nom. 5° mempecha dans mon enfance de uoyr mes Parens qui m'eussent doné des memoyres contre luy, me disant qu'ils m'empoisoneroient pour me succeder. 6° me fit voyager a Paris, a Rome &^{c10} dans le temps que j'eusse pu le pousser. En cela neanmoins je ne croy pas auoir mal employé mon temps qui me suis desabusé de beaucoup de choses. voyla sa conduite. A l'age de 25 ans ie retornay de Rome a Bordeaux ou come Cameilh m'auoit fait étudier dans mon enfance et ma junesse et que j'auois fait mes actes publics en Philosophie et en Droit auec quelque aplaudissement Et que le brigand pour gagner creance sur moy m'auoit fait dire mille fois qu'il me feroit non seulement Conseiller come l'auoient este mon Pére et mes Ayeux, de l'un et l'autre côté, mais Président ou Me de Requetes[11] j'atandois qu'il me mit en offiçe. on me déterminât a estre home d'épée et me mit en équipage moy qui auois fait tous les exercices d'un gentilhomme a l'academie de Mesmond[12] et n'y étois pas mal-adroit: mais bien loin de celà après 8 mois de prieres inutiles il falut que je le plaidasse pour luy faire rendre compte.[13] Come il ne m'auoit fait conoitre dans le monde que des gens de sa Cabale mais qui luy gardoient le secret je donay d'abord dans l'intrigue et n'employay persone qui ne me trahit. Il seroit long a vous dire les faussetés et les friponeries qu'on me fit, les diuerses affaires qu'on me dona pour faire diuersion, les voyages a quoy je fus obligé: mesmement come il ne me remit que mon bien en fonds et encore en mauuais etat, il falut d'abord que je m'endétasse. voyant donc que je ne pouuois m'établir a Bordeaux ni a Paris en charge ou Office et d'ailleurs n'étant pas fort porté au Mariage je jettay les yeux sur un de mes alliés Mary d'une de mes Cousines Germaines nomé [>M[r]] de La Serre Doyen de la Cour des Aydes de Guyene[14] pour traiter auec luy de tous mes biens, et me mettre en liberté. Il me deuoit doner 10 mille francs la 1re année pour m'équiper et 2 mil écus de rente ma vie durant nous en auions conuenu et je me destinois a entrer au seruice de M[r] le Duc d'Anjou[15] dont je croyais qu'on fit la maison: quand la Serre me proposa que des enfans légitimes [>me] suruenans [>si ie me mariois] romproient le Traîté que j'aurois fait auec luy et me demanda de luy doner des seuretés que ie ne me marîrois iamais. Je n'aymois pas de me faire prestre aussi ne m'en fis ie pas: mais ne me souciant point de me marier, considerant que prendre le sous-diacre c'etoit seulement m'engager a n'estre iamais engagé par le mariage en quoy ie ne trouuois point que j'otasse de ma liberté je pris le sousdiacre sous un Titre patrimonial de deux cents liures de reuenu que La Serre luy mesme me signa come atestant ce qui montre assés que c'etoit pour traiter de mes biens ce que j'en faisois. Mais au lieu de me signer la Traîté qu'il m'auoit promis, La Serre m'ayant engagé dans l'eglise me planta là s'excusant sur les Troubles qui suruinrent dans la prouince [>de Guyene] que s'il fut uenu se mettre en possession de mes biens mes autres parans [>luy] eussent fait mauuais party, Ce qui leur eut esté aisé disoit-il le faisant passer pour [>un] Mazarin, et Pernoniste[16] (ce qui entre nous ueut dire bon et fidelle sujet. mais qui alors etoit le nom odieux au Peuple séditieux et Reuolté.) Le déplaisir que j'eus vous le jugerés. Peu de temps aprés je perdis quelques cent testes de gros betail, mes reuenus d'une année, une partie des meubles que j'auois mis ches moy aux champs; et cela sans scauoir qu'y faire autre chose qui étois malade a la mort dans ce temps de Guerre Ciuile. Releué de maladie et resolu de me sauuer a Paris les gens de bien n'étant guere en seureté a Bourdeaux je ne trouuay de ferme de mes biens que la moitié de la valeur. je les laissay donc a onze cents écus de ferme annuelle pour neuf ans de temps (ce fut en l'an 1651) a des Bourgeois només Desbats[17] et Bertail[18] les chargeant de payer a qui ie deuois et laissant Procuration pour cela au Sec[re] d'un Con[seill]er[19] nomé [>M[r] de] Sabourin[20] sur la parole de son maistre Et voicy come ie comptois. Je laisse mes biens pour la moitié de la valeur: les fermiers auront interest de s'y tenir. Je les laisse pour 9 ans, on les fera au moins les 6 ou 7 premieres années Car les fermiers ne négligent un fonds que quand le proprietaire est sur le point d'y rentrer. Je laisse procuration a Mr de Sabourin il est mon Cousin Issu de Germain, et a interest d'estre mon amy et est en office: il fera payer de simples bourgeois. Je laisse ii cents écus a prendre, on payera 50 écus de pension a ma soeur la Relligieuse vrsuline. Celà Monsieur, ne croiroit on pas que-ce fut bien compté? Je uay donc a Paris (ce que je n'oubliray iamais puis que j'eus l'honeur de vous y voyr et que vous eutes mon coeur) a Paris ie trouue Mr Bourdelot[21] mon amy intime dépuis la bataille de Rocroy[22] que j'étois a l'academie de mesmond et qui m'auoit guery icy a Bordeaux 5 medecins m'ayans abandoné dans cette longue et cruëlle maladie que je vous ay dit que J'eus aux 1^{eres} guerres.[23] Mr Bourdelot me propose d'aler auec luy en Suede ou il a esté 1er Medecin de cette Reyne et en est retorné auec de grandes recompenses. [M^r *deleted*] Je luy promets enfin d'y aler si ie puis me metre en équipage et enuoye pour cela une Procuration generale [a *deleted* >au Sage] Mr de Martel nostre amy pour lors a montauban[24] qu'il traitat auec mon Tuteur, mes autres debiteurs mes fermiers &c. et m'enuoyât 2 ou 3 mil écus. Sabourin scait la Procuration sans en scauoir le sujet et le motif. Il s'imagine que je suis a Paris dans la débauche uoulant de l'argent a quelque prix que ce soit. verdus (dit-il sans doute) se trouuant là sans argent, vray-semblablement sans credit, et en temps de guerre Ciuile si ie fais qu'il s'y trouue son bien sur les bras il en traitera auec moy qui en a uoulu traiter auec la Serre et ie l'auray pour un morceau de pain. Quoy qu'il en soit monsieur, Mr de Sabourin m'écriuit diuerses lettres si ie voulois uendre ce bien; si j'en uoulois traiter; puis [aprés *deleted*] que son Clerc luy faisoit besoin et me demandoit pardon s'il ne pouuoit uacquer a mes affaires. puis les fermiers cesserent de me payer et enfin delaisserent mes biens purement et simplement sous pretexte de la guerre Ciuile. voyla ma soeur hors du Cloitre faute de 50 écus de pension. Elle ne sçauoit point mes desseins et creut [>sans doute] qu'ayant tant de sujets de haine contre mes parens [>et m'étant mis dans l'église] ie pourrois luy pardoner si elle écoutait les propositions qu'on luy fit [>de retourner au monde]. Voicy donc une autre intrigue. vne de mes Tantes soeur de feu ma Mere nomée Mad^e Cugnos,[25] et un de mes alliés nomé Dejean[26] qui s'est fait prestre dans son veuuage ayant forçe enfans et est Curé d'une de mes Parroisses des Champs nomeé d'Ambarés[27] de six mille francs de ferme; un uray filou ayant fait banqueroute pour frauder ses creanciers, moy le premier complotant de marier cette Religieuse la suposant séculiére. Ne scachant qui luy doner ils luy donent un Cadet d'une maison de Noblesse[28] mais d'une maison de gens uiuans d'intrigue et chargés de crimes ayans eu la teste tranchée en effigie pour la fausse monoye.[29] Si ie ne fusse uenu icy sur l'auis qu'un étranger m'en dona (Car mes parens auoient tous coniuré contre moy) le dessein de la Cugnos étoit de faire décreter mon bien sur un droit cedé que luy eut doné cette maudite Renegate et cela pour dix mil écus que je luy eusse deus si elle eut demeure dans le monde; ils payoient de plus 4 mil écus que ie dois, le reste en frais de justice et en une consignation imaginaire et la Tante pretant le nom pour le lignager, un an aprés ie n'eusse rien eu dans mon bien. Cepandant si la Relligieuse le leur eut demandé ils l'eussent menaçée de la récloitrer, et son filou rauisseur de luy faire couper le cou. Et moy quand ie fusse uenu pour m'apaiser ils me uouloient doner la Cure de Dejean sous pension. Je uins; et découuris l'intrigue; Et fis comprendre a l'archeueq. de Bordeaux[30] Qu'une Relligieuse qui s'etoit enuyée 18 ans dans un Conuent dont les affaires sont en desordre auroit bien pû se trouuant en liberté faire une faute: mais de passer un Contract de mariage et fiançer cela ne se faisoit point qu'on ne fut apuyé d'une Cabale. ie fis prendre prisoniére cette malheureuse on luy prouua par temoins et par écrits qu'elle auoit 15 ans quand elle prit l'habit [> de Religieuse et] 17 quand elle fit ses veux [> qu'elle] auoit esté 18 ans sans reclamer [> qu'elle n'en auoit iamais eu de suiet s'etant mise malgré moy et ses parens en Relligion uolontairement.] sur ces entrefaites Mr de la Vie[31] auocat general de cette ville s'intrigue dans cette afaire et me fait proposer de traiter auec luy de tous mes biens. je n'y entens pas. il prend son temps Et dés que l'archeueque a doné sentence condannant cette malheureuse il la fait éuader. Enfin pour l'extreme onction come on dit les Jesuites me uienent dire que cette [fille *deleted* >femme] leur a passé par les mains. et l'archeueq. me refuse de me [doner *deleted* >faire expedier] sa sentençe [> qu'il a donée] Ce qui fait uoyr que les Jesuites ueulent mon bien et obligent l'archeueq. a ne me doner pas mes seuretés que je ne traite auec Eux. Ce que je ne dois ajouter Monsieur C'est que mes Terres labourables sont en friche sans que j'aye dequoy les leuer, que mes vignes sont perduës, que mes afaires se préscriuent, qu'ami du monde ne m'a sécourû; Que j'ay uecu dix huit mois come dans une ville assiégée reduit fort souuant au pain et a l'eau; que du peu de danrées que mon fonds a produit de luy mesme on m'en a fait banqueroute de plus de la moitié; Que presentement tout autre que moy en ma plaçe se trouueroit bien embarrassé. En cet état j'ay

reclamé souuent nostre bon amy Mr de Martel: mais en uain. il etoit
député a la Cour de la Prouince de Languedoc³² et fut uenû sans cela
me sécourir (car il me l'a écrit souuant m'exhortant a estre
uigoureux[)]³³ Je l'atens et le ueux faire mon heritier et luy doner tous
mes biens et tout mes droits qu'il me done la liberté et les moyens
d'aler a vous. Il a toutes les qualités pour cela. Il ne m'est ni parant ni
allié; et me uangera de mes parens dénaturés et alliés cabaleurs. Il est
Philosophe et sera bien aise de faire une action d'honneur en me
donant le repos pour uaquer a la Philosophie. Il est bon menager, et le
Party que je luy feray sera auantageux. Il est mon amy et qui je crois me
gardera sa parole. Il a grand credit et a son Pére le plus habile home de
Guyene pour les affaires, et luy mesme les entend bien et tirera party
des mienes. Il est de la Relligion et me uangera des Jesuites retenans
ma soeur, d'un Archeueque me refusant une sentençe qu'il a donée et
mes seuretés, et de tous les hypocrites filous qui aprés m'auoir reduit a
la faim pour m'intimider en faisant le contre-poids du crime que je suis
uenu poursuiure ont répandu premierement dans cette Prouince que
j'etois un home ayant de mauuais Prinçipes et semant de fausses
doctrines; et Puis voyant que je ne traitois point auec eux me
persécutent ouuertement, tranchans tout net le mot d'Athée, disans
partout que je le suis et m'enuoyans menaçer de m'en faire accuser en
jugement. Au reste Quoy qu'entre mes affaires il y ait a se défendre
d'une Relligieuse défroquée et que les Loix de vostre Relligion ne
souffrent ni moynes ni moynesses Toutefois come par la Loy de ce
Royaume les biens de quiconque fait des ueux ayant l'age et sans y estre
forçé sont acquis [aux *deleted*] a ses plus proches heritiers; M^r de
Martel soutiendra cela aussi bien que moy, qui suis persuädé aussi bien
que luy que moynes et moynesses sont un abus dans la Relligion et qu'a
bien dire les pauures filles qui s'y trouuent sont fort atrapées, etant
ainsi en prison perpetuëlle le tout pour auoir un heritier a son aise.
Voylà Monsieur l'état de ma fortune et de mes desseins que je ne dis
qu'a vous seul. Mr de Martel me promet secours S'il uient ce printemps
come je m'y atens et l'espère, dans tout l'esté je suis a vous. Ce qui ne
sera pas que je ne vous en done auis par auançe un mois et encore 15
jours au parauant. Cependant je vous demande deux choses. la
Premiére que vous me fassiés la faueur de me mander coment il faudra
que je me comporte, et quelles déclarations j'auray a faire en
Angleterre pour y estre en seureté puis que je me trouue dans le
sousdiacre. Car je ne uoudrois pas passer pour espion qui est un metier
indigne d'un home né gentilhome, et d'un philosophe et homme

d'honneur et que d'ailleurs ie n'ay garde de faire jamais pour le danger qu'il y a, moy qui croy que les plus grands remuëmens d'etat qui ne sont qu'un petit mouuement de quelques atomes a les considerer en contemplatif, ne nous doiuent estre rien au prix du repos de la vie et de nostre seureté. Cet auis là je l'atens de vous s'il vous plait des que vous pourrés me l'écrire. Et en second lieu je vous demande vostre response en Anglois a Wallisius, acceptant la Traduction latine que vous en ferés a mesure qu'elle s'imprimera[34] Je vous demande aussi [vostre *deleted* >la] version en Anglois de vostre liure de Corpore,[35] et sa seconde édition latine.[36] Et si ce n'est pas vous demander trop je vous prie d'y ajouter ce que Walisius a écrit et contre vous et dépuis.[37] Je ne vous demande pas neanmoins de m'enuoyer tout cela par la Poste. j'ay jugé plus a propos de vous en écrire une petite lettre séparée l'adressant a Mr Mylon qui vous la fasse tenir par quelque correspondant d'un Libraire de Paris[38] trafiquant a Londres; Et puis me les enuoye par le Messagier de cette ville. si toutefois vous ne voulés pas que tous ces Liures passent par autres mains que les mienes, et que ce soit une confidençe que vous me fassiés; en ce cas quoy que vous écriue Mr Mylon, et bien que vous reçeuiés ma petite lettre par son correspondant je vous seray autant obligé quand vous ne m'enuoyerés autre chose que vostre response Angloise et puis vos Cahyers latins a mesure qu'ils s'imprimeront.[39] Mais en ce cas aussi je desirerois que vous m'enuoyassiés cette response, en blanc, point roignée et bien conditionée, Et cela par la Poste qui porte les lettres de droiture Car je feray bien lauer ce Liure et Rellier a ma mode et en feray mon Vademécum et acheueray d'y aprendre la langue Angloise que je començay tout exprés pour entendre quelque chose de vostre Leuiathan. Je ne vous dis rien Monsieur sur ce que ie vous mets là en frais et en depense. Je croyrois vous faire injure de compter en ce présent autre chose que vostre sciençe et la bone volonté auec laquelle je fais état que vous me l'enuoyerés. vous en useriés je croy de mesme auec tout home pour qui vous auriés de l'estime. vous sçaués celle que j'ay pour vous; je vous honore infinîment, souhaitant vostre conseruation auec plus de zele que la miene propre et que vous me fassiés toujours l'honneur de m'aymer un peu qui suis et seray toujours trés fidellement

Monsieur
vostre tres humble et tres obeissant seruiteur
françois de bonneau duuerdus.

A Bordeaux le 5e Auril 1656

[*postscript:*] Monsieur

Outre les choses qui auoient esté remarquées a quoy vous aués satisfait il me reste encore deux scrupules [touchant *deleted* >sur] vostre liure du Corps. le 1er sur l'article 13e de vostre chapitre 27e de la façon que vous expliqués que s'engendrent les couleurs. le 2^d touchant la cheute des corps graues et ce que vous en dites dans l'article 4eme du chapitre dernier. Quant aux couleurs vous uoulés que dans vostre fig^e 2de du chap. 27e la reaction faite uers A trouble la lumiére 1^{ére}, et la reaction uers C. la s[econ]de^{40}. On n'entendra point cela; et ce qui embrouïlle bien fort c'est que vous décriués les lignes Daf, et EBCG come si elles ne faisoient qu'effleurer le Prisme auquel cas on ne uoit pas coment le rayon de lumiere y souffre de refraction. Il seroit a desirer que vostre explication fut plutot sur l'obseruation suyuante

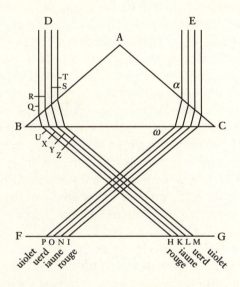

ABC est [le *deleted* >la base du] Prisme Triangulaire dont l'angle A, regarde directement le soleil dont le diametre est DE, FG est le plancher ou le paroy a l'ombre sur laquelle on recoit les rayons de [>la] lumiére. Il en tombe quatre de chaque coté qui souffrent réfraction tant en entrant [dans le prisme *deleted*] qu'au sortir du Prisme. Ceux du coté de B uont vers la paroy en hklm. et ceux du coté C en Jnop. y marquant les couleurs come je les ay écrites dans la figure. C'est a dire les quatre de chaque coté et non come dans uostre figure deux uers votre Angle A, deux uers vostre ligne BC. Il faut rendre raison 1° de ce que ces couleurs en uont iamais l'une sans l'autre. 20 de ce qu'elles sont

différentes [quoy que uenant les mesmes *deleted* >qui uient de la maniere et non du nombre de leurs] refractions chacune. Car si le rayon
Dquh (par example) qui fait le rouge en h souffre deux réfractions l'une
en q, l'autre en u: le rayon Drxk [en fait autant et *deleted* >qui fait le
jaune] en souffre aussi deux et de mesme tous les autres. 30 de ce
qu'entre z du rayon Dtzm et α du rayon EαωP il n'y a que du blanc
Car ce que vous dites Monsieur dans la ligne 6e page 265. que dans
uotre figure planum Trianguli CGK incideret in planum Trianguli
afh[41] ne satisfait pas Car on demande cela mesmes coment il se peut
que les mouuemens qui se font uers le coté B du prisme, et ceux qui se
font uers son côté C ne se confondent pas tellement que tout y soit égal
partout.

    Quand a la cheute des Corps graues On uoid bien que si le mobile E
recoit a chaque instant un coup de l'ayr, mouetur motu accelerato[42] et
que ses espaces parcourus sont en raison doublée des temps: puis que
la raison des espaces est composée de celle des temps et de celle des
uitesses, et que celle des vitesses est egale a celle des temps et sans que
j'eusse leu le Galilée je remarquay bien le paralogisme du bon M[r]
Gassendi dans l'une de ses Épitres de motu impresso a motore
translato où il done dans chaque temps deux coups a son mobile, l'un
de l'ayr l'autre de l'atraction de la Terre qu'il n'explique pas:[43] Mais il
me semble qu'il y auroit a desirer encore dans uotre explication un
petit mot de ce que l'ayr qui descend quand le graue monte pour
remplir le lieu que le graue laisse en montant ne le pousse point son
mouuement en haut, [puis qu'il ne fait *deleted* >ne faisant rien] que le
suyure et qu'au contraire ce mouuement [>en haut du graue] s'affoiblit
par la resistance de l'ayr d'en haut qu'il contraint de descendre, contre
le mouuement que luy done la Terre par le sien diurne quo altiùs
ipsum excutit.[44] Cecy neanmoins pour plus grand éclaircissement: Car
au fonds je ne trouue pas qu'on y ait tant besoin de nouuelle
explication, come a l'obseruation du Prisme et des réfractions qui font
les couleurs. Mais que dirés vous de moy Monsieur qui peut estre vous
amuse icy a ne vous dire que des bagatelles. Si je peche, c'est par bon
zele, moy qui ne puis jamais estre que vostre tres fidele et tres passioné
seruiteur.

[*endorsed by James Wheldon:*] Mon.[r] du Verdus. Aprill 5.th 1656

Translation of Letter 78

Sir,

How kind you are, and how graciously obliging! I cannot tire of reading and rereading that splendid letter of 10 March which I received from you.[1] Inviting me, as you do, to come to you, troubling yourself over the question of how I shall live there, planning for me the best kind of life that people lead there, and above all giving me that permission, which I passionately desired, to dedicate to you the one thing in the world which I am proud to have done, namely the translation of your writings:[2] after all this, you have won my heart.

But, for once in my life, I must tell you the story of my sufferings, so that you may understand what it is that prevents me from going to you for a while yet. (It will be, after all, only for a while.) Sooner or later I shall surmount all these obstacles, and shall then immediately devote myself to you for at least two years; I should be only too happy if I could spend the rest of my life with you.

I was born on 25 April 1621. The late M. du Verdus, my father, died two months later, leaving me as his sole heir, subject to the legacies which he made to my two sisters. He also appointed one of his first cousins, Lancelot de Calmeil, as my guardian.[3] My mother, Marie de Blanc, died four or five years later, having married the baron du Tirac, son of the *président* Cadillac,[4] but without having borne him any children. One of my sisters died some eighteen years later, having married the baron de Carbonnieux[5] (who has since married the marquis de Flamarens's[6] daughter), and had no children at all by him. The other sister took the veil in the Ursuline convent[7] at the age of 15. So the whole of my parents' property devolved on me, and my guardian has always had the benefit of it. The inheritance consisted of the following: my late father's office of *conseiller* of the Parlement of Bordeaux;[8] 40,000 francs in silver or in commercial bonds; an estate which yielded 150 barrels of wine and 1,600 bushels of corn, wheat, etc., which means it could be let for 6,000 livres with its furnishings, which were in excellent condition. The guardian found himself in possession of this fine booty and decreed that I should never take it from him.

First he sold all my father's furniture, after having an inventory of it drawn up to his own liking. Secondly, he caused the loss of part of the value of the office of *conseiller*[(9)] by colluding with someone who was laying a claim to it in the courts. It would normally have been worth more than 20,000 écus; but it is heavily encumbered with debts, and there are many advance-payments to be made from it. Thirdly, he came to an agreement with my father's debtors; he came to terms with them all and left them without prosecuting them (or prosecuted them collusively), having exacted whatever he could from them. Fourthly, he also colluded in allowing the estate's lands to be leased at a disgrace-fully low price to a servant of my late grandfather, who allowed him to use his name. Fifthly, when I was a child he prevented me from seeing my relations, who would have supplied me with information against him; he told me that they would poison me in order to inherit the property from me. Sixthly, he made me travel to Paris, Rome, etc.[10] at the period when I might have been able to get rid of him. But despite that, I think my time was well spent during those years, when I managed to rid myself of many illusions. That is how he behaved.

At the age of 25 I came back from Rome to Bordeaux. Since de Calmeil had made me study there in my childhood and youth; since I had taken my degrees in philosophy and law cum laude, and since that thievish man, in order to gain my confidence, had ensured that I was told a thousand times that he was going to make me not only a *conseiller*, like my father and both my grandfathers, but also a *président* or *maître de requêtes*,[11] I was now expecting him to instal me in office. But now it was decided that I should have a military career, and I was sent off for training—I who had already learned all the skills of a gentleman at the Mesmond Academy[12] and was not unaccomplished in them. Instead, after eight months of useless prayers I had to take him to court in order to force him to render his accounts.[13] The only people he had ever introduced me to were his fellow conspirators, who kept his secret; so, to begin with, I fell into his snares and was betrayed by everyone I made use of. It would take a long time to tell you of all the falsehoods and tricks which were played on me, the various affairs which they made me busy myself with in order to distract me, and the travels which I was obliged to undertake. And since he gave me back only my land, and that in poor condition, I had at first to go into debt.

Realizing therefore that I could not establish myself in any public office either in Bordeaux or in Paris, and not being very inclined to get married, I looked towards one of my relations (the husband of one of my first cousins, M. de la Serre, *doyen* of the Cour des aides of Guyenne[14]) to make an arrangement about my whole property and set me at liberty. The plan was that he should give me 10,000 francs in the first year to fit me out, and 2,000 francs' rent for the rest of my life. We agreed to this, and I decided to enter the service of the duc d'Anjou,[15] whose household, I thought, was being made up. Then de la Serre suggested to me that if I got married and had legitimate children it would break the agreement which I had made with him. He asked me to give him assurances that I would never marry. I had no desire to become a priest, so I did not become one; but since I had no intention of marrying, and as I thought that taking the subdiaconate only committed me to remaining a bachelor (which I did not think was any infringement of my liberty), I became a subdeacon with a patrimonial living of 200 livres per annum. De la Serre himself signed as a witness to my vows, which shows clearly enough that I was doing it in order to reach a settlement over my estate. But instead of signing the arrangement which he had promised me, once he had got me to join the Church he left me there, high and dry. He used as his excuse the public disorders which happened in the province of Guyenne, saying that if he had come to take possession of my property my other relations would have made things difficult for him, which they could easily have done (he said) by claiming that he was a 'Mazarin' and a 'Pernoniste'[16] (names which we would use to mean 'good and faithful subject', but which at that time were hateful to the seditious and rebellious population). You can imagine my displeasure at this.

A little later I lost some hundred head of cattle, my income for a year, part of my property which I had put out to grass on my farm. I did not know what else I could do with them; I was mortally ill during the civil war. When I was cured of my illness, I resolved to escape to Paris (men of property being hardly safe in Bordeaux); but I could only let my property at half its value. So I let it, at an annual rent of 1,100 écus, on a lease of nine years (this was in 1651), to two *bourgeois* called Desbats[17] and Bertail.[18] I directed them to pay off my creditors and assigned a power of attorney for that to the secretary of a *conseiller*[(19)] called M. de Sabourin,[20] to be used with the latter's agreement. My line of thought was as follows. I am letting my property at half its value: so it will be in the tenant's interest to stick to the agreement. I am letting it for nine years, so it will be kept up for at least six or seven: tenants neglect an estate only when the owner is about to repossess it. I am leaving a power of attorney with M. de Sabourin: he is my first cousin once removed, he has an interest in acting as my friend, and he holds an official position: he will ensure that mere commoners pay their rent. I am leaving 200 écus to be used for this, and an allowance of 50 écus will be paid to my sister, the Ursuline nun. Would one not think, Sir, that I had planned it all very well?

So I went to Paris (which I shall never forget, because it was there that I had the honour of meeting you and you won my heart). I met M. Bourdelot,[21] who had been my close friend ever since the battle of Rocroi,[22] during my time at the Mesmond Academy, when he had cured me here in Bordeaux after five doctors had abandoned me to that long and cruel illness which, as I told you, I suffered during the first wars.[23] He suggested that I should go with him to Sweden, where he had been chief physician to the Queen, and from where he had just come back richly rewarded. In the end I promised I would go with him, provided that I was able to fit myself out; for that purpose I sent a general power of attorney to our friend the wise M. de Martel, who was then at Montauban,[24] authorizing him to deal with my guardian, my other debtors, my tenants, etc., and asking him to send me two or three thousand écus. De Sabourin learned of this without knowing what it was for; he imagined that I was leading a dissolute life in Paris, in need of money at any price. 'Du Verdus', he must have said, 'is in Paris, penniless, probably without credit, and in a time of civil war; if I can make him want to get his property off his hands, he'll make a deal with me; I've always wanted to make a deal with de la Serre about it; and now I'll be able to get it for next to nothing.' Whatever the reasoning, M. de Sabourin wrote various letters to me, asking if I wanted to sell the property or if I wanted to make a deal with him; then he said that his clerk had need of his services, and that I must forgive him if he was unable to spend time on my affairs. Then the tenants stopped paying me and finally abandoned my property altogether on the pretext of the civil war.

So then my sister was forced to leave her convent because her allowance of 50 écus was not paid. She had no idea what my plans were, and no doubt thought that since there were so many matters on which I felt hatred for my relations, and since I had joined the Church, I would be able to forgive her if she listened to the proposals which were made to her that she should go back into secular life. So there was another plot. The plotters were one of my aunts (my late mother's sister, called Mme de Cugnol)[25] and one of my relations by marriage called Dejean,[26] who became a priest in his widowhood, having a large number of children, and is the priest of Ambarès,[27] a parish with a living of 6,000 francs which is one of the parishes in my country estate; he was a real swindler who had gone bankrupt in order to defraud his creditors (of whom I headed the list). Their plot was to marry off this nun, pretending that she was secular. Not knowing who to give her as a husband, they gave her a younger son from a noble family;[28] the family consists of people who live by intrigue and have criminal records—they have had their heads cut off in effigy for counterfeiting.[29] Had I not come here on the advice of a stranger (for my relations had all plotted against me), Mme de Cugnol's plan was to issue a claim to my property, based on the authorization of that cursed renegade nun, for the sum of 10,000 écus which I would have owed her if she had remained in secular life. In addition they would pay 4,000 écus which I owed; the rest would go in legal expenses and a fictitious deposit in trust; they would take my aunt's name so that it would not die out; and within a year I would have had nothing left of my property. However, if the nun had asked for it they would have threatened to put her back in the cloister, and her ravisher, the swindler, would have threatened to slit her throat. As for me, when I arrived they wanted to give me the living of Dejean's parish to appease me.

I came, and uncovered the plot. I informed the Archbishop of Bordeaux[30] that a nun who had pined for eighteen years in a convent whose affairs were in a shambles could easily have done something wrong when she found herself at liberty, but that making a marriage contract and becoming engaged could only be the result of pressure from a conspiracy. It was proved, by witnesses and written evidence, that she entered the convent at the age of 15, made her vows at the age of 17, and spent eighteen years without ever raising any objection to being made a nun, having entered the religious order voluntarily, against my wishes and those of my parents. Meanwhile M. de Lavie,[31] *avocat-général* of this town, started plotting on his own behalf in the affair, and conveyed a proposal to me that I should make an arrangement with him about all my property. I refused. He took his time, and when the Archbishop had given judgement, condemning the wretched woman, he arranged her escape. Finally, as the finishing touch, the Jesuits came and told me that the woman had got into their hands. The Archbishop refused to let me have the sentence enforced, which shows that the Jesuits wanted my property and stopped the Archbishop from giving me my sureties back because I refused to make a deal with them. I must add, Sir, that my arable lands are lying fallow as I cannot afford to have them cultivated; my vines are lost; my financial affairs are frozen by the court; I have not had the help of a single friend in the world; I have lived for eighteen months like someone in a besieged town, very often reduced to living on bread and water; because of the small income which my estate has yielded of itself I was made bankrupt for more than half of it; and anyone else in my position would be heavily in debt.

In this state I have often asked for our good friend M. de Martel, but in vain. He was sent to Court as a delegate from the province of Languedoc[32] and would have come to my aid were it not for that (for he has often written, encouraging me to take strong action)[33]. I am waiting for him: I want to make him my heir and give him all my property and all my rights if he will only let me be free and enable me to come to you. He has all the necessary qualities. He is not related to me by blood or marriage; and he will take vengeance for me on my inhuman, scheming relations. He is a philosopher and will be happy to do the worthy deed of setting me at rest so that I can devote my time to philosophy. He is financially prudent, and what I arrange for him will be to his own profit. He is my friend and, I think, will keep his promises to me. He has a high reputation; his father is the shrewdest person for business matters in the whole of Guyenne; and he himself understands business well and will be able to profit from mine. He is a Protestant, and will take my revenge on the Jesuits for holding my sister, on the Archbishop for refusing to enforce a sentence which he himself issued and for refusing to release my sureties, and on all those hypocritical swindlers. They, having reduced me to starvation to intimidate me as a counter-ploy to the crime of their own which I had come to prosecute, first of all spread it about that I am a man of loose morals and a teacher of false doctrines, and then (when they saw that I would not make any deal with them) began to persecute me quite openly, brazenly calling me an 'atheist', accusing me everywhere of atheism, and letting me know that they were threatening to have me prosecuted for it. There remains the problem of defending myself against a defrocked nun. I know that the laws of your religion permit neither monks nor nuns. But by the laws of this realm if anyone takes his vows, provided he is of age and takes them voluntarily, his property passes to his closest heirs. M. de Martel will be able to maintain that as well as I; I am as convinced as he is that monastic orders are an abuse of religion, and that to tell the truth the poor girls who are put in convents are well and truly caught—imprisoned, in effect, for ever— just so that an heir can live the good life.

That, Sir, is the state of my fortune and my plans; you are the only person to be told it. M. de Martel promises to help me. If he comes this spring, as I expect and hope he will, I can be with you for the whole summer. Which does not mean that I shall not give you notice a month in advance, and again a fortnight before I come. However, there are two things which I must ask of you.

First, I should like you to do me the favour of explaining how I must act and what declarations I shall have to make in England to ensure that my position there is safe, since I am a subdeacon. For I would not want to be thought a spy, which is a profession unworthy of someone who is a gentleman by birth, a philosopher, and a man of honour. Besides, I have no inclination ever to enter such a dangerous profession; believing that the greatest political upheavals, considered contemplatively, are nothing but a little movement of a few atoms, I think that they should count for nothing against the value of safety and a quiet life. I shall await your advice on this matter, as soon as you can write to me about it.

Secondly, I should like you to send me your reply to Wallis in English, or, as it is printed, the Latin translation which you will make of it.[34] I should also like the English translation of your book *De corpore*,[35] and the second edition of it in Latin.[36] And, if it is not too much to ask, please add what Wallis has written, both when he replied to you and since that.[37] But I am not asking you to send me all that in the post. I thought it better to write separately a little letter to you about it, addressed to M. Mylon, who will get it to you via some correspondent of a Parisian bookseller[38] who does business in London, and then have the books sent to me by the messenger from that city. However, you may feel that these dealings with me are confidential and that you do not want all those books to pass through anyone else's hands except mine. In that case, regardless of what M. Mylon tells you in his letter, and despite receiving my little letter via his correspondent, I should be grateful if you would only send me your English reply to Wallis and the proofs of your Latin book as it is printed.[39] But if you do that I should like you to send your reply to Wallis in pristine condition, uncut. Send it by the ordinary post. I shall have it cleaned and rebound to my own taste, and it will become my vade-mecum; using it, I shall finish learning English, which I began solely in order to understand something of your *Leviathan*. I do not mention, Sir, the expense I am putting you to; with such a gift it would be insulting to consider anything but your learning and the good nature with which I am sure you will send it. I am sure that you would deal similarly with anyone you admired. You know how much I admire you; I honour you infinitely, and pray for your preservation more passionately than I pray for my own. I pray too that you may continue to do me the honour of loving me a little—who am, Sir, and shall always faithfully remain

Your most humble and obedient servant
François de Bonneau du Verdus.

Bordeaux, 5 April 1656

[*postscript:*]
Sir,

Apart from the things I have already commented on, which you have adequately dealt with, I still have two queries about your book *De corpore*. The first is about XXVII. 13, and concerns the way you explain the origin of colours. The second is about the fall of heavy bodies and what you say about that in the last chapter, section 4.

On the first of these, you think that in fig. 2 of ch. XXVII the reaction towards A perturbs the first light, and the reaction towards C perturbs the second.[40] That is incomprehensible; and what makes it worse is that you describe the lines DAF and EBCG as if they merely touched the edge of the prism, in which case it is impossible to see why the ray of light should undergo any refraction. It would be preferable if your explanation were drawn instead from the following observation. Let ABC be the base of a triangular prism, of which the corner A directly faces the sun, which has the diameter DE. Let FG be the floor or wall which receives the rays of light. There are four rays which fall on each

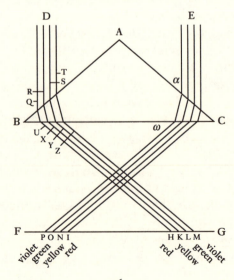

side of the prism, and which are refracted both on entering and on leaving it. The rays on the 'B' side of the prism meet the wall at H, K, L, and M, and those on the 'C' side meet it at I, N, O, and P, producing there the colours as I have noted them in the diagram. In other words all four colours are produced on each side, and not as in your diagram where you have two at your corner A and two at your line BC. One must explain, firstly, why these colours always go together; and, secondly, why they are different. The difference arises from the type of refraction they undergo, not the number of refractions. For if the ray DQUH, for example, which makes the colour red at H, undergoes two refractions, one at Q, the other at U, the ray DRXK, which makes yellow, also undergoes two—and so do all the others. Thirdly, one must explain why there is nothing but whiteness between Z of the ray DTZM and α of the ray $E\alpha\omega P$. For when you say in your book, Sir, that in your diagram 'the plane of the triangle CGK would coincide with the plane of the triangle AFH' (p. 265, line 6),[41] this is not adequate. For one must then ask how it is that the motions towards side B of the prism and those towards side C are not so mingled that everything is the same throughout.

As for the fall of heavy bodies, it is easy to see that if the moving body E receives a thrust from the air at every instant, 'it will move with an accelerated motion',[42] and that the space traversed in each unit of time will be in a ratio of 2:1 to the number of units of time elapsed. For the space traversed is a function of both time and velocity, and the velocity is equal to the time. Even before I had read Galileo I clearly saw the fallacy committed by good M. Gassendi in one of his letters *De motu impresso a motore translato*, where he said that the moving object was subject to two thrusts at each unit of time, one from the air, the other from the attraction of the earth (which he did not explain).[43] But I think it would be preferable if your explanation also included some slight account of how it is that when a heavy body is ascending, the air which descends to fill the space left by the body as it ascends does not push it from below, and in no way adds to its upward motion, doing nothing but following it. On the contrary, this upward motion of the heavy body is weakened by the resistance of the air from above which it causes to descend, contrary to the motion which the Earth imparts to it by its own motion, which 'shakes off the air higher every day'.[44] I request this only for further enlightenment, however; for really I think there is no great need for a new explanation in this matter, as there is in the observation of the prism and of the refractions which produce colours.

But Sir, what will you say of me, when perhaps you are laughing at me for making such trivial points? If I err, it is only through honest zeal, for I can never be anything other than your most faithful and most devoted servant.

The main unit of currency used by du Verdus in this letter is the écu or crown, a silver coin worth 3 livres—between 50 and 60 English pence. (A gold écu also existed, worth 6 livres, but the silver écu was the one normally referred to when stating accounts.) The livre or pound (sometimes also called 'franc') was not a coin but a notional unit of account, divided into 20 sous or shillings, with each sou divided into 12 deniers or pence. The average daily wage for a labourer was between 12 and 18 sous.

[1] This letter has not apparently survived.

[2] See Letter 76, pp. 231, 237.

[3] Lancelot de Calmeil, *escuyer*, sieur de Geneste, is mentioned in a document of 1623 (AMB MS Drouyn 275, p. 175). The de Calmeils were a *bourgeois* family of Bordeaux (Meller, *Armorial*, i). Lereine, widow of Jean de Bonneau (who was probably du Verdus's grandfather) married a de Calmeil (not Lancelot, whose wife was Anne de Maurin: perhaps Lancelot's father) in *c*.1616 (ibid.; AMB MS Drouyn 275, pp. 185, 191). Other documents refer, puzzlingly, to the guardian of the children of the late 'François' de Bonneau as 'Jean' or 'François' de Calmeil (ibid., pp. 177–9).

[4] Marie de Blanc married the sieur de Tirac in 1625, and died in 1627 (ibid., p. 179). The sieur de Tirac was a member of the d'Essenault family, who were Barons of Cadillac (Meller, *Armorial*, ii).

[5] Asdrubal de Ferron, seigneur de Carbonnieux, was a *jurat* (governing magistrate) of Bordeaux in 1599. His grandson Charles-Asdrubal de Ferron was a *bourgeois* of the city in the 1660s (le Vacher de Boisville (ed.), *Livre des bourgeois*, part 1, p. 23). Du Verdus's sister Marie died in 1639 (Bigot, 'Une lettre inédite', p. 275).

[6] Antoine-Agésilas de Grossolles, marquis de Flamarens and baron de Montastruc, was killed at the battle of Saint-Antoine in 1652 (O'Gilvy and de Bourrousse de Laffore, *Nobiliaire de Guienne*, iv).

[7] The Ursuline convent at Bordeaux was established under the patronage of Archbishop Sourdis during the years 1606–18, with very strict rules and an emphasis on education. It soon became the most important Ursuline convent in the country—and, by the mid-century, the mother convent of roughly fifty other such houses in south-west France (Boutrouche (ed.), *Bordeaux*, pp. 396–7; Salviani, *Histoire du couvent des Ursulines*, pp. 10–12).

[8] The title *conseiller* was used for any member of a judicial body such as a Parlement. Jean du Verdus's office of *conseiller* was passed, in François's name, to a Jean Dubernet in August 1621 (ADG MS 1 B 19, fo. 321ᵛ).

[9] Contraction expanded.

[10] On du Verdus's periods of residence in Paris and Rome see his entry in the Biographical Register.

[11] *Président* was the title of the presiding judge in any court; a *maître de requêtes* was a lawyer who was a member of the *conseil* of the King, especially his *conseil privé*, which exercised his private, 'reserved' justice (as opposed to the justice of the public courts).

[12] I have been unable to trace any 'Académie' of this name. It is conceivable that du

Verdus was referring to training as a gentleman in the household of the de Nesmond family, one of the most prominent families of Bordeaux (see le Vacher de Boisville (ed.), *Livre des bourgeois*, part 1, p. 115; Meller, *Armorial*, iii; Feret, *Statistique générale*); but the word is twice spelt clearly as 'Mesmond' in this letter.

[13] A copy of Lancelot de Calmeil's accounts for his management of du Verdus's estate, 1641–6, is in AMB MS Drouyn 275, pp. 185–7.

[14] Claude de Barbier (1607–74), seigneur de la Serre, married in 1633 Françoise, daughter of Florimond de Redon and Marie de Bonneau. He became *conseiller* at the Cour des aides of Guyenne (at Agen) in 1630, and *doyen* (dean) there in 1664 (O'Gilvy and de Bourrousse de Laffore, *Nobiliaire de Guienne*, iv, pp. 156–61). The Cour des aides was a court which tried both civil and criminal cases arising from the administration of various taxes and customs, such as the *taille*, *aides*, and *gabelle*.

[15] The title of duc d'Anjou had been held by Gaston, brother of Louis XIII, until 1626 (when he became duc d'Orléans); it was revived in 1640 for Philippe, younger son of Louis XIII, who was only 6 years old in 1646 (the year of du Verdus's return to Bordeaux from Rome).

[16] 'Pernoniste' was a derogatory term for those who supported the unpopular governor of Guyenne, the duc d'Espernon, who attempted to enforce the policies of the royal minister Mazarin. The chronicler Jacques Filhot recorded that in 1651, after the duc d'Espernon's departure (in May), a rumour that he would be reappointed as governor brought a crowd of 3,000 on to the streets of Bordeaux, demanding 'the annihilation of all Epernonistes and Mazarinistes' (Westrich, *Ormée of Bordeaux*, p. 21).

[17] Two merchants called Desbats held *lettres de bourgeoisie* in the early 1660s: Jacques and Joseph (le Vacher de Boisville (ed.), *Livre des bourgeois*, part 1, p. 36). Of these Joseph was the more distinguished; by the early 1660s he was *consul* of the Bourse at Bordeaux (ibid., p. 45), and in July 1653 he was one of the most prominent speakers demanding a peace settlement at a gathering of merchants in the city (Birnstiel, *Die Fronde*, p. 142).

[18] Unidentified. Possibly du Verdus meant to write 'Bertais': two lawyers, both called Jean Berthet, were *bourgeois* of Bordeaux in the early 1660s (le Vacher de Boisville (ed.), *Livre des bourgeois*, part 1, p. 4).

[19] Contraction expanded.

[20] Either Jean de Sabourin, who was a *conseiller* of the Parlement of Bordeaux in 1625 (AMB MS Delpit 42, unnumbered item for 13 Nov. 1625), was still occupying that office in 1653 (le Vacher de Boisville, 'Liste des membres du Parlement', p. 52), but had died by the early 1660s (le Vacher de Boisville (ed.), *Livre des bourgeois*, part 1, p. 135); or his son André, who was a *conseiller* in 1639 (le Vacher de Boisville, 'Liste des membres du Parlement', p. 52) and still occupied that office in 1664, when he signed a book of 'Homages' as 'Sieur de la Bouvry' (ADG MS C 2326, fo. 123).

[21] Pierre Michon (1610–85) was adopted by his uncles Jean and Edmé de Bourdelot, and took their surname. Edmé was physician to Louis XIII; Pierre studied medicine under him, and qualified as a doctor in 1642. He became physician to the Condé family, and had a successful practice in Paris. In 1650 he spent several months during the Fronde in Bordeaux. In 1651, through Saumaise, he was appointed personal physician to Queen Christina of Sweden; he rapidly became her favourite intellectual-cum-courtier (and an object of intense envy and dislike among his rivals at her Court in Stockholm). He returned to Paris in 1653, and through her influence was appointed Abbot of Macé (or 'Massay'), near Bourges; although he had taken no holy orders and

was a well-known religious sceptic, a special dispensation was made on condition that he gave free medical treatment to the poor. His 'académie', a gathering of scientists and philosophers in Paris, functioned in the 1640s in the hôtel de Condé and was revived in 1659 in Bourdelot's house. See Le Gallois, *Conversations de l'académie*; Pintard, *Libertinage*, pp. 350–5, 389–93; Gabbey, 'The Bourdelot Academy'; Stolpe, *Från Stoicism till Mystik*, pp. 163–8; Åkerman, *Queen Christina*, pp. 40–2, 106–7.

[22] The victory in May 1643 of the French army over the Spanish, outside the frontier town of Rocroi (in the north-east of France), which the Spanish had been besieging.

[23] This probably refers to the first period of the Franco-Spanish war, from 1635 to 1643; the war continued until 1659.

[24] See Letter 40 n. 3, and the Biographical Register, 'de Martel'.

[25] Marthe de Blanc, a sister of du Verdus's mother, married François de Massiot, seigneur de Cugnol (or 'Cugnols'; but not 'Cugnos', which was the estate of the Saingresse or Saint-Gresse family) in 1619. She later married François de Montferrand. In 1674 she gave a large benefaction to the director of the Congregation in Bordeaux (ADG MS G 994 (liasse); Meller, *Armorial*, iii, p. 30).

[26] François Bertrand Dejean (or 'deJean', or 'Dejehan'), who styled himself 'docteur en théologie' (ADG MS G 662, unnumbered item in file 'Affaire Dejean'); he possibly belonged to the Dejean family of which two members, a father and son, were *conseillers* of the Parlement of Bordeaux in 1653 (Birnstiel, *Die Fronde*, p. 116). He was later in trouble with the ecclesiastical authorities when, in 1674, he refused to allow priests sent by the Archbishop of Bordeaux to preach in his church at Ambarès (see n. 27). His parishioners prepared a 'denunciation of the scandalous life of M. François Bertrand Dejean' ('dénonciation contre la vie scandaleuse de M^r françois bertrand deJean'), claiming, among other things, that he kept a woman in his house, popularly known as 'la Curesse' (ADG MS G 662, unnumbered item in file 'Affaire Dejean').

[27] Dejean was curate of the church of S. Pierre at Ambarès in the canton of Carbon-Blanc, nine miles north-east of Bordeaux; du Verdus's family estate centred on this parish.

[28] Ulysse Bigot has incorrectly identified this man as Antoine de Fayard ('Une lettre inédite', p. 275). The Anne de Bonneau who married Antoine de Fayard was du Verdus's aunt, not his sister, and did so in 1599 (see ADG MS 3 E 12995, fo. 902^r, and AMB MS Drouyn 275, p. 174).

[29] Execution in effigy was a common measure applied to absconded criminals in their absence: a picture was hung up depicting the criminal undergoing the appropriate punishment (see Marion, *Dictionnaire des institutions*, 'effigie').

[30] Henri de Bethune (1604–80), who was appointed Archbishop of Bordeaux in 1646 (though he entered the diocese only in 1648). After unsuccessful attempts to mediate between the duc d'Espernon and the *frondeurs*, he issued a public condemnation of the Fronde; he went to Paris in *c*.1652, returning only after general peace had been established in Guyenne in July 1653. A competent administrator who upheld orthodox Catholicism against Jansenism, he remained Archbishop of Bordeaux until his death.

[31] Thibaud de Lavie (*c*.1608–84), whose father, Bernard, was Montaigne's nephew. Thibaud became *avocat-général* at Bordeaux in 1635; in 1648 he succeeded his father as *premier président* of the Parlement of Pau, but was allowed to retain his post as *avocat-général* at Bordeaux (Feret, *Statistique générale*). He played a prominent part as a

representative of the Parlement of Bordeaux during the Fronde (Boscheron des Portes, *Histoire du parlement de Bordeaux*, ii, pp. 64–84).

³² See the Biographical Register, 'de Martel'.

³³ ~) *omitted in MS.*

³⁴ *Six Lessons*, printed with the English translation of *De corpore*, and published in London in June–July 1656; this work was not translated into Latin.

³⁵ *Of Body* (1656). Note that du Verdus has deleted 'votre' and substituted 'la': this translation was not by Hobbes, but it was supervised and authorized by him (see the translator's preface to the reader, sig. a3).

³⁶ There was only one edn. of *De corpore* in 1655; the 2nd edn. was the one included in the *Opera philosophica* published by Blaeu in 1668. Du Verdus's request suggests that Hobbes was planning to produce another version of the Latin text to incorporate the revisions made in the English translation.

³⁷ Wallis's criticism of the mathematical sections of *De corpore* was his *Elenchus geometriae hobbianae* (1655). He also published three mathematical works in 1655–6 (see Letter 79 n. 7).

³⁸ See Letter 84 n. 10.

³⁹ Du Verdus had previously received proofs of *De homine* from Hobbes (Letter 68 n. 6), but this request is evidently referring again to the supposed Latin translation of *Six Lessons* (above, n. 34).

⁴⁰ Contraction expanded.

⁴¹ *De corpore*, XXVII. 13: 'in omni loco planum trianguli CGK incidere in planum trianguli AFH' ('the plaine of the triangle CGK would be every where coincident with the plaine of the triangle AFH').

⁴² Ibid., XXX. 4. This is apparently du Verdus's paraphrase of 'saxum ergo descendit ab E ad A motu accelerato' ('Wherefore the stone will descend from E to A with accelerated motion').

⁴³ Gassendi, *De motu*, sect. 18, pp. 69–73.

⁴⁴ *De corpore*, XXX. 4.

LETTER 79   [26 MARCH/] 5 APRIL 1656

François du Verdus to Hobbes, from Bordeaux

Chatsworth, Hobbes MSS, letter 15 (original).

Monsieur,

Dans la longue lettre que je uiens de vous écrire de droiture,[1] Je vous prie de doner a qui vous rendra celle icy [> 1.°] Vostre seconde Edition du Liure de Corpore en Latin.[2] 2° sa Traduction en Anglois.[3] 3° Vostre response en Anglois a Wallisius.[4] 4° la Traduction latine de cette response.[5] 5° Le Liure de Wallisius contre vous,[6] 6° Et ses trois traités de l'angle du Contact, de l'Aritmetique des Infinis, et des Coniques.[7] On me fera tenir bien fidelement tous ces liures, dont vous me ferés s'il vous plait l'honneur de croire que je sçauray bien user. Au reste

Monsieur, je ne vous [redis *deleted*] fais pas icy de compliment, sur ce que je vous demande ce présant là. vous ne doutés point des sentimens d'obligation que ie vous en auray. Et pour dernier abrégé de mon autre lettre de mesme date que celle icy je vous proteste de nouueau que je suis de tout mon coeur plus que persone du monde

Monsieur
Vostre tres humble et tres obeissant seruiteur et tout acquis duuerdus

A Bordeaux le 5ᵉ Auril. 1656.

[*addressed:*] For Mʳ Hobbes at the Greene Dragon in Paules Church-yerd London

[*endorsed by James Wheldon:*] Monsʳ du Verdus Ap. 5 1656.

Translation of Letter 79

Sir,

In the long letter which I have just sent you by the ordinary post,[1] I beg you to give the bearer of this letter (1) the second edition of your *De corpore* in Latin;[2] (2) the English translation of it;[3] (3) your reply to Wallis, in English;[4] (4) the Latin translation of that reply;[5] (5) Wallis's book against you;[6] and (6) his three treatises, on the angle of contact, on the arithmetic of infinite numbers, and on conics.[7] These books will be faithfully delivered to me, and please do me the honour of believing that I shall know how to make good use of them. Otherwise, Sir, I make no more compliments to you here about the fact that I am asking for this present. You do not doubt the sense of obligation which I shall have towards you on this account. And as a final summary of my other letter (of the same date as this one) I declare to you again that I am, Sir, with all my heart and more than anyone else in the world,

Your most humble and obedient servant, entirely yours,
du Verdus

Bordeaux, 5 April 1656

[*addressed: see text*]

---

[1] Letter 78.
[2] See ibid., n. 36.
[3] See ibid., n. 35.

⁴ See ibid., n. 34.

⁵ See ibid.

⁶ See ibid., n. 37.

⁷ Wallis, *De angulo contactus*, *Arithmetica infinitorum*, and *De sectionibus conicis*: these three works were published together, with separate title-pages (respectively, 1656, 1656, and 1655) but continuous signatures, under the general title *Operum mathematicorum pars altera* (1656).

LETTER 80   1 [/11] APRIL 1656

Henry Stubbe to Hobbes, from Oxford

Chatsworth, Hobbes MSS, letter 16 (original).
Printed in Thompson, 'Lettres de Stubbe à Hobbes', pp. 100–1.

S:ʳ

   I haue presumed not to satisfy my selfe but you in a further attempt upon yᵉ translation of yoʳ Leuiathan: If I miscarry, yoᵘ must blame yoʳ selfe, I reuerenced yoᵘ too much to distrust my owne abilityes, when M.ʳ Hobbes cryed, On. my onely encouragemᵗ is yᵗ you are the reviser; I haue sent you the first halfe sheet againe, I did not transcribe it because yoʳ alterations were so little yᵗ I thought I neede not put my penne to yᵗ drudgery. I haue made use of ἐλαστήριον,[1] but I haue since bethought my selfe of another word wᶜʰ is dennisoned in Latine, & yᵗ is Schasteria:[2] it is used in Plautus but not in yᵗ sense; but I haue reade it used in yᵉ description of yoʳ Oscilla or puppets, for yᵗ wᶜʰ giueth yᵐ motion being lengthened or slacked: some such thing too is in H: Stephen.[3] yoᵘ see S:ʳ yᵗ I haue something of yᵉ pedant, I loue not to Lard my writeings with Greeke wordes, I would euen erase ἰδιοσυγκρασία, & substitute out of Tully propria cujusque corporis constitutio.[4] you will pardon these things, they are yᵉ effects of an ouer-curious Zeale I haue to serue you. In these other pieces, you will see yᵗ I am tender of mistakes, where you see this asterisque (X) I doubt of yᵉ version & where you finde this (☛) I haue omitted a word which I conceiued redundant in yᵉ English. I see I shall not performe yᵉ worke so soone as I thought, but this I can assure you yᵗ wᵗ difficulty I meet with as yet (and doubtlesse greatest difficulty is in yᵉ first part) is most in yᵉ transcribeing, I writeing a very slowe hand: what you haue here was done in one day, but was two in transcribeing: you haue here yᵉ sole copy, for my first thoughts are confused, & uary much from what you see here: you may if you please keepe yᵐ by you, unlesse you would haue any thing altered: & when yᵉ whole is done, & you haue added what you please, I shall (after my usuall way) reassume yᵉ whole piece, and reade it ouer, & polish it if neede bee any where: for I professe I cannot amend ought untill it hath lien by a while, & my first thoughts bee vanished a little and giue way to second. I shall finish another sheet or two agᵗ friday and send you; & if you please but to acquaint mee with a place, I shall direct yᵐ to yoʳ hands immediately: S:ʳ you may dash or vary what you please in them, I professe I am not so confident of my selfe as yᵗ I thinke I cannot erre in any thing, unlesse it bee in professeing my selfe to bee Sʳ:

   yoʳ admirer, & humble seruant
   H: Stubbe:

Ch:ᵗ Ch: Oxon: April: I. 1656

[*addressed:*] For M:ʳ Hobbes with other papers.

[*endorsed by James Wheldon:*] M.ʳ Stubb. Apr. 10.ᵗʰ⁵ 1656

---

¹ The reins used by a charioteer. Stubbe was probably translating the word 'Strings' in the Introduction to *Leviathan*: 'For what is the *Heart*, but a *Spring*; and the *Nerves*, but so many *Strings*' (p. 1).
² σχαστηρία, the rope used in a pulley.
³ Henricus Stephanus (Henri Estienne), *Thesaurus graecae linguae*, gives 'funis, trochlea' ('rope, pulley') as the meaning of σχαστηρία.
⁴ In Greek medical writings, ἰδιοσυγκρασία means the special temperament of a body; the Ciceronian phrase means 'the peculiar constitution of each body'.
⁵ Wheldon seems to have misread the date 'I' as 'x'.

LETTER 81   [9/] 19 APRIL 1656

Claude Mylon to Hobbes, from Paris

Chatsworth, Hobbes MSS, letter 17 (original).

Monsieur
   Ayant à vous faire tenir vne Lettre ouuerte de Monsieur Du verdus¹ je prens cette occasion pour vous salüer, quoy qu'il y ait plusieurs années que vous estes retourné en Angleterre Je n'ay pas oublié les obligations que Je vous ay. Je me suis toujours souuenu de l'honneur que vous m'auez fait me donnant quelque part dans vostre amitié, et

n'ay pas manqué de demander des nouvelles de vostre santé et de vos ouurages [a celuy *deleted*] a tous ceux qui m'y ont pû dire, ça esté auec joye que J'ay appris que vous vous portiez mieux a Londres qu'a paris, et que vostre philosophie estoit Imprimeè.[2] Je l'ay estudiée aussi tost auec beaucoup de Plaisir comme vne chose que j'auois si longtemps souhaitteé, Depuis Monsieur Du verdus m'ayant demandé conte de la lecture que j'y auois faite, je luy ay temoigné l'estime que j'en faisois et luy ay enuoyé les objections qu'il vous a communiqueés.[3] J'ay sceu de luy que vous les auez receüe auec vne franchise Geometrique et tout a fait obligeante, ne doutant point qu'elles ne vinrent d'vne personne qui prend grande part a vos Interests. mais parcequ'il n'est [>pas] pleinement conuaincu De la demonstration de Mons.r Christianus hugenius de Zulichom Gentilhomme hollandais et tres bon Geometre, j'ay peur que vous ne fassiez la mesme difficulté faute d'auoir veu son traitté Imprimé de Dimensione circuli.[4] Je vous diray donc que j'ay voulu m'en asseurer, et que je l'ay leu tout Entier, j'ay trouué que dans sa 9.eme proposition Il demonstre fort bien (praemissis etiam optimé demonstratis) que duae tertiae sinus CH simul cum triente tangentis eg sunt majores arcu cg. donc doublant le tout, $\frac{2}{3}$ Chordae fg. simul cum $\frac{1}{3}$

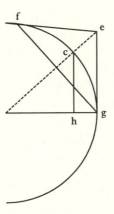

tangentis eg plus $\frac{1}{3}$ tangentis ef erunt majorae Arcu duplo fcg.[5] J'ay mis Icy vne copie d'vn Imprimé que mons.r Chr. Hugenius m'a enuoyé de la haye touchant vne satellite de saturne qu'il a découuert auec ses belles lunettes, je croy que vous serez bien aise de voir cette nouueauté[6]

On Imprimera bien tost [>en cette ville] les traittez de Monsieur Bouillaut.[7] 1°. Sa reponse a Setus Vardus Anglois. 2°. Des Spirales

d'Archimede. 3°. quelques autres opuscules et propositions Geo-
metriques.⁸

L'Angle solide de Mons.ʳ DesArgues⁹ est aussi en mesme estat. Je
vous supplie de voire que je suis de tout mon Coeur

Monsieur
Vostre treshumble et tresobeissant seruiteur
Mylon

A paris ce 19ᵉ d'Avril 1656

[*postscript:*] Si vous enuoyez quelque chose a Monsieur Du verdus
prenez la peine de me l'addresser par le moyen du marchand qui vous
aura fait tenir ce paquet, Je demeure toujours dans la rue tirechappe
pres les halles.

Ces Messieurs que j'ay nommes en ma lettre et Monsieur De
Carcaui¹⁰ vous baisent les mains.

Translation of Letter 81

Sir,

Having to forward an unsealed letter to you from M. du Verdus,[1] I
am taking this opportunity to greet you. Although it is several years
since you returned to England, I have not forgotten my obligations to
you; I have always remembered the honour you did me by giving me
some share of your friendship, and I have not failed to enquire about
your health and your works of all those who were able to tell me about
them. It gave me great happiness to learn that you were in better health
in London than in Paris, and that your philosophy had been printed.[2] I
studied it immediately with great pleasure, since it was something I had
hoped for for a long time. Then, when M. du Verdus asked me what
judgement I had come to in my study of it, I told him how highly I
valued it and sent him the objections which he has made known to you.[3]
I learned from him that you had received them with the altogether
obliging open-heartedness which befits a true geometer, and that you
did not doubt that they came from someone who is greatly concerned to
defend your interests.

But because he is not entirely convinced by the demonstration
offered by M. Christiaan Huygens of Zuylichem (a Dutch gentleman,
and an excellent geometer), I am worried that you might make the same
objection, through not having seen his printed treatise 'De dimensione

circuli'.[4] So let me tell you that I wanted to be sure about it, and read the entire treatise. I found that in his ninth proposition he demonstrated very well (from premisses which were also extremely well demonstrated) that two-thirds of the sine *ch* together with one-third of the tangent *eg* are greater than the arc *cg*. Therefore, multiplying everything by 2, two-thirds of the chord *fg*, together with one-third of the tangent *eg* plus one-third of the tangent *ef* will be greater than the double arc *fcg*.[5]

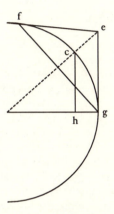

I have enclosed here a copy of a printed sheet which M. Christiaan Huygens sent me from The Hague, concerning a moon of Saturn which he has discovered with his excellent telescope; I think you will be very glad to see this new discovery.[6]

The following treatises by M. Boulliau[7] will be printed very soon here in Paris: (1) his reply to the Englishman Seth Ward; (2) on Archimedes' spirals; (3) some other short works and geometrical propositions.[8] M. Desargues's work on the solid angle[9] is also at the same stage. I beg you to believe that I am, Sir, with all my heart,

Your most humble and obedient servant,
Mylon

Paris, 19 April 1656

[*postscript:*] If you send anything to M. du Verdus, please take the trouble to address it to me via the merchant who will deliver this parcel to you. I am still living in rue Tirechappe, near les Halles.

Those gentlemen I mentioned in my letter, and M. de Carcavi,[10] send you their greetings.

The geometrical section of this letter renews Mylon's objections against Hobbes's attempted rectification of the parabola (see Letter 76, second enclosure). Hobbes's reply to Letter 81 does not survive, but its contents were reported by Mylon to Christiaan Huygens on [13/] 23 June 1656. Hobbes admitted that his attempted rectification was incorrect, but said that the fault lay not with his method, but merely with his having mistaken one line for another; and he now offered a new version of the same demonstration. (See *HOC* i, p. 439.)

¹ Possibly Letter 79.

² *De corpore*.

³ Letter 76, first enclosure.

⁴ *De circuli magnitudine inventa* (1654).

⁵ Ibid., p. 14.

⁶ Mylon enclosed with this letter a copy, in his own handwriting, of Huygens's pamphlet *De Saturni luna observatio nova* (1655). This work is printed (from the 1724 edition of Huygens's *Opera varia*) in *HOC* xv, pp. 169–77.

⁷ Ismaël Boulliau or Boulliaud (1605–94), a converted Huguenot, became a Catholic priest in c.1640. He lived in Paris from 1633, where he was befriended by Gassendi and became an accomplished astronomer. His main work, a treatise on the elliptical orbits of the planets, *Astronomia philolaica*, was published in 1645. He was a friend of both Pascal and Huygens.

⁸ (1) and (3) were published as *Exercitationes geometricae tres* (1657); (2) was published as *De lineis spiralibus demonstrationes novae* (1657). Seth Ward (on whom see Letter 75 n. 8) had criticized Boulliau's theories about the geometry of planetary orbits in his *In Ismaelis Bullialdi astronomiae philolaicae fundamenta, inquisitio brevis* (1653).

⁹ Girard Desargues (1591–1661) was best known for his *Brouillon project* on conic sections (1639). He was now living in Lyon (from c.1651 to Nov. 1656). Since 1648 his activities had been mainly in the fields of architecture and engineering, and no work of the kind mentioned here is known to have been published (see Taton, *L'Œuvre de Desargues*, pp. 55–61).

¹⁰ See Letter 67 n. 7.

LETTER 82   13–14 [/23–4] MAY 1656

Philip Tanny or Tandy to Hobbes, from London

Chatsworth, Hobbes MSS, letter 18 (original).

Sʳ

I have reade a booke of yours lately touching Liberty and necessity xc.¹ I have wondred at the indiscretion of him, that without provocation would doe any thing on this subject, I thinke there were other matters that hee might more fruitefully have busyed himselfe about but tis done, and there is noe more to bee sd of that. You, it seemes had a request for your provocation, Excuse mee, that I have spoken my mind touching it, send mee an answere to my request assoone as you can, I have bin very loath to divine your meaning and the rather beecause you seeme to blame this forwardnes in page 27th. of your booke.[2] which I hope wilbee some Excuse, that I put you to this trouble; I shall onely adde, that I am an unbyassed, and an impartiall man, and shall doe your apprehensions an impartiall right, This is all I have to say, but that I wish you well, and am

Your affectionate frend and servt,
Philip Tandy.

Stephens alley[3] May. 13. or 14th. 1656

[*addressed:*] For my much honoured frend Mr Thomas Hobs. These.

[*endorsed by James Wheldon:*] M^r. Tandy or Tanny May 14th. 1656 about Liberty & Necessity

---

[1] Hobbes's *Of Libertie and Necessitie* was published (without his authorization) in London in 1654. It was reprinted in *The Questions concerning Liberty, Necessity, and Chance*, published in London in 1656. It was probably the appearance of this edn. that prompted Tanny's letters.

[2] 'And though the *Bishops* modest entreaty had been no part of the cause of my yeilding to it, yet certainly it would have been cause enough to some civil man, to have requited me with fairer Language' (*The Questions concerning Liberty, Necessity, and Chance*, p. 27: *EW* v, p. 36).

[3] Stephen's Alley in Westminster (see the end of Letter 83).

LETTER 83   13–14 [/23–4] MAY 1656

Philip Tanny or Tandy to Hobbes, from London

BL MS Add. 32553, fos. 1–2 (original).

S^r.

  I have thought fit to passe by the epistle, it beeing done by another, and nothing concerning mee, though a minister.[1] your booke is that which I, God willing, shall take in hand, and treate with, I confesse its seeming ingenuity hath much swayed mee heretofore to thinke you a good man, and the rather because I observed in it certaine high mysterious speculations, as I thought, the best opened by you, of any man living that I ever yet saw, but S^r. I thinke you are in something short as by the sequele I hope will appeare. I doe not take upon mee to answeare you by way of opposition in all things, but rather by way of Vindication, confirmeing you in somethings, if you please to take confirmation from mee, and opposeing you onely in some other things, wherein in the modestest terms I can use, I say you come short, what those things are I shall shortly tell you, You are pleased to tell the world of the Bishop of Derryes treatise of this subject, as occasioning a request, that you should meddle with this controversy,[2] I confesse, if there were such an Embrio you had a provocation, but it had bin well notwithstanding, you had silenced your Judgement, unles your affections had bin more sweetely carryed forth to glorify Jesus Christ and not your owne wit, which doth much abound in diverse parts of your little booke. I list not to sift your subtility in examineing the many nice distinctions, which you everywhere batter, but the maine matter, which I suppose you ayme at, I shall humbly desire to weigh in the ballance of the sanctuary. You tell us that you submit your attempt in this little tract, to his Lordships the Earle of Newcastles judgemt,[3] I desire my L^d of Newcastles pardon, if I doe not soe with my answere, for though his Lordship, I make noe question bee an ingenous gentleman, yet I thinke, this subject is not by mee to bee submitted to the highest judgemt in the world, Mr Hobs himselfe not excepted, and in this I intend his Lop as well as you a provocation that I may know him if hee bee liveing.

But now, S^r to come to your selfe, there is something which dissatisfyeth mee touching your action in attempting this subject. You say, you were little concerned in it, and you give your reason, because you never d[elivere]d[4] your opinion touching it.[5] I thinke that reason is hardly strong enough to free you from beeing concerned in it were there not some other collaterall considerations that should have byassed you. But truely, S^r bee your reasons what they wil bee, it had bin well I thinke for you, if you had thought your selfe soe little concerned as not to have deliverred your opinion touching it at all, for you have made such a breach into the secret, that I assure you, S^r I had published nothing touching it, had it not bin for you but your treatise beeing abroad, I am willing, though I am not necessitated to follow you with my opinion touching yours. I adde these words 'though I am not necessitated' to let you see, I something understand the question, I thanke God for it

Now S^r I am at your booke which upon the matter beegins with the Bishop of Derryes preface, which you say, is a handsome one,[6] you allow him more than I, it may bee, would, if I should take time to reade it; But truely I cannot conveniently doe it yet tis noe matter of necessity that I forbeare it, this onely let mee say, I thinke that Bishop had wit enough to make a handsome preface, but never, that I could heare of, godlynes enough to make a good Bishop. Hee mistakes the question you say, for whereas hee sth thus, if I bee free to write this discourse, I have obteyned the cause, you deny this to bee true, and soe doe I too, but whereas you adde tis enough to his freedome of writeing, that hee had not written unles he would himselfe, and then adde withall, that if hee will obtaine the cause, hee must prove that beefore hee writ it, it was not necessary hee should write it afterwards, I must bee bold to tell you, that if by gaining the cause, you meane evincing the truth, there is noe necessity of his proving what you soe require of him, the proofe lying on your side that it was soe, which by your favour I never yet saw done. I pray you S^r doe you thinke it absolutely necessary, that I should now goe on with my examination of your treatise touching the subject and soe necessary that I cannot now forbeare it, if I will, Beleeve it, S^r, I know the liberty of my owne election, I thanke God, soe well, as that I can tell you. I can forbeare it, if I please, but truely S^r as the case stands I should bee as wicked a wretch as ever was in the world, if I should forbeare it, because I am for the present persuaded, that herein I pursue the dictates, which God hath given to my soule and yet I can forbeare it, if I would bee soe wicked. But how this will consist with the absolute decree of God, which you suppose makes a thing necessarily to bee done is the grand though not the single question, I shall, God willing and by Gods helpe cleare you in it if God shalbee pleased to give you eyes to see, otherwise I shall labour in vaine though I should speake the clearest reason in the earth, S^r I have made you a promise, take not my word, but as you shall find mee an honest man. But to goe on, you observe that it may bee his Lordship thinkes it all one to say, I was free to write it, and it was not necessary I should write it, but you thinke otherwise,[7] things are not ripe as yet for mee to speake what I thinke in this, but it little will make for you, whensoever I declare myselfe. you adde the reasons why you thinke otherwise Lets see them, Hee is free say you to doe a thing, that may doe it, if hee have the will to doe it, S^r allow mee a graine of salt here, or els I shall not digeste this, Let mee sift it a little.

You suppose that every man hath a will to doe a thing wrought in him by such strong influences, as hee cannot resist, you seeme to suppose another thing, which till I have a more evident appearance of, I will not suggest. you make freedome to consist, eyther in the not beeing hindred in the doings of things which wee have a will to doe, or els in the willingnes of the will freely chooseing to doe that which it is wrought to will, or els in some thing els, which as yet I doe not understand, which of these things, or what other thing, you ayme at in the word free, I am yet to learne, and the truth is accordingly as you meane in this poynt, I shall frame my whole discourse, and therefore I pray you spare mee till I know from your selfe, what your mind is, if you shall say, some other part of your booke cleares this, bee pleased to let mee tell you, that I find severall ambiguityes in your booke, and I may misapprehend you, if wee cleare things as wee goe, wee shall come to an ingenuous issue; Another thing let mee tell you touching my future discusse of your booke, or judgemt in this poynt, I doe not conceive my selfe bound to defend the Bishop of Derry, but to looke after the evinceing of truth, and that within as little a compasse, as rationally as I can. Hee is of age, let him speake for himselfe. S:̣ Bee cleare as words can make you, you shall find the same indeavour in my selfe, and it may please God, you may receive as much satisfaction from mee, as you indeavour to give to others, if you refuse to grant my request in the tendency of this little, (which I therefore send beefore, that I may preserve my selfe from writeing too much). you will not therein bee soe ingenuous, as the world reports you. I desire to transact all in print and let the world looke on, I feare them not; the roote of the busines will lay in the through cleareing of the coast here, which if you shall doe speedily, you shall therein much oblige.

Your affectionate frend and serv^t
Philip Tanny alias Tandy

From my study in Stephens alley neare Derby house in Westminster. May. 13. or 14th 1656.

---

[1] The 'Epistle to the Reader' placed before Hobbes's *Of Libertie and Necessitie* was by John Davies of Kidwelly (see Letter 123 n. 19), who was responsible for the unauthorized first printing of this work. It contained a number of fiercely anticlerical remarks, comparing, for example, 'the *black-coats*' to 'a sort of ignorant *tinkers*'. This epistle, however, was not reprinted in *The Questions concerning Liberty, Necessity, and Chance*, so it must be presumed that Tanny had now obtained a copy of the 1st edn. of *Of Libertie and Necessitie*.

[2] As Hobbes explains at the beginning of *Of Libertie and Necessitie*, he wrote this work in response to a 'Discourse' on liberty and necessity by John Bramhall, Bishop of Londonderry (see n. 5).

[3] *Of Libertie and Necessitie* was written at the Marquess of Newcastle's request; it is addressed to the Marquess, and in the first paragraph Hobbes writes: 'I present and submit it to your Lordships judgement' (p. 1: *EW* iv, p. 239).

⁴ Contraction expanded.

⁵ *Of Libertie and Necessitie* begins: 'Right Honourable, I had once resolved to answer my *Lord Bishop*s Objections to my book *De* CIVE in the first place as that which concerns me most, and afterwards to examine his discourse of LIBERTY and NECESSITY, which (because I had never uttered my opinion of it) concerned me the less' (p. 1: *EW* iv, p. 239).

⁶ Tanny comments here on the third paragraph of *Of Libertie and Necessitie*, where Hobbes writes: 'The *preface* is a handsome one, but it appeareth even in that, that he hath mistaken the question. For whereas he sayes thus, *If I be free to write this discourse, I have obtained the Cause*, I deny that to be true, for 'tis enough to his freedom of writing, that he had not written it unless he would himself. If he will obtain the cause, he must prove that before he writ it, it was not necessary he should [write] it afterward' (p. 2: *EW* iv, p. 239; 'write' is a MS emendation of 'prove' in Bodl. Ashmole 1325).

⁷ 'It may be his Lordship thinks it all one to say; *I was free* to write it, and *It was not necessary* I should write it, but I think otherwise, for he is *free* to do a thing that may do it if he have the will to do it, and may forbear, if he have the will to forbear. And yet if there be a *necessity* that he shall have the *will* to do it, the action is necessarily to follow' (*Of Libertie and Necessitie*, pp. 2–3: *EW* iv, pp. 239–40).

LETTER 84   [14/] 24 MAY 1656

François du Verdus to Hobbes, from Bordeaux

Chatsworth, Hobbes MSS, letter 19 (original).

Monsieur,

Je reçeus il y a quelque 15 jours vostre lettre du 1ᵉʳ May. la petite que vous auiés écrite, auparauant et adresseé a Mʳ Milon, je ne l'ay point reçeuë¹ et toute fois Mʳ Mylon m'écriuit que vous luy auiés fait response² et promis les liures pour moy,³ et qu'il me les feroit tenir seurement; et cela sans me parler de cette petite lettre; je luy écriuis la luy demandant mais ie n'en ay point de response, et ne scay a quoy il tient.

Ce que j'ay esté si long temps sans vous temoigner la joye que m'auoit doneé cette derniere dont vous m'auiés honoré [> et a vous en remercier] c'est que j'atandois de jour en jour de vous faire une response que pour mes pechés ie ne puis vous faire encore a present. j'atandois Monsieur que Mʳ de Martel m'eut écrit et m'eut promis c'est a dire confirmé son anciene promesse de me uenir mettre en liberté. Mais Monsieur que dirons nous de luy? Quand ie partis de Paris sur les memoyres que j'auois reçeu de toutes ces maudites cabales que j'ay soutenuës et soutiens de filous uoulans me rauir tous mes biens je luy dis come par esprit de Profetie tout ce qui en arriueroit et l'obligeay a me [promettre][4] qu'il uiendroit a mon secours; dépuis il a reïteré souuent sa promesse et enfin quand ie l'eus pris au mot il cessa de m'écrire. Je luy ay represanté souuent que ie uiuois au milieu de 2 ou 3 cent mille francs de bien et de droits comme dans une ville assiegée; que j'etois seul contre quatre Cabales puissantes et malignes; qu'il faloit ou que ie perisse, ou que je me rendisse ou que je me donasse; que je ne pouuois me doner a autre qu'a luy qui scait mes affaires, qui les scait bones, et mes biens beaux et grands et est mon amy et est philosophe Et que je luy ferois des conditions come a mon frere Aisné voulant estre son cadet, et le seruir et ayder: croyriés vous Monsieur qu'au fort de mes Angoisses me scachant ainsi sans consolation il a laissé passer dépuis le mois de Januier sans m'écrire et [>que] sa response que je croyois qu'il feroit a 3 ou 4 de mes lettres de ce mois icy luy disant le triste état ou je suis de me rendre a des filoux et voyr qu'ils auront plus de 100 mille francs que je luy reseruois, je ne l'ay point encore receüe? C'est donc pour cela que j'ay esté tout ce mois sans vous écrire Car ie desirois de parler décisiuement et promettre sans condition que je serois a vous cet esté. C'est une chose que je desire auec passion et qui sera s'il plait a Dieu tot ou tard. Vous me faites trop de graçe de m'y conuier et Monsieur le Comte de Déuonsire me fait plus d'honneur que je ne uaus de l'agreër et y consentir: Ce Seigneur en vous considerant comme il fait se monstre digne de la vénération de toute la Terre et pour moy je vous proteste Monsieur que pour cela seul n'eussé-je point [>eut] l'honneur de luy estre conu par ce que vous luy aués pû dire de moy je me sentois un zele extraordinaire pour son seruice et que je seray toute ma vie son tres humble seruiteur.

Mais Monsieur que ferons nous donc de Mr Martel? je sçay que le Clergé assamblé dresse des Mémoires contre Messieurs de la Religion;[5] et [>ie] juge que cela peut auoir arreté Mr Martel a la Cour où il est député du Languedoc[6] mais me traiter de mepris? me laisser si long temps sans response? cela en est il? et l'amitié est elle comme cela? Auec cela je ne me rebute pas et ne puis m'empécher de l'aymer; et croy qu'il a ses raisons qui ne seront pas mauuaises pour moy. Et Toutefois come j'en suis toujours en peine je vous conjure Monsieur que je vous aye cette obligation: je vous prie écriués luy a Paris luy disant en peu de mots Que je vous ay écrit toutes mes trauersses, la confiançe que j'auois en luy sur les paroles que je dis qu'il m'a donées, et son long silançe: Que vous le condamnés a me uenir sécourir s'il le peut; sinon a me l'écrire, et a renouër auec moy. Je vous demande cette graçe. Et vous promets de tenir bon, tout ce que feroit le plus vaillant Capitaine assiegé dans une plaçe sans secours. Mais vous scaués ce que c'est que la Guerre d'vn seul contre Tous vous en parlés dans vostre Section du Citoyen.

Qu'il est beau ce Liure là! et que je l'ayme! Toutes ces tramasseries qui me flestrissent cruëllement le corps l'esprit et les biens m'ont tellement occupé dépuis six mois que je n'auois pas trouué un quart dheure de loisir pour en comançer la verssion. Je l'ay comancée dépuis la My-May et suis auant du Titre du Comandement Imperium Mr Sorbiere dit l'Empire.[7] Mais que j'y ay de satisfaction! et que j'y passe uolontiers les jours et les nuits! Aussi Monsieur j'oseray vous dire (et cela sans vanité) j'en fais un Chef d'oeuure; je rens précisement mot pour mot dans le mesme sens et le tour françois y est; on n'a point encore ueu de telle version en françe; sur ma parole vous ne vous plaindrés pas d'y auoir esté paraphrasé. Ce que ie souhaiterois de scauoir c'est Monsieur, s'il suffit que ie traduise la premiere edition car j'ay comancé a trauailler sur l'original que vous en donates a Mr Martel, ou s'il est mieux que je traduise l'autre et toutes les notes que vous y aués ajoutées;[8] et pour cela je vous prie de me faire l'honneur de m'écrire encore une fois auant que d'aller en ce Chateau de Plaisançe de Monsieur le Comte.

Au reste Monsieur pour repondre au reste de vostre lettre. j'accepte vostre version Angloise du liure de Corpore auec la response a Wallis:[9] mais ie souhaite de l'auoir ou par la voye du libraire de Paris Mr Lyonard[10] qui Mr Mylon m'a écrit vous auoir adressé; ou par autre qui s'il vous plait ne vous coute rien. le reste que je vous auois demandé mesmement des oeuures de Walis[11] j'atandray a le uoyr que je sois de delá a Londres.

Ce que vous me dites est tout a fait galand qu'il me faudra deux maistres; l'ecriuain pour lire uos lettres; et celuy de la langue Angloise pour aprendre vostre françois ie fus rauy de uoir ce trait de vostre belle humeur et d'une imagination uiue et marquant bone santé. j'espere de reprendre mon ancienne joye prés de vous.

Celuy de mes amis qui vous écrit se nome Mr Peleau fils d'un Conseiller Secretaire du Roy; il scait l'Euclide, et a quelque teinture d'algebre; philosophe autant que vos écrits l'en ont randu mais il ne les scait pas encore bien et y a des doutes que je luy demele assés aisement au reste un esprit bien tourné et homme d'honneur. Il a couru icy une Profetie presentée, dit on par un Astrologue Italien au Roy de Suëde; moy j'ay fait courir le bruit qu'on l'auoit trouuée a Rome grauée en lettre gottique au pié d'une statuë qu'on y déterra quand j'y etois, representant la fortune qui couronoit de trois courones une teste deja couronée. Je vous en enuoye Copie; On y compte les lettres numerales, et les dates s'y trouuent justes. Il est aisé de faire trouuer tel nombre qu'on uoudra dans une phrase ayant [sens][12] complet si lon periphrase mais ce qu'il y a là de joly c'est que la chose est enoncée aux moindres termes. Je suis éternellement

Monsieur
vostre tres humble et tres obeissant seruiteur
duuerdus

A Bourdeaux le 24ᵉ May 1656

[*postscript:*]
D o   S u e c o   P o l o n i a m. 1656[13]
500   5   100   50   1   1,000

D o q u e   C o n s t a n t i n o p o l i m. 1657
500   5   100   1   50 1 1,000

D a b i t u r   t i b i   C a r o l e   R o m a 1658
500   1   5   1   1   100   50   1,000

D a b i t u r   t i b i   C a r o l e   G e r m a n i a 1659
500   1   5   1   1   100   50   1,000   1

A u s t r i a c i s   s p r e t i s   n o u u s   C a e s a r
      5   1   100 1   1   5 5   100

e l i g e t u r   f r a n c o f u r t i   n o m e n   e r i t
50 1   5   100   5   1   1,000   1

C a r o l u s   s e x t u s[14]   s u é c u s. 1661[15]
100   50 5   10   5   5   100 5

[*endorsed by James Wheldon:*] Mʳ du Verdus

Translation of Letter 84

Sir,

I received your letter of 1 May about a fortnight ago; but I have not received the note which you wrote to me earlier and sent to M. Mylon.[1] And yet M. Mylon wrote to me that you had sent him a reply[2] and promised to send the books for me,[3] and that he would find a secure way of delivering them to me—without mentioning that note. I wrote to

284

him, asking for it, but I have received no reply, and do not know what he is up to.

The reason why I have gone for so long without telling you what happiness I gained from the last letter you honoured me with, and without thanking you for it, is that I was waiting from day to day to send you a reply which, for my sins, I am still unable to send you at present. I was waiting, Sir, until M. de Martel had written to me and had promised (that is, confirmed his old promise) to come and set me free.

But, Sir, what can we say about him? When I left Paris because of the accounts I had received of all those accursed conspiracies (from which I suffered, and still suffer) of swindlers trying to rob me of all my possessions, I told him, as if in a spirit of prophecy, everything that would happen, and forced him to promise[4] that he would come to my aid. He frequently repeated his promise after that; and finally, when I had taken him at his word, he stopped writing to me. I often put it to him that I was living in the midst of my 2 or 300,000 francs' worth of possessions and entitlements, as if in a town under siege; that I was on my own against four powerful and malign conspiracies; and that I must either perish, or surrender, or entrust myself to someone else. And I told him that I could not entrust myself to anyone but him, since he is acquainted with my financial affairs, he knows that they are sound and that my estate is large and fine, and he is my friend and a philosopher. And I told him that I would treat with him as if with my elder brother, wanting to be his younger brother, to serve him and help him. Would you believe, Sir, that, at the height of my anguish, knowing me to be bereft of all support, he has gone for the whole time since January without writing to me? Nor has he replied, as I thought he would, to the three or four letters I have sent him this month telling him what a miserable state I am in, having to give in to swindlers and seeing that they will get more than 100,000 francs which I was reserving for him—to this I have received no reply whatsoever.

That is why I have been this whole month without writing to you: I wanted to be able to write in definite terms and promise unconditionally to be with you this summer. It is something I long for passionately—and which will come about, God willing, sooner or later. You do me too much honour by inviting me; and my Lord the Earl of Devonshire does me greater honour than I deserve by approving the invitation and consenting to it. In regarding you with such esteem, this Lord shows himself worthy to be venerated by the whole world. As for myself, I must tell you, Sir, that, if only because I had the honour of being known to him through what you may have told him about me, I felt an extraordinary eagerness to serve him, and for the rest of my life I shall remain his humble servant.

But, Sir, what shall we do about M. de Martel? I know that the assembly of the clergy has been drawing up accusations against the Protestants,[5] and I think that may have kept M. de Martel at Court, where he is a representative from Languedoc.[6] But to treat me with contempt! To leave me for so long with no reply! Is that what we have come to? And is that the nature of friendship? All the same, I do not lose heart, and cannot stop myself from loving him; and I believe he has his reasons, which do not signify any ill will towards me. Yet, since I am still very troubled by this matter, I urge you, Sir, to do this favour for me: write to him at Paris, I beg you, telling him briefly that I have written to you about all the set-backs I have suffered, the trust I had placed in him because of the promises he had made to me, and his long silence; and pass sentence on him, requiring him to come to my aid if he can—or, if he cannot, to write to me and renew his friendship with me. I beg this favour of you, and promise that I shall hold firm, doing everything that the most valiant commander would do under siege, in a place cut off from help. But you know what a war of one against all is like—you describe it in your *De cive*.

What a fine book that is! And how I love it! All these conspiracies, which so cruelly blight my health, spirit, and possessions, kept me so busy for six months that I had not found a quarter of an hour of leisure in which to start on my translation of it. I started after the middle of May, and am now approaching the section on 'Rule' ('Imperium'—M. Sorbière translates it as 'Empire').[7] But what satisfaction it gives me! And how willingly I spend days and nights on it! I shall also be so bold as to tell you, Sir (and this without vanity), that I am creating a masterpiece: I translate exactly, word for word, with the same meaning and with a French turn of phrase. There has never been such a translation in France before; upon my word, you will have no complaints about having been paraphrased. What I should like to know, Sir, is whether it is enough for me to translate the first edition (for I started work on the copy of it which you gave to M. de Martel), or whether it would be better if I translated the other edition, and all the notes which you added to it.[8] To answer that point, I beg you to do me the honour of writing to me once more, before you go off to my Lord the Earl's country retreat.

Otherwise, Sir, to take up the other points in your letter: I accept your English translation of *De corpore* with the reply to Wallis,[9] but should like to receive it either via the Paris bookseller M. Lyonard[10] (whom M. Mylon tells me he has put in touch with you) or through some other way which, please, should not cost you anything. As for the other books I had asked for, including Wallis's works,[11] I shall wait to see them when I am over there in London.

Your comment that I should have two teachers, a writing master to read your letters, and an English master to understand your French, is wonderfully witty; I was delighted to see this sign of your good humour and lively imagination, signifying that you are in good health. I hope to recover my old happiness when I am with you.

The friend of mine who is writing to you is called M. Peleau; his father is a *conseiller* and *secrétaire* to the King. He knows Euclid, and has a smattering of algebra; and he is a philosopher in so far as your writings have made him one. But he does not know them well yet, and has doubts from which I extricate him quite easily. Besides that, he is a man of fine intellect, and a gentleman of honour.

A prophecy has been circulating here, presented, they say, by an Italian astrologer to the King of Sweden. I myself have spread the rumour that it was found in Rome, engraved in gothic script on the base of a statue which was excavated while I was there, representing Fortune crowning an already crowned head with three more crowns. Here is a copy of it; you add up the numerical letters, and they come to the exact dates. It is easy to make whatever number one wants appear in a sentence with a full meaning[(12)] if one puts things in a roundabout way; but the nice thing about this one is that the message is presented in the briefest possible terms. I am, Sir, for ever

Your most humble and obedient servant,
du Verdus

Bordeaux, 24 May 1656

[*postscript:*]
I give Poland to Sweden: 1656.[13]
I also give Constantinople: 1657.
Rome will be given to you, Charles: 1658.
Germany will be given to you, Charles: 1659.
The divided Austrians will elect a new Emperor at Frankfurt, and his name will be Charles the Sixth,[14] the Swede: 1661.[15]

287

[1] Neither of these letters seems to have survived.

[2] See Letter 81, general note.

[3] See Letter 78 nn. 34–7, and Letter 79.

[4] *pormettre MS.*

[5] An assembly of the Catholic clergy met in Paris between 1655 and 1657, and pressed for stricter government measures against Protestantism: its demands were satisfied to some extent by a royal declaration of July 1656, and a series of decrees-in-Council in Jan. 1657 (see Garrisson, *L'Édit de Nantes*, pp. 101, 120–2; Allier, *La Cabale des dévots*, pp. 313–16).

[6] See the Biographical Register, 'de Martel'.

[7] Du Verdus's translation was published as *Les Elemens de la politique* in 1660; Sorbière's had been published as *Les Fondemens de la politique* in 1649. 'Imperium' is the general title of the second part of the book (chs. V–XIV).

[8] These notes were added by Hobbes for the 2nd edn. (1647).

[9] *Of Body* and *Six Lessons*.

[10] Probably Frédéric Lyonard (1624–96), bookseller and printer, who had set up as a bookseller in the rue Saint-Jacques in Paris in 1653 (Lepreux, *Gallia typographica*, pp. 307–20).

[11] See n. 3.

[12] *ses MS.*

[13] Charles X of Sweden had invaded Poland in the summer of 1655, capturing Warsaw and Cracow in Oct. King John Casimir of Poland then fled the country; but he returned in Dec. 1655, raised an army, and waged war against the Swedish forces until 1660.

[14] i.e. the sixth Emperor Charles.

[15] This chronogram is typical of the many astrological predictions, millenarian chronologies, and interpretations of biblical prophecies which had been applied by Protestant writers to the accession and military actions of Charles X: see Göransson, *Den Europeiska Konfessionspolitikens upplösning*, pp. 76–89, 248–60, and Åkerman, *Queen Christina*, pp. 165–70.

LETTER 85   [18/] 28 MAY 1656

François Peleau to Hobbes, from Bordeaux

Chatsworth, Hobbes MSS, letter 20 (original).

Monsieur

Il y a dix ans que ie vous admire, et il me semble que c'est vn peu trop longtemps, vous faire vn secret de la deuotion, et du culte que iay pour vostre merite extraordinaire. Ie me declare doncq aujourdhuy vostre seruiteur et vostre disciple; et i'aurois tort, si ayant appris dans uos liures, que la Reconnoissance est vne Loy Naturelle, i'en manquois enuers vous quj m'aues appris cela, et tout ce que ie scay de Philosophie. vous voyes; Monsieur, que la passion, que iay pour vous

est vne chose tres iuste, et tres raisonnable, et puisque i'aime la uerité
au point que ie fais, Il me seroit mal aisé de ne vous aimer pas, Puisque
vous me l'aues rendue aimable, apres me l'auoir monstrée si Nüe, et si
belle dans vos escrits. Que ie voudrois de tout mon coeur estre a
Londres pour baiser, et embrasser [cette *deleted* >vostre] scauante
teste, qui a donné a nostre siecle tant d'auantage sur celuy d'aristote, et
[>pour] vous traitter de Miracle, et de diuin. En effect il n'y a pas
d'asses Magnifiques superlatifs, dont ie je uous regalasse, et [quj
deleted] tous seroient mesme beaucoup au dessoubs de vous. C'est de
vostre grace, Monsieur, que nous voyons clair, et sans Nuage, dans
l'obscurité des sciences. vostre traitté de Ciue m'a parû plus beau et
plus Nouueau la trentiesme fois que ie l'ay leu, que la premiere, (s'il se
peut), et les meditations que ie fais tous les iours sur vn si rare ouurage
sont le plus doux, et le plus vtile fruit de mes etudes; c'est dans cette
agreable lecture, que ie vous ay traitté mille fois de Maximum, vel
potius vnicum philosophum omnium temporum, cuj aetas nostra
veritatem, atque suam rationem debet. malo denique vnum Hobbium,
quam trecentos socratas.[1] vous estes cause, que ie me suis rendu a la
uerité, delaquelle ie m'estois reuolté en faueur des Anciens; vostre
section, De Corpore, est vn ouurage, qui viura, et sera leu, et admiré de
la plus esloignée posterité. Jay esté fort aise de uous voir grand
Geometre, et c'est par cette qualité principalement, que vous aues
touché mon Inclination. Jay ueu ce qu'ont fait Mrs Des-Cartes,
Gassend, Galilaee, Mersenne, Mais tout cela n'est rien, au prix de ce
que i'apprens tous les iours dans vostre liure, qui est tellement deuenu
le mien, que ie n'en lis presque aucun autre, il est luy seul toute ma
Bibliotheque, et toutes mes Remarques. pour vostre Léuiathan; ie suis
resolû d'apprendre la langue de vostre paÿs, affin de l'entendre, ie scay
que [i'apprendray *altered to* i'apprendrois] l'arabe, et le Turc, si vous
auies composé en ces langues. Jattens vostre section De Homine, auec
Impatience. quand sera-ce donc, Monsieur, que vous nous la
donneres, ayes ie vous prie soin de n'exercer pas trop longtemps nostre
[impatience *altered to* patience]. on m'a enuoyé d'Hollande vne
Apologie pour vous, De principiis iusti, et Decori,[2] imprimée il y a 5
ans; Dont Monsieur Duuerdus n'a pas encore oüy parler Je serois rauy
de scauoir le Jugement que vous faittes de cette piece. iay eu quelques
doutes sur quelques endroits de uostre ouurage Dv Citoyen, ie pretens
vous en faire part, et vous sacrifier mes erreurs et les mauuaises
pensées, que iay quelquefois contre uostre raison, c'est adire, contre la
Raison mesme. [>Mais] c'est estre importun pour la premiere fois que

ie uous escris, et vous voulant persuader de faire commerce auec moy, peut-estre ie uous persuaderay de le rompre auant l'auoir commencé. Mais Monsieur [>Duuerdus] quj s'est offert a moy, pour m'offrir à vous, vous asseurera, que ce n'est pas ma coustume d'ennuyer personne, et vous dira mieux, que moy, combien ie vous aime, et vous estime, et auec quelle ardeur ie vous demande vostre amitié, que ie croy obtenir, si pour cela il suffit d'estre comme ie suis

Monsieur
Vostre tres humble et tres obeissant seruiteur
Peleau

A Bordeaux ce 28 May 1656

[*postscript:*] S'il vous [plaît de]³ me faire response mon addresse est a— Peleau escuyer sieur de saint Genes aduocat en la cour, Rue du Chapelet, a Bordeaux

[*addressed:*] For Mʳ Hobbes at the Greene Dragon in Paules Churchierd. London

Translation of Letter 85

Sir,

I have admired you for ten years; and I think that is rather too long a time in which to keep my devotion and my worship of your extra-ordinary merit a secret from you. So today I declare myself your servant and your disciple; and, since I have learned from your books that gratitude is a Law of Nature, it would be wrong of me to show a lack of gratitude towards you, who have taught me that—and all the philosophy I know. You see, Sir, that my passionate devotion to you is something very just and reasonable; and since I love truth as much as I do, I could scarcely fail to love you. For it was you who made truth lovable for me, having shown her to me, so naked and so beautiful, in your writings. How I wish, with all my heart, that I could be in London, to kiss and embrace your learned head, which has given our age such an advantage over the age of Aristotle, and to treat you as something miraculous and divine! Indeed, there are not any superlatives magnificent enough for me to shower upon you—they would all be far below what you deserve. It is thanks to you, Sir, that we can look clearly, with unclouded vision, into the darkness of the sciences.

Your treatise *De cive* struck me as more fine and more novel the thirtieth time I read it than the first (if that is possible); and my daily meditations on such an outstanding work are the sweetest and most useful product of my studies. During these delightful readings I have thought of you a thousand times as 'the greatest, or rather the only philosopher of all ages, to whom our age is indebted for its knowledge of the truth, and the explanation of it. In short, I should rather have one Hobbes than three thousand Socrates.'[1]

It is because of you that I have turned to the truth, having rebelled against it in favour of the Ancients; your section *De corpore* is a work which will live and be read and admired by the most distant of future generations. I was extremely glad to see that you are a great geometer: it was in that capacity, above all, that you touched on my own interests. I have seen the works of Descartes, Gassendi, Galileo, and Mersenne, but they all amount to nothing in comparison with what I learn every day from your book, which I have so thoroughly assimilated that I hardly read anything else: it alone is my entire library, and the subject of all my commentaries. As for your *Leviathan*, I have decided to learn your language in order to understand it; I am sure that I would learn Arabic and Turkish if you had written in those languages. I await your section *De homine* with impatience. When will you give it to us, Sir? I beg you not to strain our patience for too long. I have received from Holland an Apology for you, *De principiis iusti et decori*,[2] which was printed five years ago; M. du Verdus had never heard of it before. I should be delighted to hear your opinion of this work.

I have had some queries on some passages in your *De cive*; I aspire to share them with you, to make you a sacrificial offering of my errors, and my ill-conceived ideas which I sometimes have in opposition to your reason—that is, in opposition to Reason itself. But it would be too importunate of me, in the first letter I send you, to try to persuade you to start a correspondence with me: this might perhaps persuade you to break off the correspondence before it had even started. But M. du Verdus (who has offered me his services, to help me offer my services to you) will assure you that I am not in the habit of annoying anyone. He will tell you better than I can how much I love you, and how highly I esteem you, and how ardently I beg you for your friendship—which I hope to obtain, if for that purpose it is sufficient to be, Sir, as I am,

Your most humble and obedient servant,
Peleau

Bordeaux, 28 May 1656

[*postscript:*] If you would like to[3] reply to me, my address is: Peleau, Esquire, sieur de S. Genes and court advocate, rue du Chapelet, Bordeaux.

[*addressed: see text*]

¹ Source unidentified.
² *Epistolica dissertatio de principiis iusti et decori, continens apologiam pro tractatu clarissimi Hobbaei, de cive* (Amsterdam, 1651), by Lambert van Velthuysen.
³ plaît de *or some such construction omitted in MS.*

LETTER 86   2 [/12] JULY 1656

Philip Tanny or Tandy to Hobbes, from London

BL MS Add. 32553, fos. 3–4 (original).
Printed in Mintz, *Hunting of Leviathan*, pp. 124–5.

Sʳ

I am soe poore, that I cannot fetch my things from the presse, I pray you Excuse mee that I send to you noe sooner: my troubles are many, as well as your occasions, Excuse mee withall, that I have put the transactions in printeing,¹ I confesse I had this thought, that by this meanes I should the more clearly gaine an answere from you to my Questions which are in short these

1. whether doe you not suppose that every man hath a will to doe, or to forbeare a thing, wrought in him by such strong influences which hee cannot resist

2. Whether doe you make freedome to consist eyther
   1. In the not beeing hindred in the doing of things which wee have a will to doe. or
   2ᵈˡʸ In the willingnes of the will freely chusing to doe that which it is wrought to will. or els
   3ᵈ In any third thing, which I yet cannot imagine,

I did propound a third question for your selfe to aske your selfe, but beeing satisfyed in it, I expect noe answere, Sʳ I am heartily yours, what ever you thinke of mee. Let mee heare from you, assoone as you can, and then I shall goe about that publique satisfaction to you, which I hope will not bee grievous. Excuse mee, in Every thing, which you suspect mee in, I am a riddle, and you may bee mistaken in mee. Doe as charitably as I shall doe with you, and doe desire God to doe with my owne soule. I am, S^r, whatever you surmise,

Your affectionate humble serv.^t
Philip Tanny

From my house in Stephens alley neare Derby house.
July. 2.^d 1656.

[*addressed:*] For my much honoured frend M^r [*word deleted*] Hobbes, the author of the Treatise of liberty and necessity, at the signe of the greene Dragon, in Paules Churchyard
   These

[*endorsed by James Wheldon:*] Mr Tanny July 2. 1656

---

[1] No work on this topic by Tanny is known to have been printed.

LETTER 87   8 [/18] JULY 1656

Henry Stubbe to Hobbes, from Oxford

BL MS Add. 32553, fos. 5–6 (original).
Printed in Nicastro, *Lettere*, p. 6.

S:^r

   My occasions haue so farre engaged mee upon seuerall busynesses of late, that I had not the least time to transcribe what I had translated of yor Leuiathan; which is a tasque so pleaseing (although so great withall, that nothing could uphold mee in the prosecution of so great a worke, but the sense I haue of yor approbation:) that I shall not relinquish it, untill I shall finde some discouragement, or inhibition from M:^r Hobbes. I had not sent you these imperfect sheets had not the importunity of this gentleman extorted them from mee, that so hee might haue the greater encouragem^t: to see you: an happynesse which I cannot suddainely hope for. S:^r I suppose M:^r Shelley[1] may haue told you my request unto you, but I shall now take the liberty to reinforce my petition; & it is that you would so farre hono^r mee as to permit mee to write in yor English philosophy[2] Ex dono authoris; which is a fauo^r nothing can embolden mee to aske, but ye remembrance of yor goodnesse. I haue reade it all ouer, & if I could contribute any thing by my suffrage (or others here who haue perused yor lessons)³ I should not sticke to say it were good. I shall finish ye 8 chap: before I send you any more; in ye meane while if I can any way serue you, [or]⁴ if that proposition I acquainted M:^r Shelley with please, thinke there is no man so desirous to kisse yor hands, or so ready to approue himselfe

S:^r
Yo^r most humble seruito^r
Henry Stubbe

Oxon: July: 8. 1656.

[*addressed:*] These For his euer honoured Friend M:^r Hobbes at ye Blackmore's head in Fetterlane⁵ London.

[*endorsed by James Wheldon:*] Mr Stubb July 8 1656.

¹ Anthony Shelley (b. 1572 or 1573), of a gentry family in Sussex, matriculated at Merton College, Oxford (1589), proceeded BA from St Alban Hall (1593), and married a daughter of Cotton, Bishop of Salisbury (see Foster).
² *Of Body*.
³ *Six Lessons*.
⁴ of *MS*.
⁵ Aubrey later recorded that in the 1650s Hobbes 'lived most part in London, in Fetter lane': *ABL* i, p. 337.

LETTER 88   [late JULY 1656]

Edmund Waller to Hobbes, [from London]

Huntington Library MS HM 22641 (original).
Printed in Hardacre, 'A Letter from Edmund Waller', pp. 431–3.

Sir

On Saterday last I was att y^r Lodging by 9 a clocke in the morning (hauing ben by some vrgent occasions preuented in my intention to wayt on you the day before) but came a little too late to tell [>you] what I hope you will admitt this to doe, That I esteeme y^r Booke¹ not only as a present of the best kinde (preferring wth soloman wisdome to any other treasure) but as the best of that kinde; Had I gonn (as by this tyme I had donn) to the greene-dragone² to fetch it, I could not haue written *ex dono Authoris* vpon it, as a wittnes to posterity that I was not only in y^r

fauor but in y^r esteeme too, (gifts being proportioned to the vse & inclination of the receauer) and that wch bought would haue ben my cheifest delight only, is now that & my honor too: (S^r) one shewed mee this Morning Dr Lucys censure vpon y^r Leuiathan;[3] he subscribes himself in his Epistle to the reader William Pike w^ch (as his frend tels me) is because his name in Latine is Lucius,[4] wherein he confirms what he is offended wth you for obseruing, that a man must haue something of a scoller to bee a verier coxcomb then ordinary, for what English man that had not dabled in latine would haue changed so good a name as Lucy for that of a fish, besides it is ominous that he will proue but a pike to a leuiathan, a narrowe riuer fish to one wch deserues the whole ocean for his theater; all that I obserued in the preface of this pickrill, was, that he says y^r doctrine takes vs country-gentlemen &c:[5] sure, if wisdome comes by leasure, we may possibly be as good iudges of philosophy as country-parsons are, all whose tyme is spent in saluting those wch come into the world att gossipings,[6] takeing leaue of those that goe out of it att funerals, & vexing those that stay in it with longwinded harangs; for Wallis & his fellowe[7] (you haue handeled them so well already) that I will say nothing of them, [beside *deleted*] for if I should say [what *deleted*] all I approue in you or finde ridiculous in your adversarys I should requite y^r booke wth another; confident I am that all thay write will neuer be read ouer once, nor printed twise, [*word deleted* > so unlucky are thay to prouoake you]

> —Che reggese, & se gouerna
> Qual si gouerna, & regge l'huom, ch'é certo
> Con i posteri hauer pratica eterna;[8]
>
> Who in this Age behaue yourself, & walke,
> As one of whom posterity must talke;

W^th well applying & ill translating of wch verses, I conclude the first, & come now to the second part of what I should haue troubled you wth if I had found you in your Lodging, viz: to charge you wth my most humble seruise to the noble Lord wth whom you are,[9] as also wth my acknowledgment of the kinde message I lately receaued from his Lo^p: Letting him knowe that because I could write nothing safely wch he might not finde in print, I went to y^r Lodging perposely to haue troubled you wth my coniectures of what is like to to [*sic*] befall vs in order to satisfy his Lo^ps curiosity who honored me wth his commands therin.

Here is much talke of change both of Councills & of Councillors,[10] and both is beleued, but what or who will be next is very incertayn, & this incertenty proceeds not so much from secrecy as from irresolution, for rowling our selues vpon prouidence (as formerly) many things haue ben debated, but perhaps no one thing yet absolutely intended To me it seems that his Highnes (who sees a good way before him) had layd [longe *deleted* > sometyme] since a perfect foundation of Gouernment, I mean by the Ma: Gen^{s11} reducing vs to prouences & ruling vs by those prouincials wth the newe Leuied Army[12] &c: but fayling of the good succes hoped for abroad,[13] & these arrears & want of Mony att home,[14] may perhaps giue occasion & oportunity to such as are enemys to a settlement to retard & shocke his desseins: The generall voyse att present goes for a selected (not an elected) Parlmt[15] & that we shall very shortly see something donn therein, in the mean tyme desiring pardon for this taedious scribling (as if I were infected wth the stile of y^r frends Lucy and Wallis) I rest

> y^r humble & obliged seruant
> Waller

This letter can be dated fairly accurately on internal grounds. The fact that Waller had just received the gift of a copy of *Of Body* and *Six Lessons* suggests a date soon after publication of that volume; the dedicatory epistle of *Six Lessons* is dated 10 [/20] June; an unnamed correspondent of John Wallis mentioned in a letter of 16 [/26] June that he had just bought a copy (Wallis, *Hobbiani puncti dispunctio*, p. 11); and the earliest dated reference in Hobbes's correspondence to the receipt of a printed copy is Stubbe's letter of 8 [/18] July (Letter 87), also thanking Hobbes for the gift of a copy. And from the way in which Waller writes here about Lucy's *Examinations* (offering it as the latest news and presuming that Hobbes could not yet have seen a copy of it himself), we may assume that this letter was written very soon after the printing of that book—of which Thomason received a copy on 21 [/31] July 1656 (Fortescue (ed.), *Catalogue*, ii, p. 155).

[1] The volume consisting of *Of Body* and *Six Lessons*: identifiable here by the reference later in this letter to 'Wallis & his fellowe' and the remark that 'if I should say all I approue in you or find ridiculous in your adversarys I should requite y^r booke wth another'.

[2] Andrew Crooke's shop in St Paul's churchyard.

[3] 'William Pike', *Examinations, Censures and Confutations of Divers Errours in the two first Chapters of Mr. Hobbes his Leviathan* (1656). 'William Pike' was the pseudonym of William Lucy (1594–1677), formerly rector of the parish of Burghclere, Hants (from which he had been sequestered by the parliamentary authorities); he became Bishop of St David's at the Restoration.

[4] 'Lucius' is a word used by Ausonius for a type of fish, possibly the pike.

[5] 'Pike', *Examinations*, epistle to the reader: 'this book I find admir'd by many

Gentlemen'; 'Gentlemen, meeting with new opinions, and some shew of reason for them, are by that means furnished the next table-meeting to surprize a poor Country-Parson, such as I' (sig. A3ᵛ).

⁶ = christenings (*OED* gossiping 1).

⁷ John Wallis and Seth Ward (see Letter 75 nn. 7–8), to whom Hobbes replied in his *Six Lessons*.

⁸ Source unidentified.

⁹ Probably the third Earl of Devonshire; but possibly the Earl of Elgin or some other relation of the dowager Countess of Devonshire at Roehampton.

¹⁰ The Council was a body consisting of 13–21 men, in principle independent of Cromwell but in practice subordinate to him, set up under the 'Instrument of Government' which had become the basis of the constitution after the abdication of Parliament in Dec. 1653. In late May/early June 1656 the Major-Generals were summoned to London to consult with the members of the Council over how best to respond to popular calls for a new Parliament. 'So unusual a stir in the regions of government gave rise to the belief that important changes were at hand' (Gardiner, *History of the Commonwealth*, iv, p. 253). Cromwell acceded to demands for a new Parliament, but only on condition that no member be allowed to take his seat without a certificate from the Council. On 26 June [/6 July] it was made known that writs for the election would soon be sent out (ibid., iv, p. 256).

¹¹ The system of government by eleven Major-Generals in England and Wales had been instituted by Cromwell ('his Highnes') in Oct. 1655.

¹² The new militia which the eleven Major-Generals commanded.

¹³ This probably refers to the disastrous attempt at an invasion of Hispaniola in Apr.–May 1655.

¹⁴ The government's financial position was deteriorating rapidly. At the end of 1655 it had accumulated a debt of £230,000 (Gardiner, *History of the Commonwealth*, iv, p. 252). By Oct. 1656 the government's debts, including arrears to the Army and Navy, were estimated at between £800,000 and £900,000 (Ashley, *Financial and Commercial Policy*, p. 45, cited in Hardacre, 'A Letter from Edmund Waller', p. 433).

¹⁵ See above, n. 10.

LETTER 89   [17/] 27 AUGUST 1656

François du Verdus to Hobbes, from Bordeaux

Chatsworth, Hobbes MSS, letter 22 (original).

Monsieur,

Je dois bien vous remerçier: premierement pour les liures que vous m'enuoyés,¹ que je reçeuray sans doute Mʳ Mylon étant ponctuël, et mon amy; et en second lieu pour le conseil que vous me donnés touchant mes affaires. Je le suyuray Monsieur, s'il plait a Dieu, et me dégageray tot ou tard. fata viam inuenient, et comme j'espére aussi le chemin d'aller a vous. Il me tarde bien que cela ne soit et mesmement pour rendre mes respects a Monsieur le Comte de Deuonsire Vostre bon Patron. J'ay de la Vénération pour ce Seigneur, que quand i'imprimeray Vos Oeuures en françois, ie ne manqueray pas d'y mettre [>toutes] vos Épitres Dédicatoires a luy, comme la miene a vous de uostre Liure du Corps. Que j'aurois de joye de vous les lire auparauant! mais ie uois une disposition d'affaires que peut estre seray-j'obligé d'aller a Paris où Mr Bourdelot[2] me conuie, ce grand homme, premier Médecin de la Sérenissime Reyne de Suëde. Cepandant Monsieur je fais deux choses: pour me dégager d'icy j'imprime une Rélation de toutes mes affaires,[3] que ie vous prie de trouuer bon que je vous enuoye quand ie l'auray pour estre d'autant mieux connu de Monsieur le Comte: et pour m'engager a vous encore dauantage ie lis vos Oeuures plus que jamais. Les belles choses que j'ay trouuées dans vostre Leuiathan, des Anges, du Royaume de Dieu, de sa Parole, de celle des Prophetes et de leurs Miracles! j'auois bien les Principes de cela, que j'auois apris dans vostre Liure de Ciue: mais de remarquer tant de choses, et les ranger si bien, il n'y auoit que vous qui le peut. Sans mentir, j'ayme bien ce Liure! Et j'ay une extreme joye de uoyr comme il m'a acheué de remplir de vostre esprit! J'en dis quelque chose de temps en temps a Mr Peleau, qui l'ayme come il uous dit dans sa premiere lettre qu'il aymoit vostre Citoyen,[4] car ce qu'il fait par cette seconde lettre,[5] je croy que c'est pour se diuertir; Et en effect quand j'auray ueu vos sentimens sur ses objections, je vous écriray la response que je luy fis. Mais quand aurons nous le Traité de l'homme? Mr Bourdelot me le demande dans toutes ses lettres; Et me dit que leurs gens en sont tout a fait inquiets. Au nom de Dieu Monsieur ne nous le réfuzés pas long temps. Cepandant Et [longtemps *altered to* longues années] aprés cela, Je prie Dieu qu'il vous conserue que vous jouissiés auec joye du fruit de vos trauaux, de l'honneur et de cette grande réputation que vous vous estes acquise a si bon Titre. Je suis de toute mon Ame

Monsieur
Vostre tres humble et tres obeissant seruiteur
duuerdus

A Bourdeaux le 27e Aout 1656

[*addressed:*] For Mr Hobbes at the Greene Dragon in Paules Church-yerd London [*endorsed by James Wheldon:*] Mon.ʳ du Verdus. [Oct. *altered to* Augᵗ] 27ᵗʰ 1656

Translation of Letter 89

Sir,

I really must thank you: first for the books which you are sending me,[1] and which I shall doubtless receive (as M. Mylon is punctilious, and a friend of mine); and secondly for the advice which you give me about my affairs. God willing, I shall follow it, Sir, and shall extricate myself sooner or later. 'The fates find a way'—and, I hope, the way that leads to you. I am longing to visit you, also in order to pay my respects to your good patron, the Earl of Devonshire. I feel such veneration for this Lord that, when I print your works in French, I shall not fail to include all your dedicatory epistles to him, just as I shall include my Epistle dedicating my translation of your *De corpore* to you. What joy it will give me to read them to you beforehand! But my state of affairs is such, I see, that I may perhaps have to go to Paris, where I have an invitation from M. Bourdelot,[2] that great man, the chief physician to the Queen of Sweden.

However, Sir, I am doing two things: to extricate myself from here I am printing an Account of all my affairs,[3] of which I beg you to permit me to send you a copy, when I have one, to make myself better known to the Earl; and, to commit myself even more closely to you, I am reading your works more than ever before. What fine things I have found in your *Leviathan*, concerning angels, the Kingdom of God, the Word of God, the word of the Prophets, and their miracles! I had a good grasp of the principles of all that, having learned them from your book *De cive*; but only you could have noticed so many things, and arranged them so well. I am not lying when I say that I am in love with this book. And it gives me great joy to see how it has completed the process of inspiring me with your spirit. I talk about it from time to time with M. Peleau, who likes it as much as he liked your *De cive* (as he told you in his first letter);[4] for what he is doing in this second letter[5] is only done, I think, to amuse himself. Indeed, when I have seen your opinions on his objections, I shall write and tell you the reply I made to them.

But when shall we receive your treatise *De homine*? M. Bourdelot asks me for it in all his letters, and tells me that their learned men are all extremely anxious to see it. In the name of God, Sir, do not deny it to us for long. However, I pray that God will preserve you for long years after that, and that you may happily enjoy the fruit of your labours, the honour and the great reputation which you have so justly acquired. I am, Sir, with all my soul,

Your most humble and obedient servant,
du Verdus

Bordeaux, 27 August 1656

[*addressed: see text*]

It seems that Hobbes's reply to this letter miscarried. On 4/14 Oct. 1656 du Verdus wrote to Andrew Crooke, saying that he had 'written several times to the most distinguished Thomas Hobbes, without receiving any reply' ('Quod pluriès Clarissimo Thomae Hobbio scripserim, nec acceperim responsi quicquam'), and asking for news of Hobbes and of the printing of *De homine* (Chatsworth, Hobbes MSS, letter 23).

¹ See Letter 78 nn. 34–7.
² See Letter 78 n. 21.
³ No copy of this printed account has yet been found.
⁴ Letter 85.
⁵ Du Verdus apparently refers to Letter 90, having read it in draft.

LETTER 90   18/28 AUGUST 1656

François Peleau to Hobbes, from Bordeaux

Letter and enclosure: Chatsworth, Hobbes MSS, letter 21 (original).

Monsieur,

Vostre Ciuilité m'a tout a fait acquis a vous, et ie suis vne des choses dont vous Pouues le mieux Disposer; autrefois ie m'auöuois a M.ʳ Hobbes par les sentimens, et par les opinions; Presentement ie suis a luy par le coeur, et [il vous agreera *altered to* vous agreeres] bien que ie vous [marque *deleted*] fasse l'amour dans toutes [>mes lettres], Puisque ie ne scaurois traitter auec vous qu'auec tendresse. vostre connoissance a esté longtemps ma plus haute, et derniere curiosité, a cette heure que ie la tiens des bons offices de M.ʳ Dvuerdus, Il faut que vostre amitié acheue de me rendre heureux, Puisque ie suis le Rival tres Jaloux de mon amy dans la Passion qu'il a pour vous. Et pour ne vous dissimuler pas, iay vouleu faire le fin auec vous, vous faisant accroire que ie n'acquiessois pas a la force de vos demonstrations, et que ie trouue lieu de douter sur quelques endroits de vos escrits; mais cela ne vous surprendra pas, vous qui scaues que l'amour a d'estranges finesses, qu'il ruse, qu'il fourbe, et qu'il se sert mesme de stratageme pour mieux acquerir vne Revanche de Bonne volonté et d'estime; enfin Monsieur, Pour faire court, comme on met en oeuure les pretextes Pour faire la guerre, Je les ay uoulu aussy mettre en vsage, pour commencer vne Amitié auec vous. Non pas que ie ne vous fasse uoir par cette occasion quelques petits doutes, que iay eus, affin [de *deleted*] que [>vous] me tenies pour le moins pour homme de parole; mais ce seront des erreurs que iay condamnées, plustost que des verités [que ie *deleted*] aux quelles ie veuille m'attacher; car ie scay qu'il mest plus aisé de me tromper qu'a vous mesme, et que [ie *deleted*] n'ayant pas l'esprit si clairuoyant que le vostre, ce seroit mal a propos que ie Presumerois pouuoir obseruer dans vos escrits, des Choses que vous n'y aues pas veües; ou s'il faut parler comme ie dois, les doutes que ie vous [fais *deleted*] propose, [sont *deleted*] font mieux cognoistre mon insuffisance, et mon deffaut de raison, qu'ils ne vous accuseront d'aucune proposition auancée auec temerité. Mais pour reuenir au sujet de nostre Nouuelle connoissance Je pretens, Monsieur, que cette lettre serue d'vn Traitté D'amitié, et d'Articles de paix entre vous, et moy; et puisque vous m'aues demandé que ie vous accordasse vn Postulatum, qui est le plus raisonnable du Monde, [>Je] vous [>ay] satisfait la dessus, et bien loing de donner plus d'incommodité à vostre main, qu'elle n'en a desia, ie [soustiens *deleted*] Consens, que bien loing de prendre la peine de m'escrire, vous uous seruies, d'vn morceau de papier signé de vostre main, ou si vous ne voules, marqué seulement de l'impression de vostre cachet; ou bien si ces deux moyens ne vous plaisent pas, ie me contenteray que vous uous seruies de l'ancienne formule, *si vales, Benè est; ego quidem valeo*,[1] en mettant en titre. *Hobbius Pellaeo*. Et a la fin, Datum Londini, ou d'ailleurs ou vous seres. car ie serois tout a fait fasché de donner tant soit peu de peine a vostre Ciuilité. vostre Postulatum, est doncq plus qu'accordé, Puisque outre celuy[>-la], ie vous en accorde d'autres, Parmy lesquels vous pourres choisir. Mais puisque nous ne sommes encore qu'aux Elemens de nostre amitié, iay [des *deleted* >plusieurs] postulata,[2] que ie vous prie de maccorder, le premier que ie vous escriue souuent mesme sans suiet, et sans occasion, sans d'autre dessein que de satisfaire l'inclination que iay pour vous, et vous demander des Nouuelles de vostre santé, de vos estudes, de la Reputation de vos escrits, et de ce qui arriue de iour à autre, dans le monde touchant l'enuie[3] que l'on vous porte, et la sublimité de vostre doctrine, ie vous fairay part aussy des

Nouuelles de mes occupations, et de mille petites choses, dont les gens de lettres ont accoustumé de s'entretenir; et vous prie de me permettre de [vous escri *deleted*] faire mes lettres petites, et longues selon qu'il sera à propos; Ces postulata ne sont pas a mon auis impossibles, il est vray que si vous me les accordés, le public en souffrira, puisque i'occuperay vne partie de vostre loisir, à lire mes lettres, ou à y respondre. Mais ie vous prie de reseruer cette lecture et vos Responses aux heures de Relasche, que nous appellons en francois, heures perdües. ie vous prieray aussy, [>quand i'auray des doutes,] de construire quelque Probleme, que ie vous proposeray, et sur tout celuy-cy, que vous soudres mieux que Nostre Vieta;[4] Nullum non problema soluere; outre celuy là, ie vous en propose presentement vn autre, que ie vous proposeray toutes les fois que ie vous escriray, a scauoir Me Diligere, aequè ac ego te Diligo. il y a trop de vanité pour moy dans ce probleme, car ie scay bien que ie ne merite pas d'estre aimé de vous à mesme mesure, puisque vostre merite ne souffre Point de comparaison. ce sont là les conditions de nostre alliance; sans conter que Je vous ser-uiray, et vous rendray toutes sorte de bons offices, et iray, iusques a la plus Heroique Pieté, quand il sera question de vous obliger. Je vous enuoye mes doutes dans vne fueille a part, incluse dans cette lettre, et suis autant qu'on peut estre

Monsieur
Vostre tres humble, tres obligé et tres obeissant seruiteur
Peleau

A Bordeaux ce 18/28 Aoust 1656

[*postscript:*] Si ie n'estois extrememement occupé apres quelques ouurages, et quelques traductions en nostre langue,[5] ie vous eusse enuoyé mes doutes dans vne Epistre latine. car iay honte de traitter auec vous en autre langue, qu'en celle des sciences; mais vous-vous contenteres s'il vous plaist de mon francois, et de mes petits doutes, qui ne sont [nuls ?] rien, et que ie vous enuoye seulement pour vous tenir parole. iay grande impatience de voir vostre [derniere *deleted*] section de homine, et la Response au Docteur Walis[6] car on m'a dit que vous les acheueries bientost.

[*endorsed by James Wheldon:*] Mons.ʳ Peleau Aug. 16 1656

[*enclosed:*]

Monsieur

Me voicy en estat de vous estre importun, a force de vouloir tirer esclaircissement sur des doutes, quj n'en valent pas la peine. Je vous prie prendre patience, s'ils sont trop aisés à resoudre, car ie ne pense pas qu'on vous en puisse proposer, que de ceux-là; puisque vostre Doctrine est si asseurée, et si veritable. Je vous diray doncq.

Premierem.t au .1. Art. du .1. Chap. de la Liberté,[7] vous condamnés cette definition de l'homme: ζῶον πολιτικὸν, [siue *deleted*] ou comme vous traduises ces deux mots. *Animal aptum natum ad societatem.* et dans l'annotation du mesme chap. vous taches de confirmer vostre opinion soustenant que, *ad societatem homo aptus, non naturâ, sed disciplinâ factus est.*[8]

Et moy. Monsieur. Je pretens prouuer tout le contraire, a scauoir, que cette definition de ζῶον πολιτικὸν est tres bonne, et que vous la condamnes mal a propos; [et *deleted*] pretendant vous demonstrer sans aucun Paralogisme; (si ie ne me trompe, comme Il se peut faire fort aisément) que l'homme est vn Animal nay propre pour la societe ciuile, et que *nullâ disciplinâ, aut experientiâ eruditur ad societatem, nullumque ad hoc, habet ducem, et Magistrum, praeter ipsam Naturam.* ce que ie prouue ainsy.

N'est-il pas vray. *Monsieur*, que le desir de se conseruer est commun a tout homme, et que ce *metus mutuus*,[9] qui a porté les hommes à s'vnir entre eux en vn corps politique, vient de cette inclination Naturelle, que nous auons pour nostre conseruation; ce que ie prouue. puisque iay ce desir naturel de ma conseruation, par consequent. *Conscius mihi sum, me mihi esse amicissimum*; ie ne puis pas dire la mesme chose des autres hommes, parceque ie ne scay pas ce qui se passe dans leur coeur, et dans leur volonté; ne les ayant pas encore pratiqués. de sorteque ie ne scay pas s'ils me sont amis, ou ennemis, puisqu'ils ne m'en ont encore donné aucune marque; mais parceque ie ne les connois pas si bien, que ie me connois moy mesme, iay raison de me défier d'eux, et de les tenir pour suspects; c'est ce que i'appelle le *mutuus metus*, que cette defiance que nous auons les vns des autres. doncq Il est euident, que i'ay ce [mutuus *deleted*] metus, sans [faire *deleted*] auoir fait aucune experience de la malice, ny de l'égalité des hommes; et par consequent, iay cette crainte, cette precaution Naturellem.t, aussy bien que le desir de me conseruer; et [les *deleted*] on doit dire la mesme chose de chaque homme en particulier, qu'il aura ce Metus naturellement comme moy. mais vous aues prouué au mesme chap. que *Magnarum, et Diuturnarum societatum originem esse a mutuo metu.*[10] Doncques puisque *habemus naturaliter mutuum metum, siue prospectum futuri mali*,[11] cette Preuoyance Naturelle nous rend propres à la societé Naturellement; puisque ayant ce Metus mutuus naturellement, il paroist que nous sommes sages, et prudens Naturellement; qui sont deux qualités, qui nous rendent naturellement propres, et nés pour la societé ciuile. *Ergo. homo est Animal aptum natum ad societatem; quod erat Demonstrandum*. Ce qui pourroit affoiblir cette demonstration. c'est ce que vous dites dans l'Annotation du Mesme Chap. *omnes Homines (cum sint nati infantes) ad societatem [>ineptos] natos esse manifestum est*.[12] Je scay bien, que les enfans, et les fous, ne sont pas propres a la societé, en tant qu'enfans, et en tant que fous, a cause que les premiers, estant trop Jeunes, n'ont pas la raison asses forte, pour auoir la preuoyance & le *mutuus metus*. et que les autres ayant la raison empeschée par leur folie, agissent en aveugles, et en estourdis. Mais non obstant cela, Il ne faut pas laisser de definir l'homme. *Animal aptum natum ad societatem*. car vous scaues, par exemple, que quand on definit lhomme *animal Rationale*, les fous, ny les enfans ne peuuent pas auoir part à cette Definition si l'on entend parler de *Rationale actu*.[13] et cependant cette definition à tousiours esté receüe, et il est tousjours vray de dire que *Homo est animal Rationale*, quoyque les enfans, et les fous ne puissent estre compris à la Rigueur dans cette definition. Monsieur. Je vous prie de m'esclaircir là dessus, ie ne croiray pourtant, que ce que vous voudres, que ie croye.

En second lieu. en l'art. 3. du .1. Chap. de la liberté, vous pretendes prouuer, que tous les hommes dans l'estat de Nature sont égaux entre eux, et que l'Inegalité que nous voyons maintenant, vient de la loy Ciuile. a cause (dites-vous) *aequales sunt, qui aequalia contra se inuicem possunt, at qui Maxima possunt, nimirum occidere, aequalia possunt* ergò &c.[14]

Et Je vous soustiens, que [>tous] les hommes, *non possunt contra se inuicem aequalia, nec maxima, nimirum occidere nec vi, nec astu*.

Nest-il pas vray. Monsieur, que les Malades, les fous, les sots, les Pigmées, les Poltrons, qui sont poltrons *in gradu summo timiditatis*, iusques-là, qu'ils n'oseroient tuër leurs ennemis en ayant l'occa-sion, [non pas mesme les trouuans Endormis, ou Agonisants, sans force, et sans ruse pour se deffendre, ils n'oseroient les toucher, ny approcher d'eux, quand ils auroient la plus grande volonté de leur faire du Mal. *deleted*] Enfin tous ces gens la, empeschent qu'on puisse dire auec Verité, que tous les hommes sont égaux entre eux. Dailleurs. Les hommes ne peuuent estre égaux entre eux, que selon l'égalité des facultés de la nature humaine. Mais tous les hommes n'ont pas également de la force, de l'esperience, de la Raison, de la passion;[15]

En Troisiesme lieu . au Chap. de Regno Patrimonialj, art. 8; et au Chap. De Regno Dej per Naturam. art. 9. vous definisses l'honeur *alienae potentiae aestimatio*;[16] et au Chap. de Regno Patrimon. art. 8. vous voules qu'vn fils emancipé honore moins son pere, qu'auant l'émancipation, parceque son pere n'a plus le pouuoir qu'il auoit sur luy. Pour moy ie ne suis pas de cet auis.

Parceque cette Definition de l'honeur, n'est pas legitime; car s'il estoit vray que nous n'honorons, que ceux que Nous croyons puissants, et dont nous estimons la puissance; Il s'en suiuroit que Nous honorerions les hommes, plus ou moins; selon que Nous auons plus, ou moins d'esperance, et de crainte. Mais pourtant vous scaues, que nous auons du Respect pour des gens, de qui Nous n'esperons, ny ne craignons rien. Nous honorons la vertu, mesme quand elle est malheureuse, et qu'estant opprimée par la fortune, elle ne nous peut faire, ny mal, ny bien. Nous honorons les gens d'esprit, les vieillards, et les personnes Illustres, que nous n'auons iamais veües, et que nous ne connoissons que par reputation. Nous honorons [>souuent] les gens Beaux et Bien faits de leur personne, sans estre cogneus d'eux.

Addition
J'auois oublié d'adjouster, [>a la .1. objection] a la definition de l'homme, ces mots; *ratione sui, non sociorum, ob mutuum metum.* Desorteque je definis l'homme ainsy. *Animal natum aptum ad societatem, ratione suj, non sociorum, ob mutuum metum*.

Translation of Letter 90

Sir,

Your civility has completely won me over, and I am one of the things that are most fully yours to command. In the past I declared that I belonged to Mr Hobbes in my judgements and opinions; now I belong to him in my heart. And you will not mind at all if I deal with you like a lover in all my letters, since I could not deal with you in any way except tenderly. Your acquaintance has long been the thing I most yearned for, and now that I have it, through the good offices of M. du Verdus, your friendship must complete my happiness, since I am my friend's very jealous rival in that passion which he has for you. Not to deceive you, I wanted to have a battle of wits with you, making you think that I did not accept the cogency of your demonstrations, and that I found reasons for objecting to some passages in your writings. But that will not surprise you, you who know that love uses strange little tricks to deceive and cheat, and that it even uses stratagems to acquire more goodwill and esteem from the loved one. Finally, Sir, to be brief, just as one uses pretexts to go to war, I too wanted to use pretexts to begin a friendship with you. It is not that I did not want to take this opportunity to show you a few small objections which I had had, so that you might at least believe me to be a man of my word. But they are errors which I have condemned, rather than truths which I want to maintain; since I know that it is easier for me to make mistakes than for you, and that, not having such a penetrating intellect as you, it would be improper for me to presume to be able to detect things in your writings which you had not seen yourself. Or, to put it as I should, the objections which I am presenting to you are intended rather to make known my own inadequacy and lack of reason, than to accuse you of rashness in any of your pronouncements.

But to return to the subject of our new acquaintance: I propose, Sir, that this letter should serve as a Treaty of Friendship, and as Articles of Peace between you and me. And since you asked me to grant you one requirement ['postulatum'], which is the most reasonable thing in the world, I have satisfied you on that point; far from causing more inconvenience to your hand than it already suffers, I agree that, far from taking the trouble to write to me, you should make use of a piece of paper bearing your signature—or, if you wish, one merely stamped with your seal. Or, if you dislike both of those methods, I shall be content if you make use of the old formula, 'if you are well, that is good; at any rate, I am well',[1] under the heading 'Hobbes to Peleau', and with 'sent from London' (or wherever you are) at the foot. For I should be very upset to put your civility to any trouble, even as little as that.

So your requirement is more than granted, seeing that, besides that one, I grant you others, from which you can take your choice. But since we are still only at the 'Elements' stage of our friendship, I have several postulates[2] which I beg you to grant me. The first is that I may write to you often, even if I have no occasion to do so and no topic for my letter, with no other purpose except to satisfy my longing for you, to ask for news of your health, your studies, the reputation of your writings, and of whatever happens in the world, from day to day, to do with the envy[3] which people have for you and the sublimity of your teachings. I shall also give you news of what I am doing, and of the thousand little things which men of letters usually discuss. And I beg you to let me make my letters short or long, according to the occasion.

These postulates are not impossible, I think. It is true that if you grant them, the public will suffer, because I shall be taking up some of your free time in reading my letters or replying to them. But I beg you to reserve that reading and replying for the times when you are not at work, what we call in French 'heures perdues' ['lost time']. I shall also ask you, when I have objections, to work out a certain problem which I shall send you—and above all this one, which you will solve better than our Viète:[4] 'not to solve any problem'. Apart from that, I shall now propose another one, which I shall propose every time I write to you, namely, 'to love me as much as I love you'. There is too much vanity on my part in that problem, for I know well that I do not deserve to be loved by you to the same extent, since your merit brooks no comparison. Those are the conditions of our alliance, leaving aside the fact that I shall serve you, and do you all kinds of good offices, and shall undertake even the most heroic acts of loyalty when it is a matter of obliging you. I am sending you my objections on a separate sheet, enclosed in this letter; and I am, Sir, as much as anyone can be,

Your most humble, obliged, and obedient servant,
Peleau

Bordeaux, 18/28 August 1656

[*postscript:*] If I had not been extremely busy with certain works and certain translations in our language,[5] I would have sent you my objections in a letter in Latin. For I am ashamed to deal with you in any other language than the language of the sciences. But please be content with my French, and with my little objections, which amount to nothing, and which I am sending to you only to fulfil my promise. I am very impatient to see your *De homine*, and your reply to Dr Wallis,[6] having been told that you would finish them soon.

Translation of enclosure to Letter 90

Sir,

Here I am, being importunate in wanting you to clear up some objections, which are not worth the effort. Please be patient if they are of the kind that are too easy to solve, for I think that is the only kind that one can put to you, since your teachings are so certain and true. So let me put them as follows.

Firstly: in the first section of the first chapter 'of Liberty',[7] you condemn the definition of man as a 'political animal', or, as you translate those two words from the Greek, 'a Creature born fit for Society'. And in the note to the same chapter you try to confirm your judgement, maintaining that 'Man is made fit for Society not by Nature, but by Education.'[8] But I claim, Sir, that I can prove the exact opposite, namely that that definition, 'political animal', is perfectly good, and that you are wrong to condemn it. For I claim that I can demonstrate, without any paralogism (assuming I am not mistaken, as one easily can be) that man is an animal that is born suited to civil society, and that no teaching or experience prepares him for society, and no master or leader brings him to it, except Nature herself. Which I prove as follows.

It is true, Sir, is it not, that the desire for self-preservation is common to all men, and that this 'mutual fear'[9], which made people unite together in one body politic, arises from this natural desire for self-preservation. Here is how I prove that. Because I have this natural desire for self-preservation, it follows that I am aware of the fact that I am my own best friend; I cannot say the same of other people, because I do not know what is going on in their hearts or wills, not having associated with them yet. So I do not know whether they are my friends or enemies, since they have not yet given me any way of telling. But because I know them less well than I know myself, I have good reason to mistrust them and regard them as suspect; and that mutual mistrust is what I call 'mutual fear'. It is clear, then, that I have this fear without having had any experience either of the malice of other men, or of their equality. It follows that I have this fear and cautiousness naturally, just as much as I have the desire to preserve myself. And the same must be said of every man individually, each of whom will have this fear naturally, as I do. But in the same chapter you have proved that 'the Originall of all great, and lasting Societies consisted [. . .] in the mutual fear they had of each other'.[10] Therefore, since we naturally have this mutual fear, or 'foresight of future evil'[11], this natural foresight makes us naturally suited to society; since, having this mutual fear naturally, it seems that we are naturally wise and prudent—those being two qualities which make us naturally suited and born for civil society. Ergo 'Man is a Creature born fit for Society', QED.

The thing which might undermine this demonstration is the point you make in your note to the same chapter: 'Manifest therefore it is, that all men, because they are born in Infancy, are born unapt for Society.'[12] I fully realize that children and madmen are not suited to society, in so far as they are children and in so far as they are madmen, because the former, being too young, do not reason strongly enough to attain the foresight and mutual fear, and because the latter's reason is impaired by their madness, so that they behave giddily or blindly. All the same, it is not necessary to abandon the definition of man as 'a Creature born fit for Society'. For as you know, when (for example) one defines man as 'a rational animal', neither madmen nor children come under this definition, if one means 'actually rational'.[13] Nevertheless, this definition has always been accepted; and it is still true to say that 'man is a rational animal', even though children and madmen cannot be included, strictly speaking, under this definition. Sir, please clear up this point; despite my objection, I shall only believe what you tell me to believe.

Secondly: in the third section of the first chapter 'on Liberty', you claim to prove that all men are equal in the state of nature, and that the inequality which we see between them now comes from the civil law. The reason you give is that 'they are equalls who can doe equall things one against the other; but they who can doe the greatest things, (namely kill) can doe equall things. Therefore [...]'.[14] But I maintain that all men cannot do equal things one against the other; nor can they do the greatest things (namely kill), neither by force nor by fraud. It is true, Sir, is it not, that invalids, madmen, fools, pigmies, and poltroons (who are poltroons through extreme timidity, to the point where they would not dare kill their enemies when they had the chance)—that all these sorts of people prevent one from being able truthfully to assert that all men are equal. Besides, people cannot be equal except in terms of their equality in the faculties of human nature. But not all men are equal in strength, experience, reason, or passion.[15]

Thirdly: in the chapter on 'hereditary Government', article 8, and in the chapter 'Of the Kingdome of God, by Nature', article 9, you define honour as 'the estimation of another's power'.[16] And in the chapter on 'hereditary Government', article 8, you say that an enfranchised son honours his father less than he did before he was enfranchised, because his father no longer has the power over him which he had before. But I disagree. For this definition of honour is not valid: if it were true that we only honour those whom we think powerful, and whose power we esteem, it would follow that we would honour people more or less according to whether we had more or less hope or fear. But in fact, as you know, we have respect for people from whom we neither hope nor fear anything. We honour virtue, even when it is down on its luck and, given that it is suffering from misfortune, incapable of doing us either good or evil. We honour people of great intellect, old people, and distinguished people whom we have never met and whom we know only by reputation. And we often honour people who are beautiful and physically well proportioned, without being known to them.

Addendum In my first objection I forgot to add these words to my definition of man: 'on his own account, not that of his fellow men'. So that I define man as follows: 'a creature born fit for society, on his own account, not that of his fellow men, because of mutual fear'.

Passages presented in italics in the text (mainly quotations from Hobbes's Latin, signalled in the translation by quotation marks) are in larger script in the MS.

[1] A Latin formula used at the beginning of letters by Cicero and Seneca, and often abbreviated to SVBE, EQV.

[2] Peleau is making a kind of pun on the word 'postulatum'; having first used it in its general sense ('requirement'), he now uses the idea of a 'postulate' in Euclid's *Elements*.

[3] 'Envie' here could mean either envy or longing.

[4] François Viète or Viéta (1540–1603), one of the founders of modern algebra. Peleau alludes here to his *Zeteticorum libri quinque* (1593), which showed how to solve problems with unknown quantities of which only remote functions are given.

[5] These works and translations have not been identified.

[6] *Six Lessons*, Hobbes's reply to Wallis's *Elenchus*, had in fact been published one or two months earlier (see Letter 8, general note).

[7] 'Libertas' ('Liberty') is the general title of the first four chapters of *De cive*. The quotation given here is in fact from the second article.

[8] I. 2 n. 1

[9] I. 2 n. 2.

[10] I. 2.

[11] I. 2 n. 2.

[12] I. 2 n. 1.

[13] Peleau uses the scholastic term, meaning rational 'actually' as opposed to 'potentially' ('in potentia').

[14] I. 3.

[15] Peleau's list of the four human faculties is taken from the opening sentence of *De cive*.

[16] IX. 8; XV. 9.

Henry Stubbe to Hobbes, from Oxford

BL MS Add. 32553, fo. 8 (original).
Printed in Nicastro, *Lettere*, pp. 7–9.

S:^{r}

I receiued yor letter together with yor booke;[1] for ye late sending
whereof yo^u needed [not][2] to haue troubled yor selfe with the writeing
an apology, it could neuer come so late as to loose any thing of that
infinite obligation which so great an honour carryes with it: I confesse it
was an ambition in mee to desire it, but I hope yo^u can pardon offences
of ye right hand,[3] & dispense with insolencyes which proceed from an
excesse of respect. I haue here sent you the residue of the eighth, &
Nineth chapter. When I revised these sheetes, I found seuerall things
(especially in the 9th chap:) which might haue beene better expressed,
but I would not alter them untill I was sure I had not already prejudiced
yor sense. As for yor encouragements to proceede, did I thinke yo^u
could speake otherwise then you thinke, I should easily apprehend the
tendency of yor wordes, in ye meane while the greatest part of my ability
lyes in misgiueing that M:^{r} Hobbes thinkes mee able to goe on with it.
As for Paul's church-yard,[4] I finde them forward enough; I wish I could
in the translation either answer yor deserts or my owne intentions. But I
shall neuer hinder any from the like undertakeing. I knowe not how
long it may bee before I finish it; my occasions hitherto haue so
diuerted mee, that I haue not in 3 weekes beene able to transcribe
these. And there is now a matter of greater diuertisement happened;
wch is this: D:^{r} Wallis who is now putting out a most childish answer,[5]
(as they say) of 16 sheets in a small letter, to yor lessons, hath put out
some theses ag^t a branch of independency:[6] D:^{r} Owen hath wrote a
booke of late in the behalfe of Independency,[7] & our du Moulin
another,[8] & it is intended that ye Presbyterians shall bee mated here in
Oxon: Wallis's theses are triuiall, & so D:^{r} Owen hath desired mee to
fall upon him; & to seize him, as I thinke fit, because hee did under
hand abuse d^r Owen lately. D:^{r} Wallis hath mistooke ye question, & so I
haue order to tell him of it, & to reflect upon ye synod at westminster,
whereof hee was Scribe.[9] this will take mee up for some weekes, for I
intend to spend as good Latine as I can upon him, & I shall allow him y^e
ouerplus of one page or 2, in reuenge of yo^u, but not reflecting upon yo^u

311

nor his bookes agt you. I know not well what wee shall driue at, but I haue receiued orders to study church-gouernem^t, & a toleration, & so to oppose Presbytery: here will bee more then ordinary, for Dr Owen being sworne to day vice-chancello^r, tooke ye oath quatenus non contradicit verbo dei, legibus Angliae, principijs conscientiae et judicio proprio.^{10} Yo^u will in these papers see many markes, which showe my diffidence in ye expression. where you see ye first ☞, I conceiue there should haue beene a new breach [of a *deleted*] at Quid quaeris?^{11} seeing the subsequent wordes do not relate to ye immediate foregoeing wordes, but to the seuerall precedeing paragraphs. Where the second ☞ is, it may bee I am too jealous, but I conceiue, y^t it may not bee a true reasoning, to say ought is absurd because it cannot bee rendred in another language.^{12} there are many other things besides schoole termes y^t cannot bee expressed in other tongues, thus it is in all sciences almost: nor is ye word ineptus^{13} insignificant, because ye Greekes haue no correspondent: ye thing is true here in ye case instanced in; but I shall entreate yor pardon for suspecting ye argumt, if it bee one. I haue sent yo^u here a copy of Greeke uerses to put to yor effigies, for I hope yo^u will permit a cut^{14} to bee made: I know not how slowe I may proceede, nor yet how long I may bee in reviseing: for it is certaine I shall not acquiesce in lesse then seuerall perusalls: I shall leaue all ye papers in yor hands, & if any thing should so happen y^t yo^u should bee taken away, I shall desire y^t yo^u would bequeath mee an assistant to whome I may showe ye papers to preuent mistakes in yor sense: as also if yo^u shall please to adde any thing: I shall goe on as I can, but being obnoxious to others (for else ye Presbyterians had outed mee long agoe) I must continue their fauo^r, y^t so I may bee capable to serue you.

H: Stubbe.

Oxon: Octob: 7: 1656.

[*postscript:*] If I may know where you winter, I shall take an occasion personally to kisse yor hands for yor late fauo^r:

[*addressed:*] These For his ever honoured Friend Mr Hobbes

This was enclosed in a letter to 'M:^{r} Crooke Booke-seller at ye Shippe in Paul's church-yard', dated 9 [/19] Oct. 1656 (BL MS Add. 32553, fo. 7). The shop at the sign of the Ship was that of John Crooke (Plomer, *Dictionary of Booksellers 1641–1667*), the brother of Hobbes's publisher Andrew (on whom see the Biographical Register, 'William Crooke'); but Stubbe's later letters to Hobbes show that he wrote to Andrew Crooke at this address (see Letters 108, 119, 122–3, 125). This letter to Andrew Crooke was also forwarded to Hobbes (it is endorsed by Wheldon: 'M.ʳ Stubb, Oct. 9. 1656'). It begins: 'I desire yoᵘ would oblige mee & M.ʳ Hobbes so farre as to send him th[*half word deleted*] enclosed; & yᵗ you would by [yᵉ post *deleted* >this messenger] send mee word of yoʳ receiueall of this; for it is of some concernement to us both yᵗ yᵉ enclosed doe not miscarry. D.ʳ Wallis's booke is printing I thinke to procure some sheets of it; but as yet I could not.' Stubbe also asks Crooke for two books: *Integer theologiae cursus ad mentem Scoti* by Joannes Poncius (Paris, 1652), and any sequel or continuation to *The Reclaimed Papist; or, The Process of a Papist Knight Reformed by a Protestant Lady*, published anonymously but written by J. B. V. Canes (n.p., 1655). (No sequel is known to have been published.) He also writes: 'If yoᵘ see M.ʳ [>Antony] Shelley present my seruice to him, & let him know I should bee glad to heare from him' (cf. Letter 87 n. 1).

¹ Unidentified: possibly *The Questions concerning Liberty, Necessity, and Chance* (London, 1656). The letter has not apparently survived.

² not *omitted in MS*.

³ = offences committed through erring on the right side, or from the right motives (*OED* right hand 2c).

⁴ A reference either to Andrew or John Crooke, or to some other printer or bookseller in the area adjoining St Paul's where most of that trade was concentrated.

⁵ For Wallis see Letter 75 n. 7. His 'childish answer' was *Due Correction for Mr Hobbes* (1656): Wallis's dedicatory epistle was dated 15 [/25] Oct.

⁶ The second 'quaestio' of Wallis's *Quaestiones theologicae in vesperiis comitiorum agitatae* was 'Does the power of a Minister of the Gospel extend only to the members of one particular Church?' ('An potestas Ministri Evangelici ad unius tantum Ecclesiae particularis membra extendatur'): Wallis argued that it did not. The *Quaestiones* were published as the final part of a tripartite volume in 1657. The title of the sermon which forms the first part, and the general title of the volume, is *Mens sobria serió commendata*; the second part (a set of public lectures given by Wallis in 1654 for the degree of Doctor of Divinity) is entitled *Epistolae Pauli apostoli ad Titum expositio*. The pagination of this volume is continuous, but the three parts have separate title-pages dated 1657, 1656, and 1657 respectively. The precise date of publication is unknown (the date 20 Feb. 1656 on Thomason's copy refers surely not to publication but to the date on which the sermon *Mens sobria* was delivered); Stubbe seems to have acquired an advance copy of the *Quaestiones* from the printers (see Letters 96, 97).

⁷ Probably Owen's *Of Schisme* (not published until 1657). John Owen (1616–83), a prolific controversialist and theologian, graduated BA from Queen's College, Oxford (1632), MA (1635), and took holy orders; he left the university in 1637 rather than submit to the new Laudian statutes. Installed by parliamentary patronage in the living of Coggeshall, Essex, in 1647, he turned the church there into a model 'Independent' congregation; he was later patronized by Cromwell and, in 1650, appointed preacher to the Council of State. In 1651 he replaced the royalist Edward Reynolds as Dean of Christ Church, and a year later he was nominated Vice-Chancellor of the university by Cromwell (who was then Chancellor). He remained Vice-Chancellor, undoubtedly the most powerful and perhaps the most authoritative figure in the university, until 1658. After the Restoration, when he was ejected from Christ Church, he refused Clarendon's request that he reconcile himself to the Church of England, and remained a leading dissenter until his death.

⁸ Probably Lewis du Moulin's *Paraenesis ad aedificatores imperii in imperio* (1656). Lewis du Moulin (1606–80) was one of the two sons, both resident in England, of the eminent Huguenot Pierre du Moulin; Stubbe calls him 'our' du Moulin because he had been appointed Camden Professor of Ancient History at Oxford in 1648 by the parliamentary Visitors. After the Restoration, having been ejected from that post, he became a prominent polemicist on behalf of the Nonconformists.

⁹ Wallis had been a secretary to the Westminster Assembly of Divines, the mainly Presbyterian body set up by Parliament in 1643, which met from 1644 to 1649 and issued the Westminster Confession and the 'Directory for Church Government'.

¹⁰ 'In so far as it does not contradict the word of God, the laws of England, the principles of conscience, and my own judgement': Owen had objections, common among Puritans, to oath-taking, and to 'several superstitious rites' required of members of the university by the Laudian statutes of 1636 (see Nicastro, *Lettere*, p. 60 n. 85).

¹¹ Meaning roughly 'What more should I say?': Letter 96 shows that Stubbe had used this phrase to translate 'In summe', from the sentence in *Leviathan*, p. 36: 'In summe, all Passions that produce strange, and unusuall behaviour, are called by the generall name of Madnesse.'

¹² Ibid., p. 39.

¹³ 'Unskilled', 'inept': in its sense of 'tactless', this word was used by Cicero as an example of a Latin word for which there was no precise Greek equivalent (see Letter 96 n. 3).

¹⁴ = an engraving, i.e. of Hobbes's portrait.

LETTER 92   [11/] 21 OCTOBER 1656

Claude Mylon to Hobbes, from Paris

Chatsworth, Hobbes MSS, letter 24 (original).

Monsieur,

J'ay fait tenir a Mons.ʳ Du Verdus la lettre que vous m'auez adressé pour luy.¹ Il n'y a pas long temps que j'ay eu de ses nouuelles, vous m'obligez extremement de me communiquer vos pensées touchant la dimension du Circle, vous me faites honneur de vous fier en moy, je vous prieray de les estendre en sorte qu'elles me soient Intelligibles a present que je suis un peu hors d'eschole, je vous confesse que je n'ay pû entendre ce que vous en auez escri dans vostre Livre de Corpore,² ce que Mess.ʳˢ hughins & Auzout³ ny ont pû n'en comprendre, je vous manderay auec franchise mon sentiment, M.ʳ De Carcaui⁴ m'a dit que M.ʳ De Roberual auoit demonstrè Geometriquement la spirale egale a vne parabole, qui est vne proposition qu'il auoit autrefois démonstrée par les mouuements, vous sçauez que vous luy auez donnè sujet de la trouuer,⁵ je vous prie aussi de me mander si, le Corps politique,⁶ est la

traduction françcoise de vostre Leuiatan ou dernier ouurage que
[vous]⁷ auez fait en Anglois, & si vous approuuez cette traduction, elle
est Imprimée en Hollande. Je suis de tout mon Coeur

Monsieur
Vostre tres humble & tres affectioné seruiteur
Mylon

A paris ce 21ᵉ octob. 1656.

[*addressed:*] For Monsᵣ Hobbes At the Greene Dragon In paules
Churchyerd London

[*endorsed by James Wheldon:*] Monsʳ Mylon Oct. 21. 1656

Translation of Letter 92

Sir,

I have had delivered to M. du Verdus the letter which you sent to him
via me.¹ I had news from him recently. I am extremely grateful to you
for sending me your thoughts about the dimension of the circle; you
honour me by putting your trust in me. Please develop your thoughts at
greater length, so that I may find them comprehensible; for at present I
am slightly out of practice in my studies. I confess that I was not able to
understand what you wrote about it in your *De corpore*²—which neither
M. Huygens nor M. Auzout³ was able to understand either. I shall send
you my opinion, frankly expressed. M. de Carcavi⁴ told me that M.
Roberval had demonstrated geometrically the equality between a spiral
and a parabola, a proposition which on a previous occasion he had
demonstrated by the motion of a point. As you know, you gave him the
notion of finding it.⁵ I beg you also to let me know whether *Le Corps
politique*⁶ is the French translation of your *Leviathan*, or of a later work
which you⁽⁷⁾ have written in English, and whether you approve of this
translation: it has been printed in Holland. I am, Sir, with all my heart,

Your most humble and affectionate servant,
Mylon

Paris, 21 October 1656

¹ This letter has not apparently survived.
² *De corpore*, XX, 'De dimensione circuli'.

[3] Adrien Auzout (1622–91), mathematician and astronomer. A friend of Mylon, de Carcavi, and Boulliau, he attended meetings of Le Pailleur's post-Mersenne group of scientists; he worked with Jean Picard on the development of telescopes in the 1660s, was a member of the Académie royale des sciences (1667), and moved to Italy in 1669.

[4] See Letter 67 n. 7.

[5] On Roberval see Letter 76 n. 4. Hobbes later told the story of his discussion of the equality of a spiral and a parabola with Roberval in *Examinatio et emendatio*, pp. 121–2 (*OL* iv, pp. 188–90). As confirmation of his claim that he had given this idea to Roberval, he quoted there two sentences which he said were contained in a letter he had received from a French correspondent (whom he did not name): 'I have not seen his demonstration; but whatever he does, he cannot deny that he discovered this proposition thanks to you, since you gave him the idea and the notion of finding it. I shall always testify to that' ('Ie n'ay pas veu sa demonstration, mais quoy qu'il fasse il ne peut desnier que vous ne soyez cause quil ait trouvé cette proposition, puisque vous luy aues donné l'idee, & le suiet de la trouuer, C'est ce que ie tesmoigneray tous jours' (ibid., p. 122: *OL* iv, p. 190)). The similarity of phrasing here suggests either that Hobbes was embroidering on the relevant phrase in this letter, or that he was quoting from a further letter from Mylon on the same topic.

[6] *Le Corps politique* was a French translation of *De corpore politico* (the unauthorised printing of the second half of the *Elements of Law*), published in 1652 with no place of publication specified (Rahir suggests Rouen: *Catalogue*, no. 3366), and with a crude imitation of the engraved title-page of *Leviathan*. The printed title-page says that it was 'Traduit [. . .] par vn de ses amis'; this translation has often been attributed to Sorbière, but there is no evidence to support the attribution. Sorbière had issued a French translation of *De cive* in 1649 (*Elemens philosophiques du citoyen*, published by Blaeu in Amsterdam), signing the dedicatory epistle in his own name. It does not seem likely that he would have troubled to translate such a similar text as *De corpore politico* three years later, or that such a determined self-publicist as Sorbière would have failed to advertise his responsibility for any such translation.

[7] vous *omitted in MS*.

LETTER 93 [19/] 29 OCTOBER 1656

François Peleau to Hobbes, from Bordeaux

Chatsworth, Hobbes MSS, letter 25 (original).

Monsieur

Je desauoüe mes Erreurs, où plus-tost Je déclare, que vous auéz éclaircy tous mes doutes. C'est à cette heure, que je vous dois appeller mon Maistre; puisque iay receu de vous vne Leçon, ou le Public n'a nulle part auec moy. Je vous en remercie, comme Je dois: la franchise auec la quelle vous en auéz vsé, est vne belle chose, car, enfin vous pouuiéz [>vous] passer auec quelque bienseance, de satisfaire vn

Ignorant, et vn Importun. comme ie suis. C'est là tout le compliment que ie vous fais. M.ʳ Duuerdus scait bien, que ce que i'en [auois *deleted* >ay] fait, n'est que pour vous persuader que Je [estois *deleted* >suis] vostre disciple, en vous faisant voir que i'estudie dans vos ouurages, Puisque ie m'essaye [>de former] des doutes, affin que par leur resolution Je [suis *deleted* >sois] entierement conuaincu de la verité de vos demonstrations. Jay leu auec grand plaisir vostre logique,[1] et vostre quatriesme partie de Corpore, touchant les phenomenes de la nature, ou Je vous trouue tout à fait admirable, et j'estime infiniment ce que vous dites de la generation de la chaleur & de la lumiere.[2] Jay leu aussy quelque chose de vostre Traitté Of man, qui est inseré dans vostre Leuiathan;[3] parce que Mr. Du verdus à esté bon, et obligeant iusques-là que de me l'expliquer. Aussy-luy en suis-ie obligé, comme il faut: ie n'ay iamais n'en veu de si beau, [et *deleted* >ny] de si bien trouué, que ce que vous dites du sens, et des Imaginations, du Raisonnem.ᵗ; et du Discours de l'homme, de ses passions et de [>ses] vertus [>et puissances]: Je lis à cette heure v[ost]re[4] Metaphysique,[5] que ie trouue tres subtile, sur tout dans les definitions du Lieu, et du temps, et du Mouuement, et dans leurs proprietéz. tout cela veut dire, que bien loin de vous faire dauantage de doutes, Je [ne *deleted*] veux tout oublier, pour n'apprendre [>que] ce que vous auéz inuenté, et en faire ma science particuliere. [Quoy *deleted*] Mais pourquoy-faut-il que vous ayéz esté en france, sans que ie vous aye veu, J'enuie cette bonne fortune a M.ʳ Du verdus; Mais Je vous asseure Monsieur, que ie veux faire voyage tout expres en Angleterre pour vous vous voir, et vous ouïr; croyant par ce moyen aller puiser la philosophie, et la verité iusques dans leur source. quand vous me verréz, vous ne verréz qu'vn Jeune garçon, qui n'a pas [beaucoup *deleted*] d'esprit, et qui n'a rien en luy d[e *page torn*] bon, qu'vn grand desir pour les lettres, et vne [*page torn* gr]ande estime pour vous. Je vous souhaitte v[ne *page torn*] ferme santé, et vne belle vieillesse, et vne vie encore plus longue que la mienne; et si ie vous pouuois donner de mes années; ce seroit bien la chose que ie ferois de meilleur coeur. aiméz Moy, Monsieur, quoyque ie n'aye iamais rien merité de vous. c'est ma plus grande ambition; aussy asseuréz-vous quil n'y a personne au Monde, qui vous aime, [vous estime, et vous admire *deleted*] comme moy, Je vous ay tousiours dans l'esprit, dans le coeur et dans la bouche, et Je voudrois bien vous auoir tousiours deuant les yeux. Excusez mes longues lettres, Puisque ie n'ay autre moyen de vous parler, souffres que ie face durer vn peu cette conuersation par écrit, pour vous décharger mon coeur de l'affection que iay pour vous; et vous dire auec tous les sermens du monde, que ie veux estre toute ma vie Inuiolablement

Monsieur
Vostre tres humble & tres obeissant, et tres obligé seruiteur.
Peleau

A Bord.ˣ ce 29. octob. 1656.

[*addressed:*] For Mʳ Hobbes At the Greene Dragon In Paules Churchierd London

[*endorsed by James Wheldon:*] Monsʳ Peleau Oct. 23. 1656.

Translation of Letter 93

Sir,

I renounce my errors, or rather I declare that you have cleared up all my doubts. Now I must call you my teacher; since I have received a lesson from you, which the public did not share with me. I dutifully thank you for it: the frankness with which you have discussed the matter is a marvellous thing, since you could have ignored the requests of an ignorant and importunate person like me with perfect propriety.

Those are all the compliments I shall pay you. M. du Verdus knows well that what I did in writing to you about that was only in order to persuade you that I am your disciple, by showing you that I study your works; for I try to form doubts about them, so that by resolving them I may become completely convinced of the truth of your demonstrations. I have read your Logic[1] with great pleasure, and the fourth part of your *De corpore*, concerning natural phenomena, which strikes me as perfectly admirable; and I have an infinitely high opinion of what you say about the generation of heat and light.[2] I have also read some of your treatise 'Of Man', which is included in your *Leviathan*;[3] since M. du Verdus was so kind and obliging as to explain it to me. For that, I am dutifully obliged to him too: for I have never seen anything so fine, or so ingenious, as what you say there about sense, imagination, and reasoning, about human discourse, human passions, virtues, and powers. At the moment I am reading your[4] Metaphysics,[5] which I find very subtle, especially in the definitions of place, time, and movement, and in the account of their properties.

All of which means that, far from raising more doubts, I wish I could forget everything, so that I might learn only what you have discovered, and make it my exclusive study. Why is it that you were in France without my seeing you? I envy M. du Verdus that good fortune of his. But I assure you, Sir, that I want to travel to England purely in order to see you and listen to you; in that way, I think, I shall draw philosophy and truth from their very source. When you see me, you will see only a young boy, who has no intelligence, and nothing good about him except a great love of literature and a high esteem for you. I wish you sturdy good health and a fine old age, and a life which lasts even longer than mine; and if I could give you some of the years of my life, that is the thing I should be happiest of all to do. Love me, Sir, although I have never deserved your love. That is my highest ambition; and be assured that there is no one in the world who loves you as I do. I have you always in my thoughts, in my heart, and on my lips; and I should very much like to have you always before my eyes. Forgive my long letters, for I have no other way of speaking to you; allow me to prolong this conversation in writing for a little while, so that I may unburden my heart of the affection I feel for you, and tell you, with all the solemn oaths in the world, that I wish, Sir, to remain for all my life, unshakeably,

Your most humble, obedient, and obliged servant,
Peleau

Bordeaux, 29 October 1656

[*addressed: see text*]

1 *De corpore*, part 1, entitled 'Computatio sive logica'.
2 Ibid., XXVII, entitled 'De luce, calore, et coloribus'.
3 *Leviathan*, part 1.
4 Contraction expanded.
5 *De corpore*, part 2, entitled 'Philosophia prima'.

LETTER 94   [20/] 30 OCTOBER 1656

François du Verdus to Hobbes, from Bordeaux

Chatsworth, Hobbes MSS, letter 26 (original).

Monsieur,
   Je reçeus il y a deux jours vostre lettre du 14.eme 7.bre1 Elle me dona beaucoup de joye: car j'étois bien en peine de vous. Mr Bourdelot2

m'auoit écrit de Paris qu'un Anglois disant le sçauoir fort bien, assuroit
que vous estiés mort ce qui fut cause que j'écriuis aussi tot a M[r]
Crooke[3] vostre Imprimeur le priant de m'en éclairçir. a vous dire la
verité j'eus peine a croire que l'anglois de Mr Bourdelot fut bien
informé car dépuis l'édition d'un certain liure (intitulé si ie je me
trompe de principijs justi et decori) on m'a souuant battu les oreilles de
ce faux bruit là: l'auteur de ce liure (qui semble vous estimer
entreprenant vostre apologie, mais qui au fonds s'éloigne autant de la
uerité qu'il s'éloigne de vos Principes) ayant mis dans sa Préface en
parlant de vous, que fatis concessisti.[4] Je louë Dieu Monsieur que vous
m'ayés apris vous mesme par vostre lettre que c'est un faux bruit Je n'ay
jamais inferé de verité de vos écrits, que j'ayme tant que celle'là. Mais
que doy-j'inferer de ce que je uoy que vous uous serués d'un
amanuänse ou scribe et copiste? Est ce que vous ayés esté malade; ou
seulement pour cette incomodité que vous m'écriuites, que la main
vous tremble?[5] Si vous tombés malade Monsieur (et vous le sçaués
mieux que moy) come les maladies uienent pour l'ordinaire ou sont
acompagnées de quelque mouuement d'humeurs, il ne faut pas faire
état d'éteindre si tot ce mouuement, je ueux dire en prenant des
remedes qui donent un autre tour au sang et aux esprits; les
adoucissans sont ce qu'on a de meilleur qui amortissent peu a peu le
mouuement de la maladie, et le repos auec cela; sur tout a un homme
de uostre âge. Ce que je vous en dis c'est de tandresse et de desir que
vostre uie soit toujours douce et heureuse. Pleut a Dieu en estre le
temoin! Mais qui sçait ou le Ciel m'apelera? Mr Bourdelot [>Abbé de
Massay] l'agent de la Serenissime Reyne de Suëde [>et son premier
Médecin] m'écriuoit il y a quelque temps que si j'étois a Paris quand
cette Reyne y arriueroit je profiterois de l'occasion;[6] et depuis il m'a
écrit que si j'y eusse esté, peut-estre S. M. m'eut Elle amené en Italie
mesmement il me conuie d'y aller ce Printemps auecque luy: et si ie
puis doner ordre a mes affaires dont j'ay fait imprimer la Relation,[7]
peut estre me laisseray-je tanter a la fortune. Quoy qu'il en soit ce sera
toujours en vous honorant de tout mon coeur, portant vos Liures auec
moy; et y trauaillant auec soin. Ne craignés pas que j'imprime de
version de vos Oeuures qu'il y ait a redire. En tachant d'acquerir
quelque réputation par ce moyen [en *deleted* >et] faisant uoyr qu'au
moins ie m'aplique aux belles choses, et ay quelque intelligence de ces
matieres releuées que vous traités si bien: je suis encore plus jaloux de
vostre réputation que de la miene propre, et cela par reconoissançe
quand je tiens de vous ce que ie sçay de meilleur. J'atandray donc

vostre in folio où doiuent estre vos trois sections de Philosophie;[8] et quand je l'auray traduit, quelque part que je sois je tascheray de vous faire tenir copie de ma version, que vous l'agreiés; et s'il vous plait aussi, que vous la corrigiés auant que je la fasse imprimer. Cepandant j'étudie auec grande aplication vostre Leuiatan. Je l'auois leu une fois comme qui lit un Roman, c'est a dire parcouru sans m'y apliquer seulement pour m'en former une Idée génerale de la suitte et connection des matiéres: Maintenant je l'étudie et vous prie d'agrëer que de temps en temps je vous propose les difficultés que j'y auray ou qu'on me fera.

Présuposé mesme que vous le veuillés bien ainsi je vous propose quatre doutes entre autres qu'il me souuient que j'eus en parcourant vostre troisieme partie de cet ouurage, que vous aués intitulée Of a Christian Common-Wehalth.

Ma premiére difficulté c'est qu'entre autres choses pour prouuer que les Roys étoient sacrificateurs vous allegués l'exemple de Saul qui offrit l'holocauste au 1er liure de Samuël chap. 13.[9] Or il me semble que cet exemple fait contre vous puisque Samuël l'en reprit [et *deleted*] luy disant qu'il auoit fait sottement de n'auoir pas gardé le précepte de Dieu; et que pour cela Dieu le rejettoit. Et par quel droit Samuël [>l'en] eut-il repris; s'il eut eu droit de le faire? Il n'etoit donc pas du droit du Roy de sacrifier

Ma seconde difficulté c'est que par l'exemple d'ananias et de Sapphira[10] il semble que Jesus-Christ eut doné l'autorité souueraine a ses Apostres Car qu'est c'autre chose que cette puissance de vie et de mort.

La troisieme c'est que le passage petre amas me redit a trois diuerses fois et la Triple redite auec cela du pasce oues meas,[11] joint a l'exemple que je uiens de dire, etant quelque chose de singulier semble estre formel pour St Piere et par conséquent pour son successeur

La quatrieme ce que vous expliqués les termes that is my body: that signifieth my body[12] il me semble que cela est bien forçé que le verbe *Estre* veuille dire *signifier*. Et je ne uois point d'aparence qu'on vous le passe a moins que vous alleguiés des endroits pareils de l'écriture sainte où la copule *est* ueuïlle dire *signifie*. Je vous prie donc de me dire comment vous soutenés cela.

Je souhaiterois bien aussi que vous eussiés la bonté de m'expliquer les endroits suiuants que je vous marque et qui vous seront autant de preuues qu'effectiuement j'étudie vostre Leuiatan.

dans la page 195 dans la derniere période du 1er membre il y a ces mots. *Whereof there dependeth much upon supernatural reuelations of the Will of God*. Ces termes traduits mot a mot les uoicy. de laquelle là dépend[13] fort de surnaturelles réuelations de la volonté de Dieu. j'y trouue le verbe *dependeth*; j'y trouue le genitif *whereof* mais je n'y trouue point leur nominatif, par exemple cecy (*de laquelle la conoissance depend* &ᶜ[)]][14]. seroit ce une omission d'impression: ou un tour de phrase en vostre langue et qu'on y sous-entendit tels nominatifs?

dans la mesme page 195. Not to be folded up in the napkin of an implicite faith. Car ce sont les talens qu'il nous a mis [entre les mains *altered to* en main] pour négocier jusqu'a l'auenement derechef de nostre benit sauueur et c'est pourquoy ce n'est pas pour les tenir pliés dans la seruiette d'un serment implicite mais pour les employer a pourchasser &ᶜ.[15] Je n'ay pu trouuer de dictionaire Anglois Latin et Latin Anglois, je m'étois adressé pour cela a Mʳ Lyonard[16] un libraire de Paris, qui a (disoit-il) correspondançe auec Mʳ Crooke: Je souhaiterois donc que Mʳ Crooke m'en tint un pret, auec vostre response angloise a Walis;[17] je les luy payeray et luy écriray par quelle uoye il pourra me les faire tenir, qui deura estre celle de quelque vaisseau. Car Monsieur voyés la peine, n'ayant point de Maistre de vostre langue je n'ay que le Dictionaire de Robert Sherwood[18] qui est fort defectuëus, que seulement le mot *aith*[19] n'y est pas.

dans la mesme page. We are bidden to captiuate our understanding to ther Words; and not to labour in sifting[20] out a philosophicall truth by Logick of such mysteries as are not comprehensible. Nous somes obligés [de *deleted* >a] captiuer nostre entandement aux paroles et non a nous trauailler a cribler par logique la uérité philosophique de tels mysteres qui sont incomprehensibles. je ne sçay si cela est bien traduit ou s'il faudroit mettre *cribler tels misteres &c comme*[21] *si c'etoient des uerités philosophiques*. Mais *as* (*comme*) n'est pas dans uostre texte.

p 196. Which in sum is trust and faith reposed in him that speaketh Ce qui en somme est la croyance et la foy reposée en celuy qui parle. Cela est-il traduit mot a mot; et *trust* ueut il dire la *croyançe* Car pour le sens je le uoy bien que c'est cela qui est croire, cest cela qui est prendre Créance et ajouter foy en celuy qui parle.

dans la mesme page to win beleef. le dictionaire ne me dit point *Win* ce que c'est

P. 197. In which words two things are to be obserued first that God Wil not haue Miracles alone serue for arguments &ᶜ dans lesquels mots il y a deux choses a obseruer: la premiere que Dieu ne *ueut* pas *auoir* les miracles seuls *seruir* pour arguments &c. le tour de phrase m'embarrasse que le uerbe *ueut* [dit *deleted* >regisse] deux infinitifs, *auoir* et *seruir* Cela ne se fait pas en nostre langue et je uoudrois uos termes, traduits de uostre façon pour me seruir de modelle en cas pareils.

Ce sont là les endroits qui m'arrétent dans le 32eme Chapitre. Je vous feray de mesme le detail de ce qui m'embarrasse aux autres. Et cepandant pour n'estre pas trop long je ne uous demande plus que ces deux choses. La premiére coment vous traduiriés vostre mot *Ghost* en nostre langue car de le traduire *esprit* c'est pour uostre mot *Spirit*. La seconde en quel lieu de la Bible de l'edition Vulgate je trouuerray le passage que vous cités du 2^d liure d'esdras chap. 14. this law is burnt &^c. Car le second d'esdras de la vulgate n'ayant que 13 chapitres.[22]

Au reste Monsieur me pardonerés vous la peine que je vous donne? Mais vous m'aués defandu tout ce qui sent le Compliment; et j'ay ueu cette response galante que vous aués faite a Mr Peleau de cet échange de tant de paroles, auec ce *je dis belles*! contre une uieille et uzée.[23] Que j'ay aymé vostre ponctualité a luy répondre pié a pié a to[us][24] ses chefs! pour moy quand il me fit uoyr ses Objections qu'il vous écriuoit je luy dis que ce qu'il faisoit c'étoit come on dit pour les Dames et pour se doner carriere: et pour response plus précise j'ajoutay que de ses deux prémisses: [>la 1ere] *que l'homme se defie naturellement* et la 2de qu'en suite *on établisse la societé ciuile*;[25] on n'en inferoit pas que ce fut autrement qu'aprés beaucoup d'experiences et de l'animosité naturelle des hommes entre eux, et de leur penchant a manquer de parole. J'auois ajouté que ce qu'il vous oposoit, (qu'on ne laisse pas de définir l'homme un Animal raisonable quoy qu'en effect il y ait beaucoup de gens ne raisonans jamais actuëllement)[26] étoit contre luy etant tres naturel de dire de mesme Que Tous les hommes sont naturelement egaux entre eux c'est a dire et également indépandans l'un de l'autre par Nature et pouuans choses égales, quoy qu'en effect il y en ait de si poltrons que de s'asujetir d'abord: Mais le biais qu'il prend dans sa replique sauue galamant toutes ces choses quand il vous dit que ce qu'il en a fait c'est pour auoir de vous quelques [chefs *deleted*] instructions particuliéres. Pour moy Monsieur, je vous demande candidement la continuätion de l'honneur de vostre bienueillançe qui seray éternellement

Monsieur
vostre tres humble et tres obeissant seruiteur
duuerdus

A Bourdeaux le 30eme Octobre 1656

[*addressed:*] For Mr Hobbes at the Greene Dragon in Paules Churchyerd London

[*endorsed by James Wheldon:*] Monsr du Verdus Oct. 30. 1656

Translation of Letter 94

Sir,

I received your letter of 14 September[1] two days ago. It gave me great pleasure, since I had been very worried about you. M. Bourdelot[2] had written to me from Paris, saying that an Englishman (who said he was certain of the fact) had assured him you were dead. That was why I wrote immediately to your printer, Mr Crooke,[3] asking him to enlighten me. To tell you the truth, I found it hard to believe that M. Bourdelot's Englishman was correctly informed; for, ever since the publication of a certain book (entitled, if I am not mistaken, *De principiis iusti et decori*) I have often been pestered by that false rumour, because the author of this book (who seems to admire you, since he has undertaken to be your apologist, but who in fact strays as far from the truth as he does from your principles) has put in his preface, speaking of you, the phrase 'you have passed away'.[4] I praise God, Sir, that you yourself have let me know, by means of your letter, that the rumour is false. I have never drawn any true inference from your writings which pleased me as much as that one did.

But what am I to infer from the fact that, as I see, you are using an amanuensis or scribe and copyist? Have you been ill, or is it merely because of that infirmity which you told me about in a letter, the trembling of your hand?[5] If you fall ill, Sir (and you know this better than I), since illnesses usually come from (or are accompanied by) some movement of the humours, you should not arrange to stop this movement too soon, I mean by taking remedies which give a different cast to the blood or the spirits. Attemperating medicines are the best, which gradually subdue the movement of the illness—and, together with them, rest (especially for a man of your age). I say this out of concern for you, and out of my desire that your life should continue to be pleasant and happy—God be my witness!

But who knows where Heaven will call me to? M. Bourdelot, *abbé* of Massay, agent of Her Most Serene Highness the Queen of Sweden, and her chief physician, wrote to me some time ago to say that if I were in Paris when that Queen arrived there, I would profit from the opportunity of meeting her.[6] And since then he has written that if I had been there, perhaps Her Majesty would have taken me to Italy with her; he also invites me to go there with him this spring. And if I can put my affairs in order (having already had my 'Account' of them printed),[7] perhaps I shall let myself be tempted by fortune.

However that may turn out, I shall continue to honour you with all my heart, taking my books with me and working on them carefully. Do not be afraid that I shall print a translation of your works which will need to be corrected. Although I am trying to gain some reputation by these means, and demonstrating that I do at least apply myself to fine things, and have some understanding of those lofty subjects which you deal with so well, nevertheless I am even more keen to guard your reputation than my own—that is a matter of gratitude, since the best part of my knowledge comes from you. So I shall wait for your folio volume which must contain your three sections on philosophy;[8] and when I have translated it, wherever I am, I shall try to send a copy of my translation to you for your approval—and, if you are willing, for correction by you before I have it printed. Meanwhile I am studying your *Leviathan* with great application. I had read it once in the way that one reads a novel, that is, running through it without applying myself to it, merely to form a general impression of the way the subject-matter is laid out and organized. Now I am studying it; and I beg you to allow me, from time to time, to put to you any difficulties that I have with it, or that other people may put to me.

Assuming that you accept this request, I propose four doubts which I had (among others) when running through the third part of the work, which you entitled 'Of a Christian Common-Wealth'.

My first difficulty is that, among other reasons to show that kings performed sacrifices, you put forward the example of Saul, who offered a burnt offering in 1 Samuel 13.[9] However, I think this example goes against your argument, because Samuel reproved him for it, telling him that he had done foolishly in not keeping the commandment of God, and that for that reason God was rejecting him. And by what right could Samuel have reproved him for it, if Saul had had the right to do it? Therefore it was not within the right of the king to perform a sacrifice.

My second difficulty is that the example of Ananias and Sapphira[10] seems to show that Jesus gave sovereign authority to his Apostles; for what else is that power of life and death?

The third difficulty is that the words 'Peter, lovest thou me?', repeated three times, together with the triple repetition of 'Feed my sheep',[11] and the example which I have just given, being something exceptional, seem to be directed formally to St Peter—and, consequently, to his successor.

The fourth difficulty is with your explanation of the terms 'that is my body' as 'that signifieth my body'.[12] It strikes me as a very forced explanation that the verb 'to be' should mean 'to signify'; and I see no likelihood that anyone will grant it to you, unless you put forward similar passages from Holy Scripture in which the copula 'is' means 'signifies'. So please tell me how you will sustain that opinion.

I should also like you to have the kindness to explain the following passages which I point out to you, and which will also show you that I am indeed studying your *Leviathan*.

On p. 195, in the last sentence of the first paragraph there are these words: 'whereof there dependeth much upon Supernaturall Revelations of the Will of God'. These terms, translated word for word, are as follows: 'de laquelle là dépend[13] fort de surnaturelles réuelations de la volonté de Dieu'. I find there the verb 'dependeth'; I find the genitive 'whereof'; but I cannot find their nominative—for example, 'whereof the knowledge dependeth', etc.[14] Has something been left out by the printer, or is it a turn of phrase in your language, so that such nominatives are understood without being stated?

On the same page, p. 195: 'not to be folded up in the Napkin of an Implicite Faith': 'Car ce sont les talens qu'il nous a mis en main pour négocier jusqu'a l'auenement derechef de nostre benit sauueur et c'est pourquoy ce n'est pas pour les tenir pliés dans la seruiette d'un serment implicite mais pour les employer a pourchasser. . .'.[15] I have not been able to find an English–Latin and Latin–English dictionary; I applied for that purpose to M. Lyonard,[16] a Paris bookseller who (he said) does business with Mr Crooke. So I should like Mr Crooke to keep one ready for me, together with your English reply to Wallis;[17] I shall pay him for them, and shall write to tell him how he can have them delivered to me—no doubt by means of some ship or other. For you see, Sir, how hard it is for me, not having any teacher for your language: I have only Robert Sherwood's Dictionary,[18] which is very inadequate, only the word 'aith'[19] is not in it.

On the same page: 'wee are bidden to captivate our understanding to the Words; and not to labour in sifting[20] out a Philosophicall truth by Logick, of such mysteries as are not comprehensible'. 'Nous somes obligés a captiuer nostre entandement aux paroles et non a nous trauailler a cribler par logique la uérité philosophique de tels mysteres qui sont incomprehensibles.' I do not know whether that is a good translation, or whether I should say 'cribler tels misteres . . . *comme*[21] si c'etoient des uerités philosophiques' ['to sift such mysteries . . . *as* if they were philosophical truths']. But 'as' ('comme') is not in your text.

On p. 196: 'which in sum, is Trust, and Faith reposed in him that speaketh': 'Ce qui en somme est la croyance et la foy reposée en celuy qui parle'. Is that a word-for-word translation, and does 'trust' mean 'croyance'? So far as the meaning is concerned, I quite understand it: it means that that is belief, that is giving credence, and adding to it one's faith in the person who speaks.

On the same page: 'to win beleef'. The dictionary does not tell me what 'win' means.

On p. 197: 'In which words two things are to be observed; First, that God wil not have miracles alone serve for arguments . . .': 'Dans lesquels mots il y a deux choses a obseruer: la premiere que Dieu ne *ueut* pas *auoir* les miracles seuls *seruir* pour arguments . . .'. I have difficulty with the construction of this phrase, because the verb 'wil' governs two infinitives, 'have' and 'serve'. That does not happen in our language; and I should like to have your words in your own translation, to use as a model in similar cases.

Those are the passages which puzzle me in ch. 32. I shall also give you details of those passages which trouble me in the other chapters. However, for the sake of brevity I shall only ask you two things, as follows. The first is, how you would translate your word 'ghost' in French, since 'esprit' is used to translate your word 'spirit'. The second is, in which part of the Vulgate edition of the Bible I can find the passage which you cite from 2 Esdras 14 ('this law is burnt. . .'). For in the Vulgate, the second book of Esdras has only thirteen chapters.[22]

Otherwise, Sir, will you forgive me the trouble which I am causing you? But you have forbidden me to write anything that savours of a compliment; and I have seen that witty reply which you made to M. Peleau in that exchange of so many words, with that 'I say they are *beautiful*', against an old woman and Uzziah.[23] How I admired your punctiliousness in replying to all[(24)] his arguments point by point! For my own part, when he showed me the objections which he was writing to you, I told him that what he was doing was, as we say, to impress the ladies, and for his own promotion. And, to answer his objections more specifically, I told him that, so far as his two suppositions were concerned (first, that 'men naturally mistrust one another', and secondly, that 'it is because of that that civil society is established'),[25] one would not conclude otherwise except after frequently experiencing both the natural hostility which men have for one another, and their tendency to break their word. I added that the other objection which he had raised against you (namely, that we do not abandon the definition of man as a rational animal even though there are in fact many people who never actually reason)[26] counted against his argument. For it is still very natural to say that all men are naturally equal among themselves, that is, both equally independent of one another by nature, and capable of doing equal things, even though there may in fact be some who are so cowardly that they will subject themselves to others first. But the expedient he makes use of in his reply wittily excuses all these things, when he says that he wrote them only to get some private lessons from you. For my own part, Sir, I candidly request that you continue to do me the honour of extending your goodwill to me, who shall for ever be,

Sir,
Your most humble and obedient servant,
du Verdus

Bordeaux, 30 October 1656

[*addressed: see text*]

---

[1] This letter does not apparently survive.

[2] See Letter 78 n. 21.

[3] Andrew Crooke (see the Biographical Register, 'William Crooke').

[4] Van Velthuysen, *Epistolica dissertatio* (see Letter 85 n. 2). The preface speaks of Hobbes as dead: 'if the fates had allowed him a longer life' ('si fata illi longiorem vitam concessissent': sig. *3ᵛ).

[5] This is the first indication from one of Hobbes's correspondents that he had begun to dictate his letters to James Wheldon.

[6] Queen Christina, having abdicated in 1654, settled in Rome in December 1655. In the summer of 1656 she travelled to France to discuss with Mazarin a plan to install her as Queen of Naples; she landed at Marseille in late July, met Bourdelot at Lyon in Aug., entered Paris in early Sept., travelled to the Court at Compiègne, and set out for Italy again on 13/23 Sept. (see Masson, *Queen Christina*, pp. 272–5).

[7] See Letter 89 n. 3.

[8] No such folio volume was printed, though the three sections of Hobbes's philosophical system were eventually brought together in the (quarto) *Opera philosophica* of 1668.

[9] *Leviathan*, p. 228.

[10] Acts 5: 1–10.

[11] John 21: 15–17.

[12] *Leviathan*, p. 338.

[13] Du Verdus has failed to recognize the impersonal construction 'there dependeth', translating 'there' as an adverb instead.

[14] ~) *omitted in MS.*

[15] 'For they are the talents which he hath put into our hands to negotiate, till the coming again of our blessed Saviour; and therefore not to be folded up in the Napkin of an Implicite Faith, but employed in the purchase . . .'. Not realizing that 'aith' is a misprint (see n. 19), du Verdus seems to have taken it as an alternative form of the word 'oath', translated here as 'serment'. He has also mistakenly translated 'purchase' as 'pourchasser' ('pursue').

[16] See Letter 84 n. 10.

[17] See Letter 78 n. 34.

[18] See Letter 67 n. 12.

[19] A misprint for 'Faith', occurring in some copies of the 1st edn. of *Leviathan*, p. 195, l. 24.

[20] fifting *MS.*

[21] Underlined twice in MS.

[22] *Leviathan*, p. 283, cites Esdras 14: 21. What the Vulgate calls the second book of Esdras (i.e. Ezra) is what most Protestant texts of the Bible (including the Latin translation by Junius and Tremellius, and the Authorized Version) call the Book of Nehemiah. This book does indeed contain only thirteen chapters. Hobbes's reference is to the second of the two books of Ezra (usually entitled 'Esdras') in the Apocrypha; these are presented as books 3 and 4 of Esdras in the Vulgate. Hobbes does also refer to them as 'the third and fourth of *Esdras*' (*Leviathan*, p. 199).

[23] Hobbes had evidently replied to Letter 90; but the context of this remark is impossible to reconstruct. The translation is therefore uncertain; perhaps it should be 'I say beautiful things'.

[24] Contraction expanded.

[25] See Letter 90, enclosure.

[26] Ibid.

LETTER 95   [22 OCTOBER/] 1 NOVEMBER 1656

François Peleau to Hobbes, from Bordeaux

Chatsworth, Hobbes MSS, letter 27 (original).

Monsieur.

Le bruit [> qui] a couru En france que vous estiez mort; et la lettre, que iay receuë de vous, sans estre ny écrite, ny signée de vostre main[1] m'ont Persuadé, que pour le moins vous auiéz esté bien malade. Cette Nouuelle a mis [toute la france *altered to* tout Paris] En vne consternation publique, comme croyant auoir fait vne perte [qui *deleted*] Irreperable; les grands hommes comme vous, estant rares et vniques. Mais tout ua bien, Pourueuque vous soyéz viuant a Londres, ou en quelque autre Endroit de l'angleterre. Dieu veuille que vous ne mouriéz iamais autrement; àpeine de pleurer quelque autrefois, encore, [sur la *deleted*] sur vn faux bruit; car, sans mentir, vous estéz digne des larmes de tout le monde scauant. voila tout mon compliment.

On me persecute à force de syllogismes, pour me prouuer qu'il n'y a iamais eu dans le monde, Vn Estat de Nature, purement tel, comme vous le démontréz dans votre politique. Il ne me sert de rien, de dire, que c'et estat, estoit; auant qu'il n'y eut de villes, de cités, ny de republiques dans le monde; auant mesme qu'il n'y eut de pactes, ny de conuentions entre les hommes. Jay allegué, que parmy les Americains [il estoi *deleted*] cét estat estoit encore, et que les sauuages exercoient entre eux vne guerre de tous contre tous. qu'apres la mort de Noe; ses trois enfans, Sem, Japhet & Cham, pouuoient, s'ils eussent voulû, exercer vne telle guerre; et par consequent que cét estat de Nature estoit vne chose possible. Mais on me soustient qu'il y a tousjours eu des familles dans le monde et les familles estant de petits Royaumes; l'éstat de Nature en est exclûs, et d'ailleurs, quand il n'y auroit pas de perez de famille; L'aisné des enfans, à cause de son droit de Primogeniture, ou Préoccupation par sort, est censé Maistre du bien de son pere, et, qu'ainsy ce droit de tous sur toutes choses, est osté. pour reduire ces opiniastres à la raison, éclaircisséz-moy là dessus, je vous prie.

Au commencement de votre Logique, vous dites que la prudence, n'est pas [>comprise] dans l'estenduë de la philosophie, parce qu'elle est fondée sur l'experience, [Il *deleted* >qui] n'est autre chose qu'vn souuenir de plusieurs Choses semblables.[2] Mais Il me semble, que la prudence n'est pas seulement comme vous dites *Expectatio rerum similium* &c ... Mais vne application que la raison fait, de ces Éuenemens semblables; en disant, Cela a tousiours, ou souuent esté; Doncques il sera encore. c'est vne consequence tirée d'vne prémisse, et par consequent [Il *deleted*] c'est vn [raisonnable *altered to* raisonnement], parcequ'il faut diuiser, et composer. J'attens votre auis là dessus.

Il y a en nostre ville vn homme qui est sourd de naissance, lequel scait conter, et entend bien l'arithmetique. et vous dites que la supputation suppose vn langage, et les noms Numeraux pour les moins.[3] Mais qu'elle langue, et quels noms Numeraux, ou Chyphres peut auoir appris vn sourd, luy qui n'a jamais rien oui; et les paroles ne passant dans l'Esprit, que par l'Entremise de l'oreille.

Puisque vous m'auéz permis de vous proposer mes doutes, Je ne fais que vous obeïr, mais, Je vous prie, fiéz-vous à moy, et quoyque vous préchiez le *Mutuus metus* aux autres; vous ne le deuéz-pas pratiquer enuers moy; puisque ie suis votre amy; c'est à dire M.ʳ, que vous me fairiéz-plaisir, et grace de signer toutes vos lettres. Je suis de tout mon coeur.

Monsieur
Vostre tres humble, et tres obeissant seruiteur.
Peleau.

A Bordˣ ce 1. Nouemb. 1656

[*addressed:*] For Mʳ Hobbes. At the Greene Dragon in Paules Churchierd London

[*endorsed by James Wheldon:*] Mʳ Peleau. No. 1ˢᵗ 1656

Translation of Letter 95

Sir,

Because of the rumour of your death which ran round France and the letter I received from you which was neither written nor signed by you,[1] I have concluded that you must at least have been very ill. That rumour caused public alarm throughout Paris, as it was thought that we had suffered an irreparable loss—great men like yourself being rare and unique. But all is well, given that you are alive in London or some other part of England. God grant that you never die except in rumour, or at least that on some future occasion we should again be made to weep by false news; for, to speak the truth, you are worthy of the tears of all the learned world. There ends my compliment.

I am being hounded with syllogisms designed to prove to me that the state of nature in the strict sense (such as you show it to be in your *Politics*) has never existed in the world. It is no use if I say that this state existed before there were any towns, cities, or republics in the world, before there were even any pacts or agreements between men. I have argued that this state still exists in America; that savages wage a war of all against all among themselves; that after the death of Noah, his three sons, Shem, Japhet, and Ham, could, if they had wanted to, have waged a war of that kind; and that this state of nature is therefore possible. But they maintain that there have always been families in the world, and that since families are little kingdoms, they exclude the state of nature; besides, they say that when there are no fathers as heads of families, the eldest child is deemed owner of his father's property because of his right of primogeniture or first possession by lot: this, they say, removes the right of every man to every thing. Please enlighten me on this, so that I may force these stubborn people to see reason.

At the beginning of your Logic, you say that prudence is not a part of philosophy because it is based on experience, which is nothing but a recollection of several similar things.[2] But I think prudence is not just 'an expectation of similar things . . .', as you call it, but rather an argument applied by reason to those similar events. Reason says: this has always, or often, happened; therefore it will happen again. This is a consequence drawn from a premiss; so it is an act of reasoning, since it requires analysis and synthesis. I await your opinion about this.

In our town there is a man, deaf since birth, who can count and has a good understanding of arithmetic. You say that computation requires language and needs to make use of numerical words.[3] But what language and what words or symbols for numbers can a deaf man have learned, when he has never heard anything? Words only pass into the mind through the medium of the ear.

Since you have allowed me to put my queries to you, I am merely obeying you; but I beg you to trust me, and not to practise towards me the 'mutual fear' which you preach to others. For I am your friend; that is to say, Sir, that you would give me pleasure and honour by signing all your letters. I am, with all my heart,

Sir,
Your most humble and obedient servant
Peleau

Bordeaux, 1 November 1656

[*addressed: see text*]

---

[1] This letter has not apparently survived. On Hobbes's use of an amanuensis see Letter 94 n. 5, and the General Introduction, pp. xxiii–xxiv.

[2] *De corpore*, I. 2.

[3] Ibid., II. 1.

LETTER 96   25 OCTOBER [/4 NOVEMBER] 1656

Henry Stubbe to Hobbes, from Oxford

BL MS Add. 32553, fos. 10–11 (original).
Printed in Nicastro, *Lettere*, pp. 10–12.

S:ʳ

I receiued yoʳˢ of octob:ʳ 22ᵈ.¹ mine had ly[en *blotted*] by mee a weeke
before I sent it, & yᵗ was yᵉ occasion of so old a date. I hope you will
excuse my presumption in those remarques, wherein if yoᵘ find nothing
else, yoᵘ may reade yᵉ affection I had to serue you. Instead of *Quid
quaeris?* any of these formes [*blotted* ma]y serue, *Summa est, Ad summam,
In summâ,* all of wᶜʰ are as usuall as yᵉ English *In Summe.*² As to yᵗ of
ineptus, it was not my obseruation, but Tullye's;³ & Scaliger hath
endeauoured to finde out many wordes for it, as ἀπειρόκαλος wᶜʰ word
(as I remember doth best please Stephen) & μαψυλάκης &c. & σκαιός
may expresse it too;⁴ yᵗ yᵉ Schoole-men were a company of cheates as to
yᵉ generality of their writeings, I easily grant; yet euen in their writeings
they haue [*blotted* go]od intervalls many of yᵐ; & yᵉ new philosophy may
well bee confirmed out of their reasons. D:ʳ Wallis doth justify his
Mathematiques as to euery part, as yᵉ bookeseller telles mee;⁵ & there
will bee one brasse cut, with seuerall figures therein: yᵉ booke will bee
as bigge as his Elenchus,⁶ in yᵗ volume, & a small letter. I haue sent you
his booke agᵗ yᵉ Independents:⁷ you haue here a sermon,⁸ & if you doe
but reade where I haue put downe a leafe; you will find some pretty
interpretations in yᵉ first, & good sermon-criticismes in yᵉ second: it
was as absurd, or worse in yᵉ deliuery: in the 3ᵈ place, are passages agᵗ
Independency: but I shall onely reflect upon yᵗ: It is his Thesis at yᵉ
latter end, yᵗ I answer. In it hee hath mistooke yᵉ question, & giuen good
intelligible definitions, built yᵉ whole fabrique upon Metaphors, of a
flocke, family, body &c.⁹ & alledged impertinent proofes of yᵉ Apostles
&c. wᶜʰ are no more pertinent to us, yⁿ are all yᵉ other promises. &
unlesse hee proue yᵉ [*blotted* pre]sent ministry to bee Apostles, yᵉ
question about their commi[ssion *blotted*] hath no more influence upon
us yⁿ yᵉ debate betwixt Sigonius and Gruchius about yᵉ power of [yᵉ
blotted] Roman tribunes.¹⁰ Hee assumes an authority beyond y[ᵉ *page
torn*] Pope, extending to Infidels; & if euer they preuayle, their
jurisdiction will bee ample, for euery Parish-priest is now Oecu-
menicall, [*blotted* nor sh]all it bee a marke of AntiXᵗ to bee an vniversall

333

bishop, though yᵉ synod at Constantinople decreed it so. I shall not trouble yoᵘ any further, but his saluo's & illustration at yᵉ end,[11] are excellently triviall. D:ʳ Owen[12] hath my answer in his hands, & [>hee] being sicke, I haue not put it into Latine: I haue giuen new answers to Math: 28. & Ephes: 4.[13] such as haue not beene heretofore giuen: & dʳ: Owen is well pleased, & thereupon hath giuen mee yᵉ under-library keeper's place,[14] wᶜʰ hath made all ye Kyrke[15] madde. I intend to refute him clearely & fayrely κατὰ πόδας:[16] & to show all his defects in argueing; & in yᵉ close to make by way of Prosopopoeia[17] a Speech to D:ʳ Wallis as if hee had come to yᵉ congregation whereof I should bee a member to execute his power & in it I shall bee very smart, & I shall reduce his argumᵗˢ to syllogismes, & parallell yᵐ with some of good S. Francis's reasons, wᶜʰ are so alike, yᵗ I cannot but adopt them into yᵉ Fraternity of yᵉ Cordeliers.[18] And in this speech, wᶜʰ I haue now drawne up, but not perfected, I will bestowe as much in aggrauateing this insolent opinion as I can. And I doubt not but d:ʳ Owen will let much passe, for in yᵉ 42ᵈ page D:ʳ W: hath touched him to yᵉ quicke.[19] As to yᵉ verses,[20] I did intend no more yⁿ yᵗ πανετήτυμος should signify *verus*,[21] & yᵗ ἀνήρ should signify *vir*, wᶜʰ is a degree beyond *homo*.[22] & φερώνυμος relates to φῶτα, wᶜʰ signifyes more yⁿ ἄνθρωπος as comeing from φῶς *light*.[23] But if you shall more approue of these yoᵘ finde under-written, yoᵘ may: it is such a subject, yᵗ I can hardly hold enlargeing yᵐ. wᶜʰ made mee so order yᵉ copy: that yᵉ two last, may bee seuered from yᵉ rest, & placed under yᵉ Effigies alone, as being compleate. & then yᵉ other might bee placed ouer against it, and yᵉ same repeated as a conclusion. I thinke it hardly fitting now yᵗ I am engaged for independency, yᵗ my name stand but insteade of it, (if any, but rather none) let it bee Maternus Purefoy[24] Oxon[. *page torn*] S:ʳ I haue noe more at present to acquaint yoᵘ with, but if any opportunity permit mee to wayte upon you, or to procede in yᵗ worke: (wᶜʰ I now onely intermit) I shall not fayle to pay yᵗ respect unto you, wᶜʰ is due from

S:ʳ
yoʳ most humble seruitoʳ
H: Stubbe.

Oxon: Octob: 25. 1656

[*postscript:*]

Τίς νυ μοι εἴδεται ἔνθα μεγήρατος, Ἀγγλὸς Ὀδυσεὺς,
Καὶ πολύαινος ὁμῶς, καὶ πολύμητις Ανήρ;

[*line deleted*]

Ὠυτὸς θὴν πολλῶν ἴδεν ἄστεα, καὶ νόον ἔγνω,
καὶ γῆρυν μερόπων οἶδε πολυσπερέων.
Ἀλλ' ὄχ' ἀριστεύει ἀμός, Σειρῆνας ἐκεῖνος
Ἐξυπάλυξε φυγών, Ὁῦτος ἐπεσπάσατο.²⁵

Ὠυτὸς is used for *ille*, ὁ αὐτὸς, & not *ipse*, in Homer.²⁶ & ἀμός is *nostras*. if yoᵘ like it not yoᵘ may, substitute

Νωΐτερος δέ τ' ἀριστεύει²⁷ &c.

Or yoᵘ may use these.

Ἦ οὐκ ἀλύω ὁρόων; τίς ἐπὶ βροτοειδέι Χαλκῷ
Τεῦξε νεηγένεος (φεῦ!) σοφίης πατέρα;
Δαρδαλεήν ὄγ' ἔρυτο φύσιν,²⁸

&c as in yᵉ other.²⁹ ἀλύω is to bee madde for joy or other occasions, & to doate sometimes. It will bee I suppose 3 weekes before my piece agt d.ʳ Wallis goe to yᵉ presse, if not more: & wᵗ hintes yoᵘ shall giue mee I shall endeavour to improue yᵐ.

[*addressed:*] These For his euer honoured Friend M:ʳ Hobbes together with D:ʳ Wallis's booke London

[*endorsed by James Wheldon:*] Oct. 25ᵗʰ 1656. Mʳ Stubb

---

¹ This letter (a reply to Letter 91) has not apparently survived.
² See Letter 91 n. 11.
³ Ibid., n. 13: Cicero, *De oratore*, 2. 4. 17–18.
⁴ This reference to Scaliger has not been identified. Robertus Stephanus (Robert Estienne) gives ἀπειρόκαλος (meaning 'vulgar', 'tasteless') as one of three possible Greek equivalents of 'ineptus' (*Thesaurus linguae latinae*, ii, p. 514b). μαψυλάκας means 'idly barking'; σκαιός means 'gauche', 'clumsy'.
⁵ Wallis (see Letter 75 n. 7) was preparing his reply to Hobbes's *Six Lessons*, entitled *Due Correction*. Wallis's book was printed by Leonard Lichfield for Thomas Robinson at Oxford. Thomason's copy is dated '7ᵇᵉʳ 26', but this must be an error for '9ᵇᵉʳ', i.e. 26 Nov.: Wallis's dedicatory epistle is dated '15 October'.
⁶ Wallis, *Elenchus*.
⁷ This probably refers to the third section of *Mens sobria* (see Letters 91 n. 6, and 97 n. 2; see also the general note to Letter 97).
⁸ This probably refers to the first section of *Mens sobria*, the sermon which bears that title (see Letter 91 n. 6).
⁹ 'All believers, whether Gentiles or Jews, belong to the same family, the same flock, the same household, the same body' ('ad unam omnes familiam pertinent fideles, sive ex eis Judaeis sive Gentibus; ad eundem omnes gregem, idem domicilium, idem corpus' (*Mens sobria*, p. 142)).

¹⁰ A long-running dispute on this topic in the 1550s and 1560s between Gruchius (Nicolas de Grouchy) and Sigonius (Carlo Sigonio) culminated in the publication of *N. Gruchii et C. Sigonii [. . .] de binis comitiis et lege curiali contrariae inter se disputationes* (1566) and *N. Gruchii ad posteriorem C. Sigonii de binis magistratuum romanorum comitiis disputationem refutatio* (1567). See McCuaig, *Carlo Sigonio*, pp. 197–225.

¹¹ This probably refers to Wallis's comparison, in the final pages of the third section of *Mens sobria* (154–8), of divine ministry to the practice of medicine: an Oxford DM, he argues, is entitled to practise anywhere in England, but still cannot force his practice on a family which does not want his services.

¹² See Letter 91 n. 7.

¹³ Matt. 28: 18–20; Eph. 4: 1–16, the two key texts on the authority of the apostles.

¹⁴ Stubbe had become deputy to Thomas Barlow, Keeper of the Bodleian Library.

¹⁵ The Presbyterian Church.

¹⁶ 'Following closely in his tracks'.

¹⁷ = a rhetorical device in which an imaginary or absent person is supposed to be present and speaking.

¹⁸ The mendicant order of strict or 'observant' Franciscans, which abstained from all ownership of property.

¹⁹ In *Mens sobria*, pp. 42–3, Wallis criticized those who were intolerant and rigid over formalities, especially in a university; this was a transparent reference to Owen's campaign against academic ceremonies.

²⁰ Stubbe apparently refers here to a set of Greek verses in praise of Hobbes sent with one of his previous letters, but now lost.

²¹ The Greek term means 'all-true', the Latin, 'true'.

²² $\dot{\alpha}\nu\acute{\eta}\rho$ and 'vir' mean 'man' in the sense of 'male human being'; 'homo' means 'man' in the sense of 'human being'.

²³ $\phi\epsilon\rho\acute{\omega}\nu\nu\mu\sigma$ means 'well named'. $\phi\hat{\omega}\tau\alpha$ is from $\phi\acute{\omega}s$, meaning 'man' (usually in the sense of 'male human being'); $\acute{\alpha}\nu\theta\rho\omega\pi\sigma$ means 'man' in the sense of 'human being'. $\phi\hat{\omega}s$ means 'light'. The original conjunction of ideas seems to have been that Hobbes was well named a $\phi\acute{\omega}s$ because he was also a $\phi\hat{\omega}s$, a source of enlightenment.

²⁴ Purefoy was Stubbe's mother's maiden name.

²⁵ 'Who is this man here, excelling all others, who seems to me to be an English Odysseus, a much-praised man who is full of wise ideas? That one [the Greek Odysseus] certainly saw the cities of many men and got to know their thoughts, and understood the words of mortals far and wide. But our one [the English Odysseus] far excels him; that one escaped the Sirens by fleeing, but this one lured them to their doom.'

²⁶ This statement is incorrect; the term is also used for 'ipse' in Homer (see Autenrieth, *Homeric Dictionary*; I am grateful to Mr Nigel Hope for this reference).

²⁷ 'The one which belongs to us far excels him.'

²⁸ 'Am I not beside myself with joy when I look at you? Father of—ah!—such new-born wisdom, who fashioned you true to life in copper? For he preserved your form in his skilful work.'

²⁹ This apparently refers to Stubbe's previous set of verses, now lost (see n. 20).

LETTER 97   25 OCTOBER [/4 NOVEMBER] 1656

Henry Stubbe to Hobbes, from Oxford

BL MS Add. 32553, fo. 9 (original).
Printed in Nicastro, *Lettere*, p. 9.

S:^{r}

If upon ye perusall of D:^{r} Wallis's theses,[1] besides yor remarks upon
ye whole; if yo^u thinke fitting to penne a short letter censureing ye tract,
but instanceing at ye absurdity of one argument, or ye tendency y^t it hath
to confusion, or ye erecting a power beyond ye Papall in jurisdiction; or
his irregular proceeding, who should haue opposed ye Independent
thesis,[2] & not haue destroyed ye suppositum quaestionis.[3] besides y^t hee
doth not dispute this question, but another, wch is whither ye ministers
bee Ministri v[niversa]lis[4] Ecclesiae;[5] or rather y^t they are ministers of
Ch^t absolutely; as you may see in his conclusion: p: 152.[6] though betwixt
those two things there are [a *deleted*] great differences: for if they bee
sent to ye uniuersall church, they may preach any where: but if they bee
onely Ministers of Ch^t, his argum^t is, Christ is ye pastour of ye church,
but ye ministers are ministers of Ch:^{t} ergo of ye whole church. in w^{ch}
argumentation there bee 4 termes. I doubt not but yo^u will not finde any
line in it sounde: And if such a letter, as ye judgement of a friend from
London were in, it would doe much to disgrace ye d:^{r} together with a
short paraenesis[7] to mee to confute it. I shall print it without any name.[8]

S:^{r}
I am yor very humble seru^t
H: Stubbe.

Oxon: Octob:^{r} 25. 1656

[*addressed:*] These For his much respected Friend M:^{r} Hobbes.
together with ye booke hast:
London:

[*endorsed by James Wheldon:*] Mr Stubb. Oct. 25th 1656

The order of priority between Letters 96 and 97, which bear the same date, is hard to
establish. They were probably sent simultaneously, by the same carrier. The reference
in Letter 96 (at n. 7) to the 'book' (probably the third section of *Mens sobria*) which

337

Stubbe had already sent suggests that Letter 97 (which concerns that book, and seems from the address to have accompanied it) was written first. But on the other hand the general characters of the two letters strongly suggest the order in which they are printed here: Letter 96 begins with the usual formalities of a correspondence being renewed (references to previous letters, etc.), while Letter 97 has more the nature of a postscript.

¹ See Letter 91 n. 6.

² The second 'quaestio' of the *Quaestiones theologicae* (see Letter 91 n. 6). This is the 'Independent thesis' against which Wallis argues.

³ 'that which is supposed by the question'.

⁴ Contraction expanded.

⁵ 'Ministers of the universal Church'.

⁶ 'It is clear that the ministry of the Gospel is a ministry not of one particular Church alone, but of the whole universal Church; or rather, in absolute terms, that the ministry of Christ is ordained not for the good of one particular Church alone, but for the good of the whole universal Church' ('[est] manifestum, Ministrum Evangelicum, non unius tantum particularis Ecclesiae, sed totius potius Universalis Ministrum esse; seu potius, absolute, Christi Ministrum esse, non ad unius tantum particularis, sed totius Ecclesiae universalis commodum, ordinatum' (*Mens sobria*, p. 152)).

⁷ = exhortation.

⁸ No such work by Stubbe, with or without Hobbes's collaboration, appears to have been printed. Hobbes's own eventual attack on these arguments was published as the section on 'Scotch church politics' in *Markes* (*EW* vii, pp. 395–400).

LETTER 98   9 [/19] NOVEMBER 1656

Henry Stubbe to Hobbes, from Oxford

BL MS Add. 32553, fos. 12–13 (original).
Printed in Nicastro, *Lettere*, pp. 12–14.

S:ʳ

I receiued yoʳ letter¹ with wᵗ deuotion I beare to a person of yoʳ worth, & esteeme I haue of it's subject. I obserued therein, wᵗ I seeme still to find verifyed, (giue mee leaue so farre to undervalue yoᵘ as to speake it) a great correspondence betwixt my thoughts & yours, so yᵗ if Dʳ Owen,² who hath mine in his hands now at London, should but compare my notes with yoʳ remarques, hee would conclude them to bee but yᵉ transcript of yoʳˢ. Assoone as I shall heare further from yᵉ D:ʳ I intend to proceede: in yᵉ meane while, as I haue finished my Epilogisticall³ speech, so I am busyed in penneing yᵉ preface, wherein I shall relate with wᵗ expectation I came to reade Dʳ: W's booke,⁴ as being written by one of yᵉ Scribes of yᵉ Synod,⁵ & a Mathematician, & who had proceeded dʳ with so great solemnity at Oxon, when there happened a competition betwixt him & Ward, to whome rather then

hee would yeeld, hee chose to goe out Grand compounder;[6] & may now
upon y^t account (y^t I may phrase my speech a little after their dialect)
claime some extraordinary relation to y^e *scarlet hoore*.[7] Any one may see,
y^t his principles drawne from those Metaphors will carry us on with a
farre greater apparence to a Pope, y^n a Presbitery; & ye title of *Minister
v[niversa]lis*[8] *Ecclesiae*[9] is ye very cosen germane to y^t old mystery of
iniquity, *Episcopus Ecclesiae catholicae*,[10] wch appellation was frequent of
old, & is in some sense true, but ye people, & ye docto^{rs} whose
concernements did leade them to cherish ye phrase, & varnish ouer y^e
ambiguity, did at last serue it up higher: so *Oecumenicus*, when ascribed
to Bishops or Councells, did not signify more then a bishop of a part
τῆς οἰκυμένης,[11] yet it hath beene a cause of much trouble & scandall:
yet it did meet wth the like interpretations in those times, y^t D:^{r} W: will
giue his now, & D:^{r} Wallis's may bee improued in time if it take with y^e
vulgar, to y^t height wee see ye other to haue arriued at. you neede not
haue sent so soone, there being no urgent hast: I doubt not but you
haue laughed at ye criticall part of his sermon,[12] & his fine exposition:
there is a report (I had it from one y^t liues in ye D^r's house) y^t Roberval
hath sent a letter to London, wherein hee chargeth d^r Wallis with
plagiaryanisme,[13] as haueing stolne his quadrature of ye circle from
him. ye d^r sayth this himselfe, & boasted withall y^t hee had found it out;
& as to his present worke,[14] hee told the same gentleman y^t hee did
belieue you would not answer him, because hee should bereaue you of
all possibility of any such attempt[.][15] I confesse hee hath so pittyfully
argued in this piece of mine, y^t I can imagine him obnoxious to ye most
absurd of phantasyes, who hath betrayed so much vanity in his more
studyed contemplations. If yo^u chance to meet with any further remarke
upon ye last question,[16] (not y^t I want, but because I admire euery thing
y^t proceedes from yo^u) you may be pleased to send it at yor leasure. As
for ye verses,[17] I am glad they please you: As for ye title of y^m, I doubt not
but some of yor friends will accommodate y^m with such an inscription
as may suit with yor merit: I hope yo^u will not deny ye world at last a
sight of yor Optiques:[18] I intend shortly to resume yor Leuiathan, & to
goe as fast on with it, as I can in my nocturnall studyes. I haue since
thought upon a distick to place at y^e base of y^e Effigies, letting y^e other
to stand opposite: I am no great poet in Latine, but you may use wch you
shall like best:

> Aspice, quo fuerit celeberrimus Hobbius ore:
> Hoc referunt Tabulae, caetera nemo potest.[19] or
>
> or Caetera de scriptis, Hoc tibi charta refert.[20]

or

> $T o \hat{\iota} o \varsigma \, \dot{\epsilon} \nu \omega \pi \iota \delta \acute{\iota} \omega \varsigma \, \tau \eta \lambda \epsilon \kappa \lambda \upsilon \tau \grave{o} \varsigma \, "O \beta \beta \iota \acute{o} \varsigma \, \dot{\epsilon} \sigma \tau \iota \cdot$
> $T o \hat{\upsilon} \tau o \, \pi \acute{\iota} \nu a \xi, \, o \dot{\upsilon} \delta \epsilon \grave{\iota} \varsigma \, \tau' \, \ddot{a} \lambda \lambda a \, \sigma \kappa \iota a \gamma \rho a \phi \acute{\epsilon} \epsilon \iota$[21]

S:[r] I cannot say any more of these, then that they speake much of y[t] entire respect I haue for you, & wish I could bring so much merit as to deserue yo[r] friendship. I doe not question yo[r] being Communicative, but I perceiue yo[r] defect in writeing now;[22] so y[t] I am some what ashamed to preferre y[t] request unto you, w[ch] engages you to any trouble. You haue beene pleased in yo[r] physiques to say y[t] *first mouer is moued*:[23] w[ch] I confesse to bee true, yet I am at a losse in eternity, & scarce see how hee is first mouer being moued: for in a circulation of causes, there is no first; but such as is arbitrarily designed. If yo[u] would oblige mee with a short discourse, of w[t] yo[u] haue hinted or if you haue any discourse lyeing by you, (as I heare yo[u] haue ag[t] M[r] White seuerall pieces of seuerall subjects,)[24] if you would bee please to impart y[m] to mee when I shall finde any opportunity, I should esteeme it a singular fauour. But I shall not presume to dispose of your houres, it is an high insolency, but to haue requested such a trouble from M:[r] Hobbes; & nothing can equall it, but y[e] impudent expectation of an answer, but I hope yo[u] can pardon S:[r]

yo[r] most affectionate seruant
Henry Stubbe

Oxon: Nou: 9. 1656.

[*addressed:*] These For his much respected friend M:[r] Th: Hobbes, Leaue this at M:[r] Crookes[25] shoppe, at y[e] shippe in Paul's church-yard booke-seller London. hast

[*endorsed by James Wheldon:*] M.[r] Stubb. No. 9. 1656.

---

[1] This letter has not apparently survived; it was evidently a reply to Letters 96 and 97.

[2] See Letter 91 n. 7.

[3] = having the nature of an epilogue.

[4] *Mens sobria*, by John Wallis (see Letter 75 n. 7), on which Stubbe was planning to publish an anonymous attack (see Letter 97).

[5] See Letter 91 n. 9.

[6] John Wallis and Seth Ward (on whom see Letter 75 n. 8) proceeded Doctors of Divinity together in 1654, and both had the same number of years of 'seniority'. The university statutes provided that in such cases precedence would be given to 'grand compounders', i.e. those who paid a higher fee for their degree. In Anthony Wood's

words, 'Wallis aver'd that he was incorporated M. of A. of this university before Ward and therefore 'twas his, but it appearing that Ward stood first in the proctor's book at Cambridge (for they proceeded in arts both in one year) the Vice-chancellor Dr. Owen decided the matter on Ward's behalf: whereupon Wallis went out grand compounder, and so got seniority' (*Fasti*, ii, col. 184). See also Nicastro, *Lettere*, p. 64.

[7] The scarlet whore of Babylon, a term from Rev. 17, usually applied by Puritan and millenarian writers to the papacy. Stubbe is thinking also of the scarlet gown worn by Doctors of Divinity.

[8] Contraction expanded.

[9] 'Minister of the universal Church' (see Letter 97).

[10] 'Bishop of the Catholic Church'. 'Mystery of iniquity', a term from 2 Thess. 2: 7, was applied by Protestant writers to the papacy and its policies.

[11] 'Of the oikumene' (the New Testament term for the Christian community).

[12] See Letter 96 n. 8.

[13] Wallis had himself accused Hobbes of plagiarism from several authors, including Roberval, in *Elenchus*, pp. 132–3, and he repeated the charge in *Due Correction*, pp. 124–5, 130. On Roberval see Letter 76 n. 4. The letter from Roberval mentioned here does not apparently survive.

[14] *Hobbiani puncti dispunctio*.

[15] Concealed by binding.

[16] The second 'quaestio' of the section *Quaestiones theologicae* of Wallis's *Mens sobria* (see Letters 96, 97).

[17] See Letter 96.

[18] This probably refers to the first part of *De homine* (1658).

[19] 'See here what the most famous Hobbes looked like. Pictures can tell you this; but no one can tell you the rest.'

[20] 'The plate can show you this, but the rest must be derived from his writings.'

[21] 'This is what the far-famed Hobbes looks like face to face; the painter can sketch this, but no one can sketch the rest.'

[22] See Letter 94 n. 5.

[23] *De corpore*, XXVI. 1.

[24] This probably refers to Hobbes's *Anti-White*, fragments of which seem to have been in circulation. One such fragment, corresponding to IX. 1–9, is in Leipzig University Library, MS Stadtbibliothek Rep. IV. 47, fos. 5–7'; this appears to have belonged to Claude Guiraud of Nîmes (d. 1657), who was acquainted with Sorbière. The Catholic philosopher Thomas White (1593–1676) was ordained a priest in 1617 and taught at English seminaries in Douai and Lisbon. He was a close friend of Sir Kenelm Digby, at whose house he stayed in London, and with whom he visited Rome in the 1640s. His treatise on physics, theology, and metaphysics, *De mundo*, was published in Paris in 1642; Hobbes's long refutation of it remained in MS until this century. See H. W. Jones, 'Thomas White', and Hobbes, *Anti-White*, pp. 22–45.

[25] John Crooke (see Letter 91, general note).

LETTER 99   [12/] 22 NOVEMBER 1656

Abraham du Prat to Hobbes, from Paris

Chatsworth, Hobbes MSS, letter 28 (original).

Monsieur,

Ne pouuant apprendre de vos nouuelles, ni par la bouche de la
renommée, ni par celle de M^r du bosc, ni par vos lettres, ie prens la
liberté de vous en demander à vous mesmes. J'espere que vous excu-
serés ma curiosité, puis qu'elle n'a d'autre motif, que celui de me tirer
de la peine ou vostre long silence m'a reduit. Si les lettres que ie vous ay
escrites il y a long temps vous ont esté renduës, vous aurés sceu, que ie
n'ay point receu la Philosophie *Epicuro-Gassendo-Carletoniana*,[1] que
vous m'aués fait la faueur de m'enuoyer. Je crains que ceux à qui vous
l'auiés baillée, ne l'ayent ou retenuë ou perduë. Quoy qu'il en soit, ie
vous en suis [>aussi] obligé, que si elle estoit venuë entre mes mains.
On va imprimer à lyon toutes les oeuures de Mr Gassendi, dont ie vous
enuoye l'Elenchus,[2] que vous serés peutestre bien aise de voir. Celui
qui a soin de cette impression me prie de lui enuoyer un petit abregé de
vostre logique, pour l'inserer dans les ouurages de Mr Gassendi, dans
la place ou il auoit [>dessein] de mettre vos opinions sur cette
matiere,[3] si la mort ne l'eut preuenu. J'ay creu Monsieur qu'il faloit
s'adresser [>à vous] pour [>en] auoir un fidele abregé, et qu'il n'y
auoit personne qui fut capable de le bien dresser que vous mesmes. Je
vous prie donc de me l'enuoyer au plus tost, parce que l'on
commencera par la logique. Autrement on sera obligé de faire [>faire]
cet abregé par la main d'un autre, qui ne reussira pas si bien que vous.
Je vous prie de croire que ie suis passionnement

Vostre tres humble et tres obeissant seruiteur
Du Prat

A Paris ce 22 Nouembre 1656

[*postscript:*] Mrs Martel et Sorbiere vous baisent tres humblement les
mains.

[*addressed:*] A Monsieur
Monsieur Hobbes at the greene Dragons in pauls churchyard A
Londres.

[*endorsed by James Wheldon:*] mons.^r du Prat No. [24 *deleted* >22] 1656

Translation of Letter 99

Sir,

As I have been unable to learn any news of you, either from rumour, or from M. du Bosc, or from your letters, I am taking the liberty of asking you for it yourself. I hope you will forgive my curiosity, since its only motive is to release me from the anxiety to which your long silence has reduced me. If the letters which I wrote to you a long time ago were delivered, you will have learned that I never received the *Physiologia Epicuro-Gassendo-Carltoniana*[1] which you were so kind as to send to me. I am afraid that the people you consigned it to have either kept it or lost it. Be that as it may, I am just as grateful to you as I would have been if I had received it.

At Lyon they are going to print the complete works of M. Gassendi; I enclose a scheme of the edition,[2] which you may be glad to see. The person who is in charge of the edition has asked me to send him a short summary of your Logic, to insert it into M. Gassendi's works at the place where he had intended (if death had not prevented it) to state your opinions on that subject.[3] I have come to the conclusion, Sir, that we must turn to you for an accurate summary, and that no one apart from you is competent to do it properly. So please send it to me as soon as possible, since the edition will begin with works on logic. Otherwise it will be necessary to get someone else to make the summary, who will do it less successfully than you. I beg you to believe that I am, passionately,

Your most humble and obedient servant,
du Prat

Paris, 22 November 1656

[*postscript:*] MM. de Martel and Sorbière present their most humble compliments to you.

[*addressed: see text*]

The author of this letter is identified as Abraham du Prat by his handwriting.

[1] See Letter 74 n. 4.

[2] 'Elenchus' can mean either 'supplement' or 'refutation' or 'review'; since Gassendi did not write any work entitled *Elenchus*, I take it here to mean a review or prospectus of the edn. This edn. was Gassendi's *Opera omnia*, prepared by Sorbière and de Montmor, and published in six vols. at Lyon in 1658.

³ In Gassendi's *Syntagma*, printed for the first time in this edn. (see n. 2), chs. 9, 10, and 11 of book 1 (i, pp. 59–66) consist of summaries of the logics of Ramus, Bacon, and Descartes respectively. A summary of Hobbes's logic was evidently intended for a ch. 12; but no such summary was in fact included.

LETTER 100   [23 NOVEMBER/] 3 DECEMBER 1656

François du Verdus to Hobbes, from Bordeaux

Chatsworth, Hobbes MSS, letter 30 (original).

Monsieur,

Me le pardonerés vous, que je vous enuoye un gros pacquet de choses qui vous seront inutiles? Mais toute la vie des hommes qu'est elle qu'un enchainement de bons offices, qu'on rend a ses amis, et cela de temps en temps auec quelque incomodité. Ceux dont je vous prie de m'obliger, C'est en premier lieu de prendre en bone part que je vous aye enuoyé la Rélation de mes affaires,¹ comme je l'ay faite imprimer, c'est a dire comme elles sont en effect. Il est uray que j'y ay dissimulé mon ressentiment contre l'Archeueque de Bourdeaux,² et les Jesuites: Ceux cy m'usurpent de fort belles rentes que mon Ayeul acquit de la Baronie de Montferrand;³ et me font tenir bas par Cabales, et affaires qu'ils excitent, et norrissent, affin que je sois sans résistance contre eux: et pour l'Archeueque de Bourdeaux, il a enuie de la Cure d'Ambarés⁴ pour l'annexer a son Archeuesché; et en faisoit traiter autrefois son Oéconome auec un de nos Conseillers aux requétes nommé Mᵣ Quaysac⁵ qui en étoit pourueu; et comme le Sᵣ Dejean⁶ le Curé d'a present de cette parroisse (qui uaut six mille francs de reuenu) a grand' enuie de mes biens; et que pour me les enleuer il auoit tramé toute l'intrigue de leur Moynesse Renegate:⁷ l'Archeueque l'ayant laissé éuader (comme Vous uerrés dans la Rélation de mes affaires) c'est a dire l'ayant remise entre les mains de Déjean, il m'a fait 14 mois entiers un deny de justice de sa sentençe, qu'il me faisoit promettre sous main, à condition que je traitasse de tous mes biens auec un homme qu'il ne me nomoit pas, c'est a dire auec Déjean: Il a donc falu éclater: et me trouuant seul contre [>tous] ces ennemis, l'Archeueque, les jesuites, Dejean, les feuillas,⁸ (c'est a dire les filoux de Bourdeaux) et une grande Cabale de mes parens, j'ay soné comme on dit le tocsin sur eux; et crié au secours a l'étranger. Or Monsieur comme dans ce temps Mᵣ Bourdelot⁹ premier medecin de la Reyne de Suede et son Resident en françe, uouloit m'engager a suiure cette fortune; et que je préuoy qu'on

me poussera a autres choses: je souhaite que vous ayés entre vos mains
cette Rélation de mes affaires: que si je uay ce printemps en Angleterre,
elle me serue a estre connu de M^r le Comte de Déuonsire, et de qui
vous jugerés a propos: a quoy mesme je vous prieray de faire seruir
cette lettre-cy. L'autre chose que je vous demande, c'est s'il vous plait
Monsieur, que vous m'expliquiés les endroits de vostre Leuiathan que
je vous marque dans les feuillets ajoutés icy; que j'ay trouués difficiles.
Le *Cui bono* qui sera s'il vous plait vostre motif, c'est en premier lieu
que moyenant cette explication je vous promets vne Traduction en
francois de votre Leuiatan le plus exacte et la plus fidelle qui se puisse
faire: et cela sans uanter le Traducteur: Ce qui ne seruira pas peu a
étendre dans le monde uostre réputation déja fort grande: et en second
lieu c'est que vous y aurés la joye d'auoir instruit et enseigné un homme
désireux de profiter de vos instructions, et sur tout qui vous honore
plus que persone du Monde. J'ay compté comme vos responses uienent
que je pourrois auoyr la vostre aux étrennes. Je vous assure Monsieur
que je n'en puis réçeuoir d'aucun endroit de si agréables, et que je
cherisse tant: et vous souhaitant heureux ce qui reste de cette année, et
celle que nous alons comançer, et auec cela une longue et heureuse uie
durant le cours de plusieurs autres [>années:]: Je vous assure que je
suis de tout mon coeur

Monsieur
Vostre tres humble, et tres obeissant seruiteur
duuerdus

A Bourdeaux le 3eme x^{bre} 1656

[*endorsed by James Wheldon:*] M. du Verdus. Dec. 3. 1656

[*enclosed:*]
Endroits que je n'entans pas de vostre Leuiathan.

Postulata.

1 Quand j'auray écrit toute une phrase en Anglois et qu'aprés cela j'en
rediray quelque mot auec le point d'interrogation? ce point
d'interrogation demande qu'est ce que ce mot signifie; et signifie que
c'est là le mot que je n'entans pas.

le mesme si ie tire une ligne (comme cela) ____ au dessous du mot.

2 Quand juzeray de termes imperatifs comme je fais souuent de celluy-
cy (Traduisés) s'il vous plait de sous-entendre, *je vous prie* : Car [c'est
deleted] ce sont autant de prieres que je vous fais.

du Traité of Man

P. ueut dire page.

p. 2. but there is another saying not *of late* understood. of late?

p. 2. a 8 l. de la fin. but let one man read another by his actions *neuer so perfectly*.

p. 3 which endeauour because *outward* seemeth to be some matter without. outward?

p. 6 a 14 l. de la fin and thence[10] it is that lying cold. lying cold?

p. 7. l. 6 in case any *uncouth* and exorbitant fancy. uncouth?

p. 14. a 14 l. de la fin And men were *faun*[11] to apply their fingers. *faun?*

p. 17. sur le milieu And therefore if speech be peculiar to man (*as for ought i Know it is*) traduisés la parenthése. 2º je souhaiterois que vous me dissiés par ou vous aués connu que l'homme seul a l'usage de la parole: Car pour moy il me semble que j'entans aussi bien a, e, i, o, u, a l'aboy des chiens et au jargon des oyes qu'au bas breton

Mais ce que je dis des oyes me fait souuenir que j'ay oublié quelques endroits de vostre Épitre dédicatoire. p. A2; a 4 l. de la fin *Nor how it may reflect on those* traduisés. aussi p. A2 uerssa. between the *points* of both. *points?* plus bas il y a, offending none I think ce que j'entens bien: mais je n'entans pas ce qui suit *but those without or such within (if there be any such) as fauour them*. traduisés donc s'il vous plait et le mot outworks en suite.

Aussi p. 2. je trouue ce passage obscur as it is now used to countenance either the barbarous estate of men in power towards their inferiours: or to encourage men of low degree to a *sawcie* behauiour towards their betters. je vous prie de traduire tout cela en latin. Ce qui fait ma difficulté C'est qu'on peut dire Nosce teipsum en quatre rancontres. Aux grands Nosce teipsum qu'etans assés puissant pour dompter les petits gens qui font les suffisans. Aux grands aussi Nosce teipsum que tu n'es qu'un homme comme le petit que tu opprimes. Aux petits Nosce teipsum tu n'es pas assés fort pour tenir teste a plus grand que toy: aux petits encore Nosce teipsum puis que tu es homme aussi bien que ce Grand qui t'oprime et que tu peux estre maistre de sa vie en méprisant la tiene, empeche le de t'oprimer. Mais je retourne a la—

p. 19 l. 14. *by the claym they lay to it*. traduisés en latin ou en françois.

P 19 a 3 l. de la fin Or any free but free from being hindred by opposition. Traduisés.

[p. 20 the nature of a thing is its definition: je voy bien que la Nature de l'homme est l'accident et sa définition, un discours et qu'ainsi il est mal dit que la Nature d'une chose soit sa définition Mais quand vous dites en suite *a Mans command is his Will* ie ne uois pas lequel des deux *command* ou *Will* est accident ou nom plutot que l'autre et vous prie de me l'expliquer. *deleted* >ie comprens que *command* est le langage et *will* l'accident.]

1. derniére *but are taken up* traduisés.

p. 21 a 16 l. de la fin. an (supple according) the errours[12] of one another. traduisés.

p. 23 l. 24. for let a space be neuer so litle that which is moued ouer a greater space

et plus bas And when the endeauour is *fromward* something. fromward?

et cecy. for nature it selfe does often presse upon men those truths. traduisés en latin.

p. 25. a 13 l. de la fin As first when they one succeed another. est ce quand ces passions se succederont l'une a l'autre? [ou quand elles *deleted*]

p. 26. Admiration proper to man because it excites the appetite of Knowing the cause que sçauons nous si les autres animaux admirent? Et s'ils ne conoissent point beaucoup de causes? je vous prie repondés moy coment vous jugés qu'on peut le sçauoir?

p. 27. sudden dejection is the passion that causeth *Weeping*. Weeping? aussi *Laughter?* et a *fellow-feeling?*

Ce que vous dites p. 28. que vous ne sçauriés conceuoir qui fut possible[13] on le racconte d'un homme apelé le cheualier d'Audrieu[14] qui mourut enfin sur un Échaffaut. Cet homme prenoit un plaisir singulier de fuziller les couureurs qui recouuroient les maisons, pour rire de la grimaçe qu'ils faisoient en tombant de dessus le toit

p. 30. l. 16. There is at last an end *either by attaining or by giuing ouer*. traduisés en latin

p. 31 in so much as the plea of conscience has been always hearkened unto uery diligently in all times. traduisés en latin.

p. 33. l. 5. And whereas in this succession. ie uoudrois cet whereas en latin. a 4 lignes de là il y a similitudes in case they be such. [*they* ueut dire *elles* c'est a dire similitudes ou ueut dire *Eux* c'est a dire ceux qui obseruent. *deleted* > ueut dire elles]

347

p. 35. l. 16 There would be no lesse difference of men in their sight[15] on vous niera la mineure Car posé que ce que ie uoys rouge, un autre le uoye tanné et cela dépuis sa naissance: il ne laissera pas de l'apeler rouge aussi bien que moy; parçe qu'on luy aura apris de le nomer ainsi.

p. 35. a 15 l. de la fin *giddinesse?*

et a 3 l. de la fin. *selfe-conceit?*

p. 39 l. 28. but are fallen upon by some throug misunderstanding &ᶜ trad. en latin.

p. 41 *Worthinesse?* qu'est cela Car ce n'est pas Merite comme on uoid p. 46 sur la fin

p. 46. the Old Master that is to say in Dutch the Herealt. *Old Master? Dutch?* puis such as bare the generall company out of friendship. traduisés.

p. 49. l. 9. *to hold together.*

p. 52. are not[16] signes nor fruit of religion but in man. Qu'en sçauons nous? Et ce qu'on dit du Culte que les Elephans rendent au Soleil,[17] et les Cynocephales a la Lune?[18] Mais quand cela ne seroit pas qui peut sçauoyr ce qui se passe dans le cerueau et dans le coeur des autres animaux?

p. 53. l. 23. and therefore call them Ghosts. Ghosts?

p. 55. Contention vertue honour health rust.[19] rust?

p. 56. l. 6. And but *immates*[20] of Heauen. Immates?

et a 4 l. de la fin dipping of uerses in homer. dipping?

p. 59. a 11 l. de la fin and juggling betweene princes. juggling?

p. 60 l. 18. the fées of private Masses, and Wales[21] of purgatory. fees? Wales?

p. 64. A law of nature is a generall rule *found out* by reason. *found out?* et l. derniere when others are so too. too?

p. 66. l. 16. and in the means of so preseruing life *as not to be weary of it.*

p. 67. l. derniere. In contract i merit at the contractors hand. traduisés.

p. 68. l. 8. (hoodwinkt with carnall desires) traduisés.

p. 70. a 16 l de la fin The passion to be rekconed upon traduisés.

p. 72. somewhat like to a piece of Law in Cokes Comentaries on Litleton where he sayes if the right Heire of the Crown be attainted of treason; yet the Crown shall descend to him and eo instante *the atteynder be uoyd.* je uoudrois cela traduit, et sçauoir qui étoit ce Litleton et ce qu'il prétandoit prouuer je ueux dire quel liure il a fait et de quoy et a quel dessin.[22]

p. 73. passé le milieu. and so, as all men that contribute not to his destruction, forbear him onely out of ignorance of what is good for themselues. traduisés.

p. 74. *to be beholding?*

p. 76. l. 15. *as combersome thereunto*.

p. 80. Of Persons authors and things *personated*. de personis authoribus et rebus . . . . [>personated?] des persones autheurs et choses . . . . personated?

p. 81. l. 4. *owned* by those whom they represent. Owned?

p. 81 a 4 l. de la fin *a Bridge?*

du Traité of Common-wealth.

p. 86 a 15 l. de la fin. Qui peut assurer que les fourmis et les abeilles n'ayent pas un langage entre elles? que celles-cy ayant un Roy qu'elles reuérent ce respect et obeissançe ne leur uiene pas comme aux hommes *ex instituto?* qu'elles n'ayent nuls honneurs et dignités? Car qui sçait s'il n'y en a point quelques unes, qui par préférence aux autres se tienent plus proches de la persone de leur Roy? d'ailleurs quant a la seconde raison[23] quoy qu'elles soyent d'accord entre elles de faire leur miel en mesme ruche peut on dire que pour cela elles n'ayent nul sujet de different entre elles? n'y a t il pas des endroits dans les ruches plus commodes les uns que les autres: il faut donc faire a qui les aura, jusqu'a ce que cela soit reiglé: et qui peut dire qu'en le reiglant ne soit pas comme les hommes ob mutuum metum?

p. 89. a la marge Soweraing power cannot be *forfeited*. forfeited?

p. 91. the most sudden and roug busling in of a new truth. traduisés en latin.

p. 92. a 4. l. de la fin and persons of *infant Heires*. Infant heires?

p. 93 sur le milieu and the name of the Soweraing[24] no more giuen by the *Grantees?* et en suite if we *grant bak* the Soweraingty. *grant bak?*

p. 104. l. 18. beaten and taken or put to flight. *flight?* et, to auoyd the cruelty of their Task-masters. *Taskmasters?*

p. 106. to distinguish betweene them aright. *aright?*

p. 108. a 10 l. de la fin. traduisés cecy en latin. And did not his will assure the necessity of mans will, and consequently of all that on mans will dependeth the liberty of men would be a contradiction and impediment to the omnipotence and liberty of God.

p. 109 These *bonds* &ᶜ may neuerthelesse be made *to hold. bonds? to hold?*

p. 111. shared amongst them the soweraingty of Rome. *shared?*

p. 118. Somer-Islands?²⁵ dites le moy en latin, et aussi en françois.

p. 119. fellow-subject?

p. 120. for building &ᶜ and manning of Ships. *manning?*

p. 123 l. 13. such doctrine as was against their religion and *trade.* trade? je sçay bien qu'ailleurs il ueut dire mestier comme le métier d'un artizan: mais le mot de métier est équiuoque en uieux gaulois et ueut dire besoin, comme le fa mestierj italien.

p. 126. parlant de l'espion que vous comparés a l'oeil he is but a priuate minister; but yet a minister of the Common-wealth. dites moy je vous prie précisément s'il est ministre priué, ou ministre d'état, ou comment il est l'un et l'autre.

p. 127. the nutrition of a Common-wealth consisteth in the plenty. *plenty?*

p. 135 a 3 l. de la fin tout cecy. of their motly orations made of the diuers colored threds or shreds of authors. je ne trouue ni *motly* ni *therds* ni *shreds* dans mon dictionaire.

p. 136. that wisheth for or would accept of their pains. traduisés. en suite je trouue *wheele-barrough*, que mon dictionaire explique une *brou-ëtte* Et comme je ne uis de ma vie jouir a la paume en brouëtte, quoy que je concoiue que cela se peut en un jeu de longue-paume: je vous demande si lon y jouë ainsi en Angleterre;²⁶ et precisement comment je dois traduire *wheele-barrough*.

And therefore no great popular Common-wealth was euer *kept up.* kept up?

p. 139 a [13]²⁷ l. de la fin if it should assemble neuer so many or so wise men. traduisés.

p. 140. (as Sʳ Ed. Coke makes it) mettés s'il vous plait le nom tout au long qu'on puisse traduire.

p. 144 sur le milieu and brough to a legall triall. traduisés.

Je souhaiterois bien de sçauoir qui fut le Docteur qui fit imprimer la Loy que vous reputés a la fin de [>la mesme page]²⁸

p. 146. passé le milieu the ordinary triall²⁹ of right. traduisés. Car que triall ueuille dire le saggio italien et nostre essay, come le maistre d'hotel fait l'essay des uiandes: là il ueut dire autre chose.

p. 157. je uoudrois facti speciem des 14 lignes qui comencent if that man, et finissent upon complaint.[30] 2ᵉment je ne sçay comment traduire cecy because he might haue been righted upon complaint.

p. 160. because not onely he [was *deleted*] has wrong that falls by such judgemens. traduisés.

p. 164. As Badges Titles Offices &ᶜ. *Badges?*

p. 167. combersome points of their greatnesse.

p. 168. if Solon had not caused to be giuen out he was mad. *giuen out?*

p. 170. And for those[31] doctrines men are chiefly *beholding* &ᶜ beholding? et en suite out of an imitation of the Low Countries. traduisés.

p. 172 overwhelm the Commonwealth with oppression. *overwhelm?*

p. 173. l. 16. he is fain at last. *fain?*

p. 174. and the wens of united Conquests. *Wens?*

p. 177. so as to proclaime mariages with them in facie Ecclesiae by preachers. je vous demande doctrinae gratiâ un exemple de cela tiré de l'histoire.

p. 180 sur le milieu. may be righted of the injuries done them. *righted of?*

p. 181 l. 12. in the exercise of seuerall trades and Callings. *Callings?* Puis a 7 l. de la fin to inhabit closer together, and not range a great deal of ground, to snatch what they find, but to court each litle plot. traduisés: Car je n'y entens rien.

p. 182. unnecessary laws are trapps for mony. *trapps?*

p. 185. have been alwayes put to the trouble of contriuing their titles. traduisés tout. d'ailleurs je uoudrois que vous m'enseignassiés si *their* ueut dire d'eux les Souuerains, ou *d'Eux* des brouillons:[32] peut estre que *to contriue* bien expliqué l'expliquera.

p. [186 *deleted*] 188. l. 10. my tradings had well-nigh slipt. traduisés

p. 189. a 13 l. de la fin le premier mot est beholders. beholders?

p. 192. l. 17. to set light by his Commandemens. traduisés.

Du Traité of a Christian Common-wealth

p. 195. Whereof there dependeth much upon supernaturall reuelations of the Will of God. Ce genitif *Whereof* ne define-t-il pas un nominatif: comme *whereof notiçe* Et de mesme le uerbe *dependeth*.[33] traduisés donc en latin que je uoye ce qui est sous-entandu.

aussi. not to be folded up in the napkink of an implicite aith.[34]

aussi and not to labour in fifting[35] out a philosophicall truth by Logik of such misteries as are not comprehensible. traduisés.

p. 196. which in sum is thrust and faith in him that speaketh. traduisés. aussi to win beleef.

p. 197. first that God wil not haue miracles alone serue for arguments &c. je m'embarrasse là en ce que je voys le present du uerbe *will not* regire deux infinitifs *haue* et *serue* et cela ne se faisant ni en nostre langue, ni en latin, je ne sçay comment traduire.

p. 203. vous cités un passage d'Esdras l. 2. ch. 14. dans la Vulgate le 2^d d'Esdras n'a que 13 chapitres: et je n'ay pas icy mes Concordançes de la Bible: dites moy donc où est ce passage dans la Vulgate.[36]

p. 204. sur la fin And his claim to the Kingdome. claim?

p. 208. so that the proper signification of Spirit in common speech, is either a subtile fluid and inuisible body, or a *Ghost* or other Idol or phantasme of the imagination. *Ghost?*

p. 209 sur la fin. Ezech. 2. 30. dans la Vulgate Ezech. 2. n'a que 9 uerssets: ou donc trouueray-je ce passage.[37]

p. 210 l. 2. whereupon. *whereupon?*

aussi l. 19. submission to that *main* article of Christian faith. *main?*

l. 28. How we came to translate Spirits by the word Ghosts which signifieth nothing i examine not. ie fais icy deux questions; celle que j'ay faite déja comment traduire *Ghosts*: l'autre comment uous croyés qu'on soit uenu a dire Ghosts pour spirits.

p. 211. and out of them framed their opinions. &c *out of them*

p. 212. if it had had the form of a man or Child *of neuer so great beauty. of neuer so great beauty.* traduisés.

p. 213. to goe along With the campe. traduisés.

p. 216. from the uery creation. traduisés.

p. 219. for the claim whereof. *claim?*

aussi aprés auoyr dit il y a tant d'autres lieux &^{c} que ce seroit merueille [> &^{c}]. je n'entans pas ce qui suit that it were a wonder but that it giues too much light.[38] traduisés

aussi This they haue obserued that in stead of a sacerdotall Kingdome translate a Kingdome of Priests: for they may as well translate, a Royall Priesthood (as is[39] in St Peter) into a Priesthood of Kings. uoicy la traduction mot pour mot Cecy ils ont obserué qu'au lieu de sacerdotall royaume traduit un Royaume de Prestres[40] (et jusque-là le uerbe n'y est pas; et il n'y a point de sens) Car ils peuuent aussi bien traduire vne Royale Prestrise (comme il y a dans St Pierre) en une Prestrise des Roys. Et là effectiuement je ne trouue pas de sintaxe. Mais pour bien faire je souhaiterois tout ce nombre là traduit en latin dépuis There be, jusqu'a threasure.

Je trouue une difficulté sur la p. 219. Dieu regnoit sur les Juifs par pacte: les Juifs le détronerent pour auoyr des Roys comme les autres: Jesus-Christ uenu pour retablir ce Royaume là, déclare que son Royaume n'est pas de ce monde; ainsi ce n'est qu'a son second aduenement qu'il rétablira ce Royaume temporel: et de vray nous prions *ton Royaume aduiene* qui marque qu'il n'est pas uenu: Voylà uostre systeme: et qui est uray. Cependant vous dites a la fin de cette page et dans la 120e. Que si le Royaume de Dieu n'étoit pas un Royaume qu'il exerçe déja son royaume en Terre Car vous ne dites pas *should exercise* uous dites *did exercise* et vous dites des Roys qu'ils sont oints *under Christ* Gods ministers, Holy men. C'est donc Dieu qui regne selon vous et ainsi vous tombés ce me semble en contradiction et dites icy ou que les Juifs ne déposerent pas Dieu, ou que son Royaume est rétably.

p. 222. then Paul and Barnabas waxed bold. waxed bold?

aussi *go stand*.

aussi daily in the temple. daily est ce quotidie, tous les jours: ou tutto il giorno tout le jour?

p. 225. that in Christian Churches haue a calling to say publique prayers. a calling?

p. 228 l. 2. lest they should hear. *lest?*

aussi l. 10. of Prophets that were so by a perpetual Calling. *Calling?*

Ce que vous dites en suite After the People of the Jews had rejected God, that he should no more reign ouer them, those Kings which summitted themselues to God Gouernment, were also his Chiefs prophets; and the Hig-Priests office became ministeriall: Cela dis-je est sujet a une grande objection que font les Prestres: Que puis que par le pacte d'entre Dieu et Moyse, Dieu auoit promis vn Royaume Sacerdotall, les Roys qui se soumirent au Gouuernement de Dieu se soumirent au Grand-prestre; et que c'est d'eux des Roys que l'office became ministeriall; de sorte qu'ils ne furent aprés cela que [les *deleted*] des Generaux d'armée.

p. 229. l. 4. In the time of the new testament there was no Soveraing Prophet but our Sauiour: Cela ne contredit il point ce que vous auiés dit que Caiphe prophetiza comme Souuerain Pontife.[41]

aussi p. 229. Moyse dit a Josüé be not jealous in my *behalf*. behalf?

p. 233. Which the Almigty is about to bring to passe. [is al *deleted*] traduisés.

p. 234. When neuerthelesse there were others, could &[c]. n'y a til pas *which* ou *that* sousentandu?

p. 236. And so far from supernaturall. *so far*?

p. 238. depuis The maintenance of Ciuill Society, [jusqu'à *deleted*] traduisés en latin les 4 lignes.

p. 240. le premier mot holdeth also in this. *holdeth*?

aussi l. 4. for as death is reckoned. *reckoned*?

p. 242. l. 8 *under ground*.

p. 243. l. 17. utter darknesse. *utter*?

aussi Wedding garment. *Wedding*?

p. 246. The Lord shall be to them as a *broad mote* of swift waters. broad mote. De plus j'ay sur ce passage une grand difficulté Car s'il est uray que the lame take the prey soit que cela s'entende du boiteux par maladie ou du boiteux estropié au combat je ne uoy pas comment cet État est un État de Salut; et qu'on n'y puisse pas dire I am sicke[42]

p. 249 for as to the Morall Law they were already obliged, *and needed not haue been contracted withall*, by promise of the land of Canaan. traduisés ce qui est aligné

p. 251. l. 2. remoued and *stood afar off*.

p. 252 lest they breack throug unto the Lord to gaze.

p. 253. Samuel had an extraordinary *calling* to the gouernment. Calling?

p. 255. l. 7 *so far forth as* concerned the right.

aussi passé le milieu *they made account* they worshipped the God of Israel.

p. 261. an atonement. atonement?

a 4 l. de la. two yong goates. je trouue goate, cheureau, c'est a dire le fils de la cheure: mais comme nous disons en francois *le bouc émissaire* et non le cheureau émissaire je ne sçay coment il faudra traduire two yong goates. si c'est deux jeunes ou *boucs* ou *cheureaux*.

p. 265 There is another conjecture drawn from the Ceremonies of the Gentiles. obligés moy de me dire d'où vous aués tiré cela.

p. 267. Here we haue the person of God born now the third time. traduisés

p. 268 The spirit and the Water and the Bloud and these three agree in one. Comment traduire *agree in one*? l'édition uulgate a unum sunt.

p. 269. And not to reign in Majesty, *no not*; as his fathers Lieutenant. je n'entans pas ce, *no not*,

p. 270. l. 7. so many Nimrods. traduisés.

d'ailleurs la comparaison des pescheurs donne quelque doute. Car les pescheurs, comme on dit, pesche en eau trouble: puis quand il a le poisson il a sur luy pouuoir de vie et de mort.[43]

p. 272. l. 11. whereof some haue receiued a *calling* to preach. Calling?

p. 272. ll. 37. 38. He that to maintain &^{c}. oppose the Laws of Ciuil state: j'entans jusquelà is uery far from being a Martyr of Christ. *is uery far*? d'ailleurs le uerbe will oppose me semble deuoir regir quelque accusatif, et je n'en trouue pas là.

plus bas. to dye for euery tenet. *tenet*?

p. 275. Vous cités le passage de St Paul a Cor. 1. 5. et inferés que l'eglise assambleé jugeoit de la matiére d'excommunication:[44] si lon repond que c'est a cause que l'Apôtre étoit absent, lequel en eut jugé seul s'il eut esté présent: que faudra t-il répliquer?

p. 277. there *lyeth* excommunication for injustice. *lyeth*?

a 12 l. de la fin *to set by disputing* with [them *deleted*] him. Et a 6 l de la fin περιῖστασο *set them by* je trouue *set by* dans le dictionaire, traduit éstimer: mais là que ueut il dire?

p. 280. l. 12. *hereupon*.

p. 288 l. 19 The Holy Ghost said. Vous n'aués rien dit de la façon coment il parloit: est ce qu'on ouyt une uoix du Ciel? ou quoy?

p. 290. a 14. l. de la fin Those of the Town becomin Christians, j'entans bien cela: mais non pas cecy *should so much as haue thought on any other way*.

et a 3 l. de la fin. at such time as he went from thence to Plant the same in another place.

p. 291 l. 14. Which none could take from the Church to bestow on them. *bestow*?

p. 293. sur le milieu the good tyding. *tyding*

puis a 2 l. de la fin that it was worth their contention?

p. 296. a la fin. Les Éueques repondent[45] qu'a la uérité la puissance Coactiue ils la tienent de l'Etat from the Common-wealth: Mais que Dieu les ayant enuoyés ils disent *par la Grace de Dieu* a raison de leur Mission.

p. 297. to be continually at the Helm. *Helm?*

p. 298. a 7 l. de la fin but sometimes *oftner.*

p. 303. l. 11. This expectation of theirs. ne faudroit-il pas this their expectation, ou this expectation of them? Car theirs est adjectif où donc est son substantif?

p. 306 l. 32. No one man so much as cohering to another. traduisés.

p. 323. Contre ce que vous dites There is nothing in the Scripture &ᶜ on allégue que Portae inferi non praeualebunt.[46]

p. 324. l. 3. to afford men ordinarily. afford?

l. 19. and in others Common-wealts scarce any. scarce any?

p. 330. l. 4. et en suite *plea* que ueut dire *plea?*

p. 331 a 4 l. de la fin the main designe. *main?*

Du Traité Of the Kingdome of Darknesse

p. 334. as the land of the Goshen.[47] *Goshen?*

other matter of old *Wiues* tales. *Wiues?*

and so we come to erre by giuing heed. *heed?*

with a *seared* conscience. seared?

the greatest and *main* abuse. *main?*

p. 336. traduisés *to challenge* et a *Claime.*[48]

p. 337. a 4 l. de la fin They had faced down the King. *faced down?*

Sur la p. 338. Voicy deux difficultés This is my body dites vous sont termes de l'Écriture sainte. qu'on uoye que c'y est une façon de parler ordinaire. Puis [▷contre ce] vous dites que cela fut il, il ne s'enfuit pas que le prestre en fit autant: on objecte les termes *hoc* facite in meam commemorationem. *hoc* c'est cela mesme. Icy je me souuiens d'une question a vous faire vous m'aués dit qu'en une autre édition du Leuiatan vous mettriés la comparaison entre le prestre et le joueür de Gobelets qui montre qu'il n'y a rien puis pour cinq sols et en disant trois paroles Hoc[us][49] Boc[us][50] &ᶜ, fait uoyr que la chose y est: je souhaiterois de sçauoir en quel endroit de vostre Liure vous inseriés cela Et en quels termes.[51]

which was not aboue 500 years agoe. traduisés.

p. 339. l. 6. had[52] some set form of exorcisme. traduisés.

puis a 5 l. de la fin and *clay* into a liuing creature: *clay?*

p. 340 a 2 l. de la fin (than which there are none that make a better shew of proof) traduisés.

p. 345. Vous faites un raisonement Que Dieu étant si misericordieux it seemeth hard that God [will *deleted* >should] punish mens trans-gressions without any end. Ne peut on pas dire aussi bien qu'il semble fort rude qu'il doiue les punir comment que ce soit peu ou prou: Et cela dautant plus qu'ils ne font rien qu'aprés l'impression reçeuë de luy n'y ayant point de creature independante du Createur. Je vous prie repondés a cette difficulté

sauin that God promiseth[53] a reedimer to Adam. dites moy où lon trouue cette promesse.

p. 346. as Immates[54] of that World. *Immates?*

Dans cette page vous faites une response que Ceux qui n'auront pas creu en Jesus Christ auront grosse bodies[55] et engendreront éternelle-ment: Mais cela posé dites moy donc comment la question peut estre soluë qu'on proposa a Nostre Seigneur Et posé qu'aucun des sept maris n'eut creu un Jesus Christ Eux et leur femme deuans resusciter et puis engendrer, lequel des 7 auroit la femme?[56]

p. 347. l. 10. He brings in euery text. &c. où est l'accusatif de ce verbe?

p. 348. a 3 l. de la fin. As it were sindged off.[57] traduisés.

p. 349. a 10 l. de la fin. which he prefereth to the second place of probability. traduisés.

p. 351. a 9 l. de la fin And loosed the paines of Death; a 7 l. to loose some soules. a 6 l. Christ that was losed. *loosed. loose losed?*

p. 357. l. 13. to countenance the *setting up* of images. setting up?

p. 358. l. 3. in such manner as to forfeit them. forfeit?

p. 359. for a stone *unhewn* has been *set up* for Neptune. traduisés *unhewn*

p. 363. a 8 l. de la fin as it were by *intaile*[58] inalienable traduisés.

p. 370. l. 5. and inuentions how to puzzle such as should goe about. traduisés en latin

aussi *to pose them*

p. 371. l. 1. particular tenets. tenets?

et a 15 l. de la fin length, bredth, and lepth.[59]

357

p. 373. as men fright birds from the Corn with an empty doublet a hat and a crooked stik. traduisés.

p. 377. is not likely to haue been laid so sligthly. traduisés

p. 385. a 2. l. de la fin the ambition and canwasing. canwasing?

p. 386. a 5 l. de la fin ⎫
p. 387   ⎬ elues. *Elues?*

p. 389. l. 10. *lesse steddy.*

p. 390 sur le milieu nor how it comes about.

p. 391. passé le milieu he is *lyable to anything lyable?*

Et a 10 l. de la fin *is fain to handle.*

p. 392. a 16 l. de la fin to make them *sue* for such an office. *sue?*

p. 393 l. 13. And he the heir aparent. Traduisés.

p. 394. a 19 l. de la fin There cannot choose but be uery many.

p. 395. *when Greek and latine sentences unchewed come us again as they use to doe unchanged* traduisés cela.

Aussi a 21 l. de la fin Il y a Or to good maners, or to the disturbance of the publique tranquillity Il me semble qu'il faut ôter *disturbance* Et s'il vous plait d'y regarder et me le dire

p. derniere traduisés Et quand je dis traduisés c'est a dire s'il vous plait et en latin cette parenthése (as hauing an *angry* aspect from the dissoluers of an Old Gouernement, and seeing but the *baks* of them that erect a new.)

Je ne vous dy rien de mes [>autres] réflexions sur ce grand Ouurage Vous uerrés s'il plait a Dieu quelque jour dans quelqu'une de mes lettres le grand état que j'en fais.

[*enclosure endorsed by Hobbes:*] from Monsr du verdus quaeres Concerning his Translation of Leuiathan. Dec. 1656.

Translation of Letter 100

Sir,

   Will you forgive me for sending you a thick parcel of things which will be of no use to you? But what is human life, if not a succession of favours which one does for one's friends, and from time to time not without inconvenience to oneself?

   The first favour I should like you to do for me is to accept in a friendly spirit my sending you the 'Account' of my affairs,[1] as a printed statement—that is, as a statement of the truth. I have, admittedly, concealed my resentment of the archbishop of Bordeaux[2] and the Jesuits. The latter are usurping some very fine leases which my grandfather acquired from the Barony of Montferrand;[3] and they are oppressing me by means of conspiracies and lawsuits which they instigate and nurture, in order to make me unable to resist them. And as for the Archbishop of Bordeaux, he covets the living of Ambarès,[4] which he wants to annex to his archbishopric; on a previous occasion he made his steward negotiate about it with one of our *conseillers* at the Cour de requêtes, called M. Quaysac,[5] who had the living at the time. Since M. Dejean,[6] the present curate of that parish (which has revenues worth 6,000 francs) very much covets my property, and since he had hatched the whole plot of their 'renegade nun'[7] in order to get my property from me, the Archbishop, having let her escape (as you will see in my 'Account' of my affairs), that is, having put her back in Dejean's clutches, denied justice by withholding his sentence on her for all of fourteen months, and arranged for an under-the-counter deal to be made with me, in which he promised to deliver his sentence on condition that I negotiate the handing over of all my property to someone he would not name—in other words, Dejean. I had to break free; and, finding myself alone against all those adversaries—the Archbishop, the Jesuits, Dejean, the 'feuillas'[8] (that is, the swindlers of Bordeaux), and a large number of my relatives conspiring together—I sounded the alarm (as the saying goes) against them, and cried for help from abroad.

Now, Sir, since M. Bourdelot[9] (the first physician to the Queen of Sweden, and her Resident in France) wanted at that time to take me on as a sharer in his good fortune; and since I can foresee that I shall be led on to do other things; I should like you to have this 'Account' of my affairs in your hands—so that if I go to England this spring, it might serve as a way of telling the Earl of Devonshire (and anyone else you may think fit) about me. For that purpose, I shall also ask you to make use of this letter.

My other request, Sir, is that you would be so kind as to explain to me the passages in your *Leviathan* which I list on the enclosed sheets of paper, and which I found hard to understand. Let your motive for doing this be that the benefit will accrue as follows: first that, once provided with these explanations, I can promise you the most exact and faithful French translation that could possibly be made of your *Leviathan*—and that without boasting on behalf of the translator. This

359

will contribute not a little to advancing your reputation (which is already very great) in the world. And secondly, you will have the satisfaction of having taught and instructed someone who longs to profit from your teachings, and, above all, someone who honours you more than anyone in the world. I have calculated that, given the time it takes your replies to reach me, I might have your reply to this as a New Year's gift. I assure you, Sir, that I could not receive a New Year's gift from anywhere which would give me more pleasure, or which I would value more highly; and, hoping you will enjoy both what is left of this year, and the year to come—and for that matter a long and happy life during the course of many more years—I assure you that I am, Sir, with all my heart,

Your most humble and obedient servant,
du Verdus

Bordeaux, 3 December 1656

[*enclosure:*]
Passages which I do not understand in your *Leviathan*

Postulates

1. When I write a whole sentence in English, and repeat after it a certain word with a question mark (?), this question mark asks what the word means, and indicates that that is the word which I do not understand. If I draw a line (like this: ____) under the word, it means the same thing.

2. When I use words in the imperative, such as 'translate' (which I use frequently), please take the phrase 'I beg you' as implied there; for these are so many prayers which I address to you.

From the treatise 'Of Man'

Page 2: 'but there is another saying not of late understood': of late?

Page 2, 8 lines from the end: 'but let one man read another by his actions never so perfectly.

Page 3: 'which endeavour because Outward, seemeth to be some matter without': outward?

Page 6, 14 lines from the end: 'and hence[10] it is that lying cold': lying cold?

Page 7, line 6: 'in case any uncouth and exorbitant fancy': uncouth?

Page 14, 14 lines from the end: 'and men were <u>fayn</u>[11] to apply their fingers': <u>fayn</u>?

Page 17, half-way down: 'And therefore if Speech be peculiar to man (<u>as for ought I know it is</u>)': translate the phrase in brackets. Secondly, I should like you to tell me how you know that only man uses speech. For my own part, I think that I can hear 'a', 'e', 'i', 'o', and 'u' just as well in the barking of dogs or the tweeting of birds as in low Breton.

But what I say about birds reminds me that I have forgotten some passages in your dedicatory epistle. On sig. A2 [recto], 4 lines from the end: '<u>nor how it may reflect on those</u>': translate. Also, on p. A2 verso: 'between the <u>points</u> of both': points? Lower down: 'offending none, I think', which I fully understand; but I do not understand the passage which follows, '<u>but those without, or such within (if there be any such) as favour them</u>'. So please translate this passage, and the word 'Outworks' which follows it.

Also, on p. 2, I find this passage obscure: 'as it is now used, to countenance, either the barbarous state of men in power, towards their inferiours; or to encourage men of low degree, to a <u>sawcie</u> behaviour towards their betters'. Please translate all that into Latin. What causes difficulty for me is that the phrase 'know thyself' can be used in four different contexts. To people of high estate, 'know thyself' can mean: know that you are powerful enough to crush lowly people who give themselves airs. Again, to people of high estate, it can mean: know that you are only a man, just like the lowly person whom you are oppressing. To people of low estate, it can mean: know that you are not strong enough to challenge someone greater than yourself. And to lowly people again, it can mean: know that you too are a man, just as much as the great man who is oppressing you—you can be master of his life, if you do not mind risking your own, so stop him from oppressing you.

But I return to:

Page 19, line 14: '<u>by the claym they lay to it</u>': translate into Latin or French.

Page 19, 3 lines from the end: 'or any *Free*, but free from being hindred by opposition': translate.

[Page 20: '*the nature of a thing is its definition*': I realize that the nature of man is the accident, and the definition of man a description, and that it is therefore ill expressed to say that the nature of a thing is its definition. But when you say afterwards '*a mans command is his will*', I do not see which of the two is the accident or the description rather than the other. Please explain. *deleted* >I understand that '*command*' is the description and '*will*' the accident.]

In the last line [of p. 20]: '<u>but are taken up</u>': translate.

Page 21, 16 lines from the end: 'but specially according [...] the errors[12] of one another': translate.

Page 23, line 24: 'For let a space be never so little, that which is moved over a greater space, whereof that little one is part, must first be moved over that': translate into Latin.

Also, lower down: 'And when the Endeavour is <u>fromward</u> something': fromward?

Also: 'For Nature it selfe does often presse upon men those truths': translate into Latin.

Page 25, 13 lines from the end: 'As first, when they one succeed another': does that mean, when these passions succeed one another?

Page 26: 'admiration; proper to Man, because it excites the appetite of knowing the cause': how can we know whether other animals do not feel admiration? And how can we tell that they do not know many causes? Answer me, please: how do you think we can know this?

Page 27: '*Sudden Dejection*, is the passion that causeth weeping': weeping?

Also: '<u>Laughter</u>'? And 'a fellow-feeling'?

What you say you do not conceive possible (on p. 28)[13] is told of a man called the chevalier d'Audrieu,[14] who eventually died on the scaffold. This man took a particular delight in shooting men working on roofs, retiling houses, in order to laugh at their expression of terror when they fell off the roof.

Page 30, line 16: 'There is at last an *End*, <u>either by attaining, or by giving over</u>': translate into Latin.

Page 31: 'Insomuch that the plea of Conscience, has been alwayes hearkened unto very diligently in all times': translate into Latin.

Page 33, line 5: 'And whereas in this succession': I should like that 'whereas' translated into Latin.

Also, 4 lines further on, 'similitudes, in case they be such' [Does '<u>they</u>' mean '*elles*', in other words the similitudes, or '*eux*', in other words those that observe them? *deleted* >it means 'elles']

Page 35, line 16: 'there would be no lesse difference of men in their Sight':[15] people will deny the truth of your minor premiss here. For, if what I see as red is seen by someone else as tan, and if that has been the case since his birth, he will not fail to call it 'red' just as much as I do: he will have been taught to call it that.

Page 35, 15 lines from the end: 'GIDDINESSE'?

And 3 lines from the end: '*selfe-conceipt*'?

Page 39, line 28: 'but are fallen upon by some, through misunderstanding . . .': translate into Latin.

Page 41: 'WORTHINESSE'? What does that mean, given that you say (at the bottom of p. 46) that it does not mean merit?

Page 46: 'the Old master, that is to say in Dutch, the *Here-alt*': 'Old master? Dutch?

Further on: 'such as bare the Generall company out of friendship': translate.

Page 49, line 9: 'to hold together'.

Page 52: 'are no[16] signes, nor fruit of *Religion*, but in Man': what do we know about that? And what about the worship which (it is said) elephants render to the sun,[17] and Cynocephali to the moon?[18] But even if that were not true, who can tell what goes on in the brains and hearts of other animals?

Page 53, line 23: 'and therefore call them Ghosts': Ghosts?

Page 55: 'Contention, Vertue, Honour, Health, Rust':[19] rust?

Page 56, line 6: 'and but inmates[20] of Heaven': inmates?

Also, 4 lines from the end: 'dipping of Verses in *Homer*': dipping?

Page 59, 11 lines from the end: 'and jugling between Princes': jugling?

Page 60, line 18: 'the Fees of private Masses, and Vales[21] of Purgatory': Fees? Vales?

Page 64: 'A LAW OF NATURE [. . .] is a [. . .] generall Rule, found out by Reason': found out?

Also, in the last line: '*when others are so too*': too?

Page 66, line 16: 'and in the means of so preserving life, as not to be weary of it'.

Page 67, last line: 'In Contract, I merit at the Contractors hand': translate.

Page 68, line 8: '(hoodwinkt with carnall desires)': translate.

Page 70, 16 lines from the end: 'The Passion to be reckoned upon': translate.

Page 72: 'Somewhat like to a piece of Law in *Cokes* Commentaries on *Litleton*; where he sayes, if the right Heire of the Crowne be attainted of

Treason; yet the Crown shall descend to him, and *eo instante* the Atteynder be voyd': I should like to have that translated, and to know who this Littleton was, and what he claimed to demonstrate—I mean, what book he wrote, what it was about, and what purpose it was meant to serve.[22]

Page 73, more than half-way down: 'and so, as all men that contribute not to his destruction, forbear him onely out of ignorance of what is good for themselves': translate.

Page 74: 'to be beholding'?

Page 76, line 15: 'as combersome thereunto'?

Page 80: 'Of PERSONS, AUTHORS, and things Personated': 'de personis authoribus et rebus ... personated'; 'des persones autheurs et choses ... personated'?

Page 81, line 4: '*Owned* by those whom they represent': owned?

Page 81, 4 lines from the end: 'a Bridge'?

From the treatise 'Of Common-wealth'

Page 86, 15 lines from the end: who can be sure that ants or bees do not have a language which they use with one another? Or, since bees have a king and pay reverence to him, that this respect and obedience does not arise among them, as among men, by agreement? Or that they do not have honours and dignities? For who knows whether there are not some bees which, in preference to others, stand closer to the person of their king? Besides, as for the second reason you give:[23] although they agree amongst themselves to make their honey in the same hive, is that sufficient reason for saying that they do not disagree on anything at all? Surely there are some parts of the hive which are more pleasant than others: so something must be done to decide who will have them, until the matter is settled among them. And who can say whether, in settling this, they do not act, like men, out of mutual fear?

Page 89, in the margin: '*Sovereigne Power cannot be forfeited*': forfeited?

Page 91: 'the most sudden, and rough busling in of a new Truth': translate into Latin.

Page 92, 4 lines from the end: 'and persons of Infant heires': Infant heires?

Page 93, half-way down: 'and the name of Soveraign[24] no more given by the Grantees'?

And, further on, 'if we grant back the Soveraignty': grant back?

Page 104, line 18: 'beaten, and taken, or put to flight': <u>flight</u>?

Also: 'to avoyd the cruelty of their task-masters': <u>task-masters</u>?

Page 106: 'to distinguish between them aright': <u>aright</u>?

Page 108, 10 lines from the end: translate this into Latin: 'And did not his will assure the *necessity* of mans will, and consequently of all that on mans will dependeth, the *liberty* of men would be a contradiction, and impediment to the omnipotence and *liberty* of God.'

Page 109: 'These <u>Bonds</u> [...] may neverthelesse be made <u>to hold</u>': <u>bonds</u>? <u>hold</u>?

Page 111: 'shared amongst them the Soveraignty of *Rome*': <u>shared</u>?

Page 118: '*Sommer-Ilands*'?[25] Tell me what that is, in Latin and in French.

Page 119: 'fellow subject'?

Page 120: 'for building . . . and manning of Ships': <u>manning</u>?

Page 123, line 13: 'such doctrine, as was against their Religion, and <u>Trade</u>': trade? I know full well that elsewhere it means 'métier' ['occupation'], as in the 'métier' of an artisan. But the word 'métier' is equivocal in old French, where it also means 'need'—as in the phrase 'fa mestieri' in Italian.

Page 126: speaking of the spy, whom you compare to the eye, you say that 'he is but a Private Minister; but yet a Minister of the Common-wealth'. Please tell me precisely whether he is a private minister, or a minister of state—or how he can be both at once.

Page 127: 'The NUTRITION of a Common-wealth consisteth, in the *Plenty*': <u>*Plenty*</u>?

Page 135, 3 lines from the end, the whole of the following passage: 'of their motly orations made of the divers colored threds, or shreds of Authors': I can find neither '<u>motly</u>' nor '<u>threds</u>' nor '<u>shreds</u>' in my dictionary.

Page 136: 'that wisheth for, or would accept of their pains': translate.

Further on, I find '<u>Wheele-barrough</u>', which my dictionary translates as 'brouëtte'. And since I have never ever seen anyone playing tennis in a '<u>brouëtte</u>', although I can imagine that it is possible in a game of tennis played on a long court, I should like you to tell me whether it is played in that way in England,[26] and exactly how I should translate '<u>wheele-barrough</u>'.

'And therefore no great Popular Common-wealth was ever <u>kept up</u>': kept up?

Page 139, [13][27] lines from the end: 'if it should assemble never so many, or so wise men': translate.

Page 140: '(as Sr. *Ed. Coke* makes it)': please give the name in full, so that I may translate it.

Page 144, half-way down: 'and brought to a legall triall': translate.

I should very much like to know who the teacher of law was who published the law which you refute at the end of the same page.[28]

Page 146, more than half-way down: 'the ordinary trialls[29] of Right': translate. Given that 'trial' means 'saggio' in Italian and 'essai' in French (as when the maître d'hôtel 'tries' [i.e. samples] a dish), here it must mean something else.

Page 157: I should like an example of what you describe in the fourteen lines beginning 'If that Man . . .', and ending '. . . upon complaint'.[30]

Secondly, I do not know how to translate this: 'because he might have been righted [. . .] upon complaint'.

Page 160: 'because not onely he has wrong, that falls by such judgements': translate.

Page 164: 'as Badges, Titles, Offices . . .': <u>badges</u>?

Page 167: 'combersome points of their [. . .] greatnesse'

Page 168: 'if *Solon* had not caused to be given out he was mad': <u>given out</u>?

Page 170: 'And for these[31] doctrines, men are chiefly <u>beholding</u> . . .': 'beholding'?

Page 172: 'Overwhelm the Common-wealth with Oppression': <u>over-whelm</u>?

Page 173, line 16: 'he is fain at last': <u>fain</u>?

Page 174: 'and the *Wens*, of united conquests': <u>wens</u>?

Page 177: 'so as to proclaime Marriage with them *in facie Ecclesiae* by Preachers': please give me an example of this, drawn from history, to illustrate your teaching.

Page 180, half-way down: 'may be righted of the injuries done them': <u>righted of</u>?

Page 181, line 12: 'in the exercise of severall Trades, and Callings': <u>callings</u>?

Further on, 7 lines from the end: 'to inhabit closer together, and not range a great deal of ground, to snatch what they find; but to court each little Plot': translate—I don't understand any of it.

Page 182: 'Unnecessary Lawes are [. . .] trapps for Mony': <u>trapps</u>?

Page 185: 'have been alwayes put to the trouble of contriving their Titles': translate all that phrase.

I should also like you to instruct me as to whether 'their' refers to the sovereigns, or the disturbances;[32] perhaps a full explanation of 'to contrive' will explain that.

Page 188, line 10: '*my treadings had well-nigh slipt*': translate.

Page 189, 13 lines from the end: the first word here is 'beholders': 'beholders'?

Page 192, line 17: 'to set light by his Commandements': translate.

From the treatise 'Of a Christian Common-wealth'

Page 195: 'whereof there dependeth much upon Supernaturall Revelations of the Will of God': doesn't this genitive, '<u>whereof</u>', require a nominative—as in '<u>whereof notice</u>'? And the same goes for the verb, '<u>dependeth</u>'.[33] So translate into Latin, so that I may see what is taken as understood.

Also: 'not to be folded up in the Napkin of an Implicite Faith[34]'.

Also: 'and not to labour in sifting[35] out a Philosophicall truth by Logick of such mysteries as are not comprehensible': translate.

Page 196: 'which in sum, is Trust, and Faith reposed in him that speaketh': translate.

Also: 'to win beleef'.

Page 197: 'First, that God wil not have miracles alone serve for arguments . . .': I have difficulties here, because I observe the present-tense verb '<u>wil not</u>' governing two infinitives, '<u>have</u>' and '<u>serve</u>'. And since that is not done either in French or in Latin, I do not know how to translate it.

Page 203: you cite a passage from 2 Esdras 14. In the Vulgate, the second book of Esdras has only thirteen chapters; and I do not have my Bible concordances with me here. So tell me where this passage is in the Vulgate.[36]

Page 204, at the bottom: 'and his claim to the Kingdome': 'claim'?

Page 208: 'So that the proper signification of *Spirit* in common speech, is either a subtile, fluid, and invisible Body, or a *Ghost*, or other Idol or Phantasm of the Imagination': <u>Ghost</u>?

Page 209, at the bottom: '*Ezek* . 2. 30'. In the Vulgate, Ezekiel 2 has only nine verses; so where can I find this passage?[37]

Page 210, line 2: 'whereupon': <u>whereupon</u>?

Also, line 19: '*submission* to that <u>main</u> Article of Christian faith': <u>main</u>?

And line 28: 'How we came to translate the word Spirits by the word Ghosts, which signifieth nothing [...] I examine not'. I have two queries here, the one I have already made, namely how to translate 'ghosts', and secondly this: how is it, do you think, that people came to say 'ghosts' instead of 'spirits'?

Page 211: 'and out of them framed their opinions . . .': 'out of them'?

Page 212: 'if it had had the form of a Man, or Child <u>of never so great beauty</u>': translate 'of never so great beauty'.

Page 213: 'to goe along with the Campe': translate.

Page 216: 'From the very Creation': translate.

Page 219: 'for the claim whereof': <u>claim</u>?

Also, after you have said that there are so many other places etc., and that it were a wonder etc., I do not understand the passage which follows: 'that it were a wonder [...] but that it gives too much light'.[38] Translate.

Also: 'This they have observed, that in stead of a *Sacerdotall Kingdome*, translate, *a Kingdome of Priests*: for they may as well translate a *Royall Priesthood* (as it is[39] in St. Peter) into a *Priesthood of Kings*'. Here is a word-for-word translation: 'Cecy ils ont obserué qu'au lieu de sacerdotall royaume traduit un Royaume de Prestres'[40]—and up to this point there is no verb, and no meaning—'Car ils peuuent aussi bien tra-duire vne Royale Prestrise (comme il y a dans St Pierre) en une Prestrise des Roys'. I cannot actually find any syntax in all that. But to make a good job of it, I should like to have the whole of that paragraph translated into Latin, from 'There be' to 'Treasure'.

I have a difficulty with p. 219. God ruled the Jews by pact; the Jews dethroned him in order to have kings, like other peoples. Jesus Christ, having come to re-establish that kingdom, declares that his kingdom is not of this world. So it is only at his second coming that he will re-establish that temporal kingdom: and it is true that we pray, 'Thy kingdom come', which indicates that it has not come yet. That is your argument, and it is correct. But at the bottom of this page (and on p. 120) you say that 'If the Kingdome of God [...] were not a Kingdome which God [...] did exercise on Earth; [...] neither would many Priests have troubled themselves . . .': which seems to mean that God already exercises his kingdom on earth. For you say 'did exercise', not 'should exercise'. And you say that kings are 'anointed [. . .] <u>under Christ</u> (Gods Ministers) Holy men'. So, according to you, it is God who reigns, and I think you fall into a contradiction here, implying either that the Jews did not depose God, or that his kingdom has been re-established.

Page 222: '*Then Paul and Barnabas waxed bold*': waxed bold?

Also: '<u>*Go stand*</u>'.

Also: '*Daily in the Temple* ': does 'daily' mean 'quotidie', 'every day', or 'tutto il giorno', all day long?

Page 225: 'that in Christian Churches, have a Calling to say publique prayers': 'a calling'?

Page 228, line 2: '*lest they should hear*': <u>lest</u>?

Also, line 10: 'Of Prophets, that were so by a perpetual Calling': 'calling'?

What you say further on, 'after the people of the Jews, had rejected God, that he should no more reign over them, those Kings which submitted themselves to Gods government, were also his chief Prophets; and the High Priests office became Ministeriall'—all that, I say, is subject to the following serious objection which is raised by priests. Since, in the pact between God and Moses, God had promised a priestly kingdom, the kings who submitted themselves to God's government submitted themselves to the High Priest, and it was their office (the kings' office, that is) which 'became Ministeriall'; so that afterwards their position was no more than that of army generals.

Page 229, line 4: 'In the time of the New Testament, there was no Soveraign Prophet, but our Saviour': doesn't that contradict your earlier claim that Caiaphas prophesied as sovereign pontiff?[41]

Also on p. 229: Moses said to Joshua, 'Bee not jealous in my <u>behalf</u>': behalf?

Page 233: 'which the Almighty is about to bring to passe': translate.

Page 234: 'when neverthelesse, there were others, could . . .': isn't there a 'which' or 'that' taken as understood here?

Page 236: 'and so far from supernaturall': <u>so far</u>?

Page 238: translate into Latin the four lines beginning with 'The maintenance of Civill Society'.

Page 240, the first word: 'holdeth also in this': <u>holdeth</u>?

Also, line 4: 'For as Death is reckoned': 'reckoned'?

Page 242, line 8: <u>*under ground*</u>.

Page 243, line 17: '*Vtter Darknesse*': <u>vtter</u>?
   Also: '*Wedding garment*': <u>Wedding</u>?

Page 246: '*the Lord shall be to them as a <u>broad mote</u> of swift waters*': broad mote?

Besides that, I have one great difficulty with this passage. For if it is true that '*the lame take the prey*', whether that means those who are lame through illness, or those who are lame because they have been maimed in battle, I do not see how this state can be a state of salvation, in which no one can say '*I am sicke*'.[42]

Page 249: 'For as to the Morall law, they were already obliged, <u>and need not have been contracted withall</u>, by promise of the Land of Canaan': translate the underlined words.

Page 251, line 2: '*removed, and <u>stood a far off</u>*'.

Page 252: '*lest they break through unto the Lord to gaze*'.

Page 253: 'Samuel [...] had an [...] extraordinary <u>calling</u> to the Government': calling?

Page 255, line 7: '<u>so far forth as</u> concerned the Right'.
   Also, more than half-way down: '<u>they made account</u> they worshipped the God of Israel'.

Page 261: 'an Atonement': atonement?

Four lines further on: 'two young Goates': I can find 'goat', meaning 'chevreau', the son of a 'chèvre'; but since we say 'le bouc émissaire' ['the scapegoat'] in French, and not 'le chevreau émissaire', I do not know how one should translate 'two young Goates'—whether as 'deux jeunes boucs' or 'deux jeunes chevreaux'.

Page 265: 'There is another conjecture drawn from the Ceremonies of the Gentiles': do me the kindness of telling me your source for that.

Page 267: 'Here wee have the Person of God born now the third time': translate.

Page 268: '*the Spirit, and the Water, and the Bloud; and these three agree in one*': how should I translate '<u>agree in one</u>'? The Vulgate has 'unum sunt' ['are one'].

Page 269: 'and not to reign in Majesty, <u>no not</u>, as his Fathers Lieutenant': I do not understand this '<u>no not</u>'.

Page 270, line 7: 'so many Nimrods': translate.

Besides that, I have doubts over the comparison with fishermen. For a fisherman, as the saying goes, fishes in troubled waters: and then, when he catches a fish, he has the power of life and death over it.[43]

Page 272, line 11: 'whereof some have received a <u>Calling</u> to preach': 'calling'?

Page 272, lines 37 and 38: 'He, that to maintain . . . oppose the Laws [. . .] of [. . .] Civill State,' (I understand the meaning up to that point) 'is very far from being a Martyr of Christ': '<u>is very far</u>'? Besides that, I think that the verb 'wil oppose' ought to govern some accusative, and I cannot find any there.

    Further down: 'To die for every tenet': <u>tenet?</u>

Page 275: you cite the passage from St Paul's first letter to the Corinthians, ch. 5, and infer from it that the assembled Church judged cases involving excommunication.[44] But if people say in reply that that happened only because the apostle was absent, and that if he had been present he would have judged the case on his own, how should one answer them?

Page 277: 'There *lyeth* Excommunication for Injustice': <u>lyeth?</u>
    12 lines from the end: ' *to set by disputing with him*'. And 6 lines from the end '*περίστασο, (set them by)*': I can find 'set by' in the dictionary, where it is translated as 'éstimer' ['to esteem', 'to set store by']; but what does it mean here?

Page 280, line 12: '<u>Hereupon</u>'.

Page 288, line 19: '*the Holy Ghost said*': you have not explained how it spoke. Did people hear a voice from heaven, or what?

Page 290, 14 lines from the end: 'those of the Town becomming Christians'—I understand that all right. But I do not understand this: '<u>should so much as have thought on any other way</u>'.
    And 3 lines from the end: 'at such time as he went from thence, to plant the same in another place'.

Page 291, line 14: 'which none could take from the Church to bestow on them': <u>bestow?</u>

Page 293, half-way down: 'the good tyding': <u>tyding?</u>
    Further on, 2 lines from the end: 'that it was worth their contention'.

Page 296, at the end: the bishops' answer to this[45] is to say that they do indeed hold their coercive power from the state ('from the Commonwealth'); but that since they were sent by God they say 'by the Grace of God' by reason of their mission.

Page 297: 'to bee continually at the Helm': <u>helm?</u>

Page 298, 7 lines from the end: 'but sometimes <u>oftner</u>'.

Page 303, line 11: 'This expectation of theirs': shouldn't it be 'this their expectation', or 'this expectation of them'? For 'theirs' is an adjective—so where is the substantive?

Page 306, line 32: 'no one man so much as cohaering to another': translate.

Page 323: against your argument that 'there is nothing in the Scripture . . .', it is claimed that 'portae inferi non praevalebunt' ['the gates of hell shall not prevail'].[46]

Page 324, line 3: 'to afford men ordinarily': 'afford'?
 And line 19: 'and in other Common-wealths scarce any': 'scarce any'?

Page 330, line 4 and thereafter: '<u>plea</u>'. What does '<u>plea</u>' mean?

Page 331, 4 lines from the end: 'the main Designe': <u>main</u>?

From the treatise 'Of the Kingdome of Darknesse'

Page 334: 'as the land of the Goshen[47]': <u>Goshen</u>?
 'other matter of old <u>Wives</u> tales': <u>Wives</u>?
 'And so we come to erre, by *giving heed*': <u>heed</u>?
 '*with a <u>seared</u>* conscience': seared?
 'The greatest, and <u>main</u> abuse': <u>main</u>?

Page 336: translate '<u>to challenge</u>' and '<u>a claime</u>'.[48]

Page 337, 4 lines from the end: 'they had faced down the King': <u>faced down</u>? Here are two problems with p. 338. You say that the terms 'This is my body' are equivalent to 'this signifies, or represents, my body'. In which case, please give some examples taken from Holy Scripture, to show that it is an ordinary manner of speaking. Then, on the other hand, you say that even if it had been Christ's body, it does not follow that a priest can do the same; in objection to this, people will adduce the words 'hoc facite in commemorationem meam' ['do this in remembrance of me']. 'Hoc' means 'the very same thing'. On this point, I remember a question I wanted to ask you. You told me that you would include in another edition of Leviathan a comparison between the priest and the person who plays the game with cups, who shows you that there is nothing there, and then, for five sous, saying the three words 'Hocus[(49)] Pocus[(50)] . . .', shows you that the object is there. I should like to know where you will insert that into your book, and how you will put it.[51]
 'which was not above 500. years agoe': translate.

Page 339, line 6: 'hath[52] some set form of Exorcisme': translate.

Also, 5 lines from the end: 'and clay into a living creature': clay?

Page 340, 2 lines from the end: '(than which there are none that make a better shew of proof,)': translate.

Page 345: you argue that since God is so merciful, 'it seemeth hard [. . .] that God [. . .] should punish mens transgressions without any end'. Could one not say equally well that it seems hard that he should give them any punishment at all, long or short? And all the more so because they do nothing except through the impulse they have received from him—there being no such thing as a creature independent of the Creator. Please answer this objection.

'saving that God promised[53] a Redeemer to Adam': tell me where this promise is to be found.

Page 346: 'as inmates[54] of that world': inmates?

On this page you reply that those who did not believe in Jesus Christ will have 'grosse [. . .] bodies',[55] and will engender perpetually. But if that is granted, tell me what solution there can be to the question which was put to our Saviour: supposing that none of the seven husbands had believed in Jesus Christ, if they and their wife are all to be resurrected and then to start engendering, which of the seven will have the woman?[56]

Page 347, line 10: 'He brings in every text . . .': where is the accusative governed by this verb?

Page 348, 3 lines from the end: 'as it were sindged of[57]': translate.

Page 349, 10 lines from the end: 'which he preferreth to the second place of probability': translate.

Page 351, 9 lines from the end: '*and loosed the Paines of Death*'; 7 lines from the end: 'to loose some Soules'; 6 lines from the end: 'Christ that was loosed': loosed, loose, loosed?

Page 357, line 13: 'to countenance the setting up of Images': 'setting up'?

Page 358, line 3: 'in such manner as to forfeit them': 'forfeit'?

Page 359: 'For a Stone unhewn has been set up for Neptune': translate 'unhewn'.

Page 363, 8 lines from the end: 'as it were by entaile[58] unalienable': translate.

Page 370, line 5: 'and Inventions how to puzzle such as should goe about': translate into Latin—and also 'to pose them'.

373

Page 371, line 1: 'particular Tenets': tenets?
   And 15 lines from the end: 'Length, Bredth, and Depth[59]'.

Page 373: 'as men fright Birds from the Corn with an empty doublet, a hat, and a crooked stick': translate.

Page 377: 'is not likely to have been laid so slightly': translate.

Page 385, 2 lines from the bottom: 'the ambition, and canvasing': 'canvasing'?

Page 386, 5 lines from the bottom:⎫
Page 387   ⎬ 'Elves': Elves?

Page 389, line 10: 'lesse steddy'.

Page 390, half-way down: 'nor how it comes about'.

Page 391, more than half-way down: 'he is lyable to any thing': lyable?
   And 10 lines from the bottom: 'is fain to handle'.

Page 392, 16 lines from the end: 'to make them sue for such an Office': sue?

Page 393, line 13: 'and he the heir apparent': translate.

Page 394, 19 lines from the end: 'there cannot choose but be very many'.

Page 395: 'when Greek and Latine Sentences unchewed come up again, as they use to doe, unchanged': translate that.

   Also, 21 lines from the bottom, there is this: 'or to good Manners; or to the disturbance of the Publique Tranquillity'. I think 'disturbance' should be omitted here; please look at this and tell me whether to do so.

Last page: translate (and when I say 'translate', I mean please translate, into Latin) this passage in brackets: '(as having an angry aspect from the dissolvers of an old Government, and seeing but the backs of them that erect a new;)'.

   I shall say nothing of my other observations on this great work; one day, God willing, you will learn from one of my letters what a high opinion I have of it.

In the enclosure to this letter, the passages cited by du Verdus from *Leviathan* are presented in the translation here in their correct form, i.e. as they appear in the 1651 printed text (BL 522. k. 6). Minor formal variants between du Verdus's version and the correct version (e.g. changes in capitalization, and other minor errors of transcription) are not recorded in the notes; material variants, and major errors of transcription affecting the sense, are recorded (with the siglum '1651' for the printed text). Because the printed version already includes words and phrases in italics, the underlining of passages by du Verdus is presented as underlining in the translation of the enclosure. In the original text of the enclosure, however, where du Verdus's underlining is the only form of emphasis, it is presented as italics.

¹ See Letter 89 n. 3.

² See Letter 78 n. 30.

³ The lease of part of the Montferrand estate had been acquired by Jean de Bonneau, du Verdus's grandfather, in 1594 (AMB MS Drouyn 275, p. 174). In 1648 du Verdus let the 'moulins de Montferrand' (both windmills and water-mills) to a Bartolomé Carpentry (ibid., p. 187). In his will of 1666 du Verdus specified that 200 francs of the annual revenues from those mills should be paid to his sister, the Ursuline nun Anne de Bonneau (ADG MS 3 E 12995, fo. 903ʳ).

⁴ See Letter 78 n. 27.

⁵ Jean-Louis de Mullet, seigneur de Quayssac (or 'Queyzac', or 'Caysac'), *conseiller* of the Parlement of Bordeaux, and *commissaire aux requêtes du palais* (ADG MS G 572, fo. 176). Lancelot de Mullet, *abbé* of Verteuil and probably Jean-Louis's uncle, had been curé of the parish of S. Pierre, Ambarès since at least 1641 (ADG MS G 662, unnumbered item in file 'Affaire Dejean'), but resigned the curacy in 1648 in favour of Jean-Louis (ADG MS G 572, fo. 176).

⁶ See Letter 78 n. 26.

⁷ Anne de Bonneau, du Verdus's sister (see Letter 78).

⁸ This probably refers to the 'Feuillants', an order of reformed Cistercians, founded in 1577 by the *abbé* of Feuillant (in the diocese of Rieux). They had a convent in the centre of Bordeaux, on the rue Saint-Antoine (Lopès, *L'Église Sainct-André de Bourdeaux*, i, pp. 41–3); the calendars of the ADG *sacs à procès* for this period indicate that it was an extremely litigious institution.

⁹ See Letter 78 n. 21.

¹⁰ thence *MS*, hence *1651*.

¹¹ faun *MS*, fayn *1651*.

¹² an (supple according) the errours *MS*, but specially according to good or evill fortune, and the errors *1651*.

¹³ This refers to Hobbes's discussion of cruelty (p. 28): 'For, that any man should take pleasure in other mens great harmes, without other end of his own, I do not conceive it possible.'

¹⁴ Unidentified.

¹⁵ Hobbes argues here that 'The causes of this difference of Witts, are in the Passions: and the difference of Passions, proceedeth partly from the different Constitution of the body, and partly from different Education.' His 'minor premiss' is as follows: 'For if the difference proceeded from the temper of the brain, and the organs of Sense, either exterior or interior, there would be no lesse difference of men in their Sight, Hearing, or other Senses, than in their Fancies, and Discretions.'

¹⁶ are not *MS*, are no *1651*.

¹⁷ For the popular belief that elephants worship the sun, see Bartholomaeus Anglicus, *On the Properties of Things*, 2. 48 (ii, p. 1195): 'Of elephants Solinus speketh and seieth that he kepeth lore and discipline of the sterres [...] they saluweth and welcometh the rysyng of the sonne.' (Solinus was the 2nd- or 3rd-cent. abbreviator of Pliny.) Du Verdus's source may have been Montaigne, who commented on the same sun-greeting story: 'We may also say that elephants have some inkling of religion'

375

('Nous pouuons aussi dire que les elephans ont quelque participation de religion' (*Essais*, ii, p. 180)).

[18] The cynocephali were described by Pliny as 'a tribe of human beings with dogs' heads, who wear a covering of wild skins, and whose speech is a bark' ('genus hominum caninis ferarum pellibus velari, pro voce latratum edere' (*Historia naturalis*, 7. 2. 23)). They were also mentioned by Herodotus (*Historiae*, 4. 191) and Aulus Gellius (*Noctes atticae*, 9. 4), but none of these sources attributes religious worship to them. In medieval tradition they were regarded as idolaters (Marco Polo, *Il libro delle meraviglie*, p. 301); 'Sir John Mandeville' described them as 'full reasonable and subtle of wit. And they worship an ox for their god' (*Travels*, i, p. 140). Other medieval sources associated them with Saracens and Muslims (Friedman, *Monstrous Races*, pp. 67–70).

[19] This passage is part of a list of 'meer Accidents, and Qualities' to which the ancients ascribed divinity.

[20] immates *MS*, inmates *1651*.

[21] Wales *MS*, Vales *1651*.

[22] Hobbes refers to Sir Edward Coke's *First Part of the Institutes* (1628), a commentary on the treatise on 'Tenures' by the judge and legal author Sir Thomas Littleton (1422–81). Littleton's treatise was written for his son as a compendium of English property law; it was printed soon after Littleton's death (the date of the 1st edn. is uncertain), and became the standard textbook on the subject. Coke (1552–1634) was Chief Justice of the King's Bench (1613–17), and the leading authority of his day on the common law. His commentary on Littleton remained the standard work on property law for more than a century.

[23] Hobbes's second reason (for arguing that bees and ants can live socially without coercive power, while men cannot) is: 'that amongst these creatures, the Common good differeth not from the Private; and being by nature enclined to their private, they procure thereby the common benefit'.

[24] name of the Soweraing *MS*, name of Soveraign *1651*.

[25] 'The Summer-Islands' was a name given to the Bermudas, derived from the surname of Sir George Somers or Summers (1554–1610), who was shipwrecked there while on his way to Virginia in 1609 and claimed them for the British Crown. For Hobbes's special interest in the Bermudas see Malcolm, 'Hobbes, Sandys, and the Virginia Company'.

[26] Du Verdus's inability to recognize the deliberate absurdity of Hobbes's comparison may surprise the modern reader; but perhaps wheelbarrows in the 17th cent. had a sporting potential which they have since lost. When Peter the Great rented John Evelyn's house at Deptford, his favourite pastime consisted of being trundled round the garden in a wheelbarrow at high speed, to the ruination of Mrs Evelyn's flower-beds.

[27] 3 *MS*.

[28] Sir Edward Coke (see n. 22).

[29] triall *MS*, trialls *1651*.

[30] The argument of this paragraph is that even if the sovereign disclaims one of the rights which are essential to sovereign power, a subject who then takes advantage of that disclaimer, and seeks to exercise the right which appears to have been disclaimed, is still committing a sin: he should know that any such disclaimer which is inconsistent with sovereignty can only have been made through ignorance, and that he as a subject

has a duty to respect all the essential rights of sovereignty. And if he not only tries to take advantage of the disclaimer, but also resists an officer of the sovereign in the process, he commits a crime.

³¹ those *MS*, these *1651*.

³² The meaning of 'brouillon' is unclear here. Hobbes is discussing seizures of sovereign power by military commanders: 'those, who by violence have at any time suppressed the Power of their lawfull Soveraign, before they could settle themselves in his place, have been alwayes put to the trouble of contriving their Titles, to save the People from the shame of receiving them'. One would expect du Verdus's alternatives to be the sovereigns and the usurpers.

³³ For the origin of this confusion, see Letter 94 n. 13.

³⁴ 'aith' is a misprint (for 'Faith') occurring in some copies of the 1651 text.

³⁵ fifting *MS*, sifting *1651*.

³⁶ See Letter 94 n. 22.

³⁷ The chapter-divisions of Ezekiel do differ between the Vulgate and Protestant texts such as the Authorized Version or the Latin translation by Junius and Tremellius; but the difficulty here arises from a faulty reference in *Leviathan*, which should be to Ezek. 2: 2.

³⁸ 'There be so many other places that confirm this interpretation [sc. that the kingdom of God is a real, not a metaphorical kingdom], that it were a wonder there is no greater notice taken of it, but that it gives too much light to Christian Kings to see their right of Ecclesiasticall Government.'

³⁹ as is *MS*, as it is *1651*.

⁴⁰ Du Verdus's confusion arises from taking 'that' to refer to 'this' instead of 'they'.

⁴¹ Hobbes has argued (p. 225) that Caiaphas was a prophet by virtue of his office as High Priest.

⁴² These quotations are from Isa. 33: 23–4, which Hobbes has cited as a description of the 'state of salvation' on earth.

⁴³ Hobbes has argued that ecclesiastical power is 'compared by our Saviour, to Fishing; that is, to winning men to obedience, not by Coercion, and Punishing; but by Perswasion'.

⁴⁴ Hobbes has commented on 1 Cor. 5: 3–5 that 'Paul here pronounceth the Sentence; but the Assembly was first to hear the Cause, (for St. Paul was absent;) and by consequence to condemn him'.

⁴⁵ Hobbes has argued that 'Bishops ought to say in the beginning of their Mandates, *By the favour of the Kings Majesty, Bishop of such a Diocesse* [. . .] For in saying, *Divinâ providentiâ*, which is the same with *Dei gratiâ*, though disguised, they deny to have received their authority from the Civill State.'

⁴⁶ Hobbes has argued that 'there is nothing in the Scripture, from which can be inferred the Infallibility of the Church; much lesse, of any particular Church; and least of all, the Infallibility of any particular man'. Du Verdus cites the 'Petrine' text, Matt. 16: 18, 'thou art Peter, and on this rock I will build my church; and the gates of hell shall not prevail against it'.

⁴⁷ of the Goshen *MS*, of Goshen *1651*.

⁴⁸ The words appear as 'challenging' and 'that claime' on p. 336.

⁴⁹ Contraction expanded.

⁵⁰ Contraction expanded.

⁵¹ No such passage was added in Hobbes's final version of *Leviathan*, the Latin translation of 1668.

⁵² had *MS*, hath *1651*.

⁵³ promiseth *MS*, promised *1651*.

⁵⁴ Immates *MS*, inmates *1651*.

⁵⁵ Hobbes's claim that after the general resurrection the wicked will have 'grosse and corruptible bodies' is on the previous page, p. 345.

⁵⁶ See Matt. 22: 23–8; Mark 12: 18–23; Luke 20: 27–33.

⁵⁷ off *MS*, of *1651*.

⁵⁸ *intaile* MS, entaile *1651*.

⁵⁹ lepth *MS*, Depth *1651*.

LETTER 101   26 NOVEMBER [/6 DECEMBER] 1656

Henry Stubbe to Hobbes, from Oxford

BL MS Add. 32553, fos. 14–15 (original).
Printed in Nicastro, *Lettere*, pp. 14–15.

S.ʳ

I here send yoᵘ a long letter;¹ I doubt not but you can forgiue such faults of yᵉ right hand,² as are occasioned by excesse of zeale to serue yoᵘ. The letter, when regulated (wᶜʰ I haue not time to doe [with *deleted*], although it bee not a worke of much time: nor shall, because I may yᵉ better disauow all yᵉ libellous language wᶜʰ it carryes with it.) may bee subscribed M: P: wᶜʰ are the initiall letters of Maternus Purefoy, wᶜʰ is my mothers name.³ I leaue yᵉ busynesse wholly to yoʳ management: whither you will insert yᵐ into yᵉ maine booke: owneing what piquant language, you shall adde, retaine, or vary. or whither you will put it in a letter as an appendix; yᵉ Oeconomy whereof I haue hinted in mine: submitting to yoʳ prudence, who I doubt not will haue a care, yᵗ my zeale to serue yoᵘ bee not my ruine & undoeing. which is the onely request of

S.ʳ
yoʳ very humble seruᵗ
Henry Stubbe

Oxon: Nou: 26. 1656

[*postscript:*] S.ʳ a person of honoʳ here, an admirer of yoᵘ, hath a desire to Apollonius's Coniques in Greeke & Latine.⁴ I desire you would bid M:ʳ

Crooke[5] to send mee word if hee haue one of yᵉ best edition, & wᵗ price it is: & I shall then take care to send for it: I presume to trouble you, because I am ignorant in yᵉ editions of those bookes. yoᵘ shall oblige mee herein exceedingly.

[*addressed:*] These For his euer honoured Friend M:ʳ Thomas Hobbes. Leaue this with M:ʳ Crooke booke-seller at yᵉ Shippe[6] in Paul's church yard London hast 4d

[*endorsed by James Wheldon:*] M.ʳ Stubb. No. 26. 1656

¹ The *Letter concerning the Grammatical Part of the Controversy between Mr Hobbes and Dr Wallis*, inserted into Hobbes's *Markes*, pp. 20–30.
² See Letter 91 n. 3.
³ The letter was printed without any such subscription.
⁴ The most recent edition, with a commentary but in Latin only, was by Claude Richard: *Apollonii conicorum libri IV* (Antwerp, 1655).
⁵ Probably Andrew Crooke (see the Biographical Register, 'William Crooke').
⁶ See Letter 91, general note.

LETTER 102   29 NOVEMBER [/9 DECEMBER] 1656

Henry Stubbe to Hobbes, from Oxford

BL MS Add. 32553, fos. 16–17 (original).
Printed in Nicastro, *Lettere*, pp. 15–16.

S:ʳ

I had forgot in my last to acquaint yoᵘ with yᵉ story relateing to yᵗ passage of yᵉ D:ʳˢ *now and anon too*.¹ It is not taken out of any ballad, but referres to Obadiah Sedgewicke,² who haueing marryed for his first wife a chambermayde, presently after yᵉ marryage dinner was ended, hee took her aside into the draweing roome, and desired to anticipate those nuptiall pleasures hee was otherwise not to partake of till night. Yᵉ mayde desired him to forbeare till night; but hee replyed, *now and anon too*. and thus you haue yᵉ story as it was related by Sedgewickes brother in lawe to mee yᵉ other day. Another request I haue to put up to yoᵘ is yᵗ yoᵘ would speake fauourably of this vniuersity,³ wherein yoᵘ haue many fauourers, and wᶜʰ hath uindicated yoᵘ so much by slighting both the lectures & bookes of yoʳ Antagonists. All generally decryeing yᵉ act,⁴ & disowneing it, as an uniuersity busynesse. In particular M.ʳ Barlowe Keeper of yᵉ publique library⁵ told mee yᵗ hee had such an

379

esteeme for yoᵘ; yᵗ if yoᵘ would send him one of yoʳ physiques,[6] hee would not onely giue it entertainement in yᵉ library, but honourably register yᵉ worthy donor. Hee is a person of great repute here; & therefore I thought fit to acquaint yoᵘ with this, yᵗ so if yoᵘ pleased you might transmit one with a short letter to him, & I should see it deliuered safe. As for yᵉ Apollonius, let not M:ʳ Crooke send it downe,[7] but onely yᵉ price. S:ʳ I hope yoᵘ will excuse this boldnesse in

yoʳ most affectionate friend & seru.ᵗ
H: Stubbe

Oxon: Nov: 29. 1656

[*addressed:*] These For his much esteemed friend M:ʳ Th: Hobbes. leaue this with M:ʳ Crooke[8] booke-seller at yᵉ signe of yᵉ shippe in Paul's church-yard. London.

[*endorsed by James Wheldon:*] Nov. 29ᵗʰ 1656 M.ʳ Stubb. Now and anon too.

---

¹ This phrase was used by Wallis in his *Due Correction*, p. 96: 'unless you will say that the *same motion* may be *now, and anon too*'.

² Obadiah Sedgwick (*c.*1600–58), Puritan divine, former tutor at Magdalen Hall, Oxford, and member of the Westminster Assembly.

³ Hobbes responded to Stubbe's plea with the following passage in *Markes*: 'Concerning the Universities of *Oxford* and *Cambridge*, I ever held them for the greatest and Noblest means of advancing learning of all kinds [. . .] Nor can I yet call this your Doctrine the Doctrine of the Vniversity, but surely it wil not be unreasonable to think so, if by publick act of the Vniversity it be not disavowed, which done, and that as often as there shall be need, there can be no longer any doubt but that the Vniversities of *England* are not onely the Noblest of all Christian Vniversities, but also absolutely, & of the greatest benefit to this Common-wealth that can be imagined' (p. 19: *EW* vii, pp. 399–400).

⁴ The 'Act' was the ceremony at which degrees were awarded: this remark suggests that some public denunciation of Hobbes had been made at a recent Act.

⁵ Thomas Barlow was Keeper of the Bodleian Library from 1652 to 1660.

⁶ *Of Body* (see Letter 109 n. 1).

⁷ See Letter 101 nn. 4, 5.

⁸ John Crooke (see Letter 91, general note).

François Peleau to Hobbes, from Bordeaux

Chatsworth, Hobbes MSS, letter 31 (original).

Monsieur

Il y a long-temps que ie n'ay appris aucunes Nouuelles de vous; ie crois que mes lettres ne vous ont pas esté renduës; et Je n'adjouste aucune foy a ce que Monsieur Mylon nous a escrit de Paris touchant vostre santé. M.ʳ Du Verdus m'a prié de vous écrire, et m'a donné vn billet[1] pour renfermer dans cette lettre, ou il y a certains doutes, qu'il a eüs dans la lecture de vostre Leuiathan. Pour moy i'en ay quelques autres, dont je vous demande la résolution.

Vous dites. dans votre Metaphysique, ou philosophie premiere, que le lieu, est phantasma corporis existentis, quatenus existentis,[2] mais monsieur, vous m'avoueréz, que tout corps, est in loco [et entre phantasma *deleted*], et qu'il n'est pas, in phantasmate; doncques le lieu, non est phantasma. &c.

En second lieu, vous dites au second chapitre de la liberté, que primogenitura est sors Naturalis, seu praeoccupatio;[3] et que l'aisnesse est vn droit, [>ou Loy *deleted*] Naturel sur les choses; [>et vne Loy Naturelle] si cela est, Il me semble que [puisque *deleted*] Dans l'estat de Nature; Non potest esse ius omnium in omnia; puisque les aisnés ont préoccupé les choses, et parconsequent, minores Natu non habent aequale ius cum primogenitis, propter praeoccupationem rerum, ab ipsis primogenitis factum. Doncques Il faut que vous confessies que les aisnéz n'ont aucun droit sur les choses en vertû de leur préoccupation, ou [que *deleted*] autrement Il s'en suiura que in statu Naturae Non est aequale ius omnium in omnia. ce que destruiroit entierement l'hypothese, que vous auéz faitte dudit droit de Nature. J'attens vostre décision là dessus.

Cependant Je vous prie Nous écrire au plustost pour Nous mander de vos Nouuelles et nous tirer de l'incertitude, ou nous sommes, pour l'estat de vostre santé. Je suis de tout mon coeur

Monsieur
Vostre tres humble & tres obeissant seruiteur, et amy.
Peleau

A Bordeaux. ce 10 decemb. 1656.

[*addressed:*] For Mr Hobbes At the Greene Dragon in Paules Churchierd London

[*endorsed by Hobbes:*] M. Peleau De 10. 1656

Translation of Letter 103

Sir,

I have received no news from you for a long time. I fear that my letters have not been delivered to you; and I give no credence to what M. Mylon told us about your health in his letter from Paris. M. du Verdus has begged me to write to you, and has given me a note[1] to enclose in this letter, in which he makes some objections which have arisen during his reading of your *Leviathan*. I have a few other objections of my own, to which I request the solutions.

You say in your Metaphysics, or First Philosophy, that space is 'the phantasm of an existing body, considering it simply in so far as it exists';[2] but, Sir, you will admit that every thing is 'in space', and that it is not 'in a phantasm'. Therefore space is not a phantasm, etc.

Secondly, you say in your second chapter on Liberty that 'primogeniture and first possession are natural ways of determining ownership by lot',[3] and that the seniority of an elder child is a natural right to things; if that is so, I think that there cannot be a right of every man to every thing in the state of nature. For the elder children took first possession of things, with the result that 'the younger children do not have an equal right to that of the first-born, because of the first possession of things, carried out by the first-born themselves'. So you must admit that the elder children have no right over things by virtue of first possession, or else it would follow that 'in the state of nature there is not an equal right of every man to every thing', which would completely destroy your supposition about the said right of nature. I await your verdict on this matter.

However, I beg you to write as soon as possible, sending us your news and rescuing us from our uncertainty about the state of your health. I am, with all my heart,

Sir,
Your most humble and obedient servant, and friend,
Peleau

Bordeaux, 10 December 1656

¹ This note, which is presumably not to be identified with Letter 100, appears not to have survived.

² *De corpore* VII. 2: '*Spatium est Phantasma rei existentis, quatenus existentis.*' *Of Body* gives: '*SPACE is the Phantasme of a Thing existing without the Mind simply.*'

³ *De cive*, III. 18: '*Sors autem duplex est vel arbitraria vel naturalis.* [. . .] *Naturalis est, Primogenitura* [. . .] & *prima occupatio*' ('But all lot is twofold; *arbitrary*, or *naturall*; [. . .] Naturall is *primogeniture* [. . .] or *first possession*').

LETTER 104   8 [/18] DECEMBER 1656

Henry Stubbe to Hobbes, from Oxford

BL MS Add. 32553, fos. 18–19 (original).
Printed in Nicastro, *Lettere*, pp. 16–17.

S:ʳ

I receiued both yoʳ letters,¹ and as to yᵉ Oeconomy of those critique remarques² I leaue it wholly to your prudence, & yoᵘ may make use not onely of yᵗ one of *now & anon too*,³ but all if yoᵘ so please; & I shall thinke my selfe happy in haueing had an opportunity to oblige you. yet, it is not yᵉ thing it selfe yᵗ I am so willing to disowne (were it any way considerable) but any harsh expression, because our statutes might comprehend yᵗ under libelling:⁴ I think yᵗ origination of Empusa⁵ is cleare, & yᵉ sculptures of yᵉ Egyptian gods (from whence yᵉ Greekes borrowed all) are to be seene in our library here, being sent for a present to Bpp: Laud:⁶ & being formed so, their motion must bee like to yᵉ motion of a ship in yᵉ sea, or other motus projectorum⁷ As for yᵉ translation,⁸ D:ʳ Owen⁹ had an inkleing of it, I told him yᵗ I did make an essay at yoʳ request (to whom I was obliged for yᵗ esteeme, I had found at London; whereas yᵉ v[niversi]ᵗⁱᵉ¹⁰ had not affoorded so much countenance) but it was more to showe how unapt I was to so great a tasque, rather yⁿ to goe thorough with it: and if I had, I could say with Erasmus, non est flagitium rem malam verbis bene Latinis exprimere:¹¹ I doubted not but our Inquisition would bee as fauourable as yᵗ of Rome: & if Erasmus did not satisfy him Buchanan might, who being asked why hee penned so many fables in his scotch history, answered it was Exercitium styli.¹² And thus I scaped yᵗ brunt, & for yᵉ progresse, it shall not bee talked of here any more; for I may fairely equivocate, yᵗ I layd it aside long agoe. I cannot thinke upon any thing more of στιγμή¹³; but I belieue you haue enough. yᵗ place out of Maccabaes¹⁴ is to be so understood, στιγμή alone being neuer used for a moment: & if it bee taken in my sense yᵉ nature of the disease is most emphatically there expressed, by that authour, who is much famed for his elegancy. In Aristotle de animâ: l: 1. c. 6 there is this text, if it may doe you any good. Ἐκ τῶν δεμοκρίτου σφαιρίων, ἐὰν γένωνται στιγμαὶ, μόνον δε μένει τὸ ποσὸν, ἔσται τι ἐν αὐτῷ τὸ μὲν κινοῦν, τὸ δὲ κινούμενον. ex Democriti sphaerulis si fiant puncta, modò maneat quantitas, erit aliquid in ipsâ quod moueat et quod moueatur.¹⁵ Here στιγμή is taken a quantitatiue Atome. In yor praiseing, or rather speakeing fauourable of yᵉ v[niversi]ᵗⁱᵉ¹⁶ wᵗ you shall say, as if you heard it were now beginning to flourish after yᵉ visitation,¹⁷ will redound to D:ʳ Owens honoʳ: & if D:ʳ wallis bee bafled singly¹⁸ hee cares not; nay will bee glad to see him opposed, upon a priuate account, though not publique: because hee doth still crosse him, & back-bite him. And truely hee is of yᵉ same inclination to doctoʳ Ward, neither of yᵐ both are approued of by any Westminster scholar, who are D:ʳ Owen's creatures now of late,¹⁹ & an honourable character of yᵗ schoole will begat yoᵘ much fauour here in any occasion wherein Dʳ: Owen is not concerned, who hath undertaken our Protection agᵗ the Presbyterians: & wee haue promised to defend liberty of conscience, & [yᵉ *blotted*] other fundamentalls of this gouernemᵗ; S:ʳ in yoʳ letter to M:ʳ Barlow yoᵘ may consider whither you will take any notice of my telling you of wᵗ hee sayd, or no. or onely take notice of his ability to judge, & candour, & so passe a complement upon him: & let him guesse yᵉ rest, upon my tendering both letter & booke.²⁰ S:ʳ I had almost forgot, wᵗ it may bee impudence to desire, yᵗ when yoʳ first sheet comes out, you would bid M:ʳ Crooke²¹ send it mee: and afterwards, yᵉ chapter of critiques, yᵗ so I may see it before it bee out. S:ʳ you shall hereby infinitely oblige him, who desires onely that hee may deserue yoʳ good by some proportionate seruice & in yᵉ meane while is

S:ʳ
yoʳ most affectionate friend to serue you
H: Stubbe.

Oxon: dec: [7 *altered to* 8] 1656

[*postscript:*] As to yᵉ greeke and Latin pointing²² yᵗ it is nouell, it is cleare: Salmasius in two epistles to Sarrauius cannot make it ancienter yⁿ Ptolomeus Philadelphus:²³ Lipsius & Putean, cannot goe so farre, but make it no elder yⁿ Adrian.²⁴ & I am confident their reasons are convinceing.

[*addressed:*] These For M^r: Th. Hobbes

[*endorsed by James Wheldon:*] Mr Stubb. Dec. 8. 1656.

¹ These letters have not apparently survived.

² For the 'critique remarques' see Letter 101 n. 1; 'Oeconomy' here probably means editing and the apportioning of material between Stubbe's letter and Hobbes's own text.

³ See Letter 102 n. 1.

⁴ For the university statute against libelling, see Griffiths (ed.), *Statutes of the University of Oxford*, XV. 8, 'De famosis libellis cohibendis', which decreed that a libeller was 'to be expelled as a disturber of the peace' ('tanquam Pacis perturbator banniatur').

⁵ Hobbes had used this term in the dedicatory epistle to *De corpore*: 'a thing called *School-Divinity*, walking on one foot firmly, which is the Holy Scripture, but halted on the other rotten foot, which the Apostle *Paul* called *Vain*, & might have called *Pernicious Philosophy* [. . .] It is like that *Empusa* in the *Athenian* Comick Poet, which was taken in *Athens* for a Ghost that changed shapes, having one brazen leg, but the other was the leg of an Ass' (*Of Body*, sig. B1ᵛ–2ʳ; *De corpore*, sig. A3: '*Scholasticam* dictam θεολογίαν, pede incedentem altero quidem, quae est Scriptura sacra, firmo; altero autem putrido, quae est Philosophia illa quam Apostolus *Paulus* appellavit *vanam*, potuit *perniciosam* [. . .] Similis existens Empusae apud Comicum Atheniensem. Ea enim Athenis Daemonium habebatur, mutabili specie, pedibus altero Aeneo, altero Asinino'). Wallis had criticized this passage in *Elenchus*, p. 4, and *Due Correction*, pp. 23–4, claiming that an empusa had only one leg; Stubbe offered a lengthy refutation of this claim in the criticism of Wallis which Hobbes inserted into *Markes* (pp. 23–6: *EW* vii, pp. 410–20).

⁶ In 1636 Laud's gift of 181 MSS to the Bodleian Library was accompanied by an Arabic astrolabe, a bust of Charles I, and two 'idols', one Egyptian, the other Indian (Macray, *Annals of the Bodleian*, p. 84).

⁷ 'motion of projectiles'.

⁸ Stubbe's projected Latin translation of *Leviathan*.

⁹ See Letter 91 n. 7.

¹⁰ Contraction expanded.

¹¹ 'It is no disgrace to express a bad thing in good Latin.'

¹² 'exercise for his pen'. George Buchanan (1506–82) was a Scottish humanist, poet, historian, and political theorist: his *De rerum scoticarum historia* (1582) included material from medieval legend about the early kings of Scotland.

¹³ In *Six Lessons* Hobbes had referred to 'A mark, or as some put in stead of it στιγμη, which is a mark with a hot iron' (p. 5: *EW* vii, p. 200). Wallis claimed that this word meant a point made with a pen, and accused Hobbes of confusing στιγμή with στίγμα (*Due Correction*, pp. 28–9). This issue furnished the title of Hobbes's *Markes*, and was further pursued on pp. 28–30 of that work (*EW* vii, pp. 389–91).

¹⁴ 2 Macc. 9: 11 (cited in Stubbe's criticism of Wallis: *EW* vii, p. 425).

¹⁵ *De anima*, 409a. 11–13: 'if the atoms of Democritus become points, so long as physical quantity remains, there will be something in them which moves and is moved'. Stubbe's reference should be to bk. 1, ch. 4.

¹⁶ Contraction expanded.

¹⁷ The parliamentary Visitation of Oxford was decreed in May 1647, to correct 'the offences, abuses and disorders [. . .] of late times'. The board of Visitors began to

summon, eject, and replace members of colleges in March 1648. In the winter of 1649–50 the Visitors also required Fellows of colleges to take the Engagement oath, ejecting those who refused.

[18] That is, if Hobbes attacked only John Wallis and not Seth Ward (on whom see Letter 75 nn. 7, 8).

[19] Owen had been a Visitor of Westminster School since 1654.

[20] See Letter 102 n. 6.

[21] Andrew Crooke (see the Biographical Register, 'William Crooke').

[22] = punctuation (*OED* pointing 2).

[23] Ptolemy XII of Egypt (*c*.112–51 BC). Salmasius (Claude Saumaise) referred to him in a letter to Sarravius (Claude Sarrau), though without discussing punctuation: Sarravius, *Epistolae*, pp. 242–4.

[24] Justus Lipsius (Josse Lips) discussed the absence of accents and punctuation marks from early Latin and Greek writing in *De recta pronunciatione*, ch. 19 (pp. 94–6), though without mentioning Adrian or Hadrian. His pupil Erycius Puteanus (Errijck de Put) tentatively suggested that punctuation came in 'from the time of Hadrian' ('à temporibus Hadriani' (*Amoenitatum humanarum diatribae*, p. 279)). This refers to the Emperor Hadrian, who ruled from AD 117 to 138; Stubbe may have confused this with some other references to Adrian of Tyre (*c*. AD 113–93), a sophist who studied at Athens and taught rhetoric at Rome.

LETTER 105   [13/] 23 DECEMBER 1656

Samuel Sorbière to Hobbes, from Paris

Chatsworth, Hobbes MSS, letter 35 (original).

Viro Clarissimo et Sapientissimo THOMAE HOBBIO Samuel Sorberius χαίρειν.

Quod bene ualeas, & non solùm in tuos usus jucundé philosophando, sed, quod posteros juuet, scribendo senectutem tuam oblectes, tantò acceptius est amicis tuis omnibus, HOBBI sapientissime, et (si per ueterem amicitiam nostram licet) suauissime, quantò grauiorem de aduersa ualetudine metum incusserat tuum unius fermè anni silentium. Ex quo enim ultimam de Corpore lucubrationem tuam miseras, uix unam & alteram à te epistolam acceperant tum Bosquius, tum Prataeus[1] & Martellus, quos in primis rerum tuarum certiores facere solebas. Illud, fateor, me minus sollicitum habebat, quamuis cum uiris optimis in te amando colendoque certare soleam. Verùm minus aduertebam, ob interruptam diu istam inter nos literarum reciprocationem, sedes mutatas, itinera suscepta, & inuersam propemodum totam quam in Belgio[2] institueram uitae rationem; cum scilicet literatos inter & bonae mentis amantes honestum locum obtinens frequentissimo gaudebam tecum literarum commercio. Non alia aetas alios mores postulat, non depositum sanè philosophandi studium, nihil est detractum amicitiae nostrae per prolatas epistolas & torporem meum. Significauit identidem Prataeus quae me negotia distinerent & Musis inuitum abducerent; quare ut plurimus in me purgando sim [>omnino] necessarium non duco. Redeo igitur ad illa duo quae posteriores tuae innuunt, & nusquam tibi melius fuisse quàm nunc sit, & alacri te animo strinxisse calamum in quendam Oxoniensem maleuolum qui demonstrationes tuas acerbiùs excepit.[3] Vtrumque gratulor, & circa primum quidem, Deum opt. max. precor ut te quod superest istius seculi incolumem seruet. Quotusquisque enim est qui altiùs philosophetur, qui terram istam, ambientem aerem, sidera, mundum uniuersum oculis spectet eruditis; qui ad rerum causas, originem, nexum, seriem, & mutationes attendat; qui hominum mores, affectus, ratiocinia, & facultates minimas maximasque feliciter rimetur; qui doctrina polleat, judicio, & acumine, sine quibus philosophia illotis manibus tractatur, & authores foetus parturiunt informes sapientissimae Disciplinae dehonestamenta; quotusquisque tandem et superest, ex quo nos urget Gassendi, Cartesii, Galilaei, Verulamii, Gilberti,[4] desiderium, qui toruitatem, agrestes mores & intempestiuos, sesquipedalia uerba, tumorem, & damnatam meritò in Aula Scholae peruicaciam, philosophando procul eliminauerit? Paucissimos herculè noui, praesertim in Gallia nostra, in qua languent artes bonae, insuper habentur uiri docti, &, nisi Deus auertat, mentes posterorum irrepet uni litandum esse Mammonae, & soli incumbendum studio supinae nescio cujus, sed ui superûm nimis faustae Politices, quae diem ex die ducit, praesentia tantum uel proximè futura spectat, caeterorum unicè secura ultra limites uitae nostrae impendentium, aut quibus forsan dabitur tempus eludendis, astu scilicet uel dolo & artibus illis quae solae nunc obtinent, & solium prudentiae, candoris, fortitudinis, & caeterarum uirtutum impudentissimè, proh dolor? & maximo cum dedecore totius gentis nostrae occupauerunt. Sed quò me abripit Virtutis illius quam docent scripta tua politica, cum moribus nostris collatio? Illud urgeo, neminem nosse me qui uestigia tua premat; atque adeo tantò magis nostra interesse ut pergas adornare & perpolire quas meditando ratas sententias ex penitissimâ rerum ipsarum inspectione & tractatione, non ex solâ inanium uerborum combinatione, eruere ualuisti. Quare non possum non dolere, quod bonas horas tuas malè colloces in refutando pleniùs quam par sit homine temerario, qui dente liuido scripta tua rodit, & famae suae consulit, quam non reformidat malam, modo per te nomen suum seram transmittat in posteritatem. Suaderem ego tibi, & Viris magnis tui similibus, ut si quid aduersarij scriptitarent notatu dignum compendiosé refutarent, & addendum in proximâ editione impetiti operis reseruarent, nullâ facta authoris maleuoli [mentione][5] uel si quid alius compositae mentis blandè uerum monuisset, eo uti cum debitâ gratiarum actione ad secundas tertiasue curas emendatiores perficiendas. Est sanè interdum cum in arenam descendere necessarium sit, & quia res est maximi momenti, & quia hostis spectata uirtus eò nos prolicit; quemadmodum olim contigit Gassendo nostro cum Disquisitionem illam Metaphysicam in Cartesium instituit,[6] quam absolutissimum arbitror exemplum Controuersiae subtilissimè ornatissimeque pertractatae. Atque utinam Vir sapientissimus tempus non triuisset in Morino exagitando, idque inuerso calamo & dentatâ chartâ Apologiam, Anatomiam ridiculi muris, & Fauillam Muris cudendo,[7] quibus nihil est in Nebulonem illum φερονυμὸν accomodatius; sed quae tamen tanti philosophi grauitatem minimè decebant, & quae moriens jussit operum suorum Catalogo expungerentur. Sinas igitur, si me audis, oblatrare canes, & perge quâ capisti pandens iter ad sapientiam & rerum ueram cognitionem. Tractatum tuum de Homine ne diutiùs inuide bonis & tuarum lucubrationum amantibus; & si quid desit anatomicarum experientiarum indica mihi, uel Prataeo doctissimo qui Medicinae totus incumbit, & non solum chyli in uenas subclauias ingressum, uenas lymphaticas, sed multa alia quotidie obseruat, atque te monente obseruare plura ualerat in aegris & cadaueribus, quorum secandorum copia major est Lutetiae quam Londini. Epistola mea Sebastiani Alethophili nomine ad Joannem Pecquetum ductus chyliferi inuentorem,[8] nescio an in manus tuas uenerit. Dederam tamen ante biennium tibi tradendam Marii Conjugi[9] in Angliam proficiscenti: At nisi ad te peruenerit, in Disquisitione Anatomica Pecqueti inuenies si editionem ultimam anni quinquagesimi quarti consulas;[10] & uellem quidem de ea sententiam tuam habere; quippe circa Artem Medicam, nonnulla amoeniori stilo scripsi quae circa praecordia ludunt, & stimulo forsan esse poterunt filiis Medicorum ad grauiora demum & saniora in scriptis suis proferenda. En tibi R.P. Vaterii[11] Jesuitae Specimen de Planetarum distantiis ab sole & a Terra per opticum tubum cognoscendis. Quod laude dignissimum an assecutus te judice fuerit scire laboro: nam Tu judex rerum opticarum optimus, & in sententiam tuam ibunt facilè Mathematici nostrates, siue obseruandi modum probes calculo tuo, siue paralogismum ostendas; quod uerbo indicare poteris. Vale, Vir Maxime & me semper ama, qui nouum istum appetentem annum & sequentes multos faustos exopto; qd & trium memoratorum supra amicorum commune votum. Iterum vale.

Scribebam Lut. Par. X. Kal. Jan. A.S. MDCLVII.

Translation of Letter 105

Samuel Sorbière sends greetings to the most wise and distinguished Thomas Hobbes.

Most wise and (if I may say so, in view of our old friendship) most charming Hobbes: the fact that you are well, and that you are happily spending your old age not only engaging in philosophical studies for your own use, but also writing, to the benefit of posterity—this is all the more welcome news for all your friends, because of the rather serious fears about your health which your silence of almost a year had given rise to. For since you sent us your last treatise, *De corpore*, neither du Bosc nor du Prat[1] nor de Martel had received more than one or two letters from you, although they above all used to be the people to whom you would send news of your affairs. I confess that I was less worried by this, although I normally compete with these excellent men in loving and honouring you. However, I was less aware of it, because of the long hiatus in our own correspondence, my changes of abode, the journeys I had undertaken, and because my way of life had changed almost completely from the one I had established in The Netherlands[2]—when, that is, having a respectable position among literary people and lovers of good minds, I enjoyed a very frequent correspondence with you. A different age does not demand different customs; I have certainly not given up my zeal for philosophizing, and no damage has been done to our friendship by the delays in our correspondence and my own sloth. Du Prat has let you know several times what business it was that detained me and took me away from the Muses against my will; so I do not think it really necessary for me to excuse myself at length.

I come back, therefore, to those two remarks you made in your last letters: that you have never been better than you are now, and that you have briskly drawn your pen against some ill-willed fellow in Oxford who had made some rather acrimonious criticisms of your demonstrations.[3] I congratulate you on both points; and on the first, I pray Almighty God to keep you safe for the full term of your life. For how few people there are who philosophize at all deeply; who survey this earth, the atmosphere, the stars, and the universe with skilled eyes; who take notice of the causes of things, their origin, connection, order, and changes; who successfully probe human behaviour, emotions, reasoning, and faculties, great and small; who are strong in learning, judgement, and discrimination, without which philosophy is handled with dirty fingers, and authors give birth to malformed embryos, disgracing our most learned discipline! Now that we feel the loss of Gassendi, Descartes, Galileo, Bacon, Gilbert,[4] how few people are finally left who can fully eliminate from the study of philosophy all wildness, uncouth and unsuitable habits, long-winded terms, bombast, and that obstinacy which is rightly condemned in the universities! I know very few indeed, especially in this France of ours, where the good arts languish, learned men are held to be of no account, and, unless God prevent it, the next generation will gain the impression that they should worship only Mammon, and that the only thing worth studying is somebody or other's spineless (but, as fate would have it, all too successful) politics. A politics, that is, which proceeds day by day, looking only at things which happen in the present or the near future, utterly heedless of the other things which may happen beyond the limits of our own lives, or else hoping that it will have a chance to escape them—that is, by cunning and guile and those arts which are the only ones to be found nowadays, which, alas, have most impudently usurped the throne of prudence, honesty, fortitude, and the other virtues, to the extreme disgrace of all our people.

But where have I been driven to by that comparison I was making between the virtue taught in your political writings, and our present-day morals? The point I am making is that I do not know anyone who has come close to you; and so it is all the more important for us that you should continue to adorn and polish those settled opinions which you have been able to establish in your meditations by thoroughly inspecting and investigating the things themselves, not by merely putting meaningless words together. That is why I cannot help grieving that you are wasting your good time in producing an undeservedly thorough refutation of that presumptuous man, who nibbles enviously at your writings: he is just promoting his own reputation, not caring if it be a bad one, so long as he can use you to transmit his own name to posterity. I should like to persuade you, and great men like you, that if their opponents churn out something worth taking notice of, they should write a brief refutation, and keep it to be added to the next edition of the work which is under attack, without making any mention[5] of the ill-willed author of the criticism; or else, if some clear-headed person has kindly provided a criticism which is correct, in that case they should put it, with due acknowledgement, in the second or third editions, to make them more accurate. Of course there are times when it is necessary to descend into the arena, both because the subject is very important, and because the tried valour of our opponent draws us thither; that is what happened once to our friend Gassendi, when he began his *Disquisitio metaphysica* against Descartes,[6] which I regard as the most perfect example of how to conduct a controversy with extreme subtlety and elegance. But I wish that that most learned man had not wasted his time arguing with Morin, publishing those carefully revised and finely produced works the *Apologia, Anatomia ridiculi muris*, and *Favilla ridiculi muris*;[7] nothing could be more suitable for that suitably named worthless fellow; and yet these things were not at all suited to the dignity of such a great philosopher, and on his death-bed he ordered them to be removed from the catalogue of his works.

So if you take my advice you will let the dogs bark, and continue on your chosen broad path towards wisdom and the true knowledge of things. Do not spite good people, and those who love your works, by delaying any longer the appearance of your treatise *De homine*; and if there is any evidence from anatomical experiments which you lack, tell me. Or else tell the learned du Prat, who is devoted to the study of medicine, and is making observations every day, not only on the passage of chyle into the subclavian and lymphatic veins, but also on many other matters; at your request, he would be able to make many observations on sick people and on cadavers, the latter being more plentiful in Paris than in London. I do not know whether you have received a copy of my letter to Jean Pecquet, the discoverer of the chyle duct, which I published under the name Sebastian Alethophilus.[8] More than two years ago I gave a copy to le Maire's wife[9] to take to you when she was travelling to England. But if it did not reach you, you can find it in Pecquet's *Disquisitio anatomica*, if you consult the last edition, published in 1654.[10] I should like to have your opinion of it; for I have written several pieces on the art of medicine in a rather elegant style, which can be an amusement for the mind, and may perhaps goad the medical men into producing something more weighty and sensible in their own writings.

Here is a dissertation by Father Vatier,[11] a Jesuit, on how to find out the distances of the planets from the sun and the earth by means of a telescope. I am anxious to know whether, in your opinion, he has succeeded in this praiseworthy enterprise. For you are the best judge in optical matters, and our mathematicians here will easily follow you, whether you approve of his calculations by your own reckoning, or whether you demonstrate a fault in his argument—something you can do in a word. Farewell, great Sir, and love me always; I wish you a happy new year for the coming year, and many happy years thereafter—which is also the common wish of the three friends mentioned above. Farewell again.

Paris, 23 December in the year of our Saviour 1656.

¹ From later references in this letter, it is clear that Abraham du Prat is intended here.

² Sorbière had lived mainly in Sluys, Leiden, or The Hague from 1642 to 1650, and in Breda from 1650 to 1653 (see the entry in the Biographical Register).

³ Hobbes's replies to Wallis's *Elenchus* (*Six Lessons*) and to his *Due Correction* (*Markes*). The letters from Hobbes to Sorbière on this topic have not apparently survived.

⁴ William Gilbert (1540–1603), physician and scientist, famous for his pioneering treatise on magnetism, *De magnete* (1600).

⁵ mentior *MS*.

⁶ *Disquisitio metaphysica seu dubitationes et instantiae adversus Renati Cartesii metaphysicam et responsa* (1644): this work consisted of Gassendi's objections to Descartes's *Meditationes* (the fifth set of objections out of the series of six sets commissioned by Mersenne), with Descartes's replies, and Gassendi's responses to those replies. The printing of this work had been organized by Sorbière (see Sorbière's letter to Gassendi, 15 [/25] Oct. 1643: *MC* xii, p. 345).

⁷ Jean-Baptiste Morin (see Letter 47 n. 5) published numerous controversial works attacking Galileo and Gassendi. The *Apologia* (1649) was Gassendi's belatedly published reply to Morin's *Alae telluris fractae* (1643). *Anatomia ridiculi muris* (The Anatomy of a Ridiculous Mouse), 1651, and *Favilla ridiculi muris* (The Ashes of a Ridiculous Mouse), 1653, were replies to Morin's attacks on Gassendi's atomism (*Réponse à une longue lettre de M. Gassendi*, 1650, and *Defensio suae dissertationis*, 1651), and were published under the name of Gassendi's pupil François Bernier.

⁸ On Pecquet, see Letter 77 n. 13. Sorbière's letter was published as *Viro clarissimo D. Ioanni Pecqueto* (1654). 'Alethophilus' means 'truth-lover'.

⁹ See Letter 69 n. 4.

¹⁰ See pp. 164–80 of the 1654 edn.

¹¹ Probably Antoine Vatier (1596–1659), a Jesuit priest who taught mathematics and theology at La Flèche: he corresponded with Descartes and Mersenne in the period 1638–43 (A&T i, pp. 558–65; ii, p. 28; *MC* xi, p. 348; xii, p. 102). In 1656 Balthazar de Monconys was present at a meeting in de Montmor's house attended also by Sorbière and 'Father Vattier the Jesuit who teaches mathematics' (H. Brown, *Scientific Organizations*, pp. 71–2). A Pierre Vattier, who wrote on medicine and psychology and translated numerous works from Arabic and Persian, was later also a member of the de Montmor group: a 'discours' he pronounced at their assembly was published in 1660 as *Le Cœur déthroné*. But he was not a Jesuit, and was described on the title-page of another work (*Nouvelles pensées sur la nature des passions*) as '*conseiller* and physician to my lord the duc d'Orléans' ('Conseiller & Medecin de Monseigneur le Duc d'Orléans'). The work

referred to here by Sorbière does not appear to have been published. Nor does any version of it survive among Hobbes's papers at Chatsworth. Sorbière was circulating several copies: on [22 Dec. 1656/] 1 Jan. 1657 he wrote to Bornius: 'Here is an essay by the reverend father Vatier, a Jesuit, on the distances of the planets from the sun and the earth; I am submitting it to your judgement, and to that of van Schooten, Huygens, and other mathematicians. I have sent it to my friend Hobbes' ('En igitur tibi [. . .] Specimen R. P. Vaterij Jesuitae de Planetarum a Sole & a Terra distantijs, quod examini tuo, Schoteni, Hugenij & aliorum Mathematicorum subijcio. Misi Hobbio nostro' (BN MS f.l. 10352, part 1, fo. 238^v)).

LETTER 106   [13/23 DECEMBER 1656?]

Abraham du Prat to Hobbes [from Paris]

Chatsworth, Hobbes MSS, letter 36.

Monsieur Chanut[1] nous dit il y a quelques iours qu'il a aporté de hollande une petite [bouteille *deleted* >fiole] de verre, comme une larme,[2] dont le col est fort long. Le fonds semble estre solide, et ne se rompt point quand on frape dessus. Mais si on rompt tant soit peu de la pointe, cette fiole se dissout en mille pieces incontinent. Tous ceux qui entendent parler de cela n'en peuuent imaginer aucune cause vraisemblable. Mrs Martel et Sorbiere et moy vous aurions obligation, si vous scaués ce que c'est. Vous me feriés plaisir de me dire aussi la cause pourquoy deux cordes de deux luths estans tenduës à l'unisson, l'une estant touchée, l'autre se meut sensiblement, comme cela se remarque en mettant dessus quelque festu ou autre chose legere, et non pas les autres.

[*addressed:*] A Monsieur
Monsieur Hobbes at the greene Dragon in Pauls churchyard A Londres

[*endorsed by James Wheldon:*] Monsr Sorbierre Jan. [*blank space*] 1657

Translation of Letter 106

M. Chanut[1] told us a few days ago that he has brought back from Holland a small glass phial, like a tear-drop,[2] with a very long neck. The body of the phial seems to be solid, and does not break when you tap it. But if you break off however small a part of the tip, the phial suddenly dissolves into a thousand pieces. No one who has heard about this can imagine any probable explanation. MM. de Martel and Sorbière and I would be obliged to you if you could take the trouble of explaining this phenomenon to us, if you know what the explanation is. I shall be glad also if you can tell me the reason why, when two strings on two lutes are tuned in unison and one of them is plucked, the other moves perceptibly, as one can see if one places a straw (or other light object) on it; but the other strings do not move.

[*addressed: see text*]

Because of Wheldon's endorsement, this has been listed as a letter from Sorbière in the hand-list of the 'letters from foreign correspondents' at Chatsworth. However, Sorbière is referred to in the letter, and the handwriting is that of Abraham du Prat. The most likely explanation is that this was a note added by du Prat as a covering sheet to Letter 105, which is dated 'X Kal. Jan. 1657'—hence the hesitant and misunderstanding endorsement—and which itself lacks an outer sheet. The folds in the two MSS match exactly, confirming this explanation.

[1] Pierre Chanut (1600–62), French Resident and Ambassador in Sweden (1645–9), Minister Plenipotentiary in Lübeck (1650–3), and Ambassador to Holland (1653–5). He was famous for his knowledge of languages, and his learning was highly prized by Queen Christina of Sweden; it was at his suggestion that she invited Descartes to her Court.

[2] These hollow glass drops, later known as 'Dutch tears' ('lagrime bataviche') in Italy and as 'Rupert's drops' (after the scientifically minded Prince Rupert of the Rhine) in England, were to become one of the most famous scientific curiosities of the period. They were first discussed at a gathering in de Montmor's house in the summer of 1656, when Marin Cureau de la Chambre produced specimens he had obtained from Chanut; they were discussed again there in late July 1656, in the presence of Sorbière and Antoine Vatier, and the de Montmor 'academy' was still debating the subject in 1660 at a meeting attended by Henry Oldenburg (H. Brown, *Scientific Organizations*, pp. 71–2, 102). Balthazar de Monconys questioned Hobbes about them in London in May 1663 (*Iournal des voyages*, ii, p. 25). Robert Hooke discussed them in *Micrographia* (1665), pp. 33–4, illustrating them from his observations with a microscope (pl. 4). The fullest account was given in a book devoted to this phenomenon by Geminiano Montanari, *Speculationi fisiche* (1671). Hobbes's own explanation was published in *Problemata physica* (1662), pp. 67–71 (*OL* iv, pp. 337–8) and in *Decameron physiologicum* (1678), pp. 74–5 (*EW* vii, pp. 130–1).

LETTER 107   19[/29] DECEMBER 1656

Henry Stubbe to Hobbes, from Oxford

BL MS Add. 32553, fos. 20–1 (original).
Printed in Nicastro, *Lettere*, pp. 18–19.

S:^{r}

Yesterday there came to mee one M:^{r} Vaughan of Jesus colledge, desireing to know whither yo^u intended to answer Wallis. I assured him of it. whereupon hee told mee y^t ye Gentleman whose letters in English d.^{r} W: had inserted was his brother.^{1} & ye occasion of ye writeing y^m was this. when D.^{r} W's Elenchus came out, it was by him sent to his brother being a louer of ye Mathematiques: who upon ye perusall of it, sent him in a priuate letter y^t remarque, y^t D.^{r} W's had guessed aright, y^t such & such propositions were out of Cauallerius. Mr Vaughan being in company with Wallis, did let him know this. whereupon ye D.^{r} upon ye edition of his Arithmetica infinitorum,^{2} sent him one, together with a letter. The gentleman haueing receiued it, delayed an answer, ye letter not requireing any; untill his brother did reminde him that ye D.^{r} might expect a reply, and howeuer it would bee ciuill to returne him ye complement. Upon this account hee wrote y^t letter you see, not intending ye publication of it, or y^t euer hee should bee engaged in ye defence of a booke hee had not then examined, when hee wrote y^t hee is very much dissatisfyed with ye publishing thereof, & would bee glad to see him corrected according to his demerit, & so would his brother too, he sayth. it is giuen out here by d^r: Ward^3 & others y^t yo^u are onely publishing yor lectures in latine, & no answer to this.^{4} & y^t yo^u haue omitted w^t might reflect upon ye v[niversi]^{tie5} which all are glad of; yet yo^u may distinguish y^m both easily from our vniuersity, being Cambridge men, and not brought in by ye v[niversi]^{tie6}, but imposed in y^t ignominious Visitation.^{7} I am confident hee came on purpose to acquaint mee with this action; yet hee would not let mee tell yo^u so, or y^t yo^u might bring him upon ye stage or his brother, (who are great admirers of yo^u) but y^t yo^u might bee confident of this relation, & had hee but knowne ye D^r: would haue made such use of it, ye d.^{r} had neuer had a letter from him. S:^{r} Mr Barlow expects yor booke,^{8} & if yo^u put out any more, I hope yo^u will not forget this library. All here doe earnestly expect yor booke de Homine. S^r I am

yor uery humble and affectionate seru^t
Henry Stubbe.

Oxon. Dec: 19. 1656

[*addressed:*] These For his much esteemed Friend M:^{r} Th: Hobbes Leaue this at M:^{r} Crooke's^9 booke-seller at y^e [shippe *deleted* >Dragon]^{10} in Paul's church yarde. London.

[*endorsed by James Wheldon:*] Mr Stubb. Dec. 19th. 1656

¹ In *Due Correction*, p. 7, Wallis had printed an extract from a letter 'from a noble Gentleman' to a third party, which he introduced as follows: 'He was pleased, though wholly a stranger to mee, upon view of my *Elenchus*, to intimate to mee by a Letter directed to a third person, That D. *Wallis had unhappily guessed, that those propositions which M. Hobs had concerning the measure of Parabolasters, were not his own, but borrowed from some body else, without acknowledging his Author*: and signified withall, that *they were to be found demonstrated in an exercitation of* Cavallerius, *De usu Indivisibilium in Potestatibus Cossicis.*' (The reference is to Bonaventura Cavalieri, *Exercitationes geometricae sex* (1647), pp. 243–319.) On p. 8 Wallis also printed a further letter by the same author, sent in reply to Wallis's response to the first.

The Mr Vaughan who visited Stubbe cannot be identified with certainty, but he was very probably James Vaughan, who (according to Foster) proceeded BA at Jesus College in 1636, MA 1639, and was elected a Fellow of the college (also in 1639). According to Richards, 'The Puritan Visitation', p. 15 n., however, he had been a Fellow of Jesus since 1628. He submitted to the parliamentary Visitors in 1648 (Burrows (ed.), *Register of the Visitors*, p. 100; Foster's claim that he lost his fellowship is an error (see Richards, 'The Puritan Visitation', p. 15)). He had become Vice-Principal of the college by Aug. 1653, but was removed from that office in 1656 (ibid., pp. 57, 66–7). He came from a gentry family; Wallis's description of his brother as a 'noble gentleman' could thus have been within the bounds of polite exaggeration.

James Vaughan had four brothers, of whom one, Henry, was High Sheriff of Merionethshire in 1642 and 1654, and another, John (1603–74), was a prominent lawyer (and a friend and executor of Selden) who became Chief Justice of the Common Pleas in 1668 (see Williams, 'Sir John Vaughan', esp. p. 228 on the five brothers). John Vaughan is known to have been a friend and admirer of Hobbes: Aubrey called him Hobbes's 'great acquaintance' (*ABL* i, p. 369), and Vaughan's own legal and political philosophy was especially close to that of Hobbes (Tuck, *Natural Rights Theories*, pp. 125, 138). James Wheldon, Hobbes's amanuensis, told Aubrey that he thought it possible that Hobbes had presented the MS of his *Historia ecclesiastica* to Vaughan (*ABL* i, p. 382); this is confirmed by a MS copy of the work in the Royal Library, Copenhagen (KBK MS Thott 213 4°, fos. 1–50ʳ), the first page of which records that it was copied in 1685 from a MS signed by Hobbes which came from the library of 'My Lord Vaughan'. John Vaughan can be expected to have taken a close interest in Hobbes's public controversies, and is thus the prime candidate for identification with the author of the letters quoted by Wallis.

If these identifications are incorrect, other candidates for the Mr Vaughan of Jesus College could include the Edward Vaughan who was admitted to the college as a 'nobleman' in Dec. 1652 but whose name was removed from the Buttery books there in May 1653 (Bodl. MS Top. Oxon. c. 173, fo. 14ᵛ), or the Thomas Vaughan who was admitted as a Fellow Commoner in early 1651 (ibid., fo. 15ʳ; he is mentioned also in a document of Dec. 1651: Bodl. MS Eng. hist. c. 5, fo. 38ʳ). Another Thomas Vaughan, the occultist medical and chemical writer and brother of the poet Henry, was a Fellow of Jesus from *c.*1642 to *c.*1648 (Foster; Hutchinson, *Henry Vaughan*, pp. 30, 141 n. 3) and resided again in Oxford at some time during 1650–1 (ibid., pp. 141–2), but is not known to have been there in 1656. Finally, the only noble Vaughan who might otherwise be identified with the author of the letters cited by Wallis, John Vaughan (1640–1713), who was later fourth Earl of Carbury, a keen amateur mathematician and a Fellow of the

Royal Society, must be excluded. He was an only son, and had just matriculated at Christ Church in the summer of 1656.

[2] Wallis, *Arithmetica infinitorum* (1656).

[3] See Letter 75 n. 8.

[4] Hobbes did not in fact produce a Latin translation of *Six Lessons*; and he answered Wallis in *Markes*.

[5] Contraction expanded.

[6] Contraction expanded.

[7] See Letter 104 n. 17. Seth Ward had been a Fellow of Sidney Sussex College, Cambridge. John Wallis had been an undergraduate of Emmanuel College, Cambridge, and in *c*.1644 had been a Fellow of Queens' College, Cambridge. The Visitors installed Ward in place of John Greaves (as Savilian Professor of Astronomy) and Wallis in place of Peter Turner (as Savilian Professor of Geometry), probably in Oct. 1649 (Shapiro, *Wilkins*, p. 87).

[8] See Letter 102 n. 6.

[9] Andrew Crooke (see the Biographical Register, 'William Crooke').

[10] John Crooke's shop was at the sign of the Ship (see Letter 91, general note); Andrew's was at the sign of the Green Dragon.

LETTER 108   [22 DECEMBER 1656/] 1 JANUARY 1657

François du Verdus to Hobbes, from Bordeaux

Chatsworth, Hobbes MSS, letter 33 (original).
Enclosures (original) filed with Chatsworth, Hobbes MSS, letter 30.

Monsieur,

Comme nous comptons a Bourdeaux, d'ou j'écris présentement, c'est aujourdhuy le lundy premier jour de l'année 1657. Je la commançe en vous rendant mes deuoirs; et ne sçaurois la mieux comançer. C'est donc en premier lieu pour vous témoigner les souhaits que je fais, que cette année vous soit bonne, et une longue suitte [d'aprés *deleted* > d'autres apres;] et cela comme je fais a moy mesme: Et en second lieu, c'est pour vous marquer la joye que j'eus, quand auec uostre lettre du 20.eme Nouembre[1] je reçeus la bonne nouuelle de vostre bonne santé. Vous me parlés de [la miene *deleted* > ma lettre] latine a Mr Crooke:[2] Il est fort uray Monsieur qu'il y auoit uint ans tous entiers que je n'auois point écrit en latin; et que j'ecriuisse [> ainsi] en cette occasion, cela vous fait bien uoyr la grandeur de l'inquiétude où j'étois. Mais qui n'y auroit esté? d'un côté Mr Bourdelot[3] Abbé de Massay, mon intime Amy, et qui sçait toujours les nouuelles des qu'on les peut sçauoir, m'auoit écrit une lettre de consolation sur ce qu'au Louure on vous faisoit mort; et d'autre part Mr Mylon m'assuroit qu'il le croyoit: mais

397

pour rompre ce que je vous dis de si sérieux par une façon de parler joyeuse, Je suis trop vostre seruiteur pour refuser de vous croyre, quand vous m'assurés que vous estes en vie; et vous promets que je le croyray enuers tous et contre tous; et vous prie de me le faire croire fort long temps.

Mais aprés cette expression, que vous prendrés bien s'il vous plait, ne trouués pas mauuais Monsieur que poussé d'un bon zele je vous dise le fond de mon coeur, et ce que je pensay de vous. Mr Mylon se fondait sur ce que luy ayant promis vos pensées sur la Quadrature du Cercle, vous ne les luy auiés pas enuoyées: et moy j'alay penser, que peut estre a força de trauail et de contention d'esprit sur ce sujet là, vous seriés tombé malade. Permettés moy de vous le dire: si vous n'aués point trouué cette verité là, ne vous y aheurtés point. vostre vie en santé vous doit estre plus chere que quelque découuerte que ce soit; c'est la vie du plus grand Philosophe qui soit au monde; du Pére de la vraye Philosophie: Il faut la conseruer Monsieur; et quant a cette verité que vous cherchiés, Comme vous estes braue et genereux, il faut la mépriser brauement: Vous le sçaués mieux que moy, Cela mesme est de l'ayr du Monde qu'on apelle l'ayr galant, de dire soy mesme de soy mesme *Je pensois auoir trouué, mais je voy que non*: et quand il vous plairra de le dire, toujours aurés vous la gloyre d'estre allé aussi loin que tous les autres hommes en cela; Et plus loin qu'eux tous en tout le reste: Toute la Philosophie que vous nous aués donée étant si uraye et si bien démontrée, que des-ormais on ne peut que marcher sur vos pas, et encore, pour demeurer fort loin derriére. Mais encore une fois ce que je vous dis c'est de zele: car ce n'est pas a moy a vous donner conseil; mais s'il vous plait a le réçeuoyr de vous.

Mais pour vous dire de mes Nouuelles, et en suitte uenir a vostre lettre et au reste. Il y a quelque quinze jours qu'il me prit tout a coup enuie de comancer la Traduction de vostre Léuiathan. dépuis ce temps là J'ay traduit dépuis l'Introduction inclusiuement, toute la premiere partie qui est le Traité of Man. je n'ay jamais rien fait de ma vie auec tant de satisfaction; j'écris presque a coursse de plume, sans trouuer que peu de mots qui m'arrétent, faute d'un bon dictionaire; et ay une joye qui ne se peut dire a suyure le fil de vos pensées en ces belles matiéres. Tout de bon j'ayme cet Ouurage comme si c'étoit moy mesme qui l'eusse fait; et suis déja en peine du lieu ou je l'imprimeray; et coment je le feray seurement. Pleut a Dieu qu'il y eut icy une Comunauté de Marchands Anglois a qui je peusse doner tous mes biens, sous pension qu'ils m'enuoyeroient: je serois bien tot a Londres:

ou si je trouuois icy de Messieurs de la Relligion se chargeans de mes biens et affaires, et me faisans le mesme party: Mais comme les Maquereaux de ma Moynesse[4] sont puissants, et que l'archeueque Tampis (c'est ainsi qu'on nome le nostre[5] parçe qu'il disoit tant-pis de toutes choses) s'obstine a me prendre par famine, affin que si réduit a l'extremité par Cabales je traite de mes biens auec le Sr Déjean[6] Curé d'ambarés, le Chef d'Intrigue contre moy; Déjean traite auec luy de sa Cure [> de six mille francs de reuenu que Tampis uoudroit annéxer a l'archeueschè] je ne sçay coment j'en sortiray, ni par quelle négotiation. [Vous *deleted*] Il est certain neanmoins que de quelque façon que j'en sorte, je ne songe plus au voyage d'Italie;[7] et que ce printemps si je suis hors d'embarras, (comme j'ay quelques lumiéres que je le seray) je feray celuy d'Angleterre.

Qu'il y auroit de plaisir Monsieur d'estre apuyé de Messieurs de la Relligion; de tascher là d'estre connu [du *deleted* >de] Seigneur Protecteur; de luy dédier ma Traduction de vostre Liure; et le prier dans la Dédicatoire qu'il l'enuoyât au Roy, et le conuiât a le lire, pour s'y instruire des Droits de Souuerain que luy ont usurpé les Prestres! Cecy je vous le dis en secret: Car que scay-je le party que je prendray: Mais la Moynesse et les Prestres m'attaquent en urays filoux.

Je viens a vostre lettre et a nos matiéres. Vos quattre responses[8] m'ont satisfait a tel point, que je les souhaiterois inserées dans vostre Leuiatan. Si vous le jugés a propos mandés moy je vous prie en quels termes, et précisément en quels lieux vous les insereriés. les deux touchant St Pierre se disent en peu de mots: Que si Jesus Christ s'adressa a luy auec plus de uéhemençe qu'aux autres Apotres, c'est que le conoissant uaillant et discret il l'animoit a ayder ses freres, non a gouuerner mais a prescher. sur quoy [>dirés vous] on ne doit point aporter [>pour objection] la Mort d'ananias et de Sapphira, pour tascher de prouuer par là que St Pierre ait eu puissançe de vie et de Mort: puis que St Pierre ne fit rien que les prédire.

Celle de *Est*, et *Signifie*,[9] Il me semble qu'il est absolûment nécessaire que vous l'inseriés dans vostre Leuiatan. Et puis que les Prestres ayans trouué cette inuention de Dire au Peuple *Peuple voylà ton Dieu que nous portons entre les mains, et auons la puissançe de faire*: le Party Papiste se trouue tellement obstiné dans la croyançe de la Realité, comme ils disent, que cette seule croyançe les rend insociables auec tout autre party: certainement il est a propos d'éclairçir [la *deleted* >cette] matiére; sur tout le pouuant en peu de mots Et voicy a peu prés en quels termes je le dirois. Ce que j'ay dit que le mot *Est* veut dire *signifie*, on le uoid par la façon ordinaire de parler, quand on parle de figures. Ainsi en regardant la Carte on dit *Cecy est* Paris, et *cecy* [>est] St Denis ou par le mot *Est* on entend ce qui *signifie* Car les points qu'on montre en disant celà, sont ceux qui *signifient et representent* Paris, et St Denis: Mais d'ailleurs a uoyr les façons de parler de l'écriture, Je trouue que pour dire célebrer la solemnité et la memoyre de la Pasque, c'est a dire du passage de l'ange qui tuä les premiers nés d'Egypte sans toucher aux Israelites, cela s'apelle dans l'Ecriture *manger l'aigneau*, et *manger la pasque* Et je trouue de mesme que célebrer la sollemnité et la mémoyre de la Céne, et de la Passion, cela s'apelle dans l'Écriture *manger le pain*, et *manger le corps de Jesus-Christ*. comme donc quand il s'agit de la Pasque, *manger l'agneau* se dit a la lettre, et dans le sens litteral; Et [>que] *manger la pasque* ueut dire manger *ce qui fait ressouuenir* de la Pasque de mesme quand il s'agit de la Céne *Manger le pain* se dit a la lettre, et dans le sens litteral: et *manger Jesus-Christ* ueut dire manger *ce qui fait ressouuenir* de Jesus-Christ. Et comme il [est impossible d'entendre *deleted* >seroit trés absurde de uouloir prendre] a la lettre qu'on [mange *deleted* > *mangeât*] *la Pasque*, c'est a dire qu'on mangeât le passage, et la promenade de l'ange: il est aussi trés absurde de uouloir prendre a la lettre qu'on *mangeât le corps de Jesus-Christ*; Et de cette absurdité on tombe dans toutes ces autres, qu'un corps soit sans étanduë; qu'il soit tout en tout et tout en chaque partie du tout; que la teste les piés le reste du corps soyent en chaque endroït du pain benit, et neanmoins n'y soyent qu'une fois; qu'il y ait des accidents sans substançe; et autres telles absurdités, où il a falu tomber en suitte de la premiére.

Voylà Monsieur, ce que je juge nécessaire que vous ajoutiés a cet endroit de uostre liure: si vous uoulés qu'il fasse impression, en cela, aussi bien sur les esprits médiocres que sur les autres, qui dés la premiére ueuë seront tous a vous. Et si vous le jugés aussi a propos, vous dirés deux mots de ce que vous m'aués dit sur ce qu'on pourroit objecter que Dieu rejetta Saül pour auoyr sacrifié. Que si vous trouués a propos de faire ces petites additions (mais grandes pour l'importançe) Je vous prie écriués moy les propres termes Anglois, ausquels vous mettrés celà.

Mais ce que je dois vous dire C'est que comme je n'ay trouué persone qui sçeut que répliquer a la comparaison de manger la Pasque, et manger Nostre Seigneur: ie trouue qu'on n'est pas sans repart au reste.

Et premiérement touchant St Pierre, ils me disent qu'il y a un passage où nostre Seigneur luy dit *Compelle intrare*:[10] il est uray qu'on n'a sçeu me le montrer; et que comme je n'ay pas ma Concordance de Bible je n'ay sçeu ou le chercher: mais si vous sçaués ce que c'est, et que cela en uaille la peine Je vous prie de m'en éclairçir.

Secondement touchant [David *deleted*] Saül et Samuël comme il s'agit du droit de regner: uostre response qui me conuainc en me faisant uoyr les desseins de Samuël, je la trouue sujette a une chose; C'est que comme il est parlé de cela dans l'Écriture, Ce n'est pas tant Samuël que Dieu mesme qui rejetta Saül. Car uoyés le commançement du chapitre 16 du 1er liure de Samuel *Dixitque dominus ad Samuëlem usque quò tu luges* Saül cum *ego projecerim* eum ne regnet super Israël. la doute demeure donc, qu'il n'auoit point droit de sacrifier, n'étant pas possible que Dieu se fasche de ce qu'on fait auec droit: et a cela je vous demande encore deux mots de replique.

on presse mesme et on fait instançe (qui est la troisiéme chose que j'ay a vous proposer et je vous l'écriuis dans un morçeau de papier uolant par la uoye de Mr Peleau[11] (lequel ie vous diray par parenthese qui est un homme fort préoccupé, et qui n'aura de long temps les bons fondemens)[)][12] sur ce que le Roy Vsia fut frapé de lépre seulement pour auoyr brulé l'encens &c[13] a quoy ie vous prie de repondre.

Et passant a d'autres questions. je vous demande premierement Si selon vous une femme Souueraine d'un État est chef de son Église et de sa Relligion (pour cela je croy bien qu'ouy)[14] mais si elle auroit droit de faire toutes les fonctions de prestre? Je dis dans nostre Relligion Crétiene, ou Jesus-Christ n'a fait nuls prestres fémelles.

secondement puis que la Loy Ciuile reigle *quid suum quid alienum*, et que le Roy [>peut] de droit [peut *deleted*] tout prendre *hoc erit jus Regis*: comment on peut dire que Dauid offança Dieu, et que ce fut un adultére que de luy et Bersabée?[15] Car il n'auoit qu'a reigler qu'elle ne fut plus femme d'Vrie; et qu'elle fût la sienne; et ayant plein droit de le faire ce n'eüt pas esté un adultére que cela mais un accouplement légitime. Et de mesme tous les Roys.

3emement sur ce que vous dites que Nul n'est obligé a accuser ceux dont la mort ou la peine rendroit sa vie moins douçe, Je vous demande si celuy qui uouä de [tuer *deleted* >sacrifier] sa propre fille (Jephté je croy) étoit tenu a son ueu?[16]

La quatriéme chose que je vous demande c'est de me dire s'il vous plait vos sentimens sur ma traduction que je vous enuoye d'un de vos chapitres[17] c'est celuy du langage qui m'a semblé de taille raisonable affin que par luy vous jugeassiés du reste [>ie l'ay marqué par nombres affin que vous peussiés cotter les endroits a corriger.] La cinquiéme chose c'est s'il vous plait de m'expliquer les endroits Anglois que je vous marque, dans la derniére page de ma troisiéme feuïlle de ce pacquet:[18] Mais la derniére et la grande; Et que je vous demande de tout mon coeur; c'est que vous m'honoriés de vostre bienueillançe; Et croyiés s'il vous plait qu'il n'est pas possible d'estre plus que ie [>le] suis

Monsieur
Vostre tres humble tres obeissant et tres acquis seruiteur
duuerdus

[*endorsed by Hobbes:*] Jan. 1. 1656/57 wth the 4th chap. of Leu. in french, from mons^r du verdus

[*enclosed:*]

Chapitre Quatriéme; Du Langage

1. L'inuention de l'*Imprimerie*, quoy qu'ingenieuse, n'est pas grand chose, si on la compare a l'Inuention des *lettres*. Mais on ne sçait point qui fut le premier qui trouua l'usage des lettres: seulement on dit que ce fut *Cadmus* fils d'*Agenor* Roy de Phoenicie qui les aporta en Greçe. Inuention profitable pour continuër la mémoyre du temps passé; et réjoindre le genre humain dispersé par toute la Terre, en tant de régions différentes et éloignées les unes des autres: Mais inuention difficile; En ce qu'il y a falu une obseruation exacte de tous les mouuemens de la langue, du palais, des léures, et des autres organes de la parole, pour faire autant de différens caractéres a s'en ressouuenir. Mais la plus noble de toutes les inuentions et la plus utile, c'est celle du *Parler*: qui consiste en noms ou appellations, et dans leur connection; par quoy les hommes font régistre de leurs pensées; les rapellent dans leur souuenir quand elles sont passées; et se les déclarent l'un l'autre pour leur utilité [mutuëlle *deleted by Hobbes*], et [par *deleted by Hobbes*] conuersation [>mutuëlle *added by Hobbes*]: Et sans quoy il n'y eut jamais eu parmy les hommes ni etat, ni societé, ni Contrat, ni Paix; non plus que parmy les Lyons, [et *deleted*] les Ours, et les Loups. Le premier Auteur du langage ce fut *Dieu* luy-mesme lequel instruisit *Adam* comment il nommeroit les Créatures qu'il luy fit uoyr: Car l'Écriture sainte ne uà pas plus loin en cette matiére. Mais cela suffit pour le diriger a ajouter d'autres noms, selon que l'expériençe et l'usage qu'il auroit des Créatures luy en doneroit occasion; et a les joindre par

degrés, en sorte qu'il se fit entendre; Au moyen de quoy auec le temps il peut auoyr tout ce qu'il luy faloit de termes pour son usage, quoy qu'il n'en eut pas tout le nombre qui fait besoin a l'orateur et au Philosophe. Certes je ne trouue rien dans l'Écriture, dont on puisse receuillir ni directement ni par conséquençe, qu'*Adam* ait apris les noms de toutes les figures, des nombres, des mesures, des couleurs, des sons, des phantaisies, des Rélations: beaucoup moins qu'il ait sçeu les noms des noms, et du langage; tels que ceux-cy *Général, spécial, affirmatif, négatif, Interrogatif, Optatif, Infinitif*; tous lesquels sont en usages: Et moins encore que tout cela ceux *d'Entité, d'Intentionalité, de Quiddité*, et tels autres du jargon de l'École; qui ne signifie rien.

2. Mais tout ce langage acquis et augmenté par *Adam* et par sa posterité, se perdit [en suitte *deleted* >dépuis] a la Tour de *Babel*; quand chaque homme pour sa Rébellion fut frappé par la main de Dieu, de l'oubly de la langue qu'il sçauoit auparauant. Ainsi les hommes s'étant ueus contraints de se dispenser eux-mesmes en diuerses parties du monde, il faut nécessairement que ce soit d'eux que soit uenuë la diuersité des langues qu'il y a maintenant; et cela par degrés, selon que la Nécessité, la Mére des Inuentions, le leur enseigna: Et qu'aussi auec le temps ces langues soyent deuenuës copieuses, comme elles sont.

3. L'usage géneral du langage, c'est de transferer nostre discours mental en un Verbal; je ueux dire la suitte de nos pensées en une suitte de paroles; et cela pour deux commodités. La prémiére c'est de Régistrer les conséquençes de nos pensées, affin que nous ayant une fois échapé de la mémoyre (ce qui arriue aisément) nous n'en soyons pas en peine pour cela; mais puissions les rapeler par les paroles auec quoy nous les auions marquées. C'est donc le premier usage des noms que de seruir de *Marques* ou *Notes* pour se ressouuenir. L'autre commodité du langage; c'est [>parce *added by Hobbes*] que beaucoup de gens se [seruent *altered to* seruant *by Hobbes*] des mesmes mots [>) *added by Hobbes*] pour se signifier l'un [>a *added by Hobbes*] l'autre par leur ordre et connection ce qu'ils concoiuent, et pensent de chaque chose; et aussi ce qu'ils desirent, ce qu'ils craignent et ce pourquoy ils ont quelque autre passions; et a raison de cet usage on nomme les Paroles *Signes*. Les Vsages spéciaux de langage sont ceux-cy. Premiérement de régistrer ce que par notre pensée nous trouuons [qui est *deleted by Hobbes*] [>estre *added by Hobbes*] la cause de quelque chose présente ou passée; ou ce que nous trouuons que les choses présentes ou passées puissent produire et effectuër; Ce qui en un mot est l'acquisition des Arts. En second lieu de montrer aux autres la conoissance a laquelle

nous auons atteint; Ce qui est se conseiller, et s'enseigner les uns les autres. En troisiéme lieu de faire conoitre a autruy nos uolontés et desseins, affin de pouuoir s'entre-ayder les uns les autres. Et enfin, de nous diuertir et les autres, en nous jouänt de nos paroles par plaisir, ou les faisant seruir d'ornement: et celà innocemment.

4. A ces quatre usages il y a quatre abus qui répondent. le Premier, c'est de régistrer mal ses propres pensées, par l'inconstançe de la signification des mots qu'on y employe, par lesquels au lieu de ses propres conceptions, on régistre ce a quoy lon ne pensa jamais; et ainsi on se trompe soy mesme. le second, c'est d'user des termes par métaphore, je ueux dire de prendre les paroles en autre sens que celuy a quoy Elles ont esté ordonées; et par là on trompe les autres. le Troisiéme, c'est de déclarer par paroles, que lon ueut, ce qu'en effect on ne ueut pas. Et le quatriéme c'est de s'en seruir a gréuer autruy. Car puis que la Nature a donné d'[autres *deleted by Hobbes*] armes aux animaux, aux uns des dents [et déffançes *deleted by Hobbes*], aux autres des cornes, aux autres des mains pour nuire a leurs ennemis: c'est abuser des paroles que de faire grief de la langue; sinon que ce soit a quelqu'un qu'on soit obligé de gouuerner: Car alors ce n'est pas luy faire grief, mais le corriger et amender.

5. La façon que le langage sert a se ressouuenir de la conséquençe des causes et effects, consiste dans l'imposition des *Noms*, et [en *deleted* >dans] leur connection.

6. Des Noms les uns sont *Propres*, et singuliers a une seule chose, comme ce *Pierre, Jean, Cet homme, Cet Arbre*: et les autres communs a plusieurs choses; comme, *l'homme, le Cheual, l'Arbre*; chacun desquels quoy qu'il ne soit qu'un seul nom, l'est neanmoins de diuerses choses particuliéres, a l'egard de toutes lesquelles on l'apelle *Vniuersel*: n'y ayant rien dans le monde d'uniuersel que les noms: car quant aux choses nommées, chacune est indiuiduëlle et singuliére.

7. On impose un nom Vniuersel a plusieurs choses pour leur similitude et ressamblançe en quelque qualité, ou autre accident; et au lieu que le nom propre ne rameine dans l'esprit qu'une seule chose: chacun des [vniuersaux *altered to* uniuersels *by Hobbes*] en rapelle plusieurs.

8. Et quant a ceux-cy les uns sont de plus, les autres de moins d'étanduë; les plus étandus comprenant ceux qui les sont moins: et derechef il y en a d'égale étanduë qui se comprenent les uns les autres réciproquement. Par exemple ce nom *Le Corps* est [d'une *deleted* >de] signification plus étanduë que ce nom *l'homme*, et il le comprend: mais

ces noms *l'homme*, et *le Raisonable*, sont d'égale étanduë se comprenant mutuëllement l'un l'autre. Mais il faut estre auerty que par le nom, nous n'entandons pas toujours icy comme en Grammaire, un seul mot: mais souuent par circomlocution plusieurs mots ensemble. Car tous ces mots par exemple, *Celuy qui dans ses actions obserue les Loix de son Païs*, ne font qu'un seul nom, équivalent a ce seul mot, *Juste*.

9. Par cette imposition des noms, les uns de plus ample signification les autres de plus étroite, Nous tournons le compte et calcul des conséquences des choses imaginées dans l'ésprit, en un compte et calcul de conséquençes d'apellations. Par exemple un homme qui n'a point du tout l'usage de la parole, tel que seroit un homme [entiérement *deleted* >tout a fait] sourd et muët de naissançe, cet homme, dis-je, s'il se trouue deuant les yeux un triangle, et auec cela deux angles droits, tels que sont ceux d'un quarré ou figure faite a l'equarre, pourra bien comparer par méditation, et trouuer Que les trois angles du Triangle sont égaux aux deux Angles qu'il uoid auprés: Mais qu'on luy montre un autre Triangle, différent en forme du premier: s'il n'y trouaille tout de nouueau, il ne sçaura si ses trois angles sont égaux comme ceux de l'autre, a ces mesmes deux angles droits. Au lieu que Celuy qui a l'usage des parolles, quand il obserue que cette égalité n'est conséquente ni a la longeur des côtés, ni a aucune autre chose particuliére a ce Triangle; Mais seulement a cela que le Triangle à ses côtés droits, et ses angles trois en nombre: il pourra hardiment conclurre uniuersellement, Que telle égalité se trouue en tous Triangles quels qu'ils soyent; Et registrera son inuention en ces termes généraux, *Tout Triangle à ses trois angles égaux a deux angles droits*. Ainsi la conséquençe trouuée en un particulier uient a estre régistrée et rémémorée comme une Reigle vniuerselle; Et déchargeant de temps, et de lieu, nostre calcul mental, elle nous déliure de tout trauail d'ésprit a la reserue du premier; Et fait que ce qu'on trouue qui est uray *Icy* et *Maintenant* est uray de mesme en *tous temps*; et en *touts lieux*.

10. Mais l'usage des paroles a régistrer nos pensées n'est en rien si éuident qu'au nombre. Vn fou qui l'est de naissançe, et ne sçauroit aprendre par coeur l'ordre des noms numéraux comme *Vn, deux, trois*, &c peut bien obseruer chaque coup que frape l'horloge; et hocher la teste en l'oyant; ou dire autant de fois qu'il l'oyra de coups *un, vn, et vn*: mais non jamais sçauoir quelle heure il aura sonnée. Et il semble qu'un temps a esté que ces noms de nombrer n'étoient pas encore en usage; et que les hommes se contantoient d'apliquer les doits d'une main ou des deux aux choses qu'il uouloient tenir en compte; Et que c'est de là que

405

uient qu'il n'y a point de Nation qui ait ses noms numeraux passé dix; quelques uns mesme ne les ayant que jusqu'a cinq, aprés quoy lon recomançe a compter. Et qu'on sçache compter jusqu'a dix si lon recite les numéraux sans ordre, on se brouïllera soy-mesme et se perdra, qu'on ne sçaura ce qu'on aura fait: bien moins pourroit on donc ajouter, soustraire, et faire les autres opérations d'arithmétique. On uoid donc que sans les mots on ne pourroit faire de calcul de nombres; beaucoup moins en pourroit-on faire des grandeurs, de la vitesse, de la forçe, et des autres choses dont les comptes et calculs sont nécessaires a l'estre, ou au bien estre des hommes.

11. Quand il y a deux noms joints ensamble en une conséquence ou affirmation comme cecy *l'homme est* [*une Créature uiuante* altered to *un Animal*]; ou encor comme cecy *Si c'est un homme c'est* [une Créature uiuante *altered to* un Animal]; si le dernier nom [*Créature uiuante* deleted > *Animal*], signifie tout ce que fait le premier nom, *l'homme*, l'affirmation ou conséquençe est uraye; autrement; Elle est fausse. Car *uray* et *faux* sont attributs du langage non des choses; et où il n'y a point de langage, il n'y a ni uérité, ni fausseté. Il peut bien y auoir de l'erreur: comme quand nous attandons ce qui ne sera pas, ou soupçonons ce qui n'a pas esté: Mais en l'un ni en l'autre de ces cas, on ne peut blâmer un homme de fausseté.

12. Puis doné que la Vérité consiste a bien ranger les noms aux affirmations, Celuy qui cherche des vérités précises, doit bien se ressouuenir de ce pour quoy signifier il a étably les noms dont il se sert; Et doit les ranger conformement a celà: autrement il se trouueroit embarrassé en paroles; et seroit comme l'oyseau englüé, lequel plus il se débat, et plus il s'englüe. Aussi estre pour cela que dans la Geométrie, qui est la seule sçiençe qu'il ait pleu a Dieu de nous doner jusqu'a maintenant, on commançe d'abord a établir la signification des mots dont on se seruira; Et cet établissement là, qu'on nomme *Définitions*, on le met au commençement du compte et calcul qu'on prend a faire.

13. Cecy fait uoyr combien il est nécessaire a tout homme qui aspire a la uraye conoïssance, d'éxaminer les définitions des premiers Autheurs: Et celà soit pour les corriger quand il y a eu de la négligençe, ou mesmes pour en faire d'autres. Car les erreurs des définitions se multiplient elles mesmes a mesure que le compte et calcul s'auançe; Et font donner [les hommes *deleted*] en absurdités; de quoy [ils s'aperçoiuent *altered to* on s'aperçoit] bien enfin: mais il n'y a pas moyen de l'éuiter: sinon qu'on recomançe a [> se] compter de nouueau tout

dés le commançement, où étoit le fondement de l'érreur. De là il arriue que Ceux qui s'en fient aux liures, font justement comme qui compteroit plusieurs petites sommes en une grande, sans s'estre assuré auparauant si ces petites sommes sont bien comptées ou non: Trouuant donc enfin l'érreur uisible, et ne se défiant point de leurs premiers fondemens, ils ne sçauent comment s'éclairçir d'où celà uient: mais perdent leur temps a feüilleter leurs liures: Et vous diriés [de *deleted by Hobbes*] [>quils ressemblent *added by Hobbes*] ces oyseaux qui étans entrés par la cheminée, et se trouuans ranfermés dans une chambre, uolettent et se débattent au faux jour des uitres d'une fénétre, faute de considerer par où c'est qu'ils sont entrés. C'est donc dans la droite définition des noms que consiste le premier usage du langage, qui est d'acquerir la sciençe; Et c'est dans le défaut [>cy *added by Hobbes*] ou de définitions, ou [des définitions *deleted by Hobbes* >en ce quil y en a point *added by Hobbes*], que consiste le premier abus du langage d'où uienent tous les [doctrines *inserted by Hobbes*][19] [faux *altered by Hobbes to* fausses] et [où il n'y a point de sens *deleted by Hobbes* >absurdes *added by Hobbes*], [lesquels *altered by Hobbes to* lesquelles] font que les Gens qui tirent toute leur instruction de l'autorité des liures, et non de leur propre méditation, sont autant au dessous de la condition des hommes ignorans, que les gens sçauants sont au dessus: car entre la uraye sciençe et les doctrines erronées l'ignorançe tient le milieu. Le sens Naturel et l'Imagination ne sont point sujets a absurdité; Nature elle mesme ne sçauroit errer; Et les hommes selon qu'ils ont leur langage plus copieux et abondant, en sont ou beaucoup plus sages, ou beaucoup plus fous que l'ordinaire. Et il n'est pas possible que sans lettres l'homme deuiene excellamment sage [>comme il ne scauroit sans elles devenir *deleted by Hobbes*] [non plus qu'excellemment fou, sinon qu'il eut *deleted by Hobbes*], [>ny (sans auoir *added by Hobbes*] la mémoyre blessée par quelque maladie, ou par la mauuaise constitution des organes [) >excellement fou *added by Hobbes*]. De uray les paroles sont les gettons des gens sages, qui ne s'en seruent qu'a compter: Mais elles sont la monoye des fous, qui les estiment par l'autorité d'un *Aristote*, d'un *Ciceron*, d'un *Tomas*, ou de tel autre docteur qu'on uoudra, si seulement c'est un homme.

14. Toutes choses sont sujets aux noms (ou sujettes a estre nommées) qui peuuent entrer en un compte, ou y estre considerées, et estre ou ajoutées les unes aux autres pour faire une somme; ou soustraites les unes des autres pour laisser un résidu. Les latins nomment les Comptes d'argent *Rationes*, *Raisons*; et le compter

407

Ratiocination, ou Raisonement; et ce qu'en billets, ou sur un liure de [raisons *deleted by Hobbes* >compte *added by Hobbes*] nous apelons *Items*, ils l'apellent *Nomina*, c'est a dire *Noms*: Et de là uient-il ce semble qu'ils ont étandu le mot *Ratio*, *la Raison*, a la faculté de compter en toutes autres choses. Les Grecs n'ont que le seul mot λόγος pour les deux, le *Langage*, et la *Raison*: Et c'est qu'ils creurent qu'il n'y auoit point, je ne dis pas de langage sans raison, mais de raisonement sans langage. Aussi l'acte du raïsoner ils l'apellent *syllogisme*, qui signifie le sommer des conséquences d'un dire a un autre. Et dautant que les mesmes choses peuuent entrer en un compte pour diuers accidens; leur noms pour montrer cette diuersité sont sujets a estre diuersement tournés, et diuersifiés. Cette diuersité de noms peut estre réduite a quatre chefs géneraux.

15. Premiérement une chose peut entrer en compte pour *Matiére* ou *Corps*: comme *Viuant sansible raisonable, chaud, froid, qui se meut, qui est en repos*: où lon entend par tout ce nom *la Matiére*, ou le *Corps*: tous tels noms étant noms de la Matiére.

16. En second lieu elle peut entrer en compte, ou estre considerée pour quelque accident ou qualité, que nous conceuons qui y est, comme pour *estre meüe*; pour *estre ainsi longue*, pour *estre chaude*. &ᶜ. Et alors en tordant un peu, et détournant le nom de la chose mesme, par ce petit changement nous en faisons le nom de l'accident que nous y considerons; comme au lieu de *Viuant*, nous mettons dans le compte *Vie*; au lieu de *meu*, [>nous mettons] *mouuement* pour *chaud* [>nous mettons] *chaleur* pour *long*, *longeur*; Et ainsi des autres semblables: Et tels noms sont les noms des accidens [>et proprietés] par lesquels une Matiére ou corps est distinguée d'une autre. Et on les apelle *noms abstracts*, pour estre séparés non de la Matiére, mais du compte de la matiére.

17. En troisiéme lieu nous mettons en compte les propriétés de nos propres corps, par lesquelles nous faisons semblables distinctions. Ainsi quand nous uoyons quelque chose nous mettons en compte non *la chose ueuë*, mais *la ueuë de la chose*; sa *couleur*, son *idée* de dedans la phantaisie; Et quand nous oyons quelque chose, nous mettons en compte non *la chose ouyë*: mais *l'ouyë de la chose*; le *son* de la chose, et rien plus; ce qui n'est que la phantaisie que nous en auons, et que nous l'ayons conçeu par l'oreille. Et tels noms, le sont de nos Phantaisies.

18. En quatriéme lieu nous mettons en compte les noms mesmes, et les façons de parler; nous les considerons, et leur donnons des noms: Car *Général. vniuersel, spécial, Équiuoque*, sont noms de noms; Et

Affirmation, Interrogation, Commandement, Narration, Syllogisme, Sermon, Oraison, et tels autres noms sont noms de langages. Et c'est là toute la varieté des noms positifs, qu'on pose pour marquer quelque chose de ce qui est en Nature, ou que l'homme peut feindre par esprit, comme les corps qui sont ou qu'on peut conçeuoir qui soyent; ou les proprietés des corps, lesquelles sont en effect ou qu'on peut feindre qui soyent; ou les mots et le langage.

19. Il y a aussi d'autres noms qu'on apelle *Négatifs*, qui sont les notes pour signifier que le mot n'est pas le nom de la chose dont il est question. Comme ces mots *Rien, nul, infiny, indocile; trois-moins-quatre*, et semblables, qui sont neanmoins d'usage ou pour entrer en un compte, ou pour le corriger. Et qui pour n'estre les noms d'aucune chose, ne laissent pas de nous rapeler dans l'ésprit nos pensées passées; en ce qu'ils font que nous refusons [d'admettre *deleted* > de receuoir] aucuns noms que dans leur bon usage.

20. Tous les autres noms ne sont que des sons qui ne signifient rien, Et il y en a de deux sortes l'une de ceux qui sont nouueaux, et dont on n'a jamais expliqué le sens par aucune définition; Et de cette sorte il y en a bonne prouision qu'ont forgés les gens-d'école, et Philosophes [passés *pusled Philosophers* deleted by Hobbes > qui ont l'esprit brouille *added by Hobbes*].

21. L'autre sorte est celle des noms qu'on fait des deux, dont les significations sont contradictoires, et incompatibles. comme ce nom *Vn Corps incorporel*. Et ce qui est tout un, *Vne Substançe incorporelle*, Et grand nombre d'autres. Car quand une affirmation est fausse, les deux noms qui la composent joints ensemble et n'en faisans qu'un ne signifient rien du tout. Par exemple si c'est une affirmation fausse que de dire, *Qu'un Quadrangle soit rond* le mot *Rond-quadrangle* ne signifie rien du tout; et n'est qu'un son, et rien plus. De mesme s'il est faux de dire que la vertu puisse estre *épanchée* et *répanduë*, ou *soufflée dessus et dessous*, les mots *vertu-infuse*, et *vertu-inspirée*, sont aussi absurdes et signifient aussi peu, que le mot *rond-quadrangle*. Et c'est pourquoy mal-aysément rancontrerons nous des mots n'ayants point de sens, et ne signifians rien, qui ne soyent forgés de quelque nom latin ou Grec. Il est assés rare au françois d'ouyr nommer nostre Sauueur du nom de *Parole*, Mais si fait bien du nom de *Verbe*: Et cependant ces mots le *Verbe*, et la *Parole*, ne différent point autrement, sinon que l'un est latin, et l'autre françois.

22. Quand pour auoyr ouÿ un langage, on a les pensées pour signifier lesquelles ont esté ordonés e établis les mots [et la suitte *deleted*] de ce

langage, et leur suitte cela s'apelle *Entandre*; l'Entandement n'étant rien que la conception causée par le parler: Et c'est pourquoy si le parler est particulier a l'homme, (comme j'ay des choses qui me font conoitre qu'il l'est) en ce cas il luy est aussi particulier d'entandre. Et c'est pourquoy il n'est pas possible d'entandre les affirmations absurdes, et [> les] fausses, si elles sont uniuerselles, quoy que beaucoup de gens s'imaginent qu'ils entandent, pourueu seulement qu'ils puissent repeter douçement ou [a part eux?] les paroles qu'ils ont ouyes.

23. [> Je diray cy apres] Quelles sortes de langages signifient les Apétits, les Auersions, et passions de l'ame de l'homme; [je le diray cy apres *deleted*]. Et parleray aussi de leur usage, et de leur abus, quand j'auray parlé des passions.

24. Les Noms des choses qui nous affectent, c'est a dire, qui nous plaisent ou déplaisent, ont dans le commun discours des hommes leur signification *inconstante*: Ce qui uient de ce que les hommes ne sont pas tous semblablement affectés des mesmes choses, ni le mesme homme en tout temps. Car comme on impose les noms pour signifier ses conceptions; Et que nos affections ne sont que des conceptions: quand on conçoit différament les mesmes choses, mal-aysément peut on s'empecher de les nommer différamment. Car encore que la Nature de ce que nous conçeuons soit toujours la mesme: si est ce que la diuersité dont nous receuons les choses, en égard aux différentes constitutions du corps, et aux préjugés de l'opinion, donne a chaque chose une teinture de nos diuerses passions. C'est pour cela qu'en raisonant on doit bien prendre garde aux paroles, lesquelles outre la signification de ce que nous imaginons de leur nature, ont encore une signification de la Nature; des dispositions, et de l'interet de celuy qui parle. Tels sont les noms des vertus, et ceux des viçes. Car l'un apelle *sagesse*, ce que l'autre apelle *peur*; l'un *cruauté*, ce que l'autre apelle *justiçe*; l'un *prodigalité*, ce que l'autre apelle *magnanimité*; l'un *grauité*, ce qui n'est que *stupidité* au dire de l'autre; Et ainsi de tout le reste. C'est pour cela que tels noms ne sçauroient estre le fondement d'un bon raisonement Non plus que les Métaphores, et les Tropes ou figures du parler. Celles-cy neanmoins sont beaucoup moins dangéreuses, qui font profession ouuerte d'inconstançe, Ce que les [noms *deleted* > autres] ne font pas.

[*also enclosed:*]

1.° Dans l'Introduction du Leuiatan voicy un endroit que j'ay traduit: Nosce teipsum lis toy toy mesme dont on n'usa pas jadis comme on fait pour le present ni pour soutenir les gens puissans qui maltraitoïent leurs inférieurs ni pour encourager les petites gens a s'attaquer aux plus grands qu'eux.[20] je ne sçay si c'est bien le sens.

2.° dans l'Introduction aussi j'ay trouué ce que ueut dire le neuer qui est un anglicisme But let one man read another neuer so perfectly:[21] mais qu'un homme en lise un autre si parfaitement qu'on uoudra; ou pour parfaitement que ce soit; ou quelque parfaitement que ce soit. Et me semble que les autres façons ou il y a *never* se raportent a cette traduction. comme for let a space be neuer so litle.[22] &c.

3° aussi j'ay trouué *laughter* et *weeping*: le rire et le pleurer. Mais voicy qui m'a arrété

4.° p. 6 l. 11 and because *in sense* the brain and nerues &c are so benummed in sleep. Et dautant que dans le *sens* le cerueau et les nerfs &c sont tellement engourdis: s'il vous plait de uoyr l'endroit; car il me semble que ces mots *in sense* y sont de trop. Car c'est dans le dormir non dans l'action du sentiment qu'on est engourdy.

5.° a 7 l. plus bas. When *they* are distempered. auparauant il y a deux nominatifs pluriels inward parts; et the brayn and others organs. auquel des deux se raporte they. dans la mesme page *lying cold*. lying?

6.° p. 7 *uncouth* fancy. uncouth?[23] 7.° p. 10. sur le milieu the present onely has a being in Nature. le present seulement a un étant en Nature. *being* n'est ce pas le nom concret; et *be* l'abstrait? Nous autres francois nous disons estre ou vous dites being. comme icy nous disons le seul present a son estre en Nature: lequel des deux est le plus congru l'anglicisme ou le Gallicisme? et mettray-je *Estre* ou *Étant*?

7.°[24] p. 14 and men were faun[25] to apply their fingers. were faun?

[>8°] p. 15 false and senselesse *tenets* tenets?

9.° p. 19 j'ay peine a traduire ces trois lignes. *as it comes to bear sway in them to be taken for right reason and that in their own countrouersies bewraying their want of right reason by the claym they lay to it*.

10.° p. 27 ou vous partiés du Weeping *as some prop of their power*. je ne uoy pas le substantif de ce *their*.

11.° p. 27 a fellow feeling. traduisés.

12.° p. 29 l. 11. vnlesse it be when they serue to make others inferences besides that of the passion they proceed from déliberation is expressed subjonctiuely:[26] Ou est la syntaxe de tout cela?

13. p. 30 there is at last and end either by attaining or by *giuing ouer* traduisés.

14. p. 53. the opinion that such esprits were incorporeal[27] could neuer enter into the mind of any man by Nature. comment donc y est

elle entrée? Car ce n'est pas une chose surnaturelle qu'on parle galimatias et croye des sottises.

15. p. 54. au nombre Lastly. men are naturally *at stand*[28] at stand?

16. p. 55. vous dites que les anciens firent le Caos Dieu. Bacon dans son Cupido siue atomus dit qu'ils ne le firent point Dieu.[29] lequel est le uray?

17. p. 59. il y a 6 lignes que je ne sçay traduire elles comancent And therefore to those points of Relligion; et finissent haue Wrought into them. Je vous prie de les traduire. Et p. 59 and *whereas* in the planting. et aussi p. 59. and juggling betweene princes *juggling*? aussi p. 81. sur la fin without his counterassurançe je ne scay si je traduiray sans sa contrepromesse. Et p. 83. equality of uotes *euen* in that they condemne not do absolue. *euen* fait un equivoque en ce qu'il ueut dire *mesmes* et *pair*.

18. Enfin p. 80. 81. 82. 83. ie uoy que *to personate* c'est faire le personage ou de soy mesme ou d'autruy et le representer ie uoy que *to act* c'est faire l'acte et iouër le rollet; ie uoy que *owner* c'est s'apropier l'action, l'auouër siene et uouloir l'auoir faite en son propre et priué nom: mais ie voudrois trois mots ou françois ou latins traduisants chacun le sien *personate act* et *owner*.

Translation of Letter 108

Sir,

As we reckon the date in Bordeaux, where I am now writing from, today is Monday, the first day of the year 1657. I begin this year by fulfilling my duty to you; and I could not think of any better way of beginning it. So this letter is intended first of all to testify to my desire that you may have a good year, and a long succession of further years after this one— just as I desire the same for myself. Secondly, it is to let you know what joy I had when, thanks to your letter of 20 November,[1] I received the good news of your good health. You talk about my Latin letter to Mr Crooke:[2] it is quite true, Sir, that I had written absolutely nothing in Latin for twenty long years; and the fact that I wrote in that way on this occasion shows you how extremely worried I was. But who would not have been worried? On the one hand my close friend M. Bourdelot,[3] the *abbé* of Massay, who is always the very first with the news, had sent me a letter of condolence on the news of your death which was circulating at the Louvre; and on the other hand M. Mylon assured me that he believed it to be true. But to get away from such sombre thoughts and express things in a more high-spirited way: I am too obedient to refuse to believe you when you assure me that you are alive. And I promise you that I shall believe it no matter what other people say; and I beg you to continue to make me believe it for a very long time to come.

But after using such a manner of speaking, which I hope you will take in good part, I hope you will not be offended, Sir, if, impelled by my zeal to be of service, I tell you what I really believe, and what I have been thinking about you. M. Mylon's conjecture was founded on the fact that, having promised him your opinion about the squaring of the circle, you did not send it to him. And as for me, I was inclined to think that you might have fallen ill through working and troubling yourself so much on that subject. Allow me to say that if you have not found the solution, do not hurl yourself against the problem any more. A healthy life should be more precious to you than any discovery; for it is the life of the greatest philosopher in the world, the father of true philosophy. You must preserve it, Sir; and as for that true solution which you are hunting for, you are a noble-hearted man, and must treat it with noble disregard. As you know even better than I do, that is the correct attitude in society: it is what is called 'being gallant', saying about yourself, 'I thought I had found it, but I see that I was wrong'. And when you resolve to say that, you will still have the glory of having penetrated as far as anyone else in that matter—and further than anyone else in every other matter. For all the philosophy which you have imparted to us is so true and so well demonstrated, that henceforth all we can do is to follow in your footsteps, and still remain far behind you. But once again let me say that I am telling you this out of zealous love; it is not for me to give you advice, but rather, if you are willing, to receive it from you.

But let me give you my news, and then come to your letter, and other matters. A fortnight ago I was seized with a sudden desire to begin translating your *Leviathan*. Since then I have translated, from the Introduction onwards, the entire first part, the treatise 'Of Man'. I have never done anything so satisfying in all my life; I am doing it almost as fast as my pen can write, finding only a few words which bring me to a halt, because of my lack of a good dictionary. It gives me an indescribable joy to follow the thread of your thoughts on these splendid subjects. Seriously, I love this work as much as if I had written it myself. I am already worrying about where to have it printed, and how to find a secure way of doing so. I wish to God there were a community of English merchants here to whom I could hand over all my estate, in return for an annuity which they would send me—then I would soon be in London. Or if only I could find some Protestants here who would take care of my estate and my affairs, and join forces with me. But my nun's[4] pimps are powerful, and Archbishop Toobad (which is what they call our Archbishop,[5] because he used to say 'too bad' about everything) is determined to starve me into submission, in the hope that, reduced to extreme want by the conspiracies against me, I shall make a deal over my possessions with M. Dejean,[6] the *curé* of Ambarès, the plotter-in-chief against me. Dejean is negotiating with him about his living, which is worth 6,000 francs a year, and which Archbishop Toobad wants to annex to his see. So I do not know how I shall get clear of all this, nor what sort of negotiation will enable me to do so. It is certain, all the same, that, however I get clear, I must give up the idea of that Italian journey;[7] and if I am free of my troubles by this spring (as I have some glimmerings of hope that I shall be), I shall undertake my journey to England.

What pleasure it would give me, Sir, to be supported by Protestants; to try to become known to the Lord Protector; to dedicate my translation of your book to him; and to beg him, in my dedication, to send a copy to the King and invite him to read it, to learn from it about the rights of the sovereign which were stolen from him by the priests! I tell you this in secret; for how can I yet tell which side I shall take? But that nun and those priests are attacking me in the most scoundrelly way.

Now I come to your letter, and my arguments. Your four replies[8] satisfied me so completely that I should like to insert them into the text of your *Leviathan*. If you think it suitable to do so, please let me know in what form of words and at what points exactly you would insert them. The two replies concerning St Peter can be briefly summarized: if Christ addressed him in stronger terms than the other Apostles, it was because, knowing him to be willing and of good judgement, he was encouraging him to help his brethren—not to govern them, but to preach to them. And on that point, in your opinion, the death of Ananias and Sapphira cannot be used as an objection to prove that St Peter exercised the power of life and death, because St Peter did no more than predict that they would die.

On your point about 'is' and 'signifies',[9] I think it is absolutely necessary to insert it into your *Leviathan*. And since the priests discovered this trick of telling the people, 'People, here is your God which we carry in our hands, and which we have the power to make', the Papists' sect has become so stubborn in its belief in the Real Presence (as they call it) that that one article of belief makes them incapable of co-operating with any other sect. So there is certainly a need to clear up this matter, especially when it can be done in a few words. Here, then, is roughly how I would put it: 'My argument that "is" means "signifies" is confirmed by the ordinary way of speaking about drawings which represent something. Thus, when looking at a map, one says "This is Paris, and this is Saint-Denis"—where the word "is" means "is that which signifies". For the points on the map which one indicates when saying those words are the points which *signify* or *represent* Paris and Saint-Denis. Furthermore, to consider the way of speaking used in Holy Scripture, I observe that when it refers to celebrating the solemn memory of the Passover (that is, when the angel which killed the first-born of Egypt passed over the houses of the Israelites without touching them), the Bible calls that "eating the lamb" and "eating the Passover". And I also observe that when it refers to celebrating the solemn memory of the Last Supper and the Passion, the Bible calls that "eating the bread" and "eating the body of Christ". Now, since where the Passover is concerned, "eating the lamb" is meant literally, and "eating the Passover" means "eating *that which reminds us of* the Passover"; so where the Last Supper is concerned, "eating the bread" is meant literally, and "eating Christ" means "eating *that which reminds us of* Christ". And just as it would be quite absurd to take "eating the Passover" literally (which would mean eating the passing-by or journey of the angel); so it is also a great absurdity to want to take the phrase "eating the body of Christ" literally. And from this absurdity people are led on to all these other ones: that a body can exist without extension; that the whole of it is in the whole, and the whole of it is in each part of the whole; that the head, the feet, and the rest of the body are in every part of the consecrated bread, and that each is present nevertheless only once; that there are accidents without substance; and other absurdities of that kind, into which people necessarily fall, once they have succumbed to the first one.'

That, Sir, is what I think you must add at this point in your book—if you want it to get through, on that subject, to people of dullish intellect as well as to the others (who will all agree with you after the first glance). And if you also think it fitting, you should say a word or two of what you said to me in reply to the possible objection that God rejected Saul because of the sacrifice he had performed. If you see fit to make these minor additions (major, however, in importance), please send me the precise words in English in which you would express them.

I must tell you, however, that although I have not found anyone capable of replying to your comparison between eating the Passover and eating our Saviour, I do find that people are not so lacking in rejoinders to the other arguments.

First, where St Peter is concerned, they tell me that there is one passage where our Saviour says to him 'Compel them to enter'.[10] Admittedly, they were unable to show me the passage; and since I do not have my Bible concordance with me I have not known where to look for it. But if you know about it, and if it is worth the trouble, please clear it up for me.

Secondly, on the subject of Saul and Samuel, concerning the right to rule: although your reply convinces me in so far as it shows me what Samuel's intentions were, I find it liable to one objection, which is that since it is described in that way in the Bible, it was not so much Samuel as God himself who rejected Saul. For look at what it says at the start of 1 Samuel 16: 'And the Lord said unto Samuel, How long wilt thou mourn for Saul, seeing I have rejected him from reigning over Israel?' So the objection remains that he had no right to perform a sacrifice, since it is not possible that God should have become angry with someone for doing what he had the right to do. Please send me a word or two more in reply to that.

People also argue further and raise another objection (which is the third thing I have to put to you, and which I wrote on a sheet of paper which was sent to you by M. Peleau[11] (who, by the way, is a very busy man, and will not be fully grounded in the right principles for a long time to come)[)][(12)]. This objection concerns the fact that King Uzziah was struck with leprosy for the sole reason that he had burnt incense, etc.[13] Please give me your answer to that.

To pass on to other matters: my first question is this. Do you think that a woman who is the sovereign of a state is the head of its church and its religion? (On that point, I am convinced that the answer is 'yes'.)[14] But do you also think she would have the right to perform all the functions of a priest? (I mean in our Christian religion, where Christ did not make any female priests.)

Secondly, since the civil law regulates who owns what, and since the King can take anything by right (saying, 'This will belong to the

King'), how can one say that David offended God and committed adultery with Bathsheba?[15] For he had only to rule that she was no longer the wife of Uriah, and that she had become his wife; and as he could rightfully have done that, it would not have been adultery but a lawful coupling. And the same goes for all kings.

Thirdly, on your argument that no one is obliged to accuse those whose death or torture would make his own life less pleasant, I should like to ask you this: was the person who vowed to sacrifice his own daughter (Jephtha, I think) obliged to keep his vow?[16]

My fourth request is that you tell me your opinion of my translation of one of your chapters, which I enclose.[17] It is the chapter on language, which I thought was of an adequate length to allow you to judge the rest. (I have marked it by paragraphs, so that you can refer easily to the passages which need to be corrected.)

My fifth request is that you would please explain to me those English passages which I indicate on the last page of the third sheet of paper in this bundle.[18] But my final and most important request—which I make with all my heart—is that you will honour me with your kindly regard, and believe (I beg you) that no one could possibly be, Sir, more thoroughly than I,

Your most humble, most obedient, and most devoted servant,
du Verdus

First enclosure: du Verdus's French translation of Leviathan, *Chapter 4*

Translation of second enclosure to Letter 108

1. In the Introduction to *Leviathan*, here is a passage which I have translated as follows: 'Nosce teipsum lis toy toy mesme dont on n'usa pas jadis comme on fait pour le present pour soutenir les gens puissans qui maltraitoïent leurs inférieurs ni pour encourager les petites gens a s'attaquer a plus grand qu'eux' ['*Nosce teipsum, Read thy self*: which was not meant, as it is now used, to countenance, either the barbarous state of men in power, towards their inferiors; or to encourage men of low degree, to a sawcie behaviour towards their betters'].[20] I do not know whether that is the real meaning of it.

2. Also in the Introduction, I have noticed the meaning of 'never', which is an anglicism. 'But let one man read another [. . .] never so perfectly':[21] 'mais qu'un homme en lise un autre si parfaitement qu'on uoudra', or 'pour parfaitement que ce soit', or 'quelque parfaitement que ce soit'. I think the other ways in which 'never' is used can be

modelled on this translation—for example, 'let a space be never so little',[22] and so on.

3. I have also found '<u>laughter</u>' and '<u>weeping</u>', 'le rire' and 'le pleurer'; but this is what puzzled me:

4. Page 6, line 11: 'And because <u>in sense</u>, the Brain, and Nerves . . . are so benummed in sleep': 'Et dautant que dans le <u>sens</u> le cerueau et les nerfs . . . sont tellement engourdis'. Please look at this passage; for I think that the words '<u>in sense</u>' are superfluous there. For it is in sleep, not in the act of sensation, that one is benumbed.

5. 7 lines further down: 'when <u>they</u> be distempered': this is preceded by two nominative plurals, 'inward parts', and 'the Brayn, and other Organs'. To which of them does 'they' refer?

And on the same page, '<u>lying cold</u>': lying?

6. Page 7, '<u>uncouth</u> [. . .] fancy':[23] 'uncouth'?

7. Page 10, half-way down: 'the *Present* onely has a being in Nature': 'le Present seulement a un étant en Nature'. Isn't '<u>being</u>' the concrete noun, and '<u>be</u>' the abstract? In French we say 'estre' where you say 'being', as in this case, where we say 'le seul present a son estre en Nature'. Which of the two is more suitable, the anglicism or the gallicism? And should I write 'estre' or 'étant'?

7.[24] Page 14: 'and men were fayn[25] to apply their fingers': were fayn?

8. Page 15: 'false and senslesse <u>Tenets</u>': Tenets?

9. Page 19: I have difficulty translating these three lines: '<u>as it comes to bear sway in them, to be taken for right Reason, and that in their own controversies: bewraying their want of right Reason, by the claym they lay to it</u>'.

10. Page 27, where you discuss 'weeping': '<u>as some prop of their power</u>': I do not see what noun '<u>their</u>' refers to.

11. Page 27: please translate 'a FELLOW-FEELING'.

12. Page 29, line 11: 'unlesse it be when they serve to make other inferences, besides that of the Passion they proceed from Deliberation. is expressed *Subjunctively*'.[26] Where is the syntax of all that?

13. Page 30: 'there is at last an *End*, either by attaining, or by <u>giving over</u>': please translate.

14. Page 53: 'the opinion that such Spirits were Incorporeall [. . .]'[27] could never enter into the mind of any man by nature': so how did it enter? For it is not supernatural that one should talk nonsense and believe absurdities.

15. Page 54, in the paragraph which begins 'Lastly': 'men are naturally <u>at</u> [. . .] <u>stand</u>':[28] 'at [. . .] stand'?

LETTER 108, *December 1656/January 1657*

16. Page 55: you say that in antiquity they made Chaos a god. But Bacon says in his 'Cupido sive atomus' that they never made it a god.[29] Which is the truth?

17. Page 59: there are six lines which I do not know how to translate, beginning with 'And therefore, to those points of Religion', and ending with 'have wrought into them'. Please translate them; and, also on p. 59: 'And whereas in the planting'; and, again on p. 59, 'and jugling between Princes': jugling? Also, at the bottom of p. 81, 'without his Counter-assurance': I do not know whether I should translate that as 'sans sa contrepromesse'. And on p. 83: 'equality of votes, even in that they condemne not, do absolve': 'even' is ambiguous, meaning both 'mesme' and 'pair'.

18. Finally, on pp. 80, 81, 82, 83: I see that 'to personate' is to constitute, and represent, the person of oneself or someone else; I see that 'to act' is to perform the act and play the role; I see that 'to own' is to appropriate the action, to avow it as one's own, to wish to have made it in one's own name; but I should like you to supply three words in French or Latin, each translating one of these: 'to personate', 'to act', and 'to own'.

In the translation of the second enclosure, passages from *Leviathan* are reproduced from the 1651 printed text (BL 522. k. 6; siglum: '1651'); minor formal variants are not noted, but omissions, and major formal variants obscuring the sense, are recorded in the notes. In these quotations in the translation, the words in italics are those printed in italics in the 1651 text, and underlining is used to represent du Verdus's own emphasis.

[1] This letter has not apparently survived.
[2] Andrew Crooke (see the Biographical Register, 'William Crooke'); du Verdus's letter has not apparently survived.
[3] See Letter 78 n. 21.
[4] Du Verdus's sister Anne (see Letter 78).
[5] See Letter 78 n. 30.
[6] See Letter 78 n. 26.
[7] Du Verdus had been invited by Bourdelot to go to Italy in the spring of 1657.
[8] These were Hobbes's replies to the four queries raised by du Verdus in Letter 94.
[9] See Letter 94 n. 12.
[10] Luke 14: 23.
[11] See Letter 103 n. 1.
[12] ~) *omitted in MS*.
[13] 2 Chr. 26: 18–21.
[14] Hobbes agreed: see the passage on this subject which he added to the Latin text of *Leviathan* (p. 259 in the 1668 *Opera philosophica*), at a point corresponding to p. 299 of the English.
[15] 2 Sam. 11.
[16] Judg. 11: 30–40.

419

[17] See the first enclosure to this letter (given here in the French text only).

[18] See the second enclosure to this letter.

[19] Du Verdus has written '. . . . .', with 'tenets' above it, inviting Hobbes to fill in the space with the French for this word.

[20] p. 2.

[21] Ibid.: du Verdus omits 'by his actions'.

[22] p. 23.

[23] uncouth and exorbitant fancy *1651*.

[24] Du Verdus has duplicated '7°'.

[25] fayn *MS*, faun *1651*.

[26] Du Verdus has been confused by a printing error, which transposed the full stop which should have preceded 'Deliberation'.

[27] Incorporeall, or Immaterial could *1651*.

[28] *at stand* MS, at a stand *1651*.

[29] *De sapientia veterum*, ch. 17 (*Works*, vi, p. 654).

LETTER 109   23 DECEMBER 1656 [/2 JANUARY 1657]

Thomas Barlow to Hobbes, from Oxford

BL MS Add. 32553, fos. 22–3 (original).
Printed in Nicastro, *Lettere*, pp. 19–20.

S:.r

I receaued (by y.e hands of your seruant, and my freind, M.r Stubbs) your letter, and the rich present (for soe I doe value it, and haue good reason soe to value any thinge of yours) you were pleased to send me,[1] which I shall carefully keepe, as a monument of your (vndeserued) kindnesse, and Ciuility. You haue done me a very great honor, and though I am not in a condition to requite, yet 'tis not [>in] the power of fortune to put me out of a capacity of gratitude and thankefullnesse: soe that whensoever it shall ly in my power to serue you, you shall finde me as willinge to requite, (at least gratefully to acknowledge) as receaue a courtesy. I neuer did, nor doe thinke y.t you could condemne Vniversityes, you haue too great an vnderstandinge, absolutely to condemne the seminaries, and Nurseryes of good literature. 'Tis true, (as you well obserue) that Vniversities (and all *res mediae*)[2] are (good or bad) as they are vsed; they may be (if right managed) a happy meanes of much knowledge in all sciences sacred, or ciuil; if otherwise they are rather hinderances, then helpes. It is my hope, and prayer, y.t our Vniversityes may be such, as they should, Seminaries of all good Letters; in w.ch the youth of this Nation may (vpon just principles) be taught religion and Piety towards God, and obedience and duty to their

Gouernors. I concurre in what you say of yᵉ Scotch Diuines (as well knowinge both their Country, and Constitution of their Discipline) they challenge a transcendent power, which hath noe foundation in scripture, or Antiquity: And it infinitely concernes the Ciuil Magistrate, to Be jealous of any power superior to his owne, for whatsoeuer makes him lesse then supreme, puts him in the capacity of a subject, and soe lyable to yᵉ punishments of that power wᶜʰ pretends it selfe to be greater. I haue read your bookes constantly as they came out, and doe thankefully acknowledge to you (as I haue done, and still doe to all I discourse with) that I haue learn'd much by them, in many particulars. I confesse (at present) I doe not concurre with your judgement in euery thinge, yet I haue (as I thinke all sober men should) according to yᵉ principles of naturall reason, and Christianity, learned this much Ciuility, as to be thankefull for those discoueryes of truth, wᶜʰ any man makes to me, and where I doubt, or differ, to suspend my censure till more mature consideration. I know learned men, who publish bookes for a publique benefitt, are not bound to find me reasons, and vnderstandinge too; and therefore I am more inclined (generally) to suspect my owne judgement, then their arguments; haueing by experience found (both in yours, and other learned mens writeings) that to be true at Last, wᶜʰ at first readinge I much suspected as hereticall. I neither doe, nor euer did like your feirce censurers, who are (against all reason) more apt to censure an Author for a supposed error, then commend him for many certaine truths euidently discouered: and I haue Aristotle of my opinion, [*marginal note:* de sophisticis [*page torn* el]enchis, lib. 2 p. vlt. v[er]bis³ vltimis.] who saith 'tis reason we should be thankefull to him (or any other Author) for what is said well, and ciuilly pardon if any thinge should be impertinent . . . λοιπὸν ἄν εἴη πάντων τῶν ἀκροωμένων ἐργον, τοῖς μὲν παραλελειμμένοις [συγγνώμεν]⁴ τοῖς δ᾽ εὑρημένοις, πολλὴν χάριν ἔχειν.⁵ But if otherwise men will be censorious, and trouble themselues, yet that should not trouble you, qui iam monte potitus,⁶ beeinge gott too high to be hurt by calumnies, may rest secure of fame, (if not with this ingratefull age, yet with impartiall posterity.[)]⁷ Nay at present, I know you haue many honorers, and amongst the rest,

(S.ʳ)
Your very much obliged humble seruitor
T. Barlow

Q. Coll. Oxon. Dec. XXIII MDCLVI

[*addressed:*] For my honored freind Thomas Hobbs Esquire these

[*endorsed by James Wheldon:*] D. Barlow Dec. 23 1656.

¹ A copy of *Of Body*, inscribed 'to my friend, that most respect-worthy, distinguished, learned and candid man, Mr Thomas Barlow, Keeper of the most famous Bodleian Library, Oxford, a little present from the author' ('Amico Colendissimo Clarissimo Doctissimo Bibliothecae Bodleyanae celeberrimae, Oxonio, Bibliothecario, Munusculum ab Authore' (OQC FF. g. 517)).

² 'Intermediate things', a term from Stoic moral philosophy, meaning things which are good or bad not in themselves but in so far as they are used well or badly.

³ Contraction expanded.

⁴ συγνώμεν MS.

⁵ 'The only thing that would remain for all those who follow your work would be to pardon the faults and give many thanks for the discoveries': a condensed quotation from the appeal to the reader at the end of *De sophisticis elenchis* (184b).

⁶ 'Who have already attained the summit' (adapting Ovid, *Metamorphoses*, 5. 254).

⁷ ~) *omitted in MS.*

LETTER 110   [25 DECEMBER 1656/] 4 JANUARY 1657

François Peleau to Hobbes, from Bordeaux

Chatsworth, Hobbes MSS, letter 34 (original).

Monsieur,

Je suis tres satisfait de vostre Response à mes derniers doutes;¹ et Je suis bien aise, que vous ayéz la bonté de vous deffendre, contre des objections qui sont Moins que rien.

Je trouue que vous ne me figuréz pas asséz iustement l'estat de Nature, par les exemples des soldats, qui seruent dans diuers partis, et des Massons, qui trauaillent soubs de Differents Architectes; parceque cette guerre n'est de chacun à chacun, que [par *deleted*] successiuement, et en diuers temps; et l'autre estoit en mesme temps.

Apréz vne petite méditation là dessus, Jay trouué, s'il me semble, que presentement, et mesme tousjours, Il y a eu vne guerre D'esprits, quant aux Opinions, et aux sentimens; la quelle guerre ressemble tout à fait a l'estat de Nature. Car, (par exemple) Nest-il pas vray, que les senateurs d'vn mesme Parlement sont souuent chacun d'vn different auis, et chacun croyant estre dans le sentiment de la verité, soustient son opinion opiniastrément contre son collegue; Desorteque c'est vne guerre d'esprits de chacun contre chacun. De mesme, dans la philosophie, il y a tant de Docteurs, et de sectes differentes; chacun croit auoir trouué la Verité, et s'imagine que tous, et chacun des autres [est *deleted* > sont] dans l'erreur, et les traitte tous, comme aduersaires, et Antagonistes. semblablement dans la Religion chaque secte, prétend estre dans la veritable église, et traitte toutes les autres d'Heretiques. voila à peu prez les Images, qui me semblent représenter le plus Naïfuement Vostre estat de Nature.

D'ailleurs. Je croy qu'il y a eu vn estat de Nature dans l'estat [de Nature *deleted*] Ciuil; cette proposition paroist absurde, et Impossible en entendant seulement les termes. Mais Je vous asseure, que vous m'auouërez bien-tost qu'elle a quelque petite vraysemblance. car vous scauéz, Monsieur, que dans la Republique de Lacedemone le larcin estoit permis à toute sorte de personnes, sur tout ce qu'ils trouuoient à prendre, Doncques. Dans cette république tous auoient vn droit égal sur toutes choses.

Je pensé serieusement sur la Nature du Lieu, et il me semble qu'il [n'y *deleted*] n'en y a aucun dans la Nature, mais que seulement, ce que nous appellons Lieu. icy, ou là, ne sont [> que] certaines distances des corps entre eux. car. s'il y a vn lieu, il est finy, ou Infiny. S'il est finy. supposons, que tous les corps qui l'occupent à cette heure, ne l'occupent plus, et en soient dehors; Doncques Il restera vn [lieu *deleted* > Espace], qui aura les trois dimensions, qu'auoient les corps, qui le remplissoient auparauant. mais peut-on Imaginer des dimensions dans vn espace finy, sans [> Imaginer vne] extension, et [sans *deleted* > vne] figure, et ycelles sans parties, et icelles parties diuisibles, sans estre corps. Doncques dans cet Espace vuide, il y auroit des Corps, ce qui est contre la supposition. doncques il n'y a point de lieu finy. Je prouueray le mesme du lieu infiny. &c . . .

vous voyéz. Monsieur. que le lieu n'est rien de Réel, et que c'est seulement, la distance des corps entre eux, que nous appellons lieu pour nous pouuoir expliquer.[2] Je suis de tout mon coeur.

Monsieur
Vostre tres humble & tres obeissant seruiteur.
Peleau

A Bord^x ce 4 Januier 1657

[*addressed:*] For Mr Hobbes At the Greene Dragon In Paules Churchierd. London [*endorsed by Hobbes:*] de Monsr Peleau Jan. 4. 1656

[*endorsed by James Wheldon:*] Mon.^{r} Peleau Jan. 4. 1656

Translation of Letter 110

Sir,

I am very satisfied with your reply to my last queries,[1] and I am most gratified that you should have the kindness to defend yourself against objections which are worth less than nothing.

The examples you give of soldiers who serve in different places and masons who work under different architects fail, in my view, to illustrate accurately enough the state of nature. For these are wars of each against each only successively and at different times; whereas the one I was discussing was at one and the same time.

Having meditated a little on the subject, I found that, in my opinion, there is now and has always been a war of minds, so far as opinions and feelings are concerned, and that this war is exactly like the state of nature. For example: doesn't it often happen among the members of a single parliament that each man, having a different view and being convinced that he is right, obstinately maintains his view against each of his colleagues? So that there is a war of minds, waged by each against each. Similarly, in philosophy there are so many teachers of doctrines, and so many different sects. Each thinks he has found the truth, and imagines that each and every one of the others is wrong; he treats them all as adversaries and opponents. And in the same way, in religion each sect claims to be the true church, and treats all the others as heretics. These, more or less, are the examples which I think illustrate your state of nature as purely as possible.

Besides, I think there has been a state of nature in the civil state. This proposition does seem absurd and self-contradictory; but, I promise, you will soon admit that it is not without plausibility. For as you know, Sir, in the Republic of Sparta anyone was permitted to steal whatever he might take: in that republic, therefore, all the citizens had an equal right to all things.

I have been thinking hard about the nature of place; I believe that there is no such thing existing in nature, and that what we call place, here or there, is simply certain distances between bodies. I reason as follows: if place does exist, it must be either finite or infinite. If it is finite, let us suppose that all the bodies which occupy it cease to occupy

424

it and are outside it; there will then remain a space, which will have the dimensions of those bodies which previously occupied it. But can we imagine dimensions in a finite space without imagining extension and shape; can we imagine that extension and that shape without imagining that they have parts; and can we imagine that those parts are divisible without being bodies? So in this empty space, there would be bodies, which denies our original supposition. So there is no such thing as finite place. The same argument applies to infinite place . . .

You see, Sir, that place is nothing real, and that we simply call the distance between bodies place as an explanatory device.[2] I am, with all my heart,

Sir,
Your most humble and obedient servant
Peleau

Bordeaux, 4 January 1657

[*addressed: see text*]

The endorsements reflect the fact that the English new year was dated from 25 Mar.

[1] Letter 95; Hobbes's reply has not apparently survived.
[2] Peleau has been arguing implicitly against the theories expounded in Descartes, *Principia*, part 2, sects. 9–14 (A&T viii(1), pp. 45–8).

LETTER 111   26 DECEMBER 1656 [/5 JANUARY 1657]

Henry Stubbe to Hobbes, from Oxford

BL MS Add. 32553, fo. 24 (original).
Printed in Nicastro, *Lettere*, pp. 20–1.

S:r

I receiued yor letters, and booke;[1] ye which I did deliuer to M:r Barlowe without any alteration, saueing yt I did blot out (*openly*) where you sayd hee did as farre as might bee without offence *openly* appeare for you. There is no man more against ye jus divinum[2] of ye Clergy yn hee. hee was uery much pleased with ye present, & amicablenesse of yor letter, & did congratulate ye opportunity of commenceing any acquaintance with a person of so much merit. Hee sent mee his answer this morneing, which I here enclose;[3] I doubt not but it [is][4] as ciuill, as his comportment was when I deliuered yors. hee hath layd ye booke in

425

ye tower, untill y^t our Archiues bee emptyed and y^n hee will treasure up y^t monument in y^m.[5] I like ye Oeconomy of yor treatise,[6] & long to see a part of it. yor obseruation upon *abduxi clauem*,[7] is right. *Clauis* in Plautus's language being all one with *vectis*. So y^t it signifyes *to barre ye doore*. and so for *eduxi vinum*.[8] I cannot but applaude yor interpretation. both are to be found in eminent commentato^{rs} upon ye seuerall places: but ye D:^{r} went no farther y^n Stephen.[9] there is no man y^t knowes Plautus, but will grant y^t hee wil baulke ye elegancy of expression rather y^n loose a jest; for wch hee is commended, whilest hee doth suite his phrase to ye speaker, *vernis vernilia*.[10] neither will any scholar allowe all his language as tolerable in a learned person; so y^t if wee minde not who speakes, wee may finde as insufferable Latine in him, as any where: wch is no disparagement to ye authour, no more y^n it is to S:^{r} Ph: Sidney, y^t Damaetas doth write like Damaetas.[11] As for yor allegation of στίξας,[12] it is sufficient with any man, but such an insolent piece of Pedantry as is ye D:^{r} I shall not hasten my piece agt ye D:^{r13} till yo^{rs} bee out, because I perseiue you will as it were call for it. Our Du Moulin hath subjected ye ministry to ye Magistracy sufficiently,[14] for wch hee and Owen[15] are cryed out upon: Wilkins of Wadham,[16] maintained in his colledge y^t no forme of Church-gouernem^t is *jure diuino*. D:^{r} Ward will (it is thought) bee head of Jesus C.,[17] yo^u may consider how yo^u reflect on him; hee is much backed by Wilkins, but not by Owen. S:^{r} I haue no more at present, but y^t I am

yor most affectionate seru^t
H: Stubbe.

Oxon. dec: 26. 1656.

[*addressed:*] These For his euer honoured friend M:^{r} Th: Hobbes. Leaue this wth M:^{r} Andr: Crooke[18] at ye ship in Paul's church-yard

[*endorsement concealed by binding*]

[1] For the book see Letter 109 n. 1. The letters (one to Barlow, the other to Stubbe) have not apparently survived.

[2] 'Divine right'. For Barlow's theory of church and state, in which all jurisdictional power was derived from the civil sovereign, see his dissertation 'Imperium potestatis Supremae non solum civilia sed & sacra Complectitur', in his *Genuine Remains*, pp. 608–12.

[3] Letter 109.

[4] is *omitted in MS*.

[5] Barlow did not in fact deposit the volume in the Bodleian; it remained in his personal collection, and passed to Queen's College, Oxford (see Letter 109 n. 1).

⁶ The plan for *Markes*.

⁷ Pursuing his argument over whether the verb 'ducere' ('to bring') could be used with an inanimate object (see Letter 122 n. 7), Hobbes rejected Wallis's citation of 'abduxi clavem' from Plautus (see n. 9, below): 'if you look on the place as *Scaliger* reads it cited by the commentator, you will find it should be *obduxi*, and that *Clavis* is there used for the bolt of the lock' (*Markes*, p. 15: *EW* vii, p. 391).

⁸ 'I have knocked back the wine' (Plautus, *Stichus*, 5. 5. 18).

⁹ Robertus Stephanus (Robert Estienne), *Thesaurus*, i, p. 9a–b, has an entry: 'Abducere aliquid, pro auferre, figuratè dictum', and cites Plautus: 'Vbi intrò hanc nouam nuptam deduxi via recta, clauem abduxi.'

¹⁰ 'Buffoonish things from buffoons'.

¹¹ A doltish rustic character from Sidney's *The Countess of Pembroke's Arcadia*.

¹² Responding to Wallis's criticism of his use of στιγμή (see Letter 104 n. 13), Hobbes argued that 'στίξας and στιγματίσας signifie the same' (*Markes*, p. 15: *EW* vii, p. 390).

¹³ Stubbe's planned attack on Wallis's ecclesiastical theories was apparently never published.

¹⁴ Lewis du Moulin (see Letter 91 n. 8). The reference is probably to his *Paraenesis*, an attack on the jurisdictional claims of the Presbyterians.

¹⁵ John Owen (see Letter 91 n. 7) contributed a preface to du Moulin's book (above, n. 14).

¹⁶ John Wilkins (1614–72) proceeded BA at Magdalen Hall in 1631, was ordained in 1637, and was employed as a chaplain to several noble households. He developed his scientific interests in London in the 1640s and, as a supporter of the parliamentary cause, was appointed Warden of Wadham College, Oxford, in 1648. In 1652 he was one of the five commissioners appointed to exercise the chancellorship of the university, and in 1656 he married Cromwell's sister. From 1659 to 1660 he was Master of Trinity College, Cambridge. After the Restoration he was prominent both as co-founder and first Secretary of the Royal Society, and as a churchman who defended rational theology and Latitudinarian church politics; he became Bishop of Chester in 1668.

¹⁷ Seth Ward (see Letter 75 n. 8).

¹⁸ See the Biographical Register, 'William Crooke'.

LETTER 112   29 DECEMBER 1656/8 JANUARY 1657

Hobbes to Samuel Sorbière, from London

BN MS f.l. 10352, part 2, fos. 136ᵛ–7ʳ (transcript).

Printed in *Illustrium virorum epistolae*, pp. 575–571² (sigs. Aa12–Bb1ʳ); Tönnies, 'Siebzehn Briefe', pp. 209–10; translated (extract) in *HW* iii, p. 315.

Thomas Hobbius Samueli Sorberio Suo S.

Doctissime et Charissime Sorberi, Nollem sanè cuiquam amicorum meorum ingratus videri, aut beneficiorum (quae à te, Martello, et Prataeo¹ multa et magna accepi) immemor. Quorum beneficiorum maximum duco illud tuum, quod et in Epistola dedicatoria tua ante versionem Gallicam libelli de Ciue, et rursus in fine, dedita opera tantopere me ornare non reformidaueris[2] exosum ferè omnibus Ecclesiasticis. Itaque silentij mei tam longi reddetur tibi ratio, sed breuis haec nempe: Nullum vnquam, quod memini, Epistolam ad me, et à te, vel à Martello vel à Bosquio, vel à Prataeo perlatam esse cui non sit à me literis responsum. Nam segnitiei mei (quamquam segnis sum) praetendere negocia quae mihi faciunt aduersarij mei suis scriptis, vel quaslibet alias occupationes, non est meum. Neque tibi ob eandem rationem purgare opus erat apud me qui mearum omnium ad te ἀμοίβην acceperam. Possum enim et partes Philosophiae meae quae restant,[3] simul et Epistolas ad vos scribere, et nihilo minus nebulonem insolenter se ingerentem obiter castigare. Controuersia inter me et illum non est similis controuersiae inter Gassendum, et Morinum vel Cartesium[4] mihi res erat cum omnibus simul Ecclesiasticis totius Angliae in quorum gratiam scripsit contra me Wallis,[5] quem alioqui cui responderem indignissimum existimassem quicquid de illius scriptis sentiant quidem satis celebres Geometrae, satis quoque artis quam profitentur satis ignari, vt fortasse fiet (breui) manifestiùs.

Epistolam tuam ad Pecquetum quam innuis,[6] nunquam vidi, nisi valde oblitus sim. Quaeram autem illam Pecqueti editionem anni 1654[7] et scribam tibi quid de ea Epistola Alethophili sentiam, quamquam de rebus Anatomicis; quid ego sentiam non multum refert.

Quod attinet ad ea quae misisti mihi de Planetarum distantijs a sole[8] etiam non videtur mihi verum esse quod assumit, nempe in exiguis et remotissimis objectis, objectum videri majus vel minus in ratione distantiarum, imò falsum est, et causis videndi contrarium. Visio fit per actionem objecti siue lucidi siue illuminati, estque illa actio motus localis factus per medij pressionem ab objecto ad oculum continuam, quod autem ab eadem distantia motus fortior in oculum agat, eo major et sub majore angulo apparet. Haec ego vlterius prosequor in tractatu de Homine.[9] Interea vero vt sciamus haec Vaeterij falsa esse, sufficit experientia quotidiana cui enim vnquam duplo minor, duplo dico breuior visus est homo vel arbor à distantia duplicata? Quae tibi hoc tempore scribenda habui scripsi omnia. Sed quo modo ad te perferentur nescio, non enim scripsisti quibus verbis meae literae ad te inscribendae sunt, Charissime Sorberi. Vale et perge amare.

Tui amantissimum
Tho. Hobbes

Lond. Jan. 8. Stil. Nou. 1656

Translation of Letter 112

Thomas Hobbes to his friend Samuel Sorbière

Most learned and dearest Sorbière, naturally I do not wish to seem ungrateful to any of my friends, or forgetful of their favours—and I have received many great favours from you, de Martel, and du Prat.[1] I consider as the greatest of those favours the one you performed in your French translation of my little book *De cive*, both in the dedicatory epistle and again at the end, when you were not afraid to compliment me so greatly and so devotedly,[2] even though I am detested by almost all the ecclesiastics. So let me offer this as an explanation (albeit a brief one) for my having been silent for so long. So far as I remember, I have never received a letter from you, de Martel, du Bosc, or du Prat without sending a letter in reply. It is not my way to excuse my laziness (though I am lazy) by means of the work which my adversaries make for me with their writings, or any other tasks which have occupied my time. Nor, for the same reason, was it necessary for you to offer me excuses, since I had received a reply to everything I had sent you. I can, after all, write the remaining parts of my Philosophy,[3] and at the same time write letters to you, and moreover give a thrashing in passing to some worthless fellow who treats me impertinently. My quarrel with him is not like the quarrel between Gassendi and Morin or Descartes.[4] I was dealing at the same time with all the ecclesiastics of England, on whose behalf Wallis wrote against me.[5] Otherwise I would not consider him the least bit worthy of a reply, whatever is thought of his books by certain rather famous geometers—who are also rather ignorant of the art which they teach, as will perhaps become more obvious shortly.

I have never seen your letter to Pecquet which you refer to,[6] unless I have completely forgotten about it. However, I shall ask for that 1654 edition of Pecquet,[7] and shall tell you my opinion of that Letter of Alethophilus; although in anatomical matters my opinion is not worth very much.

As for what you sent me about the distance of the planets from the sun,[8] I do not think he is correct in assuming that minute and very distant objects seem to be greater or smaller in proportion to their distances. In fact it is untrue, and contrary to the nature of vision. Vision comes about through the action of a shining or illuminated object, and that action is a local motion caused by a continual pressing of the medium from the object to the eye. The more strongly the motion presses the eye, from the same distance, the greater it seems and the larger the angle under which it appears. I shall explain this further in my treatise *De homine*.[9] Meanwhile, our everyday experience is sufficient to disprove these claims by Vatier. For who has ever seen a man or a tree look twice as small, that is, twice as short, at twice the distance?

That is all I have to tell you at the moment. But I do not know how to get this letter to you, dearest Sorbière, since you did not tell me how to address my letter to you. Farewell, and continue to love

Your most loving
Thomas Hobbes

London, 8 January (New Style) 1656

Tönnies assigns this letter to 1656, *Illustrium virorum epistolae* to 1657. Although Hobbes writes that he is giving a New Style date, this applied only to the ten-day gap between the two calendars, not to the dating of the year from 1 Jan. or 25 Mar. Since Hobbes replies here to Letter 105, the correct year cannot be in doubt.

[1] Abraham du Prat.
[2] In his translation of *De cive*, *Elemens philosophiques du citoyen*, Sorbière praised Hobbes both in the dedicatory epistle to Cornifidz Ullefeldt, and in the 'Avertissement du traducteur' at the end of the volume.
[3] *De homine* was the only remaining part of Hobbes's tripartite philosophical system still to be published.
[4] See Letter 105 nn. 6, 7.
[5] Hobbes refers to the *Elenchus* and *Due Correction* by John Wallis (see Letter 75 n. 7).
[6] See Letter 105 n. 8.
[7] See ibid., n. 10.
[8] On this essay by Vatier see ibid., n. 11.
[9] Hobbes's account of this is in *De homine*, III.

LETTER 113   13 [/23] JANUARY 1657

Henry Stubbe to Hobbes, from Oxford

BL MS Add. 32553, fos. 25–6 (original).
Printed in Nicastro, *Lettere*, pp. 22–3.

S:[r]

I know not w[t] were y[e] contents of M:[r] Barlowe's letter,[1] but I beginne to suspect they did not please you, because I haue not receiued any thing of yo[rs] since. I assure yo[u] hee speakes uery honourably of you, as doe uery many (euen all y[t] pretend to ingenuity) in our university. I haue beene slacke in y[e] procedure of my translation[2] by reason of some particular busynesse, & also about D[r]: Wallis;[3] of y[e] latter I am of the minde to jerke[4] him by a letter,[5] & strictures, & not bestowe a full answer, wch is already drawne out to 10 sheets; I intend to speake with d:^r Owen[6] about it. Here are 2 or 3 haue proffered uerses (but to bee namelesse) upon ye controuersy betwixt yo^u & ye doctor: if yo^u please, I shall send y^m: & yo^u may adde y^m after my letter. I haue found out a place in Valla about *cum*, wch it is likely ye docto^r may occasionally produce, who sayes neuer any of ye ancients used *cum* with ye ablative of ye instrument.[7] to counterpoyse this I shall here send you ye judgem^t of Franciscus Sanctius an accurate Spanyard in his booke de causis linguae Latinae. p: 213.

De instrumenti praepositionibus

In instrumento significando deest *Cum*, graecè σὺν. sed uitandae ambiguitatis gratiâ non adhibetur. Quum enim dicis; *tetigi illum cum hastâ*, nescitur, an *illum*, et *hastam tetigeris*, an verò *instrumentum* significes. Sed ubi dubia non est oratio, *venustè* apponitur; ut *uidi gladium, cum quo se percussit*. Ouid. 1 Metam: Concussit térque quatérque caesariem, *cum quâ* terram mare, sydera mouit. Idem in ep: Aconty: Testis et Actaeon, quondam fera creditus illis, Ipse dedit letho *cum quibus* ante feras. Idem fastor: 4°. Haec modò uerrebat raro *cum pectine* pratum. Aldus aliter emendauit, quod non probo. Plin: l. 9 c: 28. Caeteri cirri, *cum quibus* venantur. Sic habet antiqua lectio. Paul: Orosius l: 7. Ipse imperator cum sagittâ saucius. Et quid elegantius quàm illud non incelebris authoris (Gladium *quî cum* se percusserat, eduxit.) quod imperitè damnat Valla libro 2. cap. 6.[8]

S:^r yo^u haue this learned man's judgement, whereof yo^u may make use yor selfe, if yo^u please; or else adde it in mine after ye judgement of Vossius.[9] I intend (if nothing diuert mee (as I thinke nothing will)[)][10] to allowe 4 houres each day to ye translation of yor Leuiathan, wch will no doubt effect ye whole next summer. & y^n nothing will remaine but to polish it. S:^r There is nothing I desire more then the finishing it, upon wch account it is y^t I haue no mind to enter a long contest upon particulars with ye D^r: about ye ministry,[11] wch is to perpetuate a quarrell of interest. yor answer is much expected here. D^r: W. ag^t Meibomius[12] is now comeing out; in ye epistle to my L:^d Broncker,[13] hee sayth Meibomius's dialogue is opus ineptum.[14] S:^r this is all from

yor most humble seru^t
H: Stubbe.

Oxon: Jan: 13. 1656.

[*addressed:*] These For his euer honoured friend M:ʳ Th: Hobbes [leaue these at M:ʳ Crooke[15] at yᵉ ship in Paul's church yard Booke-seller London *deleted*] hast.

[*endorsed by James Wheldon:*] Mʳ Stubbes Jan. 13. 1656

[1] Letter 109.

[2] Stubbe's projected translation of *Leviathan* into Latin (see Letter 87).

[3] On Wallis see Letter 75 n. 7.

[4] = to lash with satire or ridicule (*OED* jerk *v.* 1b).

[5] Published as 'An Extract of a Letter' (*Markes*, pp. 20–30: *EW* vii, pp. 401–27).

[6] See Letter 91 n. 7.

[7] Valla, *De linguae latinae elegantia*, p. 26: 'The preposition *cum* signifies an accompanying thing, or a way of acting, not an instrument' ('Cum praepositio comitem significat, aut modum actionis, non instrumentum').

[8] Sanctius (Francisco Sanchez), *Minerva*, fos. 212ᵛ–213ʳ: 'Prepositions of the instrument. *Cum* [*with*], in Greek σύν, is omitted when the instrument is meant; but the reason why it is not used is to avoid ambiguity. For when you say "I touched him with a spear", one does not know whether you touched both him and a spear, or whether you are indicating the instrument. But where the expression is not ambiguous, it may be used gracefully, as in "I saw the sword with which he struck himself". Thus Ovid, *Metamorphoses*, 1 [179–80]: "Three times, four times he shook the head of hair with which he moved the earth, the sea, and the stars." The same author in Acontius's letter [*Heroides*, 20. 103–4]: "Actaeon too will be a witness, once thought a wild beast by those with whom he himself had put wild beasts to death"; the same author in the fourth of his *Fasti*: "only seldom did she sweep the meadow with a rake" (Aldus emended this to a different reading, of which I do not approve). Pliny, [*Historia naturalis*,] 9. 28: "the other arms [of polypi] with which they hunt". (That is the old reading.) Paulus Orosius, [*Historiarum adversum paganos*,] 7: "the emperor himself, wounded with an arrow". And what could be more elegant than the phrase of that famous author, "he drew out the sword with which he had struck himself", which Valla ignorantly condemns in [*De linguae latinae elegantia*,] 2. 6?'

[9] Stubbe cited G. J. Vossius, 'De constructione' ('De sermonis constructione liber', the seventh book of his *De arte grammatica*), ch. 47, on the use of the ablative of cause, in his letter printed in *Markes*, p. 20 (*EW* vii, p. 402). The extract from Sanctius was not in fact added.

[10] ~) *omitted in MS.*

[11] See Letters 91, 96, 97.

[12] Wallis, *Adversus Marci Meibomii, dialogum* (1657). This was an attack on the *Dialogus de proportionibus* (1655) of the German classical scholar Mark Meibom (1630–1711), which had presented an imaginary discussion between several ancient Greek geometers.

[13] William Brouncker, second Viscount Brouncker (1620?–84), a skilled mathematician, linguist, and Oxford DM (1647); he corresponded with English and continental mathematicians in the 1650s (see Wallis, *Commercium epistolicum*), and became first President of the Royal Society.

[14] 'Incompetent work': the long dedicatory epistle to Brouncker does not contain the phrase, though Wallis does not conceal his contempt for Meibom.

[15] John Crooke; see Letter 91, general note.

LETTER 114   [23 JANUARY/] 2 FEBRUARY 1657

Samuel Sorbière to Hobbes, from Paris

BN MS f.l. 10352, part 1, fos. 244ᵛ–246ʳ (transcript; the discussion of physics is transcribed separately on fo. 245, and the rest of the letter is on fos. 244ᵛ and 246ʳ).

Viro celeberrimo, Doctissimóque D. Thomae Hobbio, Samuel Sorberius.

Post acceptas Epistolas posteriores tuas nos in Aula cum Prateo[1] & Martello lautè excepit heri optimus Bosquius: Interfuit & Motha Vayerius[2] Senex doctissimus. Ad noctem vsque sermo protractus de te plurimum & de rebus Philosophicis, non verò de fundis & domibus alienis fuit. Sales inspersi eruditiones abundè nec sine risu agitauimus conuiuium, quanquam nec sine profunda rerum arduarum meditatione. Verùm nosti Symposiarcham nostrum, & quàm sim ego petulanti splene cachinno.[3] Assolet Prataeus quoque nec renuit Martellus vbi nodus vindice dignus diu nos torsit animum subinde ad amaeniora diuertere; quandoquidem constet nihil magis conducere ad bonam corporis valetudinem, & Euthymiam, risu sapienti, & moderata cum interioris notae Amicis laetitia. Ridiculum acri fortius ac melius magnas plerumque secat res. Vt scias autem qua de re agebatur, En tibi Excerptum Annotatorum meorum, quod praelegebam, & nunc Examini tuo subijcio. In meum scilicet vsum, vt tibi, si detur aliquando vel Prateo & alijs proponam dubia inter legendum exorta. Annotaui in Physicam tuam permulta, quibus locus non fuisset scriptitandis te praesente & nebulas nostras deflante. Quae summa est inter tuam & Epicuri Philosophiam differentia in Vacuo, quod non admittis, posita est, & cui remouendo laboras paginâ 238. Ad tollendum Vacuum ais, Vnicum adducam Experimentum &cᵃ.[4] Epicuri Postulatum Physicum fuit, moueri Atomos in Vacuo, quod dari quaquauersùm non potest quin illuc statim corpuscula prorumpant, si quidem tale sit quod Atomos excipere queat.[5] Postulatum dico quia nunquam probauit Philosophus quod recorder, cur moueantur in Vacuo, & ideo innatum illis pondus indidit. Quanquam eò deueniendum non esset, cùm sufficiat nisus continuus vniuersarum Atomorum mutuâ factus impulsione, cui verò impulsioni non est prima quaedam assignanda in aeterna rerum duratione. Supponatur igitur impulsio quaedam, ne in immensum excurratur, vt datâ semel impulsione perpetuus motus Atomorum concipiatur, quarum aliae alias pellunt, & praesertim in dato Vacuo facillimè primipilares protrudunt. Juxta quam Hypothesim ratiocinandum erit ad tollendum Vacuum, ostendendo scilicet ex illa sequi talia & talia absurda. Haec vera est confutandi Methodus. Ergo supponenda primùm fuit Hobbio Epicuri sententia quam enarraui, & cauillatur Prataeus cùm objicit nos inter respondendum supponere quod est in quaestione manifesta cum petitione Principij. Suppono ego mentem Epicuri, quam Hobbius quoque vel ad tempus supponere debet donec euerterit Illationibus absurdis quae ex Vacuo dato plurimae sequuntur. Attendit autem ad hoc tantùm Hobbius, quòd si darentur in Aere extra hydriam minima quaedam vacua, fieri par esset vt condensaretur Aër, recipiendae aquae quae per os infernum hydriae naturali pondere decidere conatur.[6] Quod cùm minimè contingat, argumento esse plenitudinis vniuersae. Verùm inspersa minima illa spatia compresso aëre nequaquam complentur vt locus fiat aquae deciduae ob aliam quam innui causam quam non aduertit Vir Clarissimus. Neque enim tantus est nisus aquae deorsum tendentis & particulas aëris in ordinem cogere valentis, quin major sit innatus Atomorum impetus, seu inditus impulsione motus ad occupandum spatium quod primum se praebet corpore vacuum. Igitur non potest superficies superna aquae os hydriae supernum deserere, neque adeo tota moles aquae, qua ad os inferum patet vel minimum sensibiliter descendere. Non tollit ergo Vacuum Experimentum illud, Vacuum, inquam, quale Atomis inspersum supponunt Epicurei. At tollit paulo majus Vacuum cui reuerà remouendo immota manet aqua; quippe quae non ampliùs deorsum vt grauia solent, sed sursum nititur, vt superiori Naturae legi obtemperet, quae primùm jussit vt in quouis dato, atque adeo oborienti spatio statim corpuscula moueantur. Vrgere quis posset in Responsionem nostram, Nequaquam opus esse molimine tanto aquae versus partem hydriae superiorem, cùm non metuendum sit magnum Vacuum etsi locum suum humor deserat si vitream assumas hydriam, quippe repleri posset factum spatium luce quae vndiquaque vitri poros penetrat, & corporea perhibetur Epicuro. Ita quidem est; sed ne futuro magno Vacuo complendo paria sint multa prohibent. Nempe subtilissima & mobilitate vigentia corpora poros parallelos pertranseuntia sisti non possunt, & per latus oppositum rectà in aërem rùrsum patentem effundi gestiunt; insuper pauciora numero sunt penetrantia illa corpuscula complendo loco decidentis aquae. Et quamuis nisu quodam insolito, vel nouâ pernicitate confluere possent, non est tamen illud insoliti, seu noua Machina admouenda, cùm praesto sit innatum cuilibet Atomo pondus, seu in Vacuum ostentans sese impetus. Et haec sunt, Vir Clarissimè, quae referenda habui. Aliàs plura si ratio ista philosophandi non displiceat, subjungam; nec inter dissentiendum fiet vt quidquam decedat illius quam tibi debeo obseruantiae, quanquam sperem fore vt iteratâ saepius libri tui lectione, & Prataei colloquio, atque tuis Epistolis, quas per Bosquium nostrum deinceps accipiam ita volente Virorum optimo, breui lux affulgeat mihi tanta quâ possim in adyta penetrare, & quae nunc captum meum superant, intelligere. Nam vt verum fatear torquet me mirum in modum ista Vniuersi plenitudo & per inspersum Vacuum, Motum & mutationes innumeras mens mea facilius admittit; sed tuum erit omnia ista ἐνποδίσματα remouere. Vale,

Parisijs V. Non. Feb. 1657.

Translation of Letter 114

Samuel Sorbière to the very famous and learned Thomas Hobbes.

After receiving your latest letter, the excellent M. du Bosc entertained us sumptuously in his mansion, together with du Prat[1] and de Martel; that very learned old man de La Mothe le Vayer[2] was also there. Our conversation lasted till nightfall; we talked mainly about you and philosophical matters—not about other people's houses and estates. I salted our banquet with wit and erudition, and there was laughter too; but we also meditated deeply on difficult problems. You know what our host is like, and what an irreverent scoffer I am.[3] Du Prat has the same tendency; and when some knotty problem was tormenting us like a torturer's noose, de Martel did not hesitate to turn his mind immediately to lighter things. For it is well known that nothing is more conducive to good health, both in body and in mind, than wise laughter and well-tempered mirth in the company of our closest friends. Jests are stronger than bitter arguments, and they often provide a more acute analysis of important matters. To show you what the discussion was about, here is an extract from my criticism, which I read out there and now submit to your judgement. For it helps me if I sometimes tell you, or du Prat and the others, about the doubts which occur to me during my reading. I have commented on a great many things in your Physics; but there would have been no need for my scribbling about them if you had been present to dispel our uncertainties.

The main difference between your philosophy and that of Epicurus is on the existence of a vacuum, which you deny, and which you try hard to disprove on p. 238. 'For the taking away of *Vacuum*', you say, 'I will instance in onely one experiment . . .'.[4] The physical postulate of Epicurus was that atoms move in a vacuum, and that this motion cannot take place in any direction without particles immediately rushing out in that direction, if there is something there capable of receiving them.[5] I call this a postulate, because so far as I can remember the philosopher never showed why the atoms are moved in a vacuum; thus he attributed an intrinsic weight to them. However, he need not have adopted that view, since it is sufficient to suppose that there is a continual force belonging to the atoms, caused by their being impelled to hit each other; the first impulse which caused them to hit each other cannot be given, assuming that the world has existed eternally. To avoid a pursuit of causes *ad infinitum*, some impulse must therefore be postulated. When once this impulse has been given, the atoms can be understood to be perpetually in motion: some of them strike others, and the front ranks in particular are easily pushed out into the vacuum which we have assumed.

The way to remove the possibility of a vacuum is to take this hypothesis and show that such and such absurd consequences follow from it. That is the true method of disproof. So first of all Hobbes should have assumed the Epicurean doctrine which I have described; du Prat is quibbling when he objects that in my reply I am patently begging the question by assuming what is at issue. I am assuming Epicurus' opinion, which Hobbes too ought to assume—at least temporarily, until he has disproved it by showing that several absurd conclusions follow from it. But Hobbes considers only this point: if there were certain infinitesimal vacuums in the air outside the vessel, one would expect the air to become condensed to receive the water, which tries to fall by its natural weight through the lower mouth of the vessel.[6] And the fact that this does not happen at all can, he thinks, be taken as evidence for plenism.

Now, it is true that when the air is compressed those interspersed infinitesimal spaces can never be filled in such a way that the water might have room to descend; but this is for another reason, which I have mentioned, and which the distinguished Mr Hobbes has not noticed. For the force of the water which presses downwards and is able to push down the particles of air is less than the intrinsic impetus of the atoms (or the motion given to them extrinsically) to occupy the first space which presents itself as empty of matter. Therefore the upper surface of the water cannot leave the upper mouth of the vessel; nor can the whole mass of water perceptibly descend where it is exposed to the lower mouth (provided that mouth is a very small one). So that experiment does not remove the possibility of a vacuum, that is, of the vacuum interspersed with atoms as the Epicureans postulate it. It does, however, disprove the rather bigger vacuum, and indeed the water stays put in order to prevent that larger vacuum from happening; for the water will not move downwards as heavy things do, but will rise up, in accordance with a higher law of nature, whose first command was that particles of matter must move into any empty space as soon as that space appears.

The following objection might be raised against my reply. 'There is no need for the water to have such a great endeavour towards the upper part of the vessel: if you assume the vessel to be made of glass, there is no fear of a large vacuum being formed even if the liquid deserts its place, because the empty space thus created can be filled with light, which penetrates the pores of glass on all sides, and Epicurus declares that light is corporeal.' That is true; but there are many reasons why particles of light are not suitable for filling any large vacuum that might arise. For particles which are extremely fine and mobile pass right through parallel pores and cannot be contained; they will hasten to pour through the opposite side, out into the open air again. Besides, those corpuscles which penetrate the glass are too few to fill the place of the water as it falls. And although one might suppose them to flow in with some unusual force, or some new mobility, there is no need of anything unusual, no need for any new mechanism: we already have the intrinsic weight of each atom, its self-evident impetus towards a vacuum.

These, distinguished Sir, are the points I wished to make. If you do not dislike this method of reasoning, I may add many further queries. Our disagreement should not be taken to imply any lack of the deference which I owe you; but I hope that when I have reread your book more often, and when I have conferred with du Prat and read your letters (which from now on I shall get from du Bosc, if that excellent man is willing), I shall be illuminated by enough light to enable me to penetrate the mysteries, and understand that which is at present beyond my grasp. For, to tell the truth, I find that plenism of yours strangely perplexing, and it seems easier to me to explain motion and innumerable physical changes by means of an interspersed vacuum. But it will be your job to remove all those obstacles to the truth. Farewell.

Paris, 2 February 1657

---

[1] Abraham du Prat.

[2] François de La Mothe le Vayer (1588–1672), a scholar and littérateur, was a protégé of Richelieu in the 1630s and was appointed tutor to the duc d'Orléans (1649) and to Louis XIV (1652). A friend of Mersenne, he was the author of numerous works strongly influenced by classical and Montaignian scepticism.

[3] Sorbière is adapting a phrase from Persius, *Saturae*, 1. 12.

[4] *De corpore*, XXVI. 2.

[5] See the 'Epistula prima ad Herodotum', 43, in Epicurus, *Epistulae tres*.

[6] In *De corpore*, XXVI. 2 Hobbes had described a type of watering-can with many small holes at the bottom and one hole at the top: water would not flow out of the bottom when the hole at the top was stopped.

LETTER 115   [29 JANUARY/] 8 FEBRUARY 1657

François Peleau to Hobbes, from Bordeaux

Chatsworth, Hobbes MSS, letter 37 (original).

Monsieur.
Jay receu toutes vos Lettres, ensemble [>celle] de M.ʳ Crook Latine,[1] et La confirmation mise au pied par vous. [Je *deleted*] vostre Libraire est sçauant, mais ie crois que vous Luy faittes part de vostre science. M.ʳ le Cheualier Digby est depuis quelques iours en nostre ville.[2] C'est vn grand Philosophe, grand admirateur de M.ʳ Des-cartes, et on dit en france, qu'il sçait faire L'Or; Je vous écriray amplement au premier iour sur La nouvelle connoissance que iay faitte auec ce Seigneur. Je suis

Monsieur.
Vostre tres humble & tres obeissant seruiteur
Peleau

A Bord.ˣ ce .8. feburier 1657

[*addressed:*] For M.ʳ Hobbes At the greene Dragon in Paules Churchierd London

[*endorsed by James Wheldon:*] Mon.ʳ Peleau Feb. 8.ᵗʰ 1657

Translation of Letter 115

Sir,

I have received all your letters, together with the one in Latin from Mr Crooke,[1] with your confirmation at the end of it. Your bookseller is a learned man, but I think you make him partake of your own learning. Sir Kenelm Digby has been in our city for several days.[2] He is a great philosopher, a great admirer of Descartes, and in France it is said that he knows how to make gold. I shall write to you at length, at the first opportunity, about the new acquaintance I have made of this nobleman. I am, Sir,

your most humble and obedient servant,
Peleau

Bordeaux, 8 February 1657

[*addressed: see text*]

---

[1] Andrew Crooke (see the Biographical Register, 'William Crooke'). None of these letters has apparently survived.

[2] For Digby's travels in France, see the entry in the Biographical Register.

LETTER 116   30 JANUARY [/9 FEBRUARY] 1657

Henry Stubbe to Hobbes, from Oxford

BL MS Add. 32553, fos. 27–8 (original).
Printed in Nicastro, *Lettere*, pp. 23–4.

S:r

I receiued yor last letter, and since that the second sheete;[1] it was not to put you upon an answer to M:r Barlow that I hinted any thing in mine, but that I might learne how ciuill hee had beene in his answer to yor present.[2] I presented yor respects to him, which hee receiued with so much ciuility as a person could, who thinkes himselfe highly honoured in yor acquaintance: hee desired mee to returne yor complement, & tell you that if his busynesse about Bp: Vsher's bookes[3] would permit him, hee would visit you at Roe-hampton,[4] & it were onely to see one for whome hee had had great inclinations, & to whome hee hath beene so particularly obliged. I haue employed my utmost interest euen in Dr: Wallis's house to knowe the authour of that learned letter,[5] & I can almost assure you that it is Hevelius of Dantzicke to whome D:r Wallis formerly dedicated a booke,[6] & hee cannot write true Latine.

This I had from a Dutch-man who doth dyet at ye docto^{rs}, & to whome the docto^r did reade two letters, the one from —— of Paris,[7] & the other from Heuelius, & hee did not minde,[8] onely that to his best remembrance this was that of Hevelius, who hee is sure cannot write true Latine, as haueing seene diuers other letters of his to ye D^r hee promised to aske the docto^r priuately, but hath not as yet; I perceiue there are seuerall errata in this second sheet, I hope there is none in the Mathematicall part, for the doctor is so ingenuous that hee will sooner willingly mistake then amend one error. I wish you had inserted the whole sentence out of Aristophanes for [*page torn* it is sca]rce intelligible as it is now printed, without ye verbe ἀποπέμψω.[9] As for y^t non-sensicall distinction of Definitiuè & Circumscriptiuè,[10] It is rejected by others as well as yo^u, who haue not therefore beene censured, though they onely avoyded ye one absurdity to embrace another of being in loco per operationem.[11] Bodin is of yor judgemt[12] and so as to ye negatiue part are seuerall others whome hee alledgeth. I thinke it were best if in my letter y^t allegation of Vossius were left out, & that of Sanctius inserted,[13] because it had it's originall from ye like case, & is full, whereas ye other sayth it is, *non temerè imitandum*.[14] But it may bee too late now. I here send yo^u the verses I mentioned in my last[15] y^t yo^u may see ye vogue of those youths that pretend to any thing of ingenuity is against D:^{r} Wallis, & yo^u haue the good opinion of all who are judges of language, ingenuity or Mathematiques. *Pique* sent his booke to be perused here, ye 2^d part, but hee did receiue no great incouragement to print it,[16] being told, y^t many things which hee stopped at as absurd, were not onely yor principles, but admitted generally, by those who had learned to search into nature, & not to acquiesce in ye traditions of others. I heare hee is very angry at it. I pitty another enemy of yo^{rs} here a d^r in diuinity, who haueing seene ye Schoole-discipline,[17] feasted ye D:^{r} to congratulate his victory ouer yo^u: Hee was a very Zealous Presbyter, & will bee much troubled to see an answer to y^t piece whose wit hee admired. M:^{r} Barlowe told mee hee should bee glad to see yo^u here, and I doubt not but you will belieue the same of mee: I shall craue leaue to tell yo^u, that it is not any thing can happen, which shall take mee of from being

S:^{r}
yor most affectionate seru^t
H: Stubbe.

Oxon: Jan: 30. 1656.

[*addressed:*] These For his euer honoured Friend M:ʳ Th: Hobbes. leaue these at M:ʳ Andrew Crookes[18] in Paul's church-yard at yᵉ ship London

[*endorsed by James Wheldon:*] M: Stubb. Jan. 30. 1656.

¹ The second sheet of the proofs of *Markes*; Hobbes's letter has not apparently survived.

² See Letters 109, 111.

³ Barlow was preparing an edition of works by James Ussher: *Chronologia sacra* and *De romanae ecclesiae symbolo apostolico vetere* (1660).

⁴ Roehampton (in Putney, south-west of London) was the residence of Christian Cavendish, dowager Countess of Devonshire (widow of the second Earl) (see her entry in the Biographical Register).

⁵ This was a letter to Wallis, printed by him in *Due Correction*, pp. 5–6, criticizing Hobbes; Wallis had revealed only that it was sent from 'abroad' (p. 4) and that the author was 'a publick Professor of Mathematicks' (p. 5).

⁶ The astronomer Johannes Hevelius (1611–87), of Danzig, dedicatee of Wallis's *Eclipsis solaris [. . .] observatio* (1655).

⁷ This refers probably to the letter to Wallis, printed by him in *Due Correction*, pp. 4–5 (see Letter 119 n. 7).

⁸ = remember (*OED* mind *v.* 2).

⁹ *Frogs* 1509–11, quoted by Hobbes in *Markes*, p. 15 (*EW* vii, p. 390).

¹⁰ 'Definitively', 'circumscriptively': the distinction between these two terms was used in scholastic theology when referring to the presence of God, or other spiritual entities, in the physical universe: they were said to be present in a particular place 'definitivè' but not 'circumscriptivè'. Hobbes attacked this distinction in *Leviathan*, p. 373: 'For the Circumscription of a thing, is nothing else but the Determination, or Defining of its Place; and so both the Terms of the Distinction are the same.' He made the same point in *Six Lessons*, p. 6 (*EW* vii, pp. 204–5), arguing that if Seth Ward admitted, as a geometer, that circumscription and determination were the same, he could not at the same time agree with the scholastic theology of Bishop Bramhall. Wallis replied to this point in *Due Correction*, pp. 31–3.

¹¹ 'in a place by operating in it'.

¹² Jean Bodin, *Universae naturae theatrum*, bk. 4, 'De angelorum et daemonum substantia', p. 514: Bodin discusses the scholastic idea that 'separated minds' and angels can be in a place definitively, not circumscriptively, and says it is contradictory.

¹³ See Letter 113 nn. 8, 9.

¹⁴ 'not to be imitated rashly'.

¹⁵ See Letter 113.

¹⁶ William Pike's (i.e. William Lucy's) *Examinations, Censures and Confutations of Divers Errours in the two first Chapters of Mr Hobbes his Leviathan* had been published in London in 1656 (see Letter 88 n. 3). Lucy also published *Observations, Censures and Confutations of Divers Errors in the 12, 13, and 14 Chap. of Mr. Hobs his Leviathan* (London, 1658). The '2d part' referred to here may therefore have been a criticism of chs. 3–11.

¹⁷ Wallis, *Due Correction for Mr Hobbes; or, Schoole Discipline, for not saying his Lessons right*.

¹⁸ See the Biographical Register, 'William Crooke'.

Hobbes to Samuel Sorbière, from London

BN MS f.l. 10352, part 2, fos. 140ᵛ–141 (transcript).
Printed in Tönnies, 'Siebzehn Briefe', pp. 210–12.

Thomas Hobbius Samueli Sorberio suo
Vir Doctissime,

Literas tuas datas [*word deleted*] IV Non. Febr.[1] perlibenter legi, quippe quibus cognoui non solum te, sed etiam Martellum, Bosquium, Prataeum, et Clarissimum Vayerium[2] quos omnes summe colo, bene valere et conuiuium apud Bosquium hilariter agitantes etiam mei meminisse. Libenter etiam legi ea quae objicis pro sententia Epicuri circa vacuum contra sententiam meam de eadem quaestione explicatam Capite 26. art. 2°. et seqq.[3] et tanto libentius legi, quanto constantius credo veritatem a me esse, et objectionibus tuis facile posse responderi. Meum argumentum contra Vacuum ab experientia sumptum hujusmodi erat. *Aqua quae in hydria est, obturato orificio superno nulla effluit, aperto effluit omnis, nimirum per foramine inferiore.*[4] Vnde arguo sic. *Causa cur non effluit, in eo consistit, quod in locum aquae quae effluxit nullum corpus succedere potest orificio obturato, aperto autem potest. Quare causa cur aqua non effluit in eo* [*consistit*][5], *quod necesse est hydriam semper esse plenam, id est, necesse est vacuum in hydria non esse.*[6] Si quis aliam causam intelligibilem attulerit quare ex obturatione orificij aqua sistatur necessario, tum confitebor ego tam meam sententiam quam illam Epicuri vtramque esse incertam. Causa quam tu adducis quare aqua obturato orificio superno [stititur *altered to* sistitur], continetur in his tuis verbis. *Neque enim tantus nisus (inquis) est aquae deorsum tendentis et particulas aeris in ordinem cogere valentis, quin major sit innatus Atomorum impetus seu inditus impulsione motus ad occupandum spatium quod primum se praebet corpore vacuum. Igitur non potest superficies* [*inferna*][7] *aquae os hydriae deserere.*[8] Ad vim argumenti [huiusce][9] tollendam non opus est, vt, aliud dicam quam quod haec eadem causa quam tu hic exponis aeque probat aquam non deserturam summum hydriae os siue clausum siue patens; Pondus enim aquae, siue clauso siue aperto ore hydriae per naturam idem est. Quod autem non descendat obturato orificio in causa est quod descendenti, in loco jam ante omnino pleno locus vbi esse potest relictus est nullus. Sed tute videris vtrum argumentum hoc tuum non [aeque][10] militat contra omnem effluxum aquae ex hydria siue obturato siue patente orificio. In ijs quae a te ad [summam][11] rei minus pertinentia obiter scripta sunt, notabo primum, non recte se habere haec verba tua. *Attendit ad hoc tandem Hobbius quod si darentur in aere extra hydriam minima quaedam vacua fieri par esset, et condensaretur aer, vscipiendae aquae quae per os [infernum][12] hydriae naturali pondere decidere conatur; Quod cum non contingat argumento esse plenitudinis.*[13] Nam ego eo argumento nusquam vsus sum. Et si eo vsus fuissem, quo argumento potuissem euincere id non contingere? Secundum quod dicis. *Ergo Hobbio supponenda primum fuit Epicuri sententia ea quam enarraui donec eam euerterit illacionibus absurdis.*[14] Nam hoc necessarium non erat, [nec][15] vt id facerem postulabat Logica, sufficiebat probare nullam esse ad saluandum Phaenomena naturalia vacui necessitatem quorum hoc de hydria est vnum. Praeterea non videbatur mihi sententia Epicuri esse absurda, eo sensu quo is mihi vacuum videtur intellexisse. Credo enim illum, Vacuum appellasse id quod Cartesius appellat materiam subtilem, ego substantiam aetheream purissimam; cujus nulla pars est Atomus, sed secari potest (id quod dicitur de quantitate) in semper secabilia. Quin tale corpus etiam Epicurei nonnulli aquam esse putant, vt qui plurimis experimentis [incoxerunt][16] aquam nulla vi in arctiorem locum compelli posse, id est, nullum intra se continere spatium vacuum. Tertium notandum est, de Atomis non recté dici *innatum esse pondus*.[17] Pondus enim Conatus est ad terrae centrum, vel saltem ad astrum aliquod, isque certus et in se inuariabilis. Itaque si Atomis fuisset innatum pondus, diu esset, vt omnes Atomi ad Terram et Caetera Astra confluxissent, et proinde totum spatium Mundanum praeter ipsa astra hodiè esset vacuum. Postremo Quod dicis, *vbi esset vacuum illuc* statim [perrumpunt][18] corpuscula[19] quid sit non intelligo, nisi vbi sit vacuum intelligant Atomi. Vel si in factum vacuum irrumpant tantum Atomi vicinae reddenda est ratio quare Atomus locum vbi erat vacuum relinquit, vt alium impleat; vel cur non redit rursus ad implendum locum quem ipsa vacuum fecerat. Haec omnia difficilia [explicatu][20] sunt. Sed necesse est in tales difficultates incidere eos qui subtilitatem corporum aestimant [ex ea?][21] Atomorum, tanquam Aqua, aër, et caetera fluida essent vt frumentum [molitum][22], magis [minùsque *altered to* minùsue] subtilia prout in crassiores minutioresue particulas contusa et conjecta fuerant. Ego vero non modo aërem purum, sed aquam puram, etiam Hydrargy[rum] [purum][23] in partes diuisibilia esse sentio semper diuisibiles, et propter mollitiem alterum ab altero penetrari posse, aërem et aquam ab Hydrargyro facillime, Hydrargyrum ab aqua difficilius, ab aëre difficillimè,[24] sed tamen posse, vt in tubis vitreis ipso Hydrargyri pondere fieri solet. Atque haec responsa ad objectiones tuas sufficiunt. Perge hilariter viuere et me amare

Tui amantissimum
Thom. Hobbes

datae Londini. Feb. 6. 1657

Translation of Letter 117

Thomas Hobbes to his friend Samuel Sorbière.
Most learned Sir,
    I was delighted to read your letter of 2 February,[1] because I learned from it that not only you but also de Martel, du Bosc, du Prat, and the most distinguished de La Mothe le Vayer[2] (to all of whom I am utterly devoted) are in good health; and also that you even remembered me when you were merrily dining together at du Bosc's house.
    I was also glad to read what you wrote on behalf of the Epicurean theory of the vacuum, when you objected to my own theory about that subject, which I explain in chapter XXVI, arts. 2ff.[3] I read it more gladly the more sure I was that my theory is true, and that your objections could easily be answered. My argument against the existence of a vacuum was drawn from an experiment, as follows. 'When the upper orifice of a water-vessel is blocked, none of the water runs out; when it is open, it all flows out through the lower[4] hole.' From which I argue the following. 'The reason why it does not run out is that no body could replace the water while the orifice was blocked; it can be replaced when the orifice is opened. So the reason why the water does not flow out is[5] that the vessel must always be full, that is, there must not be a vacuum in the vessel.'[6] If anyone else provides an intelligible reason why the water must necessarily stay put as a result of the orifice being blocked, I shall then admit that both my theory and that of Epicurus are equally uncertain. The reason you give for the water staying put while the upper orifice is blocked is contained in these words of yours. 'The force of the water which presses downwards and is able to push down the particles of air is less than the intrinsic impetus of the atoms (or the motion given to them extrinsically) to occupy the first space which presents itself as empty of matter. Therefore the lower[7] surface of the water cannot leave the mouth of the vessel.'[8] To destroy the force of this[9] argument I need only say that the

same reason which you give here will just as well prove that the water will not leave the mouth of the vessel whether it is closed or open; for the weight of the water remains the same by nature, whether the mouth of the vessel is open or closed. But the fact that it does not descend when the orifice is blocked is due to the fact that as it descends there is no space left for it to occupy in a space which is already completely full. But you will easily see whether this argument of yours does not equally[10] militate against any flow of the water out of the vessel with the orifice closed or open.

Among the things you have written in passing which are less pertinent to the crux[11] of the matter, I shall first of all observe that these words of yours are wrong: 'Hobbes finally considers the fact that it seems equally possible that there may be certain infinitesimal vacuums in the air outside the vessel, and that the air is condensed by the water coming out, which tries to fall by its natural weight through the lower[12] mouth of the vessel. And the fact that this does not happen can be taken as evidence for plenism.'[13] For I never made use of that argument; and if I had used it, by what argument could I have shown that it does not happen? After that you say 'Therefore Hobbes should first have assumed the Epicurean theory which I have described, until he could disprove it by drawing absurd consequences from it.'[14] For that was not necessary; nor[15] did logic require me to do it. All I had to do was to show that there was no need of a vacuum to explain natural phenomena, one such phenomenon being this one of the water-vessel.

Besides, I did not think that Epicurus' theory was absurd, in the sense in which I think he understood the vacuum. For I believe that he called 'vacuum' what Descartes calls 'subtle matter', and what I call 'extremely pure ethereal substance', of which no part is an atom, and each part is divisible (as quantity is said to be) into further divisible parts. Indeed, some of the Epicureans think that water is a body of this sort, so that when they have boiled it down[16] in various experiments they think that the water cannot be compressed by any force into any smaller space, in other words that it contains no empty space within it.

The third point to note is that it is not correct to say that atoms 'have an intrinsic weight'.[17] For weight is an endeavour towards the centre of the earth, or at least towards some star, and that endeavour is fixed and invariable in itself. So if atoms had an intrinsic weight, all atoms would long ago have flowed to the earth and the other stars, and then the whole space of the world would today be empty, apart from the stars themselves.

Finally, when you say that 'where a vacuum did exist the particles of matter would immediately rush[18] into it'[19] I do not understand this, unless you think that the atoms know where the vacuum is. Or if only the neighbouring atoms rush into a vacuum which has been made, you must explain why an atom should leave empty the space where it was in order to fill another empty space; or why it does not go back and fill the space which it itself has made empty.

All these things are difficult to explain.[20] But these difficulties are necessarily incurred by those who think that the fineness of bodies arises from the fineness[21] of their atoms, as if water, air, and other fluids were like milled[22] corn, and as if they were more or less fine depending on whether they were knocked and thrown together into thicker or smaller particles. In my opinion not only pure air but also pure water and even pure[23] quicksilver are infinitely divisible. And because of their softness they are penetrable by one another: air and water are easily penetrated by quicksilver, quicksilver less easily by water, and with great difficulty[24] by air (though this is still possible, as happens in glass tubes as a result of the weight of the quicksilver).

But these are enough replies to your objections. Continue to live happily, and to love me,

Your very loving
Thomas Hobbes

London, 6 February 1657

Passages presented in italics in the text, and in inverted commas in the translation, are over-lined in the MS.

[1] Letter 114.

[2] On de La Mothe le Vayer, see ibid., n. 2; du Prat is Abraham du Prat.

[3] Of *De corpore* (see Letter 114).

[4] inferiora *MS*.

[5] *consitit* MS.

[6] Although over-lined here, this is a summary of rather than a quotation from the argument of *De corpore*, XXVI. 2.

[7] *improma* MS.

[8] Letter 114, pp. 434, 436–7.

[9] hominis *MS*. The copyist evidently had difficulty reading this word, leaving a gap and inserting 'hominis' later.

[10] aequi *MS*.

[11] sumum *MS*.

[12] infornum *MS*.

[13] This quotation differs from the original passage in Letter 114 (p. 434), because of three apparent misreadings: 'tandem' for 'tantùm', 'et' for 'vt', and 'vscipiendae' for

'recipiendae'. Since Sorbière's writing was easily legible and Hobbes's (assuming that he wrote this letter himself) was not, these probably represent misreadings of Hobbes's letter by the copyist (Sorbière's son). But since it remains possible that they represent Hobbes's misreadings of Sorbière's original letter, they are retained here and reflected in the translation.

[14] Adapting Letter 114, pp. 434, 436.
[15] me *MS*.
[16] 'incoxerunt' should perhaps be 'induxerunt', as Tönnies conjectures.
[17] Letter 114, pp. 435, 437.
[18] prerumpunt *MS*. (Tönnies emends to 'praerumpunt', which makes less sense.)
[19] The over-lining ends with 'illuc' (at the end of a line), but should evidently continue to 'corpuscula'; Hobbes is summarizing rather than quoting from Letter 114, pp. 434, 437.
[20] explicata *MS*.
[21] The copyist has written 'exsi' and left a blank, perhaps expecting 'exsistere' but seeing that it did not fit.
[22] malitum *MS*.
[23] parum *MS*.
[24] dificillime *MS*.

Hobbes to Samuel Sorbière, from London

BN MS f.l. 10352, part 2, fo. 141ᵛ (transcript).
Printed in Tönnies, 'Siebzehn Briefe', pp. 212–13.

Vir Clarissime, Amice Charissime.
    Tractatulum tuum contra Phlebotomiam nimis crebram,[1] ad me transmisit Dubosquius noster; quem tractatum decies et diligenter perlectam, a prima ad vltimam syllabam totam approbo, teneoque plurima in eo noua sunt, eademque ingeniosissima: Plurimos adjuuerit Editus, sed [non][2] sine incommodo tuo. Continget enim tibi a Medicis quod mihi (propter Politica mea) a Theologis vt te perpetuò oderint. Regnum veritatis non est hujus mundi, sed futuri. Nam valebit tandem veritas. Vale.

Londi. feb. 10 1657.

Translation of Letter 118

Most distinguished Sir, and dearest friend,
    Our friend du Bosc sent me your little treatise against too frequent phlebotomy.[1] I have read it through carefully ten times, and I approve

of it and agree with it entirely, from the first syllable to the last. There are many new and very ingenious ideas in it: its publication will help many people, but it will not[2] be without inconvenience to yourself. You will become a perpetual object of hatred to the doctors, just as I am (because of my political theory) to the theologians. The kingdom of truth is not of this world, but the next. For truth will win at last. Farewell.

London, 10 February 1657

---

[1] This MS treatise by Sorbière survives at Chatsworth (MS Hardwick, drawer 145, item 21). It is entitled 'Discours Contre la fréquente saignée' and dedicated to du Bosc. The treatise contains some strong criticism of Parisian doctors for bleeding their patients to death (fo. 2ʳ). The origins of Sorbière's animus on this point are made clear by a transparent reference to Gassendi: 'I was amazed that one of the wisest men in the world, in his sixty-third year, should have offered his arm for bleeding fourteen times—after which he succumbed to death' ('je n'ay peu assez admirer qu'vn des plus sages hommes du monde en la soixantetroisième année de son aage ait voulu tendre quatorze fois le bras aux saignées sur lesquelles il succomba' (fo. 9ᵛ)). The treatise was never published, but copies were apparently circulated by du Bosc, and Sorbière alluded to it in a letter to the Bishop of Fréjus published in *Lettres et discours*, pp. 378–80.
[2] nox *MS*.

LETTER 119   14 [/24] FEBRUARY 1657

Henry Stubbe to Hobbes, from Oxford

BL MS Add. 32553, fo. 29 (original).
Printed in Nicastro, *Lettere*, pp. 24–5.

S:ʳ

I receiued yoʳ letter, & booke[1] by M:ʳ Barlowe, I shall forbeare to speake any thing of it to yoᵘ, it being not fitting for him to commend who cannot judge. It hath already begot much talke in yᵉ v[niversi]ᵗⁱᵉ[2], although that here bee none come downe, yᵉ Dʳ[3] hath not yet seene it, but is resolued to answer it, as hee tells his booke-seller: Hee is gifted with that ungenerous quality neuer to acknowledge. But the greatest wonder is yᵗ yoᵘ doe not speake any thing to Dʳ: Ward, most like it, there being nothing considerable in his appendicula:[4] yᵉ Presbyterians grumble & say yᵗ hee hath dealt under hand with you to a peace; and Dʳ: Wallis for ought I heare is of yᵗ minde, hee being left alone in yᵉ pit, if not to fight yet to clutter[5] with his wings. yo[r] reconcilement to y[e] vniuersity pleaseth, & so I giue out y[t] du Moulin's booke & ye Vice-chancellors[6] are ye pieces y[t] haue gained yor good esteeme. yo[u] haue put y[m] to play a new game. As for ye gentleman at Paris, I meane ye author of y[t] little fragment of a letter in Latine y[t] called you *minimè defaecati ingenij*,[7] & wondered y[t] hee would take ye paines to refute you: D[r]: Ward showed mee ye whole letter, & would not let mee see ye name nor date, but sayd it was from Paris: ye latter part was about ye discouery of a new starre.[8] I cannot assure you y[t] ye letter was Heuelius's,[9] you heard the conjecture: my dutch-man asked y[e] D[r]: who it was, but hee would not tell him; The verses may bee showed y[e] Marquesse,[10] if yo[u] please. I could bee very glad to see you here, but it is hardly seasonable yet, & y[e] Presbyterians haue so filled men's eares ag[t] yo[u], y[t] none would dare to exhibite y[t] respect wch they haue for you, least they might suffer in their preferment. S[r]: I haue no more to adde at present, but y[t] assoone as D:[r] Owen returnes, & gives his *imprimatur*, I shall bee in y[e] presse ag[t] his *thesis*,[11] if I suffer no expurgation, I have mauled him, y[e] Synod[12] & London ministers, according as hee did giue mee an item. After y[t] I will make it y[e] whole busynesse of this summer to goe on with yo[r] translation, wherein if I shall please, well; if not I haue *Exercitium styli*,[13] & though successelesse, I shall haue discouered y[t] inclination I had for you, to showe my selfe

S:[r]
yo[r] most humble seru[t]
[H. Stubbe *deleted*]

Oxon: Febr: 14. 1656.

[*postscript:*] I am since informed by one y[t] sawe y[e] docto[r] write out of Rob:[t] Stephen[14] seuerall dayes together.

[*addressed:*] These For his much esteemed Friend M:[r] Tho: Hobbes. Leaue this with M:[r] Andrew Crooke[15] at y[e] ship in Paul's church-yard London.

[*endorsed by James Wheldon:*] M[r] Stubb. Feb. 14.th 1656.

---

[1] The book was *Markes*; the letter has not apparently survived.
[2] Contraction expanded.
[3] Dr John Wallis (see Letter 75 n. 7).
[4] Seth Ward's *In Thomae Hobbii philosophiam exercitatio epistolica* (1654) ends with a

'Postscriptum [. . .] sive Appendicula' replying to *Six Lessons*. On Ward see Letter 75 n. 8.

⁵ = clatter, make a confused noise (*OED* clutter *v.* 4).

⁶ See Letter 91 nn. 7, 8, and Letter 111 n. 14.

⁷ 'Extremely dim-witted': the phrase is from the fragment of a letter printed by Wallis in *Due Correction*, pp. 4–5, written, as Wallis put it, by 'a Noble Gentleman of good worth, who hath deserved better of the Mathematicks then ever M. *Hobs* is like to doe' (p. 4). The letter was in fact from Christiaan Huygens; it is printed in *HOC* i, p. 392, dated there (by reference to Wallis's reply) 5/15 Mar. 1656.

⁸ The final section of the letter (see above, n. 7) refers to Huygens's recent observations of the rings of Saturn.

⁹ See Letter 116 n. 6.

¹⁰ Henry Pierrepont, first Marquis of Dorchester (1606–80), the dedicatee of *Markes*, was a royalist who compounded for his estates in 1647 and devoted himself to scientific and medical studies in London, becoming a Fellow of the Royal College of Physicians in 1658 and a Fellow of the Royal Society in 1663.

¹¹ See Letter 91.

¹² The Westminster Assembly (see Letter 91 n. 9).

¹³ 'Exercise for my pen' (see Letter 104 n. 12).

¹⁴ R. Stephanus (Robert Estienne), *Thesaurus*.

¹⁵ See the Biographical Register, 'William Crooke'.

LETTER 120   [1/] 11 MARCH 1657

François Peleau to Hobbes, from Bordeaux

Chatsworth, Hobbes MSS, letter 38 (original).

Monsieur

Je desire vous consulter ce coup icy, Pour sçauoir si iay fait aucun Paralogisme dans vne demonstration, que ie crois auoir faitte en Physique, pour faire uoir que deux corps ne peuuent pas estre ensemble en vn mesme Lieu; non pas mesme par la Toutepuissance de Dieu; parceque Dieu auec sa toute puissance ne peut pas faire qu'vne mesme [> chose] soit égale a vne autre chose, et plus grande qu'elle, en mesme temps. cela est pour demonstrer que Dieu n'est point dans le sacrement de l'Eucharistie, comme les Catholiques Romains pretendent. Jay trouué vne belle demonstration sur vne des Plus Importantes questions de Physique; belle; c'est a dire s'il n'y a point de faux Raisonnement. Je crains de vous l'enuoyer, parceque c'est sur vne Matiere vn peu chatouilleuse, telle que la Nullité de l'existence d'vn Dieu, distinct, et different, du Monde. Je vous prie me dire si vous trouuéz a propos, que ie vous la confie. Jattens vostre response, et suis de tout mon coeur

Monsieur
Vostre tres humble & tres obeissant seruiteur
Peleau

A Bord.ˣ ce .11. Mars 1657

[*addressed:*] For M.ʳ Hobbes At the Greene-Dragon in Paules Churchierd. London.

[*endorsed by James Wheldon:*] Mʳ Peleau. Mar. 11ᵗʰ. 1657

Translation of Letter 120

Sir,

I want to consult you this time to see whether I have committed any paralogisms in a demonstration which I think I have made in physics, to show that two bodies cannot coexist in the same place, not even by the omnipotence of God. For God in his omnipotence cannot make one thing be equal to another thing which is larger than it, at one and the same time. The purpose of this is to demonstrate that God is not present at all in the sacrament of the eucharist, as the Roman Catholics claim. I have found a fine way of demonstrating it which touches on one of the most important questions in physics—fine, that is, if it does not involve any false reasoning. I am nervous of sending it to you, because it is on a rather ticklish subject, namely the non-existence of a God distinct and different from the world. Please tell me if you think it fitting for me to entrust it to you. I await your reply, and am, Sir, with all my heart,

Your most humble and obedient servant,
Peleau

Bordeaux, 11 March 1657

[*addressed: see text*]

François du Verdus to Hobbes, from Bordeaux

Chatsworth, Hobbes MSS, letter 12 (original).

Monsieur

La derniere lettre que j'aye reçeu de vous fut du 22ᵉ x.ᵇʳᵉ¹ De cela il y a trois moys. J'ay trouué ce temps fort long; ne scachant a quoy il tenoit que vous ne me fissiés doner, ou donnassiés de vos Nouuelles. d'un côté j'ay craint quelque mauuais changement dans uostre santé; d'autre [coté *deleted*] part je l'ay craint dans la bonne uolonté que vous auiés pour moy: et de quelque côté que peut estre l'alteration, elle me seroit tres sensible, vous estimant et honorant au point que je fais. Je vous prie n'allés pas vous [oublier *deleted*] auiser d'oublier ainsi l'homme du Monde qui vous considére le plus: premierement je vous accablerois de lettres; et secondement j'irois a Londres pour m'en plaindre a tous vos Amis et Amies. plutot faisons Capitulation; reiglés vous a un certain nombre de lettres; je me contente de six tous les ans: Mais tous les trois moys une fois, ce n'est pas assés: encore ne scay-je si je me plaindray si vous m'eussiés fauorisé d'un petit mot de response a mes deux derniéres.² Elles vous proposoient l'une et l'autre trois ou quattre choses. premierement une instançe contre ce que vous m'auiés si doctement et habilement repondu de Saul et Samuël³ et je repliquois que non seulement Samuël dit a Saul que Dieu l'auoyt rejetté pour auoyr sacrifié, (Car s'il n'y auoit que cela ce ne seroit point nier la uerité de l'ecriture, que de dire que pour cela Saül ne fut pas reprouué, puis qu'en ce cas l'écriture diroit seulement que Samuël le luy dit) mais l'écriture dit expressement que Saül fut reprouué.⁴

Secondement Contre ce que vous dites pour faire les Roys sacrificateurs et grands prestres en Chef je vous opposois le chapitre 26. du 2ᵈ liure Croniques où lon uoid qu'Vzià ayant uoulu bruler l'encens Azarias et 80 prestres s'oposerent a luy et pour sçauoyr qui eut raison c'est que Dieu frapa sur le champ Ozia de lepre.⁵

Troisiemement je vous demandois si posé vos principes vne Reyne telle par exemple que vostre Reyne Elizabeth auoit droit de sacrifier dans nostre Relligion je veux dire de benir le pain et prononçer dessus les paroles sacramentales pour le consacrer.⁶ Car d'un coté selon vous elle est la persone de l'etat et de son eglise et la represente seule Mais aussi d'autre part nous ne uoyons point que nostre Seigneur ait fait des prestres fémelles.

Je vous demandois encore, en quel endroit de vostre 3eme et de uostre 4.eme partie du Leuiathan vous mettiés l'addition pour expliquer que *Est* ueut dire signifie;[7] et en quels termes cela seroit et mesmes la comparaison du joueur de gobelets disant trois paroles Ocus pocus.[8] Et tout ce me semble méritoit un mot de responce aussi bien que ce que je vous demandois des nouuelles de vostre seconde section de Homine qu'il me tarde que je n'aye premierement pour en profiter et y aprendre vostre doctrine qui a pour moy la forçe des démonstrations: et secondement pour la traduire.

Si vous uoulés m'y repondre comme je le souhaite, et vous en prie, vous le pouuès mesme en Anglois. M^r le Cheualier d'Igby me fait l'honneur de m'écrire en cette langue, et je l'entans assés pour cela. Il a esté en cette ville quelque deux mois[9] faisant mention de vous tres honorable et beuuant vostre santé. Il m'a fait present de ses Oeuures et en Anglois et en Latin,[10] que j'étudie présentement. J'atans l'honneur de vos Nouuelles; et suis et seray toute ma vie

Monsieur
vostre tres humble et tres obeissant serviteur
duuerdus

A Bourdeaux le 22e Mars 1657[11]

[*addressed:*]
A Monsieur
Monsieur Hobbes

[*endorsed by James Wheldon:*] Monsr du Verdus Mar. 22th. 1655[12]

Translation of Letter 121

Sir,

The last letter I received from you was written on 22 December.[1] That was three months ago. This period of time has seemed very long to me, since I have not known what was preventing you from giving me your news, or getting someone else to give it to me. On the one hand I feared some change for the worse in your health; and on the other hand some change for the worse in your goodwill towards me. And if either of these changes were to happen, it would pain me very much, valuing and honouring you as much as I do. I beg you, do not take it into your head to ignore in this way the one person in the world who regards you the most highly. If you did, I would first of all shower you with letters, and secondly I would go to London to complain of this treatment to all gentlemen and ladies who are your friends. Rather than that, let us draw up an agreement of surrender: set yourself to write a certain number of letters. I will be content with six letters a year; but once every three months is not enough.

I still do not know whether I would have complained if you had favoured me with a few words in reply to my two last letters.[2] They both raised three or four points with you. First, a counter-example to the reply you gave so learnedly and cleverly on the subject of Saul and Samuel.[3] My reply was that not only did Samuel tell Saul that God had rejected him for having performed a sacrifice (for if that were all, it would be no denial of the truth of Scripture to say that Saul was not reproved all the same, since in that case Scripture would only be saying that Samuel told him he had been), but Scripture expressly says that Saul was reproved.[4]

Secondly, against your argument that kings are performers of sacrifices and great high priests, I countered with 2 Chronicles 26, where one can see that when Uzziah had decided to burn incense, Azariah and eighty priests opposed him, and to show which of them was right God struck Uzziah down with leprosy on the spot.[5]

Thirdly, I asked you whether, given your principles, a queen (such as, for example, your Queen Elizabeth) had the right to sacrifice in our religion, by which I mean the right to bless the bread and pronounce the sacramental words over it in order to consecrate it.[6] For on the one hand, according to you she is the person of the state, and of its Church, being its sole representative; but on the other hand we do not observe that our Saviour made any female priests at all.

I also asked you where in your third and fourth parts of *Leviathan* you would put in the additional passage to explain that 'est' means 'signifies',[7] and in what terms you would do it—also the comparison with the juggler with the cups saying 'hocus-pocus'.[8] All that, I think, deserved a word of reply, just as much as my request for news about your second section, *De homine*, which I long to have, first of all to profit from it, learning your doctrine (which in my eyes has the force of demonstrations), and secondly to translate it.

If you wish to reply (as I hope you will, and beg you to), you can do it in English too. Sir Kenelm Digby does me the honour of writing to me in that language, and I understand it well enough for that purpose. He spent two months in this town,[9] mentioning your name with much honour and drinking your health. He has given me his works in English and Latin,[10] which I am studying at the moment. I await the honour of receiving your news; and I am, and shall be for the rest of my life,

Sir,
Your most humble and obedient servant,
du Verdus

Bordeaux, 22 March 1657[11]

[*addressed:*] To Mr Hobbes

The date written by du Verdus is 1657, but the 7 could easily be mistaken for a 5; someone has added '/56' after the date on the letter, and Wheldon has made the same error in his endorsement. These details help to confirm that Wheldon's endorsements were made long after the receipt of the letters—possibly while putting Hobbes's papers in order after his death.

[1] This letter has not apparently survived.
[2] One of these was Letter 108; the other was perhaps the note sent via Peleau (see Letter 103 n. 1).
[3] See Letter 94 n. 9.
[4] 1 Sam. 13: 13–14.
[5] See Letter 108 n. 13.
[6] See ibid., n. 14.
[7] See Letter 94 n. 12; Letter 100, enclosure, query for p. 338; Letter 108 n. 9.
[8] These passages were not added in the Latin translation.
[9] See Letter 115 n. 2.
[10] This probably refers to *Two Treatises* (Paris, 1644; 2nd edn. London, 1645), and the Latin translation of it, *Demonstratio immortalitatis animae* (Paris, 1651; 2nd edn. Paris, 1655).
[11] See the general note above.
[12] See the general note above.

LETTER 122   17 [/27] MARCH 1657

Henry Stubbe to Hobbes, from Oxford

BL MS Add. 32553, fo. 30 (original).
Printed in Nicastro, *Lettere*, pp. 25–6.

S.r

I could not abstaine from writeing, haueing this day bought yͤ sight of Dr: Wallis's manuscript agt yor last piece:[1] I did not see yͤ first sheet, (but shall shortly) it will amount but to three:[2] I belieue there is little ag^t yor Mathematicks, for ye two last sheets are spent ag^t ye letter,[3] & if I may conjecture any thing by ye passage hee beginnes at, & his tedious procedure, a great part also of ye first. All hee speakes to yor politicks is but halfe a page, & impertinent;[4] yor objection ag^t his exposition in his sermon hee hath touched upon in twelue lines, wch is most triuially done.[5] Hee doth giue out y^t I wrote ye letter, & whither he names mee in his booke I know not, but all along hee calls mee yor journey-man:[6] Hee hath made us amends with *adduco*,[7] by giueing yo^u an account of traduco &c: & fero with it's compounds, as if other mens errours would justify him, or Livyes Patavinity[8] were imitable: but if hee were long before, he hath brought as much more now: & replies not, but refutes Plautus:[9] As for his *Empusa*, hee saith nothing to my ἐν ποσὶ βαίνουσα,[10] because I doe not averre it, as true. But accumulates autho^{rs} impertinently.[11] in yor place of στίξας, hee sayth ye man was out, being a stranger, y^t used it for στιγματίσας:[12] wch none in his wits would say: y^t στιγμή & στίγμα are all one hee sayth I proue not because I grant there is sometimes a difference, & sometimes not: & sayth none of my places proue στιγμή to bee a marke with an hot iron: whereas y^t is not ye proper, but more usuall signification of στίγμα.[13] Hee is not uery facete now, nor abusiue; & certainely yo^u haue done a great worke to ciuilise him: D:^{r} Owen[14] hath approued of my piece ag^t his *thesis*, with all ye harsh language agt ye Synod, I know not when it will bee printed:[15] I shall giue you an account of ye first sheet, assoone as I get it: Take notice y^t ye d^r doth take paines to proue y^t not Holyoke but D^r: Grey & some others made ye dictionary:[16] hee hath learnedly proued y^t Hobgoblin, ye latter part is french, & ye other saxon, & comes from Robert, not Hobbes, just as Richard, Richardson, Rixon; Dick, dick, Dickinson, dixon: Robert, Robinson, Robson, Hobbinall, Hobson, Hob[17]— S:^{r} I haue no more to adde but y^t I am

    yor most humble & most affectionate seru^t
    [H: Stubbe *deleted*]

Oxon. March. 17° 1656.

[*addressed:*] These For his euer honoured friend M:^{r} Thomas Hobbes. leaue this at M^r: Andrew Crookes[18] Booke-seller in Paul's church yard, at ye ship London

[*endorsed by Hobbes:*] Mr Stubb. March. 17th. 1656

[1] The MS (or more probably, given the reference to 'sheets' here, the proofs) of Wallis's *Hobbiani puncti dispunctio*, the reply to *Markes*. On Wallis see Letter 75 n. 7.

[2] The text of *Hobbiani puncti dispunctio* occupies three sheets (B–D$_8$), with an initial A1–2 for the title-page and dedicatory epistle.

[3] Ibid., pp. 3–9 are against Hobbes's mathematics, and pp. 15–46 (sigs. B8–D8^r) discuss the grammatical issues raised in Stubbe's 'Extract of a Letter' (see Letter 101 n. 1).

[4] This refers probably to remarks in ibid., pp. 42–3, where Wallis rejects Hobbes's claim that the rules of religion should be subject to civil law.

[5] Ibid., pp. 41–2.

[6] Wallis first refers to Hobbes's 'Journy-man' on p. 15 (ibid.). He does not name Stubbe, but implies that he knows his identity.

[7] For the grammatical controversy over Wallis's use of the verb 'adducere', see Hobbes, *Six Lessons*, p. 51 (*EW* vii, p. 322); Wallis, *Due Correction*, pp. 14–21; Hobbes, *Markes*, pp. 15–16 (*EW* vii, pp. 391–2); and Wallis, *Hobbiani puncti dispunctio*, pp. 18–35.

[8] The qualities of the provincial dialect of Padua (Patavium), for which Livy, a native of Padua, was censured by Pollio (Quintilian, *Institutio*, 1. 5. 56).

[9] Wallis rejected as irrelevant (*Hobbiani puncti dispunctio*, p. 23) a passage Stubbe had cited from Plautus.

[10] 'going on her foot': Stubbe offered this etymology of 'empusa' in his 'Extract of a Letter' (*Markes*, p. 25: *EW* vii, p. 414), controverting the etymology given by Wallis in *Elenchus*, p. 4. On the origins of this controversy see Letter 104 n. 5.

[11] Wallis, *Hobbiani puncti dispunctio*, pp. 35–41.

[12] Hobbes had referred to a passage in the Scholiast of Aristophanes, which described how Adimantus, who was not a native speaker of Greek, had said στίξας instead of στιγματίσας; Hobbes used this as evidence for his argument that στιγμή and στίγμα had the same meaning, but Wallis argued that it implied the opposite. On the origins of this controversy see Letter 104 n. 13.

[13] See Stubbe's 'Extract of a Letter' in *Markes*, pp. 28–30 (*EW* vii, pp. 420–7), and Wallis, *Hobbiani puncti dispunctio*, pp. 43–6.

[14] See Letter 91 n. 7.

[15] Stubbe's attack on Wallis's 'Thesis' was not in fact printed. In 1658 Dr Owen's critic Daniel Cawdrey wrote that Owen 'did imploy [. . .] Mr. *Stubbs* of Christ-Church (now advocate for Mr. Hobs) to write against it [sc. Wallis's 'Thesis']: Though indeed, when that work written, was found a *Scurrilous ridiculous piece* (for so I heare, he is since pleased to style it) he did not thinke fit to let it be made publick, because (they were his own words) "*he would not have that cause suffer so much as to be defended by such a penne*"' (*Independency further proved to be a Schism*, p. 130).

[16] Stubbe had cited Wallis's reference to 'Rider and Thomas's Dictionary' and had observed that 'Rider was onely Author of the English dictionary' (*Markes*, p. 26: *EW* vii, pp. 416–17). John Rider's English–Latin dictionary, *Bibliotheca scholastica* (1st edn. 1589) was revised and augmented by Francis Holyoke (*Riders Dictionarie Corrected*, 1st edn. 1606); a further revision was published as *Riders Dictionarie Corrected* [. . .] *to which are Joyned* [. . .] *Alterations by N. Gray* (1626). In *Hobbiani puncti dispunctio* Wallis refers to it as 'another book which I do not know how to call, (should I call it *Riders Dictionary*, you would tell mee that *Holy-oke* made part of it; should I call it *Holy-oke's*, others would say *Dr Gray*)' (p. 37).

[17] In *Elenchus* (p. 4) Wallis had compared the classical 'empusa' to the English 'Hobgoblin', which he supposed to derive its name from 'hop'. His revised etymology (from 'Robert') is in *Hobbiani puncti dispunctio*, p. 36.

[18] See the Biographical Register, 'William Crooke'.

LETTER 123   11 [/21] APRIL 1657

Henry Stubbe to Hobbes, from Oxford

BL MS Add. 32553, fos. 31–2 (original).
Printed in Nicastro, *Lettere*, pp. 27–8.

S:ʳ

    This day came out Dʳ: Wallis's booke,[1] wherein wᵗ hee hath sayd as to Mathematicks I cannot judge; But in his Critiques hee is insufferable: hee combates with shadowes, & misrepresents mee to yᵉ Marquesse:[2] yᵗ cum ferro is good, you had yᵉ judgement of Sanctius:[3] yᵗ Tully used it, it is euident, yet the dʳ reades it aduenientem cum ferro, contrary to all copyes & yᵉ intent of yᵉ authour: for Caecinna was unarmed.[4] To tell mee yᵗ I haue dealt with Ch: Stephen,[5] is a pretty excuse: I might upon yᵉ same account say all his allegations are out of a concordance, wᶜʰ hee cites in his sermons; because they are found there as well as in yᵉ authour. That *praetendo* to *pretend* is a good word, I haue proued:[6] As to my deduction of Empusa[7] hee sayth nothing but yᵗ it I confesse it a jumble: I should say so too of ἐμποδῶν, ἐμπυριβήτης,[8] & yet yᵉ deriuation stand good. As for yᵗ of νπ hee fights with his owne shadow: the changeing of yᵉ spirit[9] I valued not much: no, for from ἐ̓ cometh ἔλεγος[10] & an 100 of yᵉ like: I did not imagine a cacophony in ἔντπους or ἔμπους[11] more than in *Hempe* or *Henbane*: but I thought a Grecian would hardly change μ for ν where there was like to bee such apparent ambiguity, for in both hee would alter yᵉ *spirit*, yᵗ is certaine, & yⁿ who could know whence it was deriued? besides yᵗ it is usuall for yᵉ greekes to recede from yᵉ customary speech, rather yⁿ fall into a confusion of words. What hee sayth of their approueing his deriuation is all false, nor doth hee charge mee with altering yᵉ text: & yet hee must haue better Eyes yⁿ I yᵗ can see wᵗ the d:ʳ sayes. Suidas[12] he neuer cited; And wᵗ I deny of all is to bee understood with exception of Eustathius;[13] yoᵘ know yᵗ was put in afterwards, I could not finde it at first, when I denied it in generall: As for my wronging him in quotations, I neuer saw his *errata*, nor had time diligently to compare things with Stephen;[14]

The cause is not carryed thereby. About tanquam, hee is mad,[15] or would make others so. In στιγμή hee hath learned something from mee, but I see hee is a bad scholar, & doth not know how they used to brand heretofore: for euen their στίγματα y^t were made with a stylus, were not made by seuerall *prickeing*, but *cutting* verso *stylo*, y^t is with the broad end, wch was sharpe, & in forme like a surgeons *spatula*.[16] Duns cometh from densus, as Minshew sayes whence ye docto^r had his deriuation of Hob-goblin.[17] S:^{r} I thinke I haue giuen yo^u a confutation of all hee sayth, but *adduco*[18] wch would bee tedious: if yo^u will peruse it, & get dauies[19] to word it (for I am sensibly deficient in English) where it may stand in need, and interline it with some of his dictis melioribus,[20] hee being a great master of English, & it is belowe you, I will so lay him open as neuer man was, and giue an account of all his English quibles & adages in this and his other booke: and his other sayeings which it is pitty they should be lost. as also the whole criticall part of his sermon, wch I cited by rote as I heard it, & so wronged him something, as hee sayes,[21] which is all hee sayes to y^t fagary.[22] You know how suddainely ye letter was written, so y^t I could not attend each punctilio: if I haue wronged him in Stephen,[23] it is a great shame, y^t haueing those things before him, wch I objected, hee should euer write w^t hee did. Hee makes as if hee had not Stephen, but y^t is but to mocke ye reader, for hee was in our library[24] transcribeing him seuerall times both for his *correction*,[25] & last piece. D:^{r} Owen hath my papers still,[26] hee likes y^m, & wee are now frameing a Schisme ag^t ye Presbyters of London, who haue had an assembly to confute d:^{r} Owen of schisme, if they proceed, wee shall not spare y^m.[27] Hee did speake of yor Leuiathan, y^t it was a booke ye most full of excellent remarques of any, onely yo^u deify the magistrate, & spoyled all by yor kingdome of darknesse.[28] hee bade not meddle with ye translation;[29] hee s^d sheets of it had beene seene at London: I denyed I was about any such thing, & offered ye search of my study. but yesterday I reassumed ye worke, & did a few lines: But I haue a minde to cudgell wallis before I proceed: I submit this to yor judgem^t: I am a stranger to ye Marquesse, but I hope hee will not censure mee upon ye d^{rs} word: I am his seru^t, but will not trouble him with ye dedication, as ye d^r doth.

S:^{r}

I am yor humble seru^t

H: Stubbe.

April: 11. 1657.

459

[*addressed:*] These For his much esteemed friend M:ʳ Thomas Hobs Leaue this with M:ʳ Andrew Crooke[30] at yᵉ ship in Paul's church yard London hast

[*endorsed by Hobbes:*] M: Stubb. Apr. 11ᵗʰ 1657

[1] *Hobbiani puncti dispunctio* (on Wallis see Letter 75 n. 7).

[2] Henry Pierrepont, Marquis of Dorchester (see Letter 119 n. 10), to whom both Hobbes's *Markes* and Wallis's *Hobbiani puncti dispunctio* were addressed.

[3] See Letter 113 n. 8.

[4] In defending Hobbes's use of 'cum' with the 'ablative case of the *manner* and *cause*', Stubbe had cited Cicero's *Pro Caecina*, 25 (Hobbes, *Markes*, p. 20: *EW* vii, p. 401); Wallis replied in *Hobbiani puncti dispunctio*, p. 15, arguing that 'cum ferro' meant 'with a sword' as an accompanying object.

[5] Wallis accused Stubbe of having read the passages he cited not in the original but only in the *Thesaurus ciceronianus* of C. Stephanus (Charles Estienne) (*Hobbiani puncti dispunctio*, pp. 15, 17).

[6] Hobbes, *Markes*, pp. 20–1 (*EW* vii, pp. 402–3); Wallis, *Hobbiani puncti dispunctio*, pp. 15–16.

[7] Hobbes, Markes, pp. 24–7 (*EW* vii, pp. 410–19); Wallis, *Hobbiani puncti dispunctio*, pp. 35–41. See Letters 104 n. 5, and 122 n. 10.

[8] ἐμποδών: 'in the way' (derived from ἐν ποσὶν ὤν, 'being at one's foot'); ἐμπυρυβήτης: 'above the fire' (derived from ἐν, πῦρ, and βαίνω, 'standing on the fire').

[9] = breathing.

[10] 'Elegy'.

[11] Wallis's etymology for 'empusa' was ἕν πούς: 'one foot'. Stubbe had observed that this theory required a change of aspiration as well as a shift from νπ to μπ (Hobbes, *Markes*, p. 26: *EW* vii, p. 415).

[12] The interpretation of 'empusa' given in Suidas had been referred to by Stubbe (Hobbes, *Markes*, p. 26: *EW* vii, p. 415). 'Suidas' (ἡ Σοῦδα, or Σοῦιδα) is the name of a 10th-cent. Byzantine Greek dictionary: until the 20th cent., this was thought to have been the name of the author. It is now believed to be the name of the book—either an acronym or a mistranscription of 'guida'.

[13] A 12th-cent. Archbishop of Salonica who wrote a commentary on Homer; his authority on the meaning of 'empusa' was disputed by Stubbe (Hobbes, *Markes*, p. 24: *EW* vii, p. 412).

[14] See Letter 119 n. 14.

[15] Wallis, *Hobbiani puncti dispunctio*, pp. 16–17.

[16] Wallis countered a citation by Stubbe from Zonaras, describing the making of marks (στίγμας) on people's faces, by saying that this involved only making 'points or pricks' (ibid., p. 45).

[17] Wallis had objected to Hobbes's spelling of 'duns' (ibid., p. 10). In John Minsheu's dictionary, Ἡγεμών εἰς τὰς γλώσσας (1617), the entry for 'Dunse' begins: '*dolt, blockhead, or hardpate*, à Lat: Densus'. The entry for 'Hobgoblins' begins: '*Night-walking spirits*, quasi Robgoblins, *Robin good fellow*'. Wallis's etymology of 'hobgoblin' (see Letter 122 n. 17) is in *Hobbiani puncti dispunctio*, p. 36.

[18] Ibid., pp. 18–35.

[19] Probably John Davies of Kidwelly, Carmarthenshire (1627?-93), who was educated at Jesus College, Oxford, and St John's College, Cambridge; he travelled in France in the late 1640s, returned to England *c*.1652, settled in London, and worked prolifically as a translator from the French (see Tucker, 'John Davies of Kidwelly'). He was also responsible for the unauthorized 1st edn. of *Of Libertie and Necessitie* (1654).

[20] 'better sayings'.

[21] Wallis protested (*Hobbiani puncti dispunctio*, p. 41) at Stubbe's criticism of his Latin sermon (printed in Wallis, *Mens sobria*, pp. 1–57).

[22] = vagary.

[23] Stubbe had accused Wallis of claiming to have read Latin authors when he had merely lifted references to them from R. Stephanus (Robert Estienne), *Thesaurus* (Hobbes, *Markes*, p. 22: *EW* vii, p. 405).

[24] The Bodleian Library, of which Stubbe was Deputy Keeper.

[25] Wallis, *Due Correction*.

[26] For Stubbe's plan to publish a criticism of Wallis's ecclesiastical theories, see Letters 91, 96–8; on Owen, see Letter 91 n. 7.

[27] This seems to imply that Stubbe had a hand in Owen's *Of Schisme* (Oxford, 1657: 17 [/27] June according to Thomason's copy: BL E 1664.(2)), and/or his *A Review of the True Nature of Schisme* (Oxford, 1657: 25 Sept. [/5 Oct.] according to Thomason's copy: BL E 1664.(1)).

[28] 'Of the Kingdome of Darknesse' is the general title of part 4 of *Leviathan*.

[29] On Stubbe's projected translation of *Leviathan* into Latin, see Letters 80, 87.

[30] See the Biographical Register, 'William Crooke'.

LETTER 124   [15/] 25 APRIL 1657

Thomas de Martel to Hobbes, from Dieppe

Chatsworth, Hobbes MSS, letter 39 (original).
Printed in von Brockdorff, 'Fünf Briefe', pp. 14–15.

Monsieur

Quelque affaire m'aiant amené ici J'ai eu le boneur d'y accompagner vn honneste homme donc le nom vous est celebre c'est Mr Fermat fils de celui que vous cognoissez de reputation et de commerce.[1] Il ne faisoit pas estat non plus que moi de passer outre, mais se voiant si pres d'Angleterre Il à voulu prolonger sa promenade Jusques la auec vne extreme passion qui entra dans le dessein de son voiage de cognoistre de prez l'auteur du Liure De Ciue, et de la Ph'ie de Corpore. Son nom et l'Estime qu'il faict de vos ouurages ne demanderoient nullem.[t] d'autre voie pour l'Introduire prez de vous, mais comme toutes les fois qu'on en parle Je publie volontiers la gloire que J'ai d'estre aimé de vous, J'ai creu de la Ciuilité seule sans les autres obligations que J'en ai de l'accompagner de cette letre pour Vous aduertir seulem^t qu'il est vn tel, et qu'il vous estime auec grande cognoissance, ce qui me semble vne marque certaine de toutes les bonnes qualitez qui vous le peuuent rendre recommandable de lui mesme, ce qu'il vous confirmera si suffisam^t dans la cognoissance part.^{re} que vous aurez de lui que vous ne donnerez rien à l'amitié dont vous m'honorez pour lui accorder vos Conversations. C'est la le subiet de celle ci, ou J'adiousterai de moi que si je ne vous escris que par de semblables occasions, c'est ne in publica Commoda peccem,[2] vous scachant occupé à defendre vostre Philosophie ou à l'acheuer, car au reste ma veneration pour vous n'est pas moindre dans le silence que Je ne garde qu'auec Vous seul, n'aiant point de Conuersations auec nos amis Communs sans faire vos Eloges, vous souhaiter Longue vie et sante, cum tu si quis alius sanam mentem, et aequum animum tibi ipse parasti,[3] et sans proposer mille fois de vous aller voir pour flater au moins par la nos desirs, les miens pour cela sont si violents qu'a moins d'estre lié par de tres fortes chaisnes Je ne me serois point approché si prez de vostre Isle que vous ne m'y eussiez attiré veritablemt comme on la conte de celle des sirenes, cela me seroit Infailliblemt arriué si J'auois les mouuemts de mon Inclination aussi libres que Mr. fermat qui vous Confirmera ces sentiments, en attendant que tost ou tard vous cognoissiez par quelque grand effect cette force que vous auez sur moi m'attirant peut estre de plus loin, sans autre motif que celui de vous voir, car J'enuie peu à Mr. fermat qu'il aille voir le dernier acte de la revolution de vostre pais ou l'experience respond si parfaictemt à ce que vous auez demonstré de l'autorité souueraine, Je suis de tout mon coeur

Monsieur
Vostre treshumble et tres obeissant seruiteur
De Martel

A Diepe ce 25 April 1657

[*addressed:*] À Monsieur
   Monsieur Hobbes au Dragon Vert au cloistre de l'Eglise S. Paul. A Londres.

[*endorsed by James Wheldon:*] Monsr de Martell Apr. 25. 1657

Translation of Letter 124

Sir,

Having been brought here by some business, I have had the pleasure of accompanying on the way here a worthy gentleman whose name is well known to you: he is M. Fermat, the son of the one you know by reputation and by correspondence.[1] He was not expecting to cross the Channel any more than I was; but seeing that he was so close to England, he wanted to extend his journey to that country, and he felt a very powerful desire (which became part of the purpose of his voyage) to get to know the author of *De cive* and *De corpore* in the flesh. Given his name, and his high opinion of your works, he hardly needs any other introduction to make your acquaintance; but since, whenever the subject arises, I freely proclaim the honour I have of being loved by you, I thought that just out of civility (leaving aside my other obligations in this matter) I should send this letter with him, merely to tell you that he is as I have described him, and that he has a high opinion of you based on a great knowledge of your works. That strikes me as an infallible sign of all the good qualities which can recommend him to you on his own merit; and he will give you such thorough confirmation of that when you get to know him personally, that when you allow him to talk with you, you will not do so merely as a favour to the friendship with which you honour me.

That is what this letter is about. For my own part, I shall add that if I only write to you on occasions such as this, it is 'lest I harm the public interest',[2] knowing that you are busy defending or completing your philosophy. Otherwise my veneration for you is no smaller on account of my silence, a silence which I keep only with you, since not a conversation with our mutual friends passes without my praising you, wishing you long life and good health, since 'you, if anyone, have provided yourself with a sound mind and a calm spirit',[3] and without proposing a thousand times that I should go and visit you, at least to satisfy our own desires thereby. My desire to do that is so violent that I would not have come so close to your island without being secured by very strong chains, to stop you from drawing me towards you—just like the island of the Sirens in the story. That is what would have happened to me without fail, if I had been as free to follow my inclinations as M. Fermat—who will confirm that those are my feelings. Meanwhile I expect that sooner or later you will discover, from some great effect which it will produce, the power which you have over me, which will

draw me towards you perhaps from a greater distance, without any
other purpose than that of seeing you. For I do not envy M. Fermat very
much the fact that he is going to see the last act of your country's
revolution, where experience corresponds so exactly to your demonstrations on the subject of sovereign authority.

[*addressed:*] To Mr Hobbes, at the Green Dragon in St Paul's
churchyard, London

¹ On Pierre Fermat (father of Samuel), see Letter 67 n. 8; no letters between Pierre
Fermat and Hobbes are known to have survived. On Samuel Fermat see the
Biographical Register.
² Horace, *Epistolae*, 2. 1. 3.
³ Source unidentified.

LETTER 125   6 [/16] MAY 1657

Henry Stubbe to Hobbes, from Oxford

BL MS Add. 32553, fos. 33–4 (original).
Printed in Nicastro, *Lettere*, pp. 28–30.

S:ʳ

I receiued yoʳ last,¹ but yoʳ specifyeing nothing concerneing the
receipt of mine, makes mee feare yoᵘ haue not receiued it: I haue beene
so engaged in disputes of diuinity in our priuate colledge,² yᵗ I could
not till now reuise³ the doctour's last piece;⁴ I haue concluded upon an
answer so much to our aduantage, yᵗ it were a thousand pityes to
suppresse it. All yᵉ v[niversi]ᵗⁱᵉ⁵ lookes upon mee as yᵉ authour of yᵗ
Letter,⁶ and expect a reply, not yᵗ there is neede, but to giue checke to yᵉ
Dʳˢ pride: though there are them yᵗ thinke euery thing unanswerable agᵗ
wᶜʰ they doe not see a title-page posted up: I communicated yᵉ title with
M:ʳ Oldenburgh, & it is this

Clamor, rixa, joci, mendacia, furta, cachinni:⁷
or
an account
of
Eudaemon-Joannes⁸ Wallis, grammar-reader in Oxon:
his
Oneirocritica;⁹ together with a collection of seuerall prouerbes,

464

quibles, quiblets[10] & other ornaments of speech, for the benefit of
those y^t admire him.

'Goe tell ye assembly of diuines
'Tell Adoniram blew
'Tell Marshall, Burges, Case & Vines
'Tell *Now* and *Anon* too.[']'[11]

I giue out y^t I intend onely to satisfye him, to whome I sent the former,
& y^t hee (who is a good droller) will prefixe this title. D:^{r} Ward[12]
requested mee earnestly not to meddle in it, for ye v[niversi]^{tie}[13] sake: I
professed I would insert nothing of ill language, nay I would disavow
all, but it could not bee expected y^t I should giue lawes to him who
published ye other letter, or prohibite him enterlineing it, no more y^n
from prefixeing a title. I haue so euidently maintained all ye parts unto
y^t of *adducis malleum*,[14] (wch hee makes ye last of ye Latine) y^t it pleaseth
mee, & I haue enterlaced a discourse concerneing ye rule of
Language,[15] & two long passages, one out of Scaliger, ye other out of
Doletus, about Tullye's soloecismes,[16] & choyce of wordes: wch haue an
incredible influence upon ye whole controuersy: besides much more
out of other authors, so as to render it usefull to others, as well as
reuengefull ag^t him. I haue halfe finished *adducis malleum*, & I doubt not
but I shall satisfy my selfe in y^t as well as other parts. About Empusa, I
shall question-lesse expose him, notwithstanding *νπ*.[17] and for
στιγμή[18] I hope for ye like successe, but I haue not as yet considered w^t
hee hath objected there. After I haue finished this, I will make a
collection, of his pretty storyes, proverbes, &c: and y^n adde yor
objections about obscoenity, & *Lurry*:[19] to wch I shall adde a considerable criticisme. And then I shall conclude y^t haueing so clearely
demonstrated his mistakes, it cannot but seeme conuenient y^t hee
should recant in S: Maryes[20] his false doctrine in critickes, wch hee may
doe takeing for his text stigmata porto in corpore,[21] much more pertinently then hee inserted y^t philology lecture of *σόφρων*,[22] wch I shall
then subjoine. I doe not thinke y^t I leaue any part unanswered, no not a
title, & I insert y^t text of ye letter, & then his references: & where occasion requires, I write downe his text in *due correction*: you would not
thinke how I am pleased with ye reply, & if you will interline it any
where occasionally, with another hand, it will passe under ye name of y^e
Gentleman y^t communicated ye letter to you. I shall haue finished it by
y^t time I heare from you, & I sh[all *page torn* re]ferre ye Oeconomy of it
wholly to you: though ye apprehension I perceiue they haue of it will

put y^m upon urgeing mee to cease: but I shall so put ye papers into yor hands y^t they may be irrevocable: and after they are printed I will prefixe a chartell,²³ disowneing all contumely, as not proceeding from mee, & giue an account of the occasion of my first writeing, & how it was a sense of ye honour of the v[niversi]^{tie24} made mee penne y^t, & not any extraordinary inclination I had to those works of yo^{rs} y^t I had not reade: yet yor Thucydides²⁵ did oblige mee to haue an esteeme of yor polite learning, & to this purpose: for this must bee done, y^t so I may haue ye opportunity to continue

S:^r
yor most humble & most affectionate seru^t
H: Stubbe.

Oxon. May. 6. 1657.

[*addressed:*] These For his euer honoured Friend M:^r Thomas Hobbes, Leaue this at M:^r Andrew Crooke's²⁶ at y^e ship in Paul's church-yard, Booke-seller, to bee sent with speed. London hast:
hast

[*endorsed by James Wheldon:*] Mr. Stubb. May 6.th 1657

¹ Hobbes's letter to Stubbe has not apparently survived.
² Christ Church, Oxford.
³ = look at again (*OED* revise *v.* 2).
⁴ *Hobbiani punctio dispunctio* by John Wallis (on whom see Letter 75 n. 7).
⁵ Contraction expanded.
⁶ The 'Extract of a Letter' by Stubbe, printed in Hobbes, *Markes*, pp. 20–30.
⁷ 'Shouting, brawling, tricks, lies, deceit, and jeering'.
⁸ This is an allusion to the Jesuit theologian (of Greek origin) Andreas Eudaemon-Joannes (literally, 'Happy-John'), alias L'Heureux (1560–1625), author of numerous polemical anti-Protestant works.
⁹ The Greek term for a book on the interpretation of dreams.
¹⁰ = quibbles.
¹¹ ~' *omitted in MS.* Stephen Marshall (1594?–1655), Cornelius Burges (1589?–1665), Thomas Case (1598–1682), Richard Vines (1600?–56), and Obadiah Sedgwick ('Now and anon': see Letter 102) were members of the Westminster Assembly; Adoniram Byfield (d. 1660) was one of the scribes to the Assembly, and Wallis was his amanuensis.
¹² See Letter 75 n. 8.
¹³ Contraction expanded.
¹⁴ Stubbe, *Clamor, rixa*, p. 16.
¹⁵ Ibid., pp. 17–18.
¹⁶ Ibid., pp. 8–10. Julius Caesar Scaliger (1484–1558), the Italian-born humanist

scholar, and Étienne Dolet (1509–46), the humanist scholar and polemicist, were both critics of the cult of Ciceronianism.

[17] See Letter 123 n. 11.

[18] See Letter 104 n. 13.

[19] In *Markes*, p. 14 (*EW* vii, pp. 387–9), Hobbes had commented on Wallis's use of colloquial proverbs ('*just the same to a cow's thumb*, a pretty adage') and his use of the word 'lurry' (a slang or dialect word for a patter, jingle or lesson learned by rote), and had rebutted Wallis's accusation of obscenity (against Hobbes's reference to the 'Devil's Arse' cavern in his poem *De mirabilibus pecci* (*Due Correction*, p. 3)) by citing Wallis's own use of the phrase 'now and anon too'.

[20] The university church of St Mary's, where official recantations were performed.

[21] 'I bear in my body the marks [of the Lord Jesus]' (Gal. 6: 7).

[22] Wallis, *Mens sobria*, pp. 15–17.

[23] = a written challenge, a letter of defiance (*OED* cartel 1).

[24] Contraction expanded.

[25] Hobbes's translation, *Eight Bookes of the Peloponnesian Warre*.

[26] See the Biographical Register, 'William Crooke'.

LETTER 126   [17/] 27 MAY 1657

François du Verdus to Hobbes, from Bordeaux

Chatsworth, Hobbes MSS, letter 40 (original).

Monsieur,

Il est bien de mon deuoyr que je vous rende mes remercimens tres humbles pour le beau present que vous m'aués fait de vostre Premiére Section des Elemens de la Philosophie traduite en Anglois auec les leçons de Wallis et Wardens, de leur pretandu Elencus de vostre Geometrie Et de leur Arithmétique des infinis.[1] vous croyiés peut estre que j'eusse reçeu ces liures il y a long temps Et si vous l'aués crû vous aués pû m'accuser de peu de reconoissançe de ne vous en auoyr pas rendu graçes. Mr Mylon m'écriuit ces fétes de Paques derniéres qu'encore qu'ils fussent partis de Londres depuis lan passé, il ne uenoit que de les receuoyr alors; Et moy je n'ay fait que traduire vos six Leçons depuis les auoyr reçeus. Il est uray que premierement je leus le libelle intitulé Elenchus &c. Et qu'a vous dire toutes choses je me sentis fort échauffé contre ces coquins; d'estre ainsi des gens de mauuaise foy de faire a tout bout de champ les sophistes; de déclamer et prescher. Et quand ils errent mesme dans les principes les plus simples s'attaquer ainsi à vous qui demontrés les verités les plus profondes: Mais j'en fus bien tot dehors: il me tardoit que je ne courasse a la uangeançe et a uray dire apres auoyr leu vos six Leçons je me trouué si bien uangé de leur insolançe qu'il me sambloit qui chocquoit tout homme aymant la verité: que bien loin d'y auoyr plus de mal de coeur; je fus rauy que par leur témérité ils vous eussent doné occasion d'écrire de si dignes choses. Certes il n'est pas possible a l'esprit de l'homme de prendre la chose de plus haut que ce que vous aués fait. Vous leur enseignés et a tout le Monde (persone ne l'ayant encore enseigné) qu'est ce que la Geometrie; quoy la dimension, et quelle chose la quantité. vous montrés vostre dessein plus uaste que celuy d'Euclide qui ne songeoit qu'aux cincq corps dont auoit parlé Platon:[2] Puis ayant trouué a redire a celles de ses definitions ou en effect il s'est trouué embarrassé, et expliqué le dessein des vostres, vous faites uoyr ce qu'il me souuient que je vous écriuis une fois Que c'est vous qui aués jetté les bons fondemens de toute la Geometrie. J'ay eté rauy en lisant ce bel Opuscule (opuscule pour le volume mais qui pour les choses merite le nom d'excellent Ouurage) d'y uoyr que je m'etois rancontré dans vos sentimens qund j'auois dit que la définition qu'Euclide done de point, a la prendre a la lettre definit le Rien; et que celle de la ligne droite est conceuë en des termes qui [>n'en] excitent point d'idée claire et distincte.[3] j'ay esté rauy quand j'ay trouué qu'alleguant le jugement de Mr Mylon sur uostre definition des par-alleles, et autres endroits qu'il auoit remarqués, vous luy ayiés fait justiçe le qualifiant un des premiers Geometres de Paris et vous louänt de ses maniéres;[4] Et pour ne vous rien dire de vos autres meditations profondes Comme de celle de la sciençe de la Composition des Raisons[5] que vous expliqués si bien; pour ne vous rien dire de vos railleries fines a vos sottes gens d'aduersaires comme quand vous leur faites doner des pieces de dix sols condensées en pieces de cincq;[6] pour ne point defendre au detail de cette belle Morale qui fait uostre sixiéme leçon: enfin pour dire tout en un mot J'ay eté rauy de tout. Dieu soit loüé qu'a cet age vous ayés tant de uigeur: J'inf ére de là Que vous aués encore une grande partie de vostre carriére a courir. Continués donc (Grand Homme) et nous donés bien tot vostre seconde Section.[7] Mais quand Elle sera imprimée ou quelque autre chose de vous que ce soit, quoy que j'aye dessein de traduire tout vous n'aués que faire de me mettre en peine de me l'enuoyer: Mais je vous oblige s'il vous plait par la bonté que vous aués pour moy [(][8]quoy que ie ne la mérite pas) que vous me doniés auis par lettre quand l'impression en sera acheuée. Et cela me suffira ayant trouué icy un Anglois de conoissance qui me les fera uenir seurement dans un vaisseau. Mais nous doneriés vous point encore autre chose? Je lisois naguere dans vostre Leuiatan vostre Table of the seuerall subjects of Knowledge:[9] Ne vous prendroit il point enuie de nous donner toute cette Philosophie? Ne fut ce qu'en quelques leçons (comme les six a Wallis) que vous nous donassiés un plan et un dessein des Traités d'Architecture, de Nauigation d'optique de Musique de Poetique de Rhetorique &c; Cela ouuriroit l'esprit aux gens de ce Siecle et tout le monde vous en seroit obligé. Car je ne vous parle pas de ranger en meilleur ordre les premiéres propositions de la Geometrie ce que vous apelés *actum agere* quand vous renuoyés vos lecteurs a Euclide a Archimede &c. Et toutefois il seroit a desirer qu'on eut ces choses bien digerées. Vous diray-j'icy une reflection que je fis sur ces deux propositions: la 1.ere Que la raison des espaces parcourus est composée de celle des uitesses et de celle des temps a les prendre directement; et la 2de que la raison des Temps est composée de la raison des espaces pris directement et de celle des uitesses prises au contraire? Considerant les espaces parcourus comme le produit de la multiplication des uitesses par les temps je reduis la premiere de ces propositions a la vostre Generale au Chapitre de l'analogisme[10] que la raison des effects est composée de celles de leurs causes: et la seconde fait uoyr que la raison de deux causes partiales de deux effects qui ont chacun deux causes, est composée de la raison des effects pris directement et de celle des deux autres causes prises au contraire. Cette reflection me poussa a desirer de sçauoyr [quelle][11] seroit la raison d'une Cause, a la Cause homologue d'un autre effect ou les effects auroient 3, 4, 5, 6 &c tel nombre qu'on uoudroit de coefficientes et je souhaiterois que vous me donassiés cette proposition en termes generaux et que vous la donassiés au public la jugeant come je fais de tres grand usage. Ce que j'ay encor a desirer de vous Monsieur c'est que vous m'expliquiés s'il vous plait les textes suyuants de l'anglois de vos Leçons ou mon Dictionaire est court.

A proportion is a what shall-i-call-it Isnesse or Sonesse of 1000 magnitudes &c[12] La proportion est une je ne sçay si je diray . . . . . . de deux grandeurs: je voy bien que vous composés Isnesse et Sonesse de Is et de So et qu'a ce compte Sonesse se pourroit traduire en francois mesmeté mais ayant cela en latin je trouuerrois peut estre le bon biais.

p. 11. l. derniere. Why Corpus motum a Body moued. *Ile* tell you. ie n'entans pas cet Ile. Et il est aussi p. 23. lig. 12 et 13. But why say you &c Ile tell you.[13]

p. 19 A pretty argument to flesh a yong scholar &c. *to flesh*?[14]

dans la mesme p. no argument taken from thence can become a

Doctor. Nul argument pris de là ne peut deuenir un Docteur. Vn argument deuient il un docteur?[15]

Et dans la p. 22. l. penult. but fall into a *loud Oncethmus*[16] je n'entans pas ces derniers mots. A cela prés j'ay tout compris et plus ie comprens uostre doctrine plus je fais de veux que Dieu vous conserue et que vous me fassiés toujours l'honneur de me croire

Monsieur
Vostre tres humble et tres obeissant seruiteur
duuerdus.

A Bordeaux le 27e May 1657.

[*postscript:*] J'oubliois de vous dire que pour entendre une de uos railleries je souhaiterois de scauoir en quoy c'est que vostre Astronome avoit obligé son Eueq. de Bramball.[17]

[*endorsed by Hobbes:*] May 27. 1657 mons^r du verdus

Translation of Letter 126

Sir,

I am duty-bound to send you my very humble thanks for the fine present which you sent me, your First Section of the Elements of Philosophy, translated into English, with the *Lessons* to Wallis and Ward on their so-called *Elenchus* [refutation] of your geometry and their *Arithmetica infinitorum*.[1] You may have thought that I had received these books a long time ago; and if you did think so, you may have accused me of a lack of gratitude in not having thanked you for them. M. Mylon wrote to me last Easter that although they had left London the previous year, he had only just received them then; and as for me, since receiving the books I have only translated your *Six Lessons*. It is true that I read the little book called *Elenchus* first; and, to tell the truth, I felt very enraged against those rascals, for being such liars, playing the sophist at every opportunity, declaiming and preaching, and, when they make mistakes even in the simplest principles, attacking you so— you who demonstrate the most profound truths. But I quickly got past that; it was time that I set off in pursuit of vengeance. And, to tell the truth, after reading your *Six Lessons* I felt so well revenged of their insolence (which I thought would shock any lover of truth) that, far from feeling sick at heart any longer, I was delighted that their impertinence had given you an opportunity to write such worthy things.

To be sure, it is not possible for the human mind to treat the subject at a higher level than you have done. You teach them, and everyone (since no one has taught it before), what geometry is, what dimension is, and what quantity is. Your plan goes much further than that of Euclid, who considered only the five bodies mentioned by Plato;[2] then, having found a way of reformulating those definitions on which Euclid was, in fact, in theoretical difficulties, and having explained the plan for your own definitions, you demonstrate (as I remember I once told you) that you are the person who has laid the true foundations for the whole of geometry. I was delighted, when reading that little work (little in size, but in terms of its contents an excellent work), to see there that your opinions had agreed with mine when I said that Euclid's definition of a point is, if taken literally, a definition of nothing, and that his definition of a straight line is conceived in terms which do not give rise to any clear and distinct idea of it.[3] I was delighted to find that, when you cite M. Mylon's opinion on your definition of parallels, and on other passages which he had commented on, you do him the justice of calling him one of the leading geometers of Paris, and extolling his courtesy.[4] And to say nothing of your other profound reflections, such as that on the method of compounding proportions,[5] which you explain so well; to say nothing of your witty jibes at your foolish opponents, as when you let them have ten-shilling coins condensed into five-shilling ones;[6] to say nothing in detail in defence of that fine piece of moral instruction which makes up your sixth lesson; finally, to sum it all up in a word, I was delighted by everything.

God be praised that you are so vigorous at your age: it makes me think that you still have a large part of your career ahead of you. So carry on, great man, and give us your Second Section[7] soon! But when it (or anything else by you) is printed, although I am planning to translate all your works, you need not bother to send it to me; but I require you, please, in your kindness towards me ([8]even though I do not deserve it), to let me know by a letter when the book has been printed. And that will be enough for me; for I have an English acquaintance here who will have them sent to me by boat, in safety. But won't you give us anything more? I was recently reading your 'Table of the several subjects of knowledge' in your *Leviathan*:[9] wouldn't you like to give us this entire body of philosophy? If you gave us an outline plan of treatises on architecture, navigation, optics, music, poetry, rhetoric, etc., even if it were only in a few lessons (like those six lessons to Wallis), it would awaken the minds of the people of this age, and everyone would be obliged to you for it. I do not mention arranging the first propositions of geometry in a better order, what you call 'doing that which has been done', when you send your readers back to Euclid, Archimedes, etc. Nevertheless it would be a desirable thing for these matters to be properly arranged.

Shall I tell you what I thought about the following two propositions: (1) the proportion of the distances traversed is composed of the direct proportion of the velocities and the direct proportion of the times; and (2) the proportion of the times is composed of the direct proportion of the distances and the inverse proportion of the velocities? Considering the distances traversed as the product of multiplying the velocities by the times, I reduce the first of these propositions to your general proposition, in your chapter on analogisms,[10] that the proportion of the effects is compounded of the proportions of their causes. And the second shows that the proportion of two partial causes of two effects, each of which has two causes, is compounded of the direct proportion of the effects and the inverse proportion of the two other causes. This thought made me want to know what[(11)] the proportion would be of one cause to the homologous cause of another effect, where the effects had three, four, five, six, or any number of coefficients. And I should like you to give me this proposition in general terms, and to give it to the public, since I think it would be of great use.

What I also wish, Sir, is that you would please explain to me the following passages from the English used in your Lessons, where my dictionary is inadequate.

'A proportion is a what-shall-I-call-it *Isnesse or Sonesse* of two magnitudes, etc.'[12]: I fully understand that you are compounding 'Isnesse' and 'Sonesse' out of 'Is' and 'So', and that on this account I could translate 'Sonesse' as 'mêmeté' in French; but if I had it in Latin I might perhaps be able to work out the best way of doing it.

Page 11, last line: 'Why "Corpus motum" a Body moved. *Ile* tell you'. I do not understand that 'Ile'. And it also occurs on page 23, lines 12 and 13: 'But why say you', etc. . . . 'Ile tell you'.[13]

Page 19 'A pretty argument to flesh a yong scholar', etc. *To flesh?*[14]

On the same page: 'no argument taken from thence can become a Doctor'. Does an argument turn into a Doctor?[15]

And on page 22, the penultimate line: 'but fall into a *loud Oncethmus*'.[16] I do not understand these last words.

Apart from that, I have understood everything. And the more I understand your teaching, the more prayers I make that God may preserve you—and that you may always do me the honour of believing me to be,

Sir,
Your most humble and obedient servant,
du Verdus

Bordeaux, 27 May 1657

[*postscript:*] I forgot to say that in order to understand one of your witty jibes I should like to know how your astronomer had obliged Bishop Bramhall.[17]

[1] Hobbes's *Of Body* and *Six Lessons* were published as a single volume in 1656; *Six Lessons* criticizes both Wallis and Ward, but the *Elenchus* and *Arithmetica infinitorum* were by Wallis alone. On Wallis and Ward see Letter 75 nn. 7, 8.

[2] The tetrahedron, cube, octahedron, icosahedron, and dodecahedron (Plato, *Timaeus*, 54).

[3] Letter 75; Hobbes discusses Euclid's definitions of a point and a line in *Six Lessons*, pp. 5–6 (*EW* vii, pp. 200–3).

[4] See Letter 76 n. 19.

[5] *Six Lessons*, pp. 8, 21–3 (*EW* vii, pp. 209–10, 243–9).

[6] *Six Lessons*, p. 14 (*EW* vii, p. 224).

[7] *De homine*, published in 1658.

[8] ~(omitted in MS.

[9] The table in ch. 9 of *Leviathan*.

[10] *De corpore*, XII.

[11] qu'elle MS.

[12] Rejecting Euclid's definition of proportion, Hobbes wrote: 'for to render rightly the Greek definition, we are to say in English, that proportion is a what-shall-I-call-it *isness*, or *soness* of two magnitudes, &c.; than which nothing can be more unworthy of Euclid' (*Six Lessons*, p. 8: *EW* vii, p. 208).

[13] *Six Lessons*, pp. 11, 23 (*EW* vii, pp. 218, 248).

[14] *Six Lessons*, p. 19 (*EW* vii, p. 237): to flesh = to incite, to animate (*OED* flesh *v*. 2c).

[15] *Six Lessons*, p. 19 (*EW* vii, p. 238).

[16] *Six Lessons*, p. 22 (*EW* vii, p. 247), 'To the sixteenth Article you bring no Argument, but fall into a loud *Oncethmus* (the special Figure wherewith you grace your Oratory)': ὀγκηθμός = the braying of an ass.

[17] Hobbes's obscure reference is in *Six Lessons*, p. 6 (*EW* vii, p. 205), where, discussing Euclid's definition of 'figure', he addresses Ward as follows: 'if you maintain it, [you will] lose the thanks of the Favour you have shewn (you the Astronomer) to Bishop *Bramhall*'.

LETTER 127   [5/] 15 JUNE 1657

Samuel Fermat to Hobbes, from Paris

Chatsworth, Hobbes MSS, letter 41 (original).

Monsieur,

Vous m'aues traittè d'une maniere si obligeante pendan le seiour que i'ai fait a Londres, que ie uous en serai redeuable tout le temps de ma uie, si i'osois esperer quelque occasion de uous le tesmoigner par quelque chose d'effectif ie m'estimerois trop heureux, quoiqu'il en soit ma recognoissance pour estre fort inutile n'en sera pas moins ueritable et moins grande, apres cela Monsieur permettes moi de uous exhorter a executer bientost le dessein que uous aues de publier le traictè de Homine et l'optique,[1] et de les faire imprimer a paris, bienque uos ouurages soint asses bons d'eux mesmes, uous scauès neantmoins que ces ornemens externieurs ne se doibuent pas toutafait negliger, Mr Duprat[2] qui outre la capacitè et le sçauoir qu'il a est fort uostre seruiteur, ie dirois adorateur si uous ne me l'auiès deffendu, se chargera du soin de l'impression, imagines uous ie uous prie que uostre liure est las d'estre reclus paucis ostendi gemit, et qu'apres auoir estè si longtemps enfermé il est iuste qu'il se produise et prostet sosiorum pumice mundus,[3] si ie puis uous rendre quelque seruice en cela et en toute autre chose ie uous fairai cognoistre que ie suis aussi parfaitement qu'homme du monde,

Monsieur,
Vostre tres humble et tres obeissant seruiteur,
Fermat

A Paris le 15me Juin 1657

[*postscript:*] J'ai donne ordre pour faire paier au libraire du dragon uert[4] les douze pieces que uous me fistes bailler, ie uous en remercie de tout mon coeur.

[*addressed:*] A Monsieur
Monsieur Hobbes a lenseigne du dragon uert au cimetiere sainct Paul, A Londres.

[*endorsed by James Wheldon:*] Monsr. Fermat June 15. 1657.

Translation of Letter 127

Sir,

You were so obliging to me during my stay in London that I shall be in your debt for the rest of my life. I should feel only too happy if I could dare to hope for some opportunity to express my indebtedness to you in some practical way; but whatever I may do, even if I can be of no use to you my gratitude will be no less strong or genuine. After which, Sir, allow me to urge you to carry out soon your plan to publish the treatise *De homine* and the Optics,[1] and to have them printed at Paris; although your works are good enough in themselves, these external embellishments should not, as you know, be completely neglected. M. du Prat[2] will take care of the printing; besides his ability and learning he is a great admirer of you (I would say 'worshipper', had you not forbidden it). Please imagine that your book is tired of being confined and 'grieves at being shown only to a few', and that it is only right that after being shut up for so long it should come out and 'go on sale, beautifully polished by the pumice of the Sosii'.[3] If I can be of any assistance to you in that or in anything else, I shall be able to show you that I am, Sir, as completely as anyone else in the world,

Your most humble and obedient servant,
Fermat

Paris, 15 June 1657

[*postscript:*] I have given instructions for the bookseller at the Green Dragon[4] to be paid for the twelve items you sent me, for which I thank you with all my heart.

[*addressed:*] Mr Hobbes, at the sign of the Green Dragon in St Paul's churchyard, in London.

---

[1] *De homine* (of which chs. II–IX are on optics) was published in 1658.
[2] Abraham du Prat.
[3] Horace, *Epistolae*, 1. 20. 1–4:

> Vertumnum Ianumque, liber, spectare videris,
> scilicet ut prostes Sosiorum pumice mundus.
> odisti clavis et grata sigilla pudico;
> paucis ostendi gemis et communia laudas

('You seem, my book, to be gazing towards Vertumnus and Janus [the booksellers' quarter in Rome], with the hope of going on sale, beautifully polished by the pumice of the Sosii [famous booksellers; pumice was used for smoothing books]. Keys and seals are hateful to you, though they please the modest; you grieve at being shown only to a few, and praise social life'.)

⁴ Andrew Crooke (see the Biographical Register, 'William Crooke').

LETTER 128   [11/] 21 JULY 1657

Claude Mylon to Hobbes, from Paris

Chatsworth, Hobbes MSS, letter 42 (original).

Monsieur

La solution que Je vous ay enuoyeé de la question de Monsr Du Verdus,¹ est veritable, vous l'eussiez esprouuée [>telle] dans les nombres si vous n'eussiez pas changé la proposition quand vous auez mis deux couples de causes produisant deux effects, et si vous n'eussiez pas fait faute dans le Calcul.

Car soient les deux causes A, et B produisant l'effect E. et les deux autres causes C et D produisant l'effect F. Je Dis que la cause A est a son homologue la Cause C. en raison composeé de la raison de l'effect E. à l'effect F. et de la raison de la cause D a son homologue la cause B. Car A soit 2 / B. 4 / C. 3 / D. 6 / E sera 8. / F sera 18. / soit fait Comme 6 à 4. ainsi 18 a vn quatrieme qui sera 12. (et non pas 9 comme Vous m'auez escrit)² Il est euident que la raison composeé de [>la raison de] 8 à 18. plus de la raison de 6 à 4. / sera egale à la raison de 8 à 12. Laquelle est egale a celle de 2. à 3. ou de A à C.

Demesme si les trois Causes A, B, C produisent l'effect G. et si les trois autres Causes [>D, E, F,] produisent l'effect H. vous trouuerez que la Cause A est à son homologue la Cause D. en raison Composée de ces trois raisons, G à H; E à B; et F a C. car si A est 3 / B 6. / C 2 /. D. 4. / E 3 / F 6. / G sera 36. / H sera 72. Il est certain que la raison de 3 a 4 est egale a ces trois raisons 36 a 72; 3 à 6; 6 à 2. car ces trois raisons estant assemblées font la raison de 36. a 48. c'est a dire 3. à 4. Ce sont Icy vos propres termes et nombres.

Or cette proposition n'est qu'un Corolloire de celle qu'euclide donne [*two words deleted*] dans les quantitez et dans les nombres,³ et vous dans les causes et [>leurs] effects. car si A; et B produisent E. et C et D produisent F vous dites fort bien que la raison de E à F est [composee *deleted* >egale a la so[mm]e⁴] des deux raisons A à C; et B à D. donc si on oste de part et d'autre la raison de B à D. on aura la raison de E à F moins la raison de B a D egales a la seule raison de A à C.

mais la raison de E à F moins la raison de B à D. est egale à la Raison de E à F plus la raison de D à B. donc la seule raison de A à C est egale a la raison de E à F plus la raison de D a B.

Je m'estonne de vous voir si fort attaché a vostre proposition, que [l'hypo *deleted*] *La semiperiferie du Cercle* [est *deleted* >soit] *egale a l'hypotenuse d'un triangle rectangle duquel vn des costez est le Rayon du cercle et l'autre Costé soit triple du mesme rayon.*

Elle est absolument fausse puisque des le 3.eme chifre elle soit hors des Limites d'Archimede, et ny vous ny qui que ce soit au monde ne la peut pas demonstrer.

Car posant le diametre du Cercle 100. Selon Archimede la Circonference sera plus petite que 315. et elle sera plus grande que 314. or le Rayon du Cercle sera 50. / Son quarré sera 2500. / Le quarré de l'hypothenuse, [qui *deleted* >(lequel quarré] est dectuple de celuy du Rayon) sera 25000. / Sa racine quarreé foible sera 158. dont le quarré est 24964. donc 158 sera vostre hypotenuse [>foible,] laquelle estant doubleé fait 316. qui doit selon vostre Conte estre egale a la Circonference entiere, vous voyez que 316 est plus fort que 315. qui est plus grand que la Circonference selon l'Archimede. Croyez moy perdez cette penseé, ou ne la communiquez a personne si vous voulez conseruer vostre reputation a laquelle Je m'Interesse fort estant de tout mon Coeur

Monsieur
Vostre treshumble et tresobeissant seruiteur
Mylon.

A paris ce 21e Juillet 1657.

Translation of Letter 128

Sir,

The solution which I sent you to M. du Verdus's question[1] is correct; you would have seen that it was numerically correct if you had not changed the proposition when you posited two pairs of causes producing two effects, and if you had not made an error in your calculation.

For let the two causes be A and B, producing the effect E; and let the two other causes be C and D, producing the effect F. I say that the cause A is to its counterpart cause C in the compound ratio of the ratio of effect E to effect F and the ratio of cause D to its counterpart cause B.

For if A is 2; B, 4; C, 3; and D, 6; E will be 8; and F will be 18. As 6 is to 4, let 18 be to a fourth term, which will be 12 (and not 9, as you said in your letter to me).[2] It is evident that the compound ratio of the ratio of 8 to 18 and the ratio of 6 to 4 will be equal to the ratio of 8 to 12—which is equal to that of 2 to 3, or of A to C.

Similarly, if the three causes A, B, and C produce the effect G; and if the three other causes D, E, and F produce the effect H; you will find that cause A is to its counterpart, cause D, in the compound ratio of these three ratios: G to H; E to B; and F to C. For if A is 3; B, 6; C, 2; D, 4; E, 3; and F, 6; G will be 36; and H will be 72. It is certain that the ratio of 3 to 4 is equal to these three ratios: 36 to 72; 3 to 6; 6 to 2. For these three ratios, when put together, make the ratio of 36 to 48—in other words, 3 to 4. These are the terms and numbers which you yourself used.

However, this proposition is merely a corollary of the proposition which Euclid gives concerning quantities and numbers,[3] and which you give concerning causes and their effects. For if A and B produce E, and C and D produce F, you are quite correct to say that the ratio of E to F is equal to the product[4] of the two ratios A to C and B to D. So if one takes away the ratio of B to D one will be left with the ratio of E to F divided by the ratio of B to D, being equal to the sole ratio of A to C. But the ratio of E to F divided by the ratio of B to D is equal to the ratio of E to F multiplied by the ratio of D to B. So the sole ratio of A to C is equal to the ratio of E to F multiplied by the ratio of D to B.

I am very surprised to see that you are so strongly attached to your proposition that 'the semi-circumference of a circle is equal to the hypotenuse of a right-angled triangle of which one side is the radius of the circle and the other is three times that radius'.

It is absolutely false, because from as early as the third figure it exceeds the limits set by Archimedes; and neither you nor anyone in the world, whoever it may be, can demonstrate it to be true.

For suppose the diameter of the circle to be 100. According to Archimedes the circumference will be less than 315, and more than 314. Now, the radius of the circle will be 50: its square will be 2,500. The square of the hypotenuse (which is ten times that of the radius) will be 25,000. Its weak square root will be 158, the square of which is 24,964. Therefore 158 will be your weak hypotenuse, which, multiplied by 2, is 316. That, according to your calculation, must be equal to the entire circumference. As you can see, 316 is greater than 315, which according to Archimedes is greater than the circumference. Believe me, get rid of this idea, or do not communicate it to anyone, if you want to preserve your reputation—in which I have a strong interest, being, with all my heart,

Sir,
Your most humble and obedient servant,
Mylon

Paris, 21 July 1657

The parentheses in this letter are in square brackets in the MS.
    Commentary on Letter 128. 'Two causes A and B produce the effect E' means E = A.B, i.e. E is the product of the two numbers A and B. After some elementary observations about ratios, Mylon turns to Hobbes's attempt to square the circle. Hobbes believes that $\pi = \sqrt{10}$ (see Letter 200). Mylon shows that $\sqrt{10} > 3.16$, and invokes Archimedes' bounds $3.14 < \pi < 3.15$ to refute him. *G.M.*

[1] See Letter 126, pp. 469, 472.
[2] Hobbes's letter has not apparently survived.
[3] Euclid, *Elements*, 5. 17.
[4] Contraction expanded.

LETTER 129   [29 JULY/] 8 AUGUST 1657

Thomas de Martel to Hobbes, from Paris

Chatsworth, Hobbes MSS, letter 43 (original).
Printed in von Brockdorff, 'Fünf Briefe', pp. 16–17.

Monsieur

Il y à bien longtemps que Je vous escriuis sur le subiet de M.ʳ Fermat[1] auec qui Je doibs partager toutes les obligations qu'il vous a, mais aiant donné ma letre et la sienne à un honneste homme qui allant voir Londres auoit esté bien aise de se charger de vous rendre ce que Mʳ fermat vous deuoit pour auoir occasion de voir vne personne de vostre merite et de vostre reputation, en quoi J'estois bien aise de vous espargner la peine d'aller vous mesme chez un banquier receuoir cette petite somme. Il est arriué que cet honneste homme à differé de temps en temps son depart, et aiant enfin rompu son voiage m'a rendu les letres et l'argent que Je lui auois mis en main ce qui m'a obligé pour ne retarder pas plus longtemps vostre paiemᵗ de vous le remettre par letre de change sur des banquiers asses cognus pour scauoir aisemᵗ leur demeure, bien fasché de vous donner la peine d'aller chez eux,

Permettez moi au reste de vous dire ce que vous eussiez veu dans ma premiere letre sur ce subiet, que par cette generosité vous obligez tous ceux qui vous cognoissent dans la vie ciuile de publier à tous ceux qui ne vous estim^t que par vos escrits que vostre vertu esgale vostre science, et que vous en pratiquez les principes aussi bien que vous les enseignez, J'en ai plus d'experience, qu'aucun autre, mais les recentes me les rendent toutes si presentes que Je ne puis [me *deleted*] assez admirer en moi mesme et proposer aux autres vn exemple si releué de bonté, et de courtoisie, sed apud alios ista potius quam apud te Celebranda, quo nihil libentius à me semper Impetrabo,^{2} ce qui m'empesche de vous en dire dauantage, M^r. Fermat est parti il y à peu de Jours m'aiant fort recommandé de pouruoir à vostre satisfaction, et de vous asseurer de sa part qu'il n'y à personne au monde qu'il estime dauantage et à qui il se croie plus oblige de lui auoir accordé vostre conuersation si ciuilem^t, ne contant pour rien ce qu'il à veu en Angleterre apres vous, Je fais estat de le suiure bien tost pour m'aller confiner pour quelque temps chez moi ou loin d'affaires Je philosopherai à loisir auec vous, c'est à dire dans vos escrits me flatant tousiours de l'esperance de vous aller voir, et de vous faire cognoistre que J'ai faict mon plus grand estude auec vous, dans ce dessein permettez moi de vous solliciter pour mon Interest part.[iculie]r^3 de publier vostre ouurage, de Homine, et de souhaiter que vostre Leuiathan traduit soit bien tost donné au public, ut apud quamplurimos gloriâ tuâ fruaris, et que ce soit [> ad] longos annos^4 et en parfaicte santé, Je suis de tout mon coeur

Monsieur
Vostre treshumble et tresobeissant seruiteur
De Martel

A Paris ce 8 Aoust 1657

[*addressed:*] A Monsieur
    Monsieur Hobbes au Dragon vert prez le Cimetiere St Paul A Londres.

[*address endorsed in another hand:*] Je prie M.^{r} mon Frere de prendre la peine de rendre la presente en main propre
    Augier^5

[*endorsed by James Wheldon:*] Monsr Martell. Aug. 8. 1657

Translation of Letter 129

Sir,

I wrote to you rather a long time ago about M. Fermat,[1] with whom I must share all the obligations which he has received from you. I gave my letter and his to a worthy gentleman who was going to visit London, and who was happy to take responsibility for delivering what M. Fermat owed you so that he might have the opportunity to see someone of your worth and your reputation. I was very happy with this arrangement, because it would save you from having to go to a banker in person in order to receive this small sum. But as it happened this worthy gentleman kept postponing his departure, and having finally cancelled his trip he gave me back the letters and money which I had entrusted to him. So, to prevent any further delay in paying you, I have been obliged to send you the money by a letter of exchange on some bankers. They are well known, so they will not be hard to find; but it greatly upsets me to put you to the trouble of going to them.

Otherwise, allow me to tell you what you would have read in my first letter on this topic, namely that your generosity obliges all of us who know you in civil life to declare to all those whose high opinion of you is based only on your writings, that your virtue is as great as your knowledge, and that you practise moral principles just as well as you teach them. I have had more experiences of this than anyone else; but my recent experiences make them all so vivid in my mind that I can never sufficiently admire for my own part, or propose to other people, such an exalted example of goodness and courtesy. 'But those things should be praised to others, rather than to you: and there is nothing I should rather do'[2]—which prevents me from saying anything more on that subject.

M. Fermat left a few days ago, having strongly urged me to make arrangements to pay the debt you are owed, and to assure you on his part that there is no one in the world whom he values more highly than you, or who has obliged him more by so civilly granting him his company; he says that after seeing you, the other things he saw in England were of no account. I am getting ready to follow him soon, to go and confine myself for a while at home; there, far removed from public business, I shall philosophize at leisure with you—I mean, by studying your writings. I still flatter myself with the hope that I shall come and visit you, to let you know that my deepest studies have been with you. With that in mind, allow me to urge you, out of my own

481

private[(3)] interest, to publish your work *De homine*, and allow me to wish that your *Leviathan* should be published in translation very soon, 'so that you may enjoy your fame among very many people', and that you may live 'long years'[4] and in perfect health. I am, Sir, with all my heart,

Your most humble and obedient servant,
de Martel

Paris, 8 August 1657

[*addressed:*] To Mr Hobbes, at the Green Dragon near St Paul's churchyard, London.

[*address endorsed in another hand:*] I beg my brother to take the trouble to deliver this letter in person.
Augier.[5]

---

[1] This refers not to Letter 124, but to some subsequent letter, now apparently lost.
[2] Source unidentified.
[3] Contraction expanded.
[4] Source unidentified.
[5] Probably René Augier, who had worked as an agent and chargé d'affaires at the British Embassy in Paris throughout the 1630s; he was the chief diplomatic representative of Britain in Paris, 1644–51, 1655–6 (Bell, *Handlist of British Representatives*, pp. 109, 112–13).

LETTER 130   [7/] 17 AUGUST 1657

Thomas de Martel to Hobbes, from Paris

Chatsworth, Hobbes MSS, letter 44 (original).
Printed in von Brockdorff, 'Fünf Briefe', pp. 17–18.

Monsieur
   Il me semble que Je ne scaurois mieux tesmoigner à quel prix Je mets l'honneur que J'ai de vous estre cognu qu'en le communiquant à ceux que Je desire le plus d'obliger, ce que Je fais neantmoins auec les precautions que J'y doibs apporter, ne vous demandant ces graces qu'en faueur des personnes de merite, et qui en scauent vser auec discretion, et J'ose croire que vous n'auez pas esté mal satisfaict Jusques ici de ceux qui vous ont veu de mon part, Je vous responds que vous ne le serez pas de Mr de Moncan[1] qui vous rendra celle ci, Il m'honore de son amitié, et la mienne estant trop peu de chose

J'emprunte volontiers la vostre pour recognoistre la sienne dignem! de sorte que vous m'obligerez beaucoup de la lui accorder, Il vous tesmoignera aussi bien que M.ʳ fermat le regret que J'ai de n'estre pas assez maistre de moi mesme pour passer la mer vniquemᵗ pour vous aller voir, et vous rendre cette preuue du ressentimᵗ pour vous de tant de bontez que vous auez eues pour moi, et de l'estime que Je fais de vous, Je satisfairai en cela ma passion tost ou tard, et cependᵗ Je ne cesserai de faire des voeux pour vostre santé, J'ai fort resioui M.ʳ Du Bosc des bonnes nouuelles que Je lui en ai données comme il m'escrit du 13 de Sedan, permettez au reste à mon Impatience de vous exhorter de publier vostre partie De Homine afin que nous aions vostre philosophie complete et que vostre gloire le soit aussi d'auoir trauaillé si vtilemᵗ pour le genre humain en reglant si bien sa conduite, et lui aprennant la verité, Je m'aduouerai tousiours en ces deux points le plus redevable de tous ceux qui vous prendront pour M[aîtr]ᵉ². et quand Je n'en aurois autre subiet Je serois toute ma vie plus qu'aucun autre

Monsieur
vostre treshumble et tresobeissᵗ seruiteur
De Martel

A Paris ce 17 Aoust 1657

[*postscript:*] sil faut responce [Je destran.?] chez Mʳ Louet³ tailleur d'habits pour femme aux armes de france a lescu de france

[*addressed:*] Monsieur Hobbes au dragon vert au Cimetiere Sᵗ Paul A Londres

[*endorsed by James Wheldon:*] Mons.ʳ de Martell. Aug. 17. 1657

Translation of Letter 130

Sir,

I feel that there can be no better way of showing how highly I value the honour of your acquaintance than by sharing it with those whom I am most eager to oblige. I do this, nevertheless, with due precaution, only asking this favour of you on behalf of people who are worthy of it, and who will know how to use it with discretion. I have the temerity to think that you have not been dissatisfied up till now with the people I have introduced to you. I assure you that you will not be dissatisfied either with M. de Moncan,¹ who will bring you this letter. He honours me with his friendship, and since my friendship is too slight a thing, I am glad to borrow yours in order to reciprocate properly; so you will greatly oblige me if you give him your friendship.

He, like M. Fermat, will assure you of my sadness at the fact that my time is not sufficiently at my own disposal to permit me to cross the sea just in order to visit you, and to prove to you thereby both my admiration for you and my gratitude for all the kindnesses you have shown me. My desire to do that will be satisfied sooner or later; and meanwhile I shall not cease to pray for your good health. I gave great pleasure to M. du Bosc with the good news I sent him about your health when he wrote to me on the 13th from Sedan.

Please allow my impatient spirit to urge you to publish your section *De homine*, so that we may have your complete philosophical system, and so that you may have the glory of having laboured so usefully for the human race, giving it such good guidance for its behaviour, and teaching it the truth. On those two points I shall always declare that I am the most indebted to you of all those who acknowledge you as their Master[2]; and when I had nothing else to write about I would remain for all my life, more than anyone else,

Sir,
Your most humble and obedient servant,
de Martel

Paris, 17 August 1657

[*postscript:*] In case of reply, I am staying with M. Louet,[3] a dress-maker, at the Arms of France, or the French Coat of Arms.

[*addressed:*] To Mr Hobbes, at the Green Dragon in St Paul's churchyard, London.

---

[1] Unidentified.
[2] Contraction expanded.
[3] Unidentified.

LETTER 131   29 AUGUST/8 SEPTEMBER 1657

Claude Mylon to Hobbes, from Paris

BL MS Add. 32553, fo. 35 (original).

Monsieur

Vn voyage d'un mois a retardé la response que Je deuois a la vostre du 22. Juillet, vieux stile:[1] par laquelle vous persistez a n'estre pas conuaincu de la fausseté de vostre quadrature; vous ayant reduit a l'Archimede Je croyois vous auoir entierement satisfait, mais puisque vous ne deuenez pas d'accord que luy et les autres Cyclometres ayent calculé exactement les Costez des polygones Reguliers Inscrits et circonscrits au cercle, Je n'ay plus rien a vous dire sinon que vous veriffiez vous mesme leur calcul, pour dire en quoy Ils ont faillis; Si vous trouuez leur faute, vous serez plus clairuoyant que tous les Geometres depuis deux mil ans. Je n'oppose pas l'authorité de tous ces Messieurs a vostre proposition, J'oppose la verité qui ne peut Jamais estre destruite si Ils l'ont vne fois bien demonstrée. Vous n'en serez pas plus fort quand Je vous accorderay 1°. que le quadrant est diuisible en tel nombre de secteurs egaux qu'on voudra. 2°. qu'on peut supposer vn secteur *abc* estre vne partie Centmillemillieme du quadrant. 3°. que ce

secteur *abc* est terminé en vn point *a*. 4°. que les Centmille[>mille] secteurs dont *abc* [>en] est vn, estant mis ensemble constituent le quadrant. Et enfin que les centmillemille points *a*, constituent aussi le Centre entier du quadrant. ne croyez en cecy [>Par les Indiuisibles] auoir plus d'auantage que dans les deux traittez du mesme sujet que vous m'auez enuoyé, qui commencoient par des propositions veritables, que vous auez conduites par des routes esgarées pour tomber a vostre conclusion. J'auoüe encor qu'on ne descouurira pas aysément vostre erreur par vn tastonnement Mechanique des Chordes des parties de l'arc de 45 degrez, mais vous mesme examinez le par les nombres les plus grands, trouuant la Chorde d'vne minute, ou d'vne seconde et en ayant multiplié le nombre autant de fois qu'elle est contenue dans vostre arc de 45 degrez, compariez [> en] le produit auec la droite *ca* qui est le quart de la droite qui peut dix fois le Rayon, mais Il faudra que trouuiez vous mesme le nombre de Cette Chorde d'vne minute ou d'vne seconde, Car les tables vous seront suspectes. Mais pour le plus court; vous quitterez cette meditation (si vous me croyez) qui a esté vne pierre d'achoppement a tant de personnes qui vous ont precedé, et vous appliquerez a des sujets qui sont plus ayses et me tiendrez toujours pour

Monsieur
Vostre treshumble et tresobeissant seruiteur
Mylon

A Paris ce 8ᵉ Septembre. 1657. stile Nouueau.

[*addressed:*] To Mons.ʳ Andrejo Crooke At the greene Dragon In paules Churchyeard. for mons.ʳ hobbes. London.

[*endorsed by James Wheldon:*] Mons.ʳ Mylon Sept. 8. 1657

Translation of Letter 131

Sir,
    Travelling for a month has delayed the reply which I owed to your letter of 22 July (Old Style),[1] in which you persist in your failure to be persuaded that your squaring of the circle is false. Having reduced your argument to Archimedes, I thought I must have satisfied you completely. But since you do not agree that he and the other circle-measurers calculated exactly the sides of the regular polygons which circumscribe the circle and are inscribed within it, I have nothing more to tell you except that you should check their calculation yourself, in order to say where their mistake lies. If you find their mistake, you will be more clear-sighted than all the geometers of the last two thousand years. I am not using the authority of all these people to oppose your proposition: I am using the truth, which, once they have properly demonstrated it, can never be destroyed.
    Your argument will be no stronger if I concede, first, that the quadrant can be divided into as many equal sectors as you wish; secondly, that one can posit a sector *abc*, being one hundred-millionth part of the quadrant; thirdly, that this sector *abc* terminates in the point

a; fourthly, that the hundred million sectors, of which *abc* is one, constitute the quadrant when they are put together; and finally, that the hundred million points *a* also constitute the entire centre of the quadrant. Do not think that this way of doing things, by indivisibles, will help you any more than the way you use in the two treatments of the same subject which you sent me; there you started with true propositions, which were then led astray by you in order to arrive at your conclusion. Let me tell you also that it will not be easy to discover your mistake by a mechanical exploration of the chords of parts of the arc of 45 degrees. But examine it yourself, using the largest possible numbers: find the chord of one minute, or one second, multiply that figure by the number of times it is contained in your arc of 45 degrees, and compare the product with the straight line *ca*, which is a quarter of the straight line which can be ten times the radius. But you will have to work out the figure for that chord of one minute or one second, because the printed tables will be unreliable for your purposes.

But the quickest method you should follow is this: stop thinking about this subject (if you will believe me), which has been a stumbling-block to so many of your predecessors, and apply yourself to more tractable matters. In this way you will always keep me, Sir, as

Your most humble and most obedient servant,
Mylon

Paris, 8 September (New Style)

[*addressed: see text*]

---

[1] This letter (evidently Hobbes's reply to Letter 128) has not apparently survived.

LETTER 132 [late 1657]

Claude Mylon to Hobbes [from Paris?]

Chatsworth, Hobbes MSS, letter 81 (original).

Monsieur

Je m'estonne de ce que vous ne doutez pas de la verité de vostre conclusion,[1] a laquelle vous dites auoir esté conduit par tant de voyes, Je ne voudrois point d'autre demonstration pour la combatre, Je me contenterois de scauoir qu'elle est contraire aux propositions fort bien demonstrées d'Archimede, de Snellius,[2] d'hugenius et de tant d'autres, mais [>puisque] vous desirez que J'examine encor cette 3eme proposition dont vous en auez tiré beaucoup d'autres, Je vous satisfois a La charge que vous ne vous direz pas d'Injure; vos deux premieres[3] sont vrayes quoyque dans La 1ere vous ayez obmis a prouuer que MC coupera BD au mesme point O qui est L'Intersection de BD et QS. sans tirer QS, J'en ay mis vne demonstration en mot par deux triangles semblables BOC, DON. pour venir a La 3eme qui est vostre fondamentale, J'y trouue deux fautes dont chacune suffit pour La [*word deleted*] destruire; La 1ere est qu'aprez auoir dit par supposition ou concession, *Si COM major est quam Semiperipheria BDK, erit ex parte B, recta Com minor Ipsâ semiperipheria BDK; ergò ex eadem parte B. omnis recta* [>Com] *ducta a puncto C ad rectam MB, minor erit Ipsâ semiperiph.* vous voyez que cela ne conclud pas, car entre COM et Com Je puis tirer vne Infinitè de Lignes droites de ce coste [qui *deleted* >dont les vnes] seront plus petites que La mesme demicirconference, Les autres plus grandes, [donc *deleted* >et] entre Les vnes et Les autres Il y en aura vne qui sera egale a La mesme demicirconference. c'est la mesme chose de L'autre costé de CM. La 2de faute est, quand Il seroit vray de dire, *Si COM major est semjperiph.â BDK Sequitur omnem rectam Com ductam a puncto C ad BM* [esse minorem *deleted*] *versus partes puncti B, esse minorem* [Ipsâ *deleted*] *semicircumferentiâ BDK; si autem supponatur COM minor Ipsâ semicircumf. BDK sequitur omnem rectam Com, ductam ab eodem puncto* [C *blotted*] *ad rectam BM ex alterâ parte Ipsius COM, esse majorem semicircumf.o Ergo recta COM aequalis est eaedem* [> semi] *circumferentiae.* ceste argumentation seroit fausse. mais elle seroit bonne en cette sorte, *Si recta COM talis sit vt ab vnâ parte nempe puncti B, omnis ducta recta Com semper sit minor semiperimetro, Ex altera autem parte semper major, tunc necessariô sequeretur rectam COM esse Aequalem semiperimetro:* C'est ce que vous ne demontrez pas. je me suis Icy peut estre trop estendu pour vous, et Je vous en ay assez escrit en Interligne et en marge de vostre manuscrit que Je vous renuoye; ce que J'en ay fait a esté pour ne rien Espargner a vous esclaircir, Je vous suis beaucoup obligé de La confiance que vous auez en moy et vous priant d'employer plus vtilement vos heures qu'a ce sujet ou tant de personnes ont achoppé, Je vous assure que je suis de tout mon Coeur

Monsieur
Vostre tres humble et tres obeissant Seruiteur
Mylon.

[*addressed:*] To Mons.ʳ Andreio Crooke[4] At the Greene Dragon in Paules Churyeard. For Mons.ʳ Hobbes. London.

[*endorsed by James Wheldon:*] Monsꞓ Mylon

Translation of Letter 132

Sir,
   I am amazed that you do not doubt the truth of your conclusion,[1] which you say you were drawn to by so many arguments. I should not wish for any demonstration to overturn it; I should find it sufficient to know that it is contrary to propositions which have been thoroughly demonstrated by Archimedes, Snel,[2] Huygens, and so many others. But since you want me to give further attention to that third proposition, from which you have derived many others, I am satisfying your request, on condition that you will not take offence.
   Your first two propositions[3] are true, although in the first of them you have omitted to prove that MC will intersect BD at the same point O where BD intersects QS. Without drawing QS, I have demonstrated it verbally by means of two similar triangles, BOC and DON.
   Now for the third proposition, which is your foundation. I have found two mistakes, each of which is sufficient to destroy the proposition. The first is this: after saying, as a supposition or concession, 'If COM is greater than the semi-circumference BDK', ['you say that'] 'there will be a straight line from B, the line Com, which is smaller than that semi-circumference BDK; therefore every straight line Com from B, drawn from the point C to the straight line MB, will be smaller than that semi-circumference.' You must see that that conclusion does not follow. For between COM and Com I can draw an

infinite number of straight lines from that side, of which some will be smaller than that semi-circumference, and others will be greater. And between them there will be one line which will be equal to that semi-circumference. And the same applies to the other side of CM.

The second mistake is as follows. Whilst it would be true to say, 'If COM is greater than the semi-circumference BDK, it follows that every straight line Com drawn from the point C to BM, in the direction of the point B, will be smaller than the semi-circumference BDK; if however COM is supposed to be smaller than that semi-circumference BDK, it follows that every straight line Com, drawn from the same point to the straight line BM from the other part of the same COM, will be greater than the semi-circumference. Therefore the straight line COM is equal to that same semi-circumference': this argument is false. But it would be correct if it were put like this: 'If the straight line COM is such that from one side, namely from the point B, every straight line Com is always smaller than the semi-circumference, but every straight line drawn from the other side is always greater, then it will necessarily follow that the straight line COM is equal to the semi-circumference.' That is what you fail to demonstrate. I have dwelt on this, perhaps, more than you would have liked, and I have written at quite some length about it between the lines and in the margin of your manuscript, which I am returning to you. I have done this in order to spare no effort to clear the matter up for you. I am much obliged to you for the trust you have in me; and, begging you to spend your time more usefully than on this topic, on which so many people have come to grief, I assure you that I am, Sir, with all my heart,

Your most humble and most obedient servant,
Mylon

[*addressed: see text*]

This letter, having lost its outer sheet, is undated; it evidently answers Hobbes's reply (now apparently lost) to Letter 131, and was thus probably written in Sept. or Oct. 1657.

[1] Hobbes's proposition that 'the semi-circumference of a circle is equal to the hypotenuse of a right-angled triangle of which one side is the radius of the circle and the other is three times that radius' (see Letter 128).

[2] Willebrord Snel (1591–1626), Professor of Mathematics at Leiden University (1615); his geometrical work *Cyclometrus* was published in 1621.

[3] Hobbes's three numbered propositions have not apparently survived; nor has the diagram to accompany this letter.

[4] See the Biographical Register, 'William Crooke'.

LETTER 133   [22 JANUARY/] 1 FEBRUARY 1658

Samuel Sorbière to Hobbes, from Paris

MS unknown.
Printed in Sorbière, *Lettres et discours*, pp. 631–6; *HOC* iv, pp. 513–16.

MONSIEVR,

Pendant mon seiour à Paris[1] ie n'ay cessé de vous y souhaiter, pour le particulier aduantage que i'eusse retiré de vostre conuersation: mais maintenant ie vous y souhaitterois aussi pour l'interest du Public, qui auroit occasion de se preualoir de vostre presence en l'Assemblée dont ie vous ay parlé. Ie vous ay dit en mes Lettres precedentes, que Monsieur de Montmor[2] m'ayant fait l'honneur de me communiquer le dessein qu'il auoit de receuoir chez luy vn certain nombre de personnes choisies pour s'entretenir de Questions naturelles, ou d'experiences & de belles inuentions, il me donna charge de faire vn proiect de la maniere en laquelle on pourroit former des Conferences, qui tournassent à l'vtilité publique, aussi bien qu'au diuertissement de ceux qui y entreroint. Ie dressay auec Monsieur du Prat[3] quelques Articles, qui furent presentées à la premiere Assemblée qui se trouua formée de bon nombre de personnes curieuses. Ils y furent examinés, auec quelque contestation de la part de ceux qui ne vouloient pas escrire. Ie vous les enuoye, puis que vous me les demandés; & ie seray bien aise qu'ils soient veus de tout le monde: pource qu'ils tesmoigneront nostre bonne intention, & qu'ils ne seront peut estre pas inutiles à ceux qui voudront s'appliquer aux mesmes recherches que nous nous sommes proposées. Le siecle de fer ne durera pas tousiours; la Paix reuiendra à son tour visiter la Terre; les Muses ne seront pas éternellement[4] exilées; les Arts resusciteront; les Sciences reprendront leur place; & vne plus douce influence des Astres, que celle qui ne produit auiourd'huy que des soldats & des Capitaines, produira derechef des Gilberts,[5] des Baccons, des Haruaees, des Fra Paolo,[6] des Galilées, des Mersennes, des Descartes, & des Gassendis. Il est de la gloire de nostre age que ces Illustres personnes apprenent à leur retour, que malgré la barbarie au milieu de laquelle nous auons vescu, il s'est trouué vn assés grand nombre d'honnestes gens qui n'ont pas laissé d'aimer les estudes Philosophiques, & ausquels il n'a pas tenu qu'ensuite des grandes ouuertures que ceux que ie viens de nommer nous ont faites, les choses ne soient mieux allées qu'elles ne vont pour l'aduancement de toutes nos cognoissances. Quand ie vous auray nommé vne partie de ceux qui composent nostre Assemblée, vous m'aduouërés qu'il seroit mal aisé d'en composer ailleurs vne pareille, encore qu'on la choisist parmi tout ce qu'il y a de curieux hors de Paris, & peut estre hors de ce Royaume. Mais il vaut mieux vous faire voir promptement ce que vous desirés.

Art. I. *Que le but des Conferences ne sera point le vain exercice de l'esprit à des subtilités inutiles; mais qu'on se proposera tousiours la plus claire cognoissance des oeuures de Dieu, & l'aduancement des commodités de la vie, dans les Arts & les Sciences qui seruent à les mieux establir.*

II. *Que celuy qui preside establira, de l'aduis de la Compagnie, la question pour la conference prochaine, & priera nommement deux personnes qu'il en iugera des mieux informées de rapporter leur sentiment, laissant aux autres la liberté d'en dire leurs pensees.*

III. *Que ces aduis seront leus & donnés par escrit, en termes courts & pleins de raisonnement, sans aucune amplification ny authorités.*

IV. *Qu'ils seront leus sans interruption; les deux personnes choisies ayans les premieres produit les leurs.*

V. *Qu'apres toutes les lectures chacun dira par ordre, & en peu de mots, les obiections ou les confirmations sur ce qui aura esté leu. Et qu'apres la responce, on n'insistera pas dauantage, sans la permission particuliere de celuy qui preside.*

VI. *Que l'on pourra enuoyer son aduis sur la question proposée, quand on ne pourra pas venir en personne.*

VII. *Que l'Assemblée priera ceux qui en ont occasion, d'entretenir corre-spondance auec les sçauans de France & des pays estrangers; afin d'apprendre d'eux ce qui se prepare, ou ce qui est desia publié, ou decouuert dans les Arts & les sciences; dequoy l'Assemblée sera informée en se separant.*

VIII. *Que l'Assemblée estant formée, on n'y admettra plus personne qui ne le demande,* [que][7] *par le consentement des deux tiers de la compagnie presente, lors qu'on en fera la proposition.*

IX. *Qu'on n'admettra point d'autres que les Membres de l'Assemblée dans le lieu de la Conference, qui sera toute composée de personnes curieuses des choses naturelles, de la Medecine, des Mathematiques, des Arts liberaux, & des Mechaniques; si ce n'est qu'auparauant on ait demandé permission d'y amener quelque homme de merite.*

Sur ce plan nous auons commencé de bastir nos Conferences, & desia nous y auons traicté methodiquement, & auec vne parfaicte exactitude beaucoup de choses importantes. Mais vous nous manqués au besoin, MONSIEVR, aussi bien que le bon Pere Minime,[8] & le sage Monsieur

Gassendi, auquel ie m'adresse en vne Preface que ie mettray au deuant de ses oeuures, & en laquelle ie parle de nostre Assemblée. *Adsis tu quoque praesens, optime Gassende, vt modestiae & sapientiae tuae semper omnium animis obuersetur imago!*[9] *Equidem post edita opera tua nihil deerit quominus te totum videamus; neque tantùm vigilijs tuis & [eruditione]*[10] *tua fruamur; sed & oculis perpetuo in sapientiam tuam defixis, illà potiore tui parte imitemur veram, cuius tam clarum exemplum praebuisti, philosophandi rationem. Intereris quoque, quà Terrae patent, post [innumerabilem]*[11] *annorum seriem studijs hominum ad bonam mentem contendentium, vt si qui reperiantur olim quos iuuet adhuc barbarè vel [meteoreticè]*[12] *philosophantium lectio, vnum illud Ciceronis in redargutionem vsurpari possit; Quae est autem ista inter homines tanta dementia; frugibus inuentis, vt glande vescantur.*[13] Dieu vueille que ie sois Prophete, au souhait que ie fais qu'on imite la Modestie de M. Gassendi, que son esprit doux & tranquille regne dans nostre Assemblée, & que cette nouuelle Academie ne trompe point les esperances que peuuent donner les reglemens que ie vous enuoye. Mais il est bien à craindre, comme i'auois commencé de dire, que vous ne nous manquiés au besoin, aussi bien que les deux autres Philosophes qui ne sont plus. Nous ne sçaurions nous preualoir de vostre esprit subtil & penetrant, de vostre gayeté, & de vos pensées tousiours pleines de quelque docte allusion, ou de quelque nouueauté surprenante; non plus que nous ne pourrons point profiter de la douceur, de la moderation, & du iugement exquis de celuy qui i'ay depeint & proposé en exemple, ny de la diligence & de la facilité du bon Religieux,[14] que vous nommiés si galamment le bon larron; pource qu'il estoit continuellement en action pour recueillir les raisonnemens d'autruy, & pour en faire part à tous ceux qui les vouloient entendre. Mais il me reste la consolation de vous escrire, & de receuoir quelques fois de vos Lettres, ou de voir celles qui s'adressent à nos deux chers amis, Monsieur du Bosc & Monsieur du Prat, & dans lesquelles ie trouue tousiours des marques de vostre souuenir. Ie vous supplie, Monsievr, de ne vous point lasser de m'en donner de nouuelles, & de croire que la possession de vostre amitié m'est si chere, qu'il n'y a rien que ie ne voulusse faire pour me la conseruer. Ie suis,

Monsievr,
Vostre tres-humble, & tres-obeïssant &c.

A Paris le 1. *de Feb.* 1658.

493

Translation of Letter 133

Sir,

During my stay in Paris[1] I have not ceased to wish you were here, for the particular benefit which I should have gained from your conversation. But now I would wish you were here for the benefit of the public too, which would have the opportunity to take advantage of your presence at the Assembly which I have told you about. In my previous letters I told you that M. de Montmor[2] had done me the honour of informing me about his plan to invite a certain number of selected people to his house to discuss questions of natural science, or experiments and fine discoveries, and that he had given me the task of drafting a possible procedure for discussions which would work for the public benefit, as well as the amusement of those who took part. With M. du Prat[3] I prepared some rules, and they were presented to the first meeting of the Assembly, which was composed of a good number of interested people. They were examined, and some objections were raised against them by people who did not want to write anything. Since you ask me for them, I send them to you; and I really do not mind if they are seen by everybody, since they will testify to our good intentions, and they may not be unhelpful, perhaps, to those who intend to apply themselves to the same sort of researches as the ones we have decided upon.

The age of iron will not last for ever; Peace will, in turn, come back to visit the earth; the Muses will not be exiled for all eternity[(4)]; the Arts will return to life; the Sciences will regain their proper place; and the influence of the stars—a more gentle influence than the one which nowadays produces only soldiers and captains—will produce Gilberts,[5] Bacons, Harveys, Sarpis,[6] Galileos, Mersennes, Descartes, and Gassendis once more. It is to the credit of our age that these illustrious people may learn, on their return, that, despite the barbarism in the midst of which we have lived, there have been quite a number of worthy people who have not lost their love of philosophical studies; it has not been the fault of these people if, after the great path-breaking achievements which the people I have just mentioned made for us, more progress has not been made than is being made now in the improvement of all our fields of knowledge.

When I have told you the names of some of those who make up our Assembly, you will admit that it would be hard to put together a comparable gathering, even if one could choose from among all the enquiring spirits outside Paris, and perhaps even outside this kingdom. But it would be better if I let you see straight away what you want.

Rule I. The purpose of the discussions will not consist at all of an empty parade of wit over useless subtleties; instead, they shall aim always at the clearest knowledge of the works of God, and the advancement of practical benefits, in those arts and sciences which are best suited to achieve them.

II. The person who presides will establish, according to the wishes of those present, the subject for the next discussion, and will ask the two named individuals whom he judges to be the best informed on that subject to present their opinions, leaving the rest free to express their thoughts on it.

III. These statements of opinion will be read out, and handed in in writing; they should be economically expressed, with reasons fully stated, without any rhetorical embellishment or citation of authorities.

IV. They will be read without interruption, the two chosen individuals producing theirs first.

V. After they have all been read out, each person will express, briefly and in turn, his objections to what has been read, or his confirmations of it. After a reply has been made, the matter will not be pressed any further, without the permission of the person who presides.

VI. Someone who is unable to attend in person may send in his opinion on the proposed subject.

VII. The Assembly will ask those who have the opportunity to do so to correspond with learned men in France and abroad, to learn from them about work in progress, or about things which have already been published in the arts and sciences; and the Assembly will be informed of these matters at the ends of its sessions.

VIII. Once the Assembly has been convened, no applicants will be admitted unless [7] two-thirds of those present agree when the proposal is put to them.

IX. Only members of the Assembly will be allowed into the room where the discussion takes place, the Assembly being composed of people who have an interest in natural science, medicine, mathematics, the liberal arts, and mechanics, unless permission has been asked in advance to bring some worthy person there.

We have started work on our discussions according to this plan, and we have already dealt with many important subjects there, methodically and with great precision. But we have need of you, Sir, as well as of the good Minim father,[8] and the wise M. Gassendi, whom I address in a Preface which I shall put in front of his works, in which I speak about our Assembly:

'Be present too, Gassendi, best of men, so that the image of your modesty and wisdom may always be seen by everyone!(9) Truly, once your works have been published we shall have everything we need in order to see you in your entirety; we shall not only have the benefit of your acuity and learning(10), but also, by keeping our eyes constantly fixed on your wisdom, we shall, by means of your superior ability, be able to follow the true method of philosophizing, of which you gave us such a distinguished example. And as long as the world lasts, after the passage of countless(11) years, you will still be studied by those who strive after good sense; so that if there is anyone then who enjoys reading authors who philosophize in a barbarous or abstruse(12) way, it will be possible to use that phrase of Cicero's to oppose them: "What is this madness men suffer from, that having found grain they feed on acorns?" '13

May God make me a true prophet, when I say I hope that people will imitate M. Gassendi's modesty, that his gentle and tranquil spirit will reign over our Assembly, and that this new Academy will not disappoint the hopes which may be raised by the rules I am sending you. But we have good reason to suspect, as I had begun to say, that we shall have need of you, as well as of those two other philosophers who are no longer with us. We shall not be able to avail ourselves of your subtle and penetrating mind, your lively humour, and those judgements of yours which are always full of some learned allusion or some surprising novelty; no more than we shall be able to enjoy the gentleness, moderation, and perfect judgement of the person I have described and put forward as an example, or the diligence and talent of the good friar,14 whom you used to call so jokingly 'the good thief', because he was constantly at work collecting other people's arguments, to share them with all those who wanted to hear them. But I still have the consolation of writing to you, and of sometimes receiving your letters, or seeing the ones which are addressed to our two dear friends M. du Bosc and M. du Prat, in which I still find signs of your remembrance of me. I beg you, Sir, never to tire of sending me your news, and to believe that the possession of your friendship is so dear to me, that there is nothing I would not do in order to retain it. I am,

Sir,
your most humble and obedient servant . . .

Paris, 1 February 1658.

The copy-text used here is Bodl. Lister C 156; it has been collated with BL 636. h. 10 (siglum: 'BL'), and CUL W. 8. 7 (siglum: 'CUL'). Where these three copies agree, the siglum is '1660'. The passage Sorbière cites from his introduction to Gassendi, *Opera omnia* (i, sig. i5ʳ) has been collated with a copy of that edition (CUL M. 1. 25, siglum: '1658').

¹ Sorbière had been living in Paris since early 1654 (except during part of 1655, when he travelled to Rome) (see the Biographical Register).

² Henri Louis Habert de Montmor (c.1600–79) came from a prosperous family of high-ranking government officials; he became a *conseiller* of the Parlement of Paris (c.1625) and a *maître de requêtes* (1632). He was elected a member of the Académie française (1634). De Montmor possessed a fine library, and was a generous patron; he once offered Descartes the use of his country house (Baillet, *Vie de Descartes*, ii, p. 462), and Gassendi lived in his Paris house (on the rue du Temple) for the last two years of his life (1653–5). From the mid-1650s until the early 1660s this house was the usual meeting-place of the gatherings of scientists, physicians, and philosophers which were formalized as this letter describes. De Montmor also co-edited (with Sorbière and Antoine de la Poterie) the 6-vol. *Opera omnia* of Gassendi.

³ Abraham du Prat.

⁴ eternellement *BL, CUL*.

⁵ See Letter 105 n. 4.

⁶ Paolo Sarpi (1552–1623), the Venetian Servite friar, best known as the author of the *Istoria del concilio tridentino* (1619), published little on science, but was renowned during his lifetime for his researches in anatomy (especially on veins and the eye), which he communicated to the Paduan scientist Fabrizio Acquapendente, and for his work in astronomy, on which he corresponded with Galileo.

⁷ *&* 1660 (presumably a printer's misreading of a contraction for 'que').

⁸ Mersenne.

⁹ ~? 1658; ~! 1660.

¹⁰ *eruditone* 1660; *eruditione* 1658.

¹¹ *innumerailem* 1660; *innumerabilem* 1658.

¹² *meteoraticè* 1660; *meteoreticè* 1658.

¹³ Cicero, *De oratore*, 9. 31 ('Quae est autem in hominibus tanta perversitas, ut inventis frugibus glande vescantur').

¹⁴ Mersenne.

LETTER 134   1 [/11] MARCH 1658

Edward Bagshaw to Hobbes, from Westminster

Chatsworth, Hobbes MSS, letter 45 (original).

Honoured Sʳ

Though I am very sensible how much injury they doe to yᵉ Commonwealth of Learning, who doe in yᵉ least manner, divert you from those great designes you are now upon; yet when I have related my reason of

Troubling you, I shall with some confidence not onely request your Pardon, but likewise your Assistance. The Occasion is this; discoursing yesterday with a Lady (of Eminent both Quality and Understanding) concerning your Excellent Tract about Necessity,[1] I did represent your Opinion, and ye Reasons which moved me to assent to it, to ye best Advantage I could. But notwithstanding any Rhetoricke of mine, I could not satisfy her, in y^t Inevitable Inconvenience which followes ye Doctrine of Freewill—That if ye Will be free, God cannot foresee ye Operacions of it. (upon which score ye Socinians[2] doe altogether deny Prescience). This Proposition, though it seeme cleare to me, yet for my life I cannot make it cleare to another: whether it bee [indeed *deleted*] that I doe not fully understand it; or that it bee of ye Nature of these Truths, which being cleare in themselves, become intricate by [>Larger] explaining; such as that is, that Nothing can move it selfe:[3] which is another Absurdity in this Tenet, and yet so farre from being looked upon as such that it is Obstinately asserted: S^r, Having this Taske imposed upon me by ye Lady, and she being a Person infinitely deserving ye Effects of my Obedience: I thought it but justice to light my Candle at your Sunne; and to seeke from y^t Person, Solucion of all Doubts, from whom [>alone] I have [totally *deleted*] derived ye full Knowledge of ye Opinion. If therfore you please in a few lines, to demonstrate—that Prescience and Freewill are Inconsistent: besides ye clearing up a Controverted Truth, you will gaine an Excellent Person for your Proselyte: who is as great an Ornament to her owne Sexe, as you are to Ours: and when I have said that, I am sure I thinke her Incomparable. As for my selfe, though your Condescension herein will be very great, yet you cannot, by any Future Act of Favour, oblige me to be more, then by your Merit I already am

Honoured S^r
Your most humble and most Affectionately devoted Servt
Edw: Bagshawe.

Deanes-yard[4] March: 1°

[*postscript:*] S^r I have made bold to send you a small Treatise of my owne Making,[5] which in no respect is fit for your Reading (ye Subjects being put upon me and not my owne choice in ye University) But I could not have satisfied my selfe, if I had not, since I printed onely a few copies for my [*word deleted*] Friends, presented one to you, as ye person I most honour.

[*addressed:*] These For my Ever honoured Friend Mr Thomas Hobbes Present at my Lord of Devonshires house in Bedford Street.

[*endorsed by James Wheldon:*] M^r. Ed. Bagshaw. March 1st. 1658.

The year of this letter is supplied only by the endorsement. The possible ambiguity of 'March 1st. 1658' (which could mean 1659) is removed by the fact that this letter was written from Westminster School, which Bagshaw left later in 1658 (see the Biographical Register).

¹ *Of Libertie and Necessitie.*
² Adherents to a tradition of anti-Trinitarian rationalist theology founded by the 16th-cent. theologians Lelio and Fausto Sozini or Sozzini.
³ Bagshaw developed this argument in *A Letter to Mr Pierce*, p. 10.
⁴ Dean's Yard, Westminster.
⁵ Probably *Dissertationes duae anti-socinianae*.

LETTER 135   [22 JULY/] 1 AUGUST 1658

Samuel Sorbière to Hobbes, from Paris

BN MS f.l. 10352, part 1, fo. 273^r (transcript).

Clarissimo Viro D. Thomae Hobbio, Samuel Sorberius.

Quod dudum nihil ad te literarum scripserim, nescio quomodo factum, cùm nihil jucundius mihi sit quàm de te cogitare, de te cum Amicis confabulari, tuam in Musaeo meo Iconem intueri, mentem verò in scriptis suspicere, & in Epistolis familiaribus amoenitatem ingenij exosculari. Sed multis sanè impeditus fui negotiis, quae inter annumeranda est illa Praefatio mea in Opera Petri Gassendi,¹ cujus Exemplar credidi nescio cui Nobili Anglo qui tibi deferendam suscepit. Mentio de te obiter facta² ostendet satis quàm non sim tuarum virtutum segnis cultor, licet rariùs ad te scribam, imò rescribam, qui debitor sum Responsi ad illam, in qua de Dissertatiuncula mea ad Dubosquium contra Phlebotomiam nimis frequentem³ animi tui sensa aperuisti. Hujuscemodi plures institui Velitationes, quae forsan in vnum signa si contulissent⁴ ornatiùs incederent. Sed tuum de Homine librum ecquando transmittes? Alterum verò Angliae editum Leuiathan nemore Latio⁵ donabit? Equidem Latina circa res naturales Opera tua ego libenter Gallicâ veste donarem si satis intelligerem, vel ea me maneret felicitas, quam in interpretandis Politicis⁶ sum consecutus. Ita enim & me & alios docerem, nec renuerem iter in Angliam facere vt tecum philosopharer si possem tricis me expedire, quod tamen non despero futurum quandoquidem video te septuagenario majorem tam firmâ vti bonâ valetudine, atque animi tantâ alacritate. Seculum vtinam pariter impleas vt per istam inter homines moram locus detur, & mihi & Prataeo[7] & Martello transfretandi in Patriam tuam & te amplectandi nostri semper memorem & redamantem.

Vale

Lutetiae Parisiorum Kal. Augusti 1658.

Translation of Letter 135

Samuel Sorbière to the most distinguished Mr Thomas Hobbes.

I do not know how it has happened that I have not sent you any letters for such a long time; nothing gives me greater pleasure than thinking about you, talking about you with my friends, looking at your portrait in my collection, contemplating your mind in your writings, and fondly admiring the sweetness of your wit in your friendly letters. But I have been entangled in a great many chores, among them that Preface which I wrote to the Works of Pierre Gassendi:[1] I gave a copy of the book to some English nobleman or other, who undertook to deliver it to you. The mention which I make of you there in passing[2] should show that I am not an idle admirer of your virtues, even though I seldom write to you—I should say, write back to you, since I owe you a reply to the letter in which you gave me your opinion of that little dissertation which I wrote for du Bosc against too frequent phlebotomy.[3] I have made several skirmishes of this kind, and perhaps if I had combined all my troops into a single regiment[4] they might march along more elegantly.

But when will you send your book *De homine*? Will *Leviathan* present another edition printed in England to the groves of Latium?[5] I should be happy to give a French garb to your Latin works on physics if I understood them well enough, or if I still had that felicitousness in interpreting them which I experienced with your Politics.[6] In that way I should educate both myself and others; I should be willing to travel to England in order to discuss philosophy with you, if only I could extricate myself from my troubles—and I do not despair of doing so, since I see that at more than 70 you enjoy such sound good health and such alertness of mind. I wish you may live to be 100, so that during your lifetime there will be a chance for me, du Prat,[7] and de Martel to cross the seas to your country and embrace you, finding you always mindful of us and returning our love.

Farewell

Paris, 1 August 1658

¹ Published in Gassendi, *Opera omnia*, i.
² Ibid., i, sigs. e5ᵛ, i1ᵛ.
³ See Letter 118 n. 1.
⁴ Alternative translation: 'if they had all engaged with a single foe'; but the probable meaning is, if they had been published together as one book.
⁵ Meaning, 'in Latin'; 'nemore' may perhaps be a copyist's error for 'nemoroso'.
⁶ Sorbière's translation of *De cive*, *Elemens philosophiques du citoyen*.
⁷ Probably Abraham du Prat.

LETTER 136   15 [/25] MAY 1659

Pierre Guisony to Hobbes, from Oxford

Chatsworth, Hobbes MSS, letter 46 (original).

Monsieur

Je n'ay point eu de plus principal dessein dans mon voïage d'angleterre, que d'auoir l'honneur de faire la reuerance aux habiles gens qui ỳ viuent; & comme pas un d'entre eux ne vous dispute aueq raison le premier rang, la passion qui m'animoit visoit d'autantplus a vostre personne. Messieurs de Sorbiere & du Prat¹ sçauent l'estime que ie fais de vostre illustre nom & de ces beaux escrits qui instruisent maintenant toute l'Europe; & Monsʳ Stubbe cautionnera toujours, qu'apres ne vous auoir pas rencontré à Londres, ie n'étois uenu à oxford que pour piquer a Deuonshire, ou ie uous croiois par vn bruict commun, & que ça été aueq tous les regrets imaginables, que i'ay appris, que Vostre sejour est trop eloigné² à vn Etranger dans l'etat des affaires presentes, pour vous ỳ aller asseurer de ses tres humbles respects. Cependant, Monsieur, ie prens la liberté de le faire par vne mechante lettre, puisque ie ne le puis en seurté de viue uoix, & de vous randre vne partie des deuoirs, auxquels, la veneration que i'ay pour vostre vertu, m'incline. faites moy (s'il uous plaict) la Justice, Monsieur, de croire qu'il n'y à personne qui uous honnore plus que moy, & qui pense auoir moins ueu en angleterre, lorsqu'il n'a pas eu le bonheur de vous approcher. Ce me seroit extrememement glorieux, si par la voye de

501

Mons.ʳ Stubbe i'etois honnoré de vos Commandemens, afin que vos amis sceussent, que ie n'ay pas esté tout a faict mal-heureux que de ne vous persuader, que ie suis autant qu'on le pùt estre

> Monsieur
> Vostre tres humble & tres obeiss.ᵗ seruiteur
> Guisony

à Oxford le 15.ᵉ de may 1659.

[*postscript:*] La proposition, par laquelle uous soutenes que le foetus uit de la vie de la mere,[3] m'embarrasse beaucoup dans les animaux (qu'on appelle, ouipara) ou le poussin se trouue toutafaict separé de la poule; & dans ceux mesme, (qu'on nomme viuipara) ou par plusieurs dissections i'ay toujours ueu separation entre le placenta de la mere, & celluy du foetus. J'ay encore quelque petite difficulté de conceuoir certaines propositions d'optique, mais comme il faudroit des figures, ie n'en dis mot. il me tomba à Paris entre les mains, [des *deleted* >quelques] obiections que M.ʳ Descartes faisoit autrefois contre l'excellent traité de la Politique:[4] elles sont conceües en dix ou douze lignes, en cas que vous ne les ayés pas ueües, ie ne scay si vous en series curieux quelque jour. M.ʳ Du Prat nous faisoit èsperer dans l'academie de Mʳ de Montmor,[5] que vous nous eclairciriés le phoenomene de l'eleuation de l'eau dans le petit syphon; vostre lettre promettoit que vous ỳ penseriés, c'est de tout mon coeur que ie vous ỳ exhorte, si vous n'aues pas encore pris la pene de le faire, & de ne vous lasser jamais de nous instruire.

[*addressed:*] A Monsieur
  Monsieur hoobs

[*endorsed by James Wheldon:*] M. Guisony May 15ᵗʰ 1659

Translation of Letter 136

Sir,

  I had no more important aim in my English journey than to have the honour of doing homage to the great intellects who live there. And since none of them has any right to challenge you for the first rank among them, my desires were fastened all the more strongly on you. MM. Sorbière and du Prat[1] know how highly I esteem your illustrious name and those fine writings of yours by which all Europe is now instructed; and Mr Stubbe will still testify that, when I had failed to meet you in London, I came to Oxford only in order to rush off to Devonshire, where rumour made me think you were living, and that I was filled with every imaginable regret when I learned that the place where you are staying is too far away[2] to permit a foreigner, in the present state of affairs, to go there and offer you his humble service.

However, Sir, I take the liberty of doing so by means of a wretched letter, since I cannot securely do so in the flesh, and of performing a part of those obligations of honour towards you which my admiration for your virtue makes me feel. Do me the justice, Sir (I beg you), of believing that no one honours you more than I do, and that no one can think he has seen less in England, when he has not had the pleasure of visiting you. It would be an extreme honour for me if, through Mr Stubbe, you were to honour me with your requests, so that your friends might know that I have not been so unfortunate as to fail to persuade you that I am, Sir, in the utmost degree,

Your most humble and obedient servant,
Guisony

Oxford, 15 May 1659

[*postscript:*] I have great difficulty with your thesis that the foetus lives by means of the life of its mother[3] in the case of those animals (the so-called 'ovipara') where the chick lives in complete separation from the hen—and even in the case of the so-called 'vivipara', where in several dissections I have always observed a separation between the mother's placenta and the foetus's. I also have some slight difficulty in following some of your optical theories; but since I cannot discuss them without diagrams, I shall keep silent. At Paris I came across some objections which M. Descartes made in the past against your excellent treatise on politics.[4] They are stated in ten or twelve lines; if you have not seen them, I do not know whether it would interest you to look at them one day. At M. de Montmor's[5] academy M. du Prat led us to hope that you would explain to us the phenomenon of the rising of water in the small siphon. Your letter promised that you would think about it; with all my heart I beg you to do so (if you have not already taken the trouble), and never to tire of instructing us.

[*addressed:*] To Mr Hobbes

¹ Probably Abraham du Prat.
² Hobbes was in Derby., at either Hardwick or Chatsworth.
³ Guisony is referring to *De homine*, I. 2: 'It is evident that a child in its mother's womb receives the motion of its heart from the motion of its mother's blood, and its life from the life of the mother to which it is joined' ('Constat Infantem dum in utero est matris, motum cordis habere à motu sanguinis materni, & vitam à vita matris cui adhaeret').
⁴ These objections have unfortunately not been found.
⁵ See Letter 133 n. 2.

LETTER 137   5/15 SEPTEMBER 1659

Charles du Bosc to Hobbes, from Saint-Jean-de-Luz

Chatsworth, Hobbes MSS, letter 47 (original).

My most deare Cosen¹
    Though I am further from You then I haue ben since I knew You; There passeth no day, but I conuerse with You. And In this remote place, I haue no other boocks to Entertaine [>me] but Yours, and yᵉ Enchiridion of Epictete. Mʳ Andrew Croocke sent me halfe a dozen *de Homine* and one *Leuiathan* for frends. but they must be kept at Paris till I returne thether. I bestowed already heretofore good many of them, specially to foure or fiue of Your good frends, mess.ʳˢ de la Mote,² Sorbiere, Martel, & my deare condisciple Mʳ du Prat.³ I gaue one also to Mʳ Pecquet.⁴ Mʳ Lantin⁵ of dijon while we were there had the reading de Homine. Three of these I sent for, are for him, and the Leuiatan. All yᵉ learned men I know desire that Leuiathan were in french or Latine. And I desire your workes were in a faire print, as things of that worth should be. The two great ministers of france & spane haue already had twelue Conferences about peace & mariage.⁶ We think that both will be effected; but as they are of highest Importance, so there must be much time In the treatings. I am very sorry that we are too long without hearing from one another. I would faine settle so yᵗ I should heare of your health once a month. I wish it as my owne. which is not bad I thancke God. My hearty commendations to Mʳ Hallily.⁷ Mʳ Andrew Croocke writ to me yᵗ you haue ben both In darbyshire about a Yeare. I Know not if my Lord⁸ be there. if so I desire you to present my duty & obedience to his lordᵖ. I am euermore

    Your most humble and most assured frend & seruant
    Du Bosc

S.ᵗ Jean de luz yᵉ 15.ᵗʰ 7.ᵇᵉʳ 1659. St. Nᵒ.

[*addressed:*] For My most deare Cosen M.ʳ Thomas Hobbes Esquire.

[*endorsed by James Wheldon:*] Mons.ʳ du Bos Sept 15ᵗʰ 1659.

[1] This is evidently used here as a term of endearment, not of relatedness.

[2] François de La Mothe le Vayer (see Letter 114 n. 2).

[3] Abraham du Prat.

[4] See Letter 77 n. 13.

[5] Jean-Baptiste Lantin (1620–95), born at Dijon, the son of a well-known lawyer and scholar; he trained as a lawyer and was *conseiller* of the Parlement of Bourgogne, 1652–92. A man of wide scholarly interests, he corresponded with Saumaise and prepared for publication the latter's *Praefatio in librum de homonymis hyles intricae* (1668). His own unpublished work included a translation of the Greek mathematician Pappus into Latin, and annotations on Diogenes Laertius. Auzout so admired his skill in mathematics that he asked him to revise his works. From a surviving volume of Lantin's MS notes ('Lantiniana': BN MS f.fr. 23253), it is evident that he knew Hobbes personally.

[6] The negotiations between France and Spain (conducted by Mazarin and Don Luis de Haro respectively) culminated in the signing of the Treaty of the Pyrenees on 28 Oct./7 Nov. 1659.

[7] Christopher Hallely, an employee of the Earls of Devonshire. He received an annual wage of £10 in 1636 (Chatsworth, MS Hardwick 28), and was steward at Hardwick in 1639 (MS Hardwick 30). In the 1674 draft of Hobbes's will (MS Hardwick 19) he received a bequest of £10. Hallely outlived Hobbes, and was described by Aubrey in 1680 as 'his intimate friend, an old gent' (*ABL* i, p. 366).

[8] William Cavendish, third Earl of Devonshire.

LETTER 138   9 [/19] OCTOBER 1659

Henry Stubbe to Hobbes, from Oxford

Chatsworth, Hobbes MSS, letter 48 (original).
Printed in Thompson, 'Lettres de Stubbe', p. 102.

S.ʳ

I receiued yoʳˢ, & no lesse resent[1] the fauour you doe mee by yoʳ returnes, then the Honour my Lord[2] does mee in his remembrances: if wee can ouerthrowe presbytery, it shall not bee indifferent any longer to mee which side after preuayles, if that to which I joyne can put mee into a capacity to expresse my acknowledgements to his Lordship. I shall conuey yoʳ enclosed to Mʳ Guisony;[3] that John Owen is not our D.ʳ but another of Deuon-shire:[4] hee was placed in yᵉ front, not as the most considerable, but that people might mistake it for our Deane, who durst not publiquely disowne the busynesse for feare of disgusting yᵉ

fifth-Monarchy men:⁵ I haue a paper comeing out against yᵉ Presbyterians directed to the army,⁶ that they may not bee admitted to
places of trust, I shall send my Lord one of them next weeke it may bee:
in the meane while I beseech you to render my Lord the greatest
assurances possible that I owne not lesse inclinations for his Lordship
then those are wherewith I am

S:ʳ yoʳ most humble seruᵗ
H: Stubbe.

Ch: Ch: Octob: 9. 1659

[*addressed:*] These For his highly honoured friend Mʳ Thomas Hobbes.
Leaue this with Mʳ Andrew Crooke⁷ booke-seller at yᵉ Greene-dragon
in Pauls yard London

[*endorsed by James Wheldon:*] M.ʳ Stubb. Oct. 9ᵗʰ 1659

---

¹ = feel grateful for, appreciate (*OED* resent *v*. 9).
² William Cavendish, third Earl of Devonshire.
³ Cf. Letter 136; Hobbes's reply to Guisony has not apparently survived.
⁴ Hobbes had evidently referred in his letter to a recently published broadside, *An
Essay toward Settlement upon a Sure Foundation* (dated 19 [/29] Sept. by Thomason: BL 669.
f. 21. 73). The list of twenty signatories at the foot of the page begins with 'John Owen'.
(For 'our D:ʳ' see Letter 91 n. 7.) It also includes the Welsh Nonconformist divine and
republican Vavasor Powell (1617–70), and Robert Overton, the former military
commander who was imprisoned for his opposition to Cromwell. The main aim of the
broadside was to 'witnesse against the setting up or introducing any Person whatsoever,
as King, or chiefe Magistrate, or a House of Lords, [. . .] apprehending that the great
work of taking the Kingdome from Man, and giving it to Christ, hath had its beginning
in the revolutions wee have been under'. It also demanded that 'the Rulers over men
forbeare for ever to impose any nationall, parochiall Ministry, so as to inforce any forme
of Worship suited to their interest'.
⁵ A radical sect whose members believed in the imminence of the thousand-year
reign of Christ on earth (the fifth such empire after the empires of Assyria, Persia,
Greece, and Rome (see Dan. 2: 44)). Several of the signatories of *An Essay toward
Settlement upon a Sure Foundation* (above, n. 4) were members of this sect (see Capp, *Fifth
Monarchy Men*, p. 126).
⁶ *A Letter to an Officer of the Army* (1659; received by Thomason on 26 Oct. [/5 Nov.]
(Fortescue, *Catalogue*, ii, p. 262)).
⁷ See the Biographical Register, 'William Crooke'.

M. de la Moulinière to Samuel Sorbière for Hobbes, enclosed in a letter from Samuel Sorbière to Hobbes from Paris

Chatsworth, Hobbes MS F. 2 (original). This is the enclosure only; Sorbière's letter does not survive.

Les Scribes et Phariziens sont assis en la cheze de Moyse faittes tout ce qu'ils vous commanderont &c[1]

M. de B.[2] soustient que ce passage ne prouue point l'obeissance deue aux Souuerains mais seulement celle qui est deue en matiere de Religion a Ceux qui en ont la direction parceque les Scribes et Phariziens n'auoyent pas la puissance souueraine estants eux mesme comme le reste de la Judée subiets a l'Empire de Rome. Joint que M. Hobbes senueloppe luy mesme dans vne manifeste contradiction quand il dit vn peu plus bas que J.C. a qui par droit hereditaire le Royaume des Juifs estoit deub ne laissoit pas viuant en personne priuée de payer le tribut a Cezar[3] et de dire qu'il luy appartenoit rendes dit J.C. a Cezar &c.[4]

Pour respondre a cette obiection Je croy selon mon petit sens qu'il fault examiner qui estoient ces Scribes et Phariziens et en quoy consistoit leur puissance. Josephe[5] dit si ie ne me trompe que cestoit vne secte des plus puissantes entre les Juifs qui faisoit profession de fuir les mollesses et les delices et de viure fort saintement, qu'ils portoient ordinairement des philacteres qui estoient de certaines peaux deliées ou le decalogue ou autres passages de l'Ecriture estoient escrits et les lioient a leur front ou a leurs brads, qu'ils se faisoient plus aimer de la Commune que les autres sectes et comme plus doctes et plus riches auoyent presque tousiours le gouuernem.t Cest pourquoy J.C. dit qu'ils sont assis en la cheze de Moyse entendant par cette cheze la domination temporelle quoy que limitée par l'Empire des Romains non la spirituelle quoy qu'elle fust reunie auec la temporelle en la personne de Moyse. Car nostre Seigneur n'eust pas recommandé l'obeissance aux choses spirituelles a des personnes qui n'estoient pas prestres ny sacrez Les Scribes et Phariziens n'estant ny l'vn ny l'autre dou sensuit que leur authorité ne sestendoit que sur les chozes temporelles, joint qu'il y auoit lors vn souuerain sacrificateur qui auoit la direction des choses spirituelles qui eust esté jaloux que d'autre que luy sen fussent mesles.

Quant a ce qui regarde la Contradiction qui se trouue dans le raisonnem^t de M. Hobbes ie dy que cest a J.C. a y respondre puis que luy mesme sestant serui de ce passage pour prouuer l'obeissance deue aux souuerains ne laisse pas de recommander qu'on paye le tribut a Cezar et de reconnoistre sa domination au mesme temps quil recommandoit aux juifs d'obeir aux Scribes et Phariziens

Ces Commandements neanmoins qui semblent contradictoires ne sont pas difficiles a concilier si on demeure daccord jusques à quel point les Romains auoyent voullu estendre leur domination sur les Juifs, Il semble qu'ils se contentoient de les auoir soubsmis a leur Empire, dexiger deux des tributs et de prononcer par la bouche de leurs gouuerneurs les sentences de mort contre ceux qui en auoyent esté juges dignes par les Juifs, leur permettant dailleurs de viure selon leurs loix tant Ceremonielle morale que Politique, mesme de connoistre de la qualité des Crimes selon leurs loix non pas de prononcer sentence de mort moins encor de lexecuter ce qui estoit reserué a leurs gouuerneurs comme il se justiffie par le 1 et 2 v. du chap. 27 de St Mathieu par lequel appert que les Sacrificateurs et les principaux du peuple (qui estoient les Scribes et Phariziens) tinrent conseil pour faire mourir J.C. et que l'ayant pris ils le lierent et menerent a Pilate leur gouuerneur pour prononcer sentence de mort contre luy et en St Jean chap. 18. Les Juifs ayants mené J. a Pilate pour le condamner il leur dit prenes le vous et le juges selon vostre loy et ils responderent il ne nous est pas loisible de faire mourir aucun.[6]

De tout ce que dessus il semble que lon peut inferer que le pouuoir des Scribes et Phariziens ne sestendoit particulierement que sur les choses temporelles Et que J.C. ayant recommandé aux Juifs de faire ce qu'ils leur diroient il a entendu vne obeissance telle que les Phariziens la pouuoient exiger deux et conformement au pouuoir que les Romains leur auoyent laissé sur ceux de leur nation.

Ce n'est pas que les Scribes et Phariziens ne se meslassent aussy des choses spirituelles mais comme ce n'estoit que par vsurpation sur lauthorité du souuerain sacrificateur il y a apparence que J.C. n'auroit pas donné le nom de cheze de Moyse a vne authorité vsurpée.

Jay tant de veneration pour Monsieur Hobbes et tant de deference a ces puissants raisonnemens que ie n'ay pu les voir choquer sans les deffendre mais j'ay peur de les auoir affoiblis par ma trop foible deffence je supplie monsieur de sorbiere de la fortiffier des siens et de mayder a soustenir les fondements d'vne si belle politique qu'est celle de ce grand personnage.

Translation of Letter 139 (enclosure)

'The scribes and the Pharisees sit in Moses' seat: All therefore whatsoever they bid you observe, that observe and do . . .'.[1]

Monsieur de B.[2] maintains that this passage does not prove in the slightest that people should obey their sovereigns, merely that they should obey, in matters of religion, those who are in charge of those matters. For, he says, the scribes and the Pharisees did not hold sovereign power; they themselves, like the rest of Judaea, were subject to Roman rule. And besides, he says, Mr Hobbes entangles himself in an evident contradiction when he says, a little later, that Jesus Christ (who was the rightful heir to the Kingdom of the Jews) did not fail as a private citizen to pay tribute to Caesar[3] and to say that it belonged to him: 'Render', said Christ, 'unto Caesar . . .'.[4]

In order to reply to this objection, it is necessary, I think (according to my slender understanding), to consider who the scribes and Pharisees were and what was the nature of their power. Josephus[5] says, if I am not mistaken, that they were one of the most powerful sects among the Jews, and that they made a point of spurning all luxuries and pleasures and living in a very holy way; he says that they usually wore phylacteries, which were thin pieces of leather on which the Ten Commandments or other passages from Scripture were written, and which they tied to their foreheads or their arms. And he says that they made themselves more popular in the community than the other sects, and that, being the most learned and the richest, they nearly always governed. That is why Jesus Christ says that they sit in Moses' seat, by which seat he means the exercise of temporal dominion, even though it was limited by Roman rule; he does not mean spiritual dominion, even though it was united with temporal dominion in the person of Moses. For Our Lord would not have recommended obedience in spiritual matters to people who were not priests or consecrated men—and the scribes and the Pharisees were neither. So it follows that their authority extended only to temporal matters, since there was at that time a sovereign High Priest who was in charge of spiritual matters, and who would have been jealous of anyone else interfering in such things.

As for the contradiction in Mr Hobbes's argument, I reply that Jesus Christ must answer for that, since he himself, having used this passage

509

in order to prove that sovereigns must be obeyed, did not fail to recommend that people pay tribute to Caesar, recognizing Caesar's rule at the same time as he recommended the Jews to obey the scribes and the Pharisees.

Nevertheless, although these commandments may seem contradictory, they are not difficult to reconcile, if one can agree on how far the Romans meant to extend their dominion over the Jews. They limited themselves, it seems, to having made the Jews submit to their rule, to demanding tributes from them, and to requiring that death sentences which had been passed by the Jews should be pronounced by the Roman governors. Otherwise they allowed them to live under their own laws—ceremonial and moral as well as political—and even to consider the gravity of offences in accordance with their own laws, but not to pronounce the death sentence, and still less to carry it out (which was reserved for their governors). This is proved by Matthew 27: 1–2, which shows that the chief priests and elders of the people (i.e. the scribes and the Pharisees) took counsel against Jesus to put him to death, and that having taken him they bound him and delivered him to Pilate, their governor, so that he could pronounce the death sentence against him. And in John 18 it says that when the Jews had taken Jesus to Pilate to condemn him, he said: 'Take ye him, and judge him according to your law'; and they replied, 'It is not lawful for us to put any man to death.'[6]

From all the foregoing one can infer that the power of the scribes and the Pharisees extended specifically to temporal matters only. So that when Jesus Christ recommended to the Jews that they should do what the scribes and Pharisees told them, he had in mind the kind of obedience which the Pharisees could demand of them, in accordance with the power over their own countrymen which the Romans had left to them.

Admittedly, the scribes and the Pharisees did also interfere in spiritual matters; but they did so only by usurping the authority of the chief High Priest, and it does not seem likely that Jesus Christ would have used the phrase 'Moses' seat' to refer to a usurped authority.

I feel so much veneration for Mr Hobbes, and so much deference towards his powerful arguments, that I could not see them attacked without trying to defend them. But I fear that my defence may have weakened them by being too feeble. I beg M. Sorbière to strengthen my defence with his own arguments, and to help me to shore up the foundations of that great man's splendid political theory.

The identification of this document, and the dating of the letter from Sorbière which enclosed it, are made possible by Hobbes's reply, which is Letter 140.

¹ Matt. 23: 2–3, cited by Hobbes in *Leviathan*, p. 262.

² Unidentified; possibly Bourdelot.

³ In *Leviathan*, p. 263, Hobbes argued that the time of Christ's preaching on earth was 'not properly a Kingdome, and thereby a warrant to deny obedience to the Magistrates that then were, (for hee commanded to obey those that sate then in Moses chaire, and to pay tribute to Caesar;)'.

⁴ Matt. 22: 21; Mark 12: 17.

⁵ Flavius Josephus (d. AD 93) describes the Pharisees in his *De bello judaico*, 1. 110–13; 2. 162–3.

⁶ John 18: 31.